Listen In

BOOK 2

Second Edition

David Nunan

THE URBANA FREE LIBRARY

3 1230 00665 1018

D0144412

The Urbana Free Library

To renew materials call
217-367-4057

DISCARDED BY THE
URBANA FREE LIBRARY

DATE DUE		
JUL 08 2010		
AUG 09 2011		

THOMSON

HEINLE

Australia · Canada · Mexico · Singapore · Spain · United Kingdom · United States

THOMSON
HEINLE

Listen In, Second Edition, Student Book 2
David Nunan

Publisher, Global ELT: Christopher Wenger
Editorial Manager: Sean Bermingham
Development Editors: Ross Wallace, Derek Mackrell
Production Editor: Tan Jin Hock
ELT Directors: John Lowe (Asia),
    Francisco Lozano (Latin America)

Director of Marketing, ESL/ELT: Amy Mabley
Marketing Manager: Ian Martin
Interior/Cover Design: Christopher Hanzie, TYA Inc.
Illustrations: Raketshop Design Studio, Philippines
Composition: Stella Tan, TYA Inc.
Printer: Seng Lee Press

Copyright © 2003 by Heinle, a part of the Thomson Corporation. Heinle, Thomson and the Thomson logo are trademarks used herein under license.

All rights reserved. No part of this work covered by the copyright hereon may be reproduced or used in any form or by any means—graphic, electronic, or mechanical, including photocopying, recording, taping, Web distribution or information storage and retrieval systems—without the written permission of the publisher.

Printed in Singapore
1 2 3 4 5 6 7 8 9 10   06 05 04 03 02

For permission to use material from this text or product, contact us in the United States:
Tel   1-800-730-2214
Fax   1-800-730-2215
Web   www.thomsonrights.com

For more information, contact Heinle, 25 Thomson Place, Boston, Massachusetts 02210 USA, or you can visit our Internet site at http://www.heinle.com

ISBN 0-8384-0434-0

Photo Credits

Unless otherwise stated, all photos are from PhotoDisc, Inc. Digital Imagery © copyright 2002 PhotoDisc, Inc.

Photos on the cover, title page, pages 7, 11 (top), 15 (top), 19 (top), 23 (top), 27 (top), 31 (top), 37 (top), 38 (top left), 41 (top), 45 (top), 49 (top), 53 (top), 59 (top), 63 (top), 67 (top), 71 (top), 75 (top), 81 (top), 85 (top), 89 (top), 93 (top), and 97 (top) are the exclusive property of Heinle.

Photos on pages 36, 68 (top right and bottom right), 70, and 86 are from Associated Press. Photo on page 68 (left) is from Fashion Wire Daily/Associated Press.

Source of information for page 71: http://www.usaweekend.com/98_issues/980503/980503teen_survey_results.html

Every effort has been made to trace all sources of illustrations/photos/information in this book, but if any have been inadvertently overlooked, the publisher will be pleased to make the necessary arrangements at the first opportunity.

Author's Acknowledgments

First and foremost, I would like to thank Chris Wenger, whose vision for this project matched mine, and who readily understood what I was trying to achieve. Sean Bermingham and Ross Wallace have made a great editorial team, and really took the pain out of the revision process. Heartfelt thanks are also due to the friends, colleagues, and acquaintances who helped in the collection of the authentic data on which the materials are based—you all helped in the creation of a truly special series. Thanks to Dennis Hogan and Tan Tat Chu for their support in paving the way for the second edition, and also to Bob Cullen who astonishes me with his ability to monitor the many projects and initiatives that Thomson Learning has under development.

In addition to the above, I extend my appreciation to the following people, all of whom have helped to make this series a pleasure to work on: Amy Mabley, John Lowe, Ian Martin, Francisco Lozano, Tan Jin Hock, and Derek Mackrell at Thomson Learning; Christopher Hanzie, Stella Tan, and the staff at T.Y.A.; Leo Cultura and the staff at Raketshop Design Studio.

I am also very grateful to the following professionals who provided invaluable comments and suggestions during the development of this series:

Brett Bowie	Konkuk University, Korea	Jui-hsiang Lu	Van Nung Institute of Technology, Taiwan
Marlene Brenes	Benemerita University, Mexico		
Grace Chang	Tak Ming College, Taiwan	Shiona MacKenzie	Gakashuin Boys' Senior High School, Japan
Grace Chao	Soochow University, Taiwan		
Jim Chou	National Chengchi University, Taiwan	Rhona McCrae	Freelance English Instructor, Japan
		Michael Noonan	Kookmin University, Korea
Susana Christie	San Diego State University, USA	Maria Ordoñez	Universidad de Celaya, Mexico
Karen Cisney	Soochow University, Taiwan	Daisy Pan	Van Nung Institute of Technology, Taiwan
Carla Diez	ITESM, Mexico		
Michael Fox	Seoul National University of Education, Korea	Jason Park	Korea University of Foreign Studies, Korea
Chiu-hua Fu	Van Nung Institute of Technology, Taiwan	Young Park	Dankook University, Korea
		Kerry Read	Blossom English Center, Japan
Pierre Gauvin	Sung Dong ECC, Korea	Lesley Riley	Kanazawa Institute of Technology, Japan
Frank Graziani	Tokai University, Japan		
Ann-Marie Hadzima	National Taiwan University, Taiwan	Cathy Rudnick	Hanyang University, Korea
		Kathy Sherak	San Francisco State University, USA
Patti Hedden	Yonsei University, Korea		
Angela Hou	Fu-Jen Catholic University, Taiwan	Yoshiko Shimizu	Osaka College of Foreign Languages, Japan
Yu-chen Hso	Soochow University, Taiwan		
Ju-ying Vinia Huang	Tamkang University, Taiwan	John Smith	International Osaka Owada Koko, Japan
Yuko Iwata	Tokai University, Japan		
Inga Jelescheff	Saguragaoka High School, Japan	Sue Sohn	Sung Dong ECC, Korea
Monica Kamio	AEON Amity, Japan	May Tang	National Taiwan University, Taiwan
Alexis Kim	English City Institute, Korea		
Mia Kim	Kyunghee University, Korea	Yu-hsin Tsai	Chinese Culture University, Taiwan
Jane King	Soochow University, Taiwan		
Mary Ying-hsiu Ku	Taipei Municipal First Girl's High School, Taiwan	Melanie Vandenhoeven	Sungshin University, Korea
		Holly Winber	Senzoku Gakuen Fuzoku Koko, Japan
Balk-eum Lee	Aju University Education Center, Korea		
		Jane Wu	Fu-Jen Catholic University, Taiwan
Cheri Lee	One World Language Institute, Korea		
		Hsiao-tsui Yang	Shih Chien University, Taiwan
Jenny Lee	Seoul National University of Education, Korea	Hai-young Yun	Korea Development Institute, Korea
Li-te Li	Tung Fang B & E Vocational High School, Taiwan		

Scope and Sequence

Unit	Title/Topic	Goals	Sources	Pronunciation
Starter *Page 8*	*Listening for meaning.* **Listening skills**	Identifying types of listening Identifying ways to improve listening skills	Voice mail message Classroom lecture Store conversation Survey interviews	Intonation for clarification and apology
1 *Page 12*	*Can I ask you some questions?* **At the airport**	Understanding personal information questions Understanding airport announcements	Airport announcements Conversation on a plane Survey interview	Reduced forms of *can* in questions
2 *Page 16*	*He's handsome and intelligent.* **Dating**	Understanding personal descriptions Identifying personal preferences	Casual conversations Dating agency interview Self-introductions	Word stress
3 *Page 20*	*That's the bride's mother.* **Family events**	Identifying people at an event Identifying family relationships	Casual conversations	Intonation for sarcasm
4 *Page 24*	*I'm pretty good at math.* **School subjects**	Identifying school subjects Identifying abilities	Classroom lectures Conversation with counselor University automated telephone system	Intonation for *OK*
5 *Page 28*	*Where in the world is it?* **Geography**	Identifying geographical information Understanding travel ads	Quiz show TV show preview Travel advertisement Casual conversations	Syllable stress
1–5 *Page 32*	**Review**		Casual conversations Airport announcement Office conversation Travel advertisement	
6 *Page 34*	*It has a great view of the ocean.* **Housing**	Understanding descriptions of housing Identifying advantages and disadvantages	Conversation with an estate agent TV program	Vowel sounds
7 *Page 38*	*How about a genuine gold watch?* **Buying and selling**	Identifying consumer goods Understanding sales pitches	Shopping conversations Casual conversation	Word stress
8 *Page 42*	*That's an unusual job.* **Job preferences**	Identifying occupations Understanding job descriptions	Workplace conversations Classroom conversations	Intonation for requesting information and checking for understanding
9 *Page 46*	*Could you fax this for me?* **Office work**	Identifying requests Understanding excuses	Office conversation Telephone answering machine message	Sentence stress
10 *Page 50*	*We spent three days in New York.* **Tours**	Identifying tourist information Understanding descriptions of places	Casual conversation Tour narration Conversation with travel agent	Contrast of tag question intonation for certainty and uncertainty
6–10 *Page 54*	**Review**		Casual conversations Voice mail message Tour narration	

Unit	Title/Topic	Goals	Sources	Pronunciation
11 *Page 56*	*Let's get take-out.* **Ordering food**	Understanding restaurant descriptions Identifying food orders	Radio advertisements Casual conversation Telephone conversation	Reduced forms of *get any* and *got any*
12 *Page 60*	*What do you do to relax?* **Stress and relaxation**	Identifying stress-related problems Identifying methods of relaxation	Casual conversation Telephone conversation	Rising and falling intonation in questions
13 *Page 64*	*This is the news.* **News**	Understanding news reports Understanding sequence of events	Radio broadcast Office conversation	Pauses in speech to indicate relative clauses
14 *Page 68*	*I really admire her.* **Famous personalities**	Understanding interviews and surveys Identifying personal qualities	Casual conversations Interview	Contrast of stressed syllables in nouns and adjectives
15 *Page 72*	*Where does it hurt?* **Health**	Identifying medical problems Understanding medical consultations	Conversation at medical clinic Medical consultations Radio broadcast	Contrast of intonation in open and closed questions
11–15 *Page 76*	**Review**		Conversation with waiter Medical consultations Helicopter traffic report Radio advertisements	
16 *Page 78*	*You'll never believe this!* **Amazing stories**	Identifying main points of a story Recognizing surprising information	Casual conversations TV news report Media interview	Syllable stress to show surprise
17 *Page 82*	*We want someone who's reliable.* **Interviews**	Identifying personal qualities Understanding interviews	Casual conversations Job interviews	Sentence stress in questions
18 *Page 86*	*Let's go to the movies.* **Movies**	Understanding survey questions Understanding movie descriptions	Casual conversations Radio broadcasts Survey interview	Word stress
19 *Page 90*	*Is he ready to quit?* **Advice**	Understanding problems Identifying advice and solutions	Radio conversations Casual conversation Telephone conversation	Rising intonation to show annoyance
20 *Page 94*	*Who did you see today?* **Social networks**	Understanding social interactions Identifying a sequence of events	Casual conversations Office conversations Classroom lecture	Pronunciation of *s* in a sentence
16–20 *Page 98*	**Review**		Casual conversations Office conversations Classroom lecture	

To the Student

Dear Student,

Welcome to *Listen In*. This three-level series will give you many opportunities to develop your listening skills. It will also help you improve your speaking skills. There are several important features of the series that may be unfamiliar to you. They include real-life tasks, real-life language, and learning strategies.

Real-life tasks
The tasks you do in *Listen In* are all based on the kinds of listening that you do in real life, such as following directions, listening to telephone messages, and understanding the news and weather.

Real-life language
The listening materials are also taken from real life. You will hear many different kinds of recorded language, including conversations, telephone messages, store announcements, news and weather broadcasts, and public announcements.

Learning strategies
In addition to teaching you language, *Listen In* also focuses on learning strategies. In completing the tasks, you will use strategies that will improve your listening inside and outside the classroom.

Each level of *Listen In* consists of a Starter Unit to get you thinking about the listening strategies in the book, as well as giving you some practice using those strategies. There are 20 main units and four Review units. Linked to each of the main units is a page of Self-Study Practice at the back of the book. Here is what each unit contains:

Warm-up Task
This section is designed to introduce you to the topic for the unit and present some of the important vocabulary and expressions that you will hear and eventually use in the unit.

Listening Tasks
You will then hear a number of different listening passages, all of which relate to the target language of that unit. One of the listening tasks in each unit focuses on pronunciation; another type of task allows you to decide on your own response. The *Listen for it* boxes highlight useful words and expressions commonly used in everyday speech. The teacher will ask you to listen to most passages more than once. This will give you the chance to understand more of what you hear, use a variety of listening strategies, and check your answers to the listening tasks.

Your Turn!
The last page gives you the opportunity to practice the target language you have been listening to. *Try this . . .* is a communicative task that you complete in pairs or in groups. The sample language in the box will help you to complete this task. *In Focus* gives you cultural information that you can discuss as a class.

Self-Study Practice
After class, you can get extra listening practice by turning to the back of the book (pages 107–127) and completing the Self-Study Practice Units.

The main thing to remember when you are using these materials is to relax and enjoy yourself as you learn. In some units, you will hear conversations in which you will not understand every word. This does not matter. Not even native English speakers understand or listen for every single word. This series will help you develop strategies for understanding the most important information.

I had a great time creating *Listen In*. I hope that you enjoy using these materials as much as I enjoyed writing them.

Good luck!

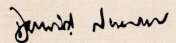

Classroom Language

Could you repeat that, please?

Could you play it again, please?

Could you turn up the volume, please?

How do you say . . . in English?

What does . . . mean?

How do you spell . . . ?

I'm not sure.

Sorry, I don't understand.

What did you get for question number one?

What's your answer for number two?

Listening for meaning.

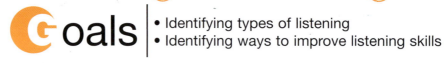

G oals
- Identifying types of listening
- Identifying ways to improve listening skills

1 *Before you listen, it's a good idea to think about the TYPE of listening that you will do. Here are some of the types of listening you will do in this course.*

A **Which of the following do you think are the most difficult to understand in English? Which are less difficult? Rank them in order (1 = most difficult). Then share your opinions with a partner.**

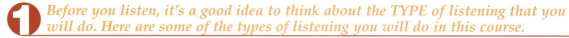

Types of listening

3	Public announcements	2	Formal conversations/interviews
4	Radio and TV programs	5	Medical consultations
4	News reports	1	Voice mail messages
4	English-language movies	1	Telephone conversations
2	Academic lectures	5	Conversations in stores
2	Casual conversations	2	Tour guide commentaries

B **Look through the units in this book. Find places where you can practice the types of listening above. Write the page numbers next to each one.**

C **Brainstorm!** **Work with a partner. Think of some situations when you had difficulty understanding spoken English. What was the situation? What type of listening did it involve (e.g., a conversation, a TV or radio broadcast, an announcement)? Why was it difficult? Note details below.**

2

Sometimes we listen for gist, or to get the main idea of what we are hearing.

A You will hear four types of listening. Listen and number the pictures (1–4).

The woman is calling about
travel plans / work.

The dress is **too expensive /
the wrong size**. *mid*

This is **a history lecture /
an English lecture**.

The man had **a good day /
a bad day**.

B Listen again for the main ideas. Circle the correct words under each picture.

3

Sometimes information is not stated directly but can be inferred.

A Listen to three people talk about movies they have seen. What did each person think about the movie? Circle *good* (😊), *OK* (😐), or *poor* (🙁) for each.

1. 😊 😐 (🙁)   *I don't understanding movie. avoid. poor direction. slow story*   *Kno what is* *special effect*
2. (😊) 😐 🙁   *excellent Amazing Can wonderful really recommert*   *special effect*
3. 😊 (😐) 🙁   *It's ok. The ending is disapointing*   *really*

B Listen again and write the key words that helped you decide.

4

Some words can have different meanings depending on how they are spoken.

A Listen to the examples.

Example 1   Sorry?   (asking for clarification)   **Example 2**   Sorry.   (apologizing)

Listen. Is each person asking for clarification (C) or apologizing (A)?

1. C   A   **2.** C   A   **3.** C   A   **4.** C   A   **5.** C   A   **6.** C   A

B Listen again and check your answers.

C Work with a partner. What other expressions can you use when you need to ask for clarification or repetition? Make a list. (Some examples are on page 7.)

Listening for meaning.

5 *As well as listening for gist or for inference, we can also listen for specific information.*

A   **Four students are talking about how they practice listening outside the classroom. Listen and number the people (1–4).**

	_____ uses English listening sites on the Web
	_____ downloads English songs from the Web
	_____ records and listens to her own voice
	_____ listens to English language news reports
	_____ watches music TV in English
	_____ watches English language movies on TV
	_____ chats with English speakers
	_____ goes to an English-speaking club
	_____ travels to English-speaking countries
	_____ downloads English songs from the Web
	_____ practices English songs at home
	_____ uses English listening sites on the Web

B   **What do the people do to improve their listening ability? Listen again and check (✔) two methods for each person.**

Which method(s) do you think would work best for you? _____

6 *In interactive types of listening, such as conversations, surveys, and interviews, people typically respond to what they hear.*

Listen and circle the answers that are right for you.

1. Announcements and messages.   TV programs and movies.   Conversations.

2. Understand TV and radio.   Talk with English speakers.   Understand lectures.

3. To pass an exam or get a job.   To communicate with English speakers.   For fun.

Your Turn!

Talking about reasons for studying English

- Why are you studying English?
- What's the main reason you're studying English?

  I'm studying it so I can **get a job**.

  So I can **talk with English speakers**.

  I want to use English **when I travel abroad**.

- Are you studying English to **pass an exam**?

  Yes, I need it to **pass a university entrance exam**.

  No, I'm **just studying it for fun**.

- How do you think studying English will help you?

  I'll be able to use my English skills to **get a job**.

Reasons for studying English

- [ ] Pass an exam
- [ ] Get a job using English
- [ ] Talk with English speakers
- [ ] Travel easily overseas
- [ ] Understand movies/TV
- [ ] Understand news reports
- [ ] Understand lectures
- [ ] Understand/sing English songs
- [ ] Live in an English-speaking country
- [ ] _____
- [ ] _____

Try this . . .
What are the main reasons you are studying English? Rank the reasons listed above in order (1 = most important reason). You can add other reasons to the list. Tell your partner and ask about his/her reasons.

In Focus: *Learning to listen*

People sometimes think that listening is not as important as speaking, reading, and writing. It is like a baby sister that no one pays attention to. This is because more attention has been paid to its three "elder sisters"—speaking, reading, and writing. For many people, being able to use a foreign language means being able to speak and write the language, or being able read foreign-language books or newspapers. In recent years, however, more and more attention has been paid to the importance of listening. People who argue in favor of teaching listening say that learners cannot start using another language effectively until they have heard lots of authentic, comprehensible examples of the language. *Why is listening important to you? What listening skills do you want to develop during the course?*

> When you're traveling, you need to be able to listen well so you can understand what people are saying to you.

> I'm hoping to study overseas one day. I need to improve my listening skills so I'll be able to understand lectures in English.

> I can understand OK when people speak slowly, but I need to be able to understand when they talk fast.

Listening for meaning.

11

UNIT

Can I ask you some questions?

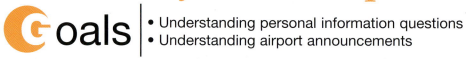

Goals · Understanding personal information questions
· Understanding airport announcements

1

A **What are these parts of an airport called? Use the words in the box to label the photos. Two are extra.**

baggage claim area	immigration counter	duty-free shop
check-in counter	security checkpoint	departure lounge

B **In which of the places above might you see or hear the following words? Write at least one word under each photo.**

boarding pass	passport	carry-on bag	boarding call
credit card	gate	carousel	luggage

C **Brainstorm!** Work with a partner. Imagine you've arrived at a U.S. airport. What questions might you be asked at Immigration? Make a list.

2

 A Listen and number the pictures (1–4).

B Listen again. Circle the titles you hear.

Ms.   Dr.   Prof.   Mr.   Mrs.

3

 A Listen and fill in the arrival card.

Singapore Immigration Service   Arrival Card

Welcome to Singapore

Arrival Card Number

000 , 0000 , 00 , 000

Family Name

First (Given) Name(s)

Sex   Passport Number
☐ Male   ☐ Female

Flight No./Vessel Name/Vehicle No.

Last City/Port of Embarkation

Address in Singapore

Length of Stay
☐ Days _____ Signature

B Listen again and check your answers.

Listen for it

There you go is used when a person hands something to someone. Other expressions with similar meaning are *there you are*, *here you are*, and *here you go*.

4

 A Imagine you are at Immigration in the United States. Listen and circle the best response.

1. Sure. There you go.   No, I'm sorry.   Yes, I had one issued recently.
2. Yes, I've been here before.   No, I haven't.   No, this is my second time.
3. In the United States.   For five days.   At the Downtown Hotel.
4. In the United States.   For five days.   At the Downtown Hotel.
5. Yes, I do. Here it is.   On the 16th.   Here's my passport.
6. My next stop is Montreal.   I'm not sure.   I'm attending a conference.

B Listen again and practice.

Can I ask you some questions?

5

A Oliver is answering questions about the services at an airport. Listen to Part 1 of the conversation. What does the airport official ask about? Check (✔) the boxes.

Listen for it

You're telling me, with stress on *me*, is used to agree strongly with something another person says.

☐ Name ☐ Address ☐ Where from

☐ Age ☐ Nationality

B Listen to Part 2 of the conversation. Is Oliver happy with the items on the list? Check (✔) *Yes* or *No* and note his comments.

About the airport

	Satisfied?		
	Yes	**No**	**Comments**
Arrival area	☐	☐	
Immigration	☐	☐	
Duty free	☐	☐	
General appearance	☐	☐	

6

A Questions like *Can you fill in this card for me?* are often reduced. Listen to the example.

> **Example:** Can you fill in this card for me?   *C'n y' fill in this card for me?*

Now listen and circle *Reduced* or *Not reduced*.

1. Reduced	Not reduced		**4.** Reduced	Not reduced
2. Reduced	Not reduced		**5.** Reduced	Not reduced
3. Reduced	Not reduced		**6.** Reduced	Not reduced

B Listen again and check your answers.

7

Listen and circle the answers that are right for you.

1. Yes, I do.	No, I don't.	I don't know.
2. I like it.	I've never flown.	I don't like it.
3. Yes, I am.	No, I'm not.	I've never thought about it.
4. Yes, I would.	No, I wouldn't.	I'm not sure.
5. Yes, a lot.	Yes, I've bought some.	No, I haven't bought any.

Your Turn! 🔊

Asking and answering personal information questions

- What's your name?
  Jill. My last name is **Davis**.
- Can you tell me your nationality?
- Where do you come from?
  I'm from **Canada**.
  I'm **Canadian**.
- Where do you live?
- Do you still live in **Canada**?
  Yes, I live in **Montreal**.
  No, I live in **Hong Kong** now.
- Where are you planning to stay in the United States?
  I'm staying at the **San Francisco Marriott**. It's on **4th Street**.

Immigration Service U.S.A.   **Arrival Card**

Welcome to the United States
Admission Number

000 0000 00 000

Family Name

First (Given) Name

Birth Date (Day/Month/Year)

Sex
☐ Male ☐ Female

Country of Citizenship

Passport Number

Airline and Flight Number

Country Where You Live

City Where You Boarded

Address While in the United States

Signature

Try this . . .

Imagine you are an airline passenger. You've lost your glasses and can't read the arrival card. Ask your partner to fill it in for you.

In Focus: *The future of travel*

To some people, taking a "dream vacation" might mean suntanning on the beach in Bali, trekking through the Himalayas, or skiing in the Swiss Alps. But how about spending a relaxing week at the bottom of the ocean or blasting off for a fun-filled trip into outer space? Sound impossible? Many experts predict that vacations like these could be widely available within as little as 20 years—albeit at a very high price. *What's your vision of the future of travel? What sorts of vacations will people be taking 20, 50, or 100 years from now?*

In a few years, it'll be possible to travel really long distances in less than an hour.

In 50 years, I think they'll have luxury cruise ships that actually fly.

Someday I think we'll be able to take trips to the moon and even Mars.

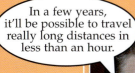

He's handsome and intelligent.

Goals • Understanding personal descriptions
• Identifying personal preferences

1

A How would you describe the people below? Use the words in the box or your own ideas.

slim/slender ④	muscular ②	heavyset ③	handsome ②
pretty ④	average-looking ②④	bearded ①	clean-shaven ②③
(un)healthy ② ③	longhaired ④	shorthaired ②③	balding/bald ①

1.

2.

3.

4.

B Now use the words below to describe what you think each person is like.

He/She looks . . .	(kind of) *kinda*	creative	intelligent	funny	energetic
He/She seems . . .	(sort of) *sorta*	kind	interesting	boring	shy
He/She's probably . . .		serious	talkative	quiet	gentle

C Brainstorm! Work with a partner. Think of three people you both know. Make a list of ways you could describe each one.

16

A Listen and number the pictures (1–3).

Listen for it

Pretty + adjective means *quite . . .* or *kind of . . .*

B Listen again. How do the women describe the men? Circle the words you hear in each conversation.

1. interesting	intelligent	creative	shy	gentle
2. smart	kind	funny	nice	boring
3. interesting	intelligent	handsome	talkative	strange

 A Listen and circle the words that are stressed.

1. Are any members of your family shy?

2. Would you describe yourself as slender?

3. Are you an energetic type of person?

4. Do you think you'll ever be bald?

5. Do you like to meet people who are talkative?

B Listen again and practice.

 He's handsome and intelligent.

4

A Megan is talking to someone from a dating agency. Listen and complete the form.

Listen for it

Mm-hmm is used to express agreement, understanding, or to express an affirmative answer.

PerfectMatch Inc.

○

Name: *Megan Johnson*

Interests:

☐ Books Kinds: *biographies*
☐ Music Kinds: _____
☐ Movies Kinds: _____
☐ Sports Kinds: _____

○

Person looking for:

Shares same interests?   Yes   No   Doesn't matter

Personal qualities: _____

Appearance: important   not important

B Listen again and check your answers.

5

A Listen to the descriptions and write what each person likes.

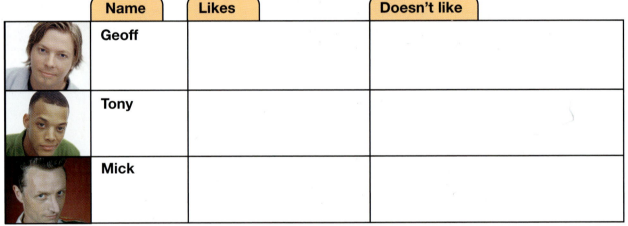

Name	Likes	Doesn't like
Geoff		
Tony		
Mick		

B Listen again and write what each person doesn't like.
Who do you think is the best person for Megan to go out with? Why?

_____

6

Listen and circle the answers that are right for you.

1. No, they aren't.   Some are.   Yes.

2. I guess I am.   Not really.   Not at all.

3. Yes, I am.   Kind of.   No, I'm not.

4. No way!   I might be.   Probably.

5. Definitely.   Doesn't matter.   No, I don't.

Describing people

- What does the person look like?
  He's **kind of average-looking.**
- Does he have **a beard or mustache**?
  Yes, he has **both**. And he **wears glasses**.
- Is he **tall**?
  Not really. He's **average height**.
- What is he like?
  Well, he's **intelligent**, and he's **very talented**.
- How old is he?
  I guess he's **in his early fifties.**
- Is it **Steven Spielberg**?
  Yes, that's right. It is!
  No, keep trying!

Try this . . . Think of someone famous in your country. Your partner will ask you questions about the person and try to guess who it is. Ask your partner about his/her famous person and make notes. Try to guess whom your partner is describing.

In Focus: *Celebrity lookalikes*

When someone witnesses a crime, police generally ask for a description of the criminal: age, height, hair color, visible scars. Sometimes a police artist draws a picture based on the description that is sent out to other police departments and the media. In a science fiction novel by William Gibson, police get descriptions of criminals by asking what famous stars they look like. Witnesses might say someone looks like "Mick Jagger with a beard" or "a young Frank Sinatra." *Does anyone in your class look like a celebrity? How would you describe yourself, your best friend, or someone in your family?*

Some people think my best friend looks like Michelle Yeoh, but with glasses.

My brother looks a little like Mel Gibson. Maybe that's why he's so popular!

My older brother has cut his hair short, and he now looks like Michael Jordan without the mustache.

He's handsome and intelligent.

That's the bride's mother.

Goals · Identifying people at an event
· Identifying family relationships

1

A Look at the invitations and use the words in the box to complete them.

| anniversary | birthday | reunion | wedding |

❶
Mr. and Mrs. John Lee request the pleasure of your company at the _____ of their daughter Jennifer to Albert Goldsmith on Saturday, September 8 at 4:30 p.m. at St. Lawrence Church

❷ Peggy is turning 40!

Come celebrate her _____
Date: Sunday March 5th
Time: 7—11 p.m.
Place: Michael's on the Thames
RSVP by February 20th

❸ **CLASS OF '84**

The E.J. Beale High School
Class of 1984 will hold its
20th annual _____
on Saturday, October 25th.
If you're from our class, please
make plans to be there!

❹ 25

*Help Us Celebrate
Mark & Gail's 25th _____
Sat., Aug. 19th
Crenshaw Country Club
RSVP by July 28th*

B Look at these relationship words. Write *M* (for *Male*), *F* (for *Female*), or *B* (for *Both*) next to each.

_____ parent-in-law _____ grandchild _____ uncle _____ spouse _____ aunt

_____ cousin _____ niece _____ sibling _____ stepson _____ nephew

C **Brainstorm!** Work with a partner. What are some other words associated with weddings? Make a list.

2

A Listen. Where are the speakers? Check (✔) the correct event.

☐ family reunion   ☐ wedding   ☐ birthday party   ☐ office party

B Listen again. Circle the names you hear.

Paul	Tommy	Roger	Philip
Betsy	Bobby	Mark	Manny

3

A Listen to the conversations at a wedding reception. Where does each person live now? Match the people with the places. One place is extra.

> **Listen for it**
>
> *Gosh* is an informal way of expressing mild surprise or delight.

Aunt Gertrude •   ◄ Bermuda

Cousin Emily •   ◄ Chicago

Uncle Morty •   ◄ Atlantic City

Aunt Jean •   ◄ New York

          ◄ Boston

B Listen again. Draw lines from the names to the correct people.

Cousin Emily   Aunt Gertrude   Aunt Jean   Uncle Morty

That's the bride's mother.

4

A **You can use intonation to mean the opposite of what you say. Listen to the examples.**

Example 1 **A:** How was the wedding?
   B: Great! (The wedding was great.)

Example 2 **A:** How was the wedding?
   B: Great! (The wedding wasn't great.)

Now listen and circle the correct meaning.

1. The reception . . .	was great.	wasn't great.
2. The band . . .	was talented.	wasn't talented.
3. The food . . .	was good.	wasn't good.
4. The bride's mother . . .	was excited.	wasn't excited.
5. In general, it . . .	was fun.	wasn't fun.

B **Listen again and practice.**

5

A **Corey is at her cousin's wedding. Who do you think is talking to her? Listen and circle the correct answer.**

1. Mother	Aunt	Friend
2. Mother	Aunt	Friend
3. Mother	Aunt	Friend

Listen for it

To *get out of here* is an informal expression meaning to leave the place you are in.

B **Listen again. Write the words that helped you decide.**

1. _____   2. _____   3. _____

_____   _____   _____

6

Listen and circle the answers that are right for you.

1. Sure, they're great.	Not really.	I've never been to one.
2. Traditional.	Western-style.	I'm not sure.
3. I love them.	They're alright.	I don't really like them.
4. With my family.	With my friends.	I don't celebrate it.
5. Yes, I really enjoy it.	It's OK.	No, not particularly.

Your Turn!

Asking and talking about special events

- Have you been to a family event recently?
  Yes, I went to **my cousin's wedding**.
- What was the **reception** like?
  Well, the **food was really good**.
- How many people turned up?
  I guess around **two hundred**. It was **really crowded**.
- Did anything funny happen?
  No, not really. It was **really serious**.
  Yeah, **my uncle gave a really funny speech**.
- So, was it fun?
  Yes, **everyone enjoyed it**.
  No, it was **pretty boring actually**.

Event: _____

Try this . . .

Think of a family event you attended. Write three good and three not-so-good things about it. Tell a partner about the event. Ask about your partner's event.

In Focus: *Crying in the chapel*

Is marriage obsolete? Since the 1950s, declining numbers of married couples and growing divorce rates have led some to believe that it is. But huge numbers of people continue to value marriage as an important life goal, and the vast majority will marry at least once in their lifetime. One reason people regard marriage so highly is that it can provide people with a source of emotional support, mutual trust, and lasting commitment. *What is the attitude toward marriage among young people in your country? Do you think marriage has a future?*

Most people my age want to get married but they also want successful careers.

People will always want to get married, but weddings will become a lot less formal.

I think marriage as a long-term commitment will disappear. It's an old-fashioned idea.

That's the bride's mother.

I'm pretty good at math.

oals | • Identifying school subjects
• Identifying abilities

1

A In which of these school subjects would you use the items below? Write the number(s) next to each item.

> 1. geography   3. physical education   5. mathematics   7. English
> 2. science   4. computer science   6. home economics   8. industrial arts

B How difficult is each of the subjects in Task A for you? Write the numbers (1–8) on the scale. Then rank them from most interesting to least interesting. Compare with a partner.

Very difficult   OK   Very easy

Least interesting   OK   Most interesting

C **Brainstorm!** Work with a partner. Think of at least five other subjects that people study in college/university. Add them to the list.

engineering, architectural design, business studies, . . .

2

◄)) **A** Listen to the lessons. Which subjects are being taught? Number the subjects (1–3).

☐ Home Economics ☐ Mathematics ☐ History ☐ English

☐ Geography ☐ Computer Science ☐ Science ☐ Industrial Arts

B Listen again and write the words that helped you decide.

1. _____ 2. _____ 3. _____

3

◄)) **A** Listen to the two counseling interviews. Write what each student wants to be.

Listen for it

OK has many uses, for example, to begin a sentence, to show understanding, and to ask for or express acceptance.

Student	Wants to be	Strengths	Weaknesses
Jenny Tan			
Julie Morris			

B Listen again and write their strengths and weaknesses.

4

◄)) **A** Depending on the intonation, *OK* can have many different meanings. Listen to the intonation of *OK* and match each one with the correct ending.

1. OK, •   • Just stop asking me!

2. OK . . . •   • I'll see you there on Monday night.

3. OK! •   • Good. Let's move to the next question.

4. OK? •   • If you're sure that's what you want.

B Listen and check your answers. Then practice saying the sentences using the correct intonation.

I'm pretty good at math.   **25**

5

A Listen to the descriptions of classes offered at Stamford Junior College. Write the correct class names in the chart. One is extra.

Listen for it

A *high-flying* career means a very successful career.

(English Proficiency)   (Architectural Design)

(Computer Programming)   (Music Composition)   (Sports Medicine)

Class name:				
Instructor:	Matt Harper	Ellen Carter	Carol Warren	Ben Keating
Classroom:	447A		744C	
Class time:	Tue–Fri 9 a.m.–12:30 p.m.	Mon–Thu 9 a.m.–3 p.m.		Wednesdays 1–5 p.m.

B Listen again and fill in the missing information in the chart. Which classes would be suitable for the people in Task 3?

Jenny Tan: _____   Julie Morris: _____

6

Listen and circle the answers that are right for you.

1. Yes, I'm pretty good.   Kind of.   No, not really.
2. Yes, I'm very good.   I'm OK.   No, I'm not very good.
3. Very interested.   Not really.   Not at all.
4. Yes, I would.   Maybe.   No, I wouldn't.
5. It's very important.   It's kind of important. It's not really important.

Your Turn! 🔊

Asking and talking about school subjects

- What were your best subjects in high school?
  My best subjects were **math** and **science**.
  I was really keen on **languages**.
- Are you more interested in **sciences** or **arts**?
  Oh, definitely **sciences**.
  I guess I prefer **arts**.
- Which types of subjects interest you now?
  I really enjoy **computer science**.
- What sort of career are you interested in?
  I'd like to be a **computer programmer**.
- Have you thought about **working for a big software company**?
  Yes, I'd love to.
  No, I'd prefer to **work for a smaller company**.

Try this . . . Imagine you're a career counselor for students. Interview your partner. Take notes on his/her strengths, weaknesses, favorite school subjects, and future career plans. Then, recommend some possible career choices.

In Focus: *Back to school*

For generations in the United States, a nineteenth century invention known as the public school system was seen as the best way to give students the knowledge and skills to become productive citizens. Around the 1960s, experts began questioning the system, citing the need for new types of schools to meet the changing demands of the twentieth century. These reformers eventually won for parents a much broader range of educational choices—including religious, alternative, and charter schools and home schooling—but they also sparked a debate on teaching and learning that still divides experts to this day. *How do you feel about the state of education in your country? What (if anything) would you do to change or improve the school system?*

> I'd like to change the system so that there's less emphasis on rote learning.

> I think schools should focus more on real-world subjects like politics and economics.

> Schools could attract more qualified teachers by paying higher salaries.

I'm pretty good at math.

UNIT 5

Where in the world is it?

Goals • Identifying geographical information
• Understanding travel ads

A How much do you know about the world around you?
Try this quiz, then compare your answers with a partner's.

MILLIONAIRE CHALLENGE!

$500
Q1. Which is the highest mountain in the world?
a. Mt. Fuji b. Mt. Everest c. K2

$1,000
Q2. In which country can you find the Great Pyramid at Giza?
a. Egypt b. Mexico c. Indonesia

$2,000
Q3. What is the world's longest river?
a. The Amazon b. The Mississippi c. The Nile

$5,000
Q4. In which country can you find the ruined city of Machu Picchu?
a. Brazil b. Argentina c. Peru

$10,000
Q5. In which Japanese city can you find the world's oldest wooden temple?
a. Kyoto b. Nara c. Tokyo

$50,000
Q6. Which is the world's highest waterfall?
a. Angel Falls, Venezuela b. Victoria Falls, Zimbabwe c. Niagara
Falls, United States/Canada

$100,000
Q7. Which skyscraper became the world's tallest building in 1998?
a. Sears Tower, Chicago b. Petronas Towers, Kuala Lumpur
c. Bank of China Tower, Hong Kong

$250,000
Q8. The area near Tienhsiang in Taiwan is famous for which natural feature?
a. A volcano b. A gorge c. A rain forest

$500,000
Q9. Mammoth Cave National Park, the world's largest cave system, is in
which U.S. state?
a. Kentucky b. North Dakota c. California

$1 million
Q10. South Korea's highest mountain is Mt. Halla, on Jeju island. How high is it?
a. 1,450 m b. 1,950 m c. 2,450 m

B **Brainstorm!** Work with a partner. What are some well-known natural features in your
country? How about man-made features? Make a list of the top ten. Rank them (1 =
most impressive).

28

2

A **Listen to the quiz program and check your answers in Task 1.**

How much money could you have won? $ _____

B **Listen again and complete the sentences.**

1. The world's highest mountain is _____ meters high.

2. The Great Pyramid is _____ years old.

3. The world's longest river is _____ kilometers long.

4. Horyuji Temple is _____ years old.

5. The total length of the Mammoth Cave system is _____ kilometers.

3

A **Listen and number the places in the order you hear them described (1–4). One is extra.**

Listen for it

If something is *out of this world* it means it's amazing or unique.

B **How does the speaker describe the places? Listen again and circle the adjectives you hear.**

incredible	amazing	stunning	awesome	unbelievable
spectacular	awe-inspiring	indescribable	beautiful	phenomenal

4

A **Listen and circle the stressed syllable in each adjective.**

1. stun-ning   3. a-ma-zing   5. in-cred-i-ble   7. in-de-scrib-a-ble

2. awe-some   4. beau-ti-ful   6. spec-tac-u-lar   8. un-be-lie-va-ble

B **Listen again and check your answers. Then practice saying the sentences using the correct stress.**

5

A

Listen and check the correct statement.

Listen for it

To *get away from it all* means to go somewhere far away and remote.

This is . . .

_____ a weather report for Australia.

_____ a travel ad for Australia.

_____ a quiz show about Australia.

_____ a news report about Australia.

_____ a documentary about Australia.

B

Listen again and complete the statements.

Australia is the _____ continent and the _____ island on earth. It's also

the _____ country. The Great Barrier Reef is the _____ reef in the world.

Uluru, or Ayer's Rock, is the world's _____ monolith.

6

A

Listen and trace Ed's route on the map.

Great Barrier Reef

Kakadu National Park

Sydney

The Pinnacles

Melbourne

Uluru

B

Listen again. Which of the places Ed visited was . . .

1. the most fun? _____

2. the most beautiful? _____

3. the most exciting? _____

4. the most unusual? _____

7

Listen and circle the answers that are right for you.

1. Several.	A few.	I haven't.	**3.** Africa.	Antarctica.	Europe.
2. Natural.	Man-made.	Either.	**4.** Alone.	With friends.	In a group.

Your Turn!

Asking and talking about a trip

- So, where did you go?
  We took a trip to **South America**.
- How long did you go for?
  We went for **two weeks**.
  For about **a fortnight**.
- What countries did you visit?
  We traveled through **Brazil and Argentina**.
- What did you do in **Brazil**?
  We went to **Rio** first, then went **on a tour of the Amazon**.
- How about in **Argentina**?
  We visited **Iguazú Falls**, and then traveled to **Buenos Aires**.
- So, what was the most **exciting** thing you did?
  Going up the Amazon was the highlight of the trip.

Try this . . . Work with a partner. Imagine you've just come back from a trip. Decide where you went and what each place was like. Describe your trip to another pair. Ask questions and makes notes about their trip.

In Focus: *The World Heritage List*

The World Heritage List is a list of the most important natural and cultural sites around the world, compiled and updated annually by the United Nations Educational, Scientific, and Cultural Organization (UNESCO). In 2002, a total of 730 sites were featured on the list, including the Statue of Liberty in the United States, Iguazú National Park in Argentina, the Great Barrier Reef in Australia, the Great Wall of China, and the Acropolis in Athens, Greece. Many of these sites are threatened by tourism and pollution. UNESCO works for the protection of each of the sites on the list, to ensure that future generations may experience the natural and cultural treasures we enjoy today. *What are the most impressive natural or man-made places in your country? Which deserve to be on the UNESCO World Heritage List? Why?*

Himeji Castle is probably the most important historical building in Japan, and it's also the most beautiful.

The Grand Canyon should be top of any list of sites in the United States —it's spectacular and there's nothing like it!

Stonehenge deserves its place on the list, because it was built so long ago.

Review

Units 1–5

1

A Listen and number the pictures (1–3). One picture is extra.

B Listen again. Write the words that helped you decide.

1. _____ 2. _____ 3. _____

2

A Listen and circle the word that best completes each response.

1. lazy	**2.** bearded	**3.** heavyset	**4.** tall	**5.** fit
energetic	clean-shaven	slim	short	unfit

B Listen again and check your answers.

3

 A **Listen to the tourism advertisement. Check (✔) the things the person talks about.**

☐ scenery ☐ nightclubs ☐ restaurants ☐ historical sites ☐ prices
☐ transport ☐ skyscrapers ☐ festivals ☐ accommodation ☐ climate

B **Listen again. Circle the words used to describe each place.**

Chicago

incredible   indescribable

unbelievable   unusual

New York

phenomenal   awe-inspiring

awesome   amazing

Boston

beautiful   unique

spectacular   stunning

4

A **Listen to the conversation. Which of the cities in Task 3 is each person from? Write the city next to the person's name.**

Bob Price _____   Nancy Jordan _____   Steve Maglieri _____

B **Listen again and find the three people described. Label each one with the correct name.**

5

Listen and circle the answers that are right for you.

1. A few times a year.   Not very often.   I never have.

2. Yes, I think so.   It depends on the situation.   No, not at all.

3. Yes, I do.   I don't mind them.   I try to avoid them.

4. Yes, I think it is.   I'm not sure.   No, I don't think it is.

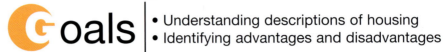

UNIT

It has a great view of the ocean.

 oals
- Understanding descriptions of housing
- Identifying advantages and disadvantages

1

A **Use the information in the real estate brochure to answer the questions.**

1. Which homes are close to transportation?

   _1,_____

2. Which homes have views of a park?

   _____

3. Which homes are best for students?

   _____

4. Which homes are for rent? For sale?

   rent: _____ sale: _____

5. Which homes are furnished?

   _____

6. Which homes are apartments? Houses?

   apts: _____ houses: _____

Summerhill Real Estate

This week's listings:

1. Apt. for rent

Spacious two-bedroom with balcony. High floor, across from park. Near stores, subway station. Tel: 555-5691.

2. Fully renovated

Huge 21st floor penthouse overlooking Montclair Park. Close to subway, downtown shopping. Priced to sell. Mr. Lee 555-0808. *No agents please.*

3. Gated community

Newly built houses for sale in suburban community. Large family rm & master bedrm. Playground, public pool nearby. 24-hour security. Phone 555-0160.

4. Condominium living

Furnished 3rd/4th floor units for lease. Ideal for professional couples. In downtown business district. Full facilities, ample parking. Call 555-3883.

5. House to share

Professional woman seeks two others to share two-floor house. Quiet, convenient. Short drive to city. Rent negotiable. Sabrina 555-9383.

6. Studio apt.

Fully furnished, steps from university, bus routes. Avail. Sept 1. Affordable rent. Rick at 555-0098.

B **Underline the parts of the descriptions that helped you decide.**

C **Brainstorm!** Work with a partner. Imagine you are looking for a new place to live. Think of a list of questions you would ask about one of the homes above.

2

 A Read the statements (1–5). Listen to the conversation and circle *True* or *False*.

1. The front door needs to be repaired.	True	False
2. The apartment has a good view of the ocean.	True	False
3. There's a gym in the apartment building.	True	False
4. There's a shopping center nearby.	True	False
5. The second bedroom is spacious.	True	False

B Listen again. Make a list of the good points (pros) and bad points (cons) of the apartment.

Pros	Cons
1.	
2.	
3.	

Listen for it

That's a plus is used informally to point out a positive aspect of a thing or situation.

3

 A Listen and circle the best response.

1. But I always drive to work.	But I don't own a car.
2. It's really convenient.	You can see it from the back.
3. It looks kind of small to me.	It needs to be fixed.
4. You can use the one next door.	The rent is eight hundred a month.
5. We'll get it fixed.	But it's very small.

B Listen again and check your answers.

4

 A Listen. Are the words the same or different in each pair? Check (✔) the correct column.

Same	Different		Same	Different
1.		4.		
2.		5.		
3.		6.		

B Listen again and practice.

It has a great view of the ocean.

A You will hear descriptions of three luxury homes. Match the description of each home to the correct celebrity owner.

Samuel L. Jackson

Madonna

Frank Sinatra

Spectacular 2-storey mansion	*Beautiful 2-storey Tudor-style house*	*Stunning 4-storey Georgian mansion*
• 9,000 square ft, close to Sunset Blvd.	• 4,200 square ft	• central London location
• 5 bdrm, 6 bthrm	• 4 bdrm, 5 bthrm, 3-car garage	• 6 bdrm, 5 bthrm
• master suite incls. gym, outdoor terrace	• swimming pool, patio, putting green	• library, sweeping staircase
• garden with pools, patio, waterfall	• location: Encino, California	• separate servants' apartment

Price: US$_____   Price: US$_____   Price: US$_____

B What is the asking price for each property? Listen again and fill in the price.

6

Listen and circle the answers that are right for you.

1. That would be great.   I'd consider it.   No, I'm happy where I am.

2. Yes, it is.   Kind of close.   Not at all.

3. Yes, a lot.   Quite a few.   No, not many.

4. Very nice.   Not bad.   Not very good.

5. Yes, there is.   There's some space.   No, not much.

Your Turn!

Asking about and describing homes

- How many **rooms** does it have?
  There are **sixteen rooms** altogether.
- Does it have **a swimming pool**?
  Yes. There's **a pool in the backyard**.
  No, but there's **a putting green**.
- How many **cars does the garage hold**?
  It's a **three-car garage**.

- What's the square footage?
  It's **a 4,000-square-foot** home.
- Is there **a tennis court**?
  Yes, there's **an indoor court**.
  No, just **a squash court**.
- What other amenities does it have?
  There's **a Jacuzzi and sauna**.

Try this . . .

Imagine you're a real estate agent for the stars. Your partner is a celebrity looking for a new home. Describe one of the homes in Task 4 (or make up your own information) and answer your partner's questions. Switch roles and make notes.

In Focus: *Dream homes*

In 1919, multi-millionaire publisher William Randolph Hearst decided to do something with a huge tract of land in California he had inherited from his mother. "We are tired of camping out in the open at the ranch in San Simeon," Hearst is said to have written. "I would like to build a little something." Years and millions of dollars later, that "little something" turned out to be Hearst Castle, a 165-bedroom mansion that features a marble and 22-carat-gold swimming pool, 1,000-year-old artifacts, and even its own zoo. Hearst may never have been satisfied with his dream home—he made countless renovations—but tourists still flock to the castle to marvel at its spectacular grandeur. *What would your dream home look like? What kinds of things would it include?*

I'd have a home theater in my dream home so I could watch videos on the big screen.

I'd build it in a place where I could go downhill skiing one day and scuba diving the next.

My dream home would have 365 rooms so I could sleep in a different one every night.

It has a great view of the ocean.

How about a genuine gold watch?

oals
• Identifying consumer goods
• Understanding sales pitches

1

A **What are the items below? Which do you already own? Check (✔) them. Circle the items you would like to have. Use the prompts to make sentences.**

I already have . . .

I'd like to buy . . .

I don't really need . . .

B **Brainstorm!** Work with a partner. How much would each item cost if you bought it at a department store? How about secondhand? Make a list of prices. What other items would you like to buy in the next year? How much would they cost?

2

A Listen. What are the people trying to sell? Listen and number the items (1–3). One is extra.

_____ electronic diary   _____ sunglasses   _____ cell phone   _____ wristwatch

B Listen again and write the key words that helped you decide.

1. _____

2. _____

3. _____

> **Listen for it**
>
> *Look* is sometimes used to interrupt someone or encourage the person to pay close attention to what you're about to say.

3

A Listen to the conversation and number the sentences (1–7) in the order you hear them.

_____ I won't pay more than $50.   _____ What if I buy two?

_____ Have you got anything cheaper?   _____ Could you give me a discount?

_____ Would you take $40?   _____ Sorry, that's too much.

_____ You can't lower the price at all?

B Listen again. How many necklaces does Peter agree to buy? How much do they cost in total?

How many? _____   How much? _____

4

A Listen and circle the best response.

1. **a.** No, thanks. I'm not interested.
   b. No, thanks. They're not silk.
   c. No, thanks. I'm not wearing a watch.

2. **a.** I wear sunglasses.
   b. They're too expensive.
   c. I've already got one.

3. **a.** I have a CD player.
   b. I'll give you twelve fifty.
   c. Sorry, that's too much.

4. **a.** Could you give me a discount?
   b. Could you give me fifty dollars?
   c. Could you give me your last CD?

5. **a.** I don't need it quickly.
   b. I don't need a bike.
   c. I don't need to sell it.

6. **a.** What if I buy two?
   b. Would you take four fifty?
   c. Do you have any ties?

B Listen again and check your answers.

How about a genuine gold watch?   **39**

5

A Read the statements (1–4). Listen and circle *True, False,* or *Unknown*.

Listen for it

Stuff is a general term used informally to refer to unspecified items or objects.

1. Lisa is meeting a friend.   True   False   Unknown
2. Lisa arrives late.   True   False   Unknown
3. They're in a restaurant.   True   False   Unknown
4. Lisa met a salesman.   True   False   Unknown

B Listen again. Answer each question (1–3) in a few words.

1. What was Lisa doing just before she arrived?

   _____

2. What does the other person think of what Lisa bought?

   _____

3. What might Lisa have to do with her purchase?

   _____

6

A Listen and underline the stressed words.

1. I already have a gold watch.
2. I don't need another pair of sunglasses.
3. I don't want a new MP3 player.
4. I don't wear scarves.
5. I've already bought one of those.
6. I can't stand listening to cheap CDs.

B Listen again and practice.

7

Listen and circle the answers that are right for you.

1. Sure, I'd like one.   I already have one.   Not at all.
2. Most of the time.   Sometimes I do.   Not usually.
3. Yes, I still do.   I used to have one.   No, I never have.
4. I could use another pair.   I don't own any.   No, I don't think so.
5. Sounds good.   I'd like to see it first.   Not interested.

Your Turn!

Discussing and bargaining for consumer goods

- Can I interest you in an **MP3 player**?
  That looks good. How much is it?
  No, thanks. I've already got one.
- These **gold bracelets** are just **$35** each.
  Would you take **$30**?
- These **sunglasses** are the best on the market.
  Have you got anything cheaper?
  Could you give me a discount?
- I can let you have the **watch** for $95.
  OK. It's a deal.
  Sorry, that's too much.
- This is top quality. Look at these features.
  Thanks but I don't really need it.
- You can have them all for **$55**.
  Forty dollars. That's my best offer.
  I'll give you **forty** for it.

Try this . . .
Imagine you are a salesperson. Write the names of three different consumer goods that you want to sell. List an asking price and note details for each. Negotiate until your partner agrees to buy what you're selling. Switch roles.

In Focus: *Too good to be true*

In the 1920s, small-time crook Charles Ponzi began a moneymaking scheme that made him America's most infamous swindler. The method was simple: Ponzi told people that by giving him their money, they could double their investment in just 45 days. Over 10,000 people did so and Ponzi soon amassed almost $10 million. What investors didn't know was that Ponzi was taking money from the second round of investors and using it to repay the first. He used the remaining cash to bankroll his lavish lifestyle. Predictably, Ponzi soon ran out of takers and was unable to repay all of his investors. Ponzi's scheme—for which he was sent to prison—helped popularize the saying, "If something looks too good to be true, it probably is." *Have you ever bought or invested in something that was "too good to be true?" What happened?*

I once bought a great bike for a really low price and then found out it was stolen.

My brother spent $5,000 on a used car and it broke down the very next day.

My friend invested all his money in stocks— and then the stock market crashed!

How about a genuine gold watch?

That's an unusual job.

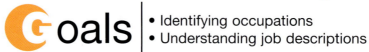

Goals
- Identifying occupations
- Understanding job descriptions

A Complete the job ads using the words in the box. Two are extra.

newscaster	veterinarian	salesperson	cleaner
teacher	bodyguard	childcare worker	laborer

Classifieds
The Marketplace for Jobs

Help Wanted

Immediate opening
for _____ at McClane Frozen Foods. Duties include: driving, loading, unloading trucks. Minimum wage. 555-6379.

Herriott Animal Hospital
is currently accepting applications for position of _____. Duties: sweeping up and maintaining animal cages. Tel: 555-3434.

Opportunity for _____. WorldLink Language School seeks experienced instructor. Must be good with children, willing to travel. Generous salary. Call (700) 555-8100.

Wanted: _____ Del's Shoe Emporium seeks individual with proven sales record to work at its Westdale Mall location. References a must. Call 555-0097.

Have you got what it takes?
Stinson Security Services is looking for a _____ to protect dignitaries, VIPs during official visits to city. Prior experience is a must. Call D. Stinson @ 555-9945.

Looking for a rewarding career?
Geisel House invites applications for position of _____. Responsible for overseeing kids, ages 3–8. Experience preferred but not essential. 555-7741.

B Would you be interested in any of these jobs? Which one is most suitable for you?

C **Brainstorm!** Work with a partner. Think of at least two pros (positive aspects) and two cons (negative aspects) of each of the jobs above.

2

A Listen. Who's talking? Write the occupation of the first person in each conversation.

	Occupation	Key Words
Conversation 1		
Conversation 2		
Conversation 3		

B Listen again and write the key words that helped you decide.

3

A Read the statements (1–4). Listen and check (✔) the statement that is closest in meaning to what each person says.

> **Listen for it**
>
> *Weird* is an informal way of saying *strange* or *unusual*.

Statement	Occupation
1. _____ **a.** A lot of women want to do this job. _____ **b.** Very few women do this kind of work.	
2. _____ **a.** The worst thing about my job is having to get up early. _____ **b.** I don't like being on TV.	
3. _____ **a.** My job is terrible, because my manager is always complaining. _____ **b.** I don't like it when customers are dissatisfied.	
4. _____ **a.** I get satisfaction from helping people to be successful. _____ **b.** My former students are all successful.	

B Listen again. What do these people do? Write the occupations.

That's an unusual job.

4

A Listen and write the correct name (Nick, Jim, or Linda) to complete each sentence.

1. _____ doesn't want to have a pet.   4. _____ worked as a cleaner.

2. _____ wants to be a teacher.   5. _____ wore a winter coat at work.

3. _____ had a really cool job.

B Can you find Nick, Jim, and Linda? Write each name under the correct picture. Three are extra.

_____

_____

_____

_____

_____

_____

5

A Are these people requesting information or checking for understanding? Listen to the examples.

Ex. 1 What did you do in the summer?   (requesting information)
Ex. 2 What did you do in the summer?   (checking for understanding)

1. _____ Where did Jim work last summer?   4. _____ How did you get the job?

2. _____ Where did you say Jim worked?   5. _____ How old were the kids you looked after?

3. _____ What was the worst thing about your job?

B Listen again and practice.

6

Listen and circle the answers that are right for you.

1. Yes, I would.	Depends on the job.	No, I wouldn't.
2. Yes, I do.	I kind of enjoy it.	Not at all.
3. That would be great.	I wouldn't mind it.	I'd rather not.
4. I'd like that.	That would be OK.	Not really.
5. Definitely.	They're equally important.	I don't think so.

Your Turn!

Asking about and describing jobs

- What are the main job responsibilities?
  The job mainly involves **doing medical exams** and **prescribing medicine**.
- Do you have to use any special equipment?
  I use **a lot of medical instruments** and **medicines**.
- What kinds of clothes do you wear at work?
  I always wear **a white lab coat** and **rubber gloves**.
- What's the best part of the job?
  The best part is **helping sick pets** and **making people happy**.
- What's the worst part of the job?
  The worst part is **having to give people bad news about their pet**.
- About how much does the job pay?
  Anywhere from about **$40,000 to $60,000 a year**.

Try this . . . Think of an occupation and write down as many statements as you can about what you do. Describe your job and answer your partner's questions. See if your partner can guess the job. Switch roles.

In Focus: *Someone's got to do it . . .*

Wanted: Three people to sniff armpits. Must have a good nose. Easy work for good pay.
Think this is a joke? Jobs like this are actually offered by companies that make deodorants and other personal hygiene products. When chemists in the hygiene industry develop deodorants with new and different scents, they have to determine which ones the public likes best. They typically have around twenty sweaty men apply different formulas to their underarms and then subject their armpits to an intensive inspection—not with the eyes but with the nose. That's where the armpit-sniffers come in. Yes, it's a smelly job, but somebody has to do it. It could be you! *What are some unusual occupations in your country? Would you be willing to hold an unusual job if the price was right?*

I spent a whole summer wearing a Goofy costume at Disneyland in California.

My father used to clean up after circus elephants. The pay was actually pretty good.

My best friend earns a lot of money each year by acting as Santa Claus in department stores.

That's an unusual job.

Could you fax this for me?

Goals • Identifying requests
• Understanding excuses

A Use the words in the box to number the pictures (1–9).

1. print a document	4. make a phone call	7. send an SMS message
2. send an e-mail message	5. download a file	8. send a fax
3. check voice mail	6. send a letter	9. make a photocopy

B Which of the things above have you done in the past week? Check (✔) them.

C Brainstorm! Work with a partner. What kinds of electronic items might you find in a typical office? What can you do with each item? Make a list.

2

A Listen and number the pictures (1–5). One is extra.

Listen for it

If something or someone is *due any second*, it means the event or person will arrive very shortly.

Done   In progress

Done

In progress

Done

In progress

Done

In progress

Done

In progress

Done

In progress

Done   In progress

B Listen again. Is the task already done, or in progress? Circle the correct answer for each.

3

Listen and circle the correct response.

1. Yes, I did.   Yes, I will.   **4.** Yes, she did.   She wasn't in.

2. The store was closed. Yes, I will.   **5.** Yes, I will.   No, I didn't.

3. The line was busy.   Yes, he did.   **6.** I'm just checking.   It's on your desk.

4

A Listen. What is the main focus of the statement? Circle the correct answer.

1. Place   Date   Time   **4.** Place   Date   Time

2. Place   Date   Time   **5.** Place   Date   Time

3. Place   Date   Time

B Listen again and practice.

Could you fax this for me?   **47**

5

A Listen to Jenny's voice mail and check (✔) the things her boss asks her to do.

Listen for it

Mess up is an informal way of saying "make a mistake."

☐ reconfirm flight ☐ copy speech ☐ call a doctor for boss

☐ change flight ☐ print out itinerary ☐ send assistant to pharmacy

☐ reserve aisle seat ☐ call boss's wife

☐ get file ☐ send fax to boss's wife

B Read the statements. Listen again and circle **T** for *True* or **F** for *False*.

1. Her boss is going to Seoul. T F 4. He is staying in a hotel. T F

2. He has to give a speech T F 5. He needs to take along his medicine. T F

3. His wife is going with him. T F 6. His wife's name is Connie. T F

6

A Listen and check (✔) the things Jenny did.

reconfirm flight _____

reserve aisle seat _____

make copies of speech _____

fax itinerary to wife _____

pick up medicine _____

B Listen again. Why did some things not get done?

_____

_____

_____

7

Listen and circle the answers that are right for you.

1. Yes, a lot of time. Not too much time. Not really.

2. All the time. Occasionally. Never.

3. Sure, it's easy. I think so. I have no idea.

4. No problem. I probably could. Definitely not.

5. Yeah, lots. Quite a lot. Hardly any.

Your Turn! 🔊

Asking for information and making excuses

- Did you **do everything on the list** yesterday?
  Yes, everything's done.
  No, I didn't get everything done.
- Did you **print out my itinerary**?
  Sorry, **the printer was broken**.
- What about **the calls I asked you to make**?
  None of the people were available.
- Did you have time to **mail those letters**?
  Yes, **I mailed them at lunch**.
  Sorry, I forgot all about it.
- Where's the **package** I asked you to **pick up**?
  I'll **pick it up tomorrow**.
- Why didn't you **send these faxes**?
  I didn't have enough time.

To Do List

Try this . . .
Imagine your partner works for you. Make a list of things your partner was supposed to do for you yesterday but didn't. Find out why these tasks weren't done. Switch roles.

In Focus: *Houston, we have a problem*

Few would deny that technology has brought huge benefits to humanity in terms of better health, improved communications, and a better quality of life for millions. Without advances in medical technology, we might never have found cures for once dreaded diseases like polio and tuberculosis. Without breakthroughs in engineering, we might never have reached outer space or even conquered the skies. But what about the other side of the issue? Some experts claim that the ill effects of our growing dependence on technology could actually outweigh the positive results. As examples, they typically cite the toll on the environment often attributed to the rise in use of the automobile, and the decline of community and literacy resulting from the introduction of television. *What do you see as the pros and cons of technological progress? Do you have any concerns that technology might actually be diminishing our quality of life?*

Even if there's a negative side to advances in technology, you can't stop progress.

Technology is meant to bring us closer together but sometimes I think it pushes us farther apart.

There's nothing wrong with technology, only with the way people use it.

UNIT 10

We spent three days in New York.

Goals
- Identifying tourist information
- Understanding descriptions of places

1

A Read the statements (1–5). Which of the places in the brochure is each person referring to? Number the places.

Highlights of New York City

🍎 **Empire State Building**
Still the most famous building in New York. A must for all visitors.

🍎 **Guggenheim Museum**
Designed by renowned U.S. architect Frank Lloyd Wright, this remarkable building houses one of the world's great collections of modern art and sculpture.

🍎 **St. Patrick's Cathedral**
This gothic-style cathedral is the headquarters of the Roman Catholic Church in New York.

🍎 **Central Park Zoo**
Located on the East Side at 65th Street, this zoo has many architectural innovations. Make sure you visit the indoor rain forest.

🍎 **Chrysler Building**
When built in 1930, it was the tallest building in the world. It's still considered New York's finest by many people.

🍎 **Barnes and Noble Bookstore**
An ornate iron and glass building that began life in 1913 as a bookstore and has been a bookstore ever since.

🍎 **Carnegie Hall**
Built in 1891, this is one of the most popular concert halls in New York.

🍎 **Rockefeller Center**
Art Deco business and entertainment center popular with tourists and office workers alike.

🍎 **Grand Central Station**
Constructed between 1903 and 1913, this is a wonderful place to just wander around.

1 Oh, it's not just a place where you catch trains. It's much more than that.

2 A new Picasso exhibition just opened there. Do you want to go?

3 My wife and I saw Pavarotti perform there last year—the acoustics are amazing.

4 It's a great place to take the kids—they really love the primate enclosure.

5 My friend and his wife had their marriage ceremony there last year.

B **Brainstorm!** Work with a partner. What other famous places do you know in the United States? Which would you most like to visit? Make a list and rank the places (1 = most want to visit). Share your list with another pair.

50

2

A **Listen to the conversations. Which places are the people talking about? Number the places (1–3). One is extra.**

Statue of Liberty

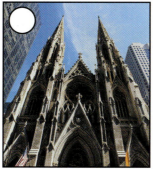
St. Patrick's Cathedral

Empire State Building

Grand Central Station

B **Listen again. Write the words in each conversation that helped you decide.**

1. _____ 2. _____ 3. _____

3

A **Listen to the conversation. Are the statements (1–4) true or false? Circle *T* for *True* or *F* for *False*.**

> ### Listen for it
> *Ends up at . . .* is another way to say *finishes at . . .*

1. Cindy works for a tour operator.   T   F

2. Both tours take three hours.   T   F

3. The woman plans to take a tour next week. T   F

4. The woman decides on the afternoon tour.   T   F

B **Listen again and write *A* for places on the Architectural Tour and *C* for places on the Cultural Tour.**

Empire State Building	_____	Central Park Zoo	_____	Carnegie Hall	_____
Guggenheim Museum	_____	Chrysler Building	_____	Rockefeller Center	_____
St. Patrick's Cathedral	_____	Barnes and Noble Bookstore	_____	Grand Central Station	_____

4

A **Intonation in tag questions can vary according to how sure the speaker is. Listen to the examples.**

Ex. It's on Fifth, isn't it? (sure/confirming)   It's on Fifth, isn't it? (not sure/questioning)

Listen to the questions. Circle *S* for *Sure* or *NS* for *Not Sure*.

1. It's pretty new, isn't it?	S NS	4. You're going tomorrow, aren't you? S NS
2. That's it over there, isn't it?	S NS	5. They've bought tickets, haven't they? S NS
3. She's been before, hasn't she?	S NS	6. We're meeting at two, aren't we? S NS

We spent three days in New York.   **51**

5

A
A tour guide is describing a tour through New York. Listen and trace the route on the map.

Listen for it

Feel free (to . . .) is an informal way to allow or encourage someone to do something.

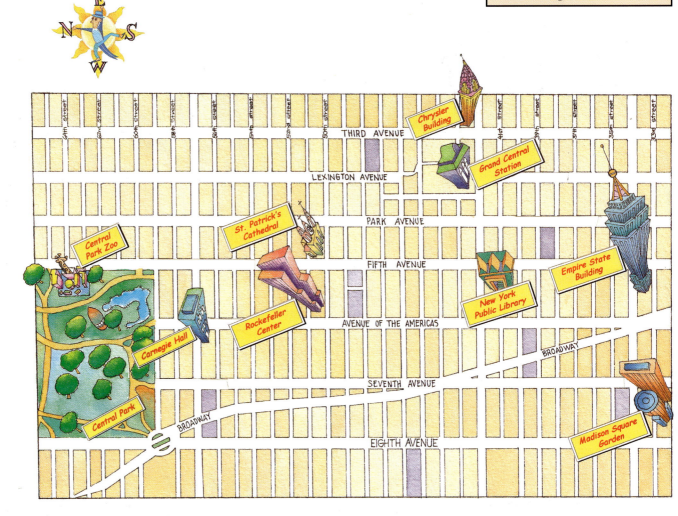

B
Listen again and check the route you have drawn.

Which tour did Jane pick? _____

6

Listen and circle the answers that are right for you.

1. Yes, I'd love to.   Yeah, I wouldn't mind.   No, I don't like tall buildings.

2. Yes, definitely.   Maybe.   No, I'd go somewhere else first.

3. Yes, it probably is.   It might be. I don't know.   No, I disagree.

4. So would I.   I'm not sure.   No, I'd rather do something else.

5. Architectural.   Cultural.   I wouldn't take a group tour.

Your Turn!

Asking for and giving tour information

- What kind of tour are you going to take?
  It's **an afternoon coach tour**.
- Where does your tour start?
  It begins at **the Empire State Building**.
- Then where do you go?
  We travel down **Fifth Avenue** to **Central Park**.
- What are you going to see along the way?
  We'll stop off at **the Rockefeller Center** and **St. Patrick's Cathedral**.
- Where does the tour finish?
  We end up **on Broadway**. We're going to **see a play there**.

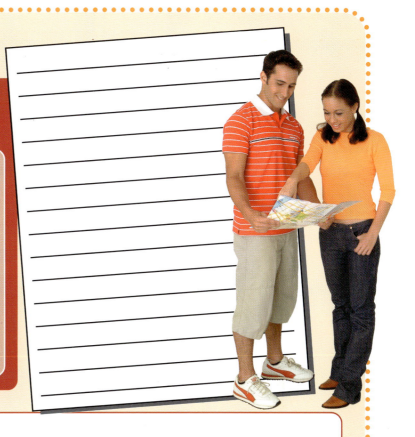

Try this . . .

Bring a map of your city to class (or use the map on page 52). Plan a tour. Note the tour details. Give the map to another pair. Tell them about the tour. They will ask questions and trace the route. Switch roles.

In Focus: *A landmark remembered*

Few people will forget where they were when they heard the news of the World Trade Center attack on September 11th, 2001. Completed in 1976, the twin towers of the World Trade Center were one of the most recognizable landmarks in the New York City skyline. Designed by Japanese-American architect Minoru Yamasaki, the WTC was the highest skyscraper in New York, a giant steel, concrete, and glass structure with 110 floors in each tower and more than nine million square feet of office space. Yamasaki hoped his most famous creation would become "a living symbol of man's dedication to world peace;" although now destroyed, the symbol lives on in people's memories. *The World Trade Center attack shocked people around the world. What news events have shocked or surprised you? Do you remember where you were or what you were doing when you heard the news?*

I heard about the World Trade Center attack on the radio. I just couldn't believe it.

One of my friends told me about the death of Princess Diana. That was a real shock.

I was a 15-year-old girl in 1970 when the Beatles split up. I remember crying when I heard the news.

We spent three days in New York.

Review

Units 6–10

1

A Listen to the conversations and number the pictures (1–3). One picture is extra.

B Listen again and circle the words you hear.

beautiful	fabulous	convenient	exciting	friendly
fantastic	interesting	adorable	expensive	spacious

2

A Listen. Check (✔) the things Sandy needs to do.

- ☐ call airline
- ☐ cancel newspaper
- ☐ reconfirm flight
- ☐ put sweater in bag
- ☐ buy some medicine
- ☐ book taxi
- ☐ get extra cash from ATM
- ☐ call the man's mother

B Listen again. What is happening at these times? Fill in Sandy's planner.

3:30	
4:00	
5:30	

3

A Listen. What is Steve's job? Check (✔) the correct answer.

- [ ] swimming instructor
- [ ] fitness instructor
- [ ] lifeguard
- [ ] security guard

B Listen again. What are the pros (good points) and cons (bad points) of Steve's job? Complete the chart.

Pros	Cons
1.	1.
2.	2.
3.	3.

4

A Listen to the guide describing a tour of Sydney. Which places are included on today's tour? Check (✔) them.

- [ ] Olympic Site
- [ ] Darling Harbour
- [ ] Harbour Bridge
- [ ] Centrepoint Tower
- [ ] Paddington
- [ ] Chinatown
- [ ] Opera House
- [ ] Botany Bay
- [ ] Bondi Beach
- [ ] The Rocks
- [ ] Royal Botanic Gardens

B Listen again. Where and at what time does *tomorrow*'s tour start? Where and when does it finish?

Starting time: _____ Place: _____

Finishing time: _____ Place: _____

5

Listen. A friend is going on vacation and wants you to do some things for her. Circle the more polite response.

1. Sure—anything.   It depends on what they are.

2. I'm sorry, but I'm not going downtown today.   No, it isn't very convenient.

3. Oh, all right. If you don't have the time.   I'll try. Let me have the details.

4. No. I don't like dogs.   I'm sorry, but I really can't.

5. No problem—if it's every couple of days.   You don't need me to do it every day, do you?

6. No, it's OK. Don't bother.   OK. Have a great time.

UNIT 11

Let's get take-out.

Goals
- Understanding restaurant descriptions
- Identifying food orders

1

A Read the restaurant review and circle the words that refer to food or cooking.

Food for Thought
by Beth Mitchell, *Times Food Critic*

A Taste of China in City's Heart

Hungry for a Chinese feast but worried about prices only an emperor could afford? Then good fortune has come your way in the form of Wong's Chinese Restaurant, a newly-opened dining venue in the downtown area.

During a recent visit for dinner, I had a chance to sample Wong's diverse range of authentic Chinese dishes. Menu selections include traditional favorites like beef with broccoli, steamed fish, stir-fried vegetables, lemon chicken, and a wide variety of Chinese dumplings—all high quality dishes offered at surprisingly low prices. Where else but Wong's could you get delicious garlic prawns for just $5.00?

The other dishes on the menu are just as affordable. My dinner companion and I sampled the corn soup, steamed lobster, roasted pork, and the lamb with green onions and were pleasantly surprised at how little it cost us. We topped things off with a generous serving of fried rice and washed it all down with cups of hot tea.

Simply put, Wong's Chinese Restaurant serves up great dishes at very reasonable prices. And the atmosphere is just as warm and inviting as the food.

Wong's is located at 735 Bleeker Street. Dress is casual and reservations are recommended.

B Use words from the restaurant review to complete the chart.

Meat	Vegetables	Seafood	Cooking methods
beef	*broccoli*	*fish*	*steamed*
lemon chicken	stir-fried vegetable	steamed fish	roasted
pork	green onions	lobster	fried.
lamb.		garlic prawn.	
beef			

C **Brainstorm!** Work with a partner. Add at least two more words to each column of the chart.

2

 A Listen to the radio ads. What types of food are being described? Number the pictures (1–3).

Listen for it

Pull up a chair is an informal way of inviting someone to join you.

Chinese

Italian

Mexican

 B Listen again. Complete the ads with the restaurant names, addresses, and phone numbers.

Authentic Mexican Food
Super value meals and best quality service. Find us at:
_____
Tel: _____

Old-Style Italian Eatery
"Pasta and pizza like Mamma used to make!"
Conveniently located at:
_____
Tel: _____

Chinese Food Restaurant
City's #1 Chinese Buffet
as Voted by the Editors of Dining Out magazine
Location:
_____
Tel: _____

 3

 A Listen and circle the best response.

1. Sure. How much is it?	Sure. What time is it?	✓Sure. What would you like?
2.✓No, just chicken and pork.	Chicken or pork?	There's chicken in it.
3. Do you have any soup?	How's the soup?	✓Would you like anything else?
4. Just vegetables.	✓Stir-fried or steamed?	Do you like vegetables?
5. Five of them.	✓Five dollars.	Table for five?

4

A In spoken English, words such as *any, anything,* and *anyone* are sometimes reduced when they follow *get* or *got*. Listen to the example. Then listen and circle *Reduced* or *Not Reduced*.

Ex. Didn't you get any napkins?   Didn't you get'ny napkins?

1. Reduced	Not Reduced	**4.** Reduced	Not Reduced
2. Reduced	Not Reduced	**5.** Reduced	Not Reduced
3. Reduced	Not Reduced	**6.** Reduced	Not Reduced

 B Listen again and practice.

Let's get take-out.

A Look at the menu and listen to the conversation. Check (✔) the items Joe and Margaret ordered.

Listen for it

That should do it is an informal way of saying you don't need anything else.

Wong's Chinese Restaurant
MENU

Soups

Corn Soup $1.50

Hot & Sour Soup $2.00

Wonton Soup $1.50

Seafood

Garlic Prawns $5.00

Steamed Lobster $6.00

Fried Fish $4.50

Steamed Fish $5.00

Meat Dishes

Lemon Chicken $4.50

Ginger Chicken $5.00

Beef in Oyster Sauce $5.00

Beef with Broccoli $5.50

Sweet & Sour Pork $5.00

Roasted Pork $4.50

Lamb w. Green Onions $5.00

Chinese Dumplings

Various kinds from $1.50

Vegetable Dishes

Stir-fried Vegetables $3.50

Steamed Vegetables $3.50

Rice & Noodles

Steamed Rice $2.00

Fried Rice $3.50

Fried Noodles $3.00

Drinks

Hot Tea $0.50   Soft Drinks $1.00

B Listen again and check your answers. How much will they have to pay? $ _____ .

6

A Look at the menu in Task 5 and circle the items Joe and Margaret received.

B Listen again and circle *True*, *False,* or *Unknown*.

1. Joe ordered sweet and sour pork.	True	False	Unknown
2. Margaret is allergic to pork.	True	False	Unknown
3. Joe doesn't eat lamb.	True	False	Unknown
4. Margaret will just eat the steamed rice.	True	False	Unknown
5. They're going to eat out instead.	True	False	Unknown

7

Listen and circle the answers that are right for you.

1. It's good.	I'm not sure.	I don't care for it.
2. I think so, too.	It's alright.	I don't think so.
3. That's true.	I don't know about that.	I disagree.
4. Yes, there is.	I don't know.	No, there's not.
5. Sure you can.	Maybe. I'm not sure.	No, I don't think so.

Your Turn! 🔊

Placing and taking orders for take-out food

- **Wong's Chinese Restaurant**, how may I help you?
  I'd like to place an order for delivery, please.
- Do you have **chicken** dishes?
  Yes, we have **lemon** and **ginger** chicken.
- Could you give me two orders of rice, please?
  Sure. Would you like **steamed** or **fried rice**?
- What kind of **pork** dishes do you have?
  We have **sweet and sour** and **roasted pork**.
- How much is the **steamed lobster**?
  The **steamed lobster** is **$6.00** per order.
- What's the grand total on that?
  That'll be **$13.50** plus tax and delivery charge.

Try this . . .

Read the menu in Task 5. Work with a partner. Take turns being an employee of Wong's Chinese Restaurant and a customer phoning to place a food order for delivery. Note your partner's order.

In Focus: *Is meat murder?*

Just as in the animal kingdom of carnivores, omnivores, and herbivores, humanity can be divided into those who eat meat and those who don't. The broad term for people who don't eat meat is vegetarian, but there are differences in eating habits even among the members of this group. Some people call themselves vegetarians because they avoid red meat, mainly beef. Others choose not to eat any kind of fish or meat. Strict vegetarians, sometimes called "vegans," also prefer not to eat animal products like eggs or dairy foods. Why do people become vegetarians? Some do it out of concern for their health, some because of their religious beliefs, and others for humanitarian reasons. *Is vegetarianism very popular in your country? If you're not a vegetarian, do you think you would ever consider giving up meat? Why or why not?*

It's not easy being a vegetarian in this country since so many popular dishes contain meat.

I don't think I could become a vegetarian because I'd miss eating hamburgers and steak.

I became a vegetarian after I heard that raising cattle harms the environment.

What do you do to relax?

Goals
- Identifying stress-related problems
- Identifying methods of relaxation

1

A Read the survey and check (✔) the answers that are true for you.

Are You Stressed?

Strongly disagree ←——→ Strongly agree

	1	2	3	4	5	
1	☐	☐	☐	☐	☐	I sometimes have trouble sleeping and feel tired during the day.
2	☐	☐	☐	☐	☐	I find I'm working really hard but not achieving enough.
3	☐	☐	☐	☐	☐	I often forget appointments, deadlines, and personal items.
4	☐	☐	☐	☐	☐	I sometimes get angry with my friends and argue with them.
5	☐	☐	☐	☐	☐	I don't have much time to relax or do things that I like.
6	☐	☐	☐	☐	☐	I often get ill with things like colds, headaches, and upset stomach.
7	☐	☐	☐	☐	☐	I often have to study or work late into the evening.
8	☐	☐	☐	☐	☐	I don't have much time to eat, and I often eat fast food.
9	☐	☐	☐	☐	☐	I worry a lot about my weight and looks.
10	☐	☐	☐	☐	☐	I often leave assignments to the last minute and then rush them.
11	☐	☐	☐	☐	☐	I often get annoyed at little things like missing a bus.
12	☐	☐	☐	☐	☐	I think I'm more stressed than most other people.

B Count up your score, and see how stressed you are on the scale below.
Share your answers and score with a partner.

12–20:	You're lucky—you have a pretty stress-free life!
21–40:	You need to take care with your stress levels, but overall you're OK.
41–60:	You'd better find some time to relax—you're way too stressed!

C Brainstorm! Work with a partner. What things stress you out?
What are some ways to reduce stress? Make a list.

2

A Joe is taking the survey in Task 1. Listen and circle his responses on the survey form.

B Listen again to check your answers. What is Joe's stress level score? _____

3

A Joe is asking his friends for advice. Listen and match each piece of advice to the correct person. One is extra.

Lisa

Ken

Geri

(Take a vacation)   (Try self-hypnosis)   (Go for a massage)

(Go to a spa)   (Listen to music)

(Go to bed early)   (Give up smoking)   (Attend a yoga class)

B Listen again and circle the activities Joe plans to do.

4

A Is the intonation rising or falling? Listen and circle (↗) or (↘).

1. Could you teach me how to do it?   ↗ ↘
2. Where did you go on vacation?   ↗ ↘
3. What do you do to unwind?   ↗ ↘
4. Can I ask you a few questions?   ↗ ↘
5. Would you say you're pretty healthy?   ↗ ↘
6. How did you get started in that?   ↗ ↘

B Listen again and practice.

What do you do to relax?   **61**

A Look at the ad for Spa Heaven. Listen and circle the things Joe asks about.

Spa Heaven
Your Downtown Oasis

Is the pace of modern life stressing you out? Do you find you have no time to unwind and relax? Take a break from the daily grind at Spa Heaven, a newly-opened relaxation complex in a convenient downtown location. Spa Heaven is the perfect place to get away from it all. Come and revitalize yourself at our city oasis!

Our wide range of relaxation facilities includes:

Fitness Our extensive fitness center offers state-of-the-art strength training equipment. Next to the gym is our aerobics room, where classes are held every morning. Come and experience a total work-out!

Sports Spa Heaven's sporting facilities include two 25-meter swimming pools. Jacuzzi facilities and steam and sauna rooms are also available. Tennis fans will appreciate our six full-size tennis courts, including two indoor courts—so you can play whatever the weather!

Meditation In this oasis of quiet, you'll be able to find a place of total relaxation. Yoga classes are offered every day, to help you achieve a perfect balance of body, mind, and soul.

Massage Our individual massage rooms provide total privacy. Feel the everyday effects of modern-day stress disappear at the hands of our experienced masseurs. We offer a wide range of professional massage techniques including reflexology, aromatherapy, and shiatsu.

Acupuncture If you suffer from aches, tense muscles, or tiredness, try our acupuncture sessions. The traditional techniques of acupuncture are painless and soothing. They will help reduce tension and bring you deep relaxation.

Call 555-7967 for membership details.

B Listen again. Note on the ad the cost of the activities Joe is interested in.
Which activity does he decide to do?

_____

> ### Listen for it
>
> If a person says he or she *could really do* with something, it means he or she would really like to have or do it.

6

A Listen and circle the answers that are right for you.

1. Yes, I do.   No, I'm about average.   No, I'm pretty relaxed.

2. Yes, I think so.   Not really.   Not at all.

3. I watch TV.   I do some exercise.   I talk with friends or family.

4. Sure I would.   Maybe. I'm not sure.   No way!

Your Turn!

Asking and talking about stress and relaxation

- What's the most stressful thing for you?
  I worry about **money** the most. **I never seem to have enough.**
- I think **school problems** are the most stressful, like **preparing for exams**.
  Yeah, **exams** really stress me out.
  Really? I think **relationship problems** are the worst.
- So how do you deal with stress?
  I find that **doing exercise** helps me to **focus and overcome stress.**
  What usually works best for me is to **talk over my problems with my family or friends.**
- What do you do when you want to unwind?
  For me, the best way to unwind is to **relax at home and just watch TV.**

Try this . . .

What causes you stress? Complete the survey by ranking the items 1–5 (1 = causes the most stress). Interview your partner and complete his/her results. How does he or she deal with stress?

	You	Partner	Partner's solutions
Problems with study and school			
Things that happen at work			
Money worries			
Relationship problems			
Health worries			

In Focus: *Putting your best foot forward*

Massage has long been a popular method of alleviating stress. A wall painting found in a tomb at Saqqara, Egypt, clearly shows that foot massage, also known as reflexology, was practiced more than 4,000 years ago. Reflexology is a natural healing art based on the principle that there are reflexes in the feet, and also in the hands and ears, that correspond to every other part of the body (see picture). It is believed that by applying pressure to these reflexes, tension can be reduced and body circulation improved. *Do you believe that traditional methods such as reflexology can improve health and reduce stress? What do you think are the most effective ways to fight stress?*

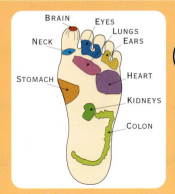

BRAIN EYES LUNGS EARS NECK STOMACH HEART KIDNEYS COLON

I don't believe that having someone pressing my feet will reduce stress in my life. Taking a vacation is the only way I can really relax!

I think that traditional techniques like reflexology and acupuncture still have value today. People have been practicing them for so long because they really work.

This is the news.

Goals | • Understanding news reports
• Understanding sequence of events

1

A Match each headline with the correct category.

1. Sports   3. Crime   5. International News

2. Business   4. Local News

World Cup winners return home

Dollar strengthens as other currencies fall

Mayor says he won't quit
Mayor Walters stated yesterday the [...] intends to f[...]

UN Security Council meets on crisis

The Sunday Times
Houses destroyed in weekend storms

Universities told to raise fees

Miss World Contest turns ugly

Bank robbers escape with $1M

Stock markets lower at year end

Olympic skater nabbed for drug use
Controversial Olympic [...] Monic[...] Ker[...]ton was

B Choose one of the headlines. What would you like to know about the story? Make a list of questions.

Who? _____   Where? _____

What? _____   Why? _____

When? _____   How? _____

C **Brainstorm!** Work with a partner. Think of another headline for each of the categories in Task A.

A Listen and match the radio news items with the newspaper headlines in Task 1.
Number the headlines (1–5).

B Listen again. Write the words that helped you decide.

1. _____

2. _____

3. _____

4. _____

5. _____

Listen for it

Late-breaking is a word used in news reports to indicate a story or fact that has just been reported.

A Listen and number the photos (1–3) in the order you hear the news reports.
One photo is extra.

_____   _____   _____   _____

_____   _____   _____   _____

B Listen again. What are the basic facts of each news item? Write details under each photo.

A Listen. Insert commas (,) when you hear the announcers pause.

1. The suspect who was serving time for armed robbery escaped last Thursday in a laundry truck.

2. A fight which broke out during the first round of judging has led to renewed calls for the event to be called off.

3. The earthquake which measured 6.5 on the Richter Scale caused extensive damage.

4. The president who is currently touring Asia rejected calls for him to return home.

5. The Security Council decision which is currently under debate is likely to cause problems.

B Listen again and practice.

5

A **Listen and number the pictures (1–5).**

> **Listen for it**
>
> *Made off with* is an expression used in reports of robberies that means *escaped with*.

B **Listen again and check your answers. Repeat the story to a partner.**

6

A **Listen to Nick tell his coworker about the robbery. What information does he get wrong? Fill in the chart.**

	Where?	What?	How many robbers?	Who was hurt?	What happened?
News account	Center Street	Jewelry store	Three	Woman bystander	Caught by police
Nick's account					

B **Listen again and check your answers. Where does he think the robbers are now?**

7

Listen and circle the answers that are right for you.

1. TV and radio.   The Internet.   Newspapers.

2. Every day.   Sometimes.   Never.

3. Very interested.   Somewhat interested.   Not at all.

4. Yes, I do.   Yeah, a little.   Not really.

5. Very important.   Kind of important.   Not important.

Your Turn! 🔊

Asking and talking about news stories

- Which types of news interest you most?
  I'm interested in **the local news** because **I like to know what's going on right here.**
- Is there any type of news that doesn't interest you at all?
  I'm not really interested in **watching sports or reading about them.**
- What has been the biggest news story so far this year?
  I think it was the **controversy over the national elections.**
- Which is the best source for news: TV or newspapers?
  I prefer **newspapers**, because **you don't get enough information on TV.**

Try this . . .
Ask a partner the questions below. Add a question of your own. Ask follow-up questions to find out more information.

News Survey	Details
1. What types of news interest you most?	_____
2. What types of news do not interest you?	_____
3. What's the biggest news story now?	_____
4. Which is the best source for news?	_____
5. _____?	_____

In Focus: *All the news that's fit to print*

"The real trends in journalism in the past thirty years have been toward gossip, sensationalism, manufactured controversy, and . . . the dumbing down of most American journalism."
—former *Washington Post* reporter Carl Bernstein

For years, journalists in America and elsewhere have been complaining about the so-called "tabloidization" of the media: the shift toward new and more entertainment-oriented kinds of news, and the placing of a greater emphasis on pictures than on words in both newspapers and TV news broadcasts. Opponents of "tabloidization" argue that it limits their ability to keep the public well-informed on important issues. On the other side are those who say the modern media is only giving the people what they want. *Do you think the media in your country does a good job of reporting the news? What types of stories would you like to see more often? What types would you like to see less often?*

Most people want a mix of "heavy" and "light" news and I think the media provides that.

I'd like to see less local news coverage and a greater focus on international stories.

I think the media focuses too much on the bad things and ignores all the good news that happens each day.

This is the news.

67

UNIT 14

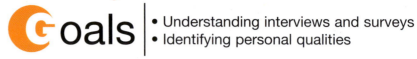
I really admire her.

Goals
- Understanding interviews and surveys
- Identifying personal qualities

1

A How would you describe these famous people? Use the words in the box, or your own ideas.

beautiful	funny	wise	calm	energetic
angry	intelligent	ambitious	humorous	original
dignified	talented	serious	courageous	generous

Whoopi Goldberg

_____

_____

Britney Spears

_____

_____

Bill Gates

_____

_____

Nelson Mandela

_____

_____

B Which of the people above do you admire most? Why? Share your reasons with a partner.

C **Brainstorm!** Work with a partner. What other people would you describe using the words in Task A? Make a list.

2

A Listen to three conversations. Which of the celebrities in Task A are the people talking about? Number the names (1–3). One is extra.

☐ Britney Spears   ☐ Bill Gates

☐ Whoopi Goldberg   ☐ Nelson Mandela

> **Listen for it**
>
> *Oh my God!* is an informal expression often used to express surprise or disbelief.

B Listen again. Write the words that helped you decide.

1. _____

2. _____

3. _____

3

A Listen. Check the words used to describe each person.

Alan

sensitive ☐   serious ☐

generous ☐   intelligent ☐

Tracy

angry ☐   ambitious ☐

friendly ☐   humorous ☐

Jenny

caring ☐   calm ☐

wise ☐   angry ☐

Greg

energetic ☐   original ☐

creative ☐   talented ☐

B Listen again. What do the speakers admire most about each person? Circle one adjective for each.

4

A Listen to the conversation and circle the correct answers.

1. This is . . .

   a. a face-to-face interview.   **b.** a survey.   **c.** a phone interview.

2. The woman is . . .

   a. an artist.   **b.** a reporter.   **c.** a photographer.

3. The man's main inspiration comes from . . .

   a. nature.   **b.** other exhibitions.   **c.** his family.

B Listen again. What does the man say about the artist Jackson Pollock? Why does he admire him?

_____

I really admire her.

5

A Read the statements (1–5). Then listen and circle *T* for *True* or *F* for *False*.

Listen for it

If someone *stands out*, it means he or she is special or different in some way.

1. Alvin is a soccer fan from Singapore.   T   F

2. Alvin is a supporter of England.   T   F

3. Alvin has met David Beckham.   T   F

4. Alvin thinks Ronaldo is the best Brazilian player ever.   T   F

5. Alvin attended the 2002 World Cup.   T   F

B Listen again. According to Alvin, what are three qualities that Ronaldo and Beckham have in common?

Both are . . .

1. _____

2. _____

3. _____

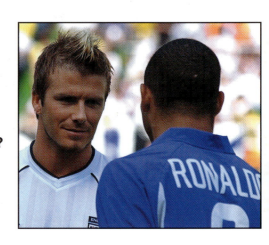

6

A Listen to the example. Pay attention to the stressed syllables.

Ex: He's cour-**a**-geous.   He has a lot of **cour**-age.

Listen and circle the stressed syllables.

1. o-rig-i-nal   o-rig-i-nal-i-ty   4. sen-si-tive   sen-si-tiv-i-ty

2. gen-er-ous   gen-er-os-i-ty   5. en-er-get-ic   en-er-gy

3. cre-a-tive   cre-a-tiv-i-ty   6. hon-est   hon-es-ty

B Listen again and practice.

7

Listen and circle the answers that are right for you.

1. Entertainers.   Sports stars.   Political and business leaders.

2. Intelligence.   Originality.   Honesty.

3. Sense of humor.   Sensitivity.   Creativity.

4. Yes, I agree.   I'm not sure.   No, I think other things are more important.

Your Turn!

Talking about people you admire

- Do you know anyone who's really **creative**? The most **creative** person I know is **my cousin. She's a talented artist.**
- Which person you know has the **best sense of humor**? My friend **Alan** is the **funniest** guy I know—**he's always playing jokes**.

- How about the most **energetic** person? I think maybe **my uncle. He's 50 years old but he still likes to go diving!**
- Who's the most **ambitious** person you know? I guess it's **Jenny—she really wants to be union president.**

Try this . . . Complete the survey with the names of people you know. Tell your partner. Ask about the people your partner has listed. Find out why your partner chose each person.

Who is the most . . . person you know?

	You	Your partner / details
creative		
humorous		
energetic		
intelligent		
ambitious		

In Focus: *The importance of being honest*

In a recent survey conducted by *USA Weekend* magazine, U.S. teenagers were asked about the things they most admire in other people of their own age. The most highly admired quality was revealed to be honesty, followed by sense of humor, intelligence, self-confidence, and kindness. Students also said they admired people who are good at sports, physically attractive, popular, and rich. When asked who was the biggest influence in their lives, the majority of respondents said that their parents were the most important influence, followed by girlfriend/boyfriend and teacher. Twenty-one percent of respondents stated that celebrities were a major influence. *Do you agree that honesty is the most admirable quality in a person? In what situations might it be OK to be dishonest?*

In some cases it's OK to be a little dishonest—like if a store clerk gives you too much change and you keep it.

I think you should always be honest, no matter what. Otherwise, you'll get into trouble.

I think kindness and generosity are more important than honesty.

Where does it hurt?

Goals
- Identifying medical problems
- Understanding medical consultations

1

A Read the list of symptoms in the doctors' notes. What diagnosis would you give? Match an illness with each set of symptoms. One is extra.

Personal info.
- *Name* - *medications*
- *Age* - *allergies*
- *phone #3*
- *Insurance*
- *Address*
- *sickness*

✱ *Symptoms*
   :problems

✱ *previous experience*

✱ *Diagnosis*
   Treatments

✱ *medicine (prescription)*

| appendicitis | cold | measles | flu | tonsillitis |

Glenmore Healthcare Center
Complete Medical Care for Families

Attending Physician: P. Chandra

Patient Reports:

Very high temperature; three days ago, red rash appeared on face, soon spread over entire body

Diagnosis

Dr. Edward Kincaid, M.D.
General Practitioner

- Patient complains of vomiting
- Loss of appetite
- Very high fever
- Sharp pains in right side of stomach

Diagnosis _____

Dr. Joanna Lin, M.D., M. Med (Ped)
Consultant Pediatrician

Patient (9 years old) has mild fever, very sore throat. Finds it hard to swallow food.

Diagnosis _____

From the Desk of:
Dr. Jacob Edelman, M.D.
Family Physician

General Symptoms

Congestion
Sneezing
Headache
No Fever

Diagnosis

B What's your medical history? Complete the survey.

1. How often do you get sick?

   never   1–2 times a year   3–4 times a year   Other: _____

2. Which of the following illnesses or medical problems have you had?

   flu   tonsillitis   measles   appendicitis   broken arm or leg   Other: _____

3. What things do you do to keep in good health?

   _____

C **Brainstorm!** Work with a partner. Make a list of other illnesses you know besides those above. What are the symptoms?

2

A Alan is talking to a receptionist at a doctor's office. Listen and complete the form.

<table>
<tr><td colspan="2">

✚ Medical Report

Official Report
</td></tr>
</table>

Name: _Allen Whitaker_
Address: _#385 A Bell st._
City: _Oakside_
Phone: _555-9009_
Date of Birth: _May 24 1958_

Health Insurance No.: _78524-601C_
Reason for Visit: _stomach pain_
Medical History: _appendix_
Taking Medication ☐ Yes ☒ No
Allergies ☒ Yes ☐ No _peanuts_

B Listen again and check your answers.

3

A Three people are telling their doctors about different medical problems. Listen and write down the problems.

Jennifer	Problem: _sore throat_
	Information: _____
Sarah	Problem: _arm didn't move_ (fell out horse)
	Information: _x-ray. pick up the form_
Mandy	Problem: _temperatue. to throw up_
(3)	Information: _aspirin. water_

father. daughter. doctor

B Listen again. Write down any other information you hear about each patient's problem.

Listen for it

Ouch! is sometimes used to express sudden pain or displeasure.

4

A Listen to the doctors and patients from Task 3. Write down the doctor's diagnosis for each patient.

Patient	Diagnosis	
Jennifer		•
Sarah		•
Mandy		•

Treatment
• cast
• operation
• medication

B Listen again. What treatment does each doctor prescribe? Match each diagnosis to the treatment.

5

A Listen to the radio broadcast. Number the topics in the order the doctor talks about them (1–4).

Listen for it

Overdo means to do too much of something, such as dieting or exercising.

Dr. Bain's
E-Z Tips for Healthy Living

☐ Exercise _____

☐ Diet _____

☐ Smoking _____

☐ Sleep _____

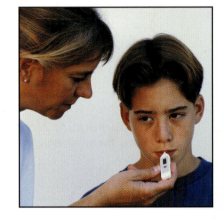

B Listen again and write down Dr. Bain's tips on maintaining good health.

6

A Questions using *or* can have rising intonation (open questions) or falling intonation (closed questions). Listen to the examples.

Example:
Have you been coughing [↗], or sneezing [↗]? Have you been coughing [↗], or sneezing [↘]?

1. Do you think it's broken, or not?

2. Have you been vomiting, or having bad headaches?

3. Does it hurt here, or here?

4. Are you taking any medication, like antibiotics or aspirin?

5. Did you hurt your hand, or your arm?

B Listen again and practice.

7

Listen and circle the answers that are right for you.

1. Yes, I do.   I'm all right.   Not, I don't think so.

2. Quite a lot, actually.   Some.   No, not very many.

3. Yes, every day.   A fair bit.   Not really.

4. Yes, I do.   Most days.   Definitely not.

5. Yeah, quite often.   Sometimes.   No, not very often.

Your Turn! 🔊

Asking and talking about medical conditions

- What seems to be the problem?
  My **head** hurts and I feel **really tired all the time.**
- How long has this been going on?
  It started about **three days** ago.
- Have you got any other symptoms?
  Yes, I also get **dizzy** sometimes and my **legs feel really weak.**
  No, those are the only ones.
- Do you have a sore **throat** or nasal congestion?
  Yes, my throat really hurts and my **nose** is **very stuffy**.
  No, I just have a **cough** and **pain in my chest.**
- What do you think the problem is, doctor?
  It sounds like you have **the flu.**
- What do you think I should do?
  Take this medicine and **get a lot of rest.**

Try this . . .
Imagine you're not feeling well. Describe your symptoms to a partner. Answer any questions about your illness. Your partner will make a diagnosis and prescribe treatment.

Medical Consultation Form

Symptoms: _____

_____

_____

Diagnosis: _____

Treatment: _____   Official Rep

In Focus: *You're making me sick!*

Have you ever received news that made you "feel like a million bucks?" Or felt physically ill upon ending a friendship or romantic relationship? If so, your experiences illustrate the impact emotions can have on a person's physical health. Medical experts have long noted the connection between physical and emotional health but many people remain skeptical that their feelings can actually make them sick. Some doctors argue that repressed emotions can help lead to the development of stomach ulcers and bladder infections among other ailments. On the other hand, there are also cases in which people given to excessive shows of emotion fall victim to diseases of the heart or circulatory system. *Do you think it's better to express your emotions openly or keep them bottled up inside? How do you feel about people taking medication to control feelings like anger and depression?*

It's always better to express yourself but you should be careful not to hurt others.

All you do when you show negative emotions is embarrass yourself.

I think people have to learn to control themselves without using drugs.

Review

Units 11–15

1

A Listen to the conversations and number the pictures (1–3).

Which conversation is a . . .

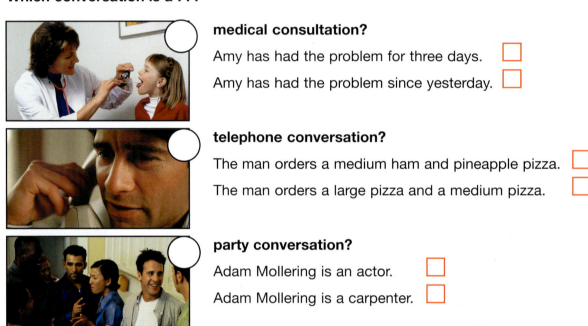

medical consultation?

Amy has had the problem for three days. ☐

Amy has had the problem since yesterday. ☐

telephone conversation?

The man orders a medium ham and pineapple pizza. ☐

The man orders a large pizza and a medium pizza. ☐

party conversation?

Adam Mollering is an actor. ☐

Adam Mollering is a carpenter. ☐

B Listen again and check the correct statement for each conversation.

2

A Listen and check the correct answer.

This is a . . .

☐ weather report.   ☐ news report.   ☐ traffic report.   ☐ sports report.

B Listen again and fill in the key information.

What is being described? _____

Where is it? _____

What advice does the person give? _____

3

 A Listen and complete the medical form.

Dr. Stephen Crouch, M.D. _____

Patient's name: _____

Symptoms: _____

_____

Diagnosis: _____

B Listen again and check your answers. What does the doctor recommend?

Doctor's recommendation: _____

4

 A Listen to the descriptions of the two spas. Fill in the information for each one.

The Pine Tree Spa

Location: _____

Facilities: _____

_____

Tel. No.: _____

The Oasis of Calm

Location: _____

Facilities: _____

_____

Tel. No.: _____

B Listen again to check your answers.

Which spa do you think Amanda should visit? Why? _____

5

 Listen and circle the answers that are right for you.

1. Either would be OK.   The vegetarian, please.   I'd rather have the seafood.

2. Yes, I agree.   I think both can be stressful.   No, work causes the most problems.

3. I look at the main news items.   I go straight to the sports pages.   I check the entertainment section.

4. Yes, I think they would.   I don't know about that.   Me? You've got to be kidding!

5. Seeing a doctor.   Going to the dentist.   They're about the same.

UNIT 16

You'll never believe this!

Goals
- Identifying main points of a story
- Recognizing surprising information

1

A Six of these headlines are true. Which ones? Share your ideas with a partner.

- ☐ Man escaping from jail eaten by crocodile
- ☐ Egyptian shepherd shot dead by one of his sheep
- ☐ Bungee-jumping monkey successfully leaps off cliff
- ☐ Empty room with light switching on and off wins art prize
- ☐ Polar bear steals toothpaste from tourist camp
- ☐ Helicopter attacked by flock of angry swans
- ☐ Exploding potato halts London ballet performance
- ☐ Horse elected mayor of U.S. town
- ☐ Mother awarded $780,000 for tripping over her own son

B **Brainstorm!** Work with a partner. For each headline you believe is true, tell what you think happened. List details for each story.

2

A Emily and Derek are talking about six stories. Listen and check (✔) the headlines in Task 1 they talk about.
Were your guesses correct?

B Listen again and answer the questions below.

1. On what date did the first incident take place? _____
2. In which country did the second story occur? _____
3. How old was the man in the third story? _____
4. What country was the man in the fourth story from? _____
5. In what kind of store did the fifth incident occur? _____
6. Where did the sixth incident take place? _____

3

A What are the people talking about? Listen to the conversations and number the events (1–5). One is extra.

◯ A wedding   ◯ A phone call   ◯ A dream

◯ A robbery   ◯ A meeting with an old school friend   ◯ A mother's first delivery

Listen for it

Get out of here! is a slang expression used between friends to express surprise.

B Listen again. What was unusual about each event? Write a few words for each.

1. _____
2. _____
3. _____
4. _____
5. _____

4

A Listen to the examples. Pay attention to the stressed syllables.

Examples: Are you **kid**ding?   You must be **jo**king!

Listen and underline the stressed syllables.

1. You've got to be kidding!
2. I can't believe it!
3. Are you serious?
4. Oh, really?
5. That's unbelievable!
6. You can't be serious!
7. That's incredible!
8. Get out of here!

B Listen again and practice.

You'll never believe this!   **79**

5

A Listen. What is this news report about?
Check the correct answer.

Listen for it

Breaking news relates to
something that has just
happened, or is
happening now.

☐ A rescue

☐ A swimming accident

☐ A helicopter crash

☐ A climbing contest

B Listen again and circle the correct answers.

1. Where did the incident take place?	on a cliff	in the sea	on a mountain
2. How old is Simon Tan?	6	15	25
3. Who was with Simon when he was found?	an older man	his father	an older woman

6

A Read the statements. Listen to the conversation and circle *True*, *False*, or *Unknown*.

1. Simon and Jake are related.	True	False	Unknown
2. The boy was going for a swim.	True	False	Unknown
3. It was a cold day.	True	False	Unknown
4. The man was scared.	True	False	Unknown
5. Jake called for help on his cell phone.	True	False	Unknown
6. The boy's parents offered a reward.	True	False	Unknown

B Listen again and check your answers. Note any other details you hear about the incident.

_____

_____

7

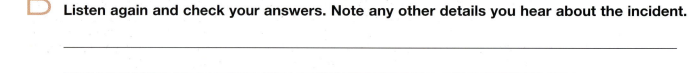

Imagine you were the person who called the rescue service. You are now being interviewed.
Listen and circle the best answer.

1. From the beach.	From the top of the cliff.	From the helicopter.
2. Just me.	About ten.	Maybe a hundred.
3. A boy and an older man.	Two older men.	Two young boys.
4. About five minutes.	About fifteen minutes.	About an hour.
5. Very scared.	Very brave.	Very interesting.

Your Turn!

Asking about and describing an incident

- Where did the incident take place?
  It took place at **a tourist camp on a Norwegian island.**
- Can you tell me what happened?
  Well, I was **sleeping in my tent** when I **heard a noise.**
- What did you see?
  I saw **a polar bear eating a tube of toothpaste.**
- You're kidding! How did you feel?
  I was **pretty scared, but it was kind of funny.**
- So, what happened then?
  Well, **the bear just ran off.**
- Why do you think **the bear took the toothpaste?**
  I don't know. Maybe **its breath smelled bad!**

Try this . . .
Choose one of the headlines on page 78. Imagine you were a witness to the incident. Your partner is a reporter and will interview you. Tell your partner what happened. Switch roles. Ask questions about the incident your partner witnessed and make notes.

In Focus: *Too good to be true*

An increasingly common phenomenon in the Internet age is the "urban legend," a type of story spread rapidly via the World Wide Web. Most urban legends share the following characteristics: they are humorous and/or shocking, they claim to be true, and they make a good story. A classic example of this phenomenon is the legend of alligators inhabiting the sewers underneath New York City. According to the legend, a number of New Yorkers brought back baby alligators from vacations in Florida, but grew tired of their pets and flushed them down the toilet. The alligators survived and bred and there is now a colony of crocodiles living under the city. Most regard the story as total fiction, but there are a few who claim it is true. Interestingly, in 1935, an 8-foot alligator was found down a manhole in East Harlem, New York, and nobody could prove where it came from. *Do you think most of what you read on the Internet is true? What are the most reliable forms of media?*

> I don't trust anything I read on the Web. I'd rather rely on TV and newspapers.

> I think you can find reliable information using the Internet, but only on the major news web sites.

> I think the information you get on the Web is more reliable. The newspapers and TV stations are too afraid to tell the truth!

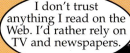

We want someone who's reliable.

Goals
- Identifying personal qualities
- Understanding interviews

1

A Look at the photos and read the words in the box. Which do you think are the most important personality traits for people in the jobs shown?

| dedicated | efficient | friendly | hardworking | honest | reliable |

teacher

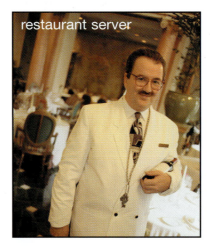

restaurant server

store clerk

bank teller

construction worker

B Think of occupations in which it's important to have the following personality traits:

1. independent: _____

2. curious: _____

3. cooperative: _____

4. brave: _____

C **Brainstorm!** Work with a partner. Make a list of other important personality traits for each of the professions in Task A.

2

A Listen to the conversation and match the personality traits to the correct people. Some words are used more than once.

Nancy

Paul

- hardworking •
- reliable •
- honest •
- curious •
- independent •
- friendly •
- efficient •
- dedicated •

John

Gina

B Listen again. What job do you think these people are being considered for? Check (✔) one column for each.

	Probably	Possibly	Probably not
Sales clerk			
Baby-sitter			
Police officer			
Singer			

Listen for it

To count on has the same meaning as *to rely on* or *depend on*.

3

A Listen to the example. Which questions have the same rhythm and stress? Listen and circle *Same* or *Different*.

Example: Why do you want the job?

1. Who do you want to see?   Same   Different
2. How did you get the job?   Same   Different
3. Why did you apply for the job?   Same   Different
4. How do you like the job?   Same   Different
5. Why do you want the position?   Same   Different

B Listen again and practice.

We want someone who's reliable.   **83**

4

A Tony and Lisa are discussing the qualities they want in a baby-sitter. Listen.
Which qualities are important? Which are not important?

Important	Not Important
1.	
2.	
3.	
4.	

B Listen again and check your answers.

Listen for it

If someone hasn't *shown up*, it means he or she hasn't arrived yet.

5

A Tony and Lisa are interviewing two people for the job. Listen and fill in the first two columns of the chart.

	Personality traits	Reason for applying	Experience	Reference letter
Tanya			Yes ☐ No ☐	Yes ☐ No ☐ From: _____
Carly			Yes ☐ No ☐	Yes ☐ No ☐ From: _____

B Listen again and complete the last two columns.
Who do you think would be best for the job? Why? _____

6

Listen and circle the answers that are right for you.

1. Yes, I would.	Most of the time.	Not really.
2. Yes, I was.	Sometimes.	Not especially.
3. Definitely.	Some people would.	I don't think so.
4. Very important.	Kind of important.	Not very important.
5. Absolutely not.	I might.	I probably would.

Your Turn!

Asking and answering job interview questions

- So, tell me, why do you want the job?
  I'm trying to **get some experience** and **save money for college.**
- Why do you think you're the right person for the job?
  I'm very **honest** and **hardworking**.
- Do you have any experience in this type of work?
  Yes, I do. I worked as an **assistant at a child care center** last year.
  No, I don't. But I **studied education at college**.
- What sorts of qualifications do you have?
  I have some experience as a **teacher**, I'm **trustworthy**, and I love **working with children**.

Try this . . .

Work with a partner. Think of a job you'd like to have. Make a list of the personal qualities and professional skills that qualify you for the job. Tell a partner. Answer your partner's interview questions. Switch roles.

In Focus: *Working to live, living to work*

In his best-selling 1987 book *The Third Wave*, futurist Alvin Toffler predicted huge growth in what he called "electronic cottagers," people who would work from home in a computerized information age. With the Internet Era now well underway, it appears that Toffler was right. According to Cyber Dialogue, a New York research and consulting firm, 15.7 million Americans worked at home during normal business hours in 1998, a figure that has no doubt grown significantly in the years since. How do most "telecommuters" feel about home-based employment? Surveys suggest the majority of these workers prefer this arrangement to the stress and inconvenience of a conventional working life. To quote a popular saying, more and more people seem to favor working to live over living to work. *What do you see as the advantages and disadvantages of working from home? Is this the type of working life you'd like to have in the future? Why or why not?*

I don't think I could work at home because there are too many distractions.

Most people would save a lot of time if they could do their jobs from home.

Traditional offices won't disappear because people like to work close to others.

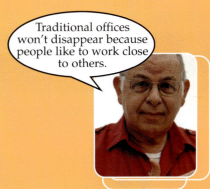

We want someone who's reliable.

Let's go to the movies.

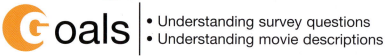oals

• Understanding survey questions
• Understanding movie descriptions

1

A Read the information about Harrison Ford. What kinds of movies are mentioned? Write the movie type next to each one. Underline the words that helped you decide.

Romantic comedy
Action/adventure
Suspense/horror
War
Science fiction

_____

_____

_____

_____

_____

MOVIE STAR BIO:
Harrison Ford

Born: *July 13, 1942*
Average salary per movie: US$25 million
Total box office revenue: US$5.65 billion
Previous occupation: *carpenter*

Career Highlights

Star Wars *(1977)* One of the most successful movies of all time. A sweeping space epic set in a distant galaxy, featuring special effects that are still impressive today. Led to two sequels and three prequels.

Apocalypse Now *(1979)* Francis Ford Coppola's masterpiece about the conflict in Vietnam. Renowned for its realistic battle scenes. Ford plays a U.S. colonel.

Working Girl *(1988)* A New York career woman (Melanie Griffith) falls in love with a charming businessman played by Ford. Also features a hilarious performance by Sigourney Weaver as Griffith's boss.

The Fugitive *(1993)* Ford plays Dr. Richard Kimble, a man on the run from the law for killing his wife. But Kimble is innocent, and is determined to find the guilty man. One of Ford's most exciting screen performances. Includes some great stunts and chase scenes.

What Lies Beneath *(2000)* In this spine-tingling thriller, Ford and Michelle Pfeiffer play a couple who move into a new house. Pfeiffer starts to see the ghost of a woman, and finds out that her husband has some dark secrets.

B Which of the words below might you use to describe each kind of movie? Write them in the columns.

funny	exciting	creepy	scary	charming	gory
tense	hilarious	entertaining	eerie	spectacular	violent

Action/adventure	Romantic comedy	Science fiction	Suspense/horror	War

C **Brainstorm!** Work with a partner. Make a list of at least five other kinds of movies. Think of an example for each and some words or phrases to describe them.

2

A Listen. What kinds of movies are the people talking about? Write the conversation number next to the movie type. One is extra.

_____ action   _____ comedy   _____ science fiction   _____ suspense

B Listen again. Did the people like the movies they saw? Circle *Yes*, *No*, or *Unknown*.

Conversation 1	Yes	No	Unknown
Conversation 2	Yes	No	Unknown
Conversation 3	Yes	No	Unknown

Listen for it

There you go can be used to point out when someone supports or reinforces something you've just said.

3

A Read the comments about the four movies listed below. Then listen to four reviews and match the comments to the correct titles.

"bad acting and bad jokes"   **Death Break**   "excellent camera work"

"a great group of actors"   **Alien Invasion**   "good story, great acting"

"violent and bloody"   **The Beguiled**   "disappointing"

"too unbelievable"   **The Crazy Professor**   "2.5 out of ten"

B Listen again and check your answers. How many points is each movie given?

Death Break: _____   Alien Invasion: _____   The Beguiled: _____   The Crazy Professor: _____

4

A Listen. Check (✔) the movies, theaters, times, and card names you hear.

Movie	Theater	Time	Card
☐ The Beguiled	☐ The Odeon	☐ 12:30	☐ Charge Plus
☐ The Crazy Professor	☐ New York Cinema	☐ 2:30	☐ Diners Express
☐ Alien Invasion	☐ ABC Theater	☐ 5:30	☐ Fastcash
☐ Death Break	☐ Vista Cineplex	☐ 8:30	☐ Mastercredit

B Listen again. What choices do Jenny and Bob make? Circle the correct answers.

Let's go to the movies.   **87**

5

A Jenny is taking part in a survey. Listen and check (✔) her responses.

Listen for it

Sci-fi is sometimes used as a short form for "science fiction."

≡: MediaWatch Surveys

Name: _____

- ○ more than once a month ○ several times a year
- ○ less than once a year

- ○ action ○ comedy ○ science fiction ○ suspense

- ○ friends ○ newspaper ○ TV

- ○ alone ○ with friends ○ with family

- ○ at the box office ○ by telephone

B Listen again and check your answers.

6

A Listen to the example. Then listen and underline the words that have the same stress as *exciting*.

Example: The film was really exciting.

1. We're going to see *The Beguiled* tomorrow.
2. *The Crazy Professor* starts at the Odeon this week.
3. *Alien Invasion* sounds like a waste of time.
4. Who's appearing in *Death Break*?
5. How do you generally find out about new movie releases?

B Listen again and practice.

7

Listen and circle the answers that are right for you.

1. Yes, I love them.   They're all right.   Not at all.
2. Sure, all the time.   Once in a while.   Never.
3. They're great.   I don't mind them.   I don't like them.
4. They're too high.   They're about right.   They're pretty low.
5. At the theater.   On video.   On TV.

Your Turn!

Asking and talking about movies

- How often do you go to the movies?
  I generally go about **once every two weeks** with **my boyfriend**.
- What's your all-time favorite movie?
  I guess it's *Philadelphia*. It's really **sad** and **it always makes me cry**.
- What are your favorite and least favorite kinds of movie?
  I like **action movies**, because they're **exciting**. I don't care much for **sci-fi** movies—I think they're **boring**.
- What was the last movie you saw?
  I saw *Psycho* on **TV last week**. It's **really scary**.

Moviegoer Profile

Basic Facts	More Information
1. Watches _____ movies per _____	_____
2. Favorite kind of movie: _____	_____
3. Doesn't like _____ movies	_____
4. Favorite movie star: _____	_____
5. Last movie seen: _____	_____
6. All-time favorite movie: _____	_____

Try this . . .
Use the prompts in the "Moviegoer Profile" to find out about a partner's taste in movies. Write your partner's answers in the spaces. Ask follow-up questions to find out more information.

In Focus: *A theater in the living room*

One of this era's most significant advances in consumer technology, the video cassette recorder (VCR) was introduced in the mid-1970s and, before its displacement by the DVD player, was among the most common electronic devices in North American homes. Although the VCR was initially seen as a means of recording TV shows for later viewing, it soon had an impact on moviemakers. Once seen as a threat to theaters, home entertainment gradually evolved into a major revenue source for the film industry and actually helped fuel the expansion of cinema chains. With both the feature film and home video industries now stronger than ever, there are still those who feel that the only way to truly experience a movie is on the big screen. *What are some of the things you like about seeing movies at the theater? What are some things you don't like? Give reasons.*

I don't think you need to see every movie at the theater, only blockbusters.

The problem with theaters is that some people like to talk during the movies.

Home video is a lot better because you can watch all the good parts again.

Let's go to the movies.

Is he ready to quit?

oals | • Understanding problems
• Identifying advice and solutions

1

A **Number the pictures (1–5) with the problems listed.**

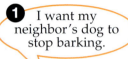 **1** I want my neighbor's dog to stop barking.

2 I want my husband to stop snoring.

3 I want to sleep at night.

4 I want my son home by 10:30 p.m.

 **5** I want to quit smoking.

B **Work with a partner. What advice would you give each person? Decide on a piece of advice for each problem.**

C **Brainstorm!** **Work with a partner. What are some other common problems for which people might need advice? Make a list.**

2

A Listen to people giving advice on solving different problems. What are the problems? Write them in the chart.

Problems	Key Words
1.	
2.	
3.	
4.	
5.	

B Listen again and write the key words that helped you decide.

3

A Listen as three people describe problems they are having. Match each person with the correct problem. Two of the problems are extra.

Listen for it

Heavy can be used to describe something a person does too much of, such as smoking or drinking.

(husband smokes too much)　　(can't afford a vacation)　　(can't sleep at night)

(husband drinks too much)　　(husband snores really loudly)

Mildred 　　**Rosie** 　　**Bill**

_____　　_____　　_____

_____　　_____　　_____

B Listen again. What advice does Dr. John give? Write the advice under each picture.

4

A Stress can be used to show annoyance. Listen to the examples.

Ex. 1 She missed her class. (not annoyed)　　**Ex. 2** She missed her class. (annoyed)

Listen and write *A* for *Annoyed* or *N* for *Not annoyed*.

1. _____ I asked you to quit.

2. _____ I wish you wouldn't snore.

3. _____ I wish that dog would stop barking.

4. _____ It's time to stop.

5. _____ I ordered fish.

B Listen again and practice.

Is he ready to quit?

5

A Listen to the conversation and check (✔) the correct answer.

Listen for it

Hold on a second can be used when you want someone to wait for a short while, or to pause while you make a point.

☐ The man is giving advice to his daughter before she gets married.

☐ The man is giving advice to his daughter before she leaves for college.

☐ The man is giving advice to his daughter before she starts a new job.

B Listen again. Circle the things they talk about.

| Dating | Travel | Housework | Money | Parties | Schoolwork | Children | Jobs |

6

A Anna has a problem. What advice does her friend give her? Listen and number the pictures in the order you hear the advice (1–6).

B Listen again and check your answers. What does Anna decide to do?

_____

7

Listen and circle the answers that are right for you.

1. Borrow the money.   Buy a cheaper one.   Save up for it.

2. Pretend you like it.   Say you don't like it.   Don't say anything.

3. Keep it.   Give it to the police.   Leave it there.

4. Talk to the person.   Tell security.   Ignore it.

Your Turn! 🔊

Asking for and giving advice

- What do you think I should do? **This guy keeps calling me on my cell phone.**
  If I were you, I'd **change my cell phone number.**
  You should just **tell him you don't want to date him.**
  Why don't you **meet up with him? He obviously likes you!**

- Do you think I'd **sleep better** if I **stopped drinking coffee?**
  Yes, that sounds like a good idea.
  No. If you want to **sleep better**, you should get **some exercise before you go to bed.**
  Have you tried **using earplugs**? That really works for me.

Try this . . .

Work with a partner. Think of a problem or dilemma. Join with another pair and ask them to suggest as many solutions as they can. Write them in the space on the right. Then switch roles.

In Focus: *Want some free advice?*

A huge best-seller upon its publication in 1988, Robert Fulghum's book *All I Really Need to Know I Learned in Kindergarten* has at its center the idea that wisdom does not come with age but "is there in the sandbox at nursery school." Among the pieces of advice for living Fulghum offers in the book are things like: "share everything," "play fair," "put things back where you found them," and "clean up your own mess." The author goes on to say that "look" is the most important word in the English language—"Everything you need to know is there somewhere"—and argues that people would be better off "if we all, the whole world, had cookies and milk about 3 o'clock every afternoon and then lay down with our blankets for a nap." *What do you think of the advice Fulghum offers in his book? Do you agree that most people have already learned everything they need to know about living life? Why or why not?*

He's got a point: if countries shared everything there would be an end to war.

It's a nice thought, but the problems of the world are more complicated than that.

If you think about it, we wouldn't need Greenpeace if everyone cleaned up their own mess.

Who did you see today?

Goals
: • Understanding social interactions
: • Identifying a sequence of events

1

A **Read the statements. Who are the people talking about? Number the photos (1–4).**

1 He told me the traffic's really bad downtown today.

2 He's usually really good, but last time he cut my ear by mistake!

3 It broke soon after I bought it, but he soon came round to fix it.

4 Whenever I go in there to buy something, he's always really friendly.

hair stylist

taxi driver

store cashier

bicycle repairman

B **How often do you talk to the people in Task A? How about the people listed below? Tell a partner. Use the words in the box.**

every day	most days	about once a week
about once a month		less than once a month

teacher or boss   best friend   bus driver   bank teller   family members

office or school secretary   doctor or nurse   dry cleaner   dentist

C **Brainstorm!** Work with a partner. What are some things you might say to each of these people? Make a list.

2

A Listen and number the pictures (1–4).

B Listen again and circle the words you hear.

> housework   homework   traffic   taxi   grease stain   gray stain   Taipei   Thailand

3

A Listen. Who is Joe talking about? Circle the correct answer.

1. His sister   His mother   **4.** His best friend   The dry cleaner

2. His secretary   His boss   **5.** A cashier   A TV repairman

3. His daughter   His wife

B Listen again and answer the questions.

1. Who is going to summer camp?   _____

2. What did Joe ask the person to do?   _____

3. What is Joe concerned about?   _____

4. What kind of event is Joe going to attend?   _____

5. What did Joe ask the person to do?   _____

4

A Listen and number the events in Joe's day in the order you hear them (1–6).

Listen for it

On the house is an informal way of saying something, usually a drink, is free of charge.

_____ Went to Tony's   _____ Took bus   _____ Picked up clothes

_____ Ate breakfast   _____ Went to clinic   _____ Got to office

B Listen again. Who did Joe speak to today? Complete the diagram.

Home	Downtown	Bus	Clinic	Work

Who did you see today?

5

A Listen to the teacher's questions and circle the best answer for each one.

Listen for it

Here we go is an informal way to say *Let's begin* or *Let's start*.

Person:	What you should say:
1. Bus driver	**a.** Can you tell me how much it is to King Street? **b.** Can you tell me when we get to King Street? **c.** Does this bus stop at King Street?
2. Doctor	**a.** I came here a couple of days ago. **b.** I took a couple of days off work this week. **c.** It's been going on for a couple of days now.
3. Restaurant server	**a.** I'll have the roast beef with green vegetables. **b.** What kind of vegetable dishes do you have? **c.** I only like certain kinds of vegetables.
4. Salesperson	**a.** It's too expensive. Do you have anything cheaper? **b.** It's too large. Do you have anything smaller? **c.** It's fine. I'll take it.
5. Bank teller	**a.** I'd like to cash this check, please. **b.** I'd like to check how much cash I have, please. **c.** I'd like to withdraw some cash from my account.
6. Travel agent	**a.** Can I book two places on the afternoon tour? **b.** What's included on the afternoon tour? **c.** How much is the afternoon tour?

B Listen again and check your answers.

 # 6

A Read the sentences. Circle the letters that have the same sound as *s* in *How's it going?* Then listen to check your answers.

1. My family's staying at some place on the coast.

2. That's what Sharon does every day.

3. We see them on Thursday evenings.

4. My husband's job takes him away a lot.

5. I just don't know what she does with her salary.

B Listen again and practice.

 # 7

Listen and circle the answers that are right for you.

1. Yes, pretty regularly.   I go, but not regularly.   No, I never go.

2. Yeah, I'd say so.   Almost every day.   No, not that often.

3. That would be great.   I wouldn't mind it.   I see them often enough.

4. More often than that.   That's about right.   Not that often.

Your Turn! 🔊

Talking to people in your social network

Example: Talking with a doctor
- Doctor, I have this really bad **sore throat**.
  OK. Do you have any other symptoms?
- Yes, I have **a fever** and I **feel really tired**.
  All right. Let me take a look at your **throat**.
- Do I need to **take some medicine**?
  Yes, I'll **give you some antibiotics**.
  No, just **get plenty of rest** and **drink a lot of water**.

Try this . . .

Work with a partner. Imagine you live in an English-speaking country. You need to talk with the people listed above. What might you say to each one? Make a list. Role-play the conversations. Switch roles.

doctor
_____
_____
salesperson
_____
_____
coworker
_____
_____
travel agent
_____
_____

In Focus: *Six degrees of separation*

Through a chain of only six friends, you can link yourself to anyone in the world. This is a claim that has become known as the "six degrees of separation" theory. The idea is that everyone in the world can be reached through a short chain of social acquaintances—you know someone in one place who knows a friend in another, who knows another person, and so on. The theory originated in 1967, when a Harvard social psychologist Stanley Milgram sent out 300 letters to people chosen at random in a city in Nebraska. Each person was asked to get the letter to a single "target" person in Boston; if they did not know the person, they could forward the letter to someone they knew (a friend, coworker, or casual acquaintance) who might be closer. The average number of steps in the chain of senders turned out to be six. Advocates argue that the theory is true also on a global scale, although it has not yet been proved. *Do you believe this theory? How many people do you think are in your own social network? How many would you regard as close friends?*

The world is getting smaller every day, so I think the theory's probably true.

I don't agree. There are still remote places in the world that you can't reach in just six steps.

With the Internet, my social network has expanded across the world, but I still just have a few close friends.

Who did you see today?

Review

Units 16–20

1

A Maggie is describing her day. Number the people (1–4) in the order she met them.

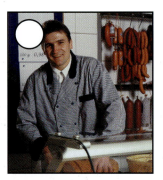   

B Listen again. Note the news that each person tells her.

1. _____   3. _____

2. _____   4. _____

2

A Three people are describing movies they have just watched. Listen and fill in the movie title and type for each person.

Name	Movie title	Type	Good points	Bad points	Rating
1. *Bill Hendrix*		___ sci-fi ___ action ___ comedy ___ suspense			___ Great! ___ So-so. ___ Terrible!
2. *Keri Yoon*		___ sci-fi ___ action ___ comedy ___ suspense			___ Great! ___ So-so. ___ Terrible!
3. *Helena Lopez*		___ sci-fi ___ action ___ comedy ___ suspense			___ Great! ___ So-so. ___ Terrible!

B What did the people think of the movies? Listen again and fill in the good and bad points, and the person's rating. Which movie would you be most interested in seeing?

3

A Listen. Jean is talking with someone from a job recruitment agency. Check (✔) the type of job they are talking about.

- ☐ designer
- ☐ office cleaner
- ☐ secretary
- ☐ manager
- ☐ computer technician

B Listen again. What type of person does Jean want to hire? Note the qualities she wants/doesn't want in the chart.

Wants someone who is . . .	Doesn't want someone who is . . .

4

A Jean is considering three people for the position in Task 3. Listen to what is said about them and make notes.

Tony

Marcia

Jill

_____   _____   _____

_____   _____   _____

_____   _____   _____

B Listen again and check your answers.

Who do you think would be the best person for the job? _____

5

A Listen to the psychology test and circle the answers that are right for you.

1. My girlfriend/boyfriend.   My husband/wife.   A close friend.

2. A small animal.   A medium-size animal.   A large animal.

3. I approach it slowly.   I attack it.   I don't do anything.

4. A small house.   A medium-size house.   A large house.

5. Paper.   Plastic.   Metal.

B Listen to what your answers mean. Do you agree with the interpretation?

Language Summaries

Unit 1

Asking and answering personal information questions
- What's your name? / Could I have your name please?
  Jill. My last name is Davis.
- Can you tell me where you're from? / What's your nationality?
  I'm from Canada.
  I'm Canadian.
- Where are you planning to stay in the United States?
  I'm staying at the San Francisco Marriott. It's on 4th Street.

Introducing yourself
- I'm Jim McGiven, by the way.
  Pleased to meet you, Jim.

Giving a message to someone
- Can you tell Professor Chen there's a call on line one in the airport office?

Asking someone for help
- Excuse me, could you help me? I need some help with this arrival card.
  Sure.

Thanking someone for their help
- Thanks very much for your help.
  You're welcome.

Handing an object to another person
- There you go. / There you are.
- Here you are. / Here you go.

Unit 2

Asking for and giving personal descriptions
- Could you describe him for me? / What's he like?
  He seems interesting. And he's pretty handsome.
  Well, he's intelligent, and he's very talented.
- What does he look like?
  He's kind of tall and average-looking.
- Does he have a beard or mustache?
  Yes, he has both. And he wears glasses.
- Is he tall?
  Not really. He's average height.
- How old is he?
  He's in his early fifties.
- Would you describe yourself as talkative?
  I guess I am.
  No, I'm a pretty quiet kind of guy.

Identifying personal preferences
- He's just my type.
- I love men with beards.
- What kind of person are you looking for?
  Well, I want someone who shares my interests.
  I'd like someone who's gentle and kind.

Asking about people's occupations
- What does he do?
  He's an engineer.

Informally introducing a topic
- So, tell me everything.
  What do you want to know?

Unit 3

Asking and talking about special events
- Have you been to a family event recently?
  Yes, I went to my cousin's wedding.
- What was the reception like? / How was the reception?
  Well, the food was really good.
- How many people turned up?
  I guess around two hundred. It was really crowded.
- So, was it fun?
  Yes, everyone enjoyed it.
  No, it was pretty boring actually.

Identifying people at an event
- Do you recognize everyone?
- Who's that in the yellow dress?
  Oh, that's Aunt Gertrude—from Chicago.
- Who's that woman over there with the long hair?
  That's Cousin Emily.

Starting and ending an informal conversation
- Hi, you're Rick, aren't you?
  Yeah, that's right. And you're Peggy Sue, aren't you?
- Hello, Corey, I haven't seen you in a long time.
  Yeah, it must've been, oh, twenty years.
- Well, it's great talking to you, but guess I should go and meet some relatives.
  OK. Great to see you, too.

Asking for clarification
- Oh, you mean the woman in the red dress?

Commenting on someone's appearance
- She looks fantastic for her age.
- Gee, she's so thin now!
- Wow! He's gotten so big.
- She's looking so old.
- Look how tall you are now!

Unit 4

Talking about school subjects and abilities
- What were your best subjects in high school?

My best subjects were math and science.

I was really keen on languages.

- Are you more interested in sciences or arts?
Oh, definitely sciences.
I guess I prefer arts.
- Which types of subjects interest you now?
I really enjoy computer science.
- How are you at science?
Not so good.
- What do you think your strengths are?
I'm good at science, and business studies.

Asking and talking about career preferences

- What sort of career are you interested in?
I'd like to be a computer programmer.
- Have you thought about working for a big software company?
Yes, I'd love to.
No, I'd prefer to work for a smaller company.

Informally finishing a set of instructions

- That's about it.
- Now, you know what you have to do?

Unit 5

Asking someone to wait while you are thinking

- Hold on.
- Let me think. / I'm thinking.
- Give me a minute.
- Just a minute. / Just a second.

Expressing surprise or disbelief

- Are you serious?
- You're joking! / You're kidding!

Saying that you don't know something

- I'm not sure.
- I've no idea.
- I wouldn't have a clue.

Asking and talking about a trip

- So, where did you go?
We took a trip to South America.
- How long did you go for?
We went for two weeks.
For about a fortnight.
- What countries did you visit?
We traveled through Brazil and Argentina.
- What did you do there?
We visited Iguazú Falls, and then traveled to Buenos Aires
- So what was the most exciting thing you did?
Going up the Amazon was the highlight of the trip.

Unit 6

Asking about and describing homes

- How many rooms does it have?
There are sixteen rooms altogether.
- Does it have a swimming pool? / Is there a pool?
Yes. There's a pool in the backyard.
No, but there's a patio.
- Is it near to public transportation?
There's a subway nearby. It's really convenient.

Describing problems with a house

- The front door needs to be repaired
- It needs to be fixed.
- This cupboard is broken.

Inviting someone into your house.

- Come on in.

Unit 7

Apologizing for being late

- Hi. Sorry I'm late.
That's OK.

Discussing and bargaining for consumer goods

- Can I interest you in an MP3 player?

That looks good. How much is it?
No, thanks. I've already got one. / No thanks, I'm not interested.
- These gold bracelets are just $35 each.
Would you take $30? / I'll give you thirty for it.
- I can let you have the watch for $95.
OK. It's a deal.
Sorry, that's too much.
Do you have anything cheaper?
Could you give me a discount?

Drawing someone's attention to something

- Hey, take a look at this jewelry. / Look at this.

Unit 8

Asking about and describing jobs

- What are the main job responsibilities?
The job mainly involves doing medical exams and prescribing medicine.
- Do you have to use any special equipment?
I use a lot of medical instruments and medicines.
- What kinds of clothes do you wear at work?
I always wear a white lab coat and rubber gloves.
- What's the best part of the job?
The best part is helping sick pets and making people happy.
- About how much does the job pay?
Anywhere from about $40,000 to $60,000 a year.

Asking if someone is ready

- OK, then, all set?

Unit 9

Asking for information and making excuses

- Did you do everything on the list yesterday?
Yes, everything's done.
No, I didn't get everything done.

- What about the calls I asked you to make?
  None of the people were available.
- Did you have time to mail those letters?
  Yes, I mailed them at lunch.
  Sorry, I forgot all about it.
- Why didn't you send these faxes?
  I didn't have enough time.

Asking someone to do something
- Can you do a few things for me?
- Can you call the airline?
- Make sure they give me an aisle seat.
- Could you make two copies of my speech?

Making a suggestion
- Look, why don't you stop on the way to the airport?
  I guess I'll have to try.

Wishing someone luck
- Have a great trip.
- I hope the speech goes well.

Unit 10

Asking for tour information
- What kind of tour are you going to take?
  It's an afternoon coach tour.
- Where does your tour start?
  It begins at the Empire State Building.
- Then where do you go?
  We travel down Fifth Avenue to Central Park.
- What are you going to see along the way?
  We'll stop off at the Rockefeller Center and St. Patrick's Cathedral.
- Where does the tour finish?
  We end up on Broadway.
- How long does it take?
  It takes about three hours.

Using tag questions to get confirmation
- That's it over there, isn't it?
- We're meeting at two, aren't we?

Using tag questions to keep a conversation going
- I'd love to go up the Empire State Building, wouldn't you?
- New York must be the most interesting city in the world, don't you think?
- I'd spend most of my time in New York shopping, wouldn't you?

Unit 11

Placing and taking orders for take-out food
- Wong's Chinese Restaurant, how may I help you?
  I'd like to place an order for delivery, please.
- Do you have any chicken dishes?
  Yes, we have lemon and ginger chicken.
- Could you give me two orders of rice please?
  Sure. Would you like steamed or fried rice?
- What kind of pork dishes do you have?
  We have sweet and sour and roasted pork.
- How much is the steamed lobster?
  It's $6 per order.
- What's the grand total on that?
  That'll be $13.50 plus tax and delivery charge.

Telling someone that you are very hungry
- I'm starved. / I'm starving.
- I'm so hungry.

Asking someone what they would like to eat
- What do you feel like having?

Identifying unknown food dishes
- What's this?
  It looks like sweet and sour pork.
- This looks like lobster.

Unit 12

Saying that you would like to have or do something
- I could really do with a massage.

Talking about stress and relaxation
- What's the most stressful thing for you?
  I worry about money the most. I never seem to have enough.
- I think school problems are the most stressful, like preparing for exams.
  Yeah, exams really stress me out.
  Really? I think relationship problems are the worst.
- So, how do you deal with stress?
  I find that doing exercise helps me to focus and overcome stress.
  What works best for me is to talk over my problems with my family.
- What do you do when you want to unwind?
  For me, the best way to unwind is to relax at home and just watch TV.

Giving and receiving advice
- You know what you should do? You should go on a vacation.
  Oh, I'd love to, but I can't afford the time.
- Why don't you try going to bed earlier?
  Actually, that's a pretty good idea.
- I think you should try self-hypnosis.
  I don't know. I just don't think it's for me.
- You know what I think? You should try yoga.
  That's a good idea. / That sounds good.

Encouraging someone to try something
- You should give it a go.
  No. I don't think so.
  Yeah, maybe I will.

Unit 13

Asking and talking about news stories

- What types of news stories interest you most?
  I'm interested in the local news because I like to know what's going on right here.
- Is there any type of news that doesn't interest you at all?
  I'm not really interested in watching sports or reading about them.
- What has been the biggest news story so far this year?
  I think it was the controversy over the national elections.
- Which is the best source for news: TV or newspapers?
  I prefer newspapers, because you don't get enough information on TV.

Unit 14

Asking about personal qualities

- What was he like?
  He was really dignified.
- What do you think of her?
  I think she's so funny.
- What do you like most about Alan?
  Hmm. I like his intelligence.

Congratulating someone

- Congratulations on the exhibition.
  Thanks very much.
- You must be very pleased.
  Yes, I am.

Expressing surprise or disbelief

- Oh, my God!
- Oh, my goodness!

Talking about people you admire

- Do you know anyone who's really creative?
  My cousin. She's a professional artist, and she's really talented.
- Who's the most ambitious person you know?
  I guess it's Jenny—she wants to be the student union president.

Unit 15

Arriving at an appointment

- Hi. I have an appointment with Dr. Lin.
  OK. Please take a seat over there, and the doctor will be with you shortly.

Asking and talking about medical conditions with a doctor

- What seems to be the problem?
  My head hurts and I feel really tired all the time.
  My throat really hurts, and my nose is very stuffy.
- How long has this been going on?
  It started about three days ago.
- Do you have any other symptoms?
  Yes, I also get dizzy sometimes, and my legs feel really weak.
  No, those are the only ones.
- Does it hurt when I touch here?
  Yes. Ouch!
  No, not so much.
- What do you think the problem is, doctor?
  It sounds like you have the flu.
- What do you think I should do?
  Take this medicine and get a lot of rest.

Unit 16

Expressing surprise

- Get out of here!
- You've got to be kidding!
- I can't believe it! / That's unbelievable!
- Are you serious? / You can't be serious!
- That's incredible!
- Oh, really?

Asking about and describing an incident

- Where did the incident take place?
  We were at a tourist camp in the Arctic.
- Can you tell me what happened?
  Well, I was sleeping in my tent when I heard a noise.
- What did you do?
  I looked out of my tent and saw a polar bear eating a tube of toothpaste!
- So what happened then?
  The bear just ran off.

Unit 17

Identifying personal qualities

- What can you tell me about John?
  Well, he sees like a friendly guy, but he doesn't seem very reliable.
- Nancy gives the impression of being someone who's efficient and reliable.

Expressing reservations about someone

- The only problem is he doesn't seem especially reliable.
- I don't know if we could count on him.
- She doesn't seem that interested in learning new things.
- The only concern I have is that she might get bored.

Expressing necessity

- They'd have to be reliable.
- We need to be able to trust them.
- Honesty is definitely important.

Asking and answering job interview questions

- So, tell me, why do you want the job?
  I'm trying to get some experience and save money for college
- Why do you think you're the right person for the job?
  I'm very honest and hardworking.
- Do you have any experience in this type of work?
  Yes, I do. I worked as an assistant at a child care center last year.
  No, I don't. But I studied education at college.

Unit 18

Responding to survey questions
- Excuse me. We're doing a survey on movies, and we'd like your opinion.
  OK. Sure.
  What would you like to know?

Making a suggestion
- Feel like seeing a movie?
  Yeah, sure. What's playing?
- How about seeing the new comedy at the Cineplex?
  Well, how about seeing a suspense movie instead?

Asking and talking about movies
- How often do you go to the movies?
  I generally go about once every two weeks with my boyfriend.
- What kinds of movie do you like?
  I like action movies, because they're exciting. I don't care much for sci-fi movies—I think they're boring.
- Would you recommend that movie? I heard it was really good.
  Oh yeah, you have to see it.
  No, I thought it was pretty boring.

Unit 19

Asking for and giving advice
- I've got a big problem and I need your advice.
- What do you think I should do? This guy keeps calling me on my cell phone.
  If I were you, I'd change my cell phone number.
  You should just tell him you don't want to date him.
  Why don't you meet up with him? He obviously likes you!
- Do you think I'd sleep better if I stopped drinking coffee?
  Yes, that sounds like a good idea.
  No. If you want to sleep better, you should get some exercise before you go to bed.

- Have you tried using earplugs? That really works for me.
  That's not a bad idea.

Starting a conversation
- Listen, . . .
- You're never going to believe this, but . . .

Asking someone to speak more slowly
- Whoa! Slow down.

Unit 20

Asking about someone's day
- How was your day?
  It was terrible. / Terrible.
  Pretty good. How about you?
  It was just one of those days, you know?

Complaining about an unfortunate event
- They ruined my jacket.
- This guy ended up cutting my ear.
- I ended up spending an hour in the clinic.
- I missed the big meeting.

Reporting what people said
- She said that she wanted to see the grandkids before they went off to summer camp.
- I asked her where she thought she was going dressed like that.
- He said I could pick it up on Friday, but then he told me it wasn't ready.
- I called him up and asked him if he would come and fix it.

Listening Skills Index

Self-Study Practice Units

Welcome to the Self-Study Practice section of *Listen In.* This section of the book will give you extra practice with the target language and listening strategies used in the main units of *Listen In.* In order to complete the Self-Study Practice section, you need to use the Self-Study Practice CD on the inside back cover of this book.

The Self-Study Practice section is made up of 20 separate units. Each one-page unit has the same title, goals, and target language as one of the 20 main units of *Listen In.* The units in the Self-Study Practice section should be completed one at a time, and only after you have covered the material in the matching main unit in class.

Each unit in the Self-Study Practice section consists of two tasks. The listening passage for each task is recorded on a separate track of the Self-Study Practice CD. See page 128 for a full listing of the CD tracks.

Here is what to do for every unit in the Self-Study Practice section:

Task 1, Part A: There are six questions or statements on the Self-Study Practice CD for this section. For each one, you will find three possible responses listed on the page. Read the list of responses and then listen to the CD. Decide which is the best response for each question or statement and circle the letter (a, b, or c).

For example, you hear:
1. *Excuse me. Are you Jason Lee?*

You see:
1. a. Nice to meet you, Jason.
   b. No, I'm Terry Phillips.
   c. Hi, Mr. Lee.

The best response is *No, I'm Terry Phillips.*, so for this question you should circle "b."

Task 1, Part B: Listen to the questions or statements again, along with the correct response to each one. Check to make sure your answers are correct.

Task 2, Part A: The listening passage is a longer dialog or monolog, such as a conversation, an announcement, or a radio broadcast. First, read the instructions and the questions you need to answer. Each unit features one of five question types: (1) Listen and circle the best answer, (2) Listen and circle *T* for *True*, *F* for *False*, or *U* for *Unknown*, (3) Listen and match, (4) Listen and complete the sentences, and (5) Listen and number. Think about what kind of information you will need to listen for. Then listen and complete your answers.

Task 2, Part B: Carefully read the instructions. Think about what type of information you need to listen for (names, descriptions, locations, etc.) and how you need to fill in your answers (filling in a chart, map, menu, survey, etc.). Play the dialog or monolog in Part A again and complete your answers.

Some listening tips:
- Complete the Self-Study Practice section in a quiet place with no distractions.
- Try to predict the words you need to listen for and make a list before you begin.
- Don't try to understand every word, just listen for the information you need.
- If you don't get all the information after listening twice, play the track again.

Good luck!

1
UNIT

Can I ask you some questions?

Student CD Track: **2**

A Listen and circle the best response.

1. **a.** Jim Jones.
   b. Yes, it's my first time.
   c. It's Jim.

2. **a.** Jones.
   b. No, that's my first name.
   c. Just call me Jim.

3. **a.** I'm from California.
   b. American.
   c. The United States.

4. **a.** I live in the United States.
   b. Bangkok.
   c. No, tomorrow.

5. **a.** Three days.
   b. The Sheraton Hotel.
   c. It's in San Francisco.

6. **a.** Yes, I've stayed here before.
   b. The Sheraton Hotel.
   c. Three days.

B Listen again and check your answers.

Student CD Track: **3**

A Listen and circle the best answer

1. **This is . . .**
   a. a survey.
   b. an interview.
   c. a face-to-face conversation.

2. **The people talking . . .**
   a. are coworkers.
   b. are friends.
   c. do not know each other.

3. **They are . . .**
   a. in an office.
   b. at an airport.
   c. at a hotel.

B Listen again and complete the information on the form.

Missing Baggage Details

Flight number: _____   From: _____

Passenger Name:

Mr./Ms. _____

Number of Bags: _____   Phone: _____

Local Address: _____

_____

UNIT 2

He's handsome and intelligent.

Student CD Track: 4

A Listen and circle the best response.

1. a. Yes, he is.
   b. I'd say I was a little shy.
   c. You would?

2. a. Yes, very.
   b. Yes, I think she is.
   c. Yes, I think I'm pretty intelligent.

3. a. He's kind of slender.
   b. Yes, he has a mustache.
   c. Yes. Is that a problem?

4. a. She's very smart.
   b. She's very tall.
   c. She likes clean-shaven men.

5. a. Yes, he is.
   b. Around 180 centimeters.
   c. Twenty-eight.

6. a. You're kidding!
   b. I love men with beards.
   c. I'm not sure.

B Listen again and check your answers.

Student CD Track: 5

A Read the statements. Then listen and circle *T* for *True*, *F* for *False*, or *U* for *Unknown*.

Claudia is intelligent.	T	F	U	She likes sports.	T	F	U
She likes people who are kind.	T	F	U	She likes the theater.	T	F	U
She's looking for someone who is handsome.	T	F	U	She is tall.	T	F	U

B Listen again, and complete the form with Claudia's information.

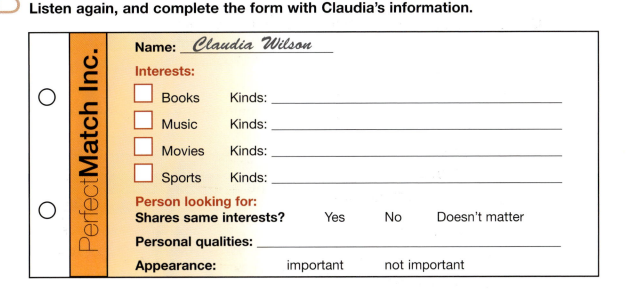

UNIT 3

That's the bride's mother.

TASK 1

Student CD Track: 6

A Listen and circle the best response.

1. a. Yeah, doesn't she look well?
   b. Her name is Gertrude.
   c. Yes, there is.

2. a. She does look young, doesn't she?
   b. She's looking at herself.
   c. I think she's 63 years old.

3. a. I like him a lot.
   b. Yes, let's say hello.
   c. Yes, Morty has two suits.

4. a. He's by the window.
   b. That's my brother, Leo.
   c. The one talking with my brothers?

5. a. Yes, she's really good-looking.
   b. She's pretty young.
   c. Yes, I think that's Emily.

6. a. His uncle's name is Joe.
   b. Yeah, Joe met my uncle.
   c. Yeah, I met him last year.

B Listen again and check your answers.

TASK 2

Student CD Track: 7

A Listen and match the person to the description.

Rachel •
John •
Simon •
Fiona •
Frank •
Judy •
Tom •

• . . . has put on weight.
• . . . has a mustache.
• . . . has lost weight.
• . . . looks friendly.
• . . . is pretty.
• . . . looks cute.
• . . . looks stylish.

B Listen again and find the people. Draw lines from the names to the correct people.

Judy •

Rachel •

John •

• Fiona

• Simon

• Tom

• Frank

NIT

I'm pretty good at math.

TASK 1

Student CD Track: **8**

A **Listen and circle the best response.**

1. **a.** Not so good.
   b. It's pretty difficult.
   c. I like it.

2. **a.** Not so good.
   b. Not bad.
   c. No, not really.

3. **a.** Not really.
   b. Not bad.
   c. No, I don't like it.

4. **a.** Something with computers.
   b. When I'm eighteen.
   c. About 5:00 in the afternoon.

5. **a.** I guess so.
   b. Every day.
   c. Oh, the usual stuff.

6. **a.** Oh, languages, definitely.
   b. Yes, they are.
   c. I'm not very good at math.

B **Listen again and check your answers.**

TASK 2

Student CD Track: **9**

A **Listen and circle the best answer.**

1. **John is talking to . . .**
   a. his dad.
   b. a teacher.
   c. an employer.

2. **John's dad thinks he should . . .**
   a. work with computers.
   b. study medicine.
   c. study languages.

3. **John's dad is . . .**
   a. a computer programmer.
   b. an engineer.
   c. a doctor.

B **Listen again and complete the chart.**

Name	Wants to be	Strengths	Weaknesses
John Lee			

Self-Study Practice

Where in the world is it?

Student CD Track: **10**

A Listen and circle the best response.

1. **a.** Australia
   b. Canada
   c. Japan

2. **a.** Asia
   b. Australia
   c. Africa

3. **a.** North Africa
   b. South America
   c. Eastern Europe

4. **a.** Australia
   b. The United States
   c. Brazil

5. **a.** The Indian Ocean
   b. The Pacific Ocean
   c. The Atlantic Ocean

6. **a.** The Philippines
   b. Denmark
   c. Mexico

B Listen again and check your answers.

Student CD Track: **11**

A Read the statements. Then listen and circle *T* for *True*, *F* for *False*, or *U* for *Unknown*.

The man and the woman went to Australia together.	T	F	U
Dave went to Australia on business.	T	F	U
He enjoyed his trip.	T	F	U
He went to the desert.	T	F	U
When he was in Cairns, he stayed on a boat.	T	F	U
He bought a lot of souvenirs.	T	F	U

B Listen again, and draw Dave's route on the map.

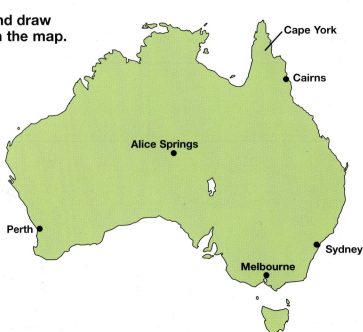

It has a great view of the ocean.

Student CD Track: **12**

A Listen and circle the best response.

1. a. It's not too far.
   b. The subway closes at 11.
   c. It's close to the park.

2. a. There are three bathrooms.
   b. Two large ones.
   c. In the basement.

3. a. I don't think so.
   b. Yes, you can play pool.
   c. That's true, but the sea is nearby

4. a. I'd like a sea view.
   b. That's OK.
   c. You can see the ocean from the back.

5. a. Yes, it's quite small.
   b. Yes, it's quite big.
   c. It could be, I guess.

6. a. We'll have it fixed.
   b. It's in front of the house.
   c. I'm glad to hear that.

B Listen again and check your answers.

Student CD Track: **13**

A Read the statements. Then listen and circle *T* for *True*, *F* for *False*, or *U* for *Unknown*.

1. Helen is talking to a real estate agent.   T   F   U

2. She is looking for a three-bedroom apartment.   T   F   U

3. The rent is more than $1,000 a month.   T   F   U

4. She wants a place that's quiet.   T   F   U

5. She decides to look at an apartment.   T   F   U

6. Helen decides to rent the place.   T   F   U

B Listen again. Which place are they talking about? Circle the correct ad.

Apartments for Rent

Two Bedroom Apt.

Spacious two-bedroom with balcony. Situated right in the heart of downtown city area. High floor, across from shopping mall. Near train station. Tel: 555-9967.

Fully Furnished Apt.

Fully furnished three-bedroom apt. for rent. Steps from university, public transportation. Avail. Dec 10th. Affordable rent. Call Jim at 555-3598.

Convenient Location

Conveniently located two-bedroom apt. for lease. Quiet suburban neighborhood, close to beach and major bus routes. Full facilities, sea views. Call 555-6298.

UNIT 7

How about a genuine gold watch?

TASK 1

Student CD Track: 14

A Listen and choose the best response.

1. a. I can make it cheaper.
   b. But it looks genuine.
   c. I already have one.

2. a. Thanks, but I don't wear them.
   b. Thanks, but I don't use them.
   c. I already have a suit.

3. a. Do they work?
   b. How much are they?
   c. Are they genuine silk?

4. a. Can I pay by credit card?
   b. Not much.
   c. I bought six pens.

5. a. What's your best price?
   b. I don't wear them.
   c. I can give you a great price.

6. a. Do you like jewelry?
   b. That's too much.
   c. I can give you a special price.

B Listen again and check your answers.

TASK 2

Student CD Track: 15

A Listen and complete the sentences:

1. Jenny has been _____.

2. She paid _____ for each item.

3. Tonight, she's going to a _____.

B Listen again. Which item will Jenny wear tonight? Check (✔) the correct item.

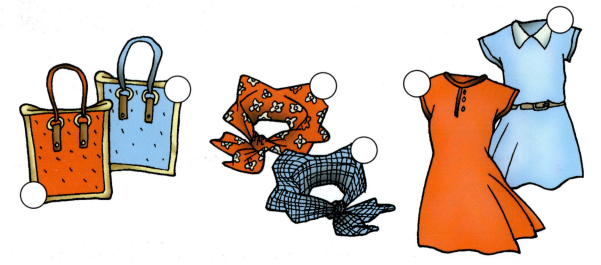

That's an unusual job.

TASK 1

Student CD Track: **16**

A Listen and circle the best response.

1. a. I took a part-time job.
   b. I prefer working outdoors.
   c. I love summer.

2. a. It's kind of boring.
   b. Working with people.
   c. Any job can be interesting.

3. a. Something part-time.
   b. I look at the ads in the newspaper.
   c. I'm working at the local pool.

4. a. It's interesting.
   b. Something part-time.
   c. Oh, job satisfaction.

5. a. Preferably weekends.
   b. Definitely.
   c. I work with a lot of people.

6. a. Something part-time.
   b. I enjoy my weekend job.
   c. I'd prefer evenings.

B Listen again and check your answers.

TASK 2

Student CD Track: **17**

A Listen and circle the best answer.

1. **Jake would like to . . .**
   a. work in a school.
   b. find a full-time job.
   c. find a part-time job.

2. **How many jobs are mentioned?**
   a. Two.
   b. Three.
   c. Four.

3. **Which job is Jake interested in?**
   a. The supermarket job.
   b. The lifeguard job.
   c. He isn't interested in any of the jobs.

B Listen again and fill in the form.

Job Search Details

Name: _Jake Campbell_ _____

Current Employment: student ___   self-employed ___   employee ___

Preferred Hours: weekdays ___   evenings ___   weekends ___

Preferred location: indoor ___   outdoor ___   doesn't matter ___

Prefers working with people?   yes ___   no ___   doesn't matter ___

Any qualifications? _____

UNIT 9

Could you fax this for me?

Student CD Track: 18

A **Listen and circle the best response.**

1. a. I've done it already.
   b. Call the airline.
   c. No, I didn't.

2. a. He wouldn't mind.
   b. Sure, I'll do it now.
   c. I would if I were you.

3. a. I invited my assistant.
   b. Can I be of assistance?
   c. OK. I'll tell her.

4. a. Sure, what's the number?
   b. Sure, I'll let you know.
   c. Sure, here you are.

5. a. That's right.
   b. I can't remember.
   c. The one I sent you yesterday?

6. a. Thanks a lot.
   b. I don't think he's in right now.
   c. He'll let you know.

B **Listen again and check your answers.**

TASK 2 **Student CD Track: 19**

A **Listen and circle the best answer.**

1. **This is . . .**
   a. a telephone conversation.
   b. an answering machine message.
   c. a public announcement.

2. **The person talking is . . .**
   a. Jenny's husband.
   b. Jenny's boss.
   c. Jenny's coworker.

3. **The person asks Jenny to . . .**
   a. do some things for him.
   b. do some things for her boss.
   c. do some things for her husband.

B **Listen again. Check (✔) the things Jenny has to do tonight.**

☐ collect medicine from pharmacy   ☐ reserve a hotel room

☐ send some faxes   ☐ make a phone call   ☐ reserve a flight

☐ buy something for dinner   ☐ reserve a seat at a restaurant

☐ buy a new fridge   ☐ pick up dry cleaning

We spent three days in New York.

TASK 1

Student CD Track: 20

A Listen and circle the best response.

1. a. Yes, that sounds great.
    b. Yes, I liked the museum.
    c. Yes, I've seen it.

2. a. I'd prefer we go today.
    b. I'd like to take a tour.
    c. I wouldn't like it.

3. a. I wouldn't either.
    b. I would, too.
    c. What was it like?

4. a. I think you'd like it a lot.
    b. I'd prefer the Architectural Tour.
    c. What's included on that?

5. a. No, I missed the bus.
    b. It gets to Stanley at 6:00.
    c. Yes, that would be fun.

6. a. Neither would I.
    b. So would I.
    c. Yes, so did I.

B Listen again and check your answers.

TASK 2

Student CD Track: 21

A Listen and circle the best answer.

1. The man and woman are . . .
   a. friends.
   b. husband and wife.
   c. brother and sister.

2. How long are they staying in Paris?
   a. Two days.
   b. Five days.
   c. Seven days.

3. What are they NOT planning to do tomorrow?
   a. See a dance show.
   b. Climb the Eiffel Tower.
   c. Visit a church.

B Listen again. Number the places (1–4) in the order they plan to visit them.

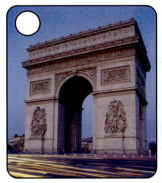
Arc de Triomphe

Louvre Museum

Eiffel Tower

Notre Dame Cathedral

UNIT 11

Let's get take-out.

Student CD Track: 22

A Listen and circle the best response.

1. a. Yes, something to eat.
   b. Why? Are you hungry?
   c. I can't decide.

2. a. It's a kind of seafood.
   b. It's 25 dollars.
   c. No thanks, I'm allergic to it.

3. a. No, I prefer it steamed.
   b. It's very cheap.
   c. No, I prefer it fried.

4. a. Fried noodles.
   b. That's right.
   c. I think it is.

5. a. Now, that's one thing I love.
   b. Sure, here's a fork.
   c. Oh, I love sweet desserts.

6. a. Yes, I do.
   b. No, I don't.
   c. I like them both.

B Listen again and check your answers.

Student CD Track: 23

A Listen and circle the best answer.

1. **The woman is . . .**
   a. ordering at a restaurant.
   b. ordering take-out.
   c. ordering dessert.

2. **How many dishes are mentioned?**
   a. Five.
   b. Six.
   c. Seven.

3. **The woman is ordering for how many people?**
   a. One.
   b. Three.
   c. Four.

B Listen again. Write the number of portions next to each dish the woman orders.

Wong's Chinese Restaurant Prices per individual portion

Meat

____ red roast pork	$5.50
____ ginger chicken	$5.80
____ honey-glazed chicken	$5.30
____ sweet and sour pork	$4.80
____ barbecued duck	$6.30

Seafood

____ stir-fried shrimp	$6.80
____ steamed lobster	$7.20

Rice and vegetables

____ steamed rice	$1.80
____ fried rice	$3.50
____ stir-fried vegetables	$5.00

What do you do to relax?

TASK 1

Student CD Track: 24

A Listen and circle the best response.

1. a. Stress causes headaches.
   b. I guess school does.
   c. Yes, it does.

2. a. I suppose so.
   b. Health is important.
   c. Don't worry about it.

3. a. I don't drink wine.
   b. By watching movies.
   c. Work is stressful.

4. a. I listen to jazz.
   b. Dancing is relaxing.
   c. So do I.

5. a. Yes, I am.
   b. I guess so.
   c. Quite healthy.

6. a. Pretty healthy, I'd say.
   b. I'm a student.
   c. Sort of.

B Listen again and check your answers.

TASK 2

Student CD Track: 25

A Listen and circle the best answer.

1. This is . . .
   a. an interview.
   b. a telephone conversation.
   c. a casual conversation.

2. The people talking . . .
   a. are sisters.
   b. are friends.
   c. do not know each other.

3. Erica's lifestyle is . . .
   a. very unhealthy.
   b. pretty healthy.
   c. very healthy.

B Listen again and fill in the survey for Erica.

1. What kinds of exercise do you do?	☐ Golf	☐ Running	☐ Swimming	☐ Other: _____
2. What do you do to relax?	☐ Movies	☐ Music	☐ Hanging out	☐ Other: _____
3 Which of the following do you eat?	☐ Meat	☐ Chicken	☐ Fish	☐ Vegetables
4. How often do you drink alcohol?	☐ Often	☐ Sometimes	☐ Never	
5. How often do you smoke?	☐ Often	☐ Sometimes	☐ Never	
6. When do you go to bed?	☐ Before 9:00	☐ 9:00–10:30	☐ 10:30–12:00	☐ After 12:00

13
UNIT

This is the news.

Student CD Track: 26

A Listen and choose the best response.

1. a. Yes, it was terrible.
    b. Yes, I read about it last week.
    c. I haven't been there.

2. a. Why did she do that?
    b. Did she lose anything valuable?
    c. Why, what was wrong with it?

3. a. It's pretty interesting.
    b. It's pretty steady.
    c. It's pretty boring.

4. a. Interesting, wasn't it?
    b. Yes, I met him yesterday.
    c. The president was on the news.

5. a. I'm going to watch it.
    b. Tell me what happened.
    c. We lost again.

6. a. There's going to be a big festival.
    b. I was downtown today.
    c. There was a robbery.

B Listen again and check your answers.

Student CD Track: 27

A Listen to the news reports and number the items 1–5 in the order that you hear them.

_____ Weather   _____ Sporting news   _____ Local news

_____ Economic news   _____ International news

B Read the statements. Then listen and circle *T* for *True*, *F* for *False*, or *U* for *Unknown*.

The Presidents of the United States and Russia met today.	T	F	U
The stock market fell.	T	F	U
People were injured in an accident.	T	F	U
Plans for the Grand Prix racing event have changed.	T	F	U
Tomorrow is Thursday.	T	F	U
It will be cold tomorrow.	T	F	U

I really admire her.

TASK 1

Student CD Track: 28

A Listen and circle the best response.

1. **a.** I think she's very talented.
   b. I'm afraid not.
   c. I think she's smart.

2. **a.** He is, isn't he?
   b. He's really smart.
   c. He's still thinking.

3. **a.** No, she's not here.
   b. Not recently.
   c. Yes, fascinating.

4. **a.** He likes playing golf.
   b. I don't like him much.
   c. He's an interesting character.

5. **a.** Thanks, that's kind of you to say so.
   b. I can't describe it.
   c. I'm not sure.

6. **a.** I love sleeping.
   b. I don't know. I just am.
   c. I guess it's interesting.

B Listen again and check your answers.

TASK 2

Student CD Track: 29

A Listen and circle the best answer.

1. This is . . .
   a. an interview.
   b. a telephone conversation.
   c. a casual conversation.

2. The speakers are . . .
   a. brother and sister.
   b. husband and wife.
   c. cousins.

3. They are talking about . . .
   a. famous family members.
   b. people in a magazine.
   c. personality traits.

B Listen again and fill in the survey for Sharon. Write each person's name and his or her relationship to Sharon.

Who is . . .

	Name	Relationship
① the funniest person you know?		
② the most energetic person you know?		
③ the most creative person you know?		
④ the most interesting person you know?		

Mr. McNeil

Sally

Debbie

Simon

15

UNIT

Where does it hurt?

Student CD Track: 30

A Listen and circle the best response.

1. **a.** I've been coughing.
   b. For about a week.
   c. Why, do you have a cold?

2. **a.** Yes, the pain is terrible.
   b. No, it's way over there.
   c. Do you think so?

3. **a.** It's a big problem.
   b. I have a bad cough.
   c. Yes, it is.

4. **a.** No, my hand.
   b. Yes, I can't stop sneezing.
   c. Yes, my foot hurts.

5. **a.** I think so.
   b. Yes, twice a day.
   c. No, we don't sell any.

6. **a.** That's great news.
   b. No problem.
   c. I'm sorry to hear that.

B Listen again and check your answers.

Student CD Track: 31

A Listen and circle the best answer.

1. **Sarah is talking to . . .**
   a. her boss.
   b. a doctor.
   c. a coworker.

2. **They are . . .**
   a. at the clinic.
   b. at home.
   c. at the office.

3. **Sarah will probably . . .**
   a. go home and rest.
   b. go to the hospital.
   c. take a vacation.

B Listen again and check (✔) Sandra's symptoms.

Symptoms

- ☐ Fever
- ✓ Sore throat
- ☐ Vomiting
- ☐ Rash
- ✓ Headache
- ✓ Sneezing
- ☐ Dizziness

UNIT

You'll never believe this!

Student CD Track: 32

A **Listen and circle the best response.**

1. a. You could say that.
    b. Yes, he did.
    c. I'm glad to hear it.

2. a. On the weekend.
    b. I nearly drowned.
    c. Near the beach.

3. a. On Saturday morning.
    b. It was pretty scary.
    c. I was on a boat and I
       fell into the ocean.

4. a. Sunday morning.
    b. I was on my own.
    c. At Marley Beach.

5. a. Some friends.
    b. Some time.
    c. Somewhere.

6. a. I'm not a good swimmer.
    b. I was interviewed by
       reporters.
    c. My friends called the
       lifeguard.

B **Listen again and check your answers.**

Student CD Track: 33

A **Listen and circle the best answer.**

1. **The man is . . .**
   a. a radio interviewer.
   b. a newspaper reporter.
   c. a police officer.

2. **The woman is describing . . .**
   a. a personal theft.
   b. a bank robbery.
   c. a murder.

3. **The incident occurred . . .**
   a. yesterday.
   b. this morning.
   c. this afternoon.

B **Listen again and fill in the details in the form.**

Incident Report

Date of incident: _Monday, September 23, 2002_

Time: _____ Location: _____

_____

Items stolen? _____ Yes _____ No

Description of item(s): _____

_____

Suspect identified? _____ Yes _____ No

Description of suspect(s): _____

_____

UNIT

We want someone who's reliable.

TASK 1

Student CD Track: **34**

A Listen and circle the best response.

1. a. Jake always shows up on time.
   b. Jake is always doing things.
   c. Jake's quite artistic.

2. a. Yes, she dances very well.
   b. No, she never lies.
   c. Oh yes. She'd never steal.

3. a. Yes, he's never lazy.
   b. No, we need someone honest.
   c. Yes, he takes a lot of time off.

4. a. That makes sense. She always works very quickly.
   b. Really? But she's so hardworking!
   c. Dave should have won—he's really generous.

5. a. She's good at making her own decisions.
   b. She's really nice.
   c. She's always on time.

6. a. He's very honest.
   b. He's a little boring.
   c. He's really creative.

B Listen again and check your answers.

TASK 2

Student CD Track: **35**

A Listen and circle the best answer.

1. This is . . .
   a. an interview.
   b. a meeting.
   c. a casual conversation.

2. The speakers are . . .
   a. parents.
   b. employers.
   c. teachers.

3. They are looking for . . .
   a. someone to be on a sports team.
   b. someone to appear in a play.
   c. someone to fill a teaching position.

B Listen again and fill in the blanks with the positive and negative characteristics of the three girls.

Name	Positives	Negatives
Nancy		
Janet		
Katie	*reliable*	

Let's go to the movies.

Student CD Track: 36

A Listen and circle the best response.

1. a. No, I haven't seen it.
   b. No, they're too scary.
   c. What's it about?

2. a. Can I come?
   b. What day are you going?
   c. What are you going to see?

3. a. It's on at 7 o'clock.
   b. That's good. Let's see it.
   c. Oh, do you think so?

4. a. How funny!
   b. I haven't seen it.
   c. I don't like comedies.

5. a. I usually go to the Odeon.
   b. Not really.
   c. It's a new movie.

6. a. Only in the evenings.
   b. Not too often.
   c. I never rent videos.

B Listen again and check your answers.

Student CD Track: 37

A Listen and circle the best answer.

1. This is . . .
   a. a recorded message.
   b. a casual conversation.
   c. a telephone conversation.

2. The speakers are . . .
   a. husband and wife.
   b. friends.
   c. coworkers at a movie theater.

3. They are talking about . . .
   a. favorite movies.
   b. the best local movie theaters.
   c. how to get movie tickets.

B Read the statements. Then listen and circle *T* for *True*, *F* for *False*, or *U* for *Unknown*.

1. Jim goes to the movies twice a week.	T F U	
2. Sally doesn't like movies.	T F U	
3. Jim uses the telephone ticketing service.	T F U	
4. He usually buys his tickets by credit card.	T F U	
5. Sally prefers dealing with people rather than machines.	T F U	
6. Jim and Sally will go to see a movie together tonight.	T F U	

UNIT 19

Is he ready to quit?

Student CD Track: 38

A Listen and circle the best response.

1. a. Are you sure?
   b. What a pain!
   c. Oh, do you?

2. a. That's a great idea.
   b. Do you think so?
   c. Why don't you quit?

3. a. You should talk to them.
   b. Ask him to stop.
   c. Tell them to stop.

4. a. Why, do I look tired?
   b. During the day.
   c. That's too bad.

5. a. No, I didn't.
   b. Well, you can borrow my notes.
   c. You'll have to give it up.

6. a. Do you drink coffee after dinner?
   b. So can I.
   c. You should stop it.

B Listen again and check your answers.

Student CD Track: 39

A Listen and circle the best answer.

1. **This is . . .**
   a. a radio call-in program.
   b. a casual conversation.
   c. a formal meeting.

2. **The speakers are . . .**
   a. neighbors.
   b. friends.
   c. real estate agents.

3. **They are talking about . . .**
   a. their own bad habits.
   b. problems with their neighbors.
   c. family problems.

B Listen again and complete the box.

Name	Problem	Possible solution
Mandy		
Jackie		
Phil		

UNIT

Who did you see today?

Student CD Track: **40**

A Listen and circle the best response.

1. **a.** On Thursday.
   b. It's tomorrow.
   c. Terrible.

2. **a.** It was great.
   b. Terrible.
   c. Just meetings.

3. **a.** I had a meeting.
   b. Oh, I met Jim Lee.
   c. I did the laundry.

4. **a.** It was very interesting.
   b. No, I forgot to do that.
   c. Not really.

5. **a.** Yes, Henry.
   b. No, this morning.
   c. No, Jack.

6. **a.** What happened?
   b. It was a great day.
   c. How was your day?

B Listen again and check your answers.

Student CD Track: **41**

A Listen and circle the best answer.

1. The speakers are . . .
   a. husband and wife.
   b. coworkers.
   c. employee and boss.

2. Tomorrow is . . .
   a. Monday.
   b. Tuesday.
   c. Wednesday.

3. Alex calls his mother . . .
   a. every day.
   b. once a week.
   c. once a month.

B Listen again and check (✔) the things Alex did today.

_____ call Mom

_____ pick up laundry at dry cleaners

_____ call boss

_____ hand in monthly report

_____ meet with boss

_____ cook dinner for Annie

_____ go to fitness center

_____ celebrate birthday

Track Listing

Track	Content	
1	Announcement	
2	Unit 1	Task 1
3	Unit 1	Task 2
4	Unit 2	Task 1
5	Unit 2	Task 2
6	Unit 3	Task 1
7	Unit 3	Task 2
8	Unit 4	Task 1
9	Unit 4	Task 2
10	Unit 5	Task 1
11	Unit 5	Task 2
12	Unit 6	Task 1
13	Unit 6	Task 2
14	Unit 7	Task 1
15	Unit 7	Task 2
16	Unit 8	Task 1
17	Unit 8	Task 2
18	Unit 9	Task 1
19	Unit 9	Task 2
20	Unit 10	Task 1
21	Unit 10	Task 2

Track	Content	
22	Unit 11	Task 1
23	Unit 11	Task 2
24	Unit 12	Task 1
25	Unit 12	Task 2
26	Unit 13	Task 1
27	Unit 13	Task 2
28	Unit 14	Task 1
29	Unit 14	Task 2
30	Unit 15	Task 1
31	Unit 15	Task 2
32	Unit 16	Task 1
33	Unit 16	Task 2
34	Unit 17	Task 1
35	Unit 17	Task 2
36	Unit 18	Task 1
37	Unit 18	Task 2
38	Unit 19	Task 1
39	Unit 19	Task 2
40	Unit 20	Task 1
41	Unit 20	Task 2

See pages 108–127 for the Self-Study Practice Tasks.

Taking Sides: Clashing Views
on Political Issues, 20/e

William J. Miller

http://create.mheducation.com

Copyright 2018 by McGraw-Hill Education. All rights
reserved. Printed in the United States of America. Except as
permitted under the United States Copyright Act of 1976, no part
of this publication may be reproduced or distributed in any form
or by any means, or stored in a database or retrieval system,
without prior written permission of the publisher.

This McGraw-Hill Create text may include materials submitted to
McGraw-Hill for publication by the instructor of this course.
The instructor is solely responsible for the editorial content of such
materials. Instructors retain copyright of these additional materials.

ISBN-10: 125988323X   ISBN-13: 9781259883231

Issue: Is Congress a Dysfunctional Institution?
YES: **Ezra Klein**, from "What Happens When Congress Fails to Do Its Job?" *Newsweek* (2010)
NO: **William Mo Cowan**, from "Cowan Farewell Address," U.S. Senate (2013)

Columnist Ezra Klein contends that institutional deadlock and partisan rancor have paralyzed Congress, causing it to lose power to the president and the bureaucracy. Former Massachusetts Senator Mo Cowan describes how he has come to view the work of Congress—along with fellow members—after fulfilling the remainder of John Kerry term upon the nomination of Governor Deval Patrick.

Issue: Should Supreme Court Justices have Term Limits?
YES: **Norm Ornstein**, from "Why the Supreme Court Needs Term Limits," *The Atlantic* (2014)
NO: **Lyle Denniston**, from "Constitution Check: Did the Founders Want Term Limits for Supreme Court Justices?" *Constitution Daily* (2015)

Writer Norm Ornstein argues that the most effective way to address the problems created by an increasingly politicized Supreme Court is to limit all justices to 18-year terms. Lyle Denniston, the National Constitution Center's constitutional literacy adviser, examines comments from one-time Republican presidential candidate Mike Huckabee about the Founders' intentions for a Supreme Court with term limits and what Alexander Hamilton said about the issue.

Issue: Should the Senate Be Able to Delay Hearings on Nominations While Waiting for a Presidential Election to Occur?
YES: **William Yeomans**, from "The Many Ways Senate Republicans can Block Obama's Supreme Court Nominee," *Reuters* (2016)
NO: **Joe Biden**, from "Joe Biden: The Senate's Duty on a Supreme Court Nominee," *The New York Times* (2016)

Former chief counsel for Senator Edward Kennedy on the Senate Judiciary Committee William Yeomans writes that whether it is the right decision or not, Republican Senators have a series of options available on how to block a potential nomination—many of which are rooted directly in the Constitution. Vice President, and former Senate Judiciary Committee member, Joe Biden, on the other hand, argues that the Constitution requires the Senate to take action and past precedent has demonstrated it is the proper thing to do.

Unit 3: Social Change and Public Policy

Issue: Does Affirmative Action Advance Racial Equality?
YES: **Anthony P. Carnevale and Jeff Strohl**, from "Separate & Unequal: How Higher Education Reinforces the Intergenerational Reproduction of White Racial Privilege," Georgetown University Public Policy Institute Center on Education and the Workforce (2013)
NO: **Dan Slater**, from "Does Affirmative Action Do What It Should?" *The New York Times* (2013)

Policy researchers Anthony P. Carnevale and Jeff Strohl show there are still wide racial and ethnic discrepancies present in education in the United States and how more direct efforts by government to achieve equality will be needed to level the playing field. Commentator Dan Slater presents information related to the mismatch theory which suggests that affirmative action can harm those it's supposed to help by placing them at schools in which they fall below the median level of ability.

Issue: Should Abortion Be Restricted?
YES: **Marco Rubio**, from "Why Abortion Is Bad for America," *The Human Life Review* (2012)
NO: **Wendy Davis**, from "Filibuster of the Texas State Senate," *Speech or Remarks* (2013)

U.S. Senator Marco Rubio discusses why abortion harms American society from multiple angles, including moral, economic, and political, during a speech at the Susan B. Anthony List Campaign for Life Gala. Texas Representative Wendy Davis presents her case for why Texas Governor Rick Perry should not sign a new abortion measure that has been deemed the most restrictive state-level effort anywhere in the United States.

Detailed Table of Contents

Unit 1: Democracy and the American Political Process

Humanities professor Jeff Madrick surveys the numerous government interventions in the economy since the end of World War II and concludes that they have been essential to America's growth and well-being. Executive Vice President of the Cato Institute David Boaz traces America's libertarian traditions and reminds readers that there are times where government's best course of action is simply deciding to do nothing.

U.S. President Barack Obama honors Martin Luther King, Jr. by discussing how King's dreams have begun to be realized and continue to fuel the actions and directions of many Americans. The 2016 State of Black America examines racial equality in the United States and ultimately finds that African Americans in America remain only 72.2 percent equal to white citizens.

Journalist Jamelle Bouie argues that the current presidential nomination system is in fact quite democratic by allowing states to determine how best to conduct elections within their borders. He notes that even outside of elections, American government has always flourished under a blend of majoritarian, nonmajoritarian, and countermajoritarian elements. William Saletan, also a journalist, acknowledges that the nomination process is not particularly democratic but reminds readers that the goals of primaries and caucuses are to select candidates that best represent party interests.

Social scientist Nicholas Eberstadt argues that the increase in entitlement programs is unprecedented in American history and has created a large dependency class that has lost the will to work. Political theorist William A. Galston sees the growth of American entitlement programs as an appropriate response to the needs of an aging population and rising costs of higher education and medicine; he sees them not as evidence of dependency but of "interdependence."

Unit 2: The Institutions of Government

John C. Yoo, a Law Professor at the University of California, Berkeley, argues that the language of the Constitution, long-accepted precedents, and the practical need for speedy action in emergencies all support broad executive power during war. American President Barack Obama examines how he has made concerted efforts during his time in the White House to expand consultations with Congress in order to provide the best opportunity for the United States to be successful in fighting terrorism.

Contents

Unit 4: America and the World

<u>**Issue: Should the United States Be More Heavily Involved in Efforts to Defeat ISIS?**</u>
YES: Max Boot, from "Defeating ISIS," *Council on Foreign Relations* (2014)
NO: Barack Obama, from "Address to the Nation by the President," *The White House* (2015)

Max Boot, Jeane J. Kirkpatrick Senior Fellow for National Security Studies at the Council for Foreign Relations, argues that the United States will need to increase its commitment in a measured way if it wishes to see ISIS defeated in the Middle East. He advocates not ruling out the option of ground-combat troops as it makes the country appear non-committed and reduces available leverage. President Barack Obama, speaking to the nation in the aftermath of the San Bernardino shooting, reiterates his desire to destroy ISIS. But, in doing so, does not appear willing to change the country's current policy, which has been judged by many to be inadequate in addressing the threat of the Islamic State terrorist group.

<u>**Issue: Is the United States Doing Enough to Address the Global Threat of Diseases like Zika?**</u>
YES: The White House, from "FACT SHEET: Preparing for and Responding to the Zika Virus at Home and Abroad," *The White House* (2016)
NO: Peter J. Hotez, from "Zika Is Coming," *The New York Times* (2016)

The White House Fact Sheet on preparing for Zika clearly delineates the steps taken across the country to help mitigate the threat of the Zika virus and handle any responses necessary if the disease were to find itself within the United States. This includes a detailed discussion of available funding and funding priorities. Peter Hotez, Dean of the National School of Tropical Medicine at Baylor College of Medicine, warns Americans, however, that Zika will likely arrive within our borders soon—especially in major Southern cities—and that we are vastly unprepared to handle any outbreak.

<u>**Issue: Should the United States Accept More Refugees from Syria?**</u>
YES: Katy Long, from "Why America Could—and Should—Admit More Syrian Refugees," *The Century Foundation* (2015)
NO: Martin Pengelly, et al., from "Cruz and Rubio Lead Republican Charge against Obama over Syria Policy," *The Guardian* (2015)

Katy Long, a visiting fellow at Stanford, argues America should work to bring more refugees that are Syrian into its borders. She contends that resettling more refugees that are Syrian quickly and equitably will lead to a moral victory, which in turn will help it persuade allies to do more to help resolve the Syrian war and the attendant humanitarian catastrophe. Three reporters, Martin Pengelly, Tom Dart, and Sabrina Siddiqui, from *The Guardian* highlight opposition arguments waged by 2016 Republican presidential hopefuls, including Ted Cruz and Marco Rubio. The major arguments against increasing the number of refugees centers on concerns for national safety and security.

<u>**Issue: Should the United States Launch a Preemptive Strike Against Iran?**</u>
YES: Matthew Kroenig, from "Time to Attack Iran," *Foreign Affairs* (2012)
NO: Colin H. Kahl, from "Not Time to Attack Iran," *Foreign Affairs* (2012)

Defense Department Adviser Matthew Kroenig believes that the United States should launch a preemptive attack on Iran because a policy of deterrence would allow Iran to develop powerful nuclear weapons that would endanger the United States and its allies. Defense Department Adviser Colin H. Kahl believes that striking Iran now would not prevent future aggression, and it is undesirable as long as economic and diplomatic means to prevent Iran's nuclear armament still hold the possibility of success.

<u>**Issue: Was President Obama's Trip to Cuba a Good Step in Normalizing Relations with the Country?**</u>
YES: Barack Obama, from "Remarks by President Obama to the People of Cuba," *The White House* (2016)
NO: Armando Valladares, from "I Was a Prisoner of Castro's Regime: Obama's Visit to Cuba Is a Mistake," *The Washington Post* (2016)

In his address from Havana, President Barack Obama explains why ceasing isolationist policies with Cuba can benefit both the United States and the island nation. He takes time to highlight the strengths of Cuban society and how he envisions normalized relations occurring in the next few years. Armando Valladares, a poet and artist who spent 22 years in Cuba as a political prisoner under Castro, writes that Obama's trip was misguided as it sends a message of favoritism for the strong at the expense of the weak. In short, he argues that common citizens will never see the benefits of normalized relations with the United States.

Preface

As I write this, the federal government is preparing for an election between Hillary Clinton and Donald Trump, the Tea Party is trying to determine its purpose and future, Barack Obama is spending his last weeks attempting to shape his legacy, the FDA is inspecting food I'll consume next week, my Homeowner's Association is measuring my grass, a parent is lamenting the loss of their child to gun violence, the FCC is monitoring the National Football League game on television, a college football player is being ejected for a clean hit in the name of safety, the Social Security bathtub is ebbing and flowing, a young African female is being taught how to pull the detonating device on a suicide vest, the NSA is watching my text messages, my institution is screening my e-mails, and I am unable to kick the urge to pull the tag off of my mattress. In short, public policy is happening around me. And I cannot possibly imagine in all the ways it is doing so.

In recent years, the world has seen how important political issues truly are. From the impact of a death on the Supreme Court to international reactions to terrorism and immigrants alike, we have witnessed enough chasing of views on political issues to fill volumes, let alone a single reader. At the end of the day, we work to frame issues in macro-level terms when possible to assure applicability and continued relevancy, even after the initial moment of interest has passed. We strive to encourage dialogue on these ever important issues occurring around us in our daily lives. And we hope to hearten a more meaningful debate than the one Americans witness among talking heads every evening. Rather than simply observing two ships as they pass in the night, this volume aims to provide a groundwork that allows all readers to critically assess the political world around them.

If Americans are forced to rely on talking heads, they will likely fail to ever grasp the complexities of government and policy in the democratic context. Talking heads, after all, have both an audience and an agenda. Consequently, it is highly unlikely that they will provide the necessary context and clarity for a given issue so that the average viewer can formulate their own opinion. As debate continues, everyone involved will typically utilize vague, emotion-laden language and tend to speak past many viewers, in some cases intentionally. If the conversation gets too heated, they may rely on epithets or simply spewing party-based rhetoric meant to win over viewers with an impressive dose of partisanship. For example, when the discussion of affirmative action comes down to both sides accusing the other of "racism," or when the controversy over abortion degenerates into taunts and name-calling, then no one really listens and learns from the other side.

I still believe there is value in learning from an opponent. No matter how diametrically opposed two sides may be, there is knowledge to be gained from fully comprehending the arguments made against you. Your own case, after all, can be made significantly stronger if you account for your own potential weaknesses. Sometimes, after listening to others, we change our view entirely. But in most cases, we either incorporate some elements of the opposing view—thus making our own richer—or else learn how to answer the objections to our viewpoint. Either way, we gain from the experience. For these reasons, I believe that encouraging dialogue between opposed positions is the most certain way of enhancing public understanding.

The purpose of this 20th edition of *Taking Sides* is to continue to work toward the revival of political dialogue in America while encouraging the development of a sense of relevancy. As has occurred in the past 19 editions, I examine leading issues in American politics from the perspective of sharply opposed points of view. I have tried to select authors who argue their points vigorously but in such a way as to enhance comprehension of the issue. In short, I have aimed to include works that will stimulate interest and encourage understanding of multiple angles in any given issue.

I hope that readers who confront lively and thoughtful statements on vital issues will be stimulated to ask some of the critical questions about American politics. What are the highest priority issues with which government must deal today? What positions should be taken on these issues? What should be the attitude of Americans toward their government? I firmly believe that in order to be a truly great, stable democracy, citizens must be willing to consider such questions, even if they are unsure of where they stand. Acknowledging a need to become more informed will forever be favored as opposed to apathy, passivity, or misunderstood resentment.

Editor of This Volume

WILLIAM J. MILLER is executive director of institutional analytics, effectiveness, and planning at Flagler College and teaches courses in both political science and public administration. He is co-author of *Campaign Craft: The Strategies, Tactics, and Art of Political Campaign Management* (Praeger, 2015). He is also the editor of *Tea Party Effects on 2010 U.S. Senate Elections: Stuck in the Middle to Lose* (Lexington, 2012), *Taking Sides: Clashing Views on Public Administration & Policy* (McGraw Hill, 2012), *The Election's Mine—I Draw the Line: The Political Battle over Congressional Redistricting at the State Level* (Lexington, 2013), *The Battle to Face Obama: The 2012 Republican Nomination and the Future of* *the Republican Party* (Lexington, 2013), and *Handbook on Teaching and Learning in Political Science and International Relations* (Edward Elgar, 2015). His research appears in *Journal of Political Science Education, Journal of Political Marketing, Political Science Quarterly, Studies in Conflict & Terrorism, International Studies Quarterly, Nonproliferation Review, Afro-Americans in New York Life and History, Journal of South Asian and Middle Eastern Studies, American Behavioral Scientist, PS: Political Science and Politics*, and *Journal of Common Market Studies*.

BOOK ORGANIZATION The text is divided into four units, each addressing a different aspect of politics. At the beginning of each unit is a unit opener that briefly identifies the specific issues in the section. Next are the issues themselves, each of which starts with an introduction that sets the stage for the debate as it is argued in the YES and NO selections. An exploring the issue section follows the selections and provides some final observations and comments about the topic. The exploring the issue section contains critical thinking and reflection questions, the common ground between the two viewpoints, and print and Internet suggestions for further reading.

Acknowledgments

I must start by giving my sincere appreciation and thanks to George McKenna and Stanley Feingold who have overseen this *Taking Sides* title since its inception. I am thrilled to be taking over on my own with this edition and look forward to continuing this volume long into the future. I thank Jill Meloy for her confidence and never-ending assistance throughout the process. I look forward to hearing from readers—instructors and especially students—about their thoughts on the issues and materials selected. Feel free to reach out at any time via e-mail: wmiller@flagler.edu. It goes without saying that anything found to be incorrect throughout the book is of no one's fault but my own.

William J. Miller
Flagler College

Academic Advisory Board Members

Members of the Academic Advisory Board are instrumental in the final selection of articles for Taking Sides books. Their review of the articles for content, level, and appropriateness provides critical direction to the editor and staff. We think that you will find their careful consideration reflected in this book.

Phillip Ardoin
Appalachian State University

Bret L. Billet
Wartburg College

Steven J. Campbell
University of South Carolina, Lancaster

Gary Donato
Bentley University

Leif Johan Eliasson
East Stroudsburg University

James Hite
Clackamas Community College

Elizabeth Hull
Rutgers University – Newark

Jean-Gabriel Jolivet
Ashford University

Orin Kirshner
Florida Atlantic University

Lisa Krasner
University of Phoenix

Anne Thrower Leonard
Embry-Riddle Aeronautical University

Nancy Lind
Illinois State University

Ed Miller
University of Wisconsin-Stevens Point

Mark Miller
Clark University

Allyn Milojevich
University of Tennessee

Patrick Moore
Richland College

Derek Mosley
Meridian Community College

Lynn Paredes-Manfredi
Seminole State College

Andreas W. Reif
Manchester Community College

Joseph Romance
Fort Hays State University

David Smith
Texas A&M University Corpus Christi

Howard W. Starks Jr.
Wayne State University

Ron Vardy
University of Houston

Lowell F. Wolf
Dowling College

Introduction

Labels and Alignments in American Politics

As I write this, we are only a month from a pivotal election in the United States, pitting two strongly disliked major party candidates against each other in an effort to become leader of the free world. Whoever wins will immediately face great public scrutiny. Democrats will want to see whether Donald Trump is capable of actually behaving in a presidential manner without alienating Americans and the international community alike. Republicans, on the other hand, will undoubtedly continue to bring forth questions surrounding Benghazi and e-mail security protocols if Hillary Clinton has found herself victorious. And whoever wins will take over a country split by race more so than at any point in the past fifty years. It appears as if the democratic bargain is little more than an afterthought. There was a time in our country's history where parties put candidates up for election and accepted the election results, win or lose. Yet today both Democrats and Republicans alike take electoral losses and throw them aside while determining ways to be obstructive. And few seem willing to mention that the country loses as a whole when this happens. We often talk about right and left, red and blue. But such simple dichotomies unfortunately over simplify the political realities facing the United States today. All the while, talking heads continue to throw around ideological labels designed to help simplify our understanding and allow us to better categorize ourselves. Unfortunately, the opposite often occurs.

Liberal, conservative, moderate, pluralist, radical, right wing, left wing, "classical" economics, "progressive"—what do these terms mean? Or do they have any meaning? Some political analysts regard them as arbitrary labels slapped on by commentators seeking quick ways to sum up candidates (or in some cases to demonize them). The reaction against the ideological labels is understandable, not only because they are often used too loosely but, as we shall see, because the terms themselves can evolve over time. Nevertheless, we think there are some core meanings left, so if they are used carefully, they can help us locate positions on the political stage and the actors who occupy them. In this Introduction we shall try to spell out the meanings of these terms, at least as they are used in American politics.

Liberals versus Conservatives: An Overview

Let us examine, very briefly, the historical evolution of the terms *liberalism* and *conservatism.* By examining the roots of these terms, we can see how these philosophies have adapted themselves to changing times. In that way, we can avoid using the terms rigidly, without reference to the particular contexts in which liberalism and conservatism have operated over the past two centuries.

Classical Liberalism

The classical root of the term *liberalism* is the Latin word *libertas,* meaning "liberty" or "freedom." In the early nineteenth century, liberals dedicated themselves to freeing individuals from all unnecessary and oppressive obligations to authority—whether the authority came from the church or the state. They opposed the licensing and censorship of the press, the punishment of heresy, the establishment of religion, and any attempt to dictate orthodoxy in matters of opinion. In economics, liberals opposed state monopolies and other constraints upon competition between private businesses. At this point in its development, liberalism defined freedom primarily in terms of freedom *from.* It appropriated the French term *laissez-faire,* which literally means "leave to be." Leave people alone! That was the spirit of liberalism in its early days. It wanted government to stay out of people's lives and to play a modest role in general. Thomas Jefferson summed up this concept when he said, "I am no friend of energetic government. It is always oppressive."

Despite their suspicion of government, classical liberals invested high hopes in the political process. By and large, they were great believers in democracy. They believed in widening suffrage to include every white male, and some of them were prepared to enfranchise women and blacks as well. Although liberals occasionally worried about "the tyranny of the majority," they were more prepared to trust the masses than to trust a permanent, entrenched elite. Liberal social policy was dedicated to fulfilling human potential and was based on the assumption that this often-hidden potential is enormous. Human beings, liberals argued, were basically good and reasonable. Evil and irrationality were believed to be caused by "outside" influences; they were the result of a bad social environment.

A liberal commonwealth, therefore, was one that would remove the hindrances to the full flowering of the human personality. The basic vision of liberalism has not changed since the nineteenth century. What has changed is the way it is applied to modern society. In that respect, liberalism has changed dramatically. Today, instead of regarding government with suspicion, liberals welcome government as an instrument to serve the people. The change in philosophy began in the latter years of the nineteenth century, when businesses—once small, independent operations—began to grow into giant structures that overwhelmed individuals and sometimes even overshadowed the state in power and wealth. At that time, liberals began reconsidering their commitment to the *laissez-faire* philosophy. If the state can be an oppressor, asked liberals, can't big business also oppress people? By then, many were convinced that commercial and industrial monopolies were crushing the souls and bodies of the working classes. The state, formerly the villain, now was viewed by liberals as a potential savior. The concept of freedom was transformed into something more than a negative freedom *from;* the term began to take on a positive meaning. It meant "realizing one's full potential." Toward this end, liberals believed, the state could prove to be a valuable instrument. It could educate children, protect the health and safety of workers, help people through hard times, promote a healthy economy, and—when necessary—force business to act more humanely and responsibly. Thus was born the movement that culminated in New Deal liberalism.

New Deal Liberalism

In the United States, the argument in favor of state intervention did not win an enduring majority constituency until after the Great Depression of the 1930s began to be felt deeply. The disastrous effects of a depression that left a quarter of the workforce unemployed opened the way to a new administration—and a promise. "I pledge you, I pledge myself," Franklin D. Roosevelt said when accepting the Democratic nomination in 1932, "to a new deal for the American people." Roosevelt's New Deal was an attempt to effect relief and recovery from the Depression; it employed a variety of means, including welfare programs, public works, and business regulation—most of which involved government intervention in the economy. The New Deal liberalism relied on government to liberate people from poverty, oppression, and economic exploitation. At the same time, the New Dealers claimed to be as zealous as the classical liberals in defending political and civil liberties.

The common element in *laissez-faire* liberalism and welfare-state liberalism is their dedication to the goal of realizing the full potential of each individual. Some still questioned whether this is best done by minimizing state involvement or whether it sometimes requires an activist state. The New Dealers took the latter view, although they prided themselves on being pragmatic and experimental about their activism. During the heyday of the New Deal, a wide variety of programs were tried and—if found wanting—abandoned. All decent means should be tried, they believed, even if it meant dilution of ideological purity. The Roosevelt administration, for example, denounced bankers and businessmen in campaign rhetoric but worked very closely with them while trying to extricate the nation from the Depression. This set a pattern of pragmatism that New Dealers from Harry Truman to Lyndon Johnson emulated.

Progressive Liberalism

Progressive liberalism emerged in the late 1960s and early 1970s as a more militant and uncompromising movement than the New Deal had ever been. Its roots go back to the New Left student movement of the early 1960s. New Left students went to the South to participate in civil rights demonstrations, and many of them were bloodied in confrontations with southern police; by the mid-1960s they were confronting the authorities in the North over issues like poverty and the Vietnam War. By the end of the decade, the New Left had fragmented into a variety of factions and had lost much of its vitality, but a somewhat more respectable version of it appeared as the New Politics movement. Many New Politics crusaders were former New Leftists who had traded their jeans for coats and ties; they tried to work within the system instead of always confronting it.

Even so, they retained some of the spirit of the New Left. The civil rights slogan "Freedom Now" expressed the mood of the New Politics. The young university graduates who filled its ranks had come from an environment where "nonnegotiable" demands were issued to college deans by leaders of sit-in protests. There was more than youthful arrogance in the New Politics movement; however, there was a pervasive belief that America had lost, had compromised away, much of its idealism. The New Politics liberals sought to recover some of that spirit by linking up with an older tradition of militant reform, which went back to the time of the Revolution. These new liberals saw themselves as the authentic heirs of Thomas Paine and Henry David Thoreau, of the abolitionists, the radical populists, the suffragettes, and the great progressive reformers of the early twentieth century.

While New Deal liberals concentrated almost exclusively on bread-and-butter issues such as unemployment and poverty, the New Politics liberals introduced what came to be known as social issues into the political arena. These included the repeal of laws against abortion, the liberalization of laws against homosexuality and pornography, the establishment of affirmative action programs to ensure increased hiring of minorities and women, and the passage of the Equal Rights Amendment.

In foreign policy, too, New Politics liberals departed from the New Deal agenda. Because they had keener memories of the unpopular and (for them) unjustified war in Vietnam than of World War II, they became doves, in contrast to the general hawkishness of the New Dealers. They were skeptical of any claim that the United States must be the leader of the free world or, indeed, that it had any special mission in the world; some were convinced that America was already in decline and must learn to adjust accordingly. The real danger, they argued, came not from the Soviet Union but from the mad pace of America's arms race with the Soviets, which, as they saw it, could bankrupt the country, starve its social programs, and culminate in a nuclear Armageddon. New Politics liberals were heavily represented at the 1972 Democratic national convention, which nominated South Dakota senator

George McGovern for president. By the 1980s the New Politics movement was no longer new, and many of its adherents preferred to be called progressives.

By this time their critics had another name for them: radicals. The critics saw their positions as inimical to the interests of the United States, destructive of the family, and fundamentally at odds with the views of most Americans. The adversaries of the progressives were not only conservatives but many New Deal liberals, who openly scorned the McGovernites. This split still exists within the Democratic Party, although it is now more skillfully managed by party leaders. In 1988 the Democrats paired Michael Dukakis, whose Massachusetts supporters were generally on the progressive side of the party, with New Dealer Lloyd Bentsen as the presidential and vice presidential candidates, respectively.

In 1992 the Democrats won the presidency with Arkansas governor Bill Clinton, whose record as governor seemed to put him in the moderate-to-conservative camp, and Tennessee senator Albert Gore, whose position on environmental issues could probably be considered quite liberal but whose general image was middle-of-the-road. Both candidates had moved toward liberal positions on the issues of gay rights and abortion. By 1994 Clinton was perceived by many Americans as being "too liberal," which some speculate may have been a factor in the defeat of Democrats in the congressional elections that year. Clinton immediately sought to shake off that perception, positioning himself as a "moderate" between extremes and casting the Republicans as an "extremist" party. (These two terms will be examined presently.)

President Obama comes from the progressive liberal wing of the Democratic Party, although in his campaign for office he attempted to appeal to moderates and even some conservatives by stressing his determination to regard the country not in terms of red (Republican) states and blue (Democratic) states but as a nation united. Once in office, however, his agenda, which included an $830-billion "stimulus" expenditure to jump-start the economy and an ambitious social insurance program, came from the playbook of progressive liberalism; by 2010 it faced unanimous resistance from the Republican minority in Congress. In the 2010 congressional races its unpopularity in so-called "swing" districts and states, that had swung Democrat in the 2008 election, cost many moderate Democrats their seats in Congress. Yet by 2012, the Democrats seemed to be recovering. Headed toward 2016, it seems that the Senate may even be back in play.

Conservatism

Like liberalism, conservatism has undergone historical transformation in America. Just as early liberals (represented by Thomas Jefferson) espoused less government, early conservatives (whose earliest leaders were Alexander Hamilton and John Adams) urged government support of economic enterprise and government intervention on behalf of certain groups. But today, in reaction to the growth of the welfare state, conservatives argue strongly that more government means more unjustified interference in citizens' lives, more bureaucratic regulation of private conduct, more inhibiting control of economic enterprise, more material advantage for the less energetic and less able at the expense of those who are prepared to work harder and better, and, of course, more taxes—taxes that will be taken from those who have earned money and given to those who have not.

Contemporary conservatives are not always opposed to state intervention. They may support larger military expenditures in order to protect society against foreign enemies. They may also allow for some intrusion into private life in order to protect society against internal subversion and would pursue criminal prosecution zealously in order to protect society against domestic violence. The fact is that few conservatives, and perhaps fewer liberals, are absolute with respect to their views about the power of the state. Both are quite prepared to use the state in order to further *their* purposes. It is true that activist presidents such as Franklin Roosevelt and John Kennedy were likely to be classified as liberals. However, Richard Nixon was also an activist, and, although he does not easily fit any classification, he was far closer to conservatism than to liberalism. It is too easy to identify liberalism with statism and conservatism with antistatism: it is important to remember that it was liberal Jefferson who counseled against "energetic government" and conservative Alexander Hamilton who designed bold powers for the new central government and wrote, "Energy in the executive is a leading character in the definition of good government."

The Religious Right

The terms "right" and "left," as in "right wing of the Republican Party" and "leftist Democrats," came from an accident of seating in the French National Assembly during the Revolution of the early 1790s. It just happened that the liberals flocked to the left side of the assembly hall while conservatives went to the right. "Left" and "right," then, are almost synonyms for liberals and conservatives, the main difference being that they give a sense of continuum and degree—someone can be "center-left" or "center-right" instead of at the extremes.

Even so, the terms have a certain hard edge. To call someone a "leftist" or a "right-winger" is to give an impression that they are strident or excessively zealous. That impression is conveyed in the term "religious right," a term few of its adherents would use to describe themselves, preferring softer terms like "religious conservatives" or "cultural conservatives."

For better or worse, although, the term "religious right" has entered the media mainstream, so we shall use it here to designate observant Christians or Jews whose concerns are not so much high taxes and government spending as the decline of traditional Judeo-Christian morality, a decline they attribute in part to wrongheaded government policies and judicial decisions. They oppose many of the recent judicial decisions on socio-cultural issues such as abortion, school prayer, pornography, and gay rights, and they were outspoken critics of the Clinton administration, citing everything from President Clinton's views on gays in the military to his sexual behavior while in the White House.

Spokesmen for progressive liberalism and the religious right stand as polar opposites: The former regard abortion as a woman's right; the latter see it as legalized murder. The former tend to regard homosexuality as a lifestyle that needs protection against discrimination; the latter are more likely to see it as a perversion. The list of issues could go on. The religious right and the progressive liberals are like positive and negative photographs of America's moral landscape. Sociologist James Davison Hunter uses the term *culture wars* to characterize the struggles between these contrary visions of America. For all the differences between progressive liberalism and the religious right; however, their styles are very similar. They are heavily laced with moralistic prose; they tend to equate compromise with selling out; and they claim to represent the best and most authentic traditions of America.

This is not to denigrate either movement, for the kinds of issues they address are indeed moral issues, which do not generally admit much compromise. These issues cannot simply be finessed or ignored, despite the efforts of conventional politicians to do so

Neoconservatism

The term *neoconservatism* came into use in the early 1970s as a designation for former New Deal Democrats who had become alarmed by what they saw as the drift of their party's foreign policy toward appeasing Communists. When Senator George McGovern, the party's presidential nominee in 1972, stated that he would "crawl to Hanoi on my knees" to secure peace in Vietnam, he seemed to them to exemplify this new tendency. They were, then, "hawks" in foreign policy, which they insisted was the historic stance of their party; they regarded themselves as the true heirs of liberal presidents such as Truman and Kennedy and liberal senators such as Henry ("Scoop") Jackson of Washington State. On domestic policy, they were still largely liberal, except for their reactions to three new liberal planks added by the "progressives": gay rights, which neoconservatives tended to regard as a distortion of civil rights; abortion, which to some degree or another went against the grain of their moral sensibilities; and affirmative action, which some compared to the "quota system" once used to keep down the number of Jews admitted to elite universities. In fact, a number of prominent neoconservatives were Jews, including Norman Podhoretz, Midge Decter, Gertrude Himmelfarb, and Irving Kristol (although others, such as Michael Novak and Daniel Patrick Moynihan, were Roman Catholics, and one, Richard John Neuhaus, was a Lutheran pastor who later converted to Catholicism and became a priest).

The term *neoconservative* seemed headed for oblivion in the 1980s, when some leading neoconservatives dropped the "neo" part and classified themselves as conservatives. By the time the Soviet Union collapsed in 1991, it appeared that the term was no longer needed—the Cold War with "world Communism" was over. But the rise of Islamic terrorism in the 1990s, aimed at the West in general and the United States in particular, brought back alarms analogous to those of the Cold War period, with global terrorism now taking the place of world Communism. So, too, was the concern that liberal foreign policy might not be tough enough for the fight against these new, ruthless enemies of Western democracy. The concern was ratcheted up considerably after the events of 9/11, and now a new generation of neoconservatives was in the spotlight—some of its members literally the children of an earlier "neo" generation. They included Bill Kristol, John Podhoretz, Douglas Feith, Paul Wolfowitz, Richard Perle, David Brooks, and (although he was old enough to overlap with the previous generation) Bill Bennett.

Radicals, Reactionaries, and Moderates

The label *reactionary* is almost an insult, and the label *radical* is worn with pride by only a few zealots on the banks of the political mainstream. A reactionary is not a conserver but a backward-mover, dedicated to turning the clock back to better times. Most people suspect that reactionaries would restore us to a time that never was, except in political myth. For most Americans, the repeal of industrialism or universal education (or the entire twentieth century itself) is not a practical, let alone desirable, political program.

Radicalism (literally meaning "from the roots" or "going to the foundation") implies a fundamental reconstruction of the social order. Taken in that sense, it is possible to speak of right-wing radicalism as well as left-wing radicalism—radicalism that would restore or inaugurate a new hierarchical society as well as radicalism that calls for nothing less than an egalitarian society. The term is sometimes used in both of these senses, but most often the word *radicalism* is reserved to characterize more liberal change. While the liberal would affect change through conventional democratic processes, the radical is likely to be skeptical about the ability of the established machinery to bring about the needed change and might be prepared to sacrifice "a little" liberty to bring about a great deal more equality.

Moderate is a highly coveted label in America. Its meaning is not precise, but it carries the connotations of sensible, balanced, and practical. A moderate person is not without principles, but he or she does not allow principles to harden into dogma. The opposite of moderate is *extremist,* a label most American political leaders eschew. Yet there have been notable exceptions. When Arizona senator Barry Goldwater, a conservative Republican, was nominated for president in 1964, he declared, "Extremism in defense of liberty is no vice! . . . Moderation in the pursuit of justice is no virtue!" This open embrace of extremism did not help his electoral chances; Goldwater was overwhelmingly defeated. At about the same time, however, another American political leader also embraced a kind of extremism, and with better results. In a famous letter written from a jail cell in Birmingham, Alabama, the Reverend Martin Luther King, Jr., replied to the charge that he was an extremist not by denying it but by distinguishing between different kinds of extremists. The question, he wrote, "is not whether we will be extremist but what kind of extremist will we be. Will we be extremists for hate, or will we be extremists for love?" King aligned himself with the love extremists, in which category he also placed Jesus, St. Paul, and Thomas Jefferson, among others. It was an adroit use of a label that is usually anathema in America.

Pluralism

The principle of pluralism espouses diversity in a society containing many interest groups and in a government containing competing units of power. This implies the widest expression of competing ideas, and in this way, pluralism is in sympathy with an important element of liberalism. However, as James Madison and Alexander Hamilton pointed out when they analyzed the sources of pluralism in their *Federalist* commentaries on the Constitution, this philosophy springs from a profoundly pessimistic view of human nature, and in this respect it more closely resembles conservatism. Madison, possibly the single most influential member of the convention that wrote the Constitution, hoped that in a large and varied nation, no single interest group could control the government. Even if there were a majority interest, it would be unlikely to capture all of the national agencies of government—the House of Representatives, the Senate, the presidency, and the federal judiciary—each of which was chosen in a different way by a different constituency for a different term of office. Moreover, to make certain that no one branch exercised excessive power,

each was equipped with "checks and balances" that enabled any agency of national government to curb the powers of the others. The clearest statement of Madison's, and the Constitution's, theory can be found in the 51st paper of the *Federalist:* It may be a reflection on human nature that such devices should be necessary to control the abuses of government. But what is government itself, but the greatest of all reflections on human nature? If men were angels, no government would be necessary.

This pluralist position may be analyzed from different perspectives. It is conservative insofar as it rejects simple majority rule; yet it is liberal insofar as it rejects rule by a single elite. It is conservative in its pessimistic appraisal of human nature; yet pluralism's pessimism is also a kind of egalitarianism, holding as it does that no one can be trusted with power and that majority interests no less than minority interests will use power for selfish ends. It is possible to suggest that in America pluralism represents an alternative to both liberalism and conservatism. Pluralism is anti-majoritarian and anti-elitist and combines some elements of both.

Synthesis

Despite our effort to define the principal alignments in American politics, some policy decisions do not fit neatly into these categories. Suffice it to say that through the following pages, readers will be able to pull nuggets of the labels and alignments introduced above. Yet some will be far more obvious than others. Obviously one's position on the issues in this book will be directed by circumstances. However, we would like to think that the essays in this book are durable enough to last through several seasons of events and controversies. We can be certain that the issues will survive. The search for coherence and consistency in the use of political labels underlines the options open to us and reveals their consequences. The result must be more mature judgments about what is best for America. That, of course, is the ultimate aim of public debate and decision making, and it transcends all labels and categories.

Unit 1

Democracy and the American Political Process

*D*emocratic societies are known for allowing individuals to participate in the political process. Democracy is derived from two Greek words, demos and kratia, which mean, respectively, "people" and "rule." While there are clear differentiations between varying types of democracies, citizens have access and opportunities not present in other forms of government. For example, while a citizen in a representative democracy, such as the United States, may not get to individually vote on every issue that comes up for debate (like a citizen living in a direct democracy), they do have substantially more influence than a citizen living under a totalitarian dictator

Regardless of the type of democracy, questions still remain. Who are "the people," and how much "rule" should there be? Does big government mean better government? Do the people need more, or fewer, "rules"? Does "special interest" money in elections undermine the general interest? Are elections in America truly democratic? Some analysts of democracy believe that a viable democratic system requires widespread belief in their country's unique mission. But is that necessary?

Selected, Edited, and with Issue Framing Material by:
William J. Miller, *Flagler College*

ISSUE

Is Bigger Government Better Government?

YES: Jeff Madrick, from "The Case for Big Government," *Princeton University Press* (2008)

NO: David Boaz, from "The Return of Big Government," *Cato Policy Report* (2009)

Learning Outcomes

After reading this issue, you will be able to:

- Discuss the benefits of government expansion.
- Assess the weaknesses of limited government.
- Describe the economic benefits of government.
- Discuss the role of libertarian ideals in American society.
- Analyze how the size of government has impacted the current economic crisis.

ISSUE SUMMARY

YES: Humanities professor Jeff Madrick surveys the numerous government interventions in the economy since the end of World War II and concludes that they have been essential to America's growth and well-being.

NO: Executive Vice President of the Cato Institute David Boaz traces America's libertarian traditions and reminds readers that there are times where government's best course of action is simply deciding to do nothing.

A continuing debate about government runs through the course of American history. The debate is between those who see government as an instrument for doing good versus those who see it as a potentially oppressive institution. Those who take the latter view usually concede that, yes, we do need government for strictly limited purposes—but, in the words of Thomas Paine, government "even in its best state, is but a necessary evil."

Paine wrote those words in 1776, when America was still governed by a foreign nation. Does the situation change when a nation becomes self-governed? Alexander Hamilton thought so. Hamilton fought fiercely against the imperial government of Great Britain, but once American independence was achieved he became a champion of what he called "energetic" government, a term that included the pursuit of public programs aimed at increasing the nation's prosperity. He helped create the first federally owned Bank of the United States, encouraged the government to subsidize domestic industries, and even experimented with government-owned mills in New Jersey. Opposing him was Secretary of State Thomas Jefferson. Jefferson wanted government to stay out of the domestic economy.

Despite the protestations of Jefferson and those who followed him, government became increasingly energetic during the nineteenth century. Though Andrew Jackson killed the rechartering of the Bank of the United States with his presidential veto, the federal government passed tariffs and financed the building of roads, canals, and railroads; during and after the Civil War federal power expanded into areas such as civil rights and higher education, areas once reserved to the states. By the close of the nineteenth century, government began tentatively moving into the areas of social welfare and business regulation—though not without resistance.

In the twentieth century, government growth expanded during World War I, contracted in the 1920s, and exploded during the years of President Franklin Roosevelt, 1933–1945. A host of "alphabet" bureaucracies (e.g., WPA, PWA, NLRB, NRA, and so on) were created, government spending increased to unprecedented levels, and new entitlement programs such as Social Security and Aid to the Families of Dependent Children (AFDC) were created. During this period the terms "liberal" and "conservative" crystallized into descriptions of the two sides in the debate: liberals were those who championed government activism and conservatives were those resisting it. Today, almost 70 years later, "liberal" and "conservative" still work reasonably well, at least in the economic sphere, as thumbnail labels for those who favor government and those who don't.

Liberals and conservatives have won some and lost some since the end of the 1940s. President Dwight Eisenhower was a moderate conservative, yet it was under his administration that the Federal-Aid Highway Act was passed, which put the federal government into the business of financing the construction of 41,000 miles of instate highways throughout the nation; Eisenhower also established a new cabinet department, Health, Education and Welfare (later renamed the Department of Health and Human Services).

During President Lyndon Johnson's term, 1964–1968, the largest expansion of the federal government since the Roosevelt administration took place. Johnson boldly declared an "unconditional war on poverty." He created a variety of new federal agencies to teach job skills, stimulate community action, and dispense welfare. He pushed Medicaid and Medicare through Congress, and led Congress in passing new civil rights laws.

During Ronald Reagan's administration there was a serious challenge in the White House to liberal economic programs. The number of pages added to the *Federal Register*, which records the rules and regulations issued by federal agencies, declined each year of Reagan's presidency, breaking a sharp increase since 1960. The centerpiece of his economic program was his tax cuts, enacted in 1981, which lowered the top personal tax bracket from 70 to 28 percent in seven years. Reagan failed, however, to lower government expenditures, and the deficit soared.

What many conservative Americans today seem to be clamoring for is right-sized government. This type of government performs all functions necessary to protect life, liberty, and property of citizens. The word necessary is the key. Only those things that individuals are incapable of doing themselves should government step in to perform. Government should be practicing concerted

constraint to not become an aggressor against its citizens or compel them to do things that they either would not choose to do or would prefer not to do.

Yet conservatives who strongly disagree with Barack Obama's alleged government expansion seem to not realize how many layers of government President George W. Bush brought to the federal government through the creation of the Department of Homeland Security. Going directly against the ideals of Reagan, Bush chose to increase spending and employment in the name of security. While everything was on the table in the aftermath of September 11, the new Cabinet-level department will continue to require significant federal investments for as long as it exists.

Today's conservatives have made Reagan's approach their model, while liberals seek to build on Franklin Roosevelt's legacy. The Obama administration's decision to mandate individuals to have health insurance, first proposed as a form of universal health care by President Harry Truman in 1945, rests on assumptions about government broadly shared by liberals since Roosevelt's time but whose philosophical roots can be traced to Alexander Hamilton. Yet again, whether one believes government is inherently good or bad seemingly follows Miles' Law. Those who see the benefit of government (or who personally benefit) will be the most likely to stand up and call for expansion. Perhaps this is the great irony of American politics today. The Tea Party movement has been shown to have a significant number of elderly support. The same folks who are clamoring for government to cease to exist would also like government to keep its hands off of their Medicare. Who ever said that citizens must be consistent?

Professor Jeff Madrick takes the liberal view that activist government has done much to enhance the quality of life and increase American prosperity. However, David Boaz, of the Cato Institute, traces America's libertarian traditions and reminds readers that there are times where government's best course of action is simply deciding to do nothing—no matter how difficult this can be to admit.

YES ⬅

Jeff Madrick

The Case for Big Government

After World War II, almost all economists feared a reprise of the Depression. It was hard to imagine what could replace all the lost military demand. But the opposite occurred. After a pause in 1947, the economy grew as rapidly on average as it ever did before, and the incomes of most working Americans grew faster than ever before. The progressive turn of policy, despite a resurgence of antigovernment sensibility, did not deter growth. Nor did higher income tax rates, which were raised by Roosevelt during the Depression and were raised again to record levels during World War II, where they remained for more than a decade. The highest tax bracket reached approximately 90 percent, where it remained until 1964. To the contrary, bigger government seemed to go along with ever faster growth. Roosevelt had proposed a G.I. Bill of Rights in 1943, among other things, to provide aid for veterans to go to college and to buy a house. Congress raised objections, but in 1944 the G.I. Bill was passed. By the late 1950s, half of the returning sixteen million soldiers financed college or other training programs as a result. Millions of mortgages were guaranteed. The nation was thus directed in a particular way. The Marshall Plan under President Truman, and named after the secretary of state who strongly advocated it, provided billion of dollars of aid to rebuild Europe.

Dwight Eisenhower, as a former president, incurred the ire of the Republican right wing by proposing to expand Social Security coverage to another ten million workers—to include farm workers and professionals such as teachers, accountants, and dentists. He also increased benefits. Eisenhower said that it was simply clear that not all could save enough for retirement. Eisenhower also advocated the development and federal financing of a national highway system. He had strong support from the major auto companies, of course, and the bill passed in 1956. By the late 1950s, 90 percent of all homes in America were reachable by road, and often by highway. It was an explicit case of national government coordination and investment that deeply influenced the development of the nation into a new geography of suburbs, based on cheap gas, cheap property, and mostly free roads.

In these decades, the federal government financed and administered the antipolio vaccines. In the wake of the Soviet launch of the first space satellite, Sputnik, Congress passed the National Defense Education Act, providing billions of dollars of annual grants and loans to support higher education, technical training, and other educational programs. Young people were further spurred to go to college. The National Institutes of Health, as an extension of late nineteenth-century government investment in health research, were expanded dramatically after World War II, and accounted for a high proportion of medical breakthroughs. Research and development (R&D) was undertaken in many federal agencies, not least the Defense Department, where the Internet had its origins. The federal government accounted for most of America's R&D, in fact, through the 1960s, topping out at 67 percent of all such research in 1963. Many economists contend that such intense research efforts account for greater American economic superiority in these years than any other single factor. The Supreme Court under Eisenhower, led by Johnson's appointee as chief justice, Earl Warren, ordered that public schools be integrated.

In the 1960s, President Johnson passed Medicare and implemented his War on Poverty, including health care for the poor under Medicaid. Regulatory changes were significant, and included landmark civil rights legislation, which protected voting rights for blacks, ended Jim Crow laws once and for all, and forbade gender and racial discrimination in labor markets. Other regulatory reforms involved cigarettes, packaging, motor vehicle safety, consumer credit, and the expansion of the authority of the Food and Drug Administration.

Between 1948 and 1970, the share of spending in GDP by the federal, state, and local governments rose from 16.5 percent to 27.5 percent, nearly eleven percentage points. Most of this increase was in social expenditures. Yet productivity, wages, and overall GDP grew very rapidly, as noted. What is the complaint then in light of all this success? It is hard to escape the conclusion as noted earlier in this section that government did not hurt but significantly helped economies to grow.

The Economic Benefits of Government

. . . Few economists disagree with the theory that some measure of public investment in infrastructure, education, and health care is necessary. Because public goods such as roads and schools benefit society overall more than any individual or business, such investment would not have been adequately undertaken by private firms. . . . Government support is required for primary education, roads, and the poor.

From *The Case for Big Government* by Jeff Madrick (Princeton University Press, 2008), pp. 56–61, 128, 138–140, 142–143. Copyright © 2008 by Princeton University Press. Reprinted by permission.

Far less frequently discussed is the fact that government can be the focus of needed and useful coordination. When railroads used different size track (gauge), government was needed to standardize them. By organizing communities to use a single public water system, government creates economies of scale for such a public good. The highway system was an immense act of coordination that probably couldn't have been attained through a private network; there is no example of one in the world, in any case. The system of international trade and currency valuation is a government-led example of coordination.

Similarly, regulations can and often do make economies work better. They can make information about products and services more open. They can reduce corruption, monopolistic pricing, and anticompetitive policies regarding research, innovation, and new products. They can temper financial speculation, which distorts the flow of capital toward inefficient uses and can often lead to costly corrections and serious recessions, as occurred yet again in 2008.

Some regulations can be poorly administered and reduce economic efficiency. Others will outlive their usefullness; they should be pruned and streamlined over time. But other regulations will be a short-term cost to business that the nation chooses to bear for quality of life and even a better economy. Maintaining the safety of products that consumers cannot judge for themselves is an example; but the safety and effectiveness of products also makes consumers more confident buyers of products. Environmental regulations adopted in the early 1970s have probably been costly to all of us, but they are a cost we bear for cleaner air and water and the diminution of global warming. It is no cause for alarm that regulations have multiplied as the economy supplies so many more goods and services to the people. As economies change and grow more complex, it is only natural that more oversight is needed.

At the still more liberal end of the political spectrum, some economists will argue—though not the American mainstream—that programs that help raise and make wages more equal, such as laws that facilitate union organizing, minimum wages, and equal rights, may well aid economic growth, not undermine productivity, by creating demand for goods and services, and also reinforcing faith in workers that they will be fairly rewarded for their effort. . . .

One of the key benefits of the larger post–World War II government, if in some quarters still a controversial one, is also that it makes the economy more stable. Well before Keynes's work during the Depression there were calls for government spending to create jobs and support incomes. Massive public works projects that reignited economic growth, such as Baron Hausmann's rebuilding of Paris, are common in history. But in the post–World War II era, such activities gained new theoretical justification from Keynes's theories. Both Keynesian liberals and some Friedmanite conservatives accepted, to one degree or another, that fiscal and monetary policy—deficit spending by the treasury or the adjustment of interest rates by the central bank—could help avoid or ameliorate recessions and thereby raise the rate of growth over time. A large government is itself, despite conservative arguments cited earlier, a bulwark against rapidly declining spending. Unemployment insurance, Social Security, and government employment itself are stabilizing factors.

If the size of government truly and directly caused the inflation of the 1970s and contributed demonstrably to slower economic growth, it would be reason for concern. But we have seen that it did not in the United States, and nations with far larger governments have produced neither more rapid inflation nor substandard levels of income for their citizens. The public goods and social programs of many countries—from Sweden and Norway to France and Germany—are significantly more generous than America's. . . .

In fact, enlightened regulation has been imperative for economic growth at least since Jefferson's policies for governing the distribution of land. When done well, regulation keeps competition honest and free, enables customers to know and understand the products they receive, and fosters new ideas. When neglected, abuse becomes easy, information in markets is suppressed, capital investment is channeled to wasteful and inefficient uses, and dangerous excesses occur. The open flow of products and services information is critical to a free-market economy. The conditions for healthy competition have simply not been maintained under a free-market ideology of minimal government that professes great faith in competition. Competition requires government oversight; the wool has been pulled over our eyes.

We now know the following. If federal, state, and local governments absorb roughly 35 percent of GDP in America, rather than the current roughly 30 percent, it will not inhibit growth and undermine entrepreneurial spirits, productivity, or prosperity if the spending is well-channeled. Government absorbs much more of national income in other nations whose prosperity is the equivalent of or perhaps superior to America's. In European nations, government spending absorbs approximately 40 percent of all spending, and standards of living are high. If government programs are managed well, they will on balance enhance productivity. A rise to 35 percent will raise approximately $700 billion a year to the federal, state, and local governments to provide protections to workers, finance social programs, maintain an adequate regulatory presence, and raise significantly the level of investment in transportation, energy, education, and health care. Part and perhaps all of this $700 billion can be paid for with higher taxes. . . .

. . . The most productive way to address rising global competition is not trade restrictions per se but for the government to invest in the nation. Consumer spending leaks to foreign imports and business investment leaks across borders. But potential returns to the economy from spending on transportation projects are at this point significant, partly due to years of neglect, and the jobs created to implement them largely stay at home. The proportion of the federal budget spent on investment in the nation—including transportation, science, technology, and energy—are well down from the levels of the 1970s. Federal spending on education as a proportion of GDP fell under Clinton but was raised under his successor, George Bush, and it remains slightly higher as a proportion of GDP than it was in the 1970s. Overall, public investment equaled nearly 3 percent of GDP in the 1970s, which would come to more than $400 billion today. Under Clinton it fell to half of that proportion, and under Bush it rose but remains at less than 2 percent of GDP. Merely raising it to 1970s levels would produce $140 billion more a year to spend. To reemphasize, such spending usually creates domestic jobs and builds future productivity at the same time.

To take one estimate, a House Transportation Committee report cites a Federal Highway Administration model that claims that a $75 billion investment will create more than 3.5 million jobs and $464 billion in additional nationwide sales. Every $1 billion, in other words, yields 47,500 jobs and an other $6 billion in sales. Spending has been so inadequate that such estimates can be accepted confidently. The Society of Civil Engineers suggest that much of America's infrastructure should get a grade of D. While these studies are hardly definitive, they are suggestive of the possibilities.

The most exciting potential returns are for high-quality pre-K education. A wide range of studies has been undertaken on several high-quality programs that have long been underway in the United States. The benefits of such programs include not only improving the ability of children to learn, but also long-term reduction in crime rates, reduced need for special education and repeating grades, and lower welfare enrollment rates. A conventional conservative economist such as James Heckman, a Nobel laureate who opposes college subsidies, nevertheless favors significant funding of preschool programs. Some estimate these programs create benefits that exceed costs by five to ten times. A highly sophisticated recent analysis by two economists estimates that if a high-quality program was instituted nationwide, the federal moneys spent would be fully paid for in increased tax revenues due to improved incomes and would reduce welfare, crime, and special education expenses. In other words, it would pay for itself. . . .

As a consequence of neglect and change, an adequate agenda for America is a lengthy one, but it is not an antigrowth agenda. It favors growth. Growing personal income is more necessary to a full life than is recognized, in part because the cost of some key needs rise very fast, in part because a wealthy society can finance innovation, and in part because a wealthy populace will find it easier and more congenial to pay for communal needs through taxes. But for too long, mainstream economists have accepted the notion that more savings and technology will alone lead to faster growth. The agenda for government is therefore inappropriately limited; government spending, for example, will allegedly erode savings. America has been able to test this economic philosophy for a full generation and it has failed. Years of below-par productivity growth, low and stagnating wages, inattention to basic needs, persistent poverty, and the undermining of assets necessary to future growth, including education, health care, energy alternatives, and transportation infrastructure are the consequences.

The gap between a growing economy and falling wages is the major contemporary mystery. Global competition and off-shoring may explain part of the gap, but the trend began decades ago. Research shows that a gap in worker compensation and productivity began to open up slowly in the late 1980s: typical workers got less than their historical share, while capital (profits) and high-income workers got more. This gap widened explosively in the 2000s.

Furthermore, there was little explanation as to why male incomes in particular fared especially poorly over this long period we have described. A major reason is the withdrawal of government from its traditional purposes.

JEFF MADRICK is the editor of *Challenge* magazine, the author of *The End of Affluence* (1995) and other books, a frequent contributor to *The New York Review of Books*, and a Visiting Professor of Humanities at The Cooper Union in New York.

David Boaz    **NO**

The Return of Big Government

It's been a long time since a U.S. election generated feelings of actual joy beyond the ranks of partisan activists. If Barack Obama hasn't yet ushered in a new "era of good feelings," all Americans can take pride in the demise of yet another glass ceiling in a nation conceived in liberty and dedicated to the proposition that all of us are created equal, entitled to the inalienable rights of life, liberty, and the pursuit of happiness.

Indeed, we can take some satisfaction in observing that something normal happened: A party that had given Americans a long war and an economic crisis, led by a strikingly unpopular president, was defeated. Republican government requires that failed parties be turned out of office. The American Founders believed firmly in the principle of rotation in office. They thought that even successful officeholders should go back home to live under the laws after a short period in office. No doubt more members of the 110th Congress would have been given that privilege were it not for the vast incumbent protection complex of laws and regulations and subsidies.

George W. Bush and the Republicans promised choice, freedom, reform, and a restrained federal government. As far back as the Contract with America in 1994, congressional Republicans pledged "the end of government that is too big, too intrusive, and too easy with the public's money." But over the past eight years they delivered massive overspending, the biggest expansion of entitlements in 40 years, centralization of education, a war that has lasted longer than World War II, an imperial presidency, civil liberties abuses, the intrusion of the federal government into social issues and personal freedoms, and finally a $700 billion bailout of Wall Street that just kept on growing in the last month of the campaign. Voters who believe in limited government had every reason to reject that record.

At the Cato Institute we stand firmly on the principles of the Declaration of Independence and the Constitution, and on the bedrock American values of individual liberty, limited government, free markets, and peace. And throughout our 32 years we have been willing to criticize officials of both parties when they sought to take the country in another direction. We published papers critical of President Clinton's abuse of executive authority, his administration's misguided antitrust policies, his nation-building experiments, and his unwillingness to take on corporate welfare. Our analysts were among the first to point out the Bush administration's profligate spending, as well as the administration's policies on executive power, habeas corpus, privacy, expansion of entitlements, the federal marriage amendment, and the misbegotten war in Iraq.

But we have also been pleased to work with administrations of both parties when they seek to expand freedom or limit government—with the Clinton administration on free trade, welfare reform, and a few tentative steps toward Social Security reform; with the Bush administration on tax cuts, the initial response to the 9/11 attacks, health savings accounts, immigration reform, and Social Security accounts. We look forward to opportunities to work with the Obama administration when it moves to reverse the worst mistakes of the Bush years or otherwise to advance policies that would enhance peace, freedom, and prosperity.

The Current Crisis

In the current economic crisis, our first task is to understand it and its causes. This was a crisis caused by regulation, subsidization, and intervention, and it won't be cured by more of the same. Christopher Hitchens had a point when he wrote, "There are many causes of the subprime and derivative horror show that has destroyed our trust in the idea of credit, but one way of defining it would be to say that everybody was promised everything, and almost everybody fell for the populist bait."

The backdrop is central banking and implicit federal guarantees for risky behavior. The Federal Reserve Board creates money and adjusts interest rates, so any notion that our financial system was an example of laissez-faire fails at the start. Meanwhile, Congress and regulators pushed Fannie Mae and Freddie Mac to become a vast duopoly in the mortgage finance industry. Their debt was implicitly backed by the U.S. Treasury, and they were able to expand their debt and engage in risky transactions. As Lawrence Summers wrote, "Little wonder with gains privatized and losses socialized that the enterprises have gambled their way into financial catastrophe."

There was substantial agreement in Washington that home ownership was a good thing and that more homeownership would be even better. Thus Congress and regulators encouraged Fannie, Freddie, and mortgage lenders to extend credit to underqualified borrowers. To generate more mortgage lending to low- and

Boaz, David. "The Return of Big Government", *Cato Policy Report*, January/February 2009. Copyright © 2009 by Cato Institute. Used with permission.

moderate-income people, the federal government loosened down-payment standards, pressured lenders to increase their percentages of "affordable" loans, and implicitly guaranteed Fannie and Freddie's dramatic expansion. All that hard work paid off: The share of mortgages classified as nonprime soared, and the quality of those loans declined. And Federal Reserve credit expansion helped to make all of this lending possible, as Lawrence H. White wrote in his Cato Briefing Paper, "How Did We Get into This Financial Mess?"

"Everybody was promised everything"—cheap money, easy lending, and rising home prices. All that money and all those buyers pushed housing prices up sharply. But all good things—at least all good things based on unsustainable policies—must come to an end. When housing prices started to fall, many borrowers ran into trouble. Financial companies threatened to fall like dominos, and an ever-expanding series of bailouts began issuing from the Treasury department. And instead of the usual response to businesses that make bad decisions—let them go into bankruptcy or reorganization and let their workers and assets go to more effective companies—the federal government stepped in to keep every existing enterprise operating.

At this point it is important that the recent emergency measures be recognized as just that: emergency—if not panic—measures and not long-term policy. Congress should turn its attention to extricating the government from financial firms and basing long-term policies on a clear diagnosis of what went wrong. Congress should repeal the Community Reinvestment Act and stop pressuring lenders to make loans to underqualified borrowers. The Treasury should use its authority as conservator to liquidate Fannie Mae and Freddie Mac. The federal government should refrain from using its equity investments in companies to exercise power over their operations and should move with all deliberate speed to withdraw from corporate ownership.

One lesson of the credit crisis is that politicians prefer to "promise everybody everything"—low interest rates, affordable mortgages, higher housing prices, lower gas prices, a chicken in every pot. That's why it's important to keep politics out of such matters.

The End of Libertarianism—or a New Beginning?

Various pundits and public figures have claimed that the credit crisis means "the end of libertarianism" or even more dramatically "the end of American capitalism." As noted above, the crisis can hardly be considered a failure of laissez-faire, deregulation, libertarianism, or capitalism, since it was caused by multiple misguided government interventions into the workings of the financial system. It was and is precisely a failure of interventionism.

But could capitalism or libertarianism come to an end despite the facts? After all, the Great Depression was primarily caused by poor Federal Reserve policy and high tariffs. But a false impression that it was somehow caused by laissez-faire led to New Deal policies (pursued first by Herbert Hoover and then by Franklin D. Roosevelt) that turned a contraction into the Great Depression. What policies? Restrictive banking regulations, increases in top marginal tax rates, interventions to keep wages and prices from adjusting, and government rhetoric and activism that created (in the words of historian Robert Higgs) "pervasive uncertainty among investors about the security of their property rights in their capital and its prospective returns." That set of policies lengthened the Great Depression by eight years or more and is uncomfortably similar to recent and proposed policy responses to the 2008 credit crisis.

In *Newsweek*, Jacob Weisberg declared that the financial crisis is "the end of libertarianism." But it was in fact "progressive" interventionism that caused the crisis—just the economic philosophy that Weisberg supports. So if one big failure can kill an ideology, then let's hear it for "the end of interventionism."

If this crisis leads us to question the "American-style capitalism" in which a central monetary authority manipulates money and credit, the central government taxes and redistributes $3 trillion a year, huge government-sponsored enterprises create a taxpayer-backed duopoly in the mortgage business, tax laws encourage excessive use of debt financing, and government pressures banks to make bad loans—well, it might be a good thing to reconsider that "American-style capitalism." Or indeed, as a *Washington Post* editorial put it in October, "Government sponsored, upside-only capitalism is the kind that's in crisis today, and we say: Good riddance."

Libertarianism calls for freedom and responsibility, free markets and civil liberties, a minimal government that stays out of both boardrooms and bedrooms. Obviously libertarianism wasn't in the driver's seat in either the Clinton or the Bush administration.

Even if there are misperceptions about the causes of the crisis, both the system of capitalism and the idea of libertarianism are going to have more staying power than pundits such as Weisberg would like. There was a time when half the world rejected capitalism, and leading intellectuals in the "free world" worried that the centrally planned economies would obviously out compete the capitalist countries and that "convergence" on some sort of half-capitalist, half-socialist model was the wave of the future. But after the world got a look at the results of the two systems in East and West Germany, North and South Korea, Hong Kong and Taiwan and China, the United States and the Soviet Union, it became clear that socialism is a clumsy, backward looking prescription for stagnation at best and tyranny at worst.

Meanwhile, the half-planned economies of the West—Great Britain, New Zealand, the United States, and more—developed a milder version of economic sclerosis. Starting in the 1970s many of those countries began eliminating price controls, removing restrictions on market competition, opening up the economy, cutting tax rates, and reducing trade barriers. It came to be widely recognized—eventually on both sides of the Iron Curtain—that private property and markets are indispensable in organizing a modern economy. A nearly simultaneous cultural revolution opened up society. Women, racial minorities, and gays and lesbians entered the mainstream of society throughout the Western world. Art, literature, and lifestyles became more diverse and more individualized. The Sixties and the Eighties both led us to what Brink Lindsey in *The Age of Abundance* called "the implicit libertarian synthesis" of the United States today.

Some people see a future of ever more powerful government. Others see a future of greater freedom. *Reason* editors Nick Gillespie and Matt Welch write: "We are in fact living at the cusp of what should be called the Libertarian Moment, the dawning of . . . a time of increasingly hyper-individualized, hyper-expanded choice over every aspect of our lives. . . . This is now a world where it's more possible than ever to live your life on your own terms; it's an early rough draft version of the libertarian philosopher Robert Nozick's 'utopia of utopias. . . . This new century of the individual, which makes the Me Decade look positively communitarian in comparison, will have far-reaching implications wherever individuals swarm together in commerce, culture, or politics."

Is it possible that Congress will choose to pursue policies—tax increases, yet higher spending, continued subsidies for risky decisions, intrusion into corporate decision making—that would slow down U.S. economic growth, perhaps make us more like France, with its supposedly kinder, gentler capitalism and its GDP per capita of about 75 percent of ours? Yes, it's possible, and clearly there are proposals for such policies. But if we want economic growth—which means better health care, scientific advance, better pharmaceuticals, more leisure opportunities, a cleaner environment, better technology; in short, more well being for more people—there is no alternative to market capitalism. And if we want more growth, for more people, with wider scope for personal choice and decision making, libertarian policy prescriptions are the roadmap.

A Libertarian Agenda

Beyond the immediate financial crisis, there are many more issues confronting us. Fiscal reform, for instance. Federal spending increased by more than a trillion dollars during the Bush years, or more than 70 percent (even before the budget busting bailout and stimulus packages). The national debt rose even more sharply, from $5.727 trillion to more than $10.6 trillion, or an increase of more than 85 percent. The 2009 budget deficit may exceed $1 trillion. Trends like this are unsustainable, yet elected officials continue to promise more spending on everything from new weaponry to college tuitions. Congress and the administration must find a way to rein in this profligacy.

The current rates of spending don't yet reflect the acceleration of entitlement spending as the baby boomers start retiring. Entitlements are already about 40 percent of the federal budget. In 20 years

they may double as a share of national income. The unfunded liability of Social Security and Medicare is now over $100 trillion, an unfathomably large number. Within barely a decade, the two programs will require more than 25 percent of income tax revenues, in addition to the payroll taxes that currently fund them. Congress needs to think seriously about this problem. Are members prepared to impose the tax burden necessary to fund such levels of transfer payments? Do we want that many Americans dependent on a check from the federal government? Eventually, the projected level of entitlements will not be feasible. It would be best to start now to make changes rationally rather than in a panic a few years from now.

Private property, free markets, and fiscal restraint are important foundations for liberty, and the party that claims to uphold those values has done a poor job of it lately. But there are restrictions on liberty beyond the realm of taxes and regulations. We hope that elected officials of both parties will recognize the dangers of censorship, drug prohibition, entanglement of church and state, warrantless wiretapping, indefinite detention, government interference with lifestyle and end-of-life choices, and other such policies. Americans declared in 1776 that life, liberty, and the pursuit of happiness are inalienable rights, and in 1787 they wrote a Constitution that empowers a limited government to protect those rights.

Fidelity to those founding principles of respect for civil liberties and limited government may be easy when times are easy. The true test of our faith in those principles comes when we are beset by diabolical assaults from without and economic turmoil within, when public anxiety may temporarily make it seem expedient to put those principles aside. The importance of paying scrupulous deference to the Constitution's limits on federal power, of respecting its careful system of checks and balances, is greatest precisely when the temptation to flout them is strongest.

For those who go into government to improve the lives of their fellow citizens, the hardest lesson to accept may be that Congress should often do nothing about a problem—such as education, crime, or the cost of prescription drugs. Critics will object, "Do you want the government to just stand there and do nothing while this problem continues?" Sometimes that is exactly what Congress should do. Remember the ancient wisdom imparted to physicians: First, do no harm. And have confidence that free people, left to their own devices, will address issues of concern to them more effectively outside a political environment.

DAVID BOAZ is the Executive Vice President of the Cato Institute and has played a key role in the development of the Cato Institute and the libertarian movement. He is a provocative commentator and a leading authority on domestic issues such as education choice, drug legalization, the growth of government, and the rise of libertarianism.

EXPLORING THE ISSUE

Is Bigger Government Better Government?

Critical Thinking and Reflection

1. Madrick argues that the federal government's expansion since World War II has been good for the country. Why does he reach that conclusion? What sort of evidence does he cite?
2. Madrick often refers to the success of big government in Western Europe and cites it as a model for this country. Do you think the European model fits the United States? Why, or why not?
3. How does Boaz categorize libertarianism in the United States? Does it appear that libertarian ideals are gaining momentum today? Why or why not?
4. Why is it difficult for politicians to choose not to act on a problem facing society?
5. How do we assess whether government is working in the United States? Do different individuals utilize different metrics? Why does it matter?

Is There Common Ground?

There might be common ground between Madrick and Boaz if the latter could convince the former to limit government to (a) protecting people from other people or countries that want to harm them and (b) guaranteeing that all citizens be treated equally and fairly. But it does not seem likely that Madrick would consent to these limited functions of government, unless of course terms like "fairness" and "equality" were given very expansive definitions—which is what Boaz and other conservatives seem to complain that liberals always do!

Ultimately, America will never find agreement on the size of government. Those who need government will likely always favor expanding its power and reach, while those who do not need assistance will wonder why they are paying taxes. Unless citizens begin to look past their own self-interest and realize the larger societal goals of government, we will be faced with constant clamoring for government to both expand and condense. For elected officials and government workers, this means being stuck in a never ending tug-of-war in which nothing that is done is pleasing to half of Americans.

Additional Resources

Timothy P. Carney, *The Big Ripoff: How Big Business and Big Government Steal Your Money* (Wiley, 2006)

Milton Friedman, *Capitalism and Freedom* (University of Chicago Press, 1962)

John K. Galbraith, *The Affluent Society* (Houghton Mifflin, 1960)

Max Neiman, *Defending Government: Why Big Government Works* (Prentice Hall, 2009)

Amity Shales, *The Forgotten Man* (Harper Perennial, 2007)

Internet References . . .

Brookings Institute

www.brookings.edu

Cato Institute

www.cato.org

Center for American Progress

www.americanprogress.org

Center for Small Government

www.centerforsmallgovernment.org

Foundation for Economic Education

www.fee.org

Selected, Edited, and with Issue Framing Material by:
William J. Miller, *Flagler College*

ISSUE

Is America Approaching Equality within Society?

YES: Barack Obama, from "Remarks at the 'Let Freedom Ring' Ceremony Commemorating the 50th Anniversary of the March on Washington for Jobs and Freedom," speech delivered at Lincoln Memorial in Washington, DC (August 28, 2013)

NO: National Urban League, from "2016 State of Black America," *National Urban League* (2016)

Learning Outcomes

After reading this issue, you will be able to:

- Describe what is meant by the term equality.
- Assess whether America has become more or less equal.
- Describe how American society is currently structured economically.
- Assess differences between racial, gender, and economic inequality.
- Explain historical and modern approaches to understanding equality.

ISSUE SUMMARY

YES: U.S. President Barack Obama honors Martin Luther King, Jr. by discussing how King's dreams have begun to be realized and continue to fuel the actions and directions of many Americans.

NO: The 2016 State of Black America examines racial equality in the United States and ultimately finds that African Americans in America remain only 72.2 percent equal to white citizens.

There has always been a wide range in real income in the United States. In the first three decades after the end of World War II, family incomes doubled, income inequality narrowed slightly, and poverty rates declined. Prosperity declined in the mid-1970s, when back-to-back recessions produced falling average incomes, greater inequality, and higher poverty levels. Between the mid-1980s and the late 1990s, sustained economic recovery resulted in a modest average growth in income, but high poverty rates continued.

Defenders of the social system maintain that, over the long run, poverty has declined. Many improvements in social conditions benefit virtually all people and, thus, make us more equal. The increase in longevity (attributable in large measure to advances in medicine, nutrition, and sanitation) affects all social classes. In a significant sense, the U.S. economy is far fairer now than at any time in the past. In the preindustrial era, when land was the primary measure of wealth, those without land had no way to improve their circumstances. In the industrial era, when people of modest means needed physical strength and stamina to engage in difficult and hazardous labor in mines, mills, and factories, those who were too weak, handicapped, or too old stood little chance of gaining or keeping reasonable jobs.

In the postindustrial era, many of the manufactured goods that were once "Made in U.S.A.," ranging from clothing to electronics, are now made by cheaper foreign labor. Despite this loss, America achieved virtually full employment in the 1990s, largely because of the enormous growth of the information and service industries. Intelligence, ambition, and hard work—qualities that cut across social classes—are likely to be the determinants of success.

In the view of the defenders of the American economic system, the sharp increase in the nation's gross domestic product has resulted in greater prosperity for most Americans. Although the number of superrich has grown, so has the number of prosperous small business owners, middle-level executives, engineers, computer programmers, lawyers, doctors, entertainers, sports stars, and others who have gained greatly from the longest sustained economic growth in American history. For example, successful young pioneers in the new technology and the entrepreneurs whose capital supported their ventures have prospered, and so have the technicians and other workers whom they hired. Any change that mandated more, nearly equal income would greatly diminish the incentives for invention, discovery, and risk-taking enterprises. As a result, the standard of living would be much lower and rise much more slowly, and individual freedom would be curtailed by the degree of state interference in people's private lives.

None of these objections will satisfy those who deplore what they see as an increasing disparity in the distribution of income and wealth. In 2008 the first full year since the recession that began in 2007, the wealthiest 10 percent of Americans, those making more than $138,000 a year, earned 11.4 times the $12,000 earned by those living near or below the poverty line in 2008. Poverty jumped to 13.2 percent, an 11-year high. Nearly 10 million households used food stamps. There has been a long-term acceleration of a gap between rich and poor in the United States. Between 1979 and 2005 (the latest year for which the non-partisan Congressional Budget Office has complete statistics), the average after-tax income of the top 1 percent of households, after adjusting for inflation, increased by $745,000, or 228 percent; that of the 20 percent of Americans in the middle of the income spectrum grew an average of $8,700, or 21 percent; by contrast, that of the poorest 20 percent of Americans grew by $900, or 6 percent.

The financial wealth of the top 1 percent of households exceeds the combined household financial wealth of the bottom 98 percent. Contrary to popular cliché, a rising tide does not lift all boats; it does not lift leaky boats or those who have no boats. Advocates of more nearly equal income argue that this would produce less social conflict and crime as well as more and better social services. They maintain that more egalitarian nations (Scandinavia and Western Europe are often cited) offer more nearly equal access to education, medical treatment, and legal defense. Is democracy diminished if those who have much more also enjoy greater political power than those who have much less?

The rise of the Occupy Movement demonstrated that there is a significant amount of anger being leveled at capitalists in the United States. Consisting of younger Americans with college degrees unable to find jobs at which they can earn livable wages, the rallying cry of the 99 percent focused clearly on income inequality. While the movement fizzled out rather quickly, it nonetheless succeeded in raising awareness for the growing economic tensions in the United States today. And in his first apostolic exhortation, Pope Francis echoed many Occupy sentiments when railing against the negative impacts of capitalism on the ideals of equality, stating:

> In this context, some people continue to defend trickle-down theories which assume that economic growth, encouraged by a free market, will inevitably succeed in bringing about greater justice and inclusiveness in the world. This opinion, which has never been confirmed by the facts, expresses a crude and naive trust in the goodness of those wielding economic power and in the sacralized workings of the prevailing economic system. Meanwhile, the excluded are still waiting. To sustain a lifestyle which excludes others, or to sustain enthusiasm for that selfish ideal, a globalization of indifference has developed. Almost without being aware of it, we end up being incapable of feeling compassion at the outcry of the poor, weeping for other people's pain, and feeling a need to help them, as though all these were someone else's responsibility and not our own. The culture of prosperity deadens us; we are thrilled if the market offers us something new to purchase; and in the meantime all those lives stunted for lack of opportunity seem a mere spectacle; they fail to move us.

What Francis makes clear is that capitalism fails at assuring the safety of all within a society. As long as a nation relies on trickle-down impacts, there will always be someone left behind.

In the following selections, President Obama echoes the sentiments of Martin Luther King, Jr. in assessing how America has moved toward racial and economic equality since his assassination. While he does not believe we have accomplished everything King set out to do, he believes we are making steady progress. However, the 2016 State of Black America finds that African Americans in America remain only 72.2 percent equal to white citizens.

YES ⬅

Barack Obama

Remarks at the "Let Freedom Ring" Ceremony Commemorating the 50th Anniversary of the March on Washington for Jobs and Freedom

To the King family, who have sacrificed and inspired so much; to President Clinton; President Carter; Vice President Biden, Jill; fellow Americans.

Five decades ago today, Americans came to this honored place to lay claim to a promise made at our founding: "We hold these truths to be self-evident, that all men are created equal, that they are endowed by their Creator with certain unalienable rights, that among these are life, liberty, and the pursuit of happiness."

In 1963, almost 200 years after those words were set to paper, a full century after a great war was fought and emancipation proclaimed, that promise—those truths—remained unmet. And so they came by the thousands from every corner of our country, men and women, young and old, blacks who longed for freedom and Whites who could no longer accept freedom for themselves while witnessing the subjugation of others.

Across the land, congregations sent them off with food and with prayer. In the middle of the night, entire blocks of Harlem came out to wish them well. With the few dollars they scrimped from their labor, some bought tickets and boarded buses, even if they couldn't always sit where they wanted to sit. Those with less money hitchhiked or walked. They were seamstresses and steelworkers, students and teachers, maids and Pullman porters. They shared simple meals and bunked together on floors. And then, on a hot summer day, they assembled here, in our nation's capital, under the shadow of the Great Emancipator, to offer testimony of injustice, to petition their government for redress, and to awaken America's long-slumbering conscience.

We rightly and best remember Dr. King's soaring oratory that day, how he gave mighty voice to the quiet hopes of millions, how he offered a salvation path for oppressed and oppressors alike. His words belong to the ages, possessing a power and prophecy unmatched in our time.

But we would do well to recall that day itself also belonged to those ordinary people whose names never appeared in the history books, never got on TV. Many had gone to segregated schools and sat at segregated lunch counters. They lived in towns where they couldn't vote and cities where their votes didn't matter. They were couples in love who couldn't marry, soldiers who fought for freedom abroad that they found denied to them at home. They had seen loved ones beaten and children firehosed, and they had every reason to lash out in anger or resign themselves to a bitter fate.

And yet they chose a different path. In the face of hatred, they prayed for their tormentors. In the face of violence, they stood up and sat in with the moral force of nonviolence. Willingly, they went to jail to protest unjust laws, their cells swelling with the sound of freedom songs. A lifetime of indignities had taught them that no man can take away the dignity and grace that God grants us. They had learned through hard experience what Frederick Douglass once taught: that freedom is not given, it must be won through struggle and discipline, persistence and faith.

That was the spirit they brought here that day. That was the spirit young people like John Lewis brought to that day. That was the spirit that they carried with them, like a torch, back to their cities and their neighborhoods. That steady flame of conscience and courage that would sustain them through the campaigns to come: through boycotts and voter registration drives and smaller marches far from the spotlight; through the loss of four little girls in Birmingham and the carnage of the Edmund Pettus Bridge and the agony of Dallas and California and Memphis. Through setbacks and heartbreaks and gnawing doubt, that flame of justice flickered; it never died.

And because they kept marching, America changed. Because they marched, a civil rights law was passed. Because they marched, a voting rights law was signed. Because they marched, doors of opportunity and education swung open so their daughters and sons could finally imagine a life for themselves beyond washing somebody else's laundry or shining somebody else's shoes. Because they marched, city councils changed, and state legislatures changed, and Congress changed, and yes, eventually, the White House changed.

Because they marched, America became more free and more fair, not just for African Americans, but for women and Latinos,

Obama, Barack. From speech delivered at Lincoln Memorial in Washington, DC, August 28, 2013.

Asians and Native Americans; for Catholics, Jews, and Muslims; for gays; for Americans with disabilities. America changed for you and for me. and the entire world drew strength from that example, whether the young people who watched from the other side of an Iron Curtain and would eventually tear down that wall or the young people inside South Africa who would eventually end the scourge of apartheid.

Those are the victories they won with iron wills and hope in their hearts. That is the transformation that they wrought with each step of their well-worn shoes. That's the debt that I and millions of Americans owe those maids, those laborers, those porters, those secretaries—folks who could have run a company maybe if they had ever had a chance; those white students who put themselves in harm's way, even though they didn't have to; those Japanese Americans who recalled their own internment; those Jewish Americans who had survived the Holocaust; people who could have given up and given in, but kept on keeping on, knowing that "weeping may endure for a night, but joy cometh in the morning."

On the battlefield of justice, men and women without rank or wealth or title or fame would liberate us all in ways that our children now take for granted, as people of all colors and creeds live together and learn together and walk together and fight alongside one another and love one another and judge one another by the content of our character in this greatest nation on Earth.

To dismiss the magnitude of this progress—to suggest, as some sometimes do, that little has changed—that dishonors the courage and the sacrifice of those who paid the price to march in those years. Medgar Evers, James Chaney, Andrew Goodman, Michael Schwerner, Martin Luther King, Jr.—they did not die in vain. Their victory was great.

But we would dishonor those heroes as well to suggest that the work of this nation is somehow complete. The arc of the moral universe may bend towards justice, but it doesn't bend on its own. To secure the gains that this country has made requires constant vigilance, not complacency. Whether by challenging those who erect new barriers to the vote or ensuring that the scales of justice work equally for all and the criminal justice system is not simply a pipeline from underfunded schools to overcrowded jails, it requires vigilance.

And we'll suffer the occasional setback. But we will win these fights. This country has changed too much. People of good will, regardless of party, are too plentiful for those with ill will to change history's currents.

In some ways, though, the securing of civil rights, voting rights, the eradication of legalized discrimination, the very significance of these victories may have obscured a second goal of the march. For the men and women who gathered 50 years ago were not there in search of some abstract ideal. They were there seeking jobs as well as justice, not just the absence of oppression, but the presence of economic opportunity.

For what does it profit a man, Dr. King would ask, to sit at an integrated lunch counter if he can't afford the meal? This idea—that one's liberty is linked to one's livelihood, that the pursuit of happiness requires the dignity of work, the skills to find work, decent pay, some measure of material security—this idea was not new. Lincoln himself understood the Declaration of Independence in such terms, as a promise that in due time, "the weights should be lifted from the shoulders of all men, and that all should have an equal chance."

And Dr. King explained that the goals of African Americans were identical to working people of all races: "Decent wages, fair working conditions, livable housing, old-age security, health and welfare measures, conditions in which families can grow, have education for their children, and respect in the community."

What King was describing has been the dream of every American. It's what's lured for centuries new arrivals to our shores. And it's along this second dimension—of economic opportunity, the chance through honest toil to advance one's station in life—where the goals of 50 years ago have fallen most short.

Yes, there have been examples of success within black America that would have been unimaginable a half century ago. But as has already been noted: black unemployment has remained almost twice as high as white employment, Latino unemployment close behind. The gap in wealth between races has not lessened, it's grown. And as President Clinton indicated, the position of all working Americans, regardless of color, has eroded, making the dream Dr. King described even more elusive.

For over a decade, working Americans of all races have seen their wages and incomes stagnate, even as corporate profits soar, even as the pay of a fortunate few explodes. Inequality has steadily risen over the decades. Upward mobility has become harder. In too many communities across this country, in cities and suburbs and rural hamlets, the shadow of poverty casts a pall over our youth, their lives a fortress of substandard schools and diminished prospects, inadequate health care and perennial violence.

And so as we mark this anniversary, we must remind ourselves that the measure of progress for those who marched 50 years ago was not merely how many blacks could join the ranks of millionaires. It was whether this country would admit all people who are willing to work hard, regardless of race, into the ranks of a middle class life.

The test was not and never has been whether the doors of opportunity are cracked a bit wider for a few. It was whether our economic system provides a fair shot for the many: for the black custodian and the white steelworker, the immigrant dishwasher and the Native American veteran. To win that battle, to answer that call—this remains our great unfinished business.

We shouldn't fool ourselves: The task will not be easy. Since 1963, the economy has changed. The twin forces of technology and global competition have subtracted those jobs that once provided a foothold into the middle class, reduced the bargaining power of

American workers. And our politics has suffered. Entrenched interests, those who benefit from an unjust status quo, resisted any government efforts to give working families a fair deal, marshaling an army of lobbyists and opinion makers to argue that minimum wage increases or stronger labor laws or taxes on the wealthy who could afford it just to fund crumbling schools, that all these things violated sound economic principles. We'd be told that growing inequality was a price for a growing economy, a measure of this free market, that greed was good and compassion ineffective, and that those without jobs or health care had only themselves to blame.

And then, there were those elected officials who found it useful to practice the old politics of division, doing their best to convince middle class Americans of a great untruth: that government was somehow itself to blame for their growing economic insecurity; that distant bureaucrats were taking their hard-earned dollars to benefit the welfare cheat or the illegal immigrant.

And then, if we're honest with ourselves, we'll admit that during the course of 50 years, there were times when some of us claiming to push for change lost our way. The anguish of assassinations set off self-defeating riots. Legitimate grievances against police brutality tipped into excuse-making for criminal behavior. Racial politics could cut both ways, as the transformative message of unity and brotherhood was drowned out by the language of recrimination. And what had once been a call for equality of opportunity—the chance for all Americans to work hard and get ahead—was too often framed as a mere desire for government support, as if we had no agency in our own liberation, as if poverty was an excuse for not raising your child and the bigotry of others was reason to give up on yourself.

All of that history is how progress stalled. That's how hope was diverted. It's how our country remained divided. But the good news is, just as was true in 1963, we now have a choice. We can continue down our current path, in which the gears of this great democracy grind to a halt and our children accept a life of lower expectations; where politics is a zero-sum game; where a few do very well while struggling families of every race fight over a shrinking economic pie. that's one path. Or we can have the courage to change.

The March on Washington teaches us that we are not trapped by the mistakes of history, that we are masters of our fate. But it also teaches us that the promise of this nation will only be kept when we work together. We'll have to reignite the embers of empathy and fellow feeling, the coalition of conscience that found expression in this place 50 years ago.

And I believe that spirit is there, that truth force inside each of us. I see it when a White mother recognizes her own daughter in the face of a poor black child. I see it when the black youth thinks of his own grandfather in the dignified steps of an elderly white man. It's there when the native born recognizes that striving spirit of the new immigrant, when the interracial couple connects the pain of a gay couple who are discriminated against and understands it as their own.

That's where courage comes from: when we turn not from each other or on each other, but towards one another, and we find that we do not walk alone. That's where courage comes from. And with that courage, we can stand together for good jobs and just wages. With that courage, we can stand together for the right to health care in the richest nation on Earth for every person. With that courage, we can stand together for the right of every child, from the corners of Anacostia to the hills of Appalachia, to get an education that stirs the mind and captures the spirit and prepares them for the world that awaits them. With that courage, we can feed the hungry and house the homeless and transform bleak wastelands of poverty into fields of commerce and promise.

America, I know the road will be long, but I know we can get there. Yes, we will stumble, but I know we'll get back up. That's how a movement happens. That's how history bends. That's how, when somebody is faint of heart, somebody else brings them along and says, come on, we're marching.

There's a reason why so many who marched that day, and in the days to come, were young. for the young are unconstrained by habits of fear, unconstrained by the conventions of what is. They dared to dream differently, to imagine something better. And I am convinced that same imagination, the same hunger of purpose stirs in this generation.

We might not face the same dangers of 1963, but the fierce urgency of now remains. We may never duplicate the swelling crowds and dazzling procession of that day so long ago—no one can match King's brilliance—but the same flame that lit the heart of all who are willing to take a first step for justice, I know that flame remains.

That tireless teacher who gets to class early and stays late and dips into her own pocket to buy supplies because she believes that every child is her charge, she's marching.

That successful businessman who doesn't have to, but pays his workers a fair wage and then offers a shot to a man, maybe an ex-con who is down on his luck, he's marching.

The mother who pours her love into her daughter so that she grows up with the confidence to walk through the same doors as anybody's son, she's marching.

The father who realizes the most important job he'll ever have is raising his boy right, even if he didn't have a father—especially if he didn't have a father at home—he's marching.

The battle-scarred veterans who devote themselves not only to helping their fellow warriors stand again and walk again and run again, but to keep serving their country when they come home, they are marching.

Everyone who realizes what those glorious patriots knew on that day, that change does not come from Washington, but to Washington; that change has always been built on our willingness, we the people, to take on the mantle of citizenship, you are marching.

And that's the lesson of our past. That's the promise of tomorrow: that in the face of impossible odds, people who love their country can change it. That when millions of Americans of every race and every region, every faith and every station can join together in a spirit of brotherhood, then those mountains will be made low and those rough places will be made plain and those crooked places, they straighten out towards grace, and we will vindicate the faith of those who sacrificed so much and live up to the true meaning of our creed, as one nation, under God, indivisible, with liberty and justice for all.

BARACK OBAMA served as U.S. Senator for Illinois prior to defeating John McCain in the 2008 presidential election to become the 44th President of the United States. He is the first African American to hold the position. In 2012, President Obama defeated Republican challenger Mitt Romney to win a second term.

National Urban League  **NO**

2016 State of Black America

As we observe the 40th anniversary of the State of Black America®, the similarities in the nation in 2016 and that which then-National Urban League Executive Director Vernon Jordan documented in 1976 are disheartening. Our nation was struggling to overcome the worst economic downturn since the Great Depression. Pressure was building to slash social services for the poor, who were demonized and characterized as "chislers." Communities were rocked by hostility and violence triggered by legal challenges to the social status quo.

As with every economic downturn, communities of color bore the brunt of the decline. Black Americans remained nearly twice as likely as whites to be unemployed. Since 1976, the Black unemployment rate has consistently remained about twice that of the white rate across time, regardless of educational attainment. The household income gap remains at about 60 cents for every dollar. Black Americans are only slightly less likely today to live in poverty than they were in 1976.

On the criminal justice front, Jordan noted that Blacks were underrepresented in law enforcement in 1976. "The City of Chicago is an example: with a population that is 32.7 percent black, it has a police force that is only 16 percent black." Today, in hundreds of police departments across the nation, the percentage of whites on the force is more than 30 percentage points higher than in the communities they serve.

"The urgency of the problems that grip the American people allow no time for delay or for half-way measures," Jordan observed.

There have been times when Americans have met our shared challenges—as well as those of the international community—with full-measured urgency. When Europe found itself in physical and economic ruin after World War II, the United States invested $13 billion (or what would be approximately $130 billion today) to help rebuild Western European economies through the European Recovery Program, more commonly known as the Marshall Plan. The Marshall Plan ushered a dramatic increase in economic growth in European history. Though the plan officially ended in 1953, the unprecedented economic growth it sparked continued over two decades.

Former National Urban League President John Jacob introduced the concept of an urban Marshall Plan for America in the 15th State of Black America® in 1990. At the time, he said the nation should commit itself to completing "our unfinished revolution for democracy and human rights."

Dear Mr./Madame President, that revolution remains unfinished.

Since 2006, the United States has spent nearly $50 billion rebuilding Afghanistan through the Afghanistan Infrastructure Rehabilitation Program. The Troubled Asset Relief Program (TARP), signed into law by President George W. Bush in 2008, infused the nation's faltering financial institutions with investments of more than $400 billion. Whether we call it "recovery," "rehabilitation" or "relief," it is time for America to demonstrate that very same commitment to our own struggling urban families and communities. The necessity is as powerful and compelling as it was for Europe, Afghanistan or Wall Street.

That is why, with this milestone 40th Anniversary State of Black America®, the National Urban League proposes a sweeping and decisive solution to the nation's persistent social and economic disparities. We call it the Main Street Marshall Plan: Moving from Poverty to Prosperity.

This bold and strategic investment in America's urban communities requires a multi-annual and multi-pronged commitment of $1 trillion over the next 5 years that would course-correct our main streets. Our nation needs investments in:

- Universal early childhood education
- A federal living wage of $15 per hour, indexed to inflation
- A plan to fund comprehensive urban infrastructure
- A new Main Street small- and micro-business financing plan focusing on minority-and-women-owned businesses
- Expansion of summer youth employment programs
- Expanded homeownership strategies
- Expansion of the Earned Income Tax Credit (EITC)
- Targeted re-entry workforce training programs administered through community-based organizations
- Doubling the Pell Grant program to make college more affordable
- Expansion of financial literacy and homebuyer education and counseling
- Expansion of the low-income housing voucher "Section 8" program
- Establishment of Green Empowerment Zones in neighborhoods with high unemployment

National Urban League. "2016 State of Black America," 2016 State of Black America, 2016. Copyright © 2016 by National Urban League. Used with permission.

- Affordable high-speed broadband and technology for all
- Increased federal funding to local school districts to help eliminate resource equity gaps

As America's urban communities continue to struggle in the slow rebound from the Great Recession, we can expedite the recovery by taking a lesson from the pages of our history books and similarly focusing our efforts with great vision and purpose-filled ambition. Our economy and infrastructure have been shattered, not by bombs and tanks, but by malfeasance and indifference.

Under President Obama, the nation has made great strides in stabilizing the economy. In eight years, America has gone from losing hundreds of thousands of jobs per month to 73 consecutive months of job growth. During President Obama's term, the private sector has added 14.4 million new jobs, and the Economic Recovery and Reinvestment Act is widely credited with protecting the nation from a second Great Depression.

However, much more remains to be done. The benefits of the recovery have not reached the Main Streets of our most troubled communities. We cannot continue to rely on policies that have proven ineffective in communities with high unemployment and low income. You see, we are not asking for a new deal; we are demanding a better deal. As a nation, we must focus our resources and efforts on the neighborhoods where they are most needed.

Vernon Jordan realized in 1976 that it was incumbent upon the National Urban League to confront the problems that Washington refused to acknowledge. Forty years later, we continue on that path to progress—with a clear purpose and an even clearer plan.

Black–White

The 2016 Equality Index of Black America stands at 72.2 percent compared to a revised 2015 index of 72.0 percent. Revisions to the previous year's index are done for greater comparability across years and reflect data points that have been corrected, removed from the current year's index or re-weighted so that less emphasis is placed on older data. The largest increase in this year's index was in the area of education (from 76.1% to 77.4%), with smaller increases in economics (from 55.5% to 56.2%) and social justice (60.6% to 60.8%). The civic engagement index declined sharply over the last year (from 104.0% to 100.6%) while the health index (from 79.6% to 79.4%) declined slightly.

The increase in the education index was the result of improvements in college attainment and enrollment. The increase in the economics index came primarily through progress in closing the digital divide as well as lower denial rates for African Americans seeking mortgage and home improvement loans. The unemployment and homeownership gaps remained unchanged from the previous year. The improvements in the social justice index resulted from a decline in the Black incarceration rate, while

the percent of whites placed in prison following an arrest grew by more than the rate for Blacks.

The large drop in the civic engagement index resulted from the typical declines in voter registration and participation that are characteristic of mid- term election years.

Hispanic–White

The 2016 Equality Index of Hispanic America stands at 77.8 percent compared to a revised 2015 index of 77.3 percent. The increase in the Hispanic-White Index resulted from a major improvement in the social justice index (from 66.6% to 75.9%) and smaller gain in the economics index (from 60.8% to 61.8%) that helped to offset losses in all other categories. The greatest losses were in civic engagement (from 71.0% to 67.6%), followed by health (from 106.8% to 105.5%), and education (from 74.6% to 74.2%).

The large increase in the social justice index was the result of improvements on nearly every measure of social justice used to calculate the Equality Index. Similar to the trends in the Equality Index of Black America, the increase in the economics index came from a smaller digital divide and fewer mortgage and home improvement loan denials.

The increase in the health index was a result of lower death rates among Hispanics and increased health care coverage since the Affordable Care Act went into effect.

On the other hand, Hispanic voter registration and participation dropped sharply during the mid-term elections in 2014 (latest data available), resulting in a decline in the civic engagement index. While the Hispanic-White health index remains above 100 percent and rates of uninsurance are falling among all groups, declining index values reflect faster health insurance take-up rates among whites than Latinos

Black–White Unemployment Equality

With an index of 68.7 percent, the Providence-Warwick, RI-MA metro area once again tops the list as the metro area with the smallest Black-White unemployment gap. The Black unemployment rate in Providence was 9.9 percent (down 3.1 percentage points) and the white rate was 6.8 percent (down 1.7 percentage points). With an index of 67 percent, this year's second most equal metro area, Chattanooga, TN-GA, is up from #51 last year, reflecting a decline of more than six percentage points in the area's Black unemployment rate, while the white rate was virtually unchanged.

Similar to the 2015 rankings, the 2016 rankings reveal that metros with the greatest unemployment equality are not necessarily the metros with the best employment outcomes for either group. The metros with the lowest unemployment rate for Blacks (8.3%) were San Antonio-New Braunfels, TX and Oklahoma City, OK, #6 in the equality ranking. The metro with the lowest white unemployment rate (3.7%) was Jackson, MS, #65 in the equality ranking. The metro with the highest Black unemployment rate (20%) was Cleveland-Elyria, OH, #69 in the equality ranking. Riverside-San Bernardino- Ontario, CA registered the highest white unemployment rate (9.7%) and came in at #5 in the equality ranking.

Hispanic–White Unemployment Equality

With an index of 103.6 percent, Indianapolis-Carmel-Anderson, IN topped the Hispanic-White metro unemployment rankings this year. Indianapolis was #2 last year behind Deltona-Daytona Beach-Ormond Beach, FL, which fell to #49 this year. While there were a total of five metros in the 2015 Index with a Hispanic-White unemployment index greater than 100—indicating that the Hispanic unemployment rate was lower than the white unemployment—Indianapolis was the only metro with that distinction in this year's index.

Since unemployment disparities between Latinos and whites have narrowed more than those between Blacks and whites during the recovery, lower unemployment rates and greater unemployment equality seemed to be more closely linked. The metro with the lowest Hispanic unemployment rate (4.6%) was Tulsa, OK, #4 in the ranking. The metro with the highest Hispanic unemployment rate (21.5%) was Springfield, MA at #72 in the ranking.

Black–White Income Equality

Riverside-San Bernardino-Ontario, CA remained at the top of the Black-White Income Equality ranking this year, with the median Black household having 76 cents for every dollar of median white household income. In Riverside, Black household income rose 6.8 percent year-over-year while whites saw a decline of 1.1 percent. Black and white incomes were least equal in Minneapolis-St. Paul-Bloomington, MN-WI where the gap was 38 cents on the dollar. Minneapolis replaces San Francisco-Oakland-Hayward, CA as the metro where Black and white incomes were least equal. In Minneapolis, the median household income for Blacks was $28,138 (down 12.7% from last year's Index) compared to $74,455 for whites (up 1.7% from last year's Index).

The highest median household income for both Blacks ($66,151) and whites ($109,460) was in Washington-Arlington-Alexandria, DC-VA-MD-WV, #18 in the ranking. The lowest median Black household income ($22,386) was in Toledo, OH (#64 in the ranking). Even though Toledo had one of the lowest median white household incomes in the country, white household income in Toledo was still more than double Black household income. Toledo, OH also had the fourth highest Black unemployment rate, which would at least partly account for the low income of Black households. The lowest median white household income for whites ($47,208) was in Lakeland-Winter Haven, FL.

Hispanic–White Income Equality

For Latinos, median household incomes were closest to those of whites in Urban Honolulu, HI which was up from #7 in last year's ranking as a result of three percent income growth for Latinos and 1.3 percent growth for whites. In Urban Honolulu, the median Hispanic household had 80 cents for every dollar of median white household income. Hispanic and white incomes were least equal in Springfield, MA where the gap was 40 cents on the dollar. In Springfield, the median household income for Latinos was $23,911 (down 5.1% from the 2015 index), compared to $60,105 for whites (down 2.3%).

As was the case for Blacks and whites, the highest median Hispanic household income was in Washington-Arlington-Alexandria, DC-VA-MD- WV ($66,523), #50 in the equality ranking. The lowest median Hispanic household income was in Springfield, MA ($23,911), #72 in the equality ranking.

Note

1. The unemployment and income data used for the Metro Index rankings comes from the American Community Survey (ACS). The 2016 Metro Index is based on data from the 2014 ACS (most recent) and the 2015 Metro Index is based on data from 2013 ACS.

THE NATIONAL URBAN LEAGUE is a nonpartisan civil rights organization based in New York City that advocates on behalf of African Americans and against racial discrimination in the United States. It is the oldest and largest community-based organization of its kind in the nation.

EXPLORING THE ISSUE

Is America Approaching Equality within Society?

Critical Thinking and Reflection

1. What factors contribute to increased inequality of income and wealth in the United States?
2. Is economic inequality in America increasing or decreasing? Why? Is the process reversible?
3. Is racial inequality in America increasing or decreasing? Why? Is the process reversible?
4. How are racial and economic inequality linked? Is there a way to make inroads on both simultaneously?
5. Do you believe Martin Luther King, Jr. would be satisfied with the progress made in the United States since his assassination? Why or why not?

Is There Common Ground?

Both those who deplore increasing inequality and those who believe that Americans have achieved an impressive level of equality agree that equality of opportunity is critical. They disagree as to how much opportunity is necessary and whether American society has achieved it. Where Joseph Stiglitz and other critics of American inequality advocate much greater public investment in education, health, and other areas as the most effective means of equalizing opportunity, Barack Obama concludes that economic freedom has produced both the challenge of social ills and the development of social solutions. While he by no means would argue that our nation has become equal, he points to historical growth and reminds the country of how far it has come. The divide is between those who approach equal justice in public policies that reduce sharp areas of inequality and those who seek it in the social forces of a free society.

A study released on October 27, 2011 by the Bertelsmann Stiftung Foundation in Germany comparing poverty rates, income inequality, pre-primary education, and health rating in 32 member countries of the Organisation for Economic Co-operation and Development ranked the United States 27 among 31 countries overall in what it characterized as social justice, with the United States among the bottom five in poverty prevention, overall poverty rate,

child poverty rate, and income inequality; among the bottom 10 in senior citizen poverty rate, pre-primary education, and health rating; and in the bottom 15 in intergenerational justice, which includes family and pension policies, environmental policies, and assessment of political-economic being established for future generations. In none of the eight categories did the United States place in the top half of 31 nations.

Additional Resources

Larry Bartels, *Unequal Democracy: The Political Economy of the New Gilded Age* (Princeton University Press, 2008)

James Lardner and David A. Smith, *The Growing Economic Divide in America with Its Poisonous Consequences* (The New Press, 2006)

Ron Paul, *The Revolution: A Manifesto* (Grand Central Publishing, 2009)

Richard Rothstein, *Class and Schools: Using Social, Economic, and Educational Reform to Close the Black-White Educational Gap* (The Economic Policy Institute and Teachers College Press, 2004)

Will Wilkinson, *Thinking Clearly About Economic Inequality* (Cato Institute, 2009)

Internet References . . .

Equality and the Fourteenth Amendment

www.pbs.org/tpt/constitution-usa-peter-sagal/equality/

How Economic Inequality Harms Societies

www.ted.com/talks/richard_wilkinson.html

International Society for Peace

www.societyforpeace.com

National Association for the Advancement of Colored People

www.naacp.org

The United States of Inequality

http://billmoyers.com/segment/bill-moyers-essay-the-united-states-of-inequality/

Selected, Edited, and with Issue Framing Material by:
William J. Miller, *Flagler College*

ISSUE

Is the Current Presidential Nomination System Actually Democratic?

YES: Jamelle Bouie, from "The Process Worked," *Slate* (2016)

NO: William Saletan, from "The Primaries Aren't Democratic? They're Not Supposed to Be Democratic," *Slate* (2016)

Learning Outcomes

After reading this issue, you will be able to:

- Assess the democratic values currently embedded in the American electoral system.
- Explain the deficiencies within the American electoral system.
- Discuss electoral controversies in American presidential elections.
- Explain ways the system could be made democratic.
- List reasons why any changes to the presidential electoral system will be difficult to achieve.

ISSUE SUMMARY

YES: Journalist Jamelle Bouie argues that the current presidential nomination system is in fact quite democratic by allowing states to determine how best to conduct elections within their borders. He notes that even outside of elections, American government has always flourished under a blend of majoritarian, nonmajoritarian, and countermajoritarian elements.

NO: William Saletan, also a journalist, acknowledges that the nomination process is not particularly democratic but reminds readers that the goals of primaries and caucuses are to select candidates that best represent party interests.

The 2016 presidential nomination system for the Democratic and Republican parties in the United States produced Hillary Clinton and Donald Trump as the two candidates to vie for the nation's highest office. In August 2016, they solidified their positions as the two most unpopular presidential candidates going back more than 30 years. Among all adults, 56 percent viewed Clinton unfavorably compared with 63 percent for Trump. While with registered voters, it is 59 percent unfavorable for Clinton and 60 percent for Trump. And it's not like there were not other options: Clinton faced five other legitimate challengers while Trump shared the stage with roughly a dozen other Republican hopefuls. So how did a nomination system produce two candidates that more Americans dislike than like? And what does this suggest for future nomination cycles?

As if Democrats and Republicans do not have enough differences, they also select their presidential nominees in different ways. Both parties choose delegates to represent them. And those delegates vote for presidential nominees at their party conventions. This is an important key to remember about nominations: they are conducted by political parties for members to select nominees for general elections. They are not controlled by any national office or regulations. And the Supreme Court has supported their right to be viewed as party-specific activities.

The Democrats prefer to allocate delegates by percentage of votes won in each state's primary—a method called proportionality. Republicans lean generally, but far from exclusively, toward winner-take-all outcomes. Even so, there are many variations in different states, each of which sets its own primary voting rules. In Iowa, for example, Republican delegates were awarded proportionally, rounded to the nearest delegate. Nevada was divvied up proportionally as well.

There is a rich and convoluted history to these formulas, most of which stem from states' efforts to build up their political clout on the national scene. Politicos have always wanted an early say on who will be a presidential contender so they can ultimately shape the final outcome. And presidential candidates like it, at least usually, because they get an early start on amassing delegates and can then build momentum to lay claim to a political coronation. But when more states began to schedule their contests earlier and earlier to shore up their importance, the parties adopted changes in 2008 that required most states—with exceptions like Iowa, Nevada, New Hampshire, and South Carolina—to hold their contests after February. The rest have to follow in March or even later.

Tinkering over the years has made each party's presidential nomination process anything but simple. In a Democratic primary, candidates are awarded delegates in proportion to their share of votes in a state primary or caucus, but a candidate must first win at least 15 percent of the vote in any given state. Once that threshold is crossed, then the candidate racks up the delegates. The Republicans lack a uniform approach. Some states still stick to the traditional winner-take-all approach, but others have introduced variations. So now, some states give out delegates proportionally and—just to make things thoroughly confusing—some states mix the proportional and winner-takes-all formulas.

Before diving for the nearest spreadsheet, it is also good to know that in many states, but not all, the Republican Party requires that a candidate win at least 20 percent of the vote before actually earning delegates. But others, like Iowa, do not set a limit. So Iowa, an early voting state, parceled out its delegates to several presidential hopefuls. Setting such minimum thresholds means that fewer presidential candidates can amass many delegates. That's a surer way to abbreviate drawn-out contests and knock out those who do not latch on early to the voting public's imagination.

If that weren't complicated enough, Republicans also take into account both statewide and congressional district results. A Republican candidate could lose a statewide vote but salvage some delegates if she or he wins at least one congressional district in that state. The Democrats' proportional approach makes it harder for the party to narrow its field, as voters are seeing in the contest between Hillary Clinton and Bernie Sanders. The large number of Republican presidential contenders this cycle has also resisted winnowing.

Even so, that doesn't guarantee that they will. All kinds of variations are in play. For example, Democrats have super delegates (mostly party leaders) among their 4,765 delegates. They are free to make their own candidate choice regardless of who wins the primaries or caucus contests. Meanwhile, the 2,470 Republican delegates are bound to support their state's choice only for the first vote at the upcoming July 18 Cleveland convention. If no one achieves the 1,237 votes necessary to nail down the presidential nomination, then delegates are, at least theoretically, free to follow their personal political allegiances. Those allegiances can vary considerably.

Both parties have both primaries and caucuses throughout their nomination calendar with states choosing which method to use. Caucuses were once the most common way of choosing presidential nominees. Today, Alaska, Colorado, Hawaii, Kansas, Maine, Minnesota, Nevada, North Dakota, Wyoming, and Iowa are the only states to rely solely on the caucus, according to the Federal Election Commission. The territories of American Samoa, Guam, and the Virgin Islands use the caucus also. All other states and Puerto Rico use primary elections or a combination of the voting formats. Caucus meetings are arranged by either the state or political party to take place at a certain place and time. Caucuses are unique in that they allow participants to openly show support for candidates. Voting is often done by raising hands or breaking into groups according to the candidate participants support. The results of the caucus are used to determine the delegates present at county, state, and national nominating conventions of each political party. Most often, only registered voters can participate in a caucus, and they are limited to the caucus of the party with which they are affiliated.

Primaries are a direct, statewide process of selecting candidates and delegates. Similar to the general election process, primary voters cast secret ballots for the candidates of their choosing. The results are used to determine the configuration of delegates at the national convention of each party. Primaries come in two basic forms: In an open primary, all registered voters can vote for any candidate, regardless of their political affiliation. Registered Democrats may vote for a Republican candidate, and Republican voters may cast ballots for a Democrat, for instance. And registered Independents can participate in either party's primary. But in a closed primary, voters may vote only for candidates of the party with which they are registered.

Since the parties are permitted to control the nomination system used for picking presidential nominees, there is already a clear argument to be made that the process is not truly democratic since you have to belong to a party to vote in their primary or participate in their caucus. Unless you live in an open primary state (where you can simply request a ballot for a particular party on Election Day), you have to legally declare a party preference to participate in their primary. What becomes interesting about this scenario is that if Donald Trump and Hillary Clinton are so unpopular with voters yet still managed to win crowded primaries, it suggests there are bigger problems related to voter turnout than the actual rules in place presently.

In the following selections, journalist Jamelle Bouie argues that the current presidential nomination system is in fact quite democratic by allowing states to determine how best to conduct elections within their borders. He notes that even outside of elections, American government has always flourished under a blend of majoritarian, nonmajoritarian, and countermajoritarian elements. However, William Saletan, also a journalist, acknowledges that the nomination process is not particularly democratic but reminds readers that the goals of primaries and caucuses are to select candidates that best represent party interests.

YES ↩

Jamelle Bouie

The Process Worked

On Monday night, the Associated Press broke news. Tallying its survey of Democratic superdelegates—the cadre of party members and elected officials who help select the nominee—the AP found that Hillary Clinton had met the threshold needed for nomination. Regardless of Tuesday's outcomes in California, New Jersey, and elsewhere, Clinton will be the Democratic Party's nominee for president and the first woman to win a major party nomination.

Team Clinton was restrained at the announcement, telling an audience in California that "we are on the brink of a historic, historic, unprecedented moment, but we still have work to do.... We have six elections tomorrow, and we're going to fight hard for every single vote, especially right here in California." Team Sanders, understandably, was defiant. "It is unfortunate that the media, in a rush to judgement, are ignoring the Democratic National Committee's clear statement that it is wrong to count the votes of super delegates before they actually vote at the convention this summer," said campaign spokesman Michael Briggs in a statement.

The reactions fit the campaigns' respective attitudes toward the primary. Team Clinton wants to avoid any sense that her win was unfair or illegitimate, while Team Sanders has criticized the process as suspect and, at worst, deeply unfair to his candidacy. "What is really dumb is that you have closed primaries, like in New York state, where 3 million people who were not Democrats or Republicans could not participate," said Sanders in a recent interview with CBS News' John Dickerson. "You have a situation where over 400 superdelegates came on board Clinton's campaign before anybody else was in the race, eight months before the first vote was cast."

To this point, Sanders has offered a few reforms for the Democratic primary process, aimed at smoothing the path for future ideological candidates like himself. "In those states where it's applicable," he said, "we need same-day registration, we need open primaries." This is echoed elsewhere, from supporters who see closed primaries and superdelegates as obstacles to a candidacy like Sanders', to surrogates who slam the Democratic National Committee as an unfair lever for the Democratic "establishment." And in general, this primary season has convinced a number of observers that the Democratic Party's process for selecting a presidential nominee is broken and ripe for reform.

I'm skeptical. To say that the process is "broken" presupposes both an idea of what it's supposed to do in the first place and a general consensus that it didn't accomplish the goal. We have the former: The aim of the Democratic primary process is for the party to choose a nominee who is acceptable to all of its parts, from dedicated supporters and casual voters to elites and activists, and who could plausibly lead the party to victory in the general election. But a close look at the conversation over the nomination process shows that we don't have much of the latter—there's no consensus over the efficacy of the process. Instead, we have an argument from the losing candidate and his backers that borders on special pleading.

To wit, Sanders' supporters say the process is flawed because it harmed their candidate in critical ways: Closed primaries kept out pro-Sanders independents; superdelegates gave his opponent an appearance of inevitability; and the order of the calendar gave her an early advantage.

The problem is that these aren't flaws in the process so much as they are contingent disadvantages. Yes, Bernie Sanders flailed with stalwart Democratic voters, lacked elite party support, and couldn't win in the South. But it's a trivial task to imagine a candidate who *could* have done some combination of three, or pulled a hat trick, full stop. (In fact, we have one: Barack Obama.) That Sanders was a poor fit for some aspects of the Democratic primary doesn't mean those parts were *bad*. To make that call, we have to see if these parts are out of alignment with our stated goal.

They aren't. Well before Clinton announced her bid for the White House, she held broad support across the Democratic Party. And going into the general election, she's the clear favorite, with a modest but growing lead over her likely opponent, Donald Trump. It's possible that—per his recent argument—Sanders is the better choice for the fall, but that doesn't make Clinton a bad or unacceptable one.

If there's a stronger case for reform beyond "my preferred candidate lost," it's that the processes of the *Democratic* Party aren't especially democratic, that, together, caucuses, closed primaries, and superdelegates either preclude participation or actively subvert the "will of the people." This isn't wrong. Caucuses, which require long hours from participants, are notoriously inhospitable to voters with tough schedules or attachments. Closed primaries and strict registration deadlines are designed to remove independent voters

Bouie, Jamelle. "The Process Worked," *Slate*, June 2016. Copyright © 2016 by Slate Group. Used with permission.

from consideration. And in theory, superdelegates could overturn the decision of voters. (For weeks, in fact, Sanders was asking them to do just that.) These are real problems and dangers in the primary process as it stands. But there are virtues, too.

Closed primaries force candidates to appeal directly to loyal Democratic voters in the same way that open ones force them to win over moderates and independents. Given the degree to which this is a party selection process, that's not only fair—it's desirable. Likewise, caucuses are a proving ground for the organizational capabilities of the candidates, as well as an opportunity both for smaller constituencies to make their mark on the process and for underdog candidates to pick up momentum. Barack Obama couldn't have made ground without winning the Iowa caucus, and this year's Sanders insurgency was fueled by grass-roots activity as channeled through caucuses. They aren't the most democratic method for selecting delegates, but they serve a vital purpose nonetheless.

The same goes for superdelegates, who represent important party stakeholders and elected officials. They force candidates—who are vying to lead the party—to take another constituency into account. Yes, the fact that they always back the pledged delegate winner undermines the extent to which they're "unbound" (as we saw in 2008, when Clinton superdelegates switched sides to bring Obama to the threshold after he finished the contest with a lead). But this year's Republican presidential contest is a testament to the value of an anchor in the case of a candidate who violates core party principles; an emergency brake, to use in potentially catastrophic situations like the rise of a Trump-style figure.

That the process may benefit from "undemocratic" elements gets to a larger point. Majoritarian procedures are a necessary part of democracy, but they're not synonymous with it. And most democratic systems—including our own—are a blend of majoritarian, nonmajoritarian, and even countermajoritarian elements that translate, temper, or otherwise channel the behavior and choices of majorities. What determines if the entire system is democratic is whether it's rule-bound, transparent, and ultimately accountable to the public.

That description fits the Democratic nomination process, and insofar as it doesn't, only minor tweaks are needed. State parties—which control most on-the-ground election procedures—need to devise and follow common standards for registration, party-switching, and caucus participation (in states that use caucuses). If you need to register with the party to participate, it should be easy and straightforward (what happened ahead of the New York primary, for example, is unacceptable). Actual delegate selection—as opposed to allocation—should be as public as possible. And it might be time to restrict superdelegate status to elected officials, so that they can be held directly accountable by their voters.

JAMELLE BOUIE is the chief political correspondent for *Slate* magazine, and a political analyst for CBS News. He covers campaigns, elections, and national affairs. His work has appeared either online or in print at the *New Yorker*, the *Washington Post*, *The Nation*, and other publications.

William Saletan    **NO**

The Primaries Aren't Democratic? They're Not Supposed to Be Democratic

Donald Trump says the process of picking Republican presidential delegates is "rigged." His son compares the process to "Communist China." Bernie Sanders says unelected Democratic superdelegates are propping up Hillary Clinton. Sanders and Trump are running as populists, challenging a corrupt nomination system in the name of democracy.

It's true that the system is full of quirks. Why do some states award their delegates proportionally, others by congressional district, and others by winner-take-all? Why do some conduct open primaries, while others restrict participation to caucusgoers? Why does a Republican delegate elected by Trump supporters get to vote for Ted Cruz at the convention? You can quarrel with any of these rules. But let's not pretend that everyone deserves a say in choosing the nominees. Parties are entitled to privilege their members and choose candidates who best represent their ideas. Trump and Sanders don't necessarily fit the bill.

Last weekend, Trump's top aides went on the Sunday shows to complain about the Republican process. "What this election has shown is that when voters participate, Donald Trump wins," said Trump's convention manager, Paul Manafort. That's misleading. What the election has shown is that in a multicandidate field, Trump usually gets a plurality. So far, the only place in which he has won a majority is his home state, New York.

As the race has narrowed, Trump's advantage has shrunk. That's why he got spanked in Wisconsin. And that raises a hard question: Does Trump truly represent Republican voters? Or is his lead in the delegate race a residual artifact of a multicandidate field? Even now, John Kasich's persistence as a third candidate is propping up Trump. Look at two national polls taken this month. A Fox News poll shows that if Kasich were to drop out, 55 percent of his voters would go to Cruz. Only 24 percent would go to Trump. A CBS News poll indicates that if Kasich were to quit, Trump's lead over Cruz would shrink from 13 points to 10 points, leaving Trump still short of a majority.

So when Trump complains about multistage delegate-selection procedures that leave him with fewer delegates than he should have won based on primaries held two months ago, bear this in mind: He's complaining about a result that might have happened anyway if voters had been allowed to register their second choices and reallocate their votes accordingly. A snapshot isn't necessarily better than a deliberate process.

Trump's campaign manager, Corey Lewandowski, has another objection. On *Fox News Sunday*, he complained:

> Let me give you one example. In the state of Florida, Donald Trump dominated and won by 23 points over all of his competitors down there. He was awarded 99 delegates under the party rules. Of those 99 delegates, the chairman of the party of Florida, who is an avid and outward supporter of Marco Rubio, gets to appoint 30 of those delegates.... That's not what the rules should be. The rules should be that Donald Trump won 99 delegates, and ... we should have the opportunity to appoint those people.

Lewandowski botched the story: The Florida GOP chairman didn't take sides in the primary and doesn't appoint any delegates. But even if he did, the bigger outrage is that Trump got all 99 delegates for winning 46 percent of the vote. In three winner-take-all states—Florida, Arizona, and South Carolina—Trump won 43 percent of the combined ballots but was awarded all 207 delegates. That accounts for his entire 200-delegate lead in the nomination race. Overall, Trump has collected 48 percent of the delegates in Republican contests while winning only 37 percent of the vote.

Manafort says Trump wants Republicans and independents, "not the party bosses," to choose the nominee. Lewandowski complains that in some states, delegates are chosen based on "whether they run for statewide office and how much volunteering they have done," while other applicants are slighted "because they haven't been involved the last 25 years. That's everything that's wrong with the party system."

Everything that's wrong with the party system? Dude, that *is* the party system. A party is an organization. It has every right to award clout based on how much work you've put in over the years. Why should drive-by independents get more say than party bosses? I should know: I was one of those independents. In 2000, the Maryland Republican Party allowed people like me to vote in its presidential primary. I voted for John McCain over George W. Bush.

Saletan, William. "The Primaries Aren't Democratic? They're Not Supposed to Be Democratic," *Slate*, April 2016. Copyright © 2016 by Slate Group. Used with permission.

McCain was a better fit for people like me. But was he a better fit for the party? And isn't that the point of a Republican primary—to choose a candidate who will represent the GOP?

It's particularly rich to hear all this rhetoric about inclusion from a campaign whose core issue is sealing the nation's borders. According to Trump, we mustn't let in any Muslims, since we don't know who they are. "If you don't have borders, you don't have a country," he says. Meanwhile, Trump brags about flooding Republican primaries with independents who pledge allegiance only to him and his defiance of the Republican platform. Why shouldn't the party reassert its right to nominate someone who shares its beliefs? If you don't have ideological boundaries, you don't have a party.

Sanders shares some of Trump's gripes. Prior to New York, the Vermont senator bragged about winning "eight out of nine caucuses and primaries" since March 22. But he's trailing among superdelegates—Democratic officeholders and party officials who get to vote at the convention, just like delegates elected in primaries and caucuses. Sanders thinks that's rotten. "Hillary Clinton is the candidate of the establishment. And she has many, many times more superdelegates than we have," Sanders noted on *Face the Nation*. On Monday, he said he had "serious problems" with this system. He complained about "the establishment folks—these are elected people, these are money people, who are superdelegates." He also criticized laws in New York that tell "hundreds of thousands or more independents who would like to vote tomorrow, for me or anybody else, [that] they can't participate. I think that that's wrong."

Can't participate? Sure they can. Registering as an independent is a choice. In many states, that choice comes with a price: You don't get to vote in primaries. If you want to vote in a primary, join a party. That's what I did two weeks ago: I saw that the Democratic primary for U.S. Senate in Maryland was really close and that my vote might matter. So after 16 years, I changed my registration. On Monday, I got my new registration letter in the mail. It's that simple.

Yes, Sanders has won a bunch of caucuses and primaries. But do those wins really convey a mandate to represent the Democratic Party? Exit polls show that among self-identified Democrats, Sanders has beaten Clinton in only two primaries: his home state of Vermont (easily) and the neighboring state of New Hampshire (barely). In every other primary, Sanders has either lost to Clinton or won by padding his tally with independents. And regardless of party, Clinton has won 56 percent of all ballots cast in Democratic contests. Sanders has won only 42 percent.

As for the caucuses Sanders has won since March 22, check out the rules. You can't vote absentee. You have to show up at a specific time, usually on a Saturday morning. You're advised to reserve a seat or arrive hours early, since "there will probably be lines." If you miss the start time, you can be locked out. You have to endure "instructions and patriotic ceremonies," "speakers on behalf of all the candidates," and "general discussion and debate." The process can take hours. In most states, your ballot isn't secret: You literally "stand with your neighbors in support of your preferred candidate"—or you go to a different corner of the room and stand against them. And if your candidate doesn't get 15 percent of the vote at your caucus, you have to change your vote or throw it away.

That's why few people attend caucuses. Many states don't register voters by party, so it's hard to say how many Democrats there are. So let's use, as a rough proxy, a uniform standard that can be measured everywhere: the state-by-state vote totals for Barack Obama in the 2012 general election. The turnout in caucus states won by Sanders this year (except Utah, which has a more open process) has ranged from 9 percent to 13 percent of the Obama vote. By contrast, the turnout in primary states won by Clinton—even if you exclude the South, which Sanders claims is her base—has ranged from 40 percent to 67 percent of the Obama vote. Sanders tends to win two types of contests: ornate caucuses with very low turnout and wide-open primaries in which independents compensate for his poor showing among Democrats. Neither of these models certifies him as the candidate who best represents the Democratic Party.

Sanders doesn't even identify himself as a committed Democrat. His Senate bio calls him "the longest serving independent member of Congress." It doesn't mention any party affiliation. A year ago, when Sanders announced his presidential candidacy, he said he wouldn't join the Democratic Party. Since then, he has couched his affiliation with the party as a temporary arrangement.

WILLIAM SALETAN writes about politics, science, technology, and other stuff for *Slate*. He is the author of *Bearing Right*.

EXPLORING THE ISSUE

Is the Current Presidential Nomination System Actually Democratic?

Critical Thinking and Reflection

1. How do elections reflect political values of a society?
2. Why should we want the nomination system to be democratic?
3. How can Americans work to ensure nominations are as democratic as possible?
4. What facets of American elections could be made more democratic?
5. Do you believe American elections operate as they should? Why or why not?

Is There Common Ground?

As long as major political parties are permitted to control the nomination system, there will likely be questions regarding the relative democracy within how nominees for the president are selected. Given that the 2016 cycle produced Donald Trump and Hillary Clinton—two strongly unpopular candidates even within certain wings of their own parties—it is possible that reforms could be on the horizon; yet, it is essential to remember that those reforms would still be controlled by the Democratic and Republican parties. Democrats have been questioning the democratic nature of using superdelegates as part of the nomination system, whereas some Republicans have suggested a similar protocol moving forward to try to prevent extreme candidates from being able to take over the nomination.

If individuals are hoping to see a complete overhaul of the presidential nomination system, they are likely to be disappointed. At the end of the day, the presidential nomination system has never been directly concerned with democracy. Instead, it exists to allow political parties to select the candidate that individual party members believe will best represent the entire party in a general election. There will unquestionably be tweaks that occur prior to the 2020 presidential nomination cycle, but these will be relatively minor in nature. Bernie Sanders supporters will likely push for the Democratic Party to assure more inclusiveness in platform setting, while many non-Trump Republicans will be working to revise rules to help bring the party back to the mainstream identifier.

Additional Resources

Marty Cohen and David Karol, *The Party Decides: Presidential Nominations Before and After Reform* (University of Chicago Press, 2008)

Elaine C. Kamarck, *Primary Politics: Everything You Need to Know about How America Nominates Its Presidential Candidates* (Brookings Institution Press, 2016)

Barbara Norrander, *The Imperfect Primary: Oddities, Biases, and Strengths of U.S. Presidential Nomination Politics* (Routledge, 2015)

Internet References . . .

How the U.S. Presidential Primary System Works

http://www.cfr.org/elections/us-presidential-nominating
-process/p37522

Presidential Election Process

https://www.usa.gov/election

Understanding the Nomination Process

https://billofrightsinstitute.org/educate/educator
-resources/lessons-plans/current-events/nomination
-process/

Selected, Edited, and with Issue Framing Material by:
William J. Miller, *Flagler College*

ISSUE

Are Entitlement Programs Creating a Culture of Dependency?

YES: Nicholas Eberstadt, from "The Rise of Entitlements in Modern America, 1960–2010," *Templeton Press* (2012)

NO: William A. Galston, from "Have We Become 'A Nation of Takers'?" *Templeton Press* (2012)

Learning Outcomes

After reading this issue, you will be able to:

- Identify current entitlement programs in the United States.
- Describe what is meant by a culture of dependency.
- Assess current spending on entitlement programs on the United States budget today.
- Explain long-term concerns about entitlement spending and dependency.
- Indicate whether government can afford to maintain current entitlement programs.

ISSUE SUMMARY

YES: Social scientist Nicholas Eberstadt argues that the increase in entitlement programs is unprecedented in American history and has created a large dependency class that has lost the will to work.

NO: Political theorist William A. Galston sees the growth of American entitlement programs as an appropriate response to the needs of an aging population and rising costs of higher education and medicine; he sees them not as evidence of dependency but of "interdependence."

In a conference call with fundraisers and donors after the 2012 presidential election, Governor Mitt Romney attributed his defeat to what he called "gifts" bestowed by President Obama to selected constituencies, "especially the African-American community, the Hispanic community and young people." Similar claims were often voiced in the media. Radio talk-show host Rush Limbaugh and Fox News commentator Bill O'Reilly both talked about the election as being influenced by the prospect of "free stuff" from the White House. On the Internet, the Drudge Report posted a YouTube video of a woman in Cleveland bragging about getting a free "Obamaphone."

Central to the complaint about "free stuff" is what are called "entitlements," defined as "benefits provided by government to which recipients have a legally enforceable right" (Jack Plano and Milton Greenberg, *The American Political Dictionary*). Entitlement spending, in contrast to "discretionary spending," is spending that the

government must make to individuals based upon certain criteria. If a certain individual meets those criteria, he or she can demand payments from the government. Major examples of entitlements include Social Security, Medicare, veterans' benefits, government retirement plans, food stamps, and certain welfare programs. In 2010, the Affordable Care Act, a program of national health insurance, was enacted with some entitlement features, such as subsidies for those unable to purchase health insurance.

Entitlement spending has grown steeply over the past half-century. In 1960 it amounted to less than one-third of the total federal government outlays, the same share it occupied in 1940; today it constitutes roughly two-thirds of the total. At the present rate of growth, the risk is that it may soon crowd out other vital federal programs, from defense and internal security to national health and environmental protection. Most observers today agree that the growth of entitlement spending is a serious issue, though they may disagree on the best means of addressing the issue. Some think the best approach is through spending cuts, while others place greater emphasis on increases in revenues.

But the debate on entitlements is not just about fiscal issues. The complaint about "free stuff" touches one of the deepest nerves of American public morality. Since Puritan times, Americans have honored work as a builder of character and maturity. It follows that idleness is contemptible because it weakens character. "Idleness is the Dead Sea that swallows all virtues," wrote Ben Franklin, an appraisal repeated in various languages over the past 250 years. Idleness becomes particularly problematic in the view of most Americans when it is combined with the prospect of "free stuff." Daniel Patrick Moynihan, the 1973 U.S. Senator, addressed this issue in a discussion of "dependency." At the heart of Moynihan's thesis was a distinction between dependency and poverty. "To be poor is an objective condition; to be dependent, a subjective one as well. . . . Being poor is often combined with considerable personal qualities; being dependent rarely so." Moynihan's conclusion was that long-term dependency tends to leave a person in "an incomplete state of life: normal in a child, abnormal in an adult."

But equating entitlements with dependency is not so easy. Moynihan himself was a strong supporter of Social Security, which fits the *American Political Dictionary's* definition of an entitlement as a "legally enforceable right" to a benefit. It is hard to see how Social Security puts its recipients in "an incomplete state of life," especially since they have spent most of their life paying into it. The same is true of veterans' benefits and others considered in some sense to have been earned. Yet still other benefits such as food stamps are unearned. Entitlements, like many other government programs, are an apples-and-oranges mixture that almost defies definition.

One entitlement program that did seem to fit the category of unearned entitlements was Aid to Families with Dependent Children (AFDC) which was abolished by Congress in 1996 and replaced by Temporary Assistance for Needy Families (TANF), which left to the states much of the administration of the program but directed them to require work from recipients in order to receive benefits. Recently, the Obama administration has modified the administration of the work requirement, leaving still more discretion in the hands of individual states. Returning to Brandeis' central principles, states are

again laboratories of democracy. But in the current iteration, there is the potential for states to negatively impact the economic performance of the nation as a whole. Especially since entitlement spending takes the place of discretionary monies.

The Center on Budget and Policy Priorities examined where entitlement funds go in a February 2012 report. Their finds show, "Some conservative critics of federal social programs, including leading presidential candidates, are sounding an alarm that the United States is rapidly becoming an "entitlement society" in which social programs are undermining the work ethic and creating a large class of Americans who prefer to depend on government benefits rather than work. A new CBPP analysis of budget and Census data, however, shows that more than 90 percent of the benefit dollars that entitlement and other mandatory programs spend go to assist people who are elderly, seriously disabled, or members of working households—not to able-bodied, working-age Americans who choose not to work. This figure has changed little in the past few years." These findings directly refute much of the public perceptions—and especially conservative criticisms. Further, it complements other academic research, including a study that concluded: "The U.S. system favors groups with special needs, such as the disabled and the elderly. Groups like these which are perceived as especially deserving receive disproportionate transfers and those transfers have been increasing over time. Second, the system favors workers over non-workers and has increasingly done so over time. The rise of the EITC and the decline of AFDC/TANF is most illustrative of this trend." The study also found that "the demographic group which is most underserved by the system are non-elderly non-disabled families with no continuously-employed members." Despite these studies, public perception still seems to believe that entitlements do not always assist those in need.

In the following selections, social scientist Nicholas Eberstadt argues that the increase in entitlement programs is unprecedented in American history and has created a large dependency class that has lost the will to work. Opposing that view is political theorist William A. Galston, who sees the growth of American entitlement programs as an appropriate response to the needs of an aging population and rising costs of higher education and medicine; for him, the growth of these programs is evidence not of dependency but of "interdependence."

YES ⬅

Nicholas Eberstadt

The Rise of Entitlements in Modern America, 1960–2010

Introduction

The American republic has endured for more than two and a quarter centuries; the United States is the world's oldest constitutional democracy. But over the past fifty years, the apparatus of American governance has undergone a fundamental and radical transformation. In some basic respects—its scale, its preoccupations, even many of its purposes—the United States government today would be scarcely recognizable to a Franklin D. Roosevelt, much less an Abraham Lincoln or a Thomas Jefferson.

What is monumentally new about the American state today is the vast and colossal empire of entitlement payments that it protects, manages, and finances. Within living memory, the government of the United States of America has become an entitlements machine. As a day-to-day operation, the U.S. government devotes more attention and resources to the public transfers of money, goods, and services to individual citizens than to any other objective; and for the federal government, more to these ends than to all other purposes combined.

Government entitlement payments are benefits to which a person holds an established right under law (i.e., to which a person is entitled). A defining feature of these payments (also sometimes officially referred to as "current transfer receipts of individuals from government," or simply "transfers") is that they "are benefits received for which no current service is performed." Entitlements are a relatively new concept in U.S. politics and policy; according to Merriam-Webster, the first known use of the term was not until 1942. But entitlements have become very familiar, very fast. By the reckoning of the Bureau of Economic Analysis (BEA), the research group within the Commerce Department that prepares the U.S. government's GNP estimates and related national accounts, income from entitlement programs in the year 2010 was transferred to Americans under a panoply of over fifty separate types of programs, and accounted for almost one-fifth (18 percent) of personal income in that year.

In 1960, U.S. government transfers to individuals from all programs totaled about $24 billion. By 2010, the outlay for entitlements was almost 100 times more. Over that interim, the nominal growth in entitlement payments to Americans by their government was rising by an explosive average of 9.5 percent per annum for fifty straight years. The tempo of growth, of course, is exaggerated by concurrent inflation—but after adjusting for inflation, entitlement payments soared more than twelve-fold (1248 percent), with an implied average real annual growth rate of about 5.2 percent per annum. Even after adjusting for inflation and population growth, entitlement transfers to individuals have more than septupled (727 percent) over the past half-century, rising at an overall average of about 4 percent per annum.

These long-term spending trends mask shorter-run tendencies, to be sure. Over the past two decades, for example, the nominal growth in these entitlement outlays has slowed to an average of "only" 7.1 percent a year (or a doubling every decade). Adjusted for inflation by the Consumer Price Index, real entitlement outlays rose by an average of "just" 4.4 percent over those years—and by a "mere" 3.2 percent a year on a per capita basis. But if the pace of entitlement growth has slowed in recent decades, so has the growth in per capita income. From 1960 to 2010 real per capita income in America grew by a measured 2.2 percent on average—but over the past twenty years, it has increased by 1.6 percent per annum. In other words, total entitlement payouts on a real per capita basis have been growing twice as fast as per capita income over the past twenty years; the disparity between entitlement growth on the one hand and overall income growth on the other is greater in recent times than it was in earlier decades.

The magnitude of entitlement outlays today is staggering. In 2010 alone, government at all levels oversaw a transfer of over $2.2 trillion in money, goods, and services to recipient men, women, and children in the United States. At prevailing official exchange rates, that would have been greater than the entire GDP of Italy, roughly the equivalent of Britain's and close to the total for France—advanced economies all with populations of roughly 60 million each. (The U.S. transfer numbers, incidentally, do not include the cost of administering the entitlement programs.) In 2010 the burden of entitlement transfers came to slightly more than $7,200 for every man, woman, and child in America. Scaled against a notional family of four, the average entitlements burden

Eberstadt, Nicholas. From *A Nation of Takers: America's Entitlement Epidemic,* October 2012, pp. 3–4, 8–11, 23–25, 51–53, 58–59. Copyright © 2012 by Templeton Press. Reprinted by permission.

for that year alone would have approached $29,000. And that payout required payment from others, through taxes, borrowing, or some combination of the two.

A half-century of unfettered expansion of entitlement outlays has completely inverted the priorities, structure, and functions of federal administration, as these had been understood by all previous generations of American citizens. Until 1960 the accepted purpose of the federal government, in keeping with its constitutional charge, was governing. The federal government's spending patterns reflected that mandate. The overwhelming share of federal expenditures was allocated to defending the republic against enemies foreign and domestic (defense, justice, interest payments on the national debt) and some limited public services and infrastructural investments (the postal authority, agricultural extension, transport infrastructure, and the like). Historically, transfer payments did not figure prominently (or, sometimes, at all) in our federal ledgers. . . .

In 1960, entitlement program transfer payments accounted for well under one-third of the federal government's total outlays—about the same fraction as in 1940, when the Great Depression was still shaping American life, with unemployment running in the range of 15 percent. But then—in just a decade and a half—the share of entitlements in total federal spending suddenly spurted up from 28 percent to 51 percent. It did not surpass the 50 percent mark again until the early 1990s. But over the past two decades it rose almost relentlessly, until by 2010 it accounted for just about two-thirds of all federal spending, with all other responsibilities of the federal government— defense, justice, and all the other charges specified in the Constitution or undertaken in the intervening decades—making up barely one-third. Thus, in a very real sense, American governance has literally turned upside-down by entitlements—and within living memory. . . .

The New American Way of Life: Our National Declaration of Dependence

From the founding of our state up to the present—or rather, until quite recently—the United States and the citizens who peopled it were regarded, at home and abroad, as "exceptional" in a number of deep and important respects. One of these was their fierce and principled independence, which informed not only the design of the political experiment that is the U.S. Constitution but also the approach to everyday affairs. The proud self-reliance that struck Alexis de Tocqueville in his visit to the United States in the early 1830s extended to personal finances. The American "individualism" about which he wrote included social cooperation, and on a grand scale—the young nation was a hotbed of civic associations and voluntary organizations. Rather, it was that American men and women viewed themselves as accountable for their own situation through their own achievements in an environment bursting with

opportunity—a novel outlook at that time, markedly different from the prevailing Old World (or at least Continental) attitudes.

The corollaries of this American ethos (which might be described as a sort of optimistic Puritanism) were, on the one hand, an affinity for personal enterprise and industry; and, on the other hand, a horror of dependency and contempt for anything that smacked of a mendicant mentality. Although many Americans in earlier times were poor—before the twentieth century, practically everyone was living on income that would be considered penurious nowadays—even people in fairly desperate circumstances were known to refuse help or handouts as an affront to their dignity and independence. People who subsisted on public resources were known as "paupers," and provision for these paupers was a local undertaking. Neither beneficiaries nor recipients held the condition of pauperism in high regard.

Overcoming America's historic cultural resistance to government entitlements has been a long and formidable endeavor. But as we know today, this resistance did not ultimately prove an insurmountable obstacle to the establishment of a mass public entitlements regime or to the normalization of the entitlement lifestyle in modern America. The United States is at the verge of a symbolic threshold: the point at which more than half of all American households receive, and accept, transfer benefits from the government. From cradle (strictly speaking, from *before* the cradle) to grave, a treasure chest of government-supplied benefits is open for the taking for every American citizen—and exercising one's legal rights to these many blandishments is now part and parcel of the American way of life. . . .

From a Nation of Takers to a Nation of Gamers to a Nation of Chiselers

With the disappearance of the historical stigma against dependence on government largesse, and the normalization of lifestyles relying upon official resource transfers, it is not surprising that ordinary Americans should have turned their noted entrepreneurial spirit not simply to maximizing their take from the existing entitlement system, but to extracting payouts from the transfer state that were never intended under its programs. In this environment, gaming and defrauding the entitlement system have emerged as a mass phenomenon in modern America, a way of life for millions upon millions of men and women who would no doubt unhesitatingly describe themselves as law-abiding and patriotic American citizens.

Abuse of the generosity of our welfare state has, to be sure, aroused the ire of the American public in the past, and continues to arouse it from time to time today. For decades, a special spot in the rhetorical public square has been reserved for pillorying unemployed "underclass" garners who cadge undeserved social benefits. (This is the "welfare Cadillac" trope, and its many coded alternatives.) Public disapproval of this particular variant of entitlement misuse was sufficiently strong that Congress managed in the mid-1990s to overhaul the notorious AFDC program in a reform of welfare that replaced the old structure with Temporary Assistance for Needy Families (TANF). But entitlement fiddling in modern America is by no means the exclusive preserve of a troubled underclass. Quite the contrary: it is today characteristic of working America, and even those who would identify themselves as middle class.

Exhibit A in the documentation of widespread entitlement abuse in mainstream America is the explosion over the past half-century of disability claims and awards under the disability insurance provisions of the U.S. Social Security program. In 1960 an average of 455,000 erstwhile workers were receiving monthly federal payments for disability. By 2010 that total had skyrocketed to 8.2 million (and by 2011 had risen still further, to almost 8.6 million). Thus, the number of Americans collecting government disability payments soared eighteen-fold over the fifty years from 1960 and 2010. In the early 1960s almost twice as many adults were receiving AFDC checks as disability payments; by 2010, disability payees outnumbered the average calendar-year TANF caseload by more than four to one (8.20 million vs. 1.86 million). Moreover, "workers" who were recipients of government disability payments had jumped from the equivalent of 0.65 percent of the economically active eighteen- to sixty-four-year-old population in 1960 to 5.6 percent by 2010. In 1960, there were over 150 men and women in those age groups working or seeking employment for every person on disability; by 2010, the ratio was 18 to 1 and continuing to decrease. The ratios are even starker when it comes to paid work: in 1960, roughly 134 Americans were engaged in gainful employment for every officially disabled worker; by December 2010 there were just over 16. And by some measures, the situation today looks even more unfavorable than this.

Although the Social Security Administration does not publish data on the ethnicity of its disability payees, it does publish information on a state-by-state basis. These suggest that the proclivity to rely upon government disability payments today is at least as much a "white thing" as a tendency for any other American group. As of December 2011 the state with the very highest ratio of working-age disability awardees to the resident population ages eighteen to sixty-four was West Virginia (9.0 percent—meaning that every eleventh adult in this age group was on paid government disability). According to Census Bureau estimates, 93 percent of West Virginia's population was "non-Hispanic white" in 2011. In New England, by the same token, all-but-lily-white Maine (where ethnic minorities accounted for less than 6 percent of the population in 2011) records a 7.4 percent ratio of working-age disability payees to resident working-age population: more than one out of fourteen. . . .

In "playing" the disability system, or cheating it outright, many millions of Americans are making a living by putting their hands into the pockets of their fellow citizen—be they taxpayers now alive or as yet unborn (a steadily growing phenomenon, as we shall see in a moment). And it is not simply the disability gamers themselves who are complicit in this modern scam. The army of doctors and health-care professionals who are involved in, and paid for their services in, certifying dubious workers' compensation cases are direct—indeed indispensable—collaborators in the operation. The U.S. judicial system—which rules on disability cases and sets the standards for disability qualification—is likewise compromised. More fundamentally, American voters and their elected representatives are ultimately responsible for this state of affairs, as its willing and often knowing enablers. This popular tolerance for widespread dishonesty at the demonstrable expense of fellow citizens leads to an impoverishment of the country's civic spirit and an incalculable degradation of the nation's constituting principles. . . .

Nicholas Eberstadt is a political economist who holds the Henry Wendt Chair in Political Economy at the American Enterprise Institute (AEI). He is also a senior adviser to the National Bureau of Asian Research (NBR), a member of the visiting committee at the Harvard School of Public Health, and a member of the Global Leadership Council at the World Economic Forum.

William A. Galston

 **NO**

Have We Become "A Nation of Takers"?

Nicholas Eberstadt assembles a host of empirical trends to prove a moral conclusion: the growth of the entitlement state over the past half-century has undermined the sturdy self-reliance that has long characterized most Americans, replacing it with a culture of dependence that not only distorts our government but also threatens the American experiment. This claim raises two large questions: Do these trends represent a full and fair account of what has taken place since 1960? And do they warrant the conclusion Eberstadt urges on his readers? After some brief reflections on the former question, I devote the bulk of my remarks to the latter.

What Has Happened in the Past Half-Century?

As far as I can tell, Eberstadt's charts and statistics accurately represent the trends on which he focuses. But they are not the whole truth. In the first place, Eberstadt's accounting does not include all of the public policies that constitute entitlements as he defines them. Tax expenditures—special deductions and exemptions from, and credits against, otherwise taxable income—now constitute more than $1.1 trillion annually and they disproportionately benefit upper-income families. . . .

But suppose we consider only the list of entitlement programs on which Eberstadt focuses. Based on his presentation, one might imagine that U.S. households have become far more dependent on public programs in recent decades. This seems not to be the case, however. A Congressional Budget Report (CBO) report released in October 2011 found that government transfers did not grow as a share of household market income between 1979 (a cyclical peak in the economy) and 2007 (another such peak) but rather oscillated between 10 and 12 percent. From the beginning to the end of that period, Social Security was unchanged at 6 percent of market income; health-care programs (primary Medicare, Medicaid, and the Children's Health Insurance Program) rose from under 2 percent to a bit less than 4 percent while all other transfer programs declined.

There was a change in the distribution of these transfers, however: the share going to the poorest households declined significantly. In 1979, households in the lowest income quintile received fully 54 percent of federal transfer payments, but by 2007 that figure had fallen to only 36 percent—a reduction of one-third. Put another way, during that period, households with low-wage or nonworking adults got less, while households in the middle and upper middle classes got more. If there is a problem of growing dependence, these figures suggest that it is located more in Middle America than in the ranks of the poor and near-poor. This possibility raises the question (to which I will return in the next section) of whether transfers going to families conducting themselves in accordance with middle-class norms of work and child-rearing represent dependence in any sense that gives rise to moral concern.

At least three other long-cycle trends need to be taken into account as well if we are to understand what is happening in our society and how we might respond. In the first place, we are an aging society. The massive investments in public schools and university expansion at the height of the baby boom have given way increasingly to the funding of hospitals and nursing homes. And while we typically regard the costs of dependence at the beginning of life as primarily the responsibility of families, this is much less true for dependence at the end of life. It is easy to see why. Aging brings expanding needs for complex and costly medical procedures that exceed the resources of average families. And no matter how hard they try, middle-aged adults often find that caring for aging parents in a family setting requires strength and skills they simply do not possess.

A second trend has exacerbated the consequences of aging: the near-disappearance of the pensions and health insurance for retirees that employers provided during the decades after the World War II. America's dominance of the global industrial economy gave employers the market power to set prices high enough to fund generous contracts with unionized employees. As the devastated nations of Europe and Asia recovered and international competition intensified, the postwar bargain in the United States broke down, and government stepped into the breach. For many Americans, Social Security became the primary (not supplemental) source of retirement income, and Medicare made up the difference between having and going without health insurance.

The third trend is macroeconomic. During the generation after World War II, the economy grew briskly, and the fruits of that growth

Galston, William A. From *A Nation of Takers: America's Entitlement Epidemic,* October 2012, pp. 93–100, 105–109, 112–113. Copyright © 2012 by Templeton Press. Reprinted by permission.

were widely shared. Since then, growth has slowed, and the distribution of gains has become more concentrated at the top. Between 1947 and 1973, incomes of families in the bottom quintile rose by 117 percent; in the middle quintile, by 103 percent; at the top, by 88 percent. From 1973 to 2000, in contrast, the bottom quintile rose by only 12 percent, the middle by 25 percent, and the top by 66 percent. And in the seven years of the twenty-first century before the Great Recession struck, family incomes at the bottom actually fell by 6 percent and stagnated for everyone else (except for those at the very top). Since 1973, meanwhile, costs for big-ticket items such as higher education and health care have risen far faster than family incomes, increasing pressure on the public sector to step into the breach.

So there are reasons—in my view, compelling ones—why the federal government has undertaken major new responsibilities during the past half-century. Even so, we still have a problem: a huge gap between the promises we have made and the resources we have been willing to devote to fulfilling them. One way or another, we must close this gap. But the moral heart of this fiscal challenge is not dependence but rather a dangerous combination of self-interest, myopia, and denial.

What Is "Dependence"?

To understand why I subordinate dependence to these other concerns, we must begin by clarifying the meaning of the term. One thing is clear at the outset: the dependence/independence dyad is too crude to capture the complexity of social relations. At a minimum, we must take account of a third term, "interdependence," and the norm of reciprocity that undergirds it. When I do something for you that you would be hard-pressed to do for yourself and you respond by helping me with something I find difficult, we depend on one another and are the stronger for it.

Well-functioning societies are replete with relations of this sort and use them as models for public policy. But the move from families and small groups to large-scale collective action makes a difference. Reciprocity becomes extended not only demographically and geographically but also chronologically. Political communities exist not just for the here and now but for future generations as well. Much contemporary public policy rests on temporally extended interdependence—in other terms, on an intergenerational compact. When we consent to deductions from our salary to help fund our parents' retirement, it is with the expectation that our children will do the same for us. This compact is practically sustainable and morally acceptable, but only with the proviso that the burdens we impose on our children are not disproportionate to the burdens we ourselves are willing to bear. The terms of interdependence matter, not just the fact of it. And so—to descend to cases—if we can honor promises to the current generation of working Americans only by imposing heavier sacrifices on the next generation, then something has gone awry. But—to repeat—"dependence" is the wrong characterization of the problem.

So is the concept of "entitlement." To be entitled to something is not necessarily to be dependent on it—at least not in a way that should trouble us. Consider the definition Eberstadt provides: "Government entitlement payments are benefits to which a person holds an established right under law (i.e., to which a person is entitled). A defining feature of these payments (also sometimes officially referred to as government transfers to individuals) is that they are 'benefits received for which no current service is performed.'"

Note that many nongovernmental relations have the same structure. If I use my life savings to purchase a retirement annuity, I have a legally enforceable expectation of receiving over time the stream of income specified in the contract. When I begin receiving these payments, I am performing no "current service" in exchange for them. And I certainly "depend" on these payments to fund my living expenses when I am no longer working. But surely I am not dependent in the way that so concerned Daniel Patrick Moynihan.

I do not see why transferring this case to the public sector makes a moral difference. Suppose someone pays into a government account throughout his working life, in effect purchasing an annuity to fund his retirement. If the income stream is actuarially fair, then he can expect to get back the equivalent of what he contributed. He may do better or worse, of course. If he lives until ninety-five, he will get back more; if he dies at seventy, less. Relying on these payments doesn't make him dependent in any morally troubling sense.

Social Security works this way for millions of Americans. For many others, it is more complicated: some can expect to receive more than the actuarial value of their contributions, others less. Americans in the latter category are helping to fund retirement for those in the former. In effect, some workers are relying on others for a portion of their retirement income. But again, this quantitative premise does not imply a disturbing moral conclusion. When Moynihan worried about dependence, he was not thinking about individuals who have worked hard all their lives in low-wage jobs but whose payroll taxes do not suffice to fund what society regards as a dignified retirement. . . .

Real Problems of Dependence

Eberstadt presents no direct evidence that the growth of the federal government has changed Americans' character or weakened their moral fiber, perhaps because it is very hard to find. Indeed, in-depth examinations of public attitudes suggest the reverse. In 2009, for example, the Pew Social Mobility Project asked a representative sample of Americans what is essential or very important to getting ahead. Ninety-two percent said hard work; 89 percent, ambition; 83 percent, a good education. In contrast, factors such as race (15 percent), gender (16 percent), luck (21 percent), and family wealth (28 percent) ranked at the bottom. Asked about the role of government in fostering economic mobility, 36 percent of respondents thought it did more to help than to hurt, but many more—46 percent—endorsed the opposite view. A follow-up survey two years later revealed that the share of Americans who considered government helpful for mobility had declined to only 27 percent, while those who thought it detrimental had risen to 52 percent.

That is not to say that government has no role. Large majorities thought that public policy could do more to increase jobs in the United States and reduce college and health-care costs. But in their view, mobility-enhancing programs help individuals help themselves. If the growth of government has created a culture of dependence, it is hard to discern the evidence in these surveys, which are representative of a large body of research.

Eberstadt does offer some indirect evidence of cultural change, two instances of which warrant sustained attention. There is little doubt that the Social Security Disability Insurance program (SSDI) is subject to serious abuse. During the past decade, the number of workers receiving monthly benefits has soared from 5.3 million to 8.6 million. And because SSDI recipients qualify for Medicare after receiving benefits for two years, few working-age beneficiaries leave the program once they have entered. By 2010, annual benefits had reached $115 billion plus $75 billion in added Medicare costs. . . .

But this is not necessarily evidence of a deep cultural change. The desire to get something for nothing is a hardy perennial of human nature, not a late-twentieth-century invention. U.S. history is replete with swindles and get-rich-quick schemes. What may have changed is the willingness of taxpayers to fund programs that prefer compassion to tough love. Over the past three decades, efforts to tighten up the program have repeatedly wrecked on the shoals of public resistance. Tales of individual suffering move many voters, and a prosperous society has been willing to fund public compassion—so far. It will be interesting to see what happens when these generous instincts run up against inevitable future efforts to rein in massive budget deficits.

Far more disturbing than the abuses of a single program is the evidence Eberstadt presents of the long-term withdrawal of working-age men from the labor force. Fifty years ago, more than 85 percent of men age twenty and over were in the labor force. Ever before the Great Recession hit, that figure had declined by ten percentage points, and it has dropped more in the ensuing years. During the same period, female labor force participation rose by more than twenty points, stabilizing at around 60 percent in the late 1990s.

Why have so many men checked out? Eberstadt is sure that the "entitlement society" is responsible; without all the programs that enable men to get by without working, the flight from employment "could not have been possible." Perhaps so. Still, although men and women are equally eligible to participate in these programs, they seem to have responded quite differently, at least in the aggregate. For example, nearly as many women (4.1 million) as men (4.5 million) receive disability benefits, but that has not kept the ranks of women in the paid workforce from swelling. . . .

Conclusion

By bringing together and concisely presenting a wealth of data, Eberstadt has performed a real service. He dramatizes the remarkable rise of the entitlement state and issues warnings about its consequences that we must consider seriously. Still, there are good reasons to question the causal link between entitlement programs and dependence—at least the kind of dependence that should concern us. To be sure, Americans want a reasonable level of security in their retirement years, and they think that government programs such as Social Security and Medicare are essential to that security. But they continue to believe that government is no substitute for hard work, ambition, and the perseverance that enables young people to complete their education and put it to work in the job market. They think that government should make reasonable provision for the poor and disabled, but they do not believe that government should enable people who could be independent to depend on the efforts of others. To the extent that current programs turn out to be inconsistent with that view, they will eventually be trimmed or abolished, as was AFDC in 1996.

Left unchecked, the programs we have created in the past half-century will make it difficult to stabilize our finances, to invest in the future, and to defend the nation. These are compelling reasons to rethink the entitlement state. But they have little to do with an alleged culture of dependence, the evidence for which is thin at best. As long as we do our part, there is no harm in benefitting from programs we help sustain. As long as we contribute our share, taking is morally unproblematic. We can be a nation of takers, as long as we are a nation of givers as well. As long as we honor the norm of reciprocity for our compatriots and for posterity, we can steer a steady course.

Note

1. David H. Autor and Mark Duggan, "Supporting Work: A Proposal for Modernizing the U.S. Disability Insurance System," Center for American Progress and The Hamilton Project, December 2010, http://www.hamiltonproject.org /files/downloads_and_links/FINAL_AutorDugganPaper .pdf

---

WILLIAM A. GALSTON holds the Ezra Zilkha Chair in the Brookings Institution's Governance Studies Program, where he serves as a senior fellow. A former policy adviser to President Clinton and presidential candidates, Galston is an expert on domestic policy, political campaigns, and elections. His current research focuses on designing a new social contract and the implications of political polarization.

EXPLORING THE ISSUE

Are Entitlement Programs Creating a Culture of Dependency?

Critical Thinking and Reflection

1. Why does Nicholas Eberstadt think that the U.S. government today "would be scarcely recognizable" to Franklin Roosevelt, Abraham Lincoln, or Thomas Jefferson?
2. Eberstadt thinks that, over the last 50 years, the government has "inverted" the historic priorities of federal administration. What does he mean by that?
3. Eberstadt contends that "the United States is at the verge of a symbolic threshold." What kind of threshold?
4. William A. Galston: "If there is a problem of growing dependence . . . it is located more in Middle America than in the ranks of the poor and near-poor." Explain.
5. Galston believes that three long-term trends are better explanations than government extravagance for why entitlement spending has risen so steeply in recent years. Pick two and discuss them.
6. Instead of "dependency," Galston contends, we have moved to an era of "interdependence." Explain.

Is There Common Ground?

The common ground between Eberstadt and Galston lies in the fact that entitlement spending is indeed rising steeply. Eberstadt presents alarming statistics on this, which Galston acknowledges to be accurate "as far as I can tell." Galston also acknowledges that, "left unchecked, the programs we have created in the past half century will make it difficult to stabilize our finances, to invest in the future, and to defend the nation." What he denies is that entitlement programs are making Americans lazy and immature. Instead, he believes they serve their role as a safety net. Most Americans would agree that individuals in certain circumstances deserve help from their government in a temporary manner as they get back on their feet.

A pragmatist might argue that perhaps we can put aside the ideological arguments for the moment and bring together people of all ideologies in a nuts-and-bolts campaign to trim the unnecessary costs of these and other government programs. However, such a decision would be difficult to reach. Multiple parties would need to accept such cuts and many may in fact benefit from the programs

being trimmed. Perhaps most worrisome is how to handle a program like Social Security, in which citizens have paid into the program but may not be able to draw returns later in life. For these individuals, middle ground is difficult to find.

Additional Resources

Peter Edelman, *So Rich, So Poor: Why It's Hard to End Poverty in America* (New Press, 2012)

Barbara Ehrenreich, *Nickel and Dimed: On (Not) Getting By in America* (Picador Press, 2011)

Daniel P. Moynihan, *The Politics of a Guaranteed Family Income* (Random House, 1973)

James T. Patterson, *America's Struggle Against Poverty in the Twentieth Century* (Harvard University Press, 2000)

Leonard J. Santow and Mark E. Santow, *Social Security and the Middle-Class Squeeze: Fact and Fiction about America's Entitlement Programs* (Praeger, 2005)

Internet References . . .

Administration for Children and Families

www.acf.hhs.gov/help

Medicaid

www.medicaid.gov/

Medicare

www.medicare.gov/

Supplemental Nutrition Assistance Program

www.fns.usda.gov/snap/supplemental-nutrition
-assistance-program-snap

The United States Social Security Administration

www.ssa.gov/

Unit 2

UNIT

The Institutions of Government

*T*he Constitution divides authority between the national government and the states, delegating certain powers to the national government and providing that those not thus delegated "are reserved to the states respectively, or to the people." The national government's powers are further divided between three branches, Congress, the president, and the federal judiciary, each of which can exercise checks on the others.

Americans are familiar with these bodies—some more than others. Almost everyone is aware of who the president is, but they cannot necessarily determine whether he (or she) is doing a good job using appropriate metrics. They know their member of Congress (and overwhelmingly approve of his or her performance, in most cases), yet they rank the trustworthiness of the body as a whole to a degree comparable to lawyers and used cars salesmen. And most Americans know there is a Supreme Court that issues important decisions, but they are unaware of the rest of the federal judiciary, let alone the individuals who sit on the bench. As a result, these powerful institutions must regularly remember to show Americans how they are relevant and how they are fulfilling objectives for the betterment of society as a whole.

How vigorously and faithfully are these branches performing their respective functions? Do they remain true to the authentic meaning of the Constitution? What legitimate defenses does each branch possess against encroachment by the others? Are some branches more obstructionist than others? Does the Constitution allow for this to happen? These issues have been debated since the earliest years of the Republic, and the debate continues today.

ISSUE

Selected, Edited, and with Issue Framing Material by:
William J. Miller, *Flagler College*

Does the President Have
Unilateral War Powers?

YES: John C. Yoo, from "The President's Constitutional Authority to Conduct Military Operations Against Terrorists and Nations Supporting Them: Memorandum Opinion for the Deputy Counsel to the President," *Memorandum Opinion for the Deputy Counsel to the President* (2001)

NO: Barack Obama, from "The Future of Our Fight Against Terrorism," *Speech or Remarks* (2013)

Learning Outcomes

After reading this issue, you will be able to:

- Explain how war is declared in the United States.
- Describe the legal precedents that allow the president to have unilateral war powers.
- Assess the arguments against the president having unilateral war powers.
- Discuss how Congress and the presidency work together during times of war.
- Identify when it may be prudent for the president to have unilateral war powers.

ISSUE SUMMARY

YES: John C. Yoo, a Law Professor at the University of California, Berkeley, argues that the language of the Constitution, long-accepted precedents, and the practical need for speedy action in emergencies all support broad executive power during war.

NO: American President Barack Obama examines how he has made concerted efforts during his time in the White House to expand consultations with Congress in order to provide the best opportunity for the United States to be successful in fighting terrorism.

Dramatic and bitter as they are, the current struggles between the White House and Congress over the president's unilateral authority to conduct military operations and foreign affairs are not without precedent. Episodically, they have been occurring since the administration of George Washington.

The language of the Constitution relating to war powers almost seems to invite struggles between the two branches. Congress is given the power to declare war and "to raise and support armies." The president is authorized to serve as commander-in-chief of the armed forces "when called into actual service of the United States." While the power to "declare" or authorize war rests squarely with the U.S. Congress, the Founders gave some leeway to the president when it came to war making. At the Constitutional Convention, some delegates wanted to give Congress the exclusive power to make war,

not simply to declare it. That would have ruled out any presidential war making. But James Madison successfully argued the need for "leaving to the Executive the power to repel sudden attacks."

Down through the years, several presidents have interpreted very broadly these emergency war-making powers. In 1801, President Jefferson ordered his navy to seize the ships of Barbary pirates in the Mediterranean, and 45 years later President Polk sent American troops into territory claimed by Mexico, thus provoking the Mexican American War. A young congressman named Abraham Lincoln vigorously protested Polk's unilateral assertion of power, but when he came to office and faced the secession of the South, he went much further than Polk in the assertion of power, jailing people without trial, enlarging the size of the army and navy, withdrawing money from the Treasury, and blockading Southern ports without authorization from Congress. In more recent times,

President Truman committed America to fight in Korea without a congressional declaration, and President Kennedy ordered a naval blockade of Cuba in 1962 without even consulting Congress.

The mid-1960s marked the high-water period of unchallenged presidential war making. Between 1961 and 1963, Kennedy sent 16,000 armed "advisers" to Vietnam, and between 1964 and 1968, President Johnson escalated American involvement to 500,000 troops—all without a formal declaration of war. But that period of congressional indulgence was soon to end. By the early 1970s, Congress was starting on a course that would culminate in the cutoff of funds for Vietnam and legislative efforts to head off any more undeclared wars. In 1973, over President Nixon's veto, Congress passed the War Powers Resolution, which required the president to notify Congress within 48 hours after putting troops in harm's way, withdraw them within 60 to 90 days absent a congressional authorization, and submit periodic progress reports to Congress during that period. In practice, the War Powers Resolution has been largely ignored by Ronald Reagan when he sent troops into Grenada, by George H. W. Bush when he sent them to Panama, and by Bill Clinton when he sent them into Somalia, Haiti, and Bosnia.

Perhaps ironically, the War Powers Resolution may even have been useful to President George W. Bush in obtaining congressional authorization for the invasion of Iraq. In October 2002, Congress passed a joint resolution giving the president the authority to use the armed forces "as he determines to be necessary and appropriate" to defend national security and enforce all U.N. resolutions against Iraq. The resolution added that this constituted "specific statutory authorization" for war within the meaning of the War Powers Resolution. Such broadly worded language has come back to haunt many members of Congress who voted for it but now wish they hadn't. The new Democratic Congress elected in 2006 considered various options for challenging President Bush's war-making ability as it related to Iraq, including the repeal or modification of the 2002 authorization for going to war.

For President Barack Obama, the question of unilateral war powers surfaced most significantly when determining whether to attack Bashar al-Assad (Syrian dictator) after strong evidence emerged showing that he had used chemical weapons against his own people. In 2012, Obama had issued an ultimatum to Assad: if he used chemical weapons, the United States would have no choice but to respond. Yet with over half of Americans polled favoring an intervention (and less than 10 percent actually supporting such action), Obama had to decide whether Syria was worth going against the wishes of Americans in a way similar to his predecessor. The key is that Obama was stuck wondering whether he should or should not proceed, not whether he could or could not. Much like with Libya in 2011, there was never a question on whether Obama possessed the ability to launch attacks against a foreign enemy without a formal declaration from Congress.

Ultimately, Obama opted to move forward with diplomacy and not launch attacks despite his earlier warning. After the Bush administration's battles in Iraq and Afghanistan, many Americans began labeling the Republican Party as the one most tied to superseding Congress when deciding whether to attack foreign countries. But Obama's recent internal deliberations have reminded us that all presidents—regardless of partisanship—are forced to weight these options. Only a president with no interest in power would blindly hand off the ability to launch unilateral military action, but a wise one would find a way to work in concert with Congress to assure backing and support. Wag the Dog, after all, does not exist in reality. We cannot simply fabricate conflicts to bump polling numbers. In today's America, such actions would likely harm a leader in the polls. Instead, a majority of Americans are still looking for the branches of government to come together in an effort to solve potential problems.

In the selections that follow, John C. Yoo, a Law Professor at the University of California, Berkeley, argues that the language of the Constitution, long-accepted precedents, and the practical need for speedy action in emergencies all support broad executive power during war. Opposing that view is President Barack Obama, who points to a strong need to consult with Congress in order to assure maximum effectiveness and efficiency in dealing with foreign policy and threats to homeland security.

YES ⬅

John C. Yoo

The President's Constitutional Authority to Conduct Military Operations Against Terrorists and Nations Supporting Them: Memorandum Opinion for the Deputy Counsel to the President

Our review establishes that all three branches of the Federal Government—Congress, the Executive, and the Judiciary—agree that the President has broad authority to use military force abroad, including the ability to deter future attacks.

I.

The President's constitutional power to defend the United States and the lives of its people must be understood in light of the Founders' express intention to create a federal government "cloathed with all the powers requisite to [the] complete execution of its trust." *The Federalist* No. 23 (Alexander Hamilton). Foremost among the objectives committed to that trust by the Constitution is the security of the Nation. As Hamilton explained in arguing for the Constitution's adoption, because "the circumstances which may affect the public safety are [not] reducible within certain determinate limits, . . . it must be admitted, as a necessary consequence that there can be no limitation of that authority which is to provide for the defense and protection of the community in any matter essential to its efficiency."

"It is 'obvious and unarguable' that no governmental interest is more compelling than the security of the Nation." (1981). Within the limits that the Constitution itself imposes, the scope and distribution of the powers to protect national security must be construed to authorize the most efficacious defense of the Nation and its interests in accordance "with the realistic purposes of the entire instrument." (1948) Nor is the authority to protect national security limited to actions necessary for "victories in the field." (1946) The authority over national security "carries with it the inherent power to guard against the immediate renewal of the conflict."

We now turn to the more precise question of the President's inherent constitutional powers to use military force.

Constitutional Text

The text, structure and history of the Constitution establish that the Founders entrusted the President with the primary responsibility, and therefore the power, to use military force in situations of emergency. Article II, Section 2 states that the "President shall be Commander in Chief of the Army and Navy of the United States, and of the Militia of the several States, when called into the actual Service of the United States." He is further vested with all of "the executive Power" and the duty to execute the laws. These powers give the President broad constitutional authority to use military force in response to threats to the national security and foreign policy of the United States. During the period leading up to the Constitution's ratification, the power to initiate hostilities and to control the escalation of conflict had been long understood to rest in the hands of the executive branch.

By their terms, these provisions vest full control of the military forces of the United States in the President. The power of the President is at its zenith under the Constitution when the President is directing military operations of the armed forces, because the power of Commander in Chief is assigned solely to the President. It has long been the view of this Office that the Commander-in-Chief Clause is a substantive grant of authority to the President and that the scope of the President's authority to commit the armed forces to combat is very broad. The President's complete discretion in exercising the Commander-in-Chief power has also been recognized by the courts. In the *Prize Cases,* (1862), for example, the Court explained that, whether the President "in fulfilling his duties as Commander in Chief" had met with a situation justifying treating the southern States as belligerents and instituting a blockade, was a question "to be *decided by him*" and which the Court could not question, but must leave to "the political department of the Government to which this power was entrusted."

Some commentators have read the constitutional text differently. They argue that the vesting of the power to declare war gives

Congress the sole authority to decide whether to make war. This view misreads the constitutional text and misunderstands the nature of a declaration of war. Declaring war is not tantamount to making war—indeed, the Constitutional Convention specifically amended the working draft of the Constitution that had given Congress the power to make war. An earlier draft of the Constitution had given to Congress the power to "make" war. When it took up this clause on August 17, 1787, the Convention voted to change the clause from "make" to "declare." A supporter of the change argued that it would "leav[e] to the Executive the power to repel sudden attacks." Further, other elements of the Constitution describe "engaging" in war, which demonstrates that the Framers understood making and engaging in war to be broader than simply "declaring" war. . . . If the Framers had wanted to require congressional consent before the initiation of military hostilities, they knew how to write such provisions.

Finally, the Framing generation well understood that declarations of war were obsolete. Not all forms of hostilities rose to the level of a declared war: during the seventeenth and eighteenth centuries, Great Britain and colonial America waged numerous conflicts against other states without an official declaration of war. . . . Instead of serving as an authorization to begin hostilities, a declaration of war was only necessary to "perfect" a conflict under international law. A declaration served to fully transform the international legal relationship between two states from one of peace to one of war. Given this context, it is clear that Congress's power to declare war does not constrain the President's independent and plenary constitutional authority over the use of military force.

Constitutional Structure

Our reading of the text is reinforced by analysis of the constitutional structure. First, it is clear that the Constitution secures all federal executive power in the President to ensure a unity in purpose and energy in action. "Decision, activity, secrecy, and dispatch will generally characterize the proceedings of one man in a much more eminent degree than the proceedings of any greater number." *The Federalist* No. 70 (Alexander Hamilton). The centralization of authority in the President alone is particularly crucial in matters of national defense, war, and foreign policy, where a unitary executive can evaluate threats, consider policy choices, and mobilize national resources with a speed and energy that is far superior to any other branch. As Hamilton noted, "Energy in the executive is a leading character in the definition of good government. It is essential to the protection of the community against foreign attacks." This is no less true in war. "Of all the cares or concerns of government, the direction of war most peculiarly demands those qualities which distinguish the exercise of power by a single hand." *The Federalist* No. 74.

Second, the Constitution makes clear that the process used for conducting military hostilities is different from other government decisionmaking. In the area of domestic legislation, the Constitution creates a detailed, finely wrought procedure in which Congress plays the central role. In foreign affairs, however, the Constitution does not establish a mandatory, detailed, Congress-driven procedure for taking action. Rather, the Constitution vests the two branches with different powers—the President as Commander in Chief, Congress with control over funding and declaring war—without requiring that they follow a specific process in making war. By establishing this framework, the Framers expected that the process for warmaking would be far more flexible, and capable of quicker, more decisive action, than the legislative process. Thus, the President may use his Commander-in-Chief and executive powers to use military force to protect the Nation, subject to congressional appropriations and control over domestic legislation.

Third, the constitutional structure requires that any ambiguities in the allocation of a power that is executive in nature—such as the power to conduct military hostilities—must be resolved in favor of the executive branch. Article II, section 1 provides that "[t]he executive Power shall be vested in a President of the United States." By contrast, Article I's Vesting Clause gives Congress only the powers "herein granted." This difference in language indicates that Congress's legislative powers are limited to the list enumerated in Article I, section 8, while the President's powers include inherent executive powers that are unenumerated in the Constitution. To be sure, Article II lists specifically enumerated powers in addition to the Vesting Clause, and some have argued that this limits the "executive Power" granted in the Vesting Clause to the powers on that list. But the purpose of the enumeration of executive powers in Article II was not to define and cabin the grant in the Vesting Clause. Rather, the Framers unbundled some plenary powers that had traditionally been regarded as "executive," assigning elements of those powers to Congress in Article I, while expressly reserving other elements as enumerated executive powers in Article II. So, for example, the King's traditional power to declare war was given to Congress under Article I, while the Commander-in-Chief authority was expressly reserved to the President in Article II. Further, the Framers altered other plenary powers of the King, such as treaties and appointments, assigning the Senate a share in them in Article II itself. Thus, the enumeration in Article II marks the points at which several traditional executive powers were diluted or reallocated. Any *other*, unenumerated executive powers, however, were conveyed to the President by the Vesting Clause.

There can be little doubt that the decision to deploy military force is "executive" in nature, and was traditionally so regarded. It calls for action and energy in execution, rather than the deliberate formulation of rules to govern the conduct of private individuals. Moreover, the Framers understood it to be an attribute of the executive. "The direction of war implies the direction of the common strength," wrote Alexander Hamilton, "and the power of directing and employing the common strength forms a usual and essential part in the definition of the executive authority." *The Federalist*

No. 74 (Alexander Hamilton). As a result, to the extent that the constitutional text does not explicitly allocate the power to initiate military hostilities to a particular branch, the Vesting Clause provides that it remain among the President's unenumerated powers.

Fourth, depriving the President of the power to decide when to use military force would disrupt the basic constitutional framework of foreign relations. From the very beginnings of the Republic, the vesting of the executive, Commander-in-Chief, and treaty powers in the executive branch has been understood to grant the President plenary control over the conduct of foreign relations. As Secretary of State Thomas Jefferson observed during the first Washington Administration: "the constitution has divided the powers of government into three branches [and] has declared that the executive powers shall be vested in the president, submitting only special articles of it to a negative by the senate." Due to this structure, Jefferson continued, "the transaction of business with foreign nations is executive altogether; it belongs, then, to the head of that department, except as to such portions of it as are specially submitted to the senate. Exceptions are to be construed strictly." In defending President Washington's authority to issue the Neutrality Proclamation, Alexander Hamilton came to the same interpretation of the President's foreign affairs powers. According to Hamilton, Article II "ought . . . to be considered as intended . . . to specify and regulate the principal articles implied in the definition of Executive Power; leaving the rest to flow from the general grant of that power." As future Chief Justice John Marshall famously declared a few years later, "The President is the sole organ of the nation in its external relations, and its sole representative with foreign nations. . . . The [executive] department . . . is entrusted with the whole foreign intercourse of the nation. . . ." Given the agreement of Jefferson, Hamilton, and Marshall, it has not been difficult for the executive branch consistently to assert the President's plenary authority in foreign affairs ever since. . . .

II.

Executive Branch Construction and Practice

The position we take here has long represented the view of the executive branch and of the Department of Justice. Attorney General (later Justice) Robert Jackson formulated the classic statement of the executive branch's understanding of the President's military powers in 1941:

> "Article II, section 2, of the Constitution provides that the President "shall be Commander in Chief of the Army and Navy of the United States." By virtue of this constitutional office he has supreme command over the land and naval forces of the country and may order them to perform such military duties as, in his opinion, are necessary or appropriate for the defense of the United States. These powers exist in time of peace as well as in time of war. . . .

> "Thus the President's responsibility as Commander in Chief embraces the authority to command and direct the armed forces in their immediate movements and operations designed to protect the security and effectuate the defense of the United States. . . . [T]his authority undoubtedly includes the power to dispose of troops and equipment in such manner and on such duties as best to promote the safety of the country." . . .

Attorney General (later Justice) Frank Murphy, though declining to define precisely the scope of the President's independent authority to act in emergencies or states of war, stated that: "the Executive has powers not enumerated in the statutes—powers derived not from statutory grants but from the Constitution. It is universally recognized that the constitutional duties of the Executive carry with them the constitutional powers necessary for their proper performance. These constitutional powers have never been specifically defined, and in fact cannot be, since their extent and limitations are largely dependent upon conditions and circumstances. . . . The right to take specific action might not exist under one state of facts, while under another it might be the absolute duty of the Executive to take such action." . . .

Judicial Construction

Judicial decisions since the beginning of the Republic confirm the President's constitutional power and duty to repel military action against the United States through the use of force, and to take measures to deter the recurrence of an attack. As Justice Joseph Story said long ago, "[i]t may be fit and proper for the government, in the exercise of the high discretion confided to the executive, for great public purposes, to act on a sudden emergency, or to prevent an irreparable mischief, by summary measures, which are not found in the text of the laws." (1824). The Constitution entrusts the "power [to] the executive branch of the government to preserve order and insure the public safety in times of emergency, when other branches of the government are unable to function, or their functioning would itself threaten the public safety." (1946, Stone, C.J., concurring).

If the President is confronted with an unforeseen attack on the territory and people of the United States, or other immediate, dangerous threat to American interests and security, the courts have affirmed that it is his constitutional responsibility to respond to that threat with whatever means are necessary, including the use of military force abroad. . . .

III.

The historical practice of all three branches confirms the lessons of the constitutional text and structure. The normative role of historical practice in constitutional law, and especially with regard to separation of powers, is well settled. . . . Indeed, as the Court has observed, the role of practice in fixing the meaning of the separation of powers is implicit in the Constitution itself: "'the Constitution . . .

contemplates that practice will integrate the dispersed powers into a workable government.'" (1989). In addition, governmental practice enjoys significant weight in constitutional analysis for practical reasons, on "the basis of a wise and quieting rule that, in determining . . . the existence of a power, weight shall be given to the usage itself—even when the validity of the practice is the subject of investigation." (1915). . . .

The historical record demonstrates that the power to initiate military hostilities, particularly in response to the threat of an armed attack, rests exclusively with the President. As the Supreme Court has observed, "[t]he United States frequently employs Armed Forces outside this country—over 200 times in our history—for the protection of American citizens or national security." (1990). On at least 125 such occasions, the President acted without prior express authorization from Congress. Such deployments, based on the President's constitutional authority alone, have occurred since the Administration of George Washington. . . . Perhaps the most significant deployment without specific statutory authorization took place at the time of the Korean War, when President Truman, without prior authorization from Congress, deployed United States troops in a war that lasted for over three years and caused over 142,000 American casualties.

Recent deployments ordered solely on the basis of the President's constitutional authority have also been extremely large, representing a substantial commitment of the Nation's military personnel, diplomatic prestige, and financial resources. On at least one occasion, such a unilateral deployment has constituted full-scale war. On March 24, 1999, without any prior statutory authorization and in the absence of an attack on the United States, President Clinton ordered hostilities to be initiated against the Republic of Yugoslavia. The President informed Congress that, in the initial wave of air strikes, "United States and NATO forces have targeted the [Yugoslavian] government's integrated air defense system, military and security police command and control elements, and military and security police facilities and infrastructure. . . . I have taken these actions pursuant to my constitutional authority to conduct U.S. foreign relations and as Commander in Chief and Chief Executive." Bombing attacks against targets in both Kosovo and Serbia ended on June 10, 1999, seventy-nine days after the war began. More than 30,000 United States military personnel participated in the operations; some 800 U.S. aircraft flew more than 20,000 sorties; more than 23,000 bombs and missiles were used. As part of the peace settlement, NATO deployed some 50,000 troops into Kosovo, 7,000 of them American. . . .

Conclusion

In light of the text, plan, and history of the Constitution, its interpretation by both past Administrations and the courts, the longstanding practice of the executive branch, and the express affirmation of the President's constitutional authorities by Congress, we think it beyond question that the President has the plenary constitutional power to take such military actions as he deems necessary and appropriate to respond to the terrorist attacks upon the United States on September 11, 2001. Force can be used both to retaliate for those attacks, and to prevent and deter future assaults on the Nation. Military actions need not be limited to those individuals, groups, or states that participated in the attacks on the World Trade Center and the Pentagon: the Constitution vests the President with the power to strike terrorist groups or organizations that cannot be demonstrably linked to the September 11 incidents, but that, nonetheless, pose a similar threat to the security of the United States and the lives of its people, whether at home or overseas. In both the War Powers Resolution and the Joint Resolution, Congress has recognized the President's authority to use force in circumstances such as those created by the September 11 incidents. Neither statute, however, can place any limits on the President's determinations as to any terrorist threat, the amount of military force to be used in response, or the method, timing, and nature of the response. These decisions, under our Constitution, are for the President alone to make.

John C. Yoo, a Professor of Law at Boalt Hall, University of California, Berkeley, served as Deputy Assistant Attorney General in the Office of Legal Counsel in the U.S. Department of Justice from 2001 to 2003. He is the author of *The Powers of War and Peace* (University of Chicago, 2005) and *War by Other Means: An Insider's Account of the War on Terrorism* (Grove/Atlantic, 2006).

Barack Obama

 **NO**

The Future of Our Fight Against Terrorism

It's an honor to return to the National Defense University. Here, at Fort McNair, Americans have served in uniform since 1791—standing guard in the early days of the Republic, and contemplating the future of warfare here in the 21st century.

For over two centuries, the United States has been bound together by founding documents that defined who we are as Americans, and served as our compass through every type of change. Matters of war and peace are no different. Americans are deeply ambivalent about war, but having fought for our independence, we know that a price must be paid for freedom. From the Civil War, to our struggle against fascism, and through the long, twilight struggle of the Cold War, battlefields have changed, and technology has evolved. But our commitment to Constitutional principles has weathered every war, and every war has come to an end.

With the collapse of the Berlin Wall, a new dawn of democracy took hold abroad, and a decade of peace and prosperity arrived at home. For a moment, it seemed the 21st century would be a tranquil time. Then, on September 11th 2001, we were shaken out of complacency. Thousands were taken from us, as clouds of fire, metal and ash descended upon a sun-filled morning. This was a different kind of war. No armies came to our shores, and our military was not the principal target. Instead, a group of terrorists came to kill as many civilians as they could.

And so our nation went to war. We have now been at war for well over a decade. I won't review the full history. What's clear is that we quickly drove al Qaeda out of Afghanistan, but then shifted our focus and began a new war in Iraq. This carried grave consequences for our fight against al Qaeda, our standing in the world, and—to this day—our interests in a vital region.

Meanwhile, we strengthened our defenses—hardening targets, tightening transportation security, and giving law enforcement new tools to prevent terror. Most of these changes were sound. Some caused inconvenience. But some, like expanded surveillance, raised difficult questions about the balance we strike between our interests in security and our values of privacy. And in some cases, I believe we compromised our basic values—by using torture to interrogate our enemies, and detaining individuals in a way that ran counter to the rule of law.

After I took office, we stepped up the war against al Qaeda, but also sought to change its course. We relentlessly targeted al Qaeda's leadership. We ended the war in Iraq, and brought nearly 150,000 troops home. We pursued a new strategy in Afghanistan, and increased our training of Afghan forces. We unequivocally banned torture, affirmed our commitment to civilian courts, worked to align our policies with the rule of law, and expanded our consultations with Congress.

Today, Osama bin Laden is dead, and so are most of his top lieutenants. There have been no large-scale attacks on the United States, and our homeland is more secure. Fewer of our troops are in harm's way, and over the next 19 months they will continue to come home. Our alliances are strong, and so is our standing in the world. In sum, we are safer because of our efforts.

Now make no mistake: our nation is still threatened by terrorists. From Benghazi to Boston, we have been tragically reminded of that truth. We must recognize, however, that the threat has shifted and evolved from the one that came to our shores on 9/11. With a decade of experience to draw from, now is the time to ask ourselves hard questions—about the nature of today's threats, and how we should confront them.

These questions matter to every American. For over the last decade, our nation has spent well over a trillion dollars on war, exploding our deficits and constraining our ability to nation build here at home. Our service-members and their families have sacrificed far more on our behalf. Nearly 7,000 Americans have made the ultimate sacrifice. Many more have left a part of themselves on the battlefield, or brought the shadows of battle back home. From our use of drones to the detention of terrorist suspects, the decisions we are making will define the type of nation—and world—that we leave to our children.

So America is at a crossroads. We must define the nature and scope of this struggle, or else it will define us, mindful of James Madison's warning that "No nation could preserve its freedom in the midst of continual warfare." Neither I, nor any President, can promise the total defeat of terror. We will never erase the evil that lies in the hearts of some human beings, nor stamp out every danger to our open society. What we can do—what we must do—is dismantle networks that pose a direct danger, and make it less likely for new groups to gain a foothold, all while maintaining the freedoms and ideals that we defend. To define that strategy, we must make decisions based not on fear, but hard-earned wisdom. And that begins with understanding the threat we face.

Obama, Barack. From speech delivered at National Defense University, May 23, 2013.

Today, the core of al Qaeda in Afghanistan and Pakistan is on a path to defeat. Their remaining operatives spend more time thinking about their own safety than plotting against us. They did not direct the attacks in Benghazi or Boston. They have not carried out a successful attack on our homeland since 9/11. Instead, what we've seen is the emergence of various al Qaeda affiliates. From Yemen to Iraq, from Somalia to North Africa, the threat today is more diffuse, with al Qaeda's affiliate in the Arabian Peninsula—AQAP—the most active in plotting against our homeland. While none of AQAP's efforts approach the scale of 9/11 they have continued to plot acts of terror, like the attempt to blow up an airplane on Christmas Day in 2009.

Unrest in the Arab World has also allowed extremists to gain a foothold in countries like Libya and Syria. Here, too, there are differences from 9/11. In some cases, we confront state-sponsored networks like Hizbollah that engage in acts of terror to achieve political goals. Others are simply collections of local militias or extremists interested in seizing territory. While we are vigilant for signs that these groups may pose a transnational threat, most are focused on operating in the countries and regions where they are based. That means we will face more localized threats like those we saw in Benghazi, or at the BP oil facility in Algeria, in which local operatives—in loose affiliation with regional networks—launch periodic attacks against Western diplomats, companies, and other soft targets, or resort to kidnapping and other criminal enterprises to fund their operations.

Finally, we face a real threat from radicalized individuals here in the United States. Whether it's a shooter at a Sikh Temple in Wisconsin; a plane flying into a building in Texas; or the extremists who killed 168 people at the Federal Building in Oklahoma City—America has confronted many forms of violent extremism in our time. Deranged or alienated individuals—often U.S. citizens or legal residents—can do enormous damage, particularly when inspired by larger notions of violent jihad. That pull towards extremism appears to have led to the shooting at Fort Hood, and the bombing of the Boston Marathon.

Lethal yet less capable al Qaeda affiliates. Threats to diplomatic facilities and businesses abroad. Homegrown extremists. This is the future of terrorism. We must take these threats seriously, and do all that we can to confront them. But as we shape our response, we have to recognize that the scale of this threat closely resembles the types of attacks we faced before 9/11. In the 1980s, we lost Americans to terrorism at our Embassy in Beirut; at our Marine Barracks in Lebanon; on a cruise ship at sea; at a disco in Berlin; and on Pan Am Flight 103 over Lockerbie. In the 1990s, we lost Americans to terrorism at the World Trade Center; at our military facilities in Saudi Arabia; and at our Embassy in Kenya. These attacks were all deadly, and we learned that left unchecked, these threats can grow. But if dealt with smartly and proportionally, these threats need not rise to the level that we saw on the eve of 9/11.

Moreover, we must recognize that these threats don't arise in a vacuum. Most, though not all, of the terrorism we face is fueled by a common ideology—a belief by some extremists that Islam is in conflict with the United States and the West, and that violence against Western targets, including civilians, is justified in pursuit of a larger cause. Of course, this ideology is based on a lie, for the United States is not at war with Islam; and this ideology is rejected by the vast majority of Muslims, who are the most frequent victims of terrorist acts.

Nevertheless, this ideology persists, and in an age in which ideas and images can travel the globe in an instant, our response to terrorism cannot depend on military or law enforcement alone. We need all elements of national power to win a battle of wills and ideas. So let me discuss the components of such a comprehensive counter-terrorism strategy.

First, we must finish the work of defeating al Qaeda and its associated forces.

In Afghanistan, we will complete our transition to Afghan responsibility for security. Our troops will come home. Our combat mission will come to an end. And we will work with the Afghan government to train security forces, and sustain a counter-terrorism force which ensures that al Qaeda can never again establish a safe-haven to launch attacks against us or our allies.

Beyond Afghanistan, we must define our effort not as a boundless 'global war on terror'—but rather as a series of persistent, targeted efforts to dismantle specific networks of violent extremists that threaten America. In many cases, this will involve partnerships with other countries. Thousands of Pakistani soldiers have lost their lives fighting extremists. In Yemen, we are supporting security forces that have reclaimed territory from AQAP. In Somalia, we helped a coalition of African nations push al Shabaab out of its strongholds. In Mali, we are providing military aid to a French-led intervention to push back al Qaeda in the Maghreb, and help the people of Mali reclaim their future.

Much of our best counter-terrorism cooperation results in the gathering and sharing of intelligence; the arrest and prosecution of terrorists. That's how a Somali terrorist apprehended off the coast of Yemen is now in prison in New York. That's how we worked with European allies to disrupt plots from Denmark to Germany to the United Kingdom. That's how intelligence collected with Saudi Arabia helped us stop a cargo plane from being blown up over the Atlantic.

But despite our strong preference for the detention and prosecution of terrorists, sometimes this approach is foreclosed. Al Qaeda and its affiliates try to gain a foothold in some of the most distant and unforgiving places on Earth. They take refuge in remote tribal regions. They hide in caves and walled compounds. They train in empty deserts and rugged mountains.

In some of these places—such as parts of Somalia and Yemen—the state has only the most tenuous reach into the territory.

In other cases, the state lacks the capacity or will to take action. It is also not possible for America to simply deploy a team of Special Forces to capture every terrorist. And even when such an approach may be possible, there are places where it would pose profound risks to our troops and local civilians—where a terrorist compound cannot be breached without triggering a firefight with surrounding tribal communities that pose no threat to us, or when putting U.S. boots on the ground may trigger a major international crisis.

To put it another way, our operation in Pakistan against Osama bin Laden cannot be the norm. The risks in that case were immense; the likelihood of capture, although our preference, was remote given the certainty of resistance; the fact that we did not find ourselves confronted with civilian casualties, or embroiled in an extended firefight, was a testament to the meticulous planning and professionalism of our Special Forces—but also depended on some luck. And even then, the cost to our relationship with Pakistan—and the backlash among the Pakistani public over encroachment on their territory—was so severe that we are just now beginning to rebuild this important partnership.

It is in this context that the United States has taken lethal, targeted action against al Qaeda and its associated forces, including with remotely piloted aircraft commonly referred to as drones. As was true in previous armed conflicts, this new technology raises profound questions—about who is targeted, and why; about civilian casualties, and the risk of creating new enemies; about the legality of such strikes under U.S. and international law; about accountability and morality.

Let me address these questions. To begin with, our actions are effective. Don't take my word for it. In the intelligence gathered at bin Laden's compound, we found that he wrote, "we could lose the reserves to the enemy's air strikes. We cannot fight air strikes with explosives." Other communications from al Qaeda operatives confirm this as well. Dozens of highly skilled al Qaeda commanders, trainers, bomb makers, and operatives have been taken off the battlefield. Plots have been disrupted that would have targeted international aviation, U.S. transit systems, European cities and our troops in Afghanistan. Simply put, these strikes have saved lives.

Moreover, America's actions are legal. We were attacked on 9/11. Within a week, Congress overwhelmingly authorized the use of force. Under domestic law, and international law, the United States is at war with al Qaeda, the Taliban, and their associated forces. We are at war with an organization that right now would kill as many Americans as they could if we did not stop them first. So this is a just war—a war waged proportionally, in last resort, and in self-defense.

And yet as our fight enters a new phase, America's legitimate claim of self-defense cannot be the end of the discussion. To say a military tactic is legal, or even effective, is not to say it is wise or moral in every instance. For the same human progress that gives us the technology to strike half a world away also demands the discipline to constrain that power—or risk abusing it. That's why, over the last four years, my Administration has worked vigorously to establish a framework that governs our use of force against terrorists—insisting upon clear guidelines, oversight and accountability that is now codified in Presidential Policy Guidance that I signed yesterday.

In the Afghan war theater, we must support our troops until the transition is complete at the end of 2014. That means we will continue to take strikes against high value al Qaeda targets, but also against forces that are massing to support attacks on coalition forces. However, by the end of 2014, we will no longer have the same need for force protection, and the progress we have made against core al Qaeda will reduce the need for unmanned strikes.

Beyond the Afghan theater, we only target al Qaeda and its associated forces. Even then, the use of drones is heavily constrained. America does not take strikes when we have the ability to capture individual terrorists—our preference is always to detain, interrogate, and prosecute them. America cannot take strikes wherever we choose—our actions are bound by consultations with partners, and respect for state sovereignty. America does not take strikes to punish individuals—we act against terrorists who pose a continuing and imminent threat to the American people, and when there are no other governments capable of effectively addressing the threat. And before any strike is taken, there must be near-certainty that no civilians will be killed or injured—the highest standard we can set.

This last point is critical, because much of the criticism about drone strikes—at home and abroad—understandably centers on reports of civilian casualties. There is a wide gap between U.S. assessments of such casualties, and non-governmental reports. Nevertheless, it is a hard fact that U.S. strikes have resulted in civilian casualties, a risk that exists in all wars. For the families of those civilians, no words or legal construct can justify their loss. For me, and those in my chain of command, these deaths will haunt us as long as we live, just as we are haunted by the civilian casualties that have occurred through conventional fighting in Afghanistan and Iraq.

But as Commander-in-Chief, I must weigh these heartbreaking tragedies against the alternatives. To do nothing in the face of terrorist networks would invite far more civilian casualties—not just in our cities at home and facilities abroad, but also in the very places—like Sana'a and Kabul and Mogadishu—where terrorists seek a foothold. Let us remember that the terrorists we are after target civilians, and the death toll from their acts of terrorism against Muslims dwarfs any estimate of civilian casualties from drone strikes.

Where foreign governments cannot or will not effectively stop terrorism in their territory, the primary alternative to targeted, lethal action is the use of conventional military options. As I've said, even small Special Operations carry enormous risks. Conventional airpower or missiles are far less precise than drones, and likely to cause more civilian casualties and local outrage. And invasions of these territories lead us to be viewed as occupying armies; unleash a torrent of unintended consequences; are difficult to contain; and ultimately empower those who thrive on violent conflict. So it is false to assert that putting boots on the ground is less likely to result in civilian deaths, or to create enemies in the Muslim world. The result would be more U.S. deaths, more Black-hawks down, more confrontations with local populations, and an inevitable mission creep in support of such raids that could easily escalate into new wars.

So yes, the conflict with al Qaeda, like all armed conflict, invites tragedy. But by narrowly targeting our action against those who want to kill us, and not the people they hide among, we are choosing the course of action least likely to result in the loss of innocent life. Indeed, our efforts must also be measured against the history of putting American troops in distant lands among hostile populations. In Vietnam, hundreds of thousands of civilians died in a war where the boundaries of battle were blurred. In Iraq and Afghanistan, despite the courage and discipline of our troops, thousands of civilians have been killed. So neither conventional military action, nor waiting for attacks to occur, offers moral safe-harbor. Neither does a sole reliance on law enforcement in territories that have no functioning police or security services—and indeed, have no functioning law.

This is not to say that the risks are not real. Any U.S. military action in foreign lands risks creating more enemies, and impacts public opinion overseas. Our laws constrain the power of the President, even during wartime, and I have taken an oath to defend the Constitution of the United States. The very precision of drone strikes, and the necessary secrecy involved in such actions can end up shielding our government from the public scrutiny that a troop deployment invites. It can also lead a President and his team to view drone strikes as a cure-all for terrorism.

For this reason, I've insisted on strong oversight of all lethal action. After I took office, my Administration began brief-ing all strikes outside of Iraq and Afghanistan to the appropriate committees of Congress. Let me repeat that—not only did Con-gress authorize the use of force, it is briefed on every strike that America takes. That includes the one instance when we targeted an American citizen: Anwar Awlaki, the chief of external operations for AQAP.

This week, I authorized the declassification of this action, and the deaths of three other Americans in drone strikes, to facili-tate transparency and debate on this issue, and to dismiss some of the more outlandish claims. For the record, I do not believe it would be constitutional for the government to target and kill any U.S. citizen—with a drone, or a shotgun—without due process. Nor should any President deploy armed drones over U.S. soil.

But when a U.S. citizen goes abroad to wage war against America—and is actively plotting to kill U.S. citizens; and when neither the United States, nor our partners are in a position to capture him before he carries out a plot—his citizenship should no more serve as a shield than a sniper shooting down on an innocent crowd should be protected from a swat team.

That's who Anwar Awlaki was—he was continuously trying to kill people. He helped oversee the 2010 plot to detonate explosive devices on two U.S. bound cargo planes. He was involved in plan-ning to blow up an airliner in 2009. When Farouk Abdulmutallab—the Christmas Day bomber—went to Yemen in 2009, Awlaki hosted him, approved his suicide operation, and helped him tape a martyrdom video to be shown after the attack. His last instruc-tions were to blow up the airplane when it was over American soil. I would have detained and prosecuted Awlaki if we captured him before he carried out a plot. But we couldn't. And as President, I would have been derelict in my duty had I not authorized the strike that took out Awlaki.

Of course, the targeting of any Americans raises constitu-tional issues that are not present in other strikes—which is why my Administration submitted information about Awlaki to the Depart-ment of Justice months before Awlaki was killed, and briefed the Congress before this strike as well. But the high threshold that we have set for taking lethal action applies to all potential terrorist tar-gets, regardless of whether or not they are American citizens. This threshold respects the inherent dignity of every human life. Along-side the decision to put our men and women in uniform in harm's way, the decision to use force against individuals or groups—even against a sworn enemy of the United States—is the hardest thing I do as President. But these decisions must be made, given my responsibility to protect the American people.

Going forward, I have asked my Administration to review proposals to extend oversight of lethal actions outside of warzones that go beyond our reporting to Congress. Each option has virtues in theory, but poses difficulties in practice. For example, the estab-lishment of a special court to evaluate and authorize lethal action has the benefit of bringing a third branch of government into the process, but raises serious constitutional issues about presidential and judicial authority. Another idea that's been suggested—the establishment of an independent oversight board in the execu-tive branch—avoids those problems, but may introduce a layer of bureaucracy into national-security decision-making, without inspir-ing additional public confidence in the process. Despite these chal-lenges, I look forward to actively engaging Congress to explore these—and other—options for increased oversight.

I believe, however, that the use of force must be seen as part of a larger discussion about a comprehensive counter-terrorism strategy. Because for all the focus on the use of force, force alone cannot make us safe. We cannot use force everywhere that a radical ideology takes root; and in the absence of a strategy that reduces the well-spring of extremism, a perpetual war—through drones or Special Forces or troop deployments—will prove self-defeating, and alter our country in troubling ways.

So the next element of our strategy involves addressing the underlying grievances and conflicts that feed extremism, from North Africa to South Asia. As we've learned this past decade, this is a vast and complex undertaking. We must be humble in our expectation that we can quickly resolve deep rooted problems like poverty and sectarian hatred. Moreover, no two countries are alike, and some will undergo chaotic change before things get better. But our security and values demand that we make the effort.

This means patiently supporting transitions to democracy in places like Egypt, Tunisia and Libya—because the peaceful realization of individual aspirations will serve as a rebuke to violent extremists. We must strengthen the opposition in Syria, while isolating extremist elements—because the end of a tyrant must not give way to the tyranny of terrorism. We are working to promote peace between Israelis and Palestinians—because it is right, and because such a peace could help reshape attitudes in the region. And we must help countries modernize economies, upgrade education, and encourage entrepreneurship—because American leadership has always been elevated by our ability to connect with peoples' hopes, and not simply their fears.

Success on these fronts requires sustained engagement, but it will also require resources. I know that foreign aid is one of the least popular expenditures—even though it amounts to less than one percent of the federal budget. But foreign assistance cannot be viewed as charity. It is fundamental to our national security, and any sensible long-term strategy to battle extremism. Moreover, foreign assistance is a tiny fraction of what we spend fighting wars that our assistance might ultimately prevent. For what we spent in a month in Iraq at the height of the war, we could be training security forces in Libya, maintaining peace agreements between Israel and its neighbors, feeding the hungry in Yemen, building schools in Pakistan, and creating reservoirs of goodwill that marginalize extremists.

America cannot carry out this work if we do not have diplomats serving in dangerous places. Over the past decade, we have strengthened security at our Embassies, and I am implementing every recommendation of the Accountability Review Board which found unacceptable failures in Benghazi. I have called on Congress to fully fund these efforts to bolster security, harden facilities, improve intelligence, and facilitate a quicker response time from our military if a crisis emerges.

But even after we take these steps, some irreducible risks to our diplomats will remain. This is the price of being the world's most powerful nation, particularly as a wave of change washes over the Arab World. And in balancing the trade-offs between security and active diplomacy, I firmly believe that any retreat from challenging regions will only increase the dangers we face in the long run.

Targeted action against terrorists. Effective partnerships. Diplomatic engagement and assistance. Through such a comprehensive strategy we can significantly reduce the chances of large scale attacks on the homeland and mitigate threats to Americans overseas. As we

guard against dangers from abroad, however, we cannot neglect the daunting challenge of terrorism from within our borders.

As I said earlier, this threat is not new. But technology and the Internet increase its frequency and lethality. Today, a person can consume hateful propaganda, commit themselves to a violent agenda, and learn how to kill without leaving their home. To address this threat, two years ago my Administration did a comprehensive review, and engaged with law enforcement. The best way to prevent violent extremism is to work with the Muslim American community—which has consistently rejected terrorism—to identify signs of radicalization, and partner with law enforcement when an individual is drifting towards violence. And these partnerships can only work when we recognize that Muslims are a fundamental part of the American family. Indeed, the success of American Muslims, and our determination to guard against any encroachments on their civil liberties, is the ultimate rebuke to those who say we are at war with Islam.

Indeed, thwarting homegrown plots presents particular challenges in part because of our proud commitment to civil liberties for all who call America home. That's why, in the years to come, we will have to keep working hard to strike the appropriate balance between our need for security and preserving those freedoms that make us who we are. That means reviewing the authorities of law enforcement, so we can intercept new types of communication, and build in privacy protections to prevent abuse. That means that—even after Boston—we do not deport someone or throw someone in prison in the absence of evidence. That means putting careful constraints on the tools the government uses to protect sensitive information, such as the State Secrets doctrine. And that means finally having a strong Privacy and Civil Liberties Board to review those issues where our counter-terrorism efforts and our values may come into tension.

The Justice Department's investigation of national security leaks offers a recent example of the challenges involved in striking the right balance between our security and our open society. As Commander-in-Chief, I believe we must keep information secret that protects our operations and our people in the field. To do so, we must enforce consequences for those who break the law and breach their commitment to protect classified information. But a free press is also essential for our democracy. I am troubled by the possibility that leak investigations may chill the investigative journalism that holds government accountable.

Journalists should not be at legal risk for doing their jobs. Our focus must be on those who break the law. That is why I have called on Congress to pass a media shield law to guard against government over-reach. I have raised these issues with the Attorney General, who shares my concern. So he has agreed to review existing Department of Justice guidelines governing investigations that involve reporters, and will convene a group of media organizations to hear their concerns as part of that review. And I have directed the Attorney General to report back to me by July 12th.

All these issues remind us that the choices we make about war can impact—in sometimes unintended ways—the openness and freedom on which our way of life depends. And that is why I intend to engage Congress about the existing Authorization to Use Military Force, or AUMF, to determine how we can continue to fight terrorists without keeping America on a perpetual war-time footing.

The AUMF is now nearly twelve years old. The Afghan War is coming to an end. Core al Qaeda is a shell of its former self. Groups like AQAP must be dealt with, but in the years to come, not every collection of thugs that labels themselves al Qaeda will pose a credible threat to the United States. Unless we discipline our thinking and our actions, we may be drawn into more wars we don't need to fight, or continue to grant Presidents unbound powers more suited for traditional armed conflicts between nation states. So I look forward to engaging Congress and the American people in efforts to refine, and ultimately repeal, the AUMF's mandate. And I will not sign laws designed to expand this mandate further. Our systematic effort to dismantle terrorist organizations must continue. But this war, like all wars, must end. That's what history advises. That's what our democracy demands.

And that brings me to my final topic: the detention of terrorist suspects.

To repeat, as a matter of policy, the preference of the United States is to capture terrorist suspects. When we do detain a suspect, we interrogate them. And if the suspect can be prosecuted, we decide whether to try him in a civilian court or a Military Commission. During the past decade, the vast majority of those detained by our military were captured on the battlefield. In Iraq, we turned over thousands of prisoners as we ended the war. In Afghanistan, we have transitioned detention facilities to the Afghans, as part of the process of restoring Afghan sovereignty. So we bring law of war detention to an end, and we are committed to prosecuting terrorists whenever we can.

The glaring exception to this time-tested approach is the detention center at Guantanamo Bay. The original premise for opening GTMO—that detainees would not be able to challenge their detention—was found unconstitutional five years ago. In the meantime, GTMO has become a symbol around the world for an America that flouts the rule of law. Our allies won't cooperate with us if they think a terrorist will end up at GTMO. During a time of budget cuts, we spend $150 million each year to imprison 166 people—almost $1 million per prisoner. And the Department of Defense estimates that we must spend another $200 million to keep GTMO open at a time when we are cutting investments in education and research here at home.

As President, I have tried to close GTMO. I transferred 67 detainees to other countries before Congress imposed restrictions to effectively prevent us from either transferring detainees to other countries, or imprisoning them in the United States. These restrictions make no sense. After all, under President Bush, some 530 detainees were transferred from GTMO with Congress's support.

When I ran for President the first time, John McCain supported closing GTMO. No person has ever escaped from one of our super-max or military prisons in the United States. Our courts have convicted hundreds of people for terrorism-related offenses, including some who are more dangerous than most GTMO detainees. Given my Administration's relentless pursuit of al Qaeda's leadership, there is no justification beyond politics for Congress to prevent us from closing a facility that should never have been opened.

Today, I once again call on Congress to lift the restrictions on detainee transfers from GTMO. I have asked the Department of Defense to designate a site in the United States where we can hold military commissions. I am appointing a new, senior envoy at the State Department and Defense Department whose sole responsibility will be to achieve the transfer of detainees to third countries. I am lifting the moratorium on detainee transfers to Yemen, so we can review them on a case by case basis. To the greatest extent possible, we will transfer detainees who have been cleared to go to other countries. Where appropriate, we will bring terrorists to justice in our courts and military justice system. And we will insist that judicial review be available for every detainee.

Even after we take these steps, one issue will remain: how to deal with those GTMO detainees who we know have participated in dangerous plots or attacks, but who cannot be prosecuted—for example because the evidence against them has been compromised or is inadmissible in a court of law. But once we commit to a process of closing GTMO, I am confident that this legacy problem can be resolved, consistent with our commitment to the rule of law.

I know the politics are hard. But history will cast a harsh judgment on this aspect of our fight against terrorism, and those of us who fail to end it. Imagine a future—ten years from now, or twenty years from now—when the United States of America is still holding people who have been charged with no crime on a piece of land that is not a part of our country. Look at the current situation, where we are force-feeding detainees who are holding a hunger strike. Is that who we are? Is that something that our Founders foresaw? Is that the America we want to leave to our children?

Our sense of justice is stronger than that. We have prosecuted scores of terrorists in our courts. That includes Umar Farouk Abdulmutallab, who tried to blow up an airplane over Detroit; and Faisal Shahzad, who put a car bomb in Times Square. It is in a court of law that we will try Dzhokhar Tsarnaev, who is accused of bombing the Boston Marathon. Richard Reid, the shoe bomber, is as we speak serving a life sentence in a maximum security prison here, in the United States. In sentencing Reid, Judge William Young told him, "the way we treat you . . . is the measure of our own liberties." He went on to point to the American flag that flew in the courtroom—"That flag," he said, "will fly there long after this is all forgotten. That flag still stands for freedom."

America, we have faced down dangers far greater than al Qaeda. By staying true to the values of our founding, and by using our constitutional compass, we have overcome slavery and Civil War;

fascism and communism. In just these last few years as President, I have watched the American people bounce back from painful recession, mass shootings, and natural disasters like the recent tornados that devastated Oklahoma. These events were heartbreaking; they shook our communities to the core. But because of the resilience of the American people, these events could not come close to breaking us.

I think of Lauren Manning, the 9/11 survivor who had severe burns over 80 percent of her body, who said, "That's my reality. I put a Band-Aid on it, literally, and I move on."

I think of the New Yorkers who filled Times Square the day after an attempted car bomb as if nothing had happened.

I think of the proud Pakistani parents who, after their daughter was invited to the White House, wrote to us, "we have raised an American Muslim daughter to dream big and never give up because it does pay off."

I think of the wounded warriors rebuilding their lives, and helping other vets to find jobs.

I think of the runner planning to do the 2014 Boston Marathon, who said, "Next year, you are going to have more people than ever. Determination is not something to be messed with."

That's who the American people are. Determined, and not to be messed with.

Now, we need a strategy—and a politics—that reflects this resilient spirit. Our victory against terrorism won't be measured in a surrender ceremony on a battleship, or a statue being pulled to the ground. Victory will be measured in parents taking their kids to school; immigrants coming to our shores; fans taking in a ballgame; a veteran starting a business; a bustling city street. The quiet determination; that strength of character and bond of fellowship; that refutation of fear—that is both our sword and our shield. And long after the current messengers of hate have faded from the world's memory, alongside the brutal despots, deranged madmen, and ruthless demagogues who litter history—the flag of the United States will still wave from small-town cemeteries, to national monuments, to distant outposts abroad. And that flag will still stand for freedom.

Thank you. God Bless you. And may God bless the United States of America.

BARACK OBAMA served as U.S. Senator for Illinois prior to defeating John McCain in the 2008 presidential election to become the 44th President of the United States. He is the first African American to hold the position. In 2012, President Obama defeated Republican challenger Mitt Romney to win a second term.

EXPLORING THE ISSUE

Does the President Have Unilateral War Powers?

Critical Thinking and Reflection

1. What legal precedents does John Yoo cite to bolster his case that the president has unilateral war powers?
2. Do you believe President Obama has done enough to consult with Congress on issues related to terrorism? Why or why not?
3. The Congress has the sole power to "declare" war, but does that leave the president the sole power to "make" war? Or is there a real difference between the two?
4. Do you believe Yoo would back President Obama's utilization of drone strikes against suspected terrorists in Pakistan and Yemen? Why or why not?
5. Should the president or Congress have ultimate war-making powers? Why?

Is There Common Ground?

The only thing in common between the two sides is their tendency to occupy each other's position with a change of administration. When a Republican president faced a Democratic Congress in 2007–2009, there was much complaining from the latter about the president's unilateral war making. But a few years later, with a Democratic president, many of the same practices—targeting terrorists, holding them indefinitely, wiretapping, rendition—continued, this time with tacit approval from many Democrats in Congress. Now it was time for the Republicans to make a show of indignation.

The battle over unilateral war making is not a partisan one. Historically, we have seen both of today's major parties exercising this power at different times they deem appropriate. From a citizen's perspective, this makes any efforts at remedying the situation quite difficult. It will never be as simple as removing a president or a party. Instead, the rules of the game will need to change if citizens are that unhappy with a president's decision to act without Congress's consent. If Congress takes it upon itself to prevent a president from acting, it does little but divide the country from the elites to the masses. And as history has shown, a divided house is the most likely to fall.

Additional Resources

Mark Brandon, *The Constitution in Wartime: Beyond Alarmism and Complacency* (Duke University Press, 2005)

Louis Fisher, *Presidential War Power* (University Press of Kansas, 2004)

Richard Neustadt, *Presidential Power and the Modern Presidents: The Politics of Leadership from Roosevelt to Reagan* (Free Press, 1991)

Richard Posner, *Not a Suicide Pact: The Constitution in a Time of National Emergency* (Oxford University Press, 2006)

John C. Yoo, *The Powers of War and Peace: The Constitution and Foreign Affairs After 9/11* (University of Chicago Press, 2006)

Internet References . . .

Congressional Research Service: The War Powers Resolution: After Thirty Years

www.au.af.mil/au/awc/awcgate/crs/rl32267.htm

Department of Justice on War Powers

www.justice.gov/olc/warpowers925.htm

Liberty Classroom

www.libertyclassroom.com/warpowers/

Reclaiming the War Power

http://object.cato.org/sites/cato.org/files/serials/files
/cato-handbook-policymakers/2009/9/hb111-10.pdf

War Powers: Law Library of Congress

http://loc.gov/law/help/usconlaw/war-powers.php

Selected, Edited, and with Issue Framing Material by:
William J. Miller, *Flagler College*

ISSUE

Is Congress a Dysfunctional Institution?

YES: Ezra Klein, from "What Happens When Congress Fails to Do Its Job," *Newsweek* (2010)

NO: William Mo Cowan, from "Cowan Farewell Address," *U.S. Senate* (2013)

Learning Outcomes
After reading this issue, you will be able to: • Identify sources of institutional deadlock.   • Explain how partisan rancor impacts government.   • Describe how members of Congress view their work within the body.   • Assess whether an insider or outsider perspective is more accurate.   • Describe how Congress compares to other branches of government when it comes to power.

ISSUE SUMMARY

YES: Columnist Ezra Klein contends that institutional deadlock and partisan rancor have paralyzed Congress, causing it to lose power to the president and the bureaucracy.

NO: Former Massachusetts Senator Mo Cowan describes how he has come to view the work of Congress—along with fellow members—after fulfilling the remainder of John Kerry term upon the nomination of Governor Deval Patrick.

Those who teach introductory American government usually look forward to the unit on the American presidency. It sets off lively class participation, especially when students talk about the actions of whoever happens to be in the White House. The same happens when the topic is the Supreme Court; students can argue about controversial decisions like school prayer, flag-burning, and abortion, and the instructor sometimes has to work hard to keep the discussion from getting too hot.

But when Congress, the third branch of the federal government, comes up for discussion, it is hard to get anything going beyond a few cynical shrugs and wisecracks. Seriously intended comments, when they finally emerge, may range from skeptical questions ("What do they do for their money?") to harsh pronouncements ("Bunch of crooks!").

Students today can hardly be blamed for these reactions. They are inheritors of a rich American tradition of Congress-bashing. At the end of the nineteenth century, the novelist Mark Twain quipped that "there is no distinctly native American criminal class except Congress." In the 1930s, the humorist Will Rogers suggested that

"we have the best Congress money can buy." In the 1940s, President Harry Truman coined the term do-nothing Congress, and Fred Allen's radio comedy show had a loudmouth "Senator Claghorn" who did nothing but bluster. In the 1950s, the Washington Post's "Herblock" and other cartoonists liked to draw senators as potbellied old guys chewing cigars.

Needless to say, the drafters of the U.S. Constitution did not anticipate that kind of portrayal; they wanted Congress to stand tall in power and stature. Significantly, they listed it first among the three branches, and they gave it an extensive list of powers, 18 in all, rounding them off with the power to "make all laws which shall be necessary and proper" for executing its express powers. Given their fear of a tyrannical king, it makes sense that Congress was supposed to have the power. It was closest to the citizens, had one of its bodies directly elected, and would still be checked on all sides.

Throughout the first half of the nineteenth century, Congress played a very visible role in the business of the nation, and some of its most illustrious members, like Daniel Webster, Henry Clay, and John C. Calhoun, were national superstars. Men and women crowded into the visitors' gallery when Webster was about to deliver one of his powerful orations; during these performances they sometimes wept openly.

What, then, happened to Congress over the years to bring about this fall from grace? A number of factors have come into play, two of which can be cited immediately.

First, Congress has become a very complicated institution. In both houses, especially in the House of Representatives, legislation is not hammered out on the floor but in scores of committees and subcommittees, known to some journalists and political scientists but to relatively few others. Major bills can run hundreds of pages, and are written in a kind of lawyerspeak inaccessible to ordinary people. Congressional rules are so arcane that even a bill with clear majority support can fall through the cracks and disappear. The public simply doesn't understand all this, and incomprehension can easily sour into distrust and suspicion.

A second reason why Congress doesn't get much respect these days is connected with the increased visibility of its sometime rival, the presidency. Ever since Abraham Lincoln raised the possibility of what presidents can do during prolonged emergencies, charismatic presidents like Woodrow Wilson, Franklin Roosevelt, and Ronald Reagan, serving during such times, have aggrandized the office of the president, pushing Congress into the background. They have thus stolen much of the prestige and glamour that once attached to the legislative branch. The president has become a very visible "one" and Congress has faded into a shadowy "many." Everyone knows who the president is, but how many people can name the leaders of Congress? Can you?

The current Congress is currently being lambasted in the mainstream media for being unproductive in its term. As *USA Today* explains, "Congress is on track to beat its own low record of productivity, enacting fewer laws this year than at any point in the past 66 years." While there are obvious concerns about using such a simple metric to show productivity, it does demonstrate some of the issues currently at play in Congress. With political parties ideologically polarized like never before, it is hard to find compromises that are meaningful while still being agreeable. This was witnessed during the September/October 2013 government shutdown. Knowing that government would stop working if a compromise was not reached, neither Republicans nor Democrats would come to a middling solution prior to reaching the crisis point. One member of the Senate opted to read *Green Eggs and Ham* rather than attempt to reach a workable solution.

Further, the demands on members of Congress have increased. Citizens hold high expectations that their representative will be able and willing to fill their every need and desire. With these expectations, there is less time to spend focusing on national issues. And with the advent and development of social media, members of Congress need to have more time focused on what is occurring at the national level. Any decision leading to increased taxes, bureaucracy, or size of government will be broadcasted to the world via Twitter and blogs and used against the offending Congressperson in their next election campaign. No matter how well-intentioned or skilled a politician, it seems that Washington, DC has the ability to change people these days. The founders were careful to make sure that Congress would need consensus to accomplish any meaningful goals, but today, legislative nuances are used to stall progress in the name of politics. It is not that there is something wrong with a policy that leads to it being killed anymore. Instead, it can be just a matter of taste.

In the following selections, *Washington Post* columnist Ezra Klein blames them on the ideological polarization of our two parties in Congress, which, he believes, has virtually paralyzed the institution. Mo Cowan, a former member of Congress, takes a different position, arguing that the noisy clash of viewpoints and interests serves the public by demonstrating passion and an acknowledgment of the seriousness of each decision reached.

YES ⤹

Ezra Klein

What Happens When Congress Fails to Do Its Job?

I. In 2008 Barack Obama almost asked Evan Bayh to be his running mate. It was "a coin toss," recalls David Plouffe, Obama's campaign manager. Bayh lost that toss, but the fact that he was a finalist—much as he'd been for John Kerry four years earlier—was proof that he was doing something right in his day job as junior senator from Indiana. His future seemed bright.

Last month he announced his retirement.

There was no scandal. Bayh wasn't plagued by poor fundraising or low poll numbers. Nor is fatigue a likely explanation: at 54, Bayh is fairly young, at least when you're grading on the curve that is the United States Senate.

What drove Bayh from office, rather, was that he'd grown to hate his job. Congress, he wrote in a *New York Times* op-ed, is "stuck in an endless cycle of recrimination and revenge. The minority seeks to frustrate the majority, and when the majority is displaced it returns the favor. Power is constantly sought through the use of means which render its effective use, once acquired, impossible."

The situation had grown so grim, Bayh said, that continued service was no longer of obvious use. Americans were left with a bizarre spectacle: a member of the most elite legislative body in the most powerful country in the world was resigning because the dysfunctions of his institution made him feel ineffectual. "I simply believe I can best contribute to society in another way," Bayh explained, "creating jobs by helping grow a business, helping guide an institution of higher learning, or helping run a worthy charitable endeavor."

This is what it's come to, then: our senators envy the influence and sway held by university presidents.

II. In the months leading up to the health-care-reform vote, there was much talk that Congress is broken and serious reform is necessary. Some would say the bill's passage is a decisive refutation of that position. They are wrong.

What we have learned instead is that even in those rare moments when bold action should be easy, little can be done. Consider the position of the Democrats over the last year: a popular new president, the largest majority either party has held in the Senate since the post-Watergate wave, a 40-seat majority in the House, and

a financial crisis. Congress has managed to pass a lot of legislation, and some of it has been historic. But our financial system is not fixed and our health-care problems are not solved. Indeed, when it comes to the toughest decisions Congress must make, our representatives have passed them off to some other body or some future generation.

The architects of the health-care-reform bill, for instance, couldn't bring themselves to propose the difficult reforms necessary to assure Medicare—and the government's—solvency. So they created an independent panel of experts who will have to propose truly difficult reforms to enable the Medicare system to survive. These recommendations would take the fast track through Congress, protected from not just the filibuster but even from revision. In fact, if Congress didn't vote on them, they'd still become law. "I believe this commission is the largest yielding of sovereignty from the Congress since the creation of the Federal Reserve," says Office of Management and Budget Director Peter Orszag, and he meant it as a compliment.

Cap-and-trade, meanwhile, is floundering in the Senate. In the event that it dies, the Environmental Protection Agency has been preparing to regulate carbon on its own. Some senators would like to block the EPA from doing so, and may yet succeed. But those in Congress who want to avert catastrophic climate change, but who don't believe they can pass legislation to help do so, are counting on the EPA to act in their stead.

The financial meltdown was, in many ways, a model of quick congressional action. TARP had its problems, and the stimulus was too small, but both passed, and quickly. After they'd passed, though, it became clear they weren't sufficient, and that Congress wasn't going to be able to muster further action. So the Federal Reserve, in consultation with congressional leaders, unleashed more than a trillion dollars into the marketplace. It was still the American people's money being invested, but it didn't need 60 votes in the Senate.

Congress was reticent to do more about the financial crisis because of concern over the deficit. But even apparent bipartisan agreement wasn't sufficient to compel action. Sens. Kent Conrad (D-N.D.) and Judd Gregg (R-N.H.) [led]

From *Newsweek*, March 27, 2010. Copyright © 2010 by Newsweek, Inc. All rights reserved. Used by permission and protected by the copyright laws of the United States. The printing, copying, redistribution, or retransmission of the material without express written permission via PARS International Corp. is prohibited.

the Budget Committee, and they called for their committee—and all the other committees—to be bypassed altogether in favor of a deficit commission operating outside the normal legislative structure. "Some have argued that House and Senate committees with jurisdiction over health, retirement and revenue issues should individually take up legislation to address the imbalance," they wrote in a joint op-ed. "But that path will never work. The inability of the regular legislative process to meaningfully act on this couldn't be clearer." They were right: their proposal was defeated by a filibuster and the president formed a deficit commission by executive order instead.

As for foreign policy and national security, Congress has so abdicated its role over war and diplomacy that Garry Wills, in his new book, *Bomb Power,* says that we've been left with an "American monarch," which is only slightly scarier-sounding than the "unitary executive" theory that the Bush administration advocated and implemented.

This is not a picture of a functioning legislature.

Some might throw up their hands and welcome the arrival of outside cavalries, of rule by commissions and central banks and executive agencies. But there is a cost when Congress devolves power to others. The American public knew much more about the stimulus than about the Federal Reserve's "quantitative easing" program because Congress is much more accessible and paid more attention by the media. The EPA can impose blunt regulations on polluters, but it can't put a price on carbon in order to create a real market for cleaner energy. The debt commission's recommendations will still require a congressional vote. When Congress doesn't work, the federal government doesn't work, no matter how hard it tries.

III. So why doesn't Congress work? The simplest answer is that the country has changed, and Congress has not changed alongside it. Congress used to function despite its extraordinary minority protections because the two parties were ideologically diverse. Democrats used to provide a home to the Southern conservatives known as the Dixiecrats. The GOP used to include a bloc of liberals from the Northeast. With the parties internally divided and different blocs arising in shifting coalitions, it wasn't possible for one party to pursue a strategy of perpetual obstruction. But the parties have become ideologically coherent, leaving little room for cooperation and creating new incentives for minority obstruction.

Take the apparent paradox of the filibuster. It is easier than at any other point in our history to break a filibuster. Until 1917, there was no way to shut down debate, and until 1975, it took 67 votes rather than today's 60. And yet, the United States Senate had to break more filibusters in 2009 than in the 1950s and 1960s combined.

"It's not uncommon today to have things filibustered that, once they get past the filibuster, are passed unanimously," complains Bayh. "So it's clearly for the purpose of preventing action, not because of any underlying, substantive disagreement." Even Bill Frist, the former Republican Senate majority leader, has

been surprised by the Senate's embrace of the tactic. "Compared to 10 years ago, 15 years ago, 20 years ago," he said during an appearance on MSNBC, "it's being used way too much."

The problem has become sufficiently severe that senators, who normally cling to their institutional traditions like Vatican cardinals, are talking about addressing it. "Next Congress," Harry Reid said to a group of reporters in March, "we are going to take a look at the filibuster. And we're going to make some changes in it."

But the rise of the filibuster is not just a case of rules-gone-wild: it's evidence of a broader polarization in the United States Congress. As the party heretics lost or switched sides, Republicans and Democrats found themselves more often in agreement with themselves and less often in agreement with each other. According to the political scientists Nolan McCarty, Keith T. Poole, and Howard Rosenthal, Democrats and Republicans now vote against each other more regularly than at any time since Reconstruction.

As the Reconstruction watermark suggests, polarized parties are often the result of a polarized country. In this case, it's the opposite. We are no more divided than we were in the 1950s and '60s, when civil rights and the Vietnam War and the feminist revolution split the country. But where the legislative process once worked to harmonize those differences, today it accentuates them. "When the public sees all Democrats on one side of the issue and all Republicans on the other, it's a cue," explains Ron Brownstein, author of The Second Civil War. "And so people's opinions harden, which in turn hardens the politicians on both sides. Then you have the increasingly politicized media, and the activist groups launching primaries. It's all a machine where the whole system is working to amplify our differences."

Senate Republican leader Mitch McConnell said as much . . . in an interview with National Journal. "Whether it became the stimulus, the budget, Guantánamo, health care," he said, "what I tried to do and what John [Boehner] did very skillfully, as well, was to unify our members in opposition to it. Had we not done that, I don't think the public would have been as appalled as they became."

Minority obstruction works because voters and the media often blame the majority. If nothing is getting done and the two sides bicker ceaselessly, it seems sensible to blame the people who are running the place.

But the lesson that the minority could prosper if Washington failed was a bad one for the system to learn. The rules of the United States Congress made it possible for the minority to make the majority fail by simply obstructing their agenda. And so they did. Republicans won in 1994, after killing health-care reform. Democrats adopted the tactic a decade later, taking Congress back in 2006 after killing Social Security privatization. This year, Republicans' strategy was to kill health-care reform again. That's what Sen. Jim DeMint meant when he promised conservative activists that "if we're able to stop Obama on this, it will be his Waterloo. It will break him."

What's important about all those examples is that at no point did the minority party come to the table and propose a serious alternative. Republicans left the health-care system to deteriorate, and Bob Dole went so far as to vote against two bills that had his name on them in the mid-'90s. Democrats enforced a simple proposition in the Social Security fight: there would be no Democratic Social Security reform bill. This year Sen. Lamar Alexander gave the introductory remarks for the Republicans at the president's recent health-care summit. Alexander said the Republicans—the party that pushed No Child Left Behind, the Iraq War, the Medicare prescription-drug benefit, and a total restructuring of the tax code—had come to the conclusion that the United States Congress shouldn't attempt "comprehensive" reforms.

The strategy behind all this is to deny the other side an accomplishment, not put the minority's stamp of approval on a bill that would strengthen the majority's campaign for reelection. Obstruction, not input, has become the minority's credo. And that means gridlock, not action, has become Washington's usual signature.

IV. We like to think of American politics in terms of individuals. Candidates promise to bring a businessman's eye to Congress, or to be an independent voice from Massachusetts. They tell us about their families and their life trials. By the end of most campaigns, we could pick the winner's golden retriever out of a lineup if we had to.

This is a terrible error, because it leads us to change individuals when we need to change the system. And here is the system's problem: the minority wins when the majority fails, and the minority has the power to make the majority fail. Since the rules work no matter which party is in the minority, it means no one can ever govern.

We've become so accustomed to the current state of affairs that some think it core to the functioning of our democracy. "It's called the filibuster," Senator Gregg lectured Democrats from the floor of the Senate. "That's the way the Senate was structured. . . . The Founding Fathers realized when they structured this[;] they wanted checks and balances."

In fact, the filibuster was not an invention of the Founding Fathers. It was an accident: in the early 19th century, the Senate cleaned out its rule book and deleted the provision that let them call a vote to move from one issue to another. It took decades until anybody realized the filibuster had been created.

But Gregg is right to emphasize the importance of checks and balances to the system. The problem is that gridlock—which is partly the result of the filibuster—is eroding them. If the minority is always obstructing, then Congress can never govern. And when Congress can't act, the body cedes power to others. That worries longtime observers of the institution. "The Founders would be appalled at the notion of Congress delegating its fundamental law-making responsibilities to others," says Norm Ornstein, a congressional expert at the American Enterprise Institute.

Meanwhile, those who can act gain power at the expense of the Congress. The office of the president has grown in stature and authority. Early presidents delivered the State of the Union as a written letter because giving a big, dramatic speech to Congress would have been seen as overstepping the boundaries of the executive office. Modern presidents use the State of the Union to set the legislative agenda for Congress's next session, a development that would have shocked the Founders.

But it makes sense to us. The president is the main character in the media's retelling of our politics. His approval ratings are more important than the approval ratings of Congress even when we are voting only for congressmen. And it's getting worse: the political scientist Frances Lee has found that on average, each successive Congress spends a larger percentage of its time on the president's agenda than did its predecessor. The result is that there's the president's party in Congress, which mostly tries to help him out, and the opposition party, which tries to hinder him.

Like a parliamentary system, our politics is now defined by tightly knit teams and organized around the leader of the party or government. When Republicans controlled Congress in the early 2000s, they were so subjugated to the White House that Frist was handpicked by President Bush as the Republican Senate leader when Trent Lott, at Bush's urging, resigned over controversial comments he made.

But unlike a parliamentary system, our institutions are built to require minority cooperation. "We are operating in what amounts to a parliamentary system without majority rule," writes Brownstein in a recent National Journal column. "A formula for futility."

V. Sen. Michael Bennett, a Democrat from Colorado, is an expert at assessing and repairing failing institutions. He began in the world of corporate debt restructuring and recently ran Denver's public schools. The difficulty with saving troubled organizations, he says, is that the creditors and interests fight over the remains rather than banding together to nurse the body back to health. "Every one of those negotiations was about getting people to see their self-interest in moving the institution forward," he recalls.

Last year he was appointed to the United States Senate. After a year in the body, what he sees looks uncomfortably familiar: a culture of mistrust in an institution that requires radical transformation. Stakeholders ferociously trying to eke out every last advantage, and in doing so, destroying the very thing they all have a stake in.

Polls back him up: a recent Gallup survey found that only 18 percent of Americans approve of the job Congress is doing. Compare that with the president's approval ratings, which hover around 50 percent—despite the fact that Congress is largely just considering the president's agenda. One of the implications of these numbers: Americans are so disgusted by Congress that they don't trust it to do anything big. But our problems aren't politely waiting around until Congress gets its act together.

So how to change Congress? Well, carefully. Reform may be impossible in the day-to-day context, as the minority cannot unilaterally disarm itself. But theday-to-day context isn't the only possible context. "You have to do the John Rawls thing," says John Sides, a political scientist at George Washington University. "Go behind the veil of ignorance. Figure out the system we'd want without knowing who will be in charge or what they will be doing."

This work should start with a bipartisan group of legislators charged with reforming the rules that Congress works by, but their recommendations should only go into force in six or eight years, when no one knows who will hold the gavel. That lets everyone think of themselves as a potential majority as well as an embattled minority, and more important, it lets members of Congress focus on the health of the institution rather than their fortunes in the next election. It lets Congress be Congress again, if only in theory.

As for what the rules should say, the technical details should be hashed out by smart people from both parties. But the place to start is by ridding the Senate of the filibuster and its lesser-known friends (holds, unanimous consent to work for longer than two hours at a time, and so on), admitting that they are no longer appropriate given the polarizing realities of our politics.

That may seem like a radical change, but recall that the filibuster is an accident, and there is nothing radical or strange about majority voting: we use it for elections (Scott Brown won with 51 percent of the vote, not 60 percent), Supreme Court decisions, and the House of Representatives. As for a majority using its power unwisely, elections can remedy that. And voters can better judge Washington based on what it has done than on what it has been obstructed from doing.

The irony is that getting rid of the rules meant to ensure bipartisanship may actually discourage partisanship. Obstructionism is a good minority strategy as long as it actually works to stymie the majority's agenda and return you to power. But if it just means you sit out the work of governance while the majority legislates around you, your constituents and interest groups will eventually begin demanding that you include them in the process. And that's as it should be: we hire legislators to legislate. We need a system that encourages them to do so.

Ezra Klein is a blogger and columnist for *The Washington Post*, *Bloomberg*, *Newsweek*, and a contributor to MSNBC.

William Mo Cowan  **NO**

Cowan Farewell Address

On January 30 of this year, Governor Deval Patrick sent me to this chamber to represent the people of Massachusetts and their interests. Yesterday on June 25 those same people took to the voting booths and called me home. And in doing so, they called Senator-elect Ed Markey to the high honor of serving in this August body.

After serving in the House Senator-elect Ed Markey now has the opportunity to offer his voice, wisdom, accumulated experiences, humor and tireless devotion to justice and equality to the United States Senate. I for one believe that Massachusetts and the country will be better for it. Like the majority of Massachusetts voters who expressed themselves yesterday, I am quite confident that Senator-elect Markey will serve with distinction and act in the best interest of the citizens he's now privileged to represent. And the Senator-elect bested a strong candidate who brought a new voice and, yes, a new visage to the Massachusetts political scene. I applaud Gabriel Gomez on a well-run campaign and most importantly, his willingness to sacrifice so much in an effort to serve the people of the commonwealth. He started this journey as a relative unknown, but I suspect we have not heard the last of Mr. Gomez. I thank him and his family for their sacrifices and their willingness to engage.

Mr. President, when it comes to farewell speeches few will top the words offered by John Kerry on this floor a few months ago. After 28 years of distinguished service to the people of Massachusetts, now Secretary Kerry spent nearly an hour reflecting on his service to this body. By the same measure, Mr. President, as merely an interim Senator serving but a few short months, I probably should have ended my remarks about 45 seconds ago. But before I yield, Mr. President, I will take a few minutes to reflect on my brief time in this body and extend my gratitude to a number of folks.

First, I want to acknowledge and recognize the outstanding staff members in Boston and D.C. who have helped me serve our constituents to the best of my ability. When Governor Patrick named me as interim Senator, a few people—okay, more than a few—openly questioned whether I would be up to the task and whether I was capable of accomplishing anything other than locating the lavatory during my temporary assignment. I knew something those doubters did not know. I knew I was going to do my best for the folks back home because I came to the Senate armed with the knowledge of the issues by dint of my time in the Patrick-Murray administration and I planned to make a few key hires and convince the bulk of the

Secretary's staff to stay on and do the job the Governor sent me to do. In other words, I knew what I didn't know but I knew enough to hire the people who knew the considerable rest. Boy, have they proven me a genius. If you work in the Senate but a day—and I suspect the same is true in the House of Representatives—you will learn quickly that staff make this place hum and good staff make all the difference in the world.

I hope my team will forgive me if I do not list them all by name thereby avoiding the state of omission. But instead all of the staff will accept my heartfelt appreciation for their willingness to join my team, show me the ropes, teach a new dog some old tricks, educate me in all the rules that matter, which seem to be written nowhere, and their exhibition of the degrees of professionalism and service to our country that the public too often thinks is missing in our Congress.

To my entire staff, I have been in awe at your greatness and am forever in your debt for your immeasurable contributions to our work in the interest of Massachusetts residents. And I look forward to your many successes yet to come. To two on my team in particular, Val Young, Chief of Staff and Lauren Rich, my scheduler, who have known and worked for me for years, thank you for your continued willingness to partner with and trust in me.

And if I am being honest, Mr. President, about the people who help me look like I belonged here, I will spend a moment or two acknowledging the wonderful women and men who comprise the Senate staff. From the capitol police who protect us every day and somehow knew my name on the first day, to the subway operators who always deliver us on time and unfazed, to the elevator operators who excel in the art of cutting off reporters and annoying questions, to the cloakroom staff who field every cloying call about calling schedules, to the clerks who discreetly tell you what to say and do as presiding officer while the public and gallery silently wonders why everyone addresses you as Mr. or Madam President while sitting in that chair, to the generous food service staff who look the other way while you go back for seconds or thirds, to the others who make this engine oil and hum, to each of you who showed patience, support and grace that I know your love for this institution may trump even the members' affection for this place and will sustain the institution long after any one or all of us leave this chamber. You are tremendous resources for every new Senator, and I suspect great comfort to even the longest serving among us. The public may not

Cowan, Mo. From remarks before U.S. Senate, June 26, 2013.

know you by name or know the importance of your work, but now I do. And I have been honored to serve with you.

The next folks I recognize are the youngest and most silent among us. Of course I speak of the pages, the young women and men who spent part of a high school year dressing and acting in the formal traditions of this body. I have yet to speak with an uninteresting page or a page uninterested in the Senate and our government. These are dynamic young people who could be doing so many different things with their time, but they give their time and service to the Senate and its members. And they are indispensable to both. I look forward to the day when my young boys will be of age to follow in the footsteps of these outstanding young people.

Last and by no means least I want to thank the many family and friends who supported my family and me during my short tenure. We often say that it takes a village to raise a child, but I can attest that it also takes a village to help an interim Senator meet his duties in Congress and at home. Whether offering me a spare bedroom in Silver Spring or agreeing to last-minute baby sitting duties so my wife and I both could celebrate Black History Month at the White House, our village is vast and generous. And of course, every village needs a queen and the queen of my village is my wife, Stacy. I was able to serve because she was willing to be mom and dad and sacrifice in ways known and unknown while I have been in D.C. Over the past few months I've missed many homework assignments, some birthday dinners, pediatric appointments, school performances and parent-teacher meetings. But our sons never felt that their dad was absent and unaccounted for because their mom, a supermom, more than made up for my absence. Stacy has been my rock and salvation for nearly 20 years now, and I am better every day for it. And let the Senate record show for now and all time my love and dedication to Stacy.

Mr. President, in January of this year I planned to leave Deval Patrick's administration and transition back into private life. I was looking forward to more conventional hours, a reprieve from working under the public scrutiny of the press and spending more time with my wife and our young sons. So, I came to the United States Senate. Go figure. I was surprised but deeply honored when Governor Patrick sent me here to represent the folks back home and I'm eternally grateful for the Governor's faith and trust in my ability to serve. This floor on which I stand today and with which I have become so closely acquainted over the past five months has been occupied by some of the most dynamic and greatest political figures of our nation's history. From my own state of Massachusetts alone, names like Adams, Webster, Sumner, Kennedy, all who have come before me are enough to make anyone feel daunted when assuming a desk on this floor.

I was appointed to fill the seat of John Kerry and work alongside another great Senator, Elizabeth Warren. Thank you for being here, Elizabeth. With my work here, although my time was short, I sought to uphold not only Secretary Kerry's legacy in this body,

but the work of all the esteemed Senators who have dedicated their service to the commonwealth of Massachusetts, and I pledge to be the—pledged to be the best partner I could to Senator Warren. I entered the Senate at a vexing time in this body's history. As we all know, congressional approval levels are dismally low. People across the nation and political pundits everywhere believe that partisanship is a bridge too wide—a divide too wide to bridge and a wall too high to overcome. Yet despite the overwhelming public pessimism, I came to Washington with two achievable objectives. To serve the people of Massachusetts to the best of my ability, and to work with any Senator willing to implement smart, sensible and productive policy to advance the ideals of our nation. From the outside, the prospects for bipartisanship may seem slim. Party-line votes are the norm. The threat of the filibuster demands a supermajority of the past leading to the legislation. And the American people have come to believe Congress is more committed to obstruction than compromise.

To the everyday observer, we have reached a standstill where partisanship outweighs progress, and neither side is willing to reach across the aisle for the good of the American people. But what I have encountered in the Senate is not a body defined by vitriol but one more defined by congeniality and common respect. And that began before I even started here, Mr. President. On the day the Governor announced my appointment, I was pleasantly surprised to receive calls on my personal cell phone— I still don't know how they got those numbers—from Senators King, Hagan and Cardin, and I had the pleasure of receiving warm welcomes from majority leader Reid and Republican leader McConnell, among so many others, my first day. One of the first persons to congratulate me after Senator Warren and Secretary Kerry escorted me for my swearing in was my colleague from across the aisle, Senator Tim Scott.

Since then, Senator Rand Paul and I have recounted our days at Duke and our affection for college basketball. On a bipartisan congressional delegation to the Middle East, I traded life stories and perspectives with Senators Klobuchar and Hoeven and discussed the comedic genius of Will Ferrell with Senators Gillibrand and Graham. Senator Portman stopped by my commonwealth coffee last week to wish me well as I leave the Senate and encourage me every day during my time here. Senator Burr, my next-door neighbor in the Russell building, has always been good to remind me that I came from North Carolina before I had the privilege to serve in Massachusetts. Senator McCain invited me to cosponsor my first Senate resolution. And Senator Manchin has shown me more kindness than I can count.

The freshman Senators on both sides welcomed me to their class and offered never-ending encouragement, and indeed one of them, Heidi Heitkamp, has become the North Dakota sister I never knew I had. I wish I had time to recount every kindness each of the other 99, including the late Senator Lautenberg, gifted me while here, but I don't, but each has been recorded indelibly in my memory and is returned with gratitude.

In April, I experienced the very best of this body's character in the wake of the Boston marathon bombings when members from every corner of this nation extended their sympathies, their prayers and pledged their assistance and support to the city of Boston and to all those affected by that tragedy. In the aftermath, we all came together as Americans to honor those killed and to support the wounded during their time of recovery. And we saw the same in the wake of the terrible tornadoes that swept through Oklahoma. Upon closer inspection, it is clear that all of us here have common bonds and share similar goals. If only we are willing to seek out those bonds and focus on the goals that are in the best interests of our nation. While we may not agree on every policy, every line item or every vote, we have each embraced the role of republic servants, committed to serving the country we have pledged to support and defend. And as I have discovered in my time here, there is more opportunity for cooperation than the American public might believe.

And this cooperation has led to some noted successes. Thanks to the bipartisan work in the agriculture committee and on the Senate floor, we were able to send the farm bill to the house. Through the joint leadership of the so-called Gang of Eight, we are debating right now a workable approach to comprehensive immigration reform. We have confirmed five cabinet secretaries. And in what will remain the most memorable all-nighter of my Senate career, through a marathon session and more votes in one night than most interim Senators have in a career, the Senate passed the budget, and now we anxiously await the urgent opportunity to conference with the House.

I have seen progress, and I remain a true believer in the democratic process. The core functionality of our government endowed to us by our Founding Fathers so many decades ago. And I remain a true believer in our system of government and the Senate's role in that system. If I have been asked any question more frequently than what are you going to do next, Mo, it has been is our system of government broken? Is Congress broken? And I have answered truthfully each time—no. Our system of government is the greatest ever known, and the best example of democracy in human history. The Genius of our founding fathers is on display every day on capitol hill, in every state capital, in every city or town hall across this nation. And part of the Founders' genius was the birth of a government designed to function as the people need it to but function only as effectively as the privileged few empowered to work within it want it to work. Or as Secretary Kerry himself said when he said it best a few months ago right on this floor, and I quote—"I do not

believe the Senate is broken. There is nothing wrong with the Senate that can't be fixed by what's right with the Senate. The predominant and weighty notion that 100 American citizens, chosen by their neighbors—[or their governor, in my case]—to serve from states as different from Massachusetts to Montana can always choose to put parochial or personal interests aside and find the national interest." What an awesome responsibility and privilege. And in my scant five months, I have seen the promise of those words realized in more ways and in more interactions than the public, unfortunately, has had occasion to witness. So I believe in that unlimited promise still.

I have also been part of history while I was here. With my appointment and coincident with the appointment of Senator Scott, two African-Americans are serving in this body concurrently for the first time in our nation's history. Senator Scott and I are respectively the seventh and eighth black Senators to serve in this body. While I believe this number to be far too few, I am also hopeful that it is a sign that these United States will soon be represented by a more diverse population that more closely reflects the diverse country that we are and the diversity of opinions that exist across and within our diverse nation. With different perspectives, different backgrounds, different races, religions and creeds, we are better equipped to confront the issues that face our vast and changing nation.

America has been and always will be a nation of immigrants where religious freedom is in our DNA. Where more and more we are chipping away at the barriers preventing us from achieving true marriage equality and where people worldwide still yearn to reach our shores to enjoy our freedoms. And a Congress that is more reflective of this America as this Congress is becoming will be good for America.

Finally, Mr. President, I offer my heartfelt gratitude to the people of Massachusetts. Not one person was given the chance to vote for or against me, but I have gone about my work every day as if they had. I came to this body beholden to Massachusetts, her residents and the country only and leave confident that I have stayed true to that honor. And ladies and gentlemen of the commonwealth, it has been a true honor and privilege to represent you as your junior Senator in the United States Senate. With that, Mr. President, and for what will likely be the final time, I yield the floor.

William Mo Cowan is an American politician and lawyer who served as the junior U.S. Senator from Massachusetts in 2013. He previously served as legal counsel and Chief of Staff to Massachusetts Governor Deval Patrick. He is now a Fellow at the Institute of Politics in the Harvard Kennedy School.

EXPLORING THE ISSUE

Is Congress a Dysfunctional Institution?

Critical Thinking and Reflection

1. Do we really want a speedy system in which laws would be pushed through before a consensus develops?
2. Do we really want a system in which the viewpoint of the minority gets trampled by a rush to action by the majority?
3. How does the public tend to view the work of Congress? Do you agree or disagree? Why?
4. Why is Congress viewed as dysfunctional by some Americans?
5. How could Congress make itself appear less dysfunctional?

Is There Common Ground?

In theory, at least, there is common ground between the assertion that bills should not be hastily run through Congress and the assertion that the passage of laws should not be hamstrung indefinitely by a minority. The problem comes in trying to craft a synthesis of those two assertions in today's polarized Congress. Some hope that a temporary solution—there is never a permanent one—will come when a new election gives one of the parties decisive control of both houses of Congress. Yet that happened in 2008, and, while it did result in the passage of at least three important pieces of legislation, it also set off a powerful backlash against the majority party in the political arena.

In 2013, with a divided Congress, we have seen the smallest amount of legislative output in over a half century. Some will argue that this is a positive fact since it means that unnecessary legislation was not created. Critics, on the other hand, will point to the fact that we elect members of Congress into office to pass legislation. Instead of seeing new laws, recently we have seen little except partisan bickering and utilization of loopholes for political reasons. As a nation, we seem to be missing opportunities to take concentrated efforts to fix the problems ailing our fellow citizens.

Additional Resources

Charles B. Cushman, *An Introduction to the U.S. Congress* (Shape, 2006)

Lawrence C. Dodd and Bruce Oppenheimer, *Congress Reconsidered* (CQ Press, 2004)

Diana Evans, *Greasing the Wheels: Using Pork Barrel Projects to Build Majority Coalitions in Congress* (Cambridge University Press, 2004)

Richard Fenno, *Home Style: House Members in Their Districts* (Longman, 2002)

Sally Friedman, *Dilemmas of Representation: Local Politics, National Factors, and the Home Styles of Modern U.S. Congress Members* (State University of New York, 2007)

Internet References . . .

No Labels

www.nolabels.org/gridlock

Reclamation of the U.S. Congress

http://repositories.lib.utexas.edu/bitstream/handle
/2152/20957/FinalReclamationoftheUSCongress
_9-27.pdf?sequence=6

Steven Kull on Congressional Gridlock

www.c-spanvideo.org/program/Kul

The Gridlock Illusion

www.wilsonquarterly.com/essays/gridlock-illusion

U.S. Electoral System and Congressional Gridlock

www.c-spanvideo.org/program/316150-4

Selected, Edited, and with Issue Framing Material by:
William J. Miller, *Flagler College*

ISSUE

Should Supreme Court Justices have Term Limits?

YES: Norm Ornstein, from "Why the Supreme Court Needs Term Limits," *The Atlantic* (2014)

NO: Lyle Denniston, from "Constitution Check: Did the Founders Want Term Limits for Supreme Court Justices?" *Constitution Daily* (2015)

Learning Outcomes

After reading this issue, you will be able to:

- Explain the history of judicial term limits.
- Discuss arguments for term limiting Supreme Court justices.
- Discuss arguments against term limiting Supreme Court justices.
- Assess the potential impact term limits would have on judicial decision making.
- Discuss how term limits would impact checks and balances within the federal government.

ISSUE SUMMARY

YES: Writer Norm Ornstein argues that the most effective way to address the problems created by an increasingly politicized Supreme Court is to limit all justices to 18-year terms.

NO: Lyle Denniston, the National Constitution Center's constitutional literacy adviser, examines comments from one-time Republican presidential candidate Mike Huckabee about the Founders' intentions for a Supreme Court with term limits and what Alexander Hamilton said about the issue.

On the third season of "House of Cards," a fictional Supreme Court justice mulls retirement when he is diagnosed with Alzheimer's. Nobody is speculating that anybody on the real-life Supreme Court is suffering from a degenerative brain disease. But the show's plotline calls attention to the fact that, barring death or an impeachable offence, the justices themselves decide when to hang up their robes. And today's Supremes are no spring chickens. Ruth Bader Ginsburg, the liberal lion who has resisted calls to retire during Barack Obama's presidency, is 82. Antonin Scalia, on the right, and Anthony Kennedy, in the center, are both 79. Stephen Breyer is 77. Four justices—Clarence Thomas (67), Samuel Alito (66), Sonia Sotomayor (61), and the chief, John Roberts (60)—are sexagenarians. The new kid on the bench, Elena Kagan, is a wee 55. If nobody leaves the court in the next five years—an unlikely permutation—the average age of the justices will be 75 at the end of the next president's first term.

Article III, Section I of the United States Constitution states: "The judicial power of the United States, shall be vested in one Supreme Court, and in such inferior courts as the Congress may from time to time ordain and establish. The judges, both of the supreme and inferior courts, shall hold their offices during good behavior, and shall, at stated times, receive for their services, a compensation, which shall not be diminished during their continuance in office."

The clear implication of this statement has been for Supreme Court justices to serve life terms so long as they have avoided impeachable offenses. And Alexander Hamilton, writing *Federalist* 78, furthers this argument when saying: "According to the plan of the convention, all judges who may be appointed by the United States are to hold their offices during good behavior; which is conformable to the most approved of the state constitutions. . . . Its propriety having been drawn into question by the adversaries of that plan is no light symptom of the rage for objection which disorders their imaginations and judgments. The standard of good behavior for the continuance in office of the judicial magistracy is certainly one of the most valuable of the modern improvements in the practice of government. . . . It is the best expedient which can be devised in any government to secure a steady, upright, and impartial administrations of the laws. . . . This independence of the judges is equally requisite to guard the Constitution and the rights of individuals from the effects of those ill humors which the arts of designing men, or the influence of particular conjunctures, sometimes disseminate among the people themselves, and which, though they speedily give place to better information, and more deliberate reflection, have a tendency, in the meantime, to occasion dangerous innovations in the government, and serious oppressions of the minor party in the community."

The life term has been largely blamed for the increased politicization of the nomination and confirmation process. The idea of term-limiting justices has been brought up repeatedly—most recently after the death of Justice Antonin Scalia, who served 30 years on the Supreme Court. Many, after his death, believed that three decades on the bench was simply too long.

Most Americans would support imposing a term limit on the nine U.S. Supreme Court justices, who now serve for life, a 2016 Reuters/Ipsos opinion poll found in the aftermath of major rulings by the court on Obamacare and gay marriage. Limiting terms would be difficult, requiring an amendment to the U.S. Constitution. Congress shows no signs of taking up the idea, though Republican Senator Ted Cruz has suggested the possibility of justices being voted out of office.

Support for the 10-year term limit proposed by the poll was bipartisan, with 66 percent saying they favored such a change while 17 percent supported life tenure. Sixty-six percent of Democrats, 74 percent of Republicans, and 68 percent of independents said they favored the 10-year term limit idea, according to the poll. Respondents were not asked their preference on how long the justices' terms should last. Over the years, legal experts have debated 8-, 10-, 14-, and 18-year limits.

The poll showed broad understanding of the court, with 68 percent saying they knew justices are appointed, not elected, and 60 percent saying they knew the appointments are for life. Under the Constitution, presidents appoint the justices subject to confirmation by the U.S. Senate, a process only 32 percent of respondents backed. Forty-eight percent said justices should be elected. There was little support in the poll for tinkering with the court's role as the final arbiter of U.S. law. Only 29 percent said they would support allowing Congress or the president to overrule court decisions.

While the Constitution was clear about the Founders' intentions, many citizens have taken the opposite stance. Staying too long is not necessarily good behavior—Congress has the ability to define good behavior. But, on the other hand, the tradition in the Supreme Court of the United States that was practiced into the twentieth century was the justices would keep an eye on one another. If somebody got a little bit attenuated and fragile, the others would come to him and say, "Judge, it's time for you to quit." And he would.

But the job has become more politicized, and justices have a large sense of power. Moreover, they have got a lot of help, they've got a huge number, three or four law clerks who can do the heavy lifting. They don't have very many decisions they have to make so it's a relatively easy job in that sense. Part of what was a concern is that increasingly, the Supreme Court has been making decisions that are highly political. They are interpreting the Constitution in ways that bear heavily on a lot of decisions that people want to vote on. And that wasn't going on in the eighteenth century; it wasn't going on until the last few decades.

Justices have always been told to avoid public opinion when making decisions, and it seems like they have largely remained isolated from the views of the masses. But if they are going to be making political decisions, then it's not necessarily too bad of an idea for them to at least be thinking about, in a democratic government, what the people want or believe or would anticipate.

No matter how wise or enlightened they may be, a bench of seven or nine octogenarians will have a circumscribed perspective on the country for which they are adjudicating fundamental questions. Encrusted jurisprudence won't necessarily be bad for the country: as Alexander Hamilton pointed out in *Federalist*, vol. 79, the "danger of a superannuated bench" resulting from aged judges is "imaginary." Indeed, Justice Ginsburg shows in both her written opinions and incisive questions during oral argument that she is as vigorous intellectually as she has ever been. But breathing new life into the nation's highest court more often—even if it does not make the tribunal any less political—would bring more dynamism to the judiciary, jog the justices' decision-making patterns and narrow, even if only slightly, the yawning gap between the enrobed ones and everyday citizens.

In the following selections, writer Norm Ornstein argues that the most effective way to address the problems created by an increasingly politicized Supreme Court is to limit all justices to 18-year terms. Arguing against Ornstein is Lyle Denniston, the National Constitution Center's constitutional literacy adviser, who examines comments from one-time Republican presidential candidate Mike Huckabee about the Founders' intentions for a Supreme Court with term limits and what Alexander Hamilton said about the issue.

YES ⬅

Norm Ornstein

Why the Supreme Court Needs Term Limits

This has been quite a time for anniversaries: the 50th of the 1964 Civil Rights Act, the 50th of the Great Society, the 60th of *Brown v. Board of Education*. Each has produced a flurry of celebrations and analyses, including the latest, on *Brown*. Here's one more.

Ten years ago, on the occasion of the 50th anniversary of *Brown*, I attended one of the most interesting and moving panels ever. Yale Law School brought together six luminaries who had been clerks to Supreme Court justices during the deliberations over the *Brown* decision. They talked about the internal discussions and struggles to reach agreement, and the fact that the decision actually took two years. The justices—including Chief Justice Earl Warren and Justices Hugo Black, Felix Frankfurter, Sherman Minton, and others—tried mightily to build a consensus. Whatever their ideological predispositions, they all understood that this decision would alter the fabric of American society. They also knew it would reverberate for a long time, exacerbating some deep-seated societal divisions even as it would heal so many others and right so many wrongs.

The two terms allowed the justices to reach a unanimous conclusion. Afterward, Frankfurter penned a handwritten note to Warren that read: "Dear Chief: This is a day that will live in glory. It is also a great day in the history of the Court, and not in the least for the course of deliberation which brought about the result. I congratulate you."

As I read that letter, I thought about what would have happened if the current Supreme Court were transported back to decide *Brown*. Two years of deliberation? No way. Unanimous or even near-unanimous decision? Forget it. The decision would have been 5-4 the other way, with Chief Justice John Roberts writing for the majority, "The way to stop discrimination on the basis of race is to stop discriminating on the basis of race"—leaving separate but equal as the standard. The idea that finding unanimity or near-unanimity was important for the fabric of the society would never have come up.

Recent analyses have underscored the new reality of today's Supreme Court: It is polarized along partisan lines in a way that parallels other political institutions and the rest of society, in a fashion we have never seen. A couple of years ago, David Paul Kuhn, writing here, noted that the percentage of rulings by one-vote margins is higher under Roberts than any previous chief justice in American history. Of course, many decisions are unanimous—but it is the tough, divisive, and most important ones that end up with one-vote margins.

The *New York Times's* Adam Liptak weighed in recently with a piece called "The Polarized Court," in which he said, "For the first time, the Supreme Court is closely divided along party lines." Scott Lemieux, in *The Week*, noted further that the polarization on the Court, like the polarization in Congress, is asymmetric; conservative justices have moved very sharply to the right, liberals a bit more modestly to the left. Much of the movement did occur before Roberts was elevated to the Supreme Court, but his leadership has sharpened the divisions much more, on issues ranging from race and voting rights to campaign finance and corporate power.

How did we get here? As politics have become polarized and as two-party competition intensified, control of the courts—which are increasingly making major policy decisions—became more important. With lifetime appointments, a party in power for two or four years could have sway over policy for decades after it left power. But to ensure that sway meant picking judges who were virtual locks to rule the way the party in power wanted. That meant track records in judicial opinions, and that in turn meant choosing sitting judges to move up to the Supreme Court. It also meant choosing younger individuals with more ideology and less seasoning; better to have a justice serving for 30 years or more than for 20 or less.

The Warren Court that decided *Brown* had five members who had been elected to office—three former U.S. senators, one of whom had also been mayor of Cleveland; one state legislator; and one governor. They were mature, they understood the law, but also understood politics and the impact of their decisions on society. As a consequence, they did not always vote in predictable fashion. Only one of the justices, Sherman Minton, had served on a U.S. appellate court—and he had been a senator before that appointment.

Now, zero members of the Supreme Court have served in elective office, and only Stephen Breyer has significant experience serving on a staff in Congress. Eight of the nine justices previously were on U.S. courts of appeal. Few have had real-world experience outside of the legal and judicial realm. And few of their opinions and decisions come as surprises. That is not to say that all the justices are naïve (although Anthony Kennedy's

Ornstein, Norm. "Why the Supreme Court Needs Term Limits," *The Atlantic*, May 2014. Copyright © 2014 by Tribune Content Agency (TMS). Used with permission.

opinion in *Citizens United*, blithely dismissing the idea that there could be any corruption in campaign money spent "independently" in campaigns, was the epitome of naiveté). Roberts is political in the most Machiavellian sense; he understood the zeitgeist enough to repeatedly assure the Senate during his confirmation hearings that he would strive to issue narrow opinions that respected *stare decisis* and achieved 9-0 or 8-1 consensus, even as he lay the groundwork during his tenure for the opposite. His surprising ruling on the Affordable Care Act was clearly done with an eye toward softening the criticism that was sure to come with the series of 5-4 decisions on campaign finance and voting rights that lay ahead.

With a Court that is increasingly active in overturning laws passed by Congress and checking presidential authority when there is a president of the opposite party, that means nominations both to appeals courts and to the Supreme Court have become increasingly divisive and polarized, for both parties. And the policy future of the country depends as much on the actuarial tables and the luck of the draw for presidents as it does on the larger trends in politics and society. We could have one one-term president shaping the Court for decades, and another two-term president having zero appointments. And we could end up with a Supreme Court dramatically out of step for decades with the larger shape of the society, and likely losing much of its prestige and sense of legitimacy as an impartial arbiter, creating in turn a serious crisis of confidence in the rule of law.

For more than a decade, I have strongly advocated moving toward term limits for appellate judges and Supreme Court justices. I would like to have single, 18-year terms, staggered so that each president in a term would have two vacancies to fill. Doing so would open opportunities for men and women in their 60s, given modern life expectancies, and not just those in their 40s. It would to some degree lower the temperature on confirmation battles by making the stakes a bit lower. And it would mean a Court that more accurately reflects the changes and judgments of the society.

If we could combine term limits for justices with a sensitivity by presidents to find some judges who actually understand the real world of politics and life, and not just the cloistered one of the bench, we might get somewhere.

NORM ORNSTEIN is a contributing writer for *The Atlantic*, a contributing editor and columnist for *National Journal*, and a resident scholar at the American Enterprise Institute for Public Policy Research.

Lyle Denniston

 **NO**

Constitution Check: Did the Founders Want Term Limits for Supreme Court Justices

The Statement at Issue

"Prospective presidential nominee Mike Huckabee called Saturday for the imposition of term limits on U.S. Supreme Court justices, saying that the nation's founders never intended to create lifetime, irrevocable posts. 'Nobody should be in an unelected position for life,' the former Arkansas governor said in an interview, expanding on remarks he made during an hour-long speech at the Nixon Presidential Library in Yorba Linda. 'If the president who appoints them can only serve eight years, the person they appoint should never serve 40. That has never made sense to me; it defies that sense of public service.' Huckabee said the *Federalist Papers*, written by Alexander Hamilton, James Madison and John Jay, supported his view that the nation's founders came close to imposing judicial term limits in the Constitution; they never could have imagined people would want to serve in government for decades, he said."

> —*Story in The* Los Angeles Times, *on March 28, describing an interview with the ex-governor, who is expected to announce soon that he will again seek the presidency.*

We Checked The Constitution, And . . .

Much of the American Constitution endures, after more than two centuries, in its original form, and that is a testament to the wisdom of the founding generation that put it together. But it is sometimes true that a commentator here and there will treat the original Constitution as if it said something different from what it actually says, something more agreeable to that person.

Politicians on the stump may indulge themselves in that kind of revisionism because it better suits an aspiration they may have for America. One perhaps can expect, as America moves more deeply into the next round of presidential politics, that the Constitution will take on new meanings on the stump. Given that it is so easy to disprove such rewriting, it is surprising that even politicians eager

for votes would allow themselves to be shown to be wrong. That, however, seems not to be much of a deterrent.

One constitutional fantasy is that the Supreme Court should not really have members who can serve for their lifetimes, a choice left entirely to them personally so long as they behave themselves and do not give reasons to seek to unseat them involuntarily.

The opening words of the Constitution's Article III, describing the judiciary that the original document created at the national level, reads this way (with emphasis added): "The judicial power of the United States shall be vested in one supreme court, and in such inferior courts as the Congress may from time to time ordain and establish. The judges, both of the supreme and inferior courts, *shall hold their offices during good behavior . . .*"

The phrase "good behavior" obviously implies that there is no limit on how long a Justice may serve, once approved for serving on the court. That implication is supported by the impeachment provision of the Constitution, contained in Article II. Just as the president and vice president may be removed from office by impeachment, so, too, can federal judges, including Justices of the Supreme Court. But that can only happen if they are convicted of "treason, bribery, or other high crimes and misdemeanors." Those, surely, are words that describe the opposite of "good behavior" for a judge, so they give meaning to the question of Justices' right to continue in office indefinitely.

If former Arkansas Governor Mike Huckabee has been quoted accurately by the *Los Angeles Times*, he has a perception of what the founding generation wanted regarding judicial tenure that seems to run counter to Article III and to the history of the founding years. There is nothing in Article III, or in the impeachment provision, that supports the notion that "the nation's founders never intended to create lifetime, irrevocable posts" for Supreme Court Justices, or for other federal judges.

That part of Article III has never been revised, and the prospects that it will be—say, for example, by an amendment to impose term limits—seem quite remote if not non-existent.

But Huckabee's quarrel is not only with constitutional language, but with what that very influential document of the founding

Denniston, Lyle. "Constitution Check: Did the Founders Want Term Limits for Supreme Court Justices?" *Constitution Daily,* March 2015. Copyright © 2015 by The National Constitution Center. Used with permission.

era—the Federalist Papers—has to say on the subject of the terms of service on the Supreme Court.

The most authoritative and thorough Federalist Paper on "the judicial department" is No. 78, published on May 28, 1788. Like all other papers, it was published under the pen name "Publius," but this one was actually written by Alexander Hamilton. To suggest, as Gov. Huckabee does, that Hamilton and the other authors of the Federalist "came close to imposing judicial term limits" does not take account of Paper No. 78.

Here is some of what Hamilton wrote there, describing the sense of the Philadelphia Convention that drafted the original Constitution:

> "According to the plan of the convention, all judges who may be appointed by the United States are to hold their offices during good behavior; which is conformable to the most approved of the state constitutions. . . . Its propriety having been drawn into question by the adversaries of that plan is no light symptom of the rage for objection which disorders their imaginations and judgments. The standard of good behavior for the continuance in office of the judicial magistracy is certainly one of the most valuable of the modern improvements in the practice of government. . . . It is the best expedient which can be devised in any government to secure a steady, upright and impartial administrations of the laws. . . . This independence of the judges is equally requisite to guard the Constitution and the rights of individuals from the effects of those ill humors which the arts of designing men, or the influence of particular conjunctures, sometimes disseminate among the people themselves, and which, though they speedily give place to better information, and more deliberate reflection, have a tendency, in the meantime, to

occasion dangerous innovations in the government, and serious oppressions of the minor party in the community."

There is in those sentiments not the slightest hint that Hamilton, or Madison or Jay, "came close to imposing judicial term limits in the Constitution" or that "they never could have imagined people would want to serve in government for decades."

The Huckabee musings on this subject run into another logical barrier in the structure of the Constitution. He was quoted as saying that, if presidents who appoint members of the court can only serve eight years, the person they name should not serve 40 years. But, until the Twenty-Second Amendment was written into the Constitution in 1951, there were no term limits for those who served as president. So, for 163 years after Article III was put into the Constitution, there was no potential inconsistency between the tenure of presidents and of Supreme Court Justices.

Franklin Roosevelt, the last president not affected by the Twenty-Second Amendment, served for three full terms, plus 83 days into a fourth term. One of the eight Justices he named to the Court set the record for the longest service on the court: William O. Douglas, who served more than 36 years. While the nation turned out to be uncomfortable with a presidential term of the length of Franklin Roosevelt's, there has been no serious effort to curb the service of the Justices. And that seems to reflect the founders' true wishes.

LYLE DENNISTON has been covering the Supreme Court for fifty-eight years. In that time, he has covered one-quarter of all of the Justices ever to sit, and he has reported on the entire careers on the bench of ten of the Justices. He has been a journalist of the law for sixty-eight years, beginning that career at the Otoe County Courthouse in Nebraska City, Nebraska, in the fall of 1948

EXPLORING THE ISSUE

Should Supreme Court Justices have Term Limits?

Critical Thinking and Reflection

1. What are the benefits of Supreme Court justices not having term limits?
2. What are the negative aspects of Supreme Court justices not having term limits?
3. How do you believe term limits would change how justices behave? Why?
4. What benefits do term limits present in other offices of government?
5. Do you believe an age limit would fulfill the same purpose as term limits? Why or why not?

Is There Common Ground?

Like most things related to the courts, it's hard to imagine finding common ground on an issue like term limits. Those opposed to term limits are able to quite easily point to the Constitution's clearly defined statement of no term limits, along with the Federalist Paper discussion concerning why it's important for Supreme Court justices to not have to be concerned with leaving office after a term. Likewise, those who wish to see term limits imposed are not likely to be swayed by counter-arguments waged by those who disagree. They believe a level of accountability—along with a limit on how long a justice has the capability to determine legal decisions—is essential to making government as democratic as possible.

To reach any common ground would take an agreement that any type of term limit was desired. But what good would a hypothetical 20-year term limit serve? At that point, a judge appointed at 50 would leave the bench at 70 and have two decades to influence policy without fear of the public's sentiments. At the same time, a proposed 5-year term would make it much more difficult for judges to accept appointments since they would be out of work much more quickly.

Thus, even if there were to be an agreement reached on a desire for term limits at all, there would still be significant work needed to shape exactly what this new system would look like. Most importantly, we need to remember that the individuals who would need to make this decision are members of Congress that also do not have term limits today—and the Supreme Court would be able to determine the constitutionality of this change, barring a Constitutional amendment.

Additional Resources

Roger C. Cramton and Paul D. Carrington, *Reforming the Court: Term Limits for the Supreme Court Justices* (Carolina Academic Press, 2005)

Mark Levin, *The Liberty Amendments: Restoring the American Republic* (Threshold Editions, 2013)

James D. Zirin and Kermit Roosevelt, *Supremely Partisan: How Raw Politics Tips the Scales in the United States Supreme Court* (Rowman & Littlefield, 2016)

Internet References . . .

Running the Numbers on Supreme Court Term Limits

https://www.brennancenter.org/blog/running-numbers
-supreme-court-term-limits

Term Limits

http://fixthecourt.com/fix/term-limits/

The Supreme Court and Term Limits

https://www.termlimits.org/the-supreme-court-and
-term-limits/

Selected, Edited, and with Issue Framing Material by:
William J. Miller, *Flagler College*

ISSUE

Should the Senate Be Able to Delay Hearings on Nominations While Waiting for a Presidential Election to Occur?

YES: William Yeomans, from "The Many Ways Senate Republicans Can Block Obama's Supreme Court Nominee," *Reuters* (2016)

NO: Joe Biden, from "The Senate's Duty on a Supreme Court Nominee," *The New York Times* (2016)

Learning Outcomes
After reading this issue, you will be able to:
• Discuss the process of Supreme Court nominations.
• Explain the factors presidents consider in determining who to nominate.
• Assess the responsibilities of the Senate with regards to confirming court nominees.
• List potential impacts of the Senate choosing to not act.
• Describe the politics behind nominations and confirmations.

ISSUE SUMMARY

YES: Former chief counsel for Senator Edward Kennedy on the Senate Judiciary Committee William Yeomans writes that whether it is the right decision or not, Republican Senators have a series of options available on how to block a potential nomination—many of which are rooted directly in the Constitution.

NO: Vice President, and former Senate Judiciary Committee member, Joe Biden, on the other hand, argues that the Constitution requires the Senate to take action and past precedent has demonstrated it is the proper thing to do.

Article II, Section 2 states: "[The President] shall have power, by and with the advice and consent of the Senate, to make treaties, provided two thirds of the Senators present concur; and he shall nominate, and by and with the advice and consent of the Senate, shall appoint ambassadors, other public ministers and consuls, judges of the Supreme Court, and all other officers of the United States, whose appointments are not herein otherwise provided for, and which shall be established by law: but the Congress may by law vest the appointment of such inferior officers, as they think proper, in the President alone, in the courts of law, or in the heads of departments." Thus, Supreme Court nominations involve two parties: the President, who nominates individuals to the Court, and the Senate, who confirms the nomination.

Merrick Garland officially made Supreme Court history in July 2016—not for something he did, but for something others haven't done. President Barack Obama's choice to replace the late Justice Antonin Scalia has surpassed the record for the high court nominee who has waited the longest to be confirmed for the job. The milestone couldn't be more symbolic. Garland, who was nominated in March 2016, surpassed Louis Brandeis, one of the greatest justices to ever live, who exactly 100 years ago endured the largest gap between nomination and confirmation of any Supreme Court nominee: 125 days.

Garland has been patiently waiting much longer for a Senate hearing and a vote. And by all accounts, he is sure to keep on waiting. Congress took summer recess and then Republican leadership in the Senate—all but set on the idea to have Donald Trump fill this and other Supreme Court vacancies—has shown no intention of even granting Garland a hearing. Senate Majority Leader Mitch McConnell (R-KY) stated: "The American people should have a voice in the selection of their next Supreme Court Justice. Therefore, this vacancy should not be filled until we have a new President."

For more than 40 years, there has been an average of just over two months between a president's nominating someone to the Supreme Court and that person's receiving a hearing in Congress. What is occurring with Judge Garland appears to be quite different than the typical dysfunction one may expect from Washington, D.C. Every Supreme Court nominee since 1875 who hasn't withdrawn from the process has received a hearing or a vote. Even when the nominee was controversial. Even when the Senate and the White House were held by different parties.

But Judge Garland isn't even necessarily controversial. He has more federal judicial experience than any Supreme Court nominee in our history. He is widely respected by people of both political parties as a man of experience, integrity, and unimpeachable qualifications. The partisan decision of Senate Republicans to deny a hearing to a judge is viewed by many Democrats—including President Obama—as an unprecedented escalation of the stakes. As Obama states: "Historically, when a president nominates a Supreme Court justice—regardless of when in the presidential term this occurs—the Senate is obligated to act. Senators are free to vote their conscience. But they vote. That's their job."

If Republicans in the Senate refuse even to consider a nominee in the hopes of running out the clock until they can elect a president from their own party, so that he can nominate his own justice to the Supreme Court, then they will effectively nullify the ability of any president from the opposing party to make an appointment to the nation's highest court. They would reduce the very functioning of the judicial branch of the government to another political leverage point. And this is why many are debating whether hearings should be mandated, or perhaps required to occur within a certain period of time.

The growing politicization of the judiciary is troubling for two reasons. First, a functioning judiciary—at every level—is essential to the business of the nation. For example, in the term in which Justice Scalia died, a deadlocked Supreme Court was unable to reach a decision on several major issues, leaving the law itself in limbo. Across the country, judicial vacancies are leaving some lower courts so overwhelmed they can barely make it through their dockets. Twenty-nine judicial emergencies have been declared by lower courts across the country. This has real implications for jurisprudence, real financial costs to the judicial system, and real consequences in the lives of people awaiting the outcomes of those cases.

Second, treating the Supreme Court like a political football makes the American people more cynical about democracy. When the Supreme Court becomes a proxy for political parties, public confidence in the notion of an impartial, independent judiciary breaks down. And the resulting lack of trust can undermine the rule of law.

So here's an idea that's been proposed in recent administrations—by both major political parties. Democrats and Republicans in the Senate could agree to give every future qualified Supreme Court nominee a hearing and a vote within an established timeframe. This reasonable proposal would prevent the confirmation process from breaking down beyond repair, and help restore good faith between the two parties. Democracies depend on the institutions we build, the rules upon which the nation is founded, and the traditions, customs, and habits of heart that guide our behavior and ensure that political differences never override the founding ideals that bind us.

While the arguments for forcing Congress to act are clear, if we return to a reading of the Constitution, there is no mandate for when confirmation hearings would take place on a nominee. While it is quite unlikely that the Founders would approve of a judge waiting well over six months for a hearing for no reason other than politics, nothing they left in writing assures this to be the case. Maybe the confirmation process needs to be political. Maybe the country has reached a point where this type of dysfunction is viewed as more important politically than working together to grow the country as a whole. While this would not bode well for long-term democratic values, it may be the best way to look at the situation we find ourselves in today. Ironically, if Hillary Clinton were to win the White House in November, Senate Republicans may be the ones to try to push through a Garrick appointment given his relatively moderate tendencies and views as compared to a potentially more liberal nominee coming from a new president.

In the following selections, we take a closer look at whether the Senate should be forced to hold hearings in any particular timeframe. Former chief counsel for Senator Edward Kennedy on the Senate Judiciary Committee William Yeomans writes that whether it is the right decision or not, Republican Senators have a series of options available on how to block a potential nomination—many of which are rooted directly in the Constitution. Opposing his view is Vice President, and former Senate Judiciary Committee member, Joe Biden. He argues that the Constitution requires the Senate to take action and past precedent has demonstrated it is the proper thing to do.

YES

William Yeomans

The Many Ways Senate Republicans Can Block Obama's Supreme Court nominee

Do Senate Majority Leader Mitch McConnell (R-Ky.) and his Republican caucus have the ability simply to ignore President Barack Obama's nominee for the seat of Justice Antonin Scalia on the U.S. Supreme Court? The short answer is "yes."

Though the Constitution imposes an obligation on the president to appoint a justice, and on the Senate to give or withhold its "advice and consent" regarding the nomination, in practice there is nothing Obama can do to overcome a politically driven Senate majority.

There is no constitutional mechanism for forcing the Senate to act. Its failure to do so poses the classic disagreement between the political branches that federal courts leave to the political process for resolution. Because Republicans control the Senate, they could remain in session for the remainder of Obama's presidency, so a recess appointment would not be possible. The only real check on an obstructionist Senate is the political calculation of its membership.

Within hours of the announcement of Scalia's death, McConnell, who was immediately joined by a majority of his party, urged the president not to make a nomination and asserted that the Republican-controlled Senate would not consider any nomination that he made. This seemed an astonishing rejection of constitutional order that discredited the memory of Scalia's strict, originalist interpretation of the Constitution.

Yet, McConnell took to the Senate floor Tuesday to reaffirm his blanket opposition to considering any Obama nominee. In fact, McConnell and Senate Republican leaders announced that not only will they deny an Obama nominee a hearing and a vote, but they will not even meet with the nominee. Republican members of the Judiciary Committee took a similar stance. Only two Republican senators have broken ranks publically—Susan Collins of Maine and Mark Kirk of Illinois, who is facing a difficult election in a blue state.

Bashing Obama in the cause of preserving Scalia's crucial seat for a Republican nominee fires up the GOP base. McConnell played into the ugly far-right meme that Obama is not a legitimate president. Suggesting that it would be inappropriate for him to nominate a justice was in line with the birther movement, the shout of "You lie" during one of the president's State of the Union addresses and McConnell's announced strategy of opposing every Obama initiative to ensure he would be a one-term president.

Republicans argue, absurdly, that a president with nearly a year left in his term is a lame duck. Somehow, members of Congress become lame ducks only after the November election, but Obama is considered a lame duck roughly nine months before the actual vote.

The effort to shut down the process before it begins makes practical sense for Republicans. If they are firmly committed to opposing any nominee on principle, it simply invites political risk to go through an extended process. A hearing would allow the American people, as well as the Senate, to scrutinize the nominee. Pressure could grow on vulnerable Republican incumbents to break with the party line.

Six GOP senators are up for re-election this fall in states that Obama carried in 2012. They could face consequences for opposing a nominee who made a favorable public impression. Given the 60-vote threshold imposed by a filibuster, there is no danger of confirmation—14 Republicans would have to vote with a unanimous Democratic block to confirm. By staking out a commitment not to act, however, McConnell avoids the possibility of subjecting members of his caucus to a difficult vote.

His move carries some political risk. Democrats have responded with appropriate outrage. There was initially some softening of the Republican position, but it now appears even more unlikely that the nominee will be given a hearing.

When Republicans took control of the Senate in 2015, McConnell vowed to make the upper chamber work again by returning to regular order. He hasn't. If the Senate were to consider the nomination under regular order, here's how it would proceed:

The Nomination

The process would begin with the president's announcement of his choice for the court. The nominee's name would be transmitted formally to the Senate, where it would be referred to the Senate Judiciary Committee. The nominee, already thoroughly vetted by

---

Yeomans, William. "The Many Ways Senate Republicans Can Block Obama's Supreme Court Nominee," *Reuters*, February 2016. Copyright © 2016 by Thomson Reuters. Used with permission.

Should the Senate Be Able to Delay Hearings on Nominations While Waiting for a Presidential Election to Occur? by Miller

91

the White House, would then submit responses to an extensive Judiciary Committee questionnaire that covered early life, education, employment, professional and other memberships, speeches, writings, financial holding and family status.

This part of the process might proceed as usual. But after this step, the nomination would likely fall victim to Senate dysfunction.

The Hearing

Supreme Court confirmation hearings are invariably big and loud. Given the role that Scalia played on the court, the yawning partisan divide in American politics and the prospect that his replacement could shift the court's ideological balance in major—and politically controversial—areas, the hearing for his successor promises to be the most contested in history.

During the weeks between the nomination and the hearing, committee staffers pour over the nominee's record in search of pressure points. The Senate Judiciary Committee is the most partisan in the Senate largely because its docket includes such controversial issues as civil rights, civil liberties, abortion, crime, immigration and judges. Republican staffers look for avenues of attack against the nominee of a Democratic president, while Democratic staffers try to anticipate their arguments and develop strategies to block attacks.

During this period, staffers are bombarded by visits from, and submissions by, outside groups, which are expected to spend millions of dollars in an attempt to influence the direction of the hearing and shape public opinion of the nominee.

In the normal course, the nominee appears before the committee with great fanfare. This is one setting in which all the committee members show up. The room is packed with media, administration handlers, the nominee's family and friends and spectators. The nominee delivers an opening statement, as does each senator. Then questioning, which can last for days, begins.

It has been labeled the Kabuki-theatre portion of the process: Senators ask predictable questions, nominees respond with formulaic answers. Nominees aim to demonstrate familiarity with the law, while trying to avoid any controversial position. They often duck tough questions by saying the issue might come before the court; they refuse to respond to hypotheticals in the absence of briefs and a record. The nominee and Senate supporters work to place the appointee in the "mainstream" of judicial thought; opponents portray the prospective justice as a dangerous radical.

Equally important, the public finally sees and hears the nominee for an extended period of time, so the appointee can emerge as a person rather than an abstraction. The nominee has the opportunity to demonstrate intelligence, charm, sensitivity and basic likeability.

The 1987 nomination of Judge Robert Bork is case in point. His radically conservative views provided sufficient grounds to reject

his nomination, but his public persona as arrogant, unsympathetic and aloof sealed his fate.

Witnesses also testify at the hearing for and against the nominee—before a dwindling number of senators and a handful of compulsive C-SPAN viewers.

The decision whether to proceed with a hearing puts Senate Judiciary Committee Chairman Chuck Grassley (R-Ia.) on the spot. He has already felt pressure from his constituents, which might explain why he appears to have backed away from his initially adamant opposition to any Obama nomination. But Grassley now has the firm backing of the Republican leadership and will almost certainly deny the nominee a hearing.

Committee Consideration

If Grassley decided to place the nomination on the agenda for committee action—and he could decline to do so—the committee would have options. It could 1) refer the nomination favorably to the full Senate by majority vote, 2) reject the nomination by majority vote, thereby killing it, or 3) reject the nomination, but also vote to refer it to the full Senate. A tie vote on any of these options would be unlikely because the committee has 11 Republican and nine Democratic members. If there is a tie, it would prevent any action.

If Obama's nominee unexpectedly got a hearing, it could be the point at which the appointee would be defeated.

Floor Consideration

In the unlikely event a nomination emerged from committee, McConnell could choose not to bring it to the Senate floor for a vote, which would spare vulnerable purple-state senators the need to go on record with a vote. If McConnell calculated that he needed to relieve substantial political pressure by allowing a vote, however, he could do so. That seems highly unlikely, though.

When Democrats revised the Senate rules under then-Majority Leader Harry Reid (D-Nev.), they retained the filibuster for Supreme Court nominations. Because Republicans control the Senate and seem united in their opposition to confirming any Obama nominee, the filibuster is unlikely to come into play. It remains available, however, as the final safeguard against confirmation of a nominee.

In the end, Obama is most likely to nominate a well-qualified, moderate nominee who could become a sacrificial lamb. Republicans will almost certainly deny the nominee the courtesy of meetings, a hearing and a vote. Even if the nominee received a hearing, the prospective justice would be unlikely to emerge from committee. In the unlikely event the nominee emerged from committee, McConnell would be unlikely to allow the nomination to come to the floor for a full Senate vote. And, even if the Senate voted, Republicans would have sufficient votes to defeat the nominee—if only because Obama nominated the candidate.

The next time a Republican politician preaches about strict adherence to the Constitution, or praises regular order in the Senate, chuckle and walk away.

WILLIAM YEOMANS worked at the Department of Justice for 26 years, primarily in the civil rights division. He began his career litigating civil and criminal cases in federal courts at all levels, in cases involving voting rights, school desegregation, employment discrimination, housing discrimination, hate crimes, police misconduct, abortion clinic violence, and human trafficking.

Joseph R. Biden Jr.

 **NO**

Joe Biden: The Senate's Duty on a Supreme Court Nominee

In my 36-year tenure in the United States Senate—nearly half of it as chairman or ranking Democrat on the Judiciary Committee—I presided or helped preside over nine nominees to the Supreme Court, from both Republican and Democratic presidents. That's more than anyone else alive today.

In every instance we adhered to the process explicitly laid out in the Constitution: The president has the constitutional duty to nominate; the Senate has the constitutional obligation to provide advice and consent. It is written plainly in the Constitution that both presidents and senators swear an oath to uphold and defend.

That's why I was so surprised and saddened to see Republican leaders tell President Obama and me that they would not even consider a Supreme Court nominee this year. No meetings. No hearings. No votes. Nothing. It is an unprecedented act of obstruction. And it risks a stain on the legacy of all those complicit in carrying out this plan. I would ask my friends and colleagues—and all those who love the Senate—to think long and hard before going down this road.

Some have taken comments I made in 1992 to mean that I supported the same kind of obstructionist position as a senator. But that reading distorts the broader meaning of the speech I gave from the Senate floor that year.

It was late June, and at the time there was much speculation that a sitting justice would retire, leaving President George H.W. Bush to appoint a successor in the final months of his first term.

We had been through several highly contentious Supreme Court confirmation hearings during my tenure, and I feared that a nomination at that late date, just a few weeks before the presidential conventions, would create immense political acrimony. So I called on the president to wait until after the election to submit a nomination if a sitting justice were to create a vacancy by retiring before November. And if the president declined to do that, I recommended that the Judiciary Committee not hold hearings "until after the political campaign season is over."

Those brief statements were part of a much more extensive speech that reviewed the history of Supreme Court nomination fights during election years. My purpose was not to obstruct, but to

call for two important goals: restoring a more consultative process between the White House and the Senate in filling Supreme Court vacancies, and encouraging the nomination of a consensus candidate who could lower the partisan temperature in the country.

It is the same view I hold today.

Throughout that speech, and throughout my career, I've argued that the Senate has an important role to play. This involves the president's seeking advice from its leaders before making a nomination—as President Obama has done and will continue to do—and the Senate's examining candidates before deciding whether to consent to their appointments.

Under my chairmanship, every Supreme Court nominee was given a hearing and a vote in the Judiciary Committee. And I made sure every nominee was given a full vote on the floor of the Senate, even those whose initial vote in the Judiciary Committee had failed, and even those whom I opposed. Only those who withdrew did not get floor votes. This position earned me the anger of my own party. But I believed strongly that the Constitution, clearly and plainly, calls for all 100 senators to advise and consent on nominees—not just the handful on the Judiciary Committee.

As a senator, I zealously guarded the rights of the Senate. As vice president, I hold the same view. But the framers also intended for the president to fulfill a clear constitutional responsibility. President Obama will do that by putting forth a nominee who will be eminently qualified, who recognizes the limits of the judiciary, who is fair-minded and who has an unimpeachable record. The Senate will need to fulfill its constitutional responsibility by considering, debating and voting on that nominee.

I know there is an argument that no nominee should be voted on in the last year of a presidency. But there is nothing in the Constitution—or our history—to support this view. Justice Anthony M. Kennedy was confirmed in the last year of Ronald Reagan's second term. I know. I was chairman of the Judiciary Committee at the time. And we promptly gave him a hearing, a vote in committee and a full vote on the floor.

As I write this, nearly all Republican senators have said that they will refuse to consider any nominee—sight unseen. At a time when we need to reduce the gridlock in our politics, this would extend

Biden, Joseph R. "Joe Biden: The Senate's Duty on a Supreme Court Nominee", from *The New York Times,* March 2016. Copyright © 2016 by New York Times. All rights reserved. Used by permission and protected by the Copyright Laws of the United States. The printing, copying, redistribution, or retransmission of this Content without express written permission is prohibited.

Congress's dysfunction to the Supreme Court—preventing it from functioning as our founders intended for a year and possibly longer.

In my 1992 speech, I noted that in the five cases in which justices were confirmed in the summer of an election year, all five were filling vacancies that had arisen before the summer began. That is the case now. We still have time to proceed with hearings and a vote before we reach the summer conventions and fall campaign.

I hope that Republican leaders will take a step back and think about what they are doing. I hope they will think about the oaths they have taken. I hope they will think about their responsibility to the voters of this nation. And I hope they will think about their role in upholding the integrity of the United States Senate.

If they love the Senate as much as I do, they need to act.

JOE BIDEN at the time this book is going to press, is Vice President of the United States. He is a member of the Democratic Party and was a United States Senator from Delaware from January 3, 1973, until his resignation on January 15, 2009, following his election to the Vice Presidency. In 2012, Biden was elected to a second term alongside Obama.

EXPLORING THE ISSUE

Should the Senate Be Able to Delay Hearings on Nominations While Waiting for a Presidential Election to Occur?

Critical Thinking and Reflection

1. Does the Senate have too much power with regards to court nominations?
2. Should the Senate consider politics when deciding whether to confirm a nominee?
3. Do you believe presidents should be able to appoint court members without the Senate's approval? Why or why not?
4. How could the Senate best be enticed to hold hearings, even when they politically may not want to?
5. Why do you believe the Founders created the process that is in place today?

Is There Common Ground?

It is hard to argue that the decision to delay hearings on a nominee during a presidential election year is not something explicitly political in nature. In 2016, Republicans have more or less admitted that they are not taking action on Merrick Garland's nomination to the Supreme Court because they hope a Republican will win the presidency and bring forward a more conservative candidate. The Constitution is unfortunately silent on the question of timing, which means both sides are able to claim legal status. While the Founders were clear that the President would make a nomination to the Supreme Court and the Senate would confirm the appointment if it believed it to be in the best of the interests of the country, it makes no mention of the process of how this should occur.

What makes common ground difficult on this issue is that it has become a political, rather than a procedural, topic. Both parties believe nominees should face confirmation hearings as soon as possible—when they control the White House. While Democrats may be unhappy with the Republican-controlled Senate today, there

is little doubt they would be doing the same thing to a lame duck Republican president if they found themselves in the same situation. Thus, until both parties are willing to put their own self-interest aside and attempt to determine what would lead to the most effective appointment and confirmation process, we will likely never see common ground reached on this issue. What would common ground look like regardless? A timeline of when the Senate has to act based on how much time a president has left in office?

Additional Resources

Jan C. Greenburg, *Supreme Conflict: The Inside Story of the Struggle for Control of the United States Supreme Court* (Penguin Press, 2007)

Wil Haygood, *Showdown: Thurgood Marshall and the Supreme Court Nomination That Changed America* (Vintage, 2016)

Jeffrey Toobin, *The Nine: Inside the Secret World of the Supreme Court* (Doubleday, 2007)

Internet References . . .

Nomination and Confirmation Process

http://guides.ll.georgetown.edu
/c.php?g=365722&p=2471070

President Obama's Supreme Court Nomination

https://www.whitehouse.gov/scotus

Seven Things to Know About Presidential Appointments to the Supreme Court

http://www.npr.org/2016/02/14/466723547/7-things-to
-know-about-presidential-appointments
-to-the-supreme-court

Unit 3

UNIT

Social Change and Public Policy

*E*conomic and moral issues divide Americans along an ideological spectrum from "left" to "right." The issues are exceedingly diverse; they include economic equality, social welfare, gay rights, abortion, race relations, capital punishment, religious freedom, drug legalization, and whether there should be limits on speech activities. Disagreements break out on the floor of Congress, in state legislatures, in the nation's courtrooms, and sometimes in the streets. These controversial issues generate intense emotions because they force us to defend our most deeply held values and explain how they can be worked out in public policy.

In some cases, debate and deliberation can lead to individuals altering their views or opinions. Yet for other issues, there is no budging; this is especially true for morally centered issues. While institutions and culture may have an impact on the functioning of American government and its relationship to the citizenry, it is through policy issues where we see citizens becoming most active and involved. Look at just the past five years as the international community has experienced the power of protest. From the Tea Party Movement to Occupy to the Arab Spring to the newly emerged Black Lives Matter, citizens react when policy decisions do not reflect their perceived interests. Hence, the importance of the following debates.

Selected, Edited, and with Issue Framing Material by:
William J. Miller, *Flagler College*

ISSUE

Does Affirmative Action Advance Racial Equality?

YES: Anthony P. Carnevale and Jeff Strohl, from "Separate & Unequal: How Higher Education Reinforces the Intergenerational Reproduction of White Racial Privilege," *Georgetown University Public Policy Institute Center on Education and the Workforce* (2013)

NO: Dan Slater, from "Does Affirmative Action Do What It Should?" *The New York Times* (2013)

Learning Outcomes
After reading this issue, you will be able to: • Describe affirmative action. • Assess whether affirmative actions has worked in America. • Explain the unintended consequences of affirmative action. • Assess whether America still needs affirmative action. • Identify the successes and failures of affirmative action.

ISSUE SUMMARY

YES: Policy researchers Anthony P. Carnevale and Jeff Strohl show there are still wide racial and ethnic discrepancies present in education in the United States and how more direct efforts by government to achieve equality will be needed to level the playing field.

NO: Commentator Dan Slater presents information related to the mismatch theory which suggests that affirmative action can harm those it's supposed to help by placing them at schools in which they fall below the median level of ability.

"We didn't land on Plymouth Rock, my brothers and sisters—Plymouth Rock landed on us!" Malcolm X's observation is borne out by the facts of American history. Snatched from their native land, transported thousands of miles—in a nightmare of disease and death—and sold into slavery, blacks were reduced to the legal status of farm animals. Even after emancipation, blacks were segregated from whites—in some states by law, and by social practice almost everywhere. American apartheid continued for another century.

In 1954 the Supreme Court declared state-compelled segregation in schools unconstitutional, and it followed up that decision with others that struck down many forms of official segregation. Still, discrimination survived, and in most southern states blacks were either discouraged or prohibited from exercising their right to vote. Not until the 1960s was compulsory segregation finally and effectively challenged. Between 1964 and 1968 Congress passed the most sweeping civil rights legislation since the end of the Civil War.

But is that enough? Equality of condition between blacks and whites seems as elusive as ever. The black unemployment rate is double that of whites, and the percentage of black families living in poverty is nearly four times that of whites. Only a small percentage of blacks ever make it into medical school or law school.

Advocates of affirmative action have focused upon these de facto differences to bolster their argument that it is no longer enough just to stop discrimination. The damage done by three centuries of racism now has to be remedied, they argue, and effective remediation requires a policy of "affirmative action." At the heart of affirmative action is the use of "numerical goals." Opponents call them "racial quotas." Whatever the name, what they imply is the setting aside of a certain number of jobs or positions for blacks or other historically oppressed groups. Opponents charge that affirmative action penalizes innocent people simply because they are white, that it often results in unqualified appointments, and that it ends up harming instead of helping blacks.

Affirmative action has had an uneven history in U.S. federal courts. In *Regents of the University of California v. Allan Bakke* (1978), which marked the first time the Supreme Court directly dealt with the merits of affirmative action, a 5–4 majority ruled that a white applicant to a medical school had been wrongly excluded due to the school's affirmative action policy; yet the majority also agreed that "race-conscious" policies may be used in admitting candidates—as long as they do not amount to fixed quotas. Since *Bakke,* other Supreme Court decisions have tipped toward one side or the other, depending on the circumstances of the case and the shifting line-up of Justices. Notable among these were two cases decided by the Court on the same day in 2003, *Gratz v. Bollinger* and *Grutter v. Bollinger.* Both involved affirmative action programs at the University of Michigan; *Gratz* pertaining to undergraduate admissions and *Grutter* to the law school. The court struck down the undergraduate program in *Gratz* on grounds that it was not "narrowly tailored" enough; it awarded every black and other protected minority an extra 20 points out of a 100 point scale—which, the Court said, amounted to a "quota." But the law school admissions criteria in *Grutter* were more flexible, using race as only one criterion among others, and so the Court refused to strike them down.

The most radical popular challenge to affirmative action was the ballot initiative endorsed by California voters in 1996. Proposition 209 banned any state program based upon racial or gender "preferences." Among the effects of this ban was a sharp decline in the numbers of non-Asian minorities admitted to the elite campuses of the state's university system, especially Berkeley and UCLA. (Asian admissions to the elite campuses either stayed the same or increased, and non-Asian minority admissions to some of the less-prestigious branches increased.)

A survey from Pew Research in May 2013 shows that a majority of white and black Americans believe there is at least some discrimination against African Americans. Eighty-eight percent of black Americans saw discrimination against African Americans, with 46 percent saying that there is "a lot" of it. The percentage of white Americans who see discrimination against African Americans is smaller, but still a majority, 57 percent, says there is discrimination against African Americans, with 16 percent saying

that there is a lot. A 2008 Gallup poll found that 56 percent of adults nationally believe that there is "widespread" racism against black Americans. That includes 78 percent of black Americans who held that belief. And it's not just that Americans hold a vague sense of discrimination. Nearly 70 percent of black Americans believe that the U.S. justice system is biased against them, according to recent Gallup polling. A quarter of white Americans, and a third of all adults nationally, agree.

If this many Americans believe there are still signs of racism within society—despite the marked success of minorities in recent years—it begs the question of how we can better assure equality for all members of society. For a nation founded as a group of self-exiled individuals seeking acceptance and the ability to express individual ideals, it is essential that we offer the same for those presently in our borders. Rather than passing state laws requiring particular minorities to be ready, able, and willing to show proof of citizenship for any reason, perhaps our efforts would be better spent assuring that legal means of immigration functioned effectively and efficiently.

Today, members of the Tea Party are largely assumed to be racists due to their strong opposition to President Barack Obama. Yet, as Mark Joseph writes in *USA Today*, there is no evidence of this being true. In fact, Joseph explains how he asks white conservative friends, "If your daughter were thinking of marrying a man like Clarence Thomas or one like Chris Matthews, which would you choose?" He further explains, "The answer is quick and unanimous: They'd choose to spend their holidays with a son-in-law who looks nothing like them but shares their values rather than one who merely shares their skin color."

Affirmative action will always be a debated topic in American politics, especially with an increasing number of examples where reverse discrimination is occurring. Yet without remembering the historical context of why it came into existence, it is nearly impossible to fairly assess the success of the program and its potential moving forward.

In the following selections, Anthony Carnevale and Jeff Strohl discuss in detail disparities in education in the United States today and explain how government involvement is necessary if we hope to create a meaningful dent in current numbers and trends. On the other side, Dan Slater discusses mismatch theory and mentions how in some cases affirmative action in schools can lead to students being less likely to succeed in the long run.

YES

Anthony P. Carnevale and Jeff Strohl

Separate & Unequal: How Higher Education Reinforces the Intergenerational Reproduction of White Racial Privilege

Introduction

White flight from the center city to better neighborhood schools in the leafy green suburbs has finally arrived on the nation's ivy-covered college campuses. The racial and ethnic stratification in educational opportunity entrenched in the nation's K-12 education system has faithfully reproduced itself across the full range of American colleges and universities. Racial stratification permeates the two- and four-year college and university system among the more than 4,400 institutions analyzed in this study.

Even more striking is the growing polarization of the most selective institutions and the least selective open-access schools. White students are increasingly concentrated today, relative to population share, in the nation's 468 most well-funded, selective four-year colleges and universities while African-American and Hispanic students are more and more concentrated in the 3,250 least well-funded, open-access, two- and four-year colleges.

The American postsecondary system is a dual system of racially separate and unequal institutions despite the growing access of minorities to the postsecondary system. Polarization by race and ethnicity in the nation's postsecondary system has become the capstone for K-12 inequality and the complex economic and social mechanisms that create it. The postsecondary system mimics and magnifies the racial and ethnic inequality in educational preparation it inherits from the K-12 system and then projects this inequality into the labor market.

The education system is colorblind in theory. In fact, it operates, at least in part, as a systematic barrier to college for many minorities who finish high school unprepared for college. It also limits college and career opportunities for many African Americans and Hispanics who are well prepared for higher education but tracked into crowded and underfunded colleges where they are less likely to develop fully or to graduate. Increasing racial and ethnic polarization appears to be inseparable from the expansion of access to American educational opportunity first in K-12 education and now in the postsecondary system.

The polarization of the postsecondary system matters because resources matter. The 468 most selective colleges spend anywhere from two to almost five times as much per student. Higher spending in the most selective colleges leads to higher graduation rates, greater access to graduate and professional schools, and better economic outcomes in the labor market, when comparing with white, African-American, and Hispanic students who are equally qualified but attend less competitive schools. Greater postsecondary resources and completion rates for white students concentrated in the 468 most selective colleges confer substantial labor market advantages, including more than $2 million dollars per student in higher lifetime earnings, and access to professional and managerial elite jobs, as well as careers that bring personal and social empowerment.

Affluent white students as well as prestige seeking four-year colleges are flowing to the top tiers of selectivity while lower income minority students are flooding low tuition, open-access, two- and four-year institutions. In addition, while the number of institutions classified in the selective tiers is growing, the number of open-access, four-year colleges is declining as institutions move up the selectivity tiers. The result of this dynamic is increased spending per student at the most selective colleges and overcrowding and reduced resources per student in the open-access sector.

The postsecondary system is more and more complicit as a passive agent in the systematic reproduction of white racial privilege across generations. More college completion among white parents brings higher earnings that fuel the intergenerational reproduction of privilege by providing more highly educated parents the means to pass their educational advantages on to their children. Higher earnings buy more expensive housing in the suburbs with the best schools and peer support for educational attainment. The synergy between the growing economic value of education and the increased sorting by housing values makes parental education the strongest predictor of a child's educational attainment and future earnings. As a result, the country also has the least intergenerational educational and income mobility among advanced nations.

Carnevale, Anthony P. and Strohl, Jeff. From a report: *Separate & Unequal: How Higher Education Reinforces the Intergenerational Reproduction of White Racial Privilege,* July 2013, pp. 7–14. Copyright © 2013 by Georgetown Center on Education and the Workforce/Public Policy Institute. Used with permission.

Preparation for higher education matters in allocating access and success at the 468 most selective colleges, but it's not the whole story. Differences in access, completion, and earnings persist even among equally qualified whites, African Americans, and Hispanics. The relative lack of K-12 preparation among African Americans and Hispanics does not explain fully the growing racial and ethnic stratification in postsecondary completion and subsequent economic outcomes.

The postsecondary system does not treat similarly qualified white and African-American or Hispanic students equally and thereby blunts individual opportunity and wastes valuable talent. Many African Americans and Hispanics are unprepared for college, but whites who are equally unprepared still get more postsecondary opportunities. Moreover, African-American and Hispanic students who are prepared for college are disproportionately tracked into crowded and underfunded two-year colleges and open-access four-year colleges. The postsecondary system leaves a substantial number of qualified minorities on educational pathways that don't allow them to fulfill their educational and career potential.

- More than 30 percent of African Americans and Hispanics with a high school grade point average (GPA) higher than 3.5 go to community colleges compared with 22 percent of whites with the same GPA.
- Among African-American and Hispanic college students who score more than 1200 out of a possible 1600 points on the SAT/ACT, 57 percent eventually get a certificate, an Associate's degree, or a Bachelor's degree or better; for white students the percentage rises to 77 percent.
- Among African-American and Hispanic college students who score between 1000 and 1200 points on the SAT/ACT, 47 percent of African Americans and 48 percent of Hispanics earn a certificate, an Associate's degree, or a Bachelor's degree or better compared with 68 percent of whites.
- Among African-American and Hispanic college students who score above 1200 points on the SAT/ACT, 57 percent of African Americans and 56 percent of Hispanics graduate with a certificate, an Associate's degree, or a Bachelor's degree or better compared with 77 percent of whites.

African American and Hispanics' access to postsecondary education over the past 15 years is a good news/bad news story. The good news is that African Americans and Hispanics scored big gains in access to postsecondary education. The bad news is that both groups are losing ground in their move up to the most selective colleges relative to their growing population shares.

The absolute numbers of African Americans and Hispanics going on to postsecondary institutions have increased markedly and their share of enrollment in the top 468 colleges has increased slightly since the 1990s. But between 1995 and 2009, more than eight in 10 of net new white students have gone to the 468 most selective colleges and more than seven in 10 of net new

African-American and Hispanic students have gone to the 3,250 open-access, two- and four-year colleges.

Similarly, the larger growth in college seats has been in the most selective tiers as compared with open-access colleges. Enrollments at the most selective and better resourced colleges grew significantly (78%), reflecting increased demand for high-quality postsecondary education; the vast majority of the new seats went to white students. Among open-access, four-year colleges, growth has been significantly slower (21%), but the net increases in minority enrollments were concentrated at those schools, leading to more crowding and fewer resources per student.

Since 1995, 82 percent of new white enrollments have gone to the 468 most selective colleges, while 72 percent of new Hispanic enrollment and 68 percent of new African-American enrollment have gone to the two-year and four-year open-access schools.

As a result of these uneven flows, the white share of seats at the top 468 colleges has increased, and the white share of seats at open-access colleges has declined relative to the white share of the college-age population (ages 18–24). Conversely, the relative share of new seats going to African Americans and Hispanics at the 468 most selective colleges has declined while the African-American and Hispanic share of seats at the 3,250 open-access colleges has increased relative to their share of the college-age population.

The most telling metrics of racial polarization in postsecondary education are comparisons of white, African-American, and Hispanic enrollments to their respective shares of the college-age population. Whites have increased their enrollment share in the top 468 colleges relative to their share of the college-age population.

- In 1995, the white share of the college-age population was 68 percent, and the white share of enrollments at the top 468 colleges was 77 percent, a 9 percentage point advantage of enrollment share over population share.
- By 2009, the white share of the college-age population was 62 percent and the white share of enrollments at the top 468 colleges was 75 percent, a 13 percentage point advantage of enrollment over population share and an increase of 4 percentage points within the college-age population.

The white share of enrollment in the 3,250 open-access, two- and four-year colleges has declined relative to the white share of the college-age population.

- In 1995, the white share of the college-age population was 68 percent and the white share of enrollment at the 3,250 open-access, two- and four-year colleges was 69 percent, reflecting a balance between enrollment and population shares.
- By 2009, the white share of the college-age population was 62 percent and the white share of enrollment at the 3,250 open-access, two- and four-year colleges was 57 percent, a 5 percentage point deficit of enrollment

relative to population share and a decline of 6 percentage points within the college-age population.

The enrollment shares of African Americans and Hispanics in the top 468 colleges declined relative to their shares of the college-age population.

- In 1995, the African-American and Hispanic share of the college-age population was 27 percent, and their share of enrollments at the top 468 colleges was 12 percent, a 15 percentage point deficit of enrollment compared with population share.
- By 2009, the African-American and Hispanic share of the college-age population was 33 percent, and their share of enrollment at the top 468 colleges was 15 percent, an 18 percentage point deficit of enrollment versus population share and a decline of 3 percentage points within the college-age population.

The African-American and Hispanic share of enrollment in the 3,250 open-access, two- and four-year colleges increased relative to their share of the college-age population.

- In 1995, the African-American and Hispanic share of the college-age population was 27 percent, and their share of enrollment at the 3,250 open-access, two- and four-year colleges was 24 percent, a 3 percentage point deficit of enrollment relative to population share.
- By 2009, the African-American and Hispanic share of the college-age population was 33 percent, and their share of enrollment at the 3,250 open-access, two-and four-year colleges was 37 percent, a 4 percentage point average of enrollment relative to population share.

College readiness is important in explaining low completion rates, but the polarization of resources in the higher education system is one of the root causes of increasing college dropout rates and increasing time required to complete degrees. For every 300 college graduates, postsecondary education now produces 200 college dropouts. The completion rate for the 468 most selective four-year colleges is 82 percent, compared with 49 percent for open-access, two-and four-year colleges. Virtually all of the increase in dropout rates and the slowdown in completions are concentrated in open-access colleges; in substantial part because they are too crowded and underfunded.

African Americans and Hispanics are more likely to go to open-access, two- and four-year colleges and less likely to achieve a Bachelor's degree or better because of it. Ultimately this leads to powerful earnings differences and reduced capacity for intergenerational investments in children's education.

This dynamic leads to significant loss of talent among minorities and lower-income students. This study also found that more than 240,000 high school students every year, who graduate in the top half of their high school class and come from the bottom half of the income distribution, do not get a two- or four-year degree

within eight years of graduation from high school. The data show that roughly one in four (62,000) of these high-scoring, low-income students are African American or Hispanic.

More than 111,000 African Americans and Hispanics who graduate from high school each year in the top half of their class do not achieve a two- or four-year degree within eight years. If these students had attended one of the top 468 colleges and graduated at similar rates, 73 percent could have graduated. *Whites, African Americans, and Hispanics who score in the top half of the SAT/ACT test score distribution go to college at the same rate (90%). Yet whites have higher graduation rates and graduate school attendance because they attend more selective colleges.*

Among students who score in the top half of the test-score distribution in the nation's high schools and attend college:

- Thirty percent of white students compared with more than 48 percent of African-American students and 51 percent of Hispanic students either don't go or don't complete college; and
- Fifty-seven percent of white students get a Bachelor's degree or better compared with roughly 37 percent of African-American and 36 percent of Hispanic students.

Among those who graduate from college:

- More than 81 percent of whites get a Bachelor's degree or better compared with a little more than 72 percent of African Americans and Hispanics; and
- Less than 19 percent of whites stop with a certificate or an Associate's degree compared with roughly 27 percent of African Americans and Hispanics.

Access to the 468 most selective four-year colleges and their greater completion rates are especially important to African Americans and Hispanics.

- African Americans and Hispanics gain 21 percent in earnings advantages when they attend the more selective schools compared with 15 percent for whites who attend the same colleges.
- Among African Americans and Hispanics who score in the upper half of the SAT/ACT test-score distribution, those who attend one of the top 468 colleges graduate at a rate of 73 percent compared with a rate of 40 percent for equally qualified minorities who attend open-access colleges.
- One-third of high-scoring African Americans and Hispanics who get Bachelor's degrees at the top 468 colleges attain graduate degrees compared with 23 percent of minorities who attend open-access colleges.
- African Americans and Hispanics benefit from access to selective colleges even when their test scores are several hundred points below the averages at those colleges.

Moreover, this study's data support the axiom that the Bachelor's degree is the crucial postsecondary threshold for racial and ethnic equality. White, African-American, and Hispanic students who graduate with a Bachelor's degree from the 468 most selective colleges go on to graduate school at the same rate. African Americans and Hispanics who graduate with Bachelor's degrees from the open-access colleges go on to graduate school at slightly higher rates (23%) than their white counterparts (20%).

Stratification by income is strong. Earlier research demonstrates underrepresentation by income is quite stark. High-income students were 45 percentage points overrepresented compared to population share in the most selective colleges while white students were "only" 15 points overrepresented. African-American and Hispanic students were underrepresented in the most selective colleges, relative to population share by 9 percentage points; low-income students were underrepresented by 20 percentage points. While income stratification is strong, this fact does not take away from or mitigate strong and persistent racial stratification.

Race- and class-based inequalities in education overlap considerably, but race has a unique negative effect on college and career opportunities. African Americans and Hispanics are especially vulnerable to class-based economic disadvantages because they are more concentrated in low-income groups and because they are more isolated both spatially and socially from the general society.

African Americans and Hispanics usually remain concentrated in poorer neighborhoods, even as individual family income increases. As a result, race gives additional power to the negative effects of low-income status and limits the positive effects of income gains, better schools, and other educational improvements. Hence, minorities are disproportionately harmed by increasing income inequality and don't benefit as much as whites from generational improvements in educational attainment or income growth.

The traditional channel of intergenerational mobility, parental education, is particularly muted for African Americans and Hispanics. In comparison to white students whose parents did not go beyond high school, African-American and Hispanic students drop out of college at higher rates (34% vs. 27%), obtain certificates or Associate's degrees more often (21% vs. 18%), and do not attain Bachelor's degree as often (8% vs. 14%).

At the other end of the parental education spectrum the problem is even worse. African Americans and Hispanics benefit less than whites from their parents' educational attainment. Among students whose parents have attained at least a Bachelor's degree, African-American and Hispanic students do not attend college at twice the rate of similarly situated white students (15% vs. 7%), drop out of college much more often (37% vs. 25%), and graduate with a Bachelor's degree or better less often (35% vs. 58%).

Exacerbating this problem is the fact that low-income status appears to further dampen African-American and Hispanic educational attainment more than similarly situated whites. Compared with white students whose families are in the bottom half of the income distribution, African Americans (55%) and Hispanics

(59%) drop out of college much more often than whites (45%) while African Americans stop out with a certificate at very significant rates (24% vs. 17%). Low-income whites are more likely to graduate with a Bachelor's degree (23%) than low-income African Americans (12%) and Hispanics (13%).

It is difficult to clearly mark the point where racial discrimination ends and economic deprivation begins, but the evidence is clear that both negatively affect educational and economic opportunity and are most powerful in combination. The interaction of race and class disadvantages result in the spatial, social, and economic isolation that signify persistent hardship. This is why some class-based metrics that reflect class-based disadvantages in their most extreme form, like differences in wealth, family structure, parental education, and occupational status, can translate into proxies for race in college admissions.

Conversely, racial isolation can be an effective metric of class disadvantage. An example would be the use of class rank as an effective proxy for race in the ongoing brawl over race-based affirmative action: The current legal standard in affirmative action, established in *Grutter v. Bollinger* and affirmed in *Fisher v. University of Texas,* is that racial diversity is a legitimate goal for college admissions but race alone cannot be used as a standard for admission. Because of the spatial isolation of minorities, targeting specific geographic areas or high schools can produce racial diversity without using race alone as an admissions criterion. Spatial isolation of low-income minorities is what accounts for the relative success of the Texas affirmative action system, which guarantees admission for any student in the top 10 percent of his or her high school class. The Texas 10-percent solution does not use race alone but still allows substantial racial diversity in the Texas postsecondary system because it is predicated on continued racial and economic segregation in particular areas and high schools.

ANTHONY P. CARNEVALE is the Director and Research Professor of the Georgetown University Center on Education and the Workforce. Between 1996 and 2006, Dr. Carnevale served as Vice-President for Public Leadership at the Educational Testing Service (ETS). While at ETS, Dr. Carnevale was appointed by President George Bush to serve on the White House Commission on Technology and Adult Education.

JEFF STROHL is the Director of Research at the Georgetown University Center on Education and the Workforce where he continues his long involvement in the analysis of education and labor market outcomes and policy. He leads the Center's research, investigating the supply and demand of education and how education enhances career opportunities for today's workforce. Dr. Strohl also focuses on how to quantify skills and how to better understand competencies given the evolving nature of the U.S. workplace.

Dan Slater

 **NO**

Does Affirmative Action
Do What It Should?

What's more important to how your life turns out: the prestige of the school you attend or how much you learn while you're there? Does the answer to this question change if you are the recipient of affirmative action?

From school admissions to hiring, affirmative action policies attempt to compensate for this country's brutal history of racial discrimination by giving some minority applicants a leg up. This spring the Supreme Court will decide the latest affirmative action case, weighing in on the issue for the first time in 10 years.

The last time around, in 2003, the court upheld the University of Michigan Law School's affirmative action plan. A divided court ruled, 5 to 4, that "student body diversity is a compelling state interest that can justify the use of race in university admissions." Writing for the majority, Justice Sandra Day O'Connor said, "We expect that 25 years from now, the use of racial preferences will no longer be necessary to further the interest approved today."

In the intervening period, scholars have been looking more closely at how affirmative action works in practice. Based on how they interpret the data that have been collected, some of these scholars have come to believe that affirmative action doesn't always help the students it's supposed to. Why? Because some minority students who get into a top school with the help of affirmative action might actually be better served by attending a less elite institution to which they could gain admission with less of a boost or no boost at all.

The idea that affirmative action might harm its intended beneficiaries was suggested as early as the 1960s, when affirmative action, a phrase introduced by the Kennedy administration, began to take hold as government and corporate policy. One long-simmering objection to affirmative action was articulated publicly by Clarence Thomas years before he joined the Supreme Court in 1991. Mr. Thomas, who has opposed affirmative action even while conceding that he benefited from it, told a reporter for The New York Times in 1982 that affirmative action placed students in programs above their abilities. Mr. Thomas, who was then the 34-year-old chairman of the Equal Employment Opportunity Commission, didn't deny the crisis in minority employment. But he blamed a failed education system

rather than discrimination in admissions. "I watched the operation of such affirmative action policies when I was in college," he said, "and I watched the destruction of many kids as a result."

Scholars began referring to this theory as "mismatch." It's the idea that affirmative action can harm those it's supposed to help by placing them at schools in which they fall below the median level of ability and therefore have a tough time. As a consequence, the argument goes, these students suffer learningwise and, later, careerwise. To be clear, mismatch theory does not allege that minority students should not attend elite universities. Far from it. But it does say that students—minority or otherwise—do not automatically benefit from attending a school that they enter with academic qualifications well below the median level of their classmates.

The mismatch theory, if true, would affect many kids. According to a 2009 book, "No Longer Separate, Not Yet Equal: Race and Class in Elite College Admission and Campus Life," by Thomas J. Espenshade and Alexandria Walton Radford, a black student with an otherwise similar application to a white student receives the equivalent of a 310-point bump in SAT scores.

Mismatch theory attracted little attention until 2005, when a law professor at U.C.L.A., Richard H. Sander, published a provocative article in the Stanford Law Review, which focused on how affirmative action affected law students. Mr. Sander claimed that "a student who gains special admission to a more elite school on partly nonacademic grounds is likely to struggle more" and contended that "if the struggling leads to lower grades and less learning, then a variety of bad outcomes may result: higher attrition rates, lower pass rates on the bar, problems in the job market. The question is how large these effects are, and whether their consequences outweigh the benefits of greater prestige."

In other words, do the benefits of the connections made at, say, U.C.L.A. School of Law, and the weight U.C.L.A. carries in the job market, outweigh the cost of struggling academically there? Based on his reading of the data, Mr. Sander concluded that they did not.

Law school, as it turns out, is a somewhat natural, though imperfect, environment for studying mismatch effects. Law students

Slater, Dan. "Does Affirmative Action Do What It Should?", from *The New York Times,* March 2013. Copyright © 2013 by New York Times. All rights reserved. Used by permission and protected by the Copyright Laws of the United States. The printing, copying, redistribution, or retransmission of this Content without express written permission is prohibited.

have their knowledge tested in a fairly uniform way, first on the LSAT and then again, after graduation, on a state licensing exam, the bar.

Much of the squabble over mismatch centers on differing interpretations of the Bar Passage Study. The B.P.S. was commissioned by the Law School Admission Council in 1989 to determine whether blacks and Hispanics had disproportionately poor bar-passage rates. In 1991, more than 27,000 incoming law students—about 2,000 of them black—completed questionnaires for the B.P.S. and gave permission to track their performance in law school and later on the bar.

Among other things, the questionnaire asked students (a) whether they got into their first-choice law school, (b) if so, whether they enrolled at their first choice, and (c) if not, why not.

Data showed that 689 of the approximately 2,000 black applicants got into their first-choice law school. About three-quarters of those 689 matriculated at their first choice. The remaining quarter opted instead for their second-choice school, often for financial or geographic reasons. So, of the 689 black applicants who got into their first choice, 512 went, and the rest, 177, attended their second choice, presumably a less prestigious institution.

This data presented a plausible opportunity to gauge mismatch. The fact that 689 black students got into their first-choice law school meant that all 689 were similar in at least that one regard (though possibly dissimilar in many other ways). If mismatch theory held any water, then the 177 students who voluntarily opted for their second-choice school—and were therefore theoretically better "matched"—could be expected, on average, to have better outcomes on the bar exam than their peers who chose the more elite school. Mr. Sander's analysis of the B.P.S. data found that 21 percent of the black students who went to their second-choice schools failed the bar on their first attempt, compared with 34 percent of those who went to their first choice.

The experiment is far from ideal. Mismatch opponents argue that there are many unobservable differences between second-choice and first-choice students and that those differences, because they're unknown, cannot be accounted for in a formula. In the case of the B.P.S. data, maybe the second-choice students tended to have undergraduate majors that made them particularly well suited to flourish in the classroom and on the bar, regardless of which law school they attended. "All this work on mismatch assumes you know enough to write an algebraic expression that captures what's really going on," says Richard A. Berk, a professor of criminology and statistics at the University of Pennsylvania. "Here, there's so much we don't know. Besides, the LSAT is a very imperfect measure of performance in law school and thereafter, as is the bar exam."

Daniel E. Ho, a law professor at Stanford, also disputes the mismatch hypothesis. In a response to Mr. Sander's 2005 law review article, Mr. Ho wrote in the Yale Law Journal that "black law students who are similarly qualified when applying to law school perform equally well on the bar irrespective of what tier school they attend."

Political changes in the '90s created another opportunity to study mismatch. In 1996, California voters passed Prop 209, a ban on affirmative action. Critics of Prop 209 expected black and Hispanic enrollment at top University of California schools, like U.C.L.A. and Berkeley, to plummet—and it did, for a while. But these schools eventually saw increases in minority enrollment, particularly among Hispanics, as sophisticated new outreach programs kicked in. Enrollment has not, however, gotten back to pre-Prop 209 levels.

Recently, economists from Duke studied the effects of Prop 209, comparing undergraduate graduation rates for blacks, Hispanics and American Indians before and after the ban. In a paper being considered for publication by *The Quarterly Journal of Economics,* the Duke economists conclude that mismatch effects are strongest for students in so-called STEM majors—science, technology, engineering and math. These subjects proceed in a more regimented way than the humanities, with each topic and class building on what came before. If you don't properly learn one concept, it's easier to get knocked off track.

The Duke economists say that lower-ranked schools in the University of California system are better at graduating minority students in STEM majors. For example, they conclude that had the bottom third of minority students at Berkeley who hoped to graduate with a STEM major gone to Santa Cruz instead, they would have been almost twice as likely to earn such a degree.

"Prior to California's ban on affirmative action," Peter Arcidiacono, one of the study's authors, told me, "what Berkeley did well was switch relatively ill-prepared minority students out of the sciences and into majors where credentials are relatively less important."

Soon the Supreme Court will decide *Fisher v. University of Texas.* The case is complex, but essentially boils down to a young woman's claim that U.T. violated the Constitution's equal protection clause by denying her admission because she is white. The justices, save perhaps Clarence Thomas, are unlikely to address mismatch in their opinions. But the court could force schools to be more transparent about the racial preferences they use in admissions, and even to track the consequences for their students. For now, social scientists debate what can be gleaned from flawed data sets. They continue to argue over whether mismatch even exists and the extent of the harm it causes if it does. This raises another question: Do some of the more concrete if intangible benefits of affirmative action, like prestige and the superior connections one makes attending a fancier school, outweigh the potential cost? If affirmative-action admits are less likely to pass the bar after going to a certain type of school, or less likely to follow through with their field of choice, then the cost is potentially considerable. But are we really going to tell a kid embarking on adult life that he's better off attending a less prestigious school?

"The real question is what we want affirmative action to achieve," says Richard Brooks, a law professor at Yale. "Are we trying to maximize diversity? Engagement in the classroom? Whatever it is, I don't think the purpose of affirmative action is for everyone to have average grades." Mr. Brooks believes that mismatch exists. But he rejects the idea that it's as insidious as others claim and says that some mismatch might even be a good thing. Striving alongside people more capable than we are is a key ingredient for growth of all kinds.

In the *Fisher* case, Messrs. Brooks, Berk and Ho signed a friend-of-the-court brief disputing a brief on mismatch that was co-written by Mr. Sander and the legal journalist Stuart Taylor Jr. Messrs. Sander and Taylor also wrote a book together that was published last fall, "Mismatch: How Affirmative Action Hurts Students It's Intended to Help, and Why Universities Won't Admit It."

"Mismatch angers affirmative-action supporters because it quantifies a downside without weighing it against potential upsides," says Theodore Eisenberg, a law professor at Cornell, "such as the benefit of a diverse classroom, and the reality that some people who do attend better schools because of affirmative action are more successful in life as a result and help other minorities thrive." Mr. Eisenberg is on the board of *The Journal of Empirical Legal Studies*, which in June is publishing a paper by E. Douglass Williams, an economist at

Sewanee: The University of the South, that appears to corroborate Mr. Sander's "first-choice/second-choice" analysis of the B.P.S. data.

In essence, affirmative action is about how to fairly distribute opportunity after our long history of racial discrimination. Whether it "works" is as much an issue for school administrators as for policy makers. That is, before we tell a student to choose School B over School A, it's worth asking what schools can do to improve the experiences of students, particularly those pursuing STEM majors, who arrive less well prepared.

The upside of affirmative action might be harder to quantify. But part of the problem with the current affirmative action regime is how its supporters define the goal, what the Supreme Court calls the "compelling state interest": classroom diversity. Meanwhile, little regard is given to the actual forms of adversity that disadvantaged students of all races must overcome. If affirmative action continues—either until Justice O'Connor's 2028 horizon or beyond—then the results from California and the Bar Passage Study suggest it's worth a closer, numbers-based look at the consequences, for everyone.

DAN SLATER is a widely published author of journalism and creative nonfiction. A former legal affairs reporter for *The Wall Street Journal,* he is currently a contributor to *Fast Company* and has written for *The New York Times, The Washington Post, The Boston Globe, New York Magazine, Men's Health,* and *GQ.*

EXPLORING THE ISSUE

Does Affirmative Action Advance Racial Equality?

Critical Thinking and Reflection

1. What is the mismatch theory? Do you believe it is true? Why or why not?
2. What statistics surprised you most regarding minority performance in education?
3. Why was affirmative action initially created in the 1960s? Is that why it still exists today?
4. What is meant by "color blindness"? To what extent can our laws be color blind?
5. Is there a danger that temporary color consciousness can turn into a permanent policy? What safeguards are there?

Is There Common Ground?

In reacting against California's Proposition 209 banning the use of racial quotas in the admission policies of the state's colleges and universities, some of those on the losing side said, in effect, "OK, we won't use strict quotas, all we're saying is that admission officers can simply note the race of the applicants." But that, too, is unlikely to survive when measured against the sweeping ban in Prop 209. The best sort of common ground is to make available to all applicants some sort of pretesting tutoring program, and that has already begun in California. Police and fire departments in many cities have also initiated these programs.

It is difficult to bring together both sides of the affirmative action debate and find common ground. This particular issue brings together two difficult policies: race and employment. Racial differences—as the United States has shown historically—are difficult to smooth over, especially when being encouraged from the outside. And individuals tend to get very upset when it comes to matters of employment and the ability to support oneself and one's family. The infamous Jesse Helms ad involving the concept of a white citizen not getting a job due to a company's need to make an affirmative action hire still resonates today. Yet, oddly enough, the most recent renditions have aired on behalf of Vernon Robinson—an African American Republican who has turned the tide on illegal immigrants. As long as affirmative action is viewed through the lens of politics rather than as a civil rights (or even human rights concern), there is little hope of middle ground being reached.

Additional Resources

Barbara Bergmann, *In Defense of Affirmative Action* (Basic Books, 1996)

George E. Curry, *The Affirmative Action Debate* (Perseus, 1996)

Hugh D. Graham, *Collision Course: The Strange Convergence of Affirmative Action and Immigration Policy in America* (Oxford University Press, 2002)

Peter Schmidt, *Color and Money: How Rich White Kids Are Winning the War over College Affirmative Action* (Palgrave Macmillan, 2007)

Jim Sleeper, *Liberal Racism* (Viking, 1997)

Internet References . . .

American Civil Liberties Union

www.aclu.org

Center for Equal Opportunity

www.ceousa.org/

Equal Employment Opportunity Commission

www.eeoc.gov/

Institute for Justice

www.ij.org

U.S. Department of Labor

www.dol.gov/dol/topic/hiring/affirmativeact.htm

Selected, Edited, and with Issue Framing Material by:
William J. Miller, *Flagler College*

ISSUE

Should Abortion Be Restricted?

YES: Marco Rubio, from "Why Abortion Is Bad for America," *The Human Life Review* (2012)

NO: Wendy Davis, from "Filibuster of the Texas State Senate," *Speech or Remarks* (2013)

Learning Outcomes

After reading this issue, you will be able to:

- Identify arguments in support of abortion.
- Identify arguments in support of banning abortion.
- Assess the impact abortions have on American society.
- Discuss whether it's possible to legislate moral policy.
- Explain why Americans regularly debate the issue of abortion.

ISSUE SUMMARY

YES: U.S. Senator Marco Rubio discusses why abortion harms American society from multiple angles, including moral, economic, and political, during a speech at the Susan B. Anthony List Campaign for Life Gala.

NO: Texas Representative Wendy Davis presents her case for why Texas Governor Rick Perry should not sign a new abortion measure that has been deemed the most restrictive state-level effort anywhere in the United States.

Until 1973 the laws governing abortion were set by the states, most of which barred legal abortion except where pregnancy imperiled the life of the pregnant woman. In that year, the U.S. Supreme Court decided the controversial case *Roe v. Wade*. The *Roe* decision acknowledged both a woman's "fundamental right" to terminate a pregnancy before fetal viability and the state's legitimate interest in protecting both the woman's health and the "potential life" of the fetus. It prohibited states from banning abortion to protect the fetus before the third trimester of a pregnancy, and it ruled that even during that final trimester, a woman could obtain an abortion if she could prove that her life or health would be endangered by carrying to term. (In a companion case to *Roe*, decided on the same day, the Court defined health broadly enough to include "all factors—physical, emotional, psychological, familial, and the woman's age—relevant to the well-being of the patient.") These holdings, together with the requirement that state regulation of abortion had to survive "strict scrutiny" and demonstrate a "compelling state interest," resulted in later decisions striking down mandatory

24-hour waiting periods, requirements that abortions be performed in hospitals, and so-called informed consent laws.

The Supreme Court did uphold state laws requiring parental notification and consent for minors (though it provided that minors could seek permission from a judge if they feared notifying their parents). And federal courts have affirmed the right of Congress not to pay for abortions. Proabortion groups, proclaiming the "right to choose," have charged that this and similar action at the state level discriminate against poor women because it does not inhibit the ability of women who are able to pay for abortions to obtain them. Efforts to adopt a constitutional amendment or federal law barring abortion have failed, but antiabortion forces have influenced legislation in many states.

Can legislatures and courts establish the existence of a scientific fact? Opponents of abortion believe that it is a fact that life begins at conception and that the law must therefore uphold and enforce this concept. They argue that the human fetus is a live human being, and they note all the familiar signs of life displayed by the fetus: a beating heart, brain waves, thumb sucking, and so on. Those who defend abortion maintain that human life does not begin before the development of specifically human characteristics and possibly not until the birth of a child. As Justice Harry A. Blackmun put it in 1973, "There has always been strong support for the view that life does not begin until live birth."

Antiabortion forces sought a court case that might lead to the overturning of *Roe v. Wade*. Proabortion forces rallied to oppose new state laws limiting or prohibiting abortion. In *Webster v. Reproductive Health Services* (1989), with four new justices, the Supreme Court upheld a Missouri law that banned abortions in public hospitals and abortions that were performed by public employees (except to save a woman's life). The law also required that tests be performed on any fetus more than 20 weeks old to determine its viability. In the later decision of *Planned Parenthood v. Casey* (1992), however, the Court affirmed what it called the "essence" of the constitutional right to abortion while permitting some state restrictions, such as a 24-hour waiting period and parental notification in the case of minors.

In 2000, a five-to-four decision of the Supreme Court in *Stenberg v. Carhart* overturned a Nebraska law that outlawed "partial birth" abortions. The law defined "partial birth abortion" as a procedure in which the doctor "partially delivers vaginally a living child before killing" the child, further defining the process as "intentionally delivering into the vagina a living unborn child, or a substantial portion thereof, for the purpose of performing a procedure that the [abortionist] knows will kill the child." The Court's stated reason for striking down the law was that it lacked a "health" exception. Critics complained that the Court has defined "health" so broadly that it includes not only physical health, but also "emotional, psychological," and "familial" health, and that the person the Court has authorized to make these judgments is the attendant physician, that is, the abortionist himself.

In the past year, the United States has witnessed a rebirth of restrictive abortion measures that have yet to fully play their way through the federal court system. Perhaps the most prominent example has been the Texas abortion debate, which drew national attention; thanks to the filibustering of Texas state senator Wendy Davis. Texas HB 2 criminalizes abortions after 20 weeks and imposes harsh regulations on abortion providers that will force the vast majority of them to close their doors. HB 2 combines several pieces of antiabortion legislation that were unable to advance during Texas' regular legislative session. Perry called two special sessions specifically to give lawmakers more time to push them through.

During the first session, thousands of protesters helped delay the abortion restrictions until the last minute, giving Davis a chance to block the bill with a dramatic filibuster that lasted for more than 11 hours. But those tactics weren't enough to prevent the bill's advancement during a second special session. In November, the Supreme Court voted 5–4 to leave in effect a provision requiring doctors who perform abortions in clinics to have admitting privileges at a nearby hospital. Challenges to the bill still exist in federal appellate court, meaning the Texas law could find itself back in the court sooner rather than later.

Ohio, on the other hand, has spent the past decade enacting more restrictive controls on the availability of abortion without drawing as much negative attention at Texas. The state has become a laboratory of sorts for what antiabortion leaders call the incremental strategy. Under this plan, the state, under the leadership of Republican Governor John Kasich, has passed a series of rules aimed at pushing the limits set by the Supreme Court without directly violating them. The provisions put in place attempt to both discourage women from choosing to have an abortion and hampering clinic operations. There have been two recently passed provisions that will unquestionably make abortions more difficult to receive. First, Ohio has passed a heartbeat bill, which requires women about to have an abortion to both view an ultrasound and watch its beating heart. Through guilt the hope is the woman will have a change of heart. The second provision will perhaps be even more effective. Ohio has required abortion clinics to have formal transfer agreements with nearby hospitals for emergency care for some time despite this being largely unnecessary as hospitals must treat emergency patients. But now public hospitals are barred from signing these agreements, meaning a few clinics will likely have to shut down unless they find a suitable private hospital partner. In short, it is clear that states are still working to find ways to restrict abortion within their borders and the Supreme Court sits in waiting to consider appeals.

In the following selections, Marco Rubio discusses the moral, economic, and political arguments against abortion. He claims that each of us was a human being from conception and as a result abortion should be banned. Wendy Davis, on the other hand, asserts that the fetus removed in most abortions may not be considered a person and that women must retain the right to make decisions regarding their sexual lives.

YES ↩

Marco Rubio

Why Abortion Is Bad for America

T hank you for having me. This is such an important issue for me that I had written out a speech—some of the things I wanted to say to you tonight—and then I lost it.

So I brought my—I re-wrote it in a note here, so you'll forgive me, I'm a little disjointed. And the teleprompter was broken. We weren't able to—we sent it to the teleprompter shop but someone else in Washington was apparently in the shop ahead of us [*laughter*]. So, anyway, we're going to have to wait to get that one back. So I'll just kind of go off my notes here.

Let me just start by saying how honored I am to be a part of this event tonight, I am really blown away to see so many of you who are involved, who give not just money but time to this extraordinarily important cause. I was really inspired to see the young women who stood on the stage moments ago. Because I understand that in the culture we live in today, it's difficult to be pro-life. When I was running for office, throughout my career, I've been consistently pro-life—throughout my life—and I always laugh that some characterize that as "radical," even though all the polls show that at least, at a minimum, half of the people in this country agree with me. Other polling indicates that in fact, when you dig deeper, between 70 and 75 percent of Americans really agree with us at the end of the day in terms of seeing significant restrictions on abortions. So that alone indicates the mindset that exists among those who cover politics and make commentary on politics, that somehow being pro-life is a radical position. Being a young person who's pro-life makes those comments happen even more often, and being a young woman who is pro-life is perhaps the most—you get perhaps more pressure there, and more scorn, than any other demographic in our country when it comes to that issue. So as we look at these young women who came here tonight, not just pro-life, but working on behalf of life as a fundamental tenet of our society, I'm inspired by that, and I really want to thank them, and everyone else who wasn't recognized, but who is also part of that movement, and all of you for making it possible for them to do that.

Being in politics, being in the Senate, I give a lot of speeches about a lot of things. Tax policy, the national debt—these are all very important issues. These are important political issues, and policy decisions that confront our country. The issue of life is not a political issue, nor is it a policy issue. It's a definitional issue. It is a

basic, core issue that every society needs to answer, and the answer that it gives on this issue ends up defining what kind of society you have. That's how important the issue is. And what I wanted to do briefly tonight for a few moments is just encourage all of you who are involved in this cause, because I know that sometimes it's easy to get discouraged, especially for those who enter the public arena—you take a beating for being pro-life from those who cover politics too often. And I think sometimes it has a tendency to wear people down. Sometimes—listen, when I criticize people, I always include myself—sometimes you feel like, maybe let's just not touch that issue today, because it divides people, let's just focus on the 80 percent issues, and the stuff people want you to talk about. And I know I have, and many of you have as well, had people ask: "Why do you have to talk about that? It makes us uncomfortable. Why do you have to speak about this issue, it divides people. Just focus on the economic issues. Focus on the economy, focus on jobs, focus on the national debt. That's what people want to hear about." Well, we can't do that. Because the national debt is important, the economy is important, and it is the central political issue of our time. But this is not a political issue. In fact, this is an issue that, especially for those who enter the public arena and refuse to leave our faith behind, speaks to more than just our politics. It speaks to what we want to do with the opportunity we've been given in our life, to serve, and to glorify our Creator. And so that's what this issue is about, as well.

Let me just say at the outset that there are multiple reasons to be pro-life, not the least of which is that *Roe v. Wade* is bad Constitutional law, irrespective of how you feel about the issue. It is bad law. It is perhaps the most egregious and devastating example of a court deciding that because the political branch will not deal with an issue it believes is important, it will step in and make a policy decision. The Supreme Court literally created a Constitutional right out of nothing for the purpose of advocating a specific political position. So just on the legal grounds alone there is enough reason to be against *Roe v. Wade*.

There's one reason I won't go into in depth tonight because a) I don't have to, and b) it's not why you wanted me to speak. There's a spiritual aspect to this, which is very real. I think virtually every religion condemns the practice of abortion, recognizes that life is a gift from the Creator, and compels followers to believe that as well, as a basic tenet of faith. So, in the spiritual realm, there are

Rubio, Marco. As seen in *Human Life Review,* Winter 2012. Adapted from an address given at the Susan B. Anthony List Campaign for Life Gala, February 1, 2012, in Washington, DC. Copyright © 2012 by the Susan B. Anthony List. Reprinted by permission.

multiple ways to defend this. But what I want to focus on tonight are the pure, logical, public-policy reasons why abortion is bad for America, bad for our society, and bad for our people, and why it—why *Roe v. Wade* should be overturned.

Now, the argument is that there is a fundamental right to abortion in America. That is the argument that those in the pro-abortion, so-called pro-choice community would make, that there is a fundamental right to abortion. Women in this country have a right to have an abortion. So what's the source of this right? As you engage people in this conversation—by the way, I've never met anyone who's admitted to me that they're pro-abortion. They'll say they're pro-choice, but almost everyone I've ever met has told me they personally disagree with abortion, they just think it should be legal.

But, where does this fundamental right to abortion come from? You engage people that believe in what they call abortion rights, and sometimes here's what they'll do: They'll point to the circumstances of the pregnancy. They'll say, well it's an unwanted child. This is a child who's going to enter life and not be wanted, not be cared for. There are parents who don't want children, perhaps, but you know there are a lot of unwanted children in the world. There are a lot of unwanted children in the world who are born. We know that they exist in this country, but especially all over the world. That cannot be the justification for this. Because if it were, then that would justify by logic that somehow all those unwanted children as well should be dealt with in a similar manner, and that's a horrific conclusion. It's an indefensible position. And so that cannot be the source of this right. And quickly they move on from the argument because it's absurd and they don't want to think about it. When they say that to you, that this is an unwanted child, and you say to them, listen, there are a lot of unwanted children born all over this planet—they're orphaned, they're born disabled, they're born to families who can't afford them—you can't possibly be saying that those children should also be eliminated. And so they move quickly away from that argument because it makes no sense and it's indefensible.

The most common argument I hear next, what they quickly pivot to, is the argument of, well, it's a woman's body, and a woman has a right to do anything she wants with her body. And let's recognize right now, there is a fundamental right—there is a right to control your body, you do have a right to your body, there's no doubt about it. You do have a right to decide what to do with your body and what others can do to it, there's no doubt about it. But there is another right. And that's a right to live. And so, when you analyze this issue of pro-life vs. pro-choice in America, what we basically have are two rights which are in conflict with one another: a woman's right to choose—whatever they mean by that—is directly in conflict with an unborn child's right to live. And the question for our society is, how do you resolve a conflict like that when two fundamental rights that everyone recognizes exist are in conflict with one another?

And so immediately the other side will say, well our right to choose is more important than the right to live. And they'll say the reason why—the first argument they almost always relate—is because it's not a person, an embryo is not a person, a fetus is not a person. It's not a person yet. Well, if it's not a person, then what is it? Because if you left it alone, that's the only thing it can become. It can't develop into a cat! [*laughter*] It has the DNA of a person and it was certainly created by people. And left to nature, it will become a person, naturally. So it is a person. Then they'll argue, well, okay, maybe it is a person, but it's not a *life*. What do you mean, it's not a life? Well, it's not a life, because the first argument—the one they love to talk about—is viability. It's not a life because it cannot sustain itself without the person who has a right to choose—it cannot live outside the womb. That argument first and foremost is already a slippery slope because viability's a moving target. Viability in 1973 meant something very different than what it means today, medically. Children who were not viable back then are very viable now, and we have no idea what other advances are going to occur over the next few years, so if you build it on that, you're already on slippery sand.

Then they go on and say, well, they're not viable without the support of the mother. But that also can't be a good argument. Because a newborn isn't viable without the mother either! A one-year-old child, a two-year-old child—leave a two-year-old child by himself. [*laughter*] Leave a six-month-old child by herself; she's not viable either! Even the day you were born, and for years thereafter—some of you are chuckling because, leave a 19-year-old by him or herself! [*laughter, applause*]. My point is, this viability thing is not a good argument. Because the truth is that a child who has been born isn't viable by herself either. Just because they're not receiving nutrition through an umbilical cord doesn't mean that they can sustain themselves. And by the way, the third reason the viability thing doesn't work is because you apply it to the other spectrum of life, and you start to get scary. It starts to get scary. If in fact what we are saying is that human beings are only worthy of protection if they are able to sustain themselves independently of other people, that covers a lot of people in our society. It covers people who are disabled, it covers people who are temporarily incapacitated—it covers a lot of people. And so, there is no compelling argument for why a woman's right to choose trumps a child's right to live. There isn't any.

The fact of the matter is that we as a society, as a nation, from a political realm, have always understood that my rights, as important as they may be, . . . end where other people's rights begin. Yes, a woman should have a right to choose the kinds of things that happen to her body. But that right is not unlimited. It ends when it begins to interfere with the right of another human being to pursue life, to have a life. And that's at the core of this issue. That's really what this issue is about at its heart. And an increasing number of people are understanding that. I think the public polling shows it. And I hope that it will continue to be reflected in our political debate, because this is an essential issue. Well, let's ask ourselves, then why, if that's the case, if this is such a clear-cut argument, if it's so simple the way I've laid it out, and it's not more complex than this, then why is the law of the land what it is? Why are 50 percent of the people in this country, maybe a little less now, pro-choice? Why do they disagree with the things I've just said?

And the answer is, because in this equation, in this battle between the right to choose and the right to live, the only ones who can vote are the ones with the right to choose. The only ones who can participate in the political process are the ones with the right to choose. Unborn children can't vote; unborn children can't speak. Actually, they can. You speak for them. That's what you are. In this competition between two competing sets of rights, you are the voice of children who cannot speak for themselves. Of lives that may never have a chance to contribute to our society and make a difference. Of the unknown names of millions of children whose contributions to our world will never happen because the right to life was not respected. You vote for them when you vote. You participate in the political process for them when you participate. This is who you work for. Real people, no longer with us, who never had the chance to do what you or I did. And just as importantly, you are the voice and the vote of countless other children who have yet to be created, but whose lives will soon be challenged as well.

The truth is, I believe in all my heart that future generations will look back at this era in American history and condemn us. They'll look at what's happened here since 1973, and they will characterize this nation as barbaric. At some point, hopefully in our lifetime, but certainly at some point, people will look back at this practice and say, how could that be possible? In the way that we look back at the atrocities of the past, at things that occurred 100, 200, 300 years ago, at institutions that we as a nation have banned and now look at and say, how could people have supported this stuff? How could people have turned a blind eye to these things? How could people have ignored that these things were happening? The way we look at those things in history and condemn them, this era will be condemned for this. I have no doubt about it. Our job is to accelerate the process of getting there, to ensure that sooner rather than later, and God willing, in our lifetime, we can arrive at a consciousness in this nation that this is wrong. That the right to life is a fundamental one that trumps virtually any other right I can imagine. Because without it, none of the other rights matter. There can be no liberty without life. There can't be a Constitution without life. There can't be a nation without life. And there can't be other *lives* without life. I can't imagine any other right that we have more fundamental and more important than this one. And so the reason I'm so excited about the young people who are involved in this is because sometimes in contemporary life in America, we come to believe that all the great causes are something lost to history, that

past generations fought all the great battles: abolition, the civil rights movement, women's suffrage. That all the great causes have already been fought and won. It's not true. In fact, maybe one of the most important battles that has ever been fought is the one you're engaged in now. And so I encourage you to remain involved. Because at the end of the day, our nation can never truly become what it fully was intended to be unless it deals with this issue squarely. America cannot truly fulfill its destiny unless this issue is resolved. It's that important.

And I know that it's tough, I know. Especially for young people, I know that it's tough. When you take this position in public office or public policy, people look at you as an intolerant person. Oh, he's intolerant. Oh, they're radicals. Oh, you're trying to impose your religion on us. I understand the challenges to taking a position on this. But this issue's so important that it's different from the others. And this is where my faith comes in, and I hope most of yours as well. You see, I think our life here is important and everything we do here matters. This is now at the personal level, I'm no longer even speaking as a Senator, nor trying to impose what I believe on anybody else, I'm just sharing with you why this issue's important to me. And I'll tell you why. Because I've felt the same pressures. I've had people tell me, gosh, we love your tax policy, we love your fiscal policy, just don't do the social stuff on us, I don't want to hear about it. Turns people off, I've heard that too. And it gets to you sometimes. And I think, from now and then—probably not the people in this room—people are guilty of saying, let's just tone that one down. This is not the time for that. And then you realize that, you know, the office that we have is important, but this stuff's all fleeting. Comes and goes, you're a Senator today, you won't be tomorrow; you're in office today, you lose your next election. But at least my faith teaches that this life will end. You live—you're lucky, you live 80 years . . . you'll still be a Senator [*laughter*], and then you'll be held to account. Whatever your faith teaches you, they almost all teach the same thing: You will be held to account. At least in my case, I'm going to be asked very squarely, I know this. Look at what I gave you, God will say. I brought your family out of extraordinarily bad circumstances, and gave them opportunities. I gave you the opportunity to do things that your family never had a chance to do. I blessed you with children, who are healthy and vibrant and make a lot of noise. I blessed you with parents who encouraged you to dream, and a wife who supported you in pursuit of those dreams. I opened doors for you that you never thought were possible. When you polled below the margin of error in the first polls they took in your Senate race. When the only people who thought you could win your election all lived in your house. And when most of them were under the age of ten! I gave you the ability to speak to people and influence people. What did you do with it? And what am I going to say? Oh I had really good poll numbers? I got re-elected three times? I raised more money than anybody ever had? I was popular, people loved me; they patted me on the back, they gave me nice introductions? That's what I'm going to say I did with that? The more you are given, the more that is expected of you.

And that's not just true for us as people, that's true for us as a nation. America's not great because we're smarter than other people or we work harder than anybody else. There are smart and hard-working people all over the world. America is great because God has blessed America, and America has always honored those blessings by being an example to the world. For 230-some-odd years, there has been nothing more powerful on this planet than the American example. And the way we live our lives, and the principles we have stood for. Others don't always agree with the things we do, they disagree with our foreign policy, they get frustrated at America. But they admire us. Because when we get involved around the world, almost always it's behind principles and ideals. And so we are a blessed nation. And we're not just blessed so we can have. We're also blessed so we can give. And there's nothing that America can give this world right now more important than to show that all life, irrespective of the circumstances of its creation, irrespective of the circumstances of its birth, irrespective of the conditions it finds itself in, all life, on a planet where life is increasingly not valued, on a planet where people are summarily discarded, all life is worthy of protection, and all life enjoys God's love.

We are called to different tasks, whatever they may be. If we stand for these things, if we honor God in these things, He'll honor us. He'll bless us. He won't always give us what we want, but He'll always give us what we need. And you will know that you lived your life with purpose, and that in all the things you did, you honored the blessings that you had. And if we as a nation do this, well, God will continue to do what He has done for 230-some-odd years, bless us like no other people in all of human history. This is the great cause before us. And I encourage you to stay engaged and involved. If I falter at some point, remind me of the speech tonight. I hope not to. I don't expect to. And with your help, I won't. So thank you so much, I appreciate it. Thank you very much.

MARCO RUBIO served in the Florida House of Representatives from 2000 to 2008 and was elected to the U.S. Senate in 2010. His committee assignments currently include Commerce, Science, and Transportation; Foreign Relations; Intelligence; and Small Business and Entrepreneurship. He and his wife, Jeanette, have four young children and live in West Miami.

Wendy Davis

Filibuster of the Texas State Senate

Yes, Mr. President. I intend to speak for an extended period of time on the bill. Thank you very much.

Thank you, Mr. President and thank you members. As we began to debate this bill on the senate floor last week, we talked about the fact that we were here on this particular motion because we had taken extraordinary measures to be here, and I want to talk about that for a moment, how we wound up at this moment, on this day, on the senate floor, debating this bill. And we wound up here because extraordinary measures were taken in order to assure that we would land here. We all know that the bills that are before us today, that have been folded into this one bill, Senate Bill 5, are bills that were filed during the regular called session of the Texas Legislature, and we all know, as a body, why we did not hear this bill during the regular session. And that is because, of course, under our rules, our traditions, it takes two-thirds of the members of this body in order to suspend the regular order of business, because it is typical for a blocker bill to be filed, in order for a bill to be taken up. And we know that there were eleven members of this body who refused to allow the suspension of that particular rule. We know that there were no real courses of action on the house fight on this bill during the regular session as well. And when the session ended, and within the hour, Governor Perry called us back, he initially called us back for another matter that also could not be heard on this senate floor during the regular session because of that two-thirds rule, and of course that was our redistricting bills. And now something extraordinary has happened; we were called to a special session, our presiding officer has decided against tradition of the Texas Senate to have us convene in order to talk about bills that could not be taken up in the regular session and to not follow the tradition of the two-thirds rule in order to accommodate that occurring.

This bill, of course, is one that impacts many, many people. And it's one that took extraordinary measures in order for us to be here and to converse on it today. Members, I'm rising on the floor today to humbly give voice to thousands of Texans who have been ignored. These are Texans who relied on the minority members of this senate in order for their voices to be heard. These voices have been silenced by a governor who made blind partisanship and personal political ambition the official business of our great state. And sadly he's being abetted by legislative leaders who either share this blind partisanship, or simply do not have the strength to oppose it. Partisanship and ambition are not unusual in the state capital, but here in Texas, right now, it has risen to a level of profound irresponsibility and the raw abuse of power. The actions intended by our state leaders on this particular bill hurt Texans. There is no doubt about that. They hurt women; they hurt their families. The actions in this bill undermine the hard work and commitment of fair-minded, mainstream, Texas families, who want nothing more than to work hard, raise their children, stay healthy and be a productive part of the greatest state in our country. These mainstream Texas families embrace the challenge to create the greatest possible Texas. Yet, they are pushed back and they're held down by narrow and divisive interests that are driving our state, and this bill is an example of that narrow partisanship.

Today I'm going to talk about the paths these leaders have chosen under this bill and the dark place that the bill will take us. I will try to explain the history of the failed legislation before us, the impact of that legislation, and most importantly what history tells us about these policies and the motivations behind them. They do real damage to our state and to the families whose rights are violated, and whose personal relationship with their doctor and their creator, which should belong to them and them alone, are being violated. Most importantly today I will share with you what thousands of families have had to say about this legislation and those bringing this legislation to the floor, when the majority of Texans want us working to press upon genuine business of the state of Texas.

The legislation before you has a history, as we talked about a moment ago and I'm going to go specifically through the history of this particular bill. There was ample opportunity during the special sessions to move theses pieces of legislation and some did move, but the will of the legislature did not propel them timely through the process. And here are the basics about what happened to each of those. SB 25 by Senator Hegar was the 20 week abortion bill, filed on March the 5th. It was referred to state affairs on March the 12th; it never received a senate hearing. The house companion, House Bill 2364, by Representative Laubenberg, was filed on March the 5th, referred to state affairs on March the 11th. A hearing was held on April 10th. It was reported out of house state affairs on May the 2nd. The bill was sent to house calendars on May 7th,

Davis, Wendy. From speech delivered at the Texas State Senate, June 25, 2013.

and it was never placed on the calendar. SB 97, by Senator Patrick, regarding abortion inducing drugs and regulations on the administration of those drugs, was filed on November the twelfth, it was referred to health and human services on January 28th and the senate hearing was held on February 26th. It was reported out of the senate health and human service committee on March 28th but it died on the senate intent's calendar, and it died for the reason that I mentioned a moment ago, because a third of the members of this senate, who represented voices who deserve to be heard, prevented the bill from coming forward. There was no house companion to that bill. SB 537, by Senator Deuell, related to the regulation of abortion facilities requiring that they all have a standard met for ambulatory surgical centers. That bill was filed on February 13th. It was referred to health and human services on March 19th, excuse me, February 20th. There was a senate hearing on the bill March 19th. It was reported out of committee on March 26th and it died on the senate intent calendar. Again, it died because a third of the members of this body made it so. There was no house companion filed to that bill. SB 1198, by Senator Taylor, relating to hospital admitting privileges and the requirement that doctors who perform abortions have admitting privileges at a hospital within a certain distance. It was filed on March the sixth; it was referred to health and human services committee on March the twelfth. The senate hearing was held on April the 16th. It was reported out of committee on April 22nd and it died on the senate intent calendar for the reasons that I mentioned a moment ago, because the minority group of senators, who represent voices across the state of Texas, made it so. There was a house companion to that bill. HB 2816, by Representative Burkett. It was filed on March the seventh. It was referred to house state affairs on March 18th, the house hearing was held on March 27th. It was reported out of committee on April 24th, and sent to house calendars on April 26th, where it died.

And how did we get here? Well, of course we were called to a special session, and as I said, that session did not begin with the addition of this bill, it began with redistricting. On June the 10th, Governor Perry added transportation funding to the call, and of course, the Democrats in this chamber had indicated our intention that we would vote to advance that bill were it placed before this one today. We understand that transportation is a priority. On June the eleventh, these bills were filed, several bills were filed, um, including also a bill by Senator Huffman, SB 23, a bill again that the Democrats have indicated were it taken up today, before this bill, we would have joined our colleagues in passing it because we believe it's important. Governor Perry, of course, on that day also expanded the special session to include legislation relating to the regulation of abortion procedures, providers and facilities. He also spoke, in support of that call, about the horrors of The National Late Term Abortion Industry. He said that sadly some of those atrocities happen in our own state. And in Texas we value all life and we've worked to cultivate a culture that supports the birth of every child.

He said that we have an obligation to protect unborn children and to hold those who peddle abortions to standards that would minimize the death, disease, and pain that they cause. What he did not do was place on the call anything that would help to prevent unplanned pregnancy. What he did not do is place anything on the call that would aid women in making sure they never find themselves in need of the occasion that we meet here today to discuss. On that same day the call was broadened again. The bills were referred and put on a fast track for a hearing the following day, living—leaving little to no advance notice for a public hearing. But fortunately a procedural action forced the committee to wait an extra day; a tagging of the bill, allowing more Texans the opportunity to have their voices heard on these issues. Ultimately, the Republican leadership agreed to move only one bill on the senate floor and that was SB 5 that is before us today. Before bringing the bill up there was discussion amongst the majority and the 20 week fetal pain portion of the bill was removed by Republicans before the bill was presented to us for our consideration on the floor. As you probably remember from that night, Democratic senators offered seventeen amendments to the bill on the senate floor to address concerns from stakeholders, primarily to address concerns, again, that prevention of abortion is the surest way . . .? excuse me, that prevention of pregnancy is the surest way to decrease the demand for abortion. Included in those amendments were a request that we accept Medicaid funding from the federal level, which we knew would bring down a tremendous amount of money and assistance for women's health. Included in that was a full funding of the Women's Health Program which provides a ninety to ten match for uses of helping women who are in need of family planning services. But all of those amendments were rejected. The bill was voted out on party lines and then moved over to the house. The bill was received by the house on June 20th and was set for a public hearing the following day. The hearing also included HB 16 which was the 20-week stand-alone bill and HB 60, the omnibus bill. Hundreds of Texans from all over the state appeared to testify at the hearing, but unfortunately the hearing, which lasted sometime until the wee hours of the morning, 3:30 to 4 o'clock, was halted before all of the testimony was given by those who had waited, many of them from the prior morning, to voice their feelings on the bill. And it is my intention today to give them a voice by reading all of their testimonies on the senate floor. In committee SB 5 was changed to include the section of the bill, the 20-week ban, that was removed in the senate: also, HB 60 and HB 61. On the house floor there was minimal engagement and participation by the house author on the legislation. House D's offered thirteen amendments targeted at addressing concerns raised by stakeholders. All were rejected. And now, we find ourselves here.

This is the omnibus piece of legislation that contains these elements of bills that were filed in the 83rd session: the 20-week ban, the abortion inducing drugs provision, the ambulatory surgical center standards, and the hospital admitting privileges. The alleged reason for the bill is to enhance patient safety. But what they really do is create provisions that treat women as though they are not capable of making their own medical decisions. They weaken standards of care because as we all know, every member on this floor knows that the provisions of the ambulatory surgical center standards will immediately place 37 of the 42 abortion clinics in Texas out of compliance. And though the arguments on the senate floor were made that the reason for those standards was for patient safety, not a single instance, not a single instance, could be demonstrated to illustrate why those ambulatory surgical standards were important in assuring women's safety. Not a single example was provided where women had been provided a less safe atmosphere in the existing clinical setting today than they would receive in that setting. What this bill really does is to threaten the doctor-patient relationship, and we know that we received a great deal of information from doctors' groups which I'll read into the record in a little while about the intrusion on that relationship and we know that in no other instance has this legislature chosen to place itself between a woman and her doctor, or any patient and their doctor. We know that these additional standards are unnecessary. They're unsupported by scientific evidence, including unnecessary requirements that may be extremely difficult and in some cases impossible to meet without a basis in public health or safety.

As we've been debating this issue, we have been reminded that there was a time in our country when only the wealthy could afford to access abortion services because they had the ability to travel to places that it was legal, and that women who didn't have that access to care were relegated either to carrying a pregnancy to term or, and very sadly, to some unsafe methods that they turned to, to try to address that need. And we know that women lost their lives over that. We also know, in written testimony from the group, The National Obstetrics and Gynecologic Group, that their fear is the same thing is going to happen. In the state of Texas, through this bill, we are asking that women be forced to step back in history, back to a time when once again wealthy women who have the ability and the flexibility in their lives and their schedules to travel for these services will be accommodated, and women who will not will suffer a different and unfortunately, probably in some instances, a life-threatening consequence.

The 20-week ban on abortion, we've heard a great deal of testimony about that particular provision and I want to hit a few highlights of what has been shared with us. Number one, and most importantly, from our medical community we've heard the concern that this interferes with the practice of medicine. As important, we know that concerns have been raised that this ban interferes with a woman's healthcare decision before she and her doctor may have important health information about her own health and the health of the pregnancy. The ban will have devastating consequences when a woman is experiencing medical complications, and unfortunately it bans abortion before a woman may receive important information

about her own health and the health of her pregnancy. Fewer than two percent of abortions occur after 20 weeks and while they are uncommon, it is important that a woman and her doctor have every medical option available. On the abortion inducing drugs restrictions, some of the key concerns that we have had—heard about that: one, that it requires that the physician preferred course of treatment be replaced with a treatment that is potentially more physically harmful to the patient, and again, though asked, no one on this senate floor was able to provide information to us that demonstrated any other incidents where the legislature had taken it upon itself to interfere in such a dramatic way in a physician's decision-making as it pertains to the administration of treatment. The bill would require physicians to follow an outdated protocol, limiting women's access to safe, effective, medication abortion. It directly contradicts a physician's ability to provide the highest level of care for their patients by requiring a government prescribed course of treatment. It prohibits—prohibits physicians in Texas from providing the standard of care to their patients, subjecting physicians to disciplinary action for providing the nationally recognized standard of care endorsed by the leading medical professional association of obstetrician and gynecologists, ACOG. On the ambulatory surgical center standards, additional state government regulation on an already heavily regulated practice of medicine was one of the primary concerns raised there. Healthcare providers comply with all federal, state, and local laws and regulations, and they strongly opposed regulations that failed to make healthcare more cost effective, safer, efficient, or accessible. Texas already requires abortions performed after 16 weeks to be performed in ambulatory surgical centers. And we know, and I'll read some information in a little while about the fact, that there is a reason for that, because the incidents of problems that arise prior to that period of time at existing clinical settings is extremely low. Much lower, in fact, than any complications that arise from the live births, of which we are not subjecting to the same standards. When these facilities close, and they will, women will lose access to their trusted provider. These closed facilities cannot offer any other services that they may have been providing. And we know that in Texas sometimes these facilities are shared facilities where family planning services are also provided.

What is required of reproductive healthcare centers today? Today in the United States, reproductive healthcare services are among the safest and most commonly sought forms of care in the United States. Placing unreasonable requirements on healthcare centers that provide safe, legal abortions today is uncalled for, and again, not a hint of evidence has been offered as to why it's needed. And we know why. Governor Dewhurst's Tweet told us why. It is because the real aim of this bill is not to make women safer but it is to force the closure of multiple facilities across the state of Texas without a single care or concern for the women whose lives will be impacted by that decision. Not a single care or concern. Because our leadership has demonstrated that it is prioritizing its own political possibilities over potential and devastating consequences for individual women.

Let's talk about the parts of the bill that are medically unnecessary. First of all, I think each of us would agree that as patients we trust our doctors, not the government, to determine what medical equipment and what sized room is necessary to provide us with good care. It is medically unnecessary to require health centers to build a hospital-grade operating room for an abortion procedure when one is not required for this type of procedure. And in fact, we know there are many outpatient clinical procedures that are more invasive, have higher incidences of problems, that today are allowed to take place in clinical settings such as a doctor's office without the standards that are being required in this bill. Texas,

of course, as I said a moment ago, already requires that abortions performed after 16 weeks be performed at ambulatory surgical centers. This provision, the provision in these bills, goes further by requiring that all health centers that provide abortions comply with regulations that are equivalent to the governing places where surgery takes place. The vast majority of abortions, however, are outpatient procedures that can be performed in a health center, making those requirements inappropriate, unnecessary, and not at all about the health of women.

WENDY DAVIS is an American lawyer and Democratic politician from Fort Worth, Texas who represents District 10 of the Texas Senate. She previously served on the Fort Worth city council.

EXPLORING THE ISSUE

Should Abortion Be Restricted?

Critical Thinking and Reflection

1. What arguments are made for restricting abortion in the United States?
2. What arguments are made for not restricting abortion in the United States?
3. Do you believe the government should be involved in abortion policy? Why or why not?
4. Is being a "person" different from being a "human being"? Why does this question matter?
5. When does human life begin? Is an eight-month fetus essentially different from a two-minute old baby? If so, how? If not, what does that mean for policy moving forward?

Is There Common Ground?

There are some areas where common ground can be found. They include help for women who decide not to abort, such as medical assistance during pregnancy and after birth, care for their babies, assistance in housing, and job searches for the mothers. Pro-lifers would also like greater information about child development in the womb, so that women can make a more informed decision about whether to abort. Pro-choicers would like more information to be given to young people about methods of birth control, to which pro-lifers would rejoin that information about the advantages of "waiting until marriage" would be better. If *Roe v. Wade* is ever overturned, still other areas of common ground might be found in various states, such as banning late-term abortions, favored by large majorities of Americans.

Yet there are other areas where there can simply be no common ground. When it comes to abortions that are not medically necessary, for example, it will be difficult to convince the two sides to come to any meaningful middle point. The main issue is the absence of firm data or agreement on when life begins and at what stage a fetus is viable. If such information could be universally proven, it may be easier to convince the two sides of the argument to find neutral ground. But as the political environment stands today, it is hard to imagine circumstances in which an individual who sees an action as murder and another who views the same action as free choice will be able to agree on much of anything.

Additional Resources

Jack M. Balkin, *What Roe v. Wade Should Have Said* (New York University Press, 2005)

Francis J. Beckwith, *Defending Life: A Moral and Legal Case Against Abortion Choice* (Cambridge University Press, 2007)

Barbara H. Craig and David M. O'Brien, *Abortion and American Politics* (Chatham House, 1993)

Peter C. Hoffer, *The Abortion Rights Controversy in America: A Legal Reader* (University of North Carolina Press, 2004)

William Saletan, *Bearing Right: How Conservatives Won the Abortion War* (University of California Press, 2000)

Internet References . . .

Americans United for Life

www.aul.org

Center for Disease Control Abortion Surveillance

www.cdc.gov/mmwr/preview/mmwrhtml/ss6208a1
.htm?s_cid=ss6208a1_w

National Abortion Federation

www.prochoice.org

National Right to Life

www.nrlc.org

Planned Parenthood

www.plannedparenthood.org

Selected, Edited, and with Issue Framing Material by:
William J. Miller, *Flagler College*

ISSUE

Is Lethal Injection as a Method of Execution Still Constitutional?

YES: Samuel Alito, from *"Glossip v. Gross,"* United States Supreme Court (2015)

NO: Sonia Sotomayor, from *"Glossip v. Gross,"* United States Supreme Court (2015)

Learning Outcomes

After reading this issue, you will be able to:

- List reasons advocates have for supporting capital punishment.
- List reasons opponents have for not supporting capital punishment.
- Assess the meaning of cruel and unusual punishment.
- Explain the new processes of lethal injection used in some states.
- Assess the immediate future of capital punishment in the United States.

ISSUE SUMMARY

YES: Supreme Court Justice Samuel Alito argues that lethal injection remains a viable and constitutional method of execution despite some states experimenting with different protocols given the inability to acquire sodium thiopental or pentobarbital.

NO: Writing for the minority, Justice Sonia Sotomayor argued that she believes capital punishment, in any form, likely violates the Eighth Amendment protection against cruel and unusual punishment. As such, too much responsibility is being placed on petitioners to demonstrate certain drugs are not available, leading to a slippery slope of possible execution methods.

The Eighth Amendment to the United States Constitution states: "Excessive bail shall not be required, nor excessive fines imposed, nor cruel and unusual punishments inflicted." Whenever the Supreme Court rules on a question surrounding capital punishment, it typically examines from the lens of cruel and unusual punishment. In the issue at hand, we are focusing on whether a particular manner of executing an individual is constitutional—not whether the death penalty itself is (or should continue to be.)

In Wilkerson v. *Utah,* the Court stated: "Difficulty would attend the effort to define with exactness the extent of the constitutional provision which provides that cruel and unusual punishments shall not be inflicted; but it is safe to affirm that punishments of torture [such as drawing and quartering, embowelling alive, beheading, public dissecting, and burning alive], and all others in the same line of unnecessary cruelty, are forbidden by that amendment to the Constitution." In thus upholding capital punishment inflicted by a firing squad, the Court not only looked to traditional practices, but also examined the history of executions in the territory concerned, the military practice, and current writings on the death penalty. The Court next approved, under the Fourteenth Amendment's due process clause rather than under the Eighth Amendment, electrocution as a permissible method of administering punishment. Many years later, a divided Court, assuming the applicability of the Eighth Amendment to the States, held that a second electrocution following a mechanical failure at the first, which injured but did not kill the condemned man, did not violate the proscription.

Thus, the Supreme Court has a clear history of ruling on individual methods of execution. In some cases, such as lethal gas and the electric chair, states have turned away from methods before the Supreme Court ultimately ruled on their constitutionality. Skeptics will argue this occurred to keep the Court from possibly being able to use potentially cruel mechanisms as a means for ruling all forms of capital punishment unconstitutional. While electrocution, hanging, the gas chamber, and the firing squad are options in some states, more than 30 states authorize lethal injections with over 1250 individuals killed by lethal injection in the United States since 1976. But, today, even the lethal injection is under scrutiny.

Why is it so hard to kill someone via lethal injection? After all, veterinarians manage to euthanize pets rapidly every day, with minimal discomfort. Why aren't those drugs used in executions? Prison officials think the same way. The problem, however, is not that these drugs can't be used on humans, for the most part. It's with supply. Nearly every drug that prison officials turn to for lethal injections has been restricted from that use by manufacturers.

Until 2009, most states used a three-drug combination for lethal injections: an anesthetic (usually sodium thiopental, until pentobarbital was introduced at the end of 2010), pancuronium bromide (a paralytic agent, also called Pavulon), and potassium chloride (stops the heart and causes death). In 2011, however, Hospira Pharmaceuticals, the only U.S. manufacturer of sodium thiopental, stopped making the drug because of its use in executions. That same year, the European Union banned the export of sodium thiopental as well as other barbiturate drugs used in executions, ruling that companies had to ensure any exports would not be used for lethal injections. Pentobarbital, the barbiturate often used in animal euthanasia, was covered under the ban. Due to drug shortages, states have adopted new lethal injection methods including the following:

- Eight states have used a single-drug method for executions—a lethal dose of an anesthetic (Arizona, Georgia, Idaho, Missouri, Ohio, South Dakota, Texas, and Washington). Six other states have announced plans to use a one-drug protocol, but have not carried out such an execution (Arkansas, California, Kentucky, Louisiana, North Carolina, and Tennessee).
- Fourteen states have used pentobarbital in executions: Alabama, Arizona, Delaware, Florida, Georgia, Idaho, Mississippi, Missouri, Ohio, Oklahoma, South Carolina, South Dakota, Texas, and Virginia. Five additional states plan to use pentobarbital: Kentucky, Louisiana, Montana, North Carolina, and Tennessee. Colorado includes pentobarbital as a backup drug in its lethal injection procedure.
- One state had planned to use propofol (Diprivan), in a single-drug protocol, but has since revised its lethal injection procedure: Missouri.
- Two states have used midazolam as the first drug in a three-drug protocol: Florida and Oklahoma. Oklahoma's use of midazolam was botched, and the inmate, Clayton Lockett, died after the procedure was halted. Two states have used midazolam in a two-drug protocol: Ohio and Arizona. Both of their executions in 2014 were prolonged, accompanied by the inmate's gasping. Three states have proposed using midazolam in a two-drug protocol: Louisiana, Kentucky, and Oklahoma. Two states have proposed using midazolam in a three-drug protocol: Alabama and Virginia. Some states have proposed multiple protocols.

Missouri administered midazolam to inmates as a sedative before the official execution protocol began.

- Ten states have either used or intend to use compounding pharmacies to obtain their drugs for lethal injection. South Dakota carried out two executions in October 2012, obtaining drugs from compounders. Missouri first used pentobarbital from a compounding pharmacy in the November 20, 2013 execution of Joseph Franklin. Texas first used pentobarbital from a compounding pharmacy in the execution of Michael Yowell on October 9, 2013. Georgia used drugs from an unnamed compounding pharmacy for an execution on June 17, 2014. Ohio announced plans to obtain drugs from compounding pharmacies in October 2013. In March, 2014, Mississippi announced plans to use pentobarbital from a compounding pharmacy. Documents released in January 2014 show that Louisiana had contacted a compounding pharmacy regarding execution drugs, but it is unclear whether the drugs were obtained there. Pennsylvania may have obtained drugs from a compounder, but has not used them. Colorado sent out inquiries to compounding pharmacies for lethal injection drugs, but all executions are on hold. Oklahoma may use drugs from compounding pharmacies, if it can obtain them. Virginia first used compounded pentobarbital obtained through the Texas Department of Criminal Justice in the execution of Alfredo Prieto on October 1, 2015.
- Three states have recently passed laws allowing for alternative execution methods if lethal injection drugs are unavailable. Oklahoma's law, which becomes effective in November 2015, will allow for the use of nitrogen gas asphyxiation. Tennessee allows for the use of the electric chair. Utah allows the firing squad to be used if the state cannot obtain lethal injection drugs 30 days before an execution.

In federal executions, the method is determined by the state in which the sentencing took place. All three of the federal executions in the modern era have been by lethal injection carried out in a federal facility in Indiana. Apparently, a three-drug combination was used, though prison officials did not reveal the exact ingredients. The U.S. Military has not carried out any executions since reinstatement. It plans to use lethal injection.

The supply problem highlights a long-standing issue with the medicalization of the death penalty: Doctors are not, generally speaking, on board. The American Medical Association (AMA) opposes physician involvement in capital punishment, as does the American Board of Anesthesiology (ABA). "Patients should never confuse the death chamber with the operating room, lethal doses of execution drugs with anesthetic drugs, or the executioner with the anesthesiologist," J. Jeffrey Andrews, the secretary of the ABA, wrote in a commentary in May 2014. "Physicians should not be expected to act in ways that violate the ethics of medical practice, even if these acts are legal. Anesthesiologists are healers, not executioners."

While prisons can often find physicians to preside over executions, the involvement of the medical profession in executions does not always proceed smoothly. In 2006, executions in California halted when two anesthesiologists resigned from participation in the execution of Michael Morales. They quit after finding out that they would be expected to intervene directly if the execution procedure went wrong. "The Morales case unearthed a nagging paradox. The people most knowledgeable about the process of lethal injection—doctors, particularly anesthesiologists—are often reluctant to impart their insights and skills," wrote Deborah Denno, a professor at the Fordham University School of Law, in a 2007 paper on medicine and the death penalty.

A doctor was presiding over the June 2014 execution of Clayton D. Lockett, who died of heart failure 43 minutes after Oklahoma prison officials began his execution. But a medical technician was doing the actual procedure. Witnesses reported that it took nearly an hour of poking and prodding before the technician gave up on setting a catheter in Lockett's arms, legs, or feet, and instead tried to place a line through the femoral artery. An independent autopsy commissioned by the condemned man's lawyers found that the line was not placed properly, perhaps explaining why Lockett appeared to wake up after the first sedative drug was injected.

Thus, it is perhaps not surprising to know that the Supreme Court has taken a renewed interest in the constitutionality of lethal injection protocols across the country. In the following selections, Supreme Court Justice Samuel Alito argues that lethal injection remains a viable and constitutional method of execution despite some states experimenting with different protocols given the inability to acquire sodium thiopental or pentobarbital. While writing for the minority, Justice Sonia Sotomayor believes capital punishment, in any form, likely violates the Eighth Amendment protection against cruel and unusual punishment. As such, too much responsibility is being placed on petitioners to demonstrate certain drugs are not available, leading to a slippery slope of possible execution methods.

YES ↵

Samuel Alito

Glossip v. Gross

Prisoners sentenced to death in the State of Oklahoma filed an action in federal court under Rev. Stat. §1979, 42 U. S. C. §1983, contending that the method of execution now used by the State violates the Eighth Amendment because it creates an unacceptable risk of severe pain. They argue that midazolam, the first drug employed in the State's current three-drug protocol, fails to render a person insensate to pain. After holding an evidentiary hearing, the District Court denied four prisoners' application for a preliminary injunction, finding that they had failed to prove that midazolam is ineffective. The Court of Appeals for the Tenth Circuit affirmed and accepted the District Court's finding of fact regarding midazolam's efficacy.

For two independent reasons, we also affirm. First, the prisoners failed to identify a known and available alternative method of execution that entails a lesser risk of pain, a requirement of all Eighth Amendment method-of-execution claims. See *Baze v. Rees,* 553 U. S. 35, 61 (2008) (plurality opinion). Second, the District Court did not commit clear error when it found that the prisoners failed to establish that Oklahoma's use of a massive dose of midazolam in its execution protocol entails a substantial risk of severe pain.

I
A

The death penalty was an accepted punishment at the time of the adoption of the Constitution and the Bill of Rights. In that era, death sentences were usually carried out by hanging. The Death Penalty in America: Current Controversies 4 (H. Bedau ed. 1997). Hanging remained the standard method of execution through much of the 19th century, but that began to change in the century's later years. See *Baze, supra*, at 41–42. In the 1880's, the Legislature of the State of New York appointed a commission to find "'the most humane and practical method known to modern science of carrying into effect the sentence of death in capital cases.'" *In re Kemmler*, 136 U. S. 436, 444 (1890). The commission recommended electrocution, and in 1888, the Legislature enacted a law providing for this method of execution. *Id.*, at 444–445. In subsequent years, other States followed New York's lead in the "'belief that electrocution is less painful and more humane than hanging.'"

Baze, 553 U. S., at 42 (quoting *Malloy* v. *South Carolina*, 237 U. S. 180, 185 (1915)).

. . .

After *Gregg* reaffirmed that the death penalty does not violate the Constitution, some States once again sought a more humane way to carry out death sentences. They eventually adopted lethal injection, which today is "by far the most prevalent method of execution in the United States." *Baze, supra,* at 42. Oklahoma adopted lethal injection in 1977, see 1977 Okla. Sess. Laws p. 89, and it eventually settled on a protocol that called for the use of three drugs: (1) sodium thiopental, "a fast-acting barbiturate sedative that induces a deep, comalike unconsciousness when given in the amounts used for lethal injection," (2) a paralytic agent, which "inhibits all muscular-skeletal movements and, by paralyzing the diaphragm, stops respiration," and (3) potassium chloride, which "interferes with the electrical signals that stimulate the contractions of the heart, inducing cardiac arrest." *Baze, supra,* at 44; see also Brief for Respondents 9. By 2008, at least 30 of the 36 States that used lethal injection employed that particular three-drug protocol. 553 U. S., at 44.

While methods of execution have changed over the years, "[t]his Court has never invalidated a State's chosen procedure for carrying out a sentence of death as the infliction of cruel and unusual punishment." *Id.*, at 48. In *Wilkerson* v. *Utah*, 99 U. S. 130, 134–135 (1879), the Court upheld a sentence of death by firing squad. In *In re Kemmler, supra,* at 447–449, the Court rejected a challenge to the use of the electric chair. And the Court did not retreat from that holding even when presented with a case in which a State's initial attempt to execute a prisoner by electrocution was unsuccessful. *Louisiana ex rel. Francis* v. *Resweber*, 329 U. S. 459, 463–464 (1947) (plurality opinion). Most recently, in *Baze, supra,* seven Justices agreed that the three-drug protocol just discussed does not violate the Eighth Amendment.

. . .

B

Baze cleared any legal obstacle to use of the most common three-drug protocol that had enabled States to carry out the death

Alito, Samuel. "Glossip v. Gross," United States Supreme Court, October 2015.

penalty in a quick and painless fashion. But a practical obstacle soon emerged, as anti-death-penalty advocates pressured pharmaceutical companies to refuse to supply the drugs used to carry out death sentences. The sole American manufacturer of sodium thiopental, the first drug used in the standard three-drug protocol, was persuaded to cease production of the drug. After suspending domestic production in 2009, the company planned to resume production in Italy. Koppel, Execution Drug Halt Raises Ire of Doctors, Wall Street Journal, Jan. 25, 2011, p. A6. Activists then pressured both the company and the Italian Government to stop the sale of sodium thiopental for use in lethal injections in this country. Bonner, Letter from Europe: Drug Company in Cross Hairs of Death Penalty Opponents, N. Y. Times, Mar. 30, 2011; Koppel, Drug Halt Hinders Executions in the U. S., Wall Street Journal, Jan. 22, 2011, p. A1. That effort proved successful, and in January 2011, the company announced that it would exit the sodium thiopental market entirely. See Hospira, Press Release, Hospira Statement Regarding Pentothal™ (sodium thiopental) Market Exit (Jan. 21, 2011).

After other efforts to procure sodium thiopental proved unsuccessful, States sought an alternative, and they eventually replaced sodium thiopental with pentobarbital, another barbiturate. In December 2010, Oklahoma became the first State to execute an inmate using pentobarbital. See Reuters, Chicago Tribune, New Drug Mix Used in Oklahoma Execution, Dec. 17 2010, p. 41. That execution occurred without incident, and States gradually shifted to pentobarbital as their supplies of sodium thiopental ran out. It is reported that pentobarbital was used in all of the 43 executions carried out in 2012. The Death Penalty Institute, Execution List 2012, online at www.deathpenaltyinfo.org/execution-list-2012 (all Internet materials as visited June 26, 2015, and available in Clerk of Court's case file). Petitioners concede that pentobarbital, like sodium thiopental, can "reliably induce and maintain a comalike state that renders a person insensate to pain" caused by administration of the second and third drugs in the protocol. Brief for Petitioners 2. And courts across the country have held that the use of pentobarbital in executions does not violate the Eighth Amendment. See, e.g., *Jackson* v. *Danberg*, 656 F. 3d 157 (CA3 2011); *Beaty* v. *Brewer*, 649 F. 3d 1071 (CA9 2011); *DeYoung* v. *Owens*, 646 F. 3d 1319 (CA11 2011); *Pavatt* v. *Jones*, 627 F. 3d 1336 (CA10 2010).

Before long, however, pentobarbital also became unavailable. Anti-death-penalty advocates lobbied the Danish manufacturer of the drug to stop selling it for use in executions. See Bonner, *supra*. That manufacturer opposed the death penalty and took steps to block the shipment of pentobarbital for use in executions in the United States. Stein, New Obstacle to Death Penalty in U. S., Washington Post, July 3, 2011, p. A4. Oklahoma eventually became unable to acquire the drug through any means. The District Court below found that both sodium thiopental and pentobarbital are now unavailable to Oklahoma. App. 67–68.

C

Unable to acquire either sodium thiopental or pentobarbital, some States have turned to midazolam, a sedative in the benzodiazepine family of drugs. In October 2013, Florida became the first State to substitute midazolam for pentobarbital as part of a three-drug lethal injection protocol. Fernandez, Executions Stall As States Seek Different Drugs, N. Y. Times, Nov. 9, 2013, p. A1. To date, Florida has conducted 11 executions using that protocol, which calls for midazolam followed by a paralytic agent and potassium chloride. See Brief for State of Florida as *Amicus Curiae* 2–3; *Chavez* v. *Florida SP Warden*, 742 F. 3d 1267, 1269 (CA11 2014). In 2014, Oklahoma also substituted midazolam for pentobarbital as part of its three-drug protocol. Oklahoma has already used this three-drug protocol twice: to execute Clayton Lockett in April 2014 and Charles Warner in January 2015. (Warner was one of the four inmates who moved for a preliminary injunction in this case.)

The Lockett execution caused Oklahoma to implement new safety precautions as part of its lethal injection protocol. When Oklahoma executed Lockett, its protocol called for the administration of 100 milligrams of midazolam, as compared to the 500 milligrams that are currently required. On the morning of his execution, Lockett cut himself twice at "'the bend of the elbow.'" App. 50. That evening, the execution team spent nearly an hour making at least one dozen attempts to establish intravenous (IV) access to Lockett's cardiovascular system, including at his arms and elsewhere on his body. The team eventually believed that it had established intravenous access through Lockett's right femoral vein, and it covered the injection access point with a sheet, in part to preserve Lockett's dignity during the execution. After the team administered the midazolam and a physician determined that Lockett was unconscious, the team next administered the paralytic agent (vecuronium bromide) and most of the potassium chloride. Lockett began to move and speak, at which point the physician lifted the sheet and determined that the IV had "infiltrated," which means that "the IV fluid, rather than entering Lockett's blood stream, had leaked into the tissue surrounding the IV access point." *Warner* v. *Gross*, 776 F. 3d 721, 725 (CA10 2015) (case below). The execution team stopped administering the remaining potassium chloride and terminated the execution about 33 minutes after the midazolam was first injected. About 10 minutes later, Lockett was pronounced dead.

· · ·

II

A

In June 2014, after Oklahoma switched from pentobarbital to midazolam and executed Lockett, 21 Oklahoma death row inmates filed an action under 42 U. S. C. §1983 challenging the State's new lethal injection protocol. The complaint alleged that Oklahoma's use of midazolam violates the Eighth Amendment's prohibition of cruel and unusual punishment.

In November 2014, four of those plaintiffs—Richard Glossip, Benjamin Cole, John Grant, and Warner—filed a motion for a preliminary injunction. All four men had been convicted of murder and sentenced to death by Oklahoma juries. Glossip hired Justin Sneed to kill his employer, Barry Van Treese. Sneed entered a room where Van Treese was sleeping and beat him to death with a baseball bat. See *Glossip* v. *State*, 2007 OK CR 12, 157 P. 3d 143, 147–149. Cole murdered his 9-month-old daughter after she would not stop crying. Cole bent her body backwards until he snapped her spine in half. After the child died, Cole played video games. See *Cole* v. *State*, 2007 OK CR 27, 164 P. 3d 1089, 1092–1093. Grant, while serving terms of imprisonment totaling 130 years, killed Gay Carter, a prison food service supervisor, by pulling her into a mop closet and stabbing her numerous times with a shank. See *Grant* v. *State*, 2002 OK CR 36, 58 P. 3d 783, 789. Warner anally raped and murdered an 11-month-old girl. The child's injuries included two skull fractures, internal brain injuries, two fractures to her jaw, a lacerated liver, and a bruised spleen and lungs. See *Warner* v. *State*, 2006 OK CR 40, 144 P. 3d 838, 856–857.

The Oklahoma Court of Criminal Appeals affirmed the murder conviction and death sentence of each offender. Each of the men then unsuccessfully sought both state postconviction and federal habeas corpus relief. Having exhausted the avenues for challenging their convictions and sentences, they moved for a preliminary injunction against Oklahoma's lethal injection protocol.

B

In December 2014, after discovery, the District Court held a 3-day evidentiary hearing on the preliminary injunction motion. The District Court heard testimony from 17 witnesses and reviewed numerous exhibits. Dr. David Lubarsky, an anesthesiologist, and Dr. Larry Sasich, a doctor of pharmacy, provided expert testimony about midazolam for petitioners, and Dr. Roswell Evans, a doctor of pharmacy, provided expert testimony for respondents.

After reviewing the evidence, the District Court issued an oral ruling denying the motion for a preliminary injunction. The District Court first rejected petitioners' challenge under *Daubert* v. *Merrell Dow Pharmaceuticals, Inc.*, 509 U. S. 579 (1993), to the testimony of Dr. Evans. It concluded that Dr. Evans, the Dean of Auburn University's School of Pharmacy, was well qualified to testify about midazolam's properties and that he offered reliable testimony. The District Court then held that petitioners failed to establish a likelihood of success on the merits of their claim that the use of midazolam violates the Eighth Amendment. The court provided two independent reasons for this conclusion. First, the court held that petitioners failed to identify a known and available method of execution that presented a substantially less severe risk of pain than

the method that the State proposed to use. Second, the court found that petitioners failed to prove that Oklahoma's protocol "presents a risk that is 'sure or very likely to cause serious illness and needless suffering,' amounting to 'an objectively intolerable risk of harm.'" App. 96 (quoting *Baze*, 553 U. S., at 50). The court emphasized that the Oklahoma protocol featured numerous safeguards, including the establishment of two IV access sites, confirmation of the viability of those sites, and monitoring of the offender's level of consciousness throughout the procedure.

The District Court supported its decision with findings of fact about midazolam. It found that a 500-milligram dose of midazolam "would make it a virtual certainty that any individual will be at a sufficient level of unconsciousness to resist the noxious stimuli which could occur from the application of the second and third drugs." App. 77. Indeed, it found that a 500-milligram dose alone would likely cause death by respiratory arrest within 30 minutes or an hour.

. . .

Oklahoma executed Warner on January 15, 2015, but we subsequently voted to grant review and then stayed the executions of Glossip, Cole, and Grant pending the resolution of this case. 574 U. S.___(2015).

. . .

IV

Our first ground for affirmance is based on petitioners' failure to satisfy their burden of establishing that any risk of harm was substantial when compared to a known and available alternative method of execution. In their amended complaint, petitioners proffered that the State could use sodium thiopental as part of a single-drug protocol. They have since suggested that it might also be constitutional for Oklahoma to use pentobarbital. But the District Court found that both sodium thiopental and pentobarbital are now unavailable to Oklahoma's Department of Corrections. The Court of Appeals affirmed that finding, and it is not clearly erroneous. On the contrary, the record shows that Oklahoma has been unable to procure those drugs despite a good-faith effort to do so.

Petitioners do not seriously contest this factual finding, and they have not identified any available drug or drugs that could be used in place of those that Oklahoma is now unable to obtain. Nor have they shown a risk of pain so great that other acceptable, available methods must be used. Instead, they argue that they need not identify a known and available method of execution that presents less risk. But this argument is inconsistent with the controlling opinion in *Baze*, 553 U. S., at 61, which imposed a requirement that the Court now follows.

Petitioners contend that the requirement to identify an alternative method of execution contravenes our pre-*Baze* decision in *Hill* v. *McDonough,* 547 U. S. 573 (2006), but they misread that decision. The portion of the opinion in *Hill* on which they rely concerned a question of civil procedure, not a substantive Eighth Amendment question. In *Hill,* the issue was whether a challenge to a method of execution must be brought by means of an application for a writ of habeas corpus or a civil action under §1983. *Id.,* at 576. We held that a method-of-execution claim must be brought under §1983 because such a claim does not attack the validity of the prisoner's conviction or death sentence. *Id.,* at 579–580. The United States as *amicus curiae* argued that we should adopt a special pleading requirement to stop inmates from using §1983 actions to attack, not just a particular means of execution, but the death penalty itself. To achieve this end, the United States proposed that an inmate asserting a method-of-execution claim should be required to plead an acceptable alternative method of execution. *Id.,* at 582. We rejected that argument because "[s]pecific pleading requirements are mandated by the Federal Rules of Civil Procedure, and not, as a general rule, through case-by-case determinations of the federal courts." *Ibid. Hill* thus held that §1983 alone does not impose a heightened pleading requirement. *Baze,* on the other hand, addressed the substantive elements of an Eighth Amendment method-of-execution claim, and it made clear that the Eighth Amendment requires a prisoner to plead and prove a known and available alternative. Because petitioners failed to do this, the District Court properly held that they did not establish a likelihood of success on their Eighth Amendment claim.

Readers can judge for themselves how much distance there is between the principal dissent's argument against requiring prisoners to identify an alternative and the view, now announced by JUSTICES BREYER and GINSBURG, that the death penalty is categorically unconstitutional. *Post,* p. __ (BREYER, J., dissenting). The principal dissent goes out of its way to suggest that a State would violate the Eighth Amendment if it used one of the methods of execution employed before the advent of lethal injection *Post,* at 30–31. And the principal dissent makes this suggestion even though the Court held in *Wilkerson* that this method (the firing squad) is constitutional and even though, in the words of the principal dissent, "there is some reason to think that it is relatively quick and painless." *Post,* at 30. Tellingly silent about the methods of execution most commonly used before States switched to lethal injection (the electric chair and gas chamber), the principal dissent implies that it would be unconstitutional to use a method that "could be seen as a devolution to a more primitive era." *Ibid.* If States cannot return to any of the "more primitive" methods used in the past and if no drug that meets with the principal dissent's approval is available for use in carrying out a death sentence, the logical conclusion is clear. But we have time and again reaffirmed that capital punishment is not *per se* unconstitutional. See, *e.g.,*

Baze, 553 U. S., at 47; *id.,* at 87–88 (SCALIA, J., concurring in judgment); *Gregg,* 428 U. S., at 187 (joint opinion of Stewart, Powell, and Stevens, JJ.); *id.,* at 226 (White, J., concurring in judgment); *Resweber,* 329 U. S., at 464; *In re Kemmler,* 136 U. S., at 447; *Wilkerson,* 99 U. S., at 134–135. We decline to effectively overrule these decisions.

V

We also affirm for a second reason: The District Court did not commit clear error when it found that midazolam is highly likely to render a person unable to feel pain during an execution. We emphasize four points at the outset of our analysis.

First, we review the District Court's factual findings under the deferential "clear error" standard. This standard does not entitle us to overturn a finding "simply because [we are] convinced that [we] would have decided the case differently." *Anderson* v. *Bessemer City,* 470 U. S. 564, 573 (1985).

Second, petitioners bear the burden of persuasion on this issue. *Baze, supra,* at 41. Although petitioners expend great effort attacking peripheral aspects of Dr. Evans' testimony, they make little attempt to prove what is critical, *i.e.,* that the evidence they presented to the District Court establishes that the use of midazolam is sure or very likely to result in needless suffering.

Third, numerous courts have concluded that the use of midazolam as the first drug in a three-drug protocol is likely to render an inmate insensate to pain that might result from administration of the paralytic agent and potassium chloride. See, *e.g.,* 776 F. 3d 721 (case below affirming the District Court); *Chavez* v. *Florida SP Warden,* 742 F. 3d 1267 (affirming the District Court); *Banks* v. *State,* 150 So. 3d 797 (Fla. 2014) (affirming the lower court); *Howell* v. *State,* 133 So. 3d 511 (Fla. 2014) (same); *Muhammad* v. *State,* 132 So. 3d 176 (Fla. 2013) (same). (It is noteworthy that one or both of the two key witnesses in this case—Dr. Lubarsky for petitioners and Dr. Evans for respondents—were witnesses in the *Chavez, Howell,* and *Muhammad* cases.) "Where an intermediate court reviews, and affirms, a trial court's factual findings, this Court will not 'lightly overturn' the concurrent findings of the two lower courts." *Easley* v. *Cromartie,* 532 U. S. 234, 242 (2001). Our review is even more deferential where, as here, multiple trial courts have reached the same finding, and multiple appellate courts have affirmed those findings. Cf. *Exxon Co., U. S. A.* v. *Sofec, Inc.,* 517 U. S. 830, 841 (1996) (explaining that this Court "'cannot undertake to review concurrent findings of fact by two courts below in the absence of a very obvious and exceptional showing of error'" (quoting *Graver Tank & Mfg. Co.* v. *Linde Air Products Co.,* 336 U. S. 271, 275 (1949))).

Fourth, challenges to lethal injection protocols test the boundaries of the authority and competency of federal courts. Although we must invalidate a lethal injection protocol if it violates the Eighth Amendment, federal courts should not "embroil [them-selves] in ongoing scientific controversies beyond their expertise." *Baze, supra*, at 51. Accordingly, an inmate challenging a protocol bears the burden to show, based on evidence presented to the court, that there is a substantial risk of severe pain.

. . .

Oklahoma has also adopted important safeguards to ensure that midazolam is properly administered. The District Court emphasized three requirements in particular: The execution team must secure both a primary and backup IV access site, it must confirm the viability of the IV sites, and it must continuously monitor the offender's level of consciousness. The District Court did not commit clear error in concluding that these safeguards help to minimize any risk that might occur in the event that midazolam does not operate as intended. Indeed, we concluded in *Baze* that many of the safeguards that Oklahoma employs—including the establishment of a primary and backup IV and the presence of personnel to monitor an inmate—help in significantly reducing the risk that an execution protocol will violate the Eighth Amendment. *Id.*, at 55–56. And many other safeguards that Oklahoma has adopted mirror those that the dissent in *Baze* complained were absent from Kentucky's protocol in that case. For example, the dissent argued that because a consciousness check before injection of the second drug "can reduce a risk of dreadful pain," Kentucky's failure to include that step in its procedure was unconstitutional. *Id.*, at 119 (opinion of GINSBURG, J.). The dissent also complained that Kentucky did not monitor the effectiveness of the first drug or pause between injection of the first and second drugs. *Id.*, at 120–121. Oklahoma has accommodated each of those concerns.

. . .

Petitioners' remaining arguments about midazolam all lack merit. First, we are not persuaded by petitioners' argument that Dr. Evans' testimony should have been rejected because of some of the sources listed in his report. Petitioners criticize two of the "selected references" that Dr. Evans cited in his expert report: the Web site drugs.com and a material safety data sheet (MSDS) about midazolam. Petitioners' argument is more of a *Daubert* challenge to Dr. Evans' testimony than an argument that the District Court's findings were clearly erroneous. The District Court concluded that Dr. Evans was "well-qualified to give the expert testimony that he gave" and that "his testimony was the product of reliable principles and methods reliably applied to the facts of this case." App. 75–76. To the extent that the reliability of Dr. Evans' testimony is even before us, the District Court's conclusion that his testimony was based on reliable sources is reviewed under the deferential "abuse-of-discretion" standard. *General Elec. Co. v. Joiner*, 522 U. S. 136,

142– 143 (1997). Dr. Evans relied on multiple sources and his own expertise, and his testimony may not be disqualified simply because one source (drugs.com) warns that it "'is not intended for medical advice'" and another (the MSDS) states that its information is provided " 'without any warranty, express or implied, regarding its correctness.'" Brief for Petitioners 36. Medical journals that both parties rely upon typically contain similar disclaimers. See, *e.g.*, Anesthesiology, Terms and Conditions of Use, online at http://anes-thesiology.pubs.asahq.org/ss/terms.aspx ("None of the information on this Site shall be used to diagnose or treat any health problem or disease"). Dr. Lubarsky—petitioners' own expert—relied on an MSDS to argue that midazolam has a ceiling effect. And petitioners do not identify any incorrect statements from drugs.com on which Dr. Evans relied. In fact, although Dr. Sasich submitted a declaration to the Court of Appeals criticizing Dr. Evans' reference to drugs.com, that declaration does not identify a single fact from that site's discussion of midazolam that was materially inaccurate.

Second, petitioners argue that Dr. Evans' expert report contained a mathematical error, but we find this argument insignificant. Dr. Evans stated in his expert report that the lowest dose of midazolam resulting in human deaths, according to an MSDS, is 0.071 mg/kg delivered intravenously. App. 294. Dr. Lubarsky agreed with this statement. Specifically, he testified that fatalities have occurred in doses ranging from 0.04 to 0.07 mg/kg, and he stated that Dr. Evans' testimony to that effect was "a true statement" (though he added those fatalities occurred among the elderly). *Id.*, at 217. We do not understand petitioners to dispute the testimony of Dr. Evans and their own expert that 0.071 mg/kg is a potentially fatal dose of midazolam. Instead, they make much of the fact that the MSDS attached to Dr. Evans' report apparently contained a typographical error and reported the lowest toxic dose as 71 mg/kg. That Dr. Evans did not repeat that incorrect figure but instead reported the correct dose supports rather than undermines his testimony. In any event, the alleged error in the MSDS is irrelevant because the District Court expressly stated that it did not rely on the figure in the MSDS. See *id.*, at 75.

Third, petitioners argue that there is no consensus among the States regarding midazolam's efficacy because only four States (Oklahoma, Arizona, Florida, and Ohio) have used midazolam as part of an execution. Petitioners rely on the plurality's statement in *Baze* that "it is difficult to regard a practice as 'objectively intolerable' when it is in fact widely tolerated," and the plurality's emphasis on the fact that 36 States had adopted lethal injection and 30 States used the particular three-drug protocol at issue in that case. 553 U. S., at 53. But while the near-universal use of the particular protocol at issue in *Baze* supported our conclusion that this protocol did not violate the Eighth Amendment, we did not say that the converse was true, *i.e.*, that other protocols or methods of execution are of doubtful constitutionality. That argument, if accepted, would hamper the adoption of new and potentially more humane methods of execution and would prevent States from adapting to changes in the availability of suitable drugs.

Fourth, petitioners argue that difficulties with Oklahoma's execution of Lockett and Arizona's July 2014 execution of Joseph Wood establish that midazolam is sure or very likely to cause serious pain. We are not persuaded. Aside from the Lockett execution, 12 other executions have been conducted using the three-drug protocol at issue here, and those appear to have been conducted without any significant problems. See Brief for Respondents 32; Brief for State of Florida as *Amicus Curiae* 1. Moreover, Lockett was administered only 100 milligrams of midazolam, and Oklahoma's investigation into that execution concluded that the difficulties were due primarily to the execution team's inability to obtain an IV access site. And the Wood execution did not involve the protocol at issue here. Wood did not receive a single dose of 500 milligrams of midazolam; instead, he received fifteen 50-milligram doses over the span of two hours. Brief for Respondents 12, n. 9. And Arizona used a different two-drug protocol that paired midazolam with hydromorphone, a drug that is not at issue in this case. *Ibid.* When all of the circumstances are considered, the Lockett and Wood executions have little probative value for present purposes.

Finally, we find it appropriate to respond to the principal dissent's groundless suggestion that our decision is tantamount to allowing prisoners to be "drawn and quartered, slowly tortured to death, or actually burned at the stake." *Post*, at 28. That is simply not true, and the principal dissent's resort to this outlandish rhetoric reveals the weakness of its legal arguments.

VI

For these reasons, the judgment of the Court of Appeals for the Tenth Circuit is affirmed.

It is so ordered.

SAMUEL ALITO is tan associate justice of the United States Supreme Court. He was appointed in 2005 by President George W. Bush.

Sonia Sotomayor

 **NO**

Glossip v. Gross

Petitioners, three inmates on Oklahoma's death row, challenge the constitutionality of the State's lethal injection protocol. The State plans to execute petitioners using three drugs: midazolam, rocuronium bromide, and potassium chloride. The latter two drugs are intended to paralyze the inmate and stop his heart. But they do so in a torturous manner, causing burning, searing pain. It is thus critical that the first drug, midazolam, do what it is supposed to do, which is to render and keep the inmate unconscious. Petitioners claim that midazolam cannot be expected to perform that function, and they have presented ample evidence showing that the State's planned use of this drug poses substantial, constitutionally intolerable risks.

Nevertheless, the Court today turns aside petitioners' plea that they at least be allowed a stay of execution while they seek to prove midazolam's inadequacy. The Court achieves this result in two ways: first, by deferring to the District Court's decision to credit the scientifically unsupported and implausible testimony of a single expert witness; and second, by faulting petitioners for failing to satisfy the wholly novel requirement of proving the avail ability of an alternative means for their own executions.

On both counts the Court errs. As a result, it leaves petitioners exposed to what may well be the chemical equivalent of being burned at the stake.

I

A

The Eighth Amendment succinctly prohibits the infliction of "cruel and unusual punishments." Seven years ago, in *Baze* v. *Rees*, 553 U.S. 35 (2008), the Court addressed the application of this mandate to Kentucky's lethal injection protocol. At that time, Kentucky, like at least 29 of the 35 other States with the death penalty, utilized a series of three drugs to perform executions: (1) sodium thiopental, a "fast-acting barbiturate sedative that induces a deep, comalike unconsciousness when given in the amounts used for lethal injection"; (2) pancuronium bromide, "a paralytic agent that inhibits all muscular-skeletal movements and . . . stops respiration"; and (3) potassium chloride, which "interferes with the electrical signals that stimulate the contractions of the heart, inducing cardiac arrest." *Id.*, at 44 (plurality opinion of ROBERTS, C. J.).

In *Baze*, it was undisputed that absent a "proper dose of sodium thiopental," there would be a "substantial, constitutionally unacceptable risk of suffocation from the administration of pancuronium bromide and pain from the injection of potassium chloride." *Id.*, at 53. That is because, if given to a conscious inmate, pancuronium bromide would leave him or her asphyxiated and unable to demonstrate "any outward sign of distress," while potassium chloride would cause "excruciating pain." *Id.*, at 71 (Stevens, J., concurring in judgment). But the Baze petitioners conceded that if administered as intended, Kentucky's method of execution would nevertheless "result in a humane death," *id.*, at 41 (plurality opinion), as the "proper administration" of sodium thiopental "eliminates any meaningful risk that a prisoner would experience pain from the subsequent injections of pancuronium and potassium chloride," *id.*, at 49. Based on that premise, the Court ultimately rejected the challenge to Kentucky's protocol, with the plurality opinion concluding that the State's procedures for administering these three drugs ensured there was no "objectively intolerable risk" of severe pain. *Id.*, at 61–62 (internal quotation marks omitted).

. . .

D

The District Court denied petitioners' motion for a preliminary injunction. It began by making a series of factual findings regarding the characteristics of midazolam and its use in Oklahoma's execution protocol. Most relevant here, the District Court found that "[t]he proper administration of 500 milligrams of midazolam . . . would make it a virtual certainty that an individual will be at a sufficient level of unconsciousness to resist the noxious stimuli which could occur from the application of the second and third drugs." *Id.*, at 77. Respecting petitioners' contention that there is a "ceiling effect which prevents an increase in dosage from having a corresponding incremental effect on anesthetic depth," the District Court concluded:

> "Dr. Evans testified persuasively . . . that whatever the ceiling effect of midazolam may be with respect to anesthesia, which takes effect at the spinal cord level, there is no ceiling effect with respect to the ability of a

Sotomayor, Sonia. "Glossip v. Gross," United States Supreme Court, October 2015.

500 milligram dose of midazolam to effectively paralyze the brain, a phenomenon which is not anesthesia but does have the effect of shutting down respiration and eliminating the individual's awareness of pain." *Id.*, at 78.

Having made these findings, the District Court held that petitioners had shown no likelihood of success on the merits of their Eighth Amendment claim for two independent reasons. First, it determined that petitioners had "failed to establish that proceeding with [their] execution[s] . . . on the basis of the revised protocol presents . . . 'an objectively intolerable risk of harm.'" *Id.*, at 96. Second, the District Court held that petitioners were unlikely to prevail because they had not identified any "'known and available alternative'" means by which they could be executed—a requirement it understood *Baze* to impose. *Id.*, at 97. The District Court concluded that the State "ha[d] affirmatively shown that sodium thiopental and pentobarbital, the only alternatives to which the [petitioners] have even alluded, are not available to the [State]." *Id.*, at 98.

. . .

A

To begin, Dr. Evans identified no scientific literature to support his opinion regarding midazolam's properties at higher-than-normal doses. Apart from a Material Safety Data Sheet that was relevant only insofar as it suggests that a low dose of midazolam may occasionally be toxic, see *ante*, at 27—an issue I discuss further below—Dr. Evans' testimony seems to have been based on the Web site www.drugs.com. The Court may be right that "petitioners do not identify any incorrect statements from drugs.com on which Dr. Evans relied." *Ante*, at 27. But that is because there were *no* statements from drugs.com that supported the critically disputed aspects of Dr. Evans' opinion. If anything, the Web site supported petitioners' contentions, as it expressly cautioned that midazolam "[s]hould not be used alone for maintenance of anesthesia," App. H to Pet. for Cert. 6159, and contained no warning that an excessive dose of midazolam could "paralyze the brain," see *id.*, at 6528–6529.

Most importantly, nothing from drugs.com—or, for that matter, any other source in the record—corroborated Dr. Evans' key testimony that midazolam's ceiling effect is limited to the spinal cord and does not pertain to the brain. Indeed, the State appears to have disavowed Dr. Evans' spinal-cord theory, refraining from even mentioning it in its brief despite the fact that the District Court expressly relied on this testimony as the basis for finding that larger doses of midazolam will have greater anesthetic effects. App. 78. The Court likewise assiduously avoids defending this theory.

. . .

In sum, then, Dr. Evans' conclusions were entirely unsupported by any study or third-party source, contradicted by the extrinsic evidence proffered by petitioners, inconsistent with the scientific understanding of midazolam's properties, and apparently premised on basic logical errors. Given these glaring flaws, the District Court's acceptance of Dr. Evans' claim that 500 milligrams of midazolam would "paralyz[e] the brain" cannot be credited. This is not a case "[w]here there are two permissible views of the evidence," and the District Court chose one; rather, it is one where the trial judge credited "one of two or more witnesses" even though that witness failed to tell "a coherent and facially plausible story that is not contradicted by extrinsic evidence." *Anderson* v. *Bessemer City*, 470 U. S. 564, 574–575 (1985). In other words, this is a case in which the District Court clearly erred. See *ibid.*

B

Setting aside the District Court's erroneous factual finding that 500 milligrams of midazolam will necessarily "paralyze the brain," the question is whether the Court is nevertheless correct to hold that petitioners failed to demonstrate that the use of midazolam poses an "objectively intolerable *risk*" of severe pain. See *Baze*, 553 U. S., at 50 (plurality opinion) (internal quotation marks omitted). I would hold that they made this showing. That is because, in stark contrast to Dr. Evans, petitioners' experts were able to point to objective evidence indicating that midazolam cannot serve as an effective anesthetic that "render[s] a person insensate to pain caused by the second and third [lethal injection] drugs." *Ante*, at 23.

As observed above, these experts cited multiple sources supporting the existence of midazolam's ceiling effect. That evidence alone provides ample reason to doubt midazolam's efficacy. Again, to prevail on their claim, petitioners need only establish an intolerable *risk* of pain, not a certainty. See *Baze*, 553 U. S., at 50. Here, the State is attempting to use midazolam to produce an effect the drug has never previously been demonstrated to produce, and despite studies indicating that at some point increasing the dose will not actually increase the drug's effect. The State is thus proceeding in the face of a very real risk that the drug will not work in the manner it claims.

Moreover, and perhaps more importantly, the record provides good reason to think this risk is substantial. The Court insists that petitioners failed to provide "probative evidence" as to whether "midazolam's ceiling effect occurs below the level of a 500-milligram dose and at a point at which the drug does not have the effect of rendering a person insensate to pain." *Ante*, at 23. It emphasizes that Dr. Lubarsky was unable to say "at what dose the ceiling effect occurs," and could only estimate that it was "'[p]robably after about . . . 40 to 50 milligrams.'" *Ante*, at 23 (quoting App. 225).

But the precise dose at which midazolam reaches its ceiling effect is irrelevant if there is no dose at which the drug can, in the Court's words, render a person "insensate to pain." *Ante*, at 23. On this critical point, Dr. Lubarsky was quite clear. He explained that the drug "does not work to produce" a "lack of consciousness as noxious stimuli are applied," and is "not sufficient to produce a surgical plane of anesthesia in human beings." App. 204. He also noted that "[t]he drug would never be used and has never been used as a sole anesthetic to give anesthesia during a surgery," *id.*, at 223, and asserted that "the drug was not approved by the FDA as a sole anesthetic because after the use of fairly large doses that were sufficient to reach the ceiling effect and produce induction of unconscious ness, the patients responded to the surgery," *id.*, at 219. Thus, Dr. Lubarsky may not have been able to identify whether this effect would be reached at 40, 50, or 60 milligrams or some higher threshold, but he could specify that at no level would midazolam reliably keep an inmate unconscious once the second and third drugs were delivered.

. . .

This evidence was alone sufficient, but if one wanted further support for these conclusions it was provided by the Lockett and Wood executions. The procedural flaws that marred the Lockett execution created the conditions for an unintended (and grotesque) experiment on midazolam's efficacy. Due to problems with the IV line, Lockett was not fully paralyzed after the second and third drugs were administered. He had, however, been administered more than enough midazolam to "render an average person unconscious," as the District Court found. App. 57. When Lockett awoke and began to write and speak, he demonstrated the critical difference between midazolam's ability to render an inmate unconscious and its ability to maintain the inmate in that state. The Court insists that Lockett's execution involved "only 100 milligrams of midazolam," *ante*, at 28, but as explained previously, more is not necessarily better given midazolam's ceiling effect.

The Wood execution is perhaps even more probative. Despite being given over 750 milligrams of midazolam, Wood gasped and snorted for nearly two hours. These reactions were, according to Dr. Lubarsky, inconsistent with Wood being fully anesthetized, App. 177–178, and belie the claim that a lesser dose of 500 milligrams would somehow suffice. The Court attempts to distinguish the Wood execution on the ground that the timing of Arizona's administration of midazolam was different. *Ante*, at 28. But as Dr. Lubarsky testified, it did not "matter" whether in Wood's execution the "midazolam was introduced all at once or over . . . multiple doses," because "[t]he drug has a sufficient half life that the effect is cumulative." App. 220; see also Saari 253 (midazolam's "elimination half-life ranges from 1.7 to 3.5 h[ours]"). Nor does the fact that Wood's dose of midazolam was paired with hydromorphone rather than a paralytic and potassium chromide, see *ante*, at 29, appear to have any relevance—other than that the use of this analgesic drug may have meant that Wood did not experience the same degree of searing pain that an inmate executed under Oklahoma's protocol may face.

. . .

C

The Court not only disregards this record evidence of midazolam's inadequacy, but also fails to fully appreciate the procedural posture in which this case arises. Petitioners have not been accorded a full hearing on the merits of their claim. They were granted only an abbreviated evidentiary proceeding that began less than three months after the State issued its amended execution protocol; they did not even have the opportunity to present rebuttal evidence after Dr. Evans testified. They sought a preliminary injunction, and thus were not required to prove their claim, but only to show that they were likely to succeed on the merits. See *Winter* v. *Natural Resources Defense Council, Inc.*, 555 U. S. 7, 20 (2008); *Hill* v. *McDonough*, 547 U. S. 573, 584 (2006).

. . .

III

The Court's determination that the use of midazolam poses no objectively intolerable risk of severe pain is factually wrong. The Court's conclusion that petitioners' challenge also fails because they identified no available alternative means by which the State may kill them is legally indefensible.

A

This Court has long recognized that certain methods of execution are categorically off-limits. The Court first confronted an Eighth Amendment challenge to a method of execution in *Wilkerson* v. *Utah*, 99 U. S. 130 (1879). Although *Wilkerson* approved the particular method at issue—the firing squad—it made clear that "public dissection," "burning alive," and other "punishments of torture . . . in the same line of unnecessary cruelty, are forbidden by [the Eighth A]mendment to the Constitution." *Id.*, at 135–136. Eleven years later, in rejecting a challenge to the first proposed use of the electric chair, the Court again reiterated that "if the punishment prescribed for an offense against the laws of the State were manifestly cruel and unusual, as burning at the stake, crucifixion, breaking on the wheel, or the like, it would be the duty of the courts to adjudge such penalties to be within the constitutional prohibition." *In re Kemmler*, 136 U. S. 436, 446 (1890).

In the more than a century since, the Members of this Court have often had cause to debate the full scope of the Eighth Amendment's prohibition of cruel and unusual punishment. See, *e.g.*, *Furman* v. *Georgia*, 408 U. S. 238 (1972). But there has been little dispute that it at the very least precludes the imposition of "barbarous physical punishments." *Rhodes* v. *Chapman*, 452 U. S. 337, 345 (1981); see, *e.g.*, *Solem* v. *Helm*, 463 U. S. 277, 284 (1983); *id.*, at 312–313 (Burger, C. J., dissenting); *Baze* 553 U. S., at 97–99 (THOMAS, J., concurring in judgment); *Harmelin* v. *Michigan*,

501 U. S. 957, 976 (1991) (opinion of SCALIA, J.). Nor has there been any question that the Amendment prohibits such "inherently barbaric punishments *under all circumstances*." *Graham* v. *Florida,* 560 U. S. 48, 59 (2010) (emphasis added). Simply stated, the "Eighth Amendment *categorically* prohibits the infliction of cruel and unusual punishments." *Penry* v. *Lynaugh,* 492 U. S. 302, 330 (1989) (emphasis added).

B

The Court today, however, would convert this categorical prohibition into a conditional one. A method of execution that is intolerably painful—even to the point of being the chemical equivalent of burning alive—will, the Court holds, be unconstitutional *if*, and only if, there is a "known and available alternative" method of execution. *Ante*, at 15. It deems *Baze* to foreclose any argument to the contrary. *Ante*, at 14.

Baze held no such thing. In the first place, the Court cites only the plurality opinion in *Baze* as support for its known-and-available-alternative requirement. See *ibid*. Even assuming that the *Baze* plurality set forth such a requirement—which it did not—none of the Members of the Court whose concurrences were necessary to sustain the *Baze* Court's judgment articulated a similar view. See 553 U. S., at 71–77, 87 (Stevens, J., concurring in judgment); *id.*, at 94, 99–107 (THOMAS, J., concurring in judgment); *id.*, at 107–108, 113 (BREYER, J., concurring in judgment). In general, "the holding of the Court may be viewed as that position taken by those Members who concurred in the judgments on the narrowest grounds." *Marks* v. *United States,* 430 U. S. 188, 193 (1977) (internal quotation marks omitted). And as the Court observes, *ante*, at 14, n. 2, the opinion of JUSTICE THOMAS, joined by JUSTICE SCALIA, took the broadest position with respect to the degree of intent that state officials must have in order to have violated the Eighth Amendment, concluding that only a method of execution deliberately designed to inflict pain, and not one simply designed with deliberate indifference to the risk of severe pain, would be unconstitutional. 553 U. S., at 94 (THOMAS, J., concurring in judgment). But this understanding of the Eighth Amendment's intent requirement is unrelated to, and thus not any broader or narrower than, the requirement the Court now divines from *Baze*. Because the position that a plaintiff challenging a method of execution under the Eighth Amendment must prove the availability of an alternative means of execution did not "represent the views of a majority of the Court," it was not the holding of the *Baze Court. CTS Corp.* v. *Dynamics Corp. of America,* 481 U. S. 69, 81 (1987).

In any event, even the *Baze* plurality opinion provides no support for the Court's proposition. To be sure, that opinion contains the following sentence: "[The condemned] must show that the risk is substantial when compared to the known and available alternatives." 553 U. S., at 61. But the meaning of that key sentence and the

limits of the requirement it imposed are made clear by the sentence directly preceding it: "A stay of execution may not be granted *on grounds such as those asserted here* unless the condemned prisoner establishes that the State's lethal injection protocol creates a demonstrated risk of severe pain." *Ibid.* (emphasis added). In *Baze,* the very premise of the petitioners' Eighth Amendment claim was that they had "identified a significant risk of harm [in Kentucky's protocol] that [could] be eliminated by adopting alternative procedures." *Id.*, at 51. Their basic theory was that even if the risk of pain was only, say, 25%, that risk would be objectively intolerable if there was an obvious alternative that would reduce the risk to 5%. See Brief for Petitioners in *Baze* v. *Rees,* O. T. 2007, No. 07–5439, p. 29 ("In view of the severity of the pain risked and the ease with which it could be avoided, Petitioners should not have been required to show a high likelihood that they would suffer such pain . . ."). Thus, the "grounds . . . asserted" for relief in *Baze* were that the State's protocol was intolerably risky given the alternative procedures the State could have employed.

Addressing this claim, the *Baze* plurality clarified that "a condemned prisoner cannot successfully challenge a State's method of execution merely by showing a slightly or marginally safer alternative," 553 U. S., at 51; instead, to succeed in a challenge of this type, the comparative risk must be "substantial," *id.*, at 61. Nowhere did the plurality suggest that *all* challenges to a State's method of execution would require this sort of comparative-risk analysis. Recognizing the relevance of available alternatives is not at all the same as concluding that their absence precludes a claimant from showing that a chosen method carries objectively intolerable risks. If, for example, prison officials chose a method of execution that has a 99% chance of causing lingering and excruciating pain, certainly that risk would be objectively intolerable whether or not the officials ignored other methods in making this choice. Irrespective of the existence of alternatives, there are some risks "so grave that it violates contemporary standards of decency to expose *anyone* unwillingly to" them. *Helling* v. *McKinney,* 509 U. S. 25, 36 (1993) (emphasis in original).

That the *Baze* plurality's statement regarding a condemned inmate's ability to point to an available alternative means of execution pertained only to challenges premised on the existence of such alternatives is further evidenced by the opinion's failure to distinguish or even mention the Court's unanimous decision in *Hill* v. *McDonough,* 547 U. S. 573. *Hill* held that a §1983 plaintiff challenging a State's method of execution need not "identif[y] an alternative, authorized method of execution." *Id.*, at 582. True, as the Court notes, *ante*, at 14–15, *Hill* did so in the context of addressing §1983's pleading standard, rejecting the proposed alternative-means requirement because the Court saw no basis for the "[i]mposition of heightened pleading requirements." 547 U. S., at 582. But that only confirms that the Court in *Hill* did not view the availability of an alternative means of execution as an element of an Eighth

Amendment claim: If it had, then requiring the plaintiff to plead this element would not have meant imposing a heightened standard at all, but rather would have been entirely consistent with "traditional pleading requirements." *Ibid.*; see *Ashcroft* v. *Iqbal,* 556 U. S. 662, 678 (2009). The *Baze* plurality opinion should not be understood to have so carelessly tossed aside *Hill*'s underlying premise less than two years later.

. . .

D

In concocting this additional requirement, the Court is motivated by a desire to preserve States' ability to conduct executions in the face of changing circumstances. See *ante,* at 4–6, 27–28. It is true, as the Court details, that States have faced "practical obstacle[s]" to obtaining lethal injection drugs since *Baze* was decided. *Ante,* at 4. One study concluded that recent years have seen States change their protocols "with a frequency that is unprecedented among execution methods in this country's history." Denno, Lethal Injection Chaos Post-*Baze,* 102 Geo. L. J. 1331, 1335 (2014).

But why such developments compel the Court's imposition of further burdens on those facing execution is a mystery. Petitioners here had no part in creating the shortage of execution drugs; it is odd to punish them for the actions of pharmaceutical companies and others who seek to disassociate themselves from the death penalty—actions which are, of course, wholly lawful. Nor, certainly, should these rapidly changing circumstances give us any greater confidence that the execution methods ultimately selected will be sufficiently humane to satisfy the Eighth Amendment. Quite the contrary. The execution protocols States hurriedly devise as they scramble to locate new and untested drugs, see *supra,* at 3, are all the more likely to be cruel and unusual—presumably, these drugs would have been the States' first choice were they in fact more effective. But see Denno, The Lethal Injection Quandry: How Medicine Has Dismantled the Death Penalty, 76 Ford. L. Rev. 49, 65–79 (2007) (describing the hurried and unreasoned process by which States first adopted the original three-drug protocol). Courts' review of execution methods should be more, not less, searching when States are engaged in what is in effect human experimentation.

It is also worth noting that some condemned inmates may read the Court's surreal requirement that they identify the means of their death as an invitation to propose methods of executions less consistent with modern sensibilities. Petitioners here failed to meet the Court's new test because of their assumption that the alternative drugs to which they pointed, pentobarbital and sodium thiopental, were available to the State. See *ante,* at 13–14. This was perhaps a reasonable assumption, especially given that neighboring Texas and Missouri still to this day continue to use

pentobarbital in executions. See The Death Penalty Institute, Execution List 2015, online at www.deathpenaltyinfo.org/execution-list-2015 (as visited June 26, 2015, and available in the Clerk of the Court's case file).

In the future, however, condemned inmates might well decline to accept States' current reliance on lethal injection. In particular, some inmates may suggest the firing squad as an alternative. Since the 1920's, only Utah has utilized this method of execution. See S. Banner, The Death Penalty 203 (2002); Johnson, Double Murderer Executed by Firing Squad in Utah, N. Y. Times, June 19, 2010, p. A12. But there is evidence to suggest that the firing squad is significantly more reliable than other methods, including lethal injection using the various combinations of drugs thus far developed. See A. Sarat, Gruesome Spectacles: Botched Executions and America's Death Penalty, App. A, p. 177 (2014) (calculating that while 7.12% of the 1,054 executions by lethal injection between 1900 and 2010 were "botched," none of the 34 executions by firing squad had been). Just as important, there is some reason to think that it is relatively quick and painless. See Banner, *supra,* at 203.

Certainly, use of the firing squad could be seen as a devolution to a more primitive era. See *Wood* v. *Ryan,* 759 F. 3d 1076, 1103 (CA9 2014) (Kozinski, C. J., dissenting from denial of rehearing en banc). That is not to say, of course, that it would therefore be unconstitutional. But lethal injection represents just the latest iteration of the States' centuries-long search for "neat and non-disfiguring homicidal methods." C. Brandon, The Electric Chair: An Unnatural American History 39 (1999) (quoting Editorial, New York Herald, Aug. 10, 1884); see generally Banner, *supra,* at 169–207. A return to the firing squad—and the blood and physical violence that comes with it—is a step in the opposite direction. And some might argue that the visible brutality of such a death could conceivably give rise to its own Eighth Amendment concerns. See *Campbell* v. *Wood,* 511 U. S. 1119, 1121–1123 (1994) (Blackmun, J., dissenting from denial of stay of execution and certiorari); *Glass* v. *Louisiana,* 471 U. S. 1080, 1085 (1985) (Brennan, J., dissenting from denial of certiorari). At least from a condemned inmate's perspective, however, such visible yet relatively painless violence may be vastly preferable to an excruciatingly painful death hidden behind a veneer of medication. The States may well be reluctant to pull back the curtain for fear of how the rest of us might react to what we see. But we deserve to know the price of our collective comfort before we blindly allow a State to make condemned inmates pay it in our names.

* * *

"By protecting even those convicted of heinous crimes, the Eighth Amendment reaffirms the duty of the government to respect the dignity of all persons." *Roper* v. *Simmons,* 543 U. S. 551, 560 (2005).

Today, however, the Court absolves the State of Oklahoma of this duty. It does so by misconstruing and ignoring the record evidence regarding the constitutional insufficiency of midazolam as a sedative in a three-drug lethal injection cocktail, and by imposing a wholly unprecedented obligation on the condemned inmate to identify an available means for his or her own execution. The contortions necessary to save this particular lethal injection protocol are not worth the price. I dissent.

Sonia Sotomayor is an associate justice of the United States Supreme Court. She was appointed in 2009 by President Barack Obama.

EXPLORING THE ISSUE

Is Lethal Injection as a Method of Execution Still Constitutional?

Critical Thinking and Reflection

1. Do you believe in capital punishment? Why or why not?
2. What purpose do you believe capital punishment serves?
3. Why do you believe some states have abandoned capital punishment?
4. What do you believe would happen if capital punishment was found to be unconstitutional?
5. Do you believe lethal injection is an improvement on previous methods of capital punishment? Why or why not?

Is There Common Ground?

When it comes to an issue like capital punishment, there is little room for common ground. Societally, we either accept the right of the state to take the life of an individual who has been convicted and sentenced by a jury of peers, or we do not. Capital punishment plays out like most moral-based issues with strong advocates on both sides and fewer individuals waffling between the two sides. One either believes the state possesses a right to end the life of another as punishment for the most severe crimes, or it does not. While we have seen middle ground reached on issues pertaining to what crimes should be capital punishment eligible, the use of capital punishment against juveniles and the mentally handicapped, and the appeal rights of inmates condemned to die, we have not been able to reach it on the issue at large.

Most importantly for the question at hand is the reality that today the method of execution is not as debated as the presence of capital punishment at all. In the past, America has witnessed debates over the "cruel and unusual" aspects of the electric chair, the gas chamber, hanging, firing squads, and hangings, but today even the most staunchly opposed to the death penalty is likely to agree that lethal injection is the most humane option—if we choose to execute at all.

Additional Resources

David M. Oshinsky, *Capital Punishment on Trial: Furman v. Georgia and the Death Penalty in Modern America* (University Press of Kansas, 2010)

Jon Sorensen and Rocky L-A. Pilgrim, *Lethal Injection: Capital Punishment in Texas during the Modern Era* (University of Texas, 2013)

Carol S. Steiker and Jordan M. Steiker, *Courting Death: The Supreme Court and Capital Punishment* (Belknap, 2016)

Internet References . . .

Capital Punishment

http://www.bjs.gov/index.cfm?ty=tp&tid=18

Lethal Injection

http://www.deathpenaltyinfo.org/lethal-injection

Lethal Injection

http://www.amnestyusa.org/our-work/issues/death-penalty/lethal-injection

Selected, Edited, and with Issue Framing Material by:
William J. Miller, *Flagler College*

ISSUE

Should Colleges and Universities Be Able to Consider an Applicant's Race When Deciding Whether to Accept a Student?

YES: Anthony Kennedy, from *"Fisher v. University of Texas at Austin," United States Supreme Court* (2015)

NO: Samuel Alito, from *"Fisher v. University of Texas at Austin," United States Supreme Court (2015)*

Learning Outcomes

After reading this issue, you will be able to:

- Explain the typical college admissions process.
- Describe why race may be considered in making college admissions decisions.
- Assess the costs and benefits of including race in college admissions decisions.
- Explain support and opposition for using race as a factor in college admissions decisions.
- Assess how colleges and universities will likely respond to recent court decisions.

ISSUE SUMMARY

YES: Justice Anthony Kennedy, writing for the court, articulates that colleges and universities should be able to consider race as part of an overarching goal of assuring diversity on campus. He further notes, however, that race should play no greater role than necessary to meet this goal.

NO: Justice Samuel Alito, in a dissenting opinion, notes that the diversity goals of the university were not clearly articulated and as such should not be enough to justify race-considered admissions. He argues that race should only be counted in the decision when the reason for doing so is candidly and persuasively stated.

In a number of recent incidents across the country—perhaps most prominently during protests at the University of Missouri—black students have expressed how they continue to experience hostility because of their skin color. These students have spoken of their feelings of isolation and disempowerment. These are two values higher education are not intending to promote. Instead, all colleges and universities urgently need policies to address these challenges. One such existing policy includes the Supreme Court-endorsed limited consideration of race in admission decisions. This policy allows institutions to build a racially and ethnically diverse student body, which helps assure the development of well-rounded individual graduates

In its 2015–2016 term, the Supreme Court considered the *Fisher v. University of Texas* case. This will be the second time the court rules on the constitutionality of a race-sensitive post-secondary

admissions policy at the University of Texas. In 2008, Abigail Fisher, a white female, applied to the University of Texas at Austin and was denied admission. She then sued the university on the grounds that the university's race-conscious admissions policy violated the equal protection clause of the Fourteenth Amendment. The case is now back before the Supreme Court.

In its earlier 2013 decision, the Supreme Court had sent the case back to the lower court to conduct a more rigorous assessment of whether UT-Austin needed to consider race in admissions to advance its interest in the educational benefits of diversity. The Supreme Court was concerned that the lower court's decision had relied primarily on the university's judgment, without conducting an independent review. After reconsidering the case, the Fifth Circuit ruled that the university's policy was necessary. Court rules, however, allow the parties to appeal the decision back to the

Supreme Court, which Fisher did. In June 2015, the Court agreed to hear the case for a second time, despite her having now graduated and earned a degree from another institution.

Individuals who favor admissions that assure increased diversity in higher education believe any efforts to limit the use of race in admissions can have harmful consequences for the diversity of the student body. Research focusing on the impacts of bans on race-sensitive admissions in the field of medicine found that following these bans, underrepresented students of color at public medical schools dropped from 18.5 percent to about 15.3 percent in examined states. While the drop may seem minor, before bans on affirmative action, for every 100 students matriculated in medical schools in states with bans, there were 18 students of color, whereas after the ban, for every 100 students matriculated, about 15 were students of color. In an era where diversity grew in the general population, medical schools were becoming more homogenous—and more white.

These declines in racial student body diversity can isolate and stigmatize students of color who are admitted and make it more difficult for institutions to create a welcoming campus environment for students of color. In addition to leading to less diversity in the student body, barring the consideration of race in admissions can prevent institutions from addressing the ways in which race shapes the educational experiences of all students. We might not think that admissions policies can have an influence on the work of administrators charged with supporting students of color once they are on campus, but findings from a more recent study suggest that the influence of these laws extend beyond the composition of the student body. Bans on affirmative action can have a detrimental influence on work that is critical to the success of students of color on campus.

Race influences thoughts and behavior of individuals of all races in subconscious ways—through implicit biases, such as attitudes toward particular social groups—and other psychological phenomena such as stereotype threat, classically manifested in high-stakes test performance, involving the threatening experience of conforming to negative race-based stereotypes present in the larger society. Because race often shapes attitudes and behaviors subconsciously, not paying attention to race in admissions can further harm race relations. At the same time, permitting its consideration can lead to social cohesion. Justice Anthony Kennedy, a decisive vote in the original Fisher case, has acknowledged in past decisions how much race continues to matter. This understanding, however, needs to reflect the ways in which race matters and also take into account the impact of the court's decisions in a post-Ferguson, post–University of Missouri society. Colleges and universities need all tools they can have at their disposal to improve race relations on their campuses.

While cultivating diversity can be seen as an important virtue in higher education, there remains the question of why lesser-qualified students might be admitted over more qualified students due to the color of their skin or their ethnic background. Some ask: but without affirmative action, wouldn't our universities become all white, thus shutting off upward mobility for blacks and other minority groups? That's the sky will fall argument, but it may not stand up. The use of racial admission quotas does not lead to an increase in the total number of minority students; it only leads to their redistribution. The most academically challenging schools, such as the University of Michigan, wind up with more minority students than they would if academic preparation were all that mattered, but if Michigan just admitted students based on merit, those who didn't make it into the flagship university in Ann Arbor would instead go to some other school, where they might be a better academic fit.

If one wants to look at strong arguments against race-based admissions, they can turn to *Brown v. Board of Education*, when Thurgood Marshall, then executive director of the Legal Defense Fund of the National Association for the Advancement of Colored People, wrote: "Distinctions by race are so evil, so arbitrary and invidious that a state, bound to defend the equal protection of the laws must not invoke them in any public sphere." The argument applies to our public universities with special force because here the habits of democracy are molded. But many universities now give very marked preference by race and seek to justify what they do by the quest for diversity.

A diverse student body is an appropriate goal for a university—but that goal, as Justice Lewis F. Powell said explicitly in his opinion in *University of California v. Bakke*, is intellectual diversity, diversity of judgment and viewpoint. When our universities announce that they are striving for diversity, we know that what they are really seeking to achieve is racial proportionality; they profess an intellectual objective, but their real goal is racial balance. This passion for racial balance "misconceives"—that is Justice Powell's word—the diversity that might serve educative ends. And however meritorious those educative ends, it is worth noting that they cannot possibly serve as the "compelling" objective that is required for the constitutional use of racial classifications by the state.

In the following selections, Justice Anthony Kennedy, writing for the court, articulates that colleges and universities should be able to consider race as part of an overarching goal of assuring diversity on campus. He further notes, however, that race should play no greater role than necessary to meet this goal. Justice Samuel Alito, in a dissenting opinion, notes that the diversity goals of the university were not clearly articulated and as such should not be enough to justify race-considered admissions. He argues that race should only be counted in the decision when the reason for doing so is candidly and persuasively stated.

YES ↵

Anthony Kennedy

Fisher v. University of Texas at Austin

JUSTICE KENNEDY delivered the opinion of the Court.

The Court is asked once again to consider whether the race-conscious admissions program at the University of Texas is lawful under the Equal Protection Clause.

I

The University of Texas at Austin (or University) relies upon a complex system of admissions that has undergone significant evolution over the past two decades. Until 1996, the University made its admissions decisions primarily based on a measure called "Academic Index" (or AI), which it calculated by combining an applicant's SAT score and academic performance in high school. In assessing applicants, preference was given to racial minorities.

In 1996, the Court of Appeals for the Fifth Circuit invalidated this admissions system, holding that any consideration of race in college admissions violates the Equal Protection Clause. See *Hopwood* v. *Texas*, 78 F. 3d 932, 934–935, 948.

One year later the University adopted a new admissions policy. Instead of considering race, the University began making admissions decisions based on an applicant's AI and his or her "Personal Achievement Index" (PAI). The PAI was a numerical score based on a holistic review of an application. Included in the number were the applicant's essays, leadership and work experience, extracurricular activities, community service, and other "special characteristics" that might give the admissions committee insight into a student's background. Consistent with *Hopwood*, race was not a consideration in calculating an applicant's AI or PAI.

The Texas Legislature responded to *Hopwood* as well. It enacted H. B. 588, commonly known as the Top Ten Percent Law. Tex. Educ. Code Ann. §51.803 (West Cum. Supp. 2015). As its name suggests, the Top Ten Percent Law guarantees college admission to students who graduate from a Texas high school in the top 10 percent of their class. Those students may choose to attend any of the public universities in the State.

The University implemented the Top Ten Percent Law in 1998. After first admitting any student who qualified for admission under that law, the University filled the remainder of its incoming freshman class using a combination of an applicant's AI and PAI scores—again, without considering race.

The University used this admissions system until 2003, when this Court decided the companion cases of *Grutter* v. *Bollinger*, 539 U. S. 306, and *Gratz* v. *Bollinger*, 539 U. S. 244. In *Gratz*, this Court struck down the University of Michigan's undergraduate system of admissions, which at the time allocated predetermined points to racial minority candidates. See 539 U. S., at 255, 275–276. In *Grutter*, however, the Court upheld the University of Michigan Law School's system of holistic review—a system that did not mechanically assign points but rather treated race as a relevant feature within the broader context of a candidate's application. See 539 U. S., at 337, 343–344. In upholding this nuanced use of race, *Grutter* implicitly overruled *Hopwood*'s categorical prohibition.

In the wake of *Grutter*, the University embarked upon a year-long study seeking to ascertain whether its admissions policy was allowing it to provide "the educational benefits of a diverse student body . . . to all of the University's undergraduate students." App. 481a–482a (affidavit of N. Bruce Walker ¶11 (Walker Aff.)); see also *id.*, at 445a–447a. The University concluded that its admissions policy was not providing these benefits. Supp. App. 24a–25a.

To change its system, the University submitted a proposal to the Board of Regents that requested permission to begin taking race into consideration as one of "the many ways in which [an] academically qualified individual might contribute to, and benefit from, the rich, diverse, and challenging educational environment of the University." *Id.*, at 23a. After the board approved the proposal, the University adopted a new admissions policy to implement it. The University has continued to use that admissions policy to this day.

Although the University's new admissions policy was a direct result of *Grutter*, it is not identical to the policy this Court approved in that case. Instead, consistent with the State's legislative directive, the University continues to fill a significant majority of its class through the Top Ten Percent Plan (or Plan). Today, up to 75 percent of the places in the freshman class are filled through the Plan. As a practical matter, this 75 percent cap, which has now been fixed by statute, means that, while the Plan continues to be referenced as a "Top Ten Percent Plan," a student actually needs to finish in the top seven or eight percent of his or her class in order to be admitted under this category.

The University did adopt an approach similar to the one in *Grutter* for the remaining 25 percent or so of the incoming class. This portion of the class continues to be admitted based on a combination of their AI and PAI scores. Now, however, race is given weight as a subfactor within the PAI. The PAI is a number from 1 to 6 (6 is the best) that is based on two primary components. The first component is the average score a reader gives the applicant on two required essays. The second component is a full-file review that results in another 1-to-6 score, the "Personal Achievement Score" or PAS. The PAS is determined by a separate reader, who (1) rereads the applicant's required essays, (2) reviews any supplemental information the applicant submits (letters of recommendation, resumes, an additional optional essay, writing samples, artwork, etc.), and (3) evaluates the applicant's potential contributions to the University's student body based on the applicant's leadership experience, extracurricular activities, awards/honors, community service, and other "special circumstances."

"Special circumstances" include the socioeconomic status of the applicant's family, the socioeconomic status of the applicant's school, the applicant's family responsibilities, whether the applicant lives in a single-parent home, the applicant's SAT score in relation to the average SAT score at the applicant's school, the language spoken at the applicant's home, and, finally, the applicant's race. See App. 218a–220a, 430a.

Both the essay readers and the full-file readers who assign applicants their PAI undergo extensive training to ensure that they are scoring applicants consistently. Deposition of Brian Breman 9–14, Record in No. 1: 08–CV–00263, (WD Tex.), Doc. 96–3. The Admissions Office also undertakes regular "reliability analyses" to "measure the frequency of readers scoring within one point of each other." App. 474a (affidavit of Gary M. Lavergne ¶ 8); see also *id.,* at 253a (deposition of Kedra Ishop (Ishop Dep.)). Both the intensive training and the reliability analyses aim to ensure that similarly situated applicants are being treated identically regardless of which admissions officer reads the file.

Once the essay and full-file readers have calculated each applicant's AI and PAI scores, admissions officers from each school within the University set a cutoff PAI/AI score combination for admission, and then admit all of the applicants who are above that cutoff point. In setting the cutoff, those admissions officers only know how many applicants received a given PAI/AI score combination. They do not know what factors went into calculating those applicants' scores. The admissions officers who make the final decision as to whether a particular applicant will be admitted make that decision without knowing the applicant's race. Race enters the admissions process, then, at one stage and one stage only—the calculation of the PAS.

Therefore, although admissions officers can consider race as a positive feature of a minority student's application, there is no dispute that race is but a "factor of a factor of a factor" in the holistic-review calculus. 645 F. Supp. 2d 587, 608 (WD Tex. 2009). Furthermore, consideration of race is contextual and does not operate as a mechanical plus factor for underrepresented minorities. *Id.,* at 606 ("Plaintiffs cite no evidence to show racial groups other than African-Americans

and Hispanics are *excluded* from benefitting from UT's consideration of race in admissions. As the Defendants point out, the consideration of race, within the full context of the entire application, may be beneficial to any UT Austin applicant—including whites and Asian-Americans"); see also Brief for Asian American Legal Defense and Education Fund et al. as *Amici Curiae* 12 (the contention that the University discriminates against Asian-Americans is "entirely unsupported by evidence in the record or empirical data"). There is also no dispute, however, that race, when considered in conjunction with other aspects of an applicant's background, can alter an applicant's PAS score. Thus, race, in this indirect fashion, considered with all of the other factors that make up an applicant's AI and PAI scores, can make a difference to whether an application is accepted or rejected.

Petitioner Abigail Fisher applied for admission to the University's 2008 freshman class. She was not in the top 10 percent of her high school class, so she was evaluated for admission through holistic, full-file review. Petitioner's application was rejected.

Petitioner then filed suit alleging that the University's consideration of race as part of its holistic-review process disadvantaged her and other Caucasian applicants, in violation of the Equal Protection Clause. See U. S. Const., Amdt. 14, §1 (no State shall "deny to any person within its jurisdiction the equal protection of the laws"). The District Court entered summary judgment in the University's favor, and the Court of Appeals affirmed.

This Court granted certiorari and vacated the judgment of the Court of Appeals, *Fisher v. University of Tex. At Austin,* 570 U. S.___ (2013) (*Fisher I*), because it had applied an overly deferential "good-faith" standard in assessing the constitutionality of the University's program. The Court remanded the case for the Court of Appeals to assess the parties' claims under the correct legal standard.

Without further remanding to the District Court, the Court of Appeals again affirmed the entry of summary judgment in the University's favor. 758 F. 3d 633 (CA5 2014). This Court granted certiorari for a second time, 576 U. S.___(2015), and now affirms.

II

Fisher I set forth three controlling principles relevant to assessing the constitutionality of a public university's affirmative-action program. First, "because racial characteristics so seldom provide a relevant basis for disparate treatment," *Richmond* v. *J. A. Croson Co.,* 488 U. S. 469, 505 (1989), "[r]ace may not be considered [by a university] unless the admissions process can withstand strict scrutiny," *Fisher I*, 570 U. S., at___(slip op., at 7). Strict scrutiny requires the university to demonstrate with clarity that its "'purpose or interest is both constitutionally permissible and substantial, and that its use of the classification is necessary . . . to the accomplishment of its purpose.'" *Ibid.*

Second, *Fisher I* confirmed that "the decision to pursue 'the educational benefits that flow from student body diversity' . . . is, in substantial measure, an academic judgment to which some, but not complete, judicial deference is proper." *Id.*, at___(slip op, at 9). A university cannot impose a fixed quota or otherwise "define diversity as 'some specified percentage of a particular group merely because of its race or ethnic origin.'" *Ibid.* Once, however, a university gives "a reasoned, principled explanation" for its decision, deference must be given "to the University's conclusion, based on its experience and expertise, that a diverse student body would serve its educational goals." *Ibid.* (internal quotation marks and citation omitted).

Third, *Fisher I* clarified that no deference is owed when determining whether the use of race is narrowly tailored to achieve the university's permissible goals. *Id.*, at___(slip op., at 10). A university, *Fisher I* explained, bears the burden of proving a "nonracial approach" would not promote its interest in the educational benefits of diversity "about as well and at tolerable administrative expense." *Id.*, at___(slip op., at 11) (internal quotation marks omitted). Though "[n]arrow tailoring does not require exhaustion of every conceivable race-neutral alternative" or "require a university to choose between maintaining a reputation for excellence [and] fulfilling a commitment to provide educational opportunities to members of all racial groups," *Grutter*, 539 U. S., at 339, it does impose "on the university the ultimate burden of demonstrating" that "race-neutral alternatives" that are both "available" and "workable" "do not suffice." *Fisher I*, 570 U. S., at___(slip op., at 11).

Fisher I set forth these controlling principles, while taking no position on the constitutionality of the admissions program at issue in this case. The Court held only that the District Court and the Court of Appeals had "confined the strict scrutiny inquiry in too narrow a way by deferring to the University's good faith in its use of racial classifications." *Id.,* at___(slip op., at 12) The Court remanded the case, with instructions to evaluate the record under the correct standard and to determine whether the University had made "a showing that its plan is narrowly tailored to achieve" the educational benefits that flow from diversity. *Id.,* at___ (slip op., at 13). On remand, the Court of Appeals determined that the program conformed with the strict scrutiny mandated by *Fisher I*. See 758 F. 3d, at 659–660. Judge Garza dissented.

III

The University's program is *sui generis*. Unlike other approaches to college admissions considered by this Court, it combines holistic review with a percentage plan. This approach gave rise to an unusual consequence in this case: The component of the University's admissions policy that had the largest impact on petitioner's chances of admission was not the school's consideration of race under its holistic-review process but rather the Top Ten Percent Plan. Because petitioner did not graduate in the top 10 percent of her high school class, she was categorically ineligible for more than three-fourths of the slots in the incoming freshman class. It seems quite plausible, then, to think that petitioner would have had a better chance of being admitted to the University if the school used race-conscious holistic review to select its entire incoming class, as was the case in *Grutter*.

Despite the Top Ten Percent Plan's outsized effect on petitioner's chances of admission, she has not challenged it. For that reason, throughout this litigation, the Top Ten Percent Plan has been taken, somewhat artificially, as a given premise.

Petitioner's acceptance of the Top Ten Percent Plan complicates this Court's review. In particular, it has led to a record that is almost devoid of information about the students who secured admission to the University through the Plan. The Court thus cannot know how students admitted solely based on their class rank differ in their contribution to diversity from students admitted through holistic review.

In an ordinary case, this evidentiary gap perhaps could be filled by a remand to the district court for further fact finding. When petitioner's application was rejected, however, the University's combined percentage-plan/holistic review approach to admission had been in effect for just three years. While studies undertaken over the eight years since then may be of significant value in determining the constitutionality of the University's current admissions policy, that evidence has little bearing on whether petitioner received equal treatment when her application was rejected in 2008. If the Court were to remand, therefore, further fact finding would be limited to a narrow 3-year sample, review of which might yield little insight.

Furthermore, as discussed above, the University lacks any authority to alter the role of the Top Ten Percent Plan in its admissions process. The Plan was mandated by the Texas Legislature in the wake of *Hopwood*, so the University, like petitioner in this litigation, has likely taken the Plan as a given since its implementation in 1998. If the University had no reason to think that it could deviate from the Top Ten Percent Plan, it similarly had no reason to keep extensive data on the Plan or the students admitted under it—particularly in the years before *Fisher I* clarified the stringency of the strict-scrutiny burden for a school that employs race-conscious review.

Under the circumstances of this case, then, a remand would do nothing more than prolong a suit that has already persisted for eight years and cost the parties on both sides significant resources. Petitioner long since has graduated from another college, and the University's policy—and the data on which it first was based—may have evolved or changed in material ways.

The fact that this case has been litigated on a somewhat artificial basis, furthermore, may limit its value for prospective guidance. The Texas Legislature, in enacting the Top Ten Percent Plan, cannot much be criticized, for it was responding to *Hopwood*, which at the time was binding law in the State of Texas. That legislative response, in turn, circumscribed the University's discretion in crafting its admissions policy. These circumstances refute any criticism that the University did not make good-faith efforts to comply with the law.

That does not diminish, however, the University's continuing obligation to satisfy the burden of strict scrutiny in light of changing circumstances. The University engages in periodic reassessment of the constitutionality, and efficacy, of its admissions program. See Supp. App. 32a; App. 448a. Going forward, that assessment must be undertaken in light of the experience the school has accumulated and the data it has gathered since the adoption of its admissions plan.

As the University examines this data, it should remain mindful that diversity takes many forms. Formalistic racial classifications may sometimes fail to capture diversity in all of its dimensions and, when used in a divisive manner, could undermine the educational benefits the University values. Through regular evaluation of data and consideration of student experience, the University must tailor its approach in light of changing circumstances, ensuring that race plays no greater role than is necessary to meet its compelling interest. The University's examination of the data it has acquired in the years since petitioner's application, for these reasons, must proceed with full respect for the constraints imposed by the Equal Protection Clause. The type of data collected, and the manner in which it is considered, will have a significant bearing on how the University must shape its admissions policy to satisfy strict scrutiny in the years to come. Here, however, the Court is necessarily limited to the narrow question before it: whether, drawing all reasonable inferences in her favor, petitioner has shown by a preponderance of the evidence that she was denied equal treatment at the time her application was rejected.

IV

In seeking to reverse the judgment of the Court of Appeals, petitioner makes four arguments. First, she argues that the University has not articulated its compelling interest with sufficient clarity. According to petitioner, the University must set forth more precisely the level of minority enrollment that would constitute a "critical mass." Without a clearer sense of what the University's ultimate goal is, petitioner argues, a reviewing court cannot assess whether the University's admissions program is narrowly tailored to that goal.

As this Court's cases have made clear, however, the compelling interest that justifies consideration of race in college admissions is not an interest in enrolling a certain number of minority students. Rather, a university may institute a race-conscious admissions program as a means of obtaining "the educational benefits that flow from student body diversity." *Fisher I*, 570 U. S., at—(slip op., at 9) (internal quotation marks omitted); see also *Grutter*, 539 U. S., at 328. As this Court has said, enrolling a diverse student body "promotes cross-racial understanding, helps to break down racial stereotypes, and enables students to better understand persons of different races." *Id.*, at 330 (internal quotation marks and alteration omit ted). Equally important, "student body diversity promotes learning outcomes, and better prepares students for an increasingly diverse workforce and society." *Ibid.* (internal quotation marks omitted).

Increasing minority enrollment may be instrumental to these educational benefits, but it is not, as petitioner seems to suggest, a goal that can or should be reduced to pure numbers. Indeed, since the University is prohibited from seeking a particular number or quota of minority students, it cannot be faulted for failing to specify the particular level of minority enrollment at which it believes the educational benefits of diversity will be obtained.

. . .

The University has provided in addition a "reasoned, principled explanation" for its decision to pursue these goals. *Fisher I, supra,* at__(slip op., at 9). The University's 39-page proposal was written following a year-long study, which concluded that "[t]he use of race-neutral policies and programs ha[d] not been successful" in "provid[ing] an educational setting that fosters cross-racial understanding, provid[ing] enlightened discussion and learning, [or] prepar[ing] students to function in an increasingly diverse workforce and society." Supp. App. 25a; see also App. 481a–482a (Walker Aff. ¶¶8–12) (describing the "thoughtful review" the University undertook when it faced the "important decision . . . whether or not to use race in its admissions process"). Further support for the University's conclusion can be found in the depositions and affidavits from various admissions officers, all of whom articulate the same, consistent "reasoned, principled explanation." See, *e.g., id.,* at 253a (Ishop Dep.), 314a–318a, 359a (Walker Dep.), 415a–416a (Defendant's Statement of Facts), 478a–479a, 481a–482a (Walker Aff. ¶¶4, 10–13). Petitioner's contention that the University's goal was insufficiently concrete is rebutted by the record.

Second, petitioner argues that the University has no need to consider race because it had already "achieved critical mass" by 2003 using the Top Ten Percent Plan and race-neutral holistic review. Brief for Petitioner 46. Petitioner is correct that a university bears a heavy burden in showing that it had not obtained the educational benefits of diversity before it turned to a race-conscious plan. The record reveals, however, that, at the time of petitioner's application, the University could not be faulted on this score. Before changing its policy the University conducted "months of study and deliberation, including retreats, interviews, [and] review of data," App. 446a, and concluded that "[t]he use of race-neutral policies and programs ha[d] not been successful in achieving" sufficient racial diversity at the University, Supp. App. 25a. At no stage in this litigation has petitioner challenged the University's good faith in conducting its studies, and the Court properly declines to consider the extrarecord materials the dissent relies upon, many of which are tangential to this case at best and none of which the University has had a full opportunity to respond to. See, *e.g., post,* at 45–46 (opinion of ALITO, J.) (describing a 2015 report regarding the admission of applicants who are related to "politically connected individuals").

The record itself contains significant evidence, both statistical and anecdotal, in support of the University's position. To start, the demographic data the University has submitted show consistent stagnation in terms of the percentage of minority students enrolling at the University from 1996 to 2002. In 1996, for example, 266 African-American freshmen enrolled, a total that constituted 4.1 percent of the incoming class. In 2003, the year *Grutter* was decided, 267 African-American students enrolled—again, 4.1 percent of the incoming class. The numbers for Hispanic and Asian-American students tell a similar story. See Supp. App. 43a. Although demographics alone are by no means dispositive, they do have some value as a gauge of the University's ability to enroll students who can offer underrepresented perspectives.

. . .

Third, petitioner argues that considering race was not necessary because such consideration has had only a "'minimal impact' in advancing the [University's] compelling interest." Brief for Petitioner 46; see also Tr. of Oral Arg. 23:10–12; 24:13–25:2, 25:24–26:3. Again, the record does not support this assertion. In 2003, 11 percent of the Texas residents enrolled through holistic review were Hispanic and 3.5 percent were African-American. Supp. App. 157a. In 2007, by contrast, 16.9 percent of the Texas holistic-review freshmen were Hispanic and 6.8 percent were African-American. *Ibid.* Those increases—of 54 percent and 94 percent, respectively—show that consideration of race has had a meaningful, if still limited, effect on the diversity of the University's freshman class.

In any event, it is not a failure of narrow tailoring for the impact of racial consideration to be minor. The fact that race consciousness played a role in only a small portion of admissions decisions should be a hallmark of narrow tailoring, not evidence of unconstitutionality.

Petitioner's final argument is that "there are numerous other available race-neutral means of achieving" the University's compelling interest. Brief for Petitioner 47. A review of the record reveals, however, that, at the time of petitioner's application, none of her proposed alternatives was a workable means for the University to attain the benefits of diversity it sought. For example, petitioner suggests that the University could intensify its outreach efforts to African-American and Hispanic applicants. But the University submitted extensive evidence of the many ways in which it already had intensified its outreach efforts to those students. The University has created three new scholarship programs, opened new regional admissions centers, increased its recruitment budget by half-a-million dollars, and organized over 1,000 recruitment events. Supp. App. 29a–32a; App. 450a–452a (citing affidavit of Michael Orr ¶¶ 4–20). Perhaps more significantly, in the wake of *Hopwood*, the University spent seven years attempting to achieve its compelling interest using race-neutral holistic review. None of these efforts succeeded, and petitioner fails to offer any meaningful way in which the University could have improved upon them at the time of her application.

. . .

For all these reasons, although it may be true that the Top Ten Percent Plan in some instances may provide a path out of poverty for those who excel at schools lacking in resources, the Plan cannot serve as the admissions solution that petitioner suggests. Wherever the balance between percentage plans and holistic review should rest, an effective admissions policy cannot prescribe, realistically, the exclusive use of a percentage plan.

In short, none of petitioner's suggested alternatives—nor other proposals considered or discussed in the course of this litigation—have been shown to be "available" and "workable" means through which the University could have met its educational goals, as it understood and defined them in 2008. *Fisher I, supra*, at __(slip op., at 11). The University has thus met its burden of showing that the admissions policy it used at the time it rejected petitioner's application was narrowly tailored.

* * *

A university is in large part defined by those intangible "qualities which are incapable of objective measurement but which make for greatness." *Sweatt* v. *Painter*, 339 U. S. 629, 634 (1950). Considerable deference is owed to a university in defining those intangible characteristics, like student body diversity, that are central to its identity and educational mission. But still, it remains an enduring challenge to our Nation's education system to reconcile the pursuit of diversity with the constitutional promise of equal treatment and dignity.

In striking this sensitive balance, public universities, like the States themselves, can serve as "laboratories for experimentation." *United States* v. *Lopez*, 514 U. S. 549, 581 (1995) (KENNEDY, J., concurring); see also *New State Ice Co.* v. *Liebmann*, 285 U. S. 262, 311 (1932) (Brandeis, J., dissenting). The University of Texas at Austin has a special opportunity to learn and to teach. The University now has at its disposal valuable data about the manner in which different approaches to admissions may foster diversity or instead dilute it. The University must continue to use this data to scrutinize the fairness of its admissions program; to assess whether changing demographics have undermined the need for a race-conscious policy; and to identify the effects, both positive and negative, of the affirmative-action measures it deems necessary.

The Court's affirmance of the University's admissions policy today does not necessarily mean the University may rely on that same policy without refinement. It is the University's ongoing obligation to engage in constant deliberation and continued reflection regarding its admissions policies.

The judgment of the Court of Appeals is affirmed.

It is so ordered.

ANTHONY KENNEDY is an associate justice of the United States Supreme Court. He was appointed in 1988 by President Ronald Reagan.

Samuel Alito

 **NO**

Fisher v. University of Texas at Austin

JUSTICE ALITO, with whom THE CHIEF JUSTICE and JUSTICE THOMAS join, dissenting.

Something strange has happened since our prior decision in this case. See *Fisher* v. *University of Tex. at Austin*, 570 U.S.__ (2013) (*Fisher I*). In that decision, we held that strict scrutiny requires the University of Texas at Austin (UT or University) to show that its use of race and ethnicity in making admissions decisions serves compelling interests and that its plan is narrowly tailored to achieve those ends. Rejecting the argument that we should defer to UT's judgment on those matters, we made it clear that UT was obligated (1) to identify the interests justifying its plan with enough specificity to permit a reviewing court to determine whether the requirements of strict scrutiny were met, and (2) to show that those requirements were in fact satisfied. On remand, UT failed to do what our prior decision demanded. The University has still not identified with any degree of specificity the interests that its use of race and ethnicity is supposed to serve. Its primary argument is that merely invoking "the educational benefits of diversity" is sufficient and that it need not identify any metric that would allow a court to determine whether its plan is needed to serve, or is actually serving, those interests. This is nothing less than the plea for deference that we emphatically rejected in our prior decision. Today, however, the Court inexplicably grants that request.

To the extent that UT has ever moved beyond a plea for deference and identified the relevant interests in more specific terms, its efforts have been shifting, unpersuasive, and, at times, less than candid. When it adopted its race-based plan, UT said that the plan was needed to promote classroom diversity. See Supp. App. 1a, 24a–25a, 39a; App. 316a. It pointed to a study showing that African-American, Hispanic, and Asian-American students were underrepresented in many classes. See Supp. App. 26a. But UT has never shown that its race-conscious plan actually ameliorates this situation. The University presents no evidence that its admissions officers, in administering the "holistic" component of its plan, make any effort to determine whether an African-American, Hispanic, or Asian-American student is likely to enroll in classes in which minority students are underrepresented. And although UT's records should permit it to determine without much difficulty whether holistic admittees are any more likely than students admitted through the Top Ten Percent Law, Tex. Educ. Code Ann. §51.803 (West Cum. Supp. 2015), to enroll in the classes lacking racial or ethnic diversity, UT either has not crunched those numbers or has not revealed what they show. Nor has UT explained why the underrepresentation of Asian-American students in many classes justifies its plan, which discriminates *against* those students.

At times, UT has claimed that its plan is needed to achieve a "critical mass" of African-American and Hispanic students, but it has never explained what this term means. According to UT, a critical mass is neither some absolute number of African-American or Hispanic students nor the percentage of African-Americans or Hispanics in the general population of the State. The term remains undefined, but UT tells us that it will let the courts know when the desired end has been achieved. See App. 314a–315a. This is a plea for deference—indeed, for blind deference—the very thing that the Court rejected in *Fisher I*.

UT has also claimed at times that the race-based component of its plan is needed because the Top Ten Percent Plan admits *the wrong kind* of African-American and Hispanic students, namely, students from poor families who attend schools in which the student body is predominantly African-American or Hispanic. As UT put it in its brief in *Fisher I*, the race-based component of its admissions plan is needed to admit "[t]he African-American or Hispanic child of successful professionals in Dallas." Brief for Respondents, O. T. 2012, No. 11–345, p. 34.

After making this argument in its first trip to this Court, UT apparently had second thoughts, and in the latest round of briefing UT has attempted to disavow ever having made the argument. See Brief for Respondents 2 ("Petitioner's argument that UT's interest is favoring 'affluent' minorities is a fabrication"); see also *id.*, at 15. But it did, and the argument turns affirmative action on its head. Affirmative-action programs were created to help *disadvantaged* students.

Although UT now disowns the argument that the Top Ten Percent Plan results in the admission of the wrong kind of African-American and Hispanic students, the Fifth Circuit majority bought a version of that claim. As the panel majority put it, the Top Ten African-American and Hispanic admittees cannot match the holistic African-American and Hispanic admittees when it comes to "records of personal achievement," a "variety of perspectives" and "life experiences," and "unique skills." 758 F. 3d 633, 653 (2014). All in all, according to the panel majority, the Top

Ten Percent students cannot "enrich the diversity of the student body" in the same way as the holistic admittees. *Id.,* at 654. As Judge Garza put it in dissent, the panel majority concluded that the Top Ten Percent admittees are "somehow more homogenous, less dynamic, and more undesirably stereotypical than those admitted under holistic review." *Id.,* at 669–670 (Garza, J., dissenting).

The Fifth Circuit reached this conclusion with little direct evidence regarding the characteristics of the Top Ten Percent and holistic admittees. Instead, the assumption behind the Fifth Circuit's reasoning is that most of the African-American and Hispanic students admitted under the race-neutral component of UT's plan were able to rank in the top decile of their high school classes only because they did not have to compete against white and Asian-American students. This insulting stereotype is not supported by the record. African-American and Hispanic students admitted under the Top Ten Percent Plan receive higher college grades than the African-American and Hispanic students admitted under the race-conscious program. See Supp. App. 164a–165a.

It should not have been necessary for us to grant review a second time in this case, and I have no greater desire than the majority to see the case drag on. But that need not happen. When UT decided to adopt its race-conscious plan, it had every reason to know that its plan would have to satisfy strict scrutiny and that this meant that it would be *its burden* to show that the plan was narrowly tailored to serve compelling interests. UT has failed to make that showing. By all rights, judgment should be entered in favor of petitioner.

But if the majority is determined to give UT yet another chance, we should reverse and send this case back to the District Court. What the majority has now done—awarding a victory to UT in an opinion that fails to address the important issues in the case—is simply wrong.

. . .

II

UT's race-conscious admissions program cannot satisfy strict scrutiny. UT says that the program furthers its interest in the educational benefits of diversity, but it has failed to define that interest with any clarity or to demonstrate that its program is narrowly tailored to achieve that or any other particular interest. By accepting UT's rationales as sufficient to meet its burden, the majority licenses UT's perverse assumptions about different groups of minority students—the precise assumptions strict scrutiny is supposed to stamp out.

A

"The moral imperative of racial neutrality is the driving force of the Equal Protection Clause." *Richmond* v. *J. A. Croson Co.,* 488 U.S. 469, 518 (1989) (KENNEDY, J., concurring in part and concurring in judgment). "At the heart of the Constitution's guarantee of equal protection lies the simple command that the Government must treat citizens as individuals, not as simply components of a racial, religious, sexual or national class." *Miller* v. *Johnson,* 515 U.S. 900, 911 (1995) (internal quotation marks omitted). "Race-based assignments embody stereotypes that treat individuals as the product of their race, evaluating their thoughts and efforts—their very worth as citizens—according to a criterion barred to the Government by history and the Constitution." *Id.,* at 912 (internal quotation marks omitted). Given our constitutional commitment to "the doctrine of equality," "'[d]istinctions between citizens solely because of their ancestry are by their very nature odious to a free people.'" *Rice* v. *Cayetano,* 528 U.S. 495, 517 (2000) (quoting *Hirabayashi* v. *United States,* 320 U.S. 81, 100 (1943)).

"[B]ecause racial characteristics so seldom provide a relevant basis for disparate treatment, the Equal Protection Clause demands that racial classifications . . . be subjected to the most rigid scrutiny." *Fisher I,* 570 U.S., at___(slip op., at 8) (internal quotation marks and citations omitted). "[J]udicial review must begin from the position that 'any official action that treats a person differently on account of his race or ethnic origin is inherently suspect.'" *Ibid.*; see also *Grutter,* 539 U.S., at 388 (KENNEDY, J., dissenting) ("'Racial and ethnic distinctions of any sort are inherently suspect and thus call for the most exacting judicial examination'"). Under strict scrutiny, the use of race must be "necessary to further a compelling governmental interest," and the means employed must be "'specifically and narrowly'" tailored to accomplish the compelling interest. *Id.,* at 327, 333 (O'Connor, J., for the Court).

The "higher education dynamic does not change" this standard. *Fisher I, supra,* at___ (slip op., at 12). "Racial discrimination [is] invidious in all contexts," *Edmonson* v. *Leesville Concrete Co.,* 500 U.S. 614, 619 (1991), and "'[t]he analysis and level of scrutiny applied to determine the validity of [a racial] classification do not vary simply because the objective appears acceptable,'" *Fisher I, supra,* at___(slip op., at 12).

Nor does the standard of review "'depen[d] on the race of those burdened or benefited by a particular classification.'" *Gratz* v. *Bollinger,* 539 U.S. 244, 270 (2003) (quoting *Adarand Constructors, Inc.* v. *Peña,* 515 U.S. 200, 224 (1995)); see also *Miller, supra,* at 904 ("This rule obtains with equal force regardless of 'the race of those burdened or benefited by a particular classification'" (quoting *Croson, supra,* at 494 (plurality opinion of O'Connor, J.)). "Thus, 'any person, of whatever race, has the right to demand that any governmental actor subject to the Constitution justify any racial classification subjecting that person to unequal treatment under the strictest of judicial scrutiny.'" *Gratz, supra,* at 270 (quoting *Adarand, supra,* at 224).

In short, in "all contexts," *Edmonson, supra,* at 619, racial classifications are permitted only "as a last resort," when all else has failed, *Croson, supra,* at 519 (opinion of KENNEDY, J.). "Strict scrutiny is a searching examination, and it is the government that bears the burden" of proof. *Fisher I*, 570 U.S., at___(slip op., at 8).To meet this burden, the government must "demonstrate *with clarity* that its 'purpose or interest is both constitutionally permissible and substantial, and that its use of the classification is necessary . . . to the accomplishment of its purpose.'" *Id.,* at___ (slip op., at 7) (emphasis added).

B

Here, UT has failed to define its interest in using racial preferences with clarity. As a result, the narrow tailoring inquiry is impossible, and UT cannot satisfy strict scrutiny.

When UT adopted its challenged policy, it characterized its compelling interest as obtaining a "'critical mass'" of underrepresented minorities. *Id.,* at___(slip op., at 1). The 2004 Proposal claimed that "[t]he use of race-neutral policies and programs has not been successful in achieving a critical mass of racial diversity." Supp. App. 25a; see *Fisher* v. *University of Tex. at Austin*, 631 F. 3d 213, 226 (CA5 2011) ("[T]he *2004 Proposal* explained that UT had not yet achieved the critical mass of underrepresented minority students needed to obtain the full educational benefits of diversity"). But to this day, UT has not explained in anything other than the vaguest terms what it means by "critical mass." In fact, UT argues that it need not identify *any* interest more specific than "securing the educational benefits of diversity." Brief for Respondents 15.

UT has insisted that critical mass is not an absolute number. See Tr. of Oral Arg. 39 (Oct. 10, 2012) (declaring that UT is not working toward any particular number of African-American or Hispanic students); App. 315a (confirming that UT has not defined critical mass as a number and has not projected when it will attain critical mass). Instead, UT prefers a deliberately malleable "we'll know it when we see it" notion of critical mass. It defines "critical mass" as "an adequate representation of minority students so that the . . . educational benefits that can be derived from diversity can actually happen," and it declares that it "will . . . know [that] it has reached critical mass" when it "see[s] the educational benefits happening." *Id.,* at 314a–315a. In other words: Trust us.

This intentionally imprecise interest is designed to insulate UT's program from meaningful judicial review. As Judge Garza explained:

"[T]o meet its narrow tailoring burden, the University must explain its goal to us in some meaningful way. We cannot undertake a rigorous ends-to-means narrow tailoring analysis when the University will not define the ends. We cannot tell whether the admissions program closely 'fits' the University's goal when it fails to objectively articulate its goal. Nor can we determine whether considering race is necessary for the University to achieve 'critical mass,' or whether there are effective race-neutral alternatives, when it has not described

what 'critical mass' requires." 758 F. 3d, at 667 (dissenting opinion).

Indeed, without knowing in reasonably specific terms what critical mass is or how it can be measured, a reviewing court cannot conduct the requisite "careful judicial inquiry" into whether the use of race was "'necessary.'" *Fisher I*, *supra*, at___(slip op., at 10).

To be sure, I agree with the majority that our precedents do not require UT to pinpoint "an interest in enrolling a certain number of minority students." *Ante*, at 11. But in order for us to assess whether UT's program is narrowly tailored, the University must identify *some sort of concrete interest*. "Classifying and assigning" students according to race "requires more than . . . an amorphous end to justify it." *Parents Involved in Community Schools* v. *Seattle School Dist. No. 1*, 551 U.S. 701, 735 (2007). Because UT has failed to explain "with clarity," *Fisher I*, *supra*, at___(slip op., at 7), why it needs a race-conscious policy and how it will know when its goals have been met, the narrow tailoring analysis cannot be meaningfully conducted. UT therefore cannot satisfy strict scrutiny.

The majority acknowledges that "asserting an interest in the educational benefits of diversity writ large is insufficient," and that "[a] university's goals cannot be elusory or amorphous— they must be sufficiently measurable to permit judicial scrutiny of the policies adopted to reach them." *Ante*, at 12. According to the majority, however, UT has articulated the following "concrete and precise goals": "the destruction of stereotypes, the promot[ion of] cross-racial understanding, the preparation of a student body for an increasingly diverse workforce and society, and the cultivat[ion of] a set of leaders with legitimacy in the eyes of the citizenry." *Ibid.* (internal quotation marks omitted).

These are laudable goals, but they are not concrete or precise, and they offer no limiting principle for the use of racial preferences. For instance, how will a court ever be able to determine whether stereotypes have been adequately destroyed? Or whether cross-racial understanding has been adequately achieved? If a university can justify racial discrimination simply by having a few employees opine that racial preferences are necessary to accomplish these nebulous goals, see *ante*, at 12–13 (citing *only* self-serving statements from UT officials), then the narrow tailoring inquiry is meaningless. Courts will be required to defer to the judgment of university administrators, and affirmative-action policies will be completely insulated from judicial review.

By accepting these amorphous goals as sufficient for UT to carry its burden, the majority violates decades of precedent rejecting blind deference to government officials defending "'inherently suspect'" classifications. *Miller*, 515 U.S., at 904 (citing *Regents of Univ. of Cal.* v. *Bakke*, 438 U.S. 265, 291 (1978) (opinion of Powell, J.)); see also, *e.g., Miller*, *supra*, at 922 ("Our presumptive skepticism of all racial classifications . . . prohibits us . . . from accepting on its face the Justice Department's conclusion" (citation omitted)); *Croson*, 488 U.S., at 500 ("[T]he mere recitation of a 'benign' or legitimate purpose for a racial classification is entitled to little or no weight"); *id.*, at 501 ("The history of racial classifications in this country suggests that blind judicial deference to legislative or executive pronouncements of necessity has no place in equal protection analysis"). Most troublingly, the majority's uncritical deference to UT's self-serving claims blatantly contradicts our decision in the prior iteration of this very case, in which we faulted the Fifth Circuit for improperly "deferring to the University's good faith in its use of racial classifications." *Fisher I*, 570 U.S., at__(slip op., at 12). As we emphasized just three years ago, our precedent "ma[kes] clear that it is for the courts, not for university administrators, to ensure that" an admissions process is narrowly tailored. *Id.*, at__(slip op., at 10).

A court cannot ensure that an admissions process is narrowly tailored if it cannot pin down the goals that the process is designed to achieve. UT's vague policy goals are "so broad and imprecise that they cannot withstand strict scrutiny." *Parents Involved*, *supra*, at 785 (KENNEDY, J., concurring in part and concurring in judgment).

C

Although UT's primary argument is that it need not point to any interest more specific than "the educational benefits of diversity," Brief for Respondents 15, it has—at various points in this litigation—identified four more specific goals: demographic parity, classroom diversity, intraracial diversity, and avoiding racial isolation. Neither UT nor the majority has demonstrated that any of these four goals provides a sufficient basis for satisfying strict scrutiny. And UT's arguments to the contrary depend on a series of invidious assumptions.

. . .

D

Even assuming UT is correct that, under *Grutter*, it need only cite a generic interest in the educational bene fits of diversity, its plan still fails strict scrutiny because it is not narrowly tailored. Narrow tailoring requires "a careful judicial inquiry into whether a university could achieve sufficient diversity without using racial classifications." *Fisher I*, 570 U.S., at__(slip op., at 10). "If a ' 'nonracial approach . . . could promote the substantial interest about as well and at tolerable administrative expense,'" then the university may not consider race." *Id.*, at__(slip op., at 11) (citations omitted). Here, there is no evidence that race-blind, holistic review would not achieve UT's goals at least "about as well" as UT's race-based policy. In addition, UT could have adopted other approaches to further its goals, such as intensifying its outreach efforts, uncapping the Top Ten Percent Law, or placing greater weight on socioeconomic factors.

The majority argues that none of these alternatives is "a workable means for the University to attain the benefits of diversity it sought." *Ante*, at 16. Tellingly, however, the majority devotes only a single, conclusory sentence to the most obvious race-neutral alternative: race-blind, holistic review that considers the applicant's unique characteristics and personal circumstances. Under a system that combines the Top Ten Percent Plan with race-blind, holistic review, UT could still admit "the star athlete or musician whose grades suffered because of daily practices and training," the "talented young biologist who struggled to maintain above-average grades in humanities classes," and the "student whose freshman-year grades were poor because of a family crisis but who got herself back on track in her last three years of school." *Ante*, at 17. All of these unique circumstances can be considered without injecting race into the process. Because UT has failed to provide any evidence whatsoever that race-conscious holistic review will achieve its diversity objectives more effectively than race-blind holistic review, it cannot satisfy the heavy burden imposed by the strict scrutiny standard.

The fact that UT's racial preferences are unnecessary to achieve its stated goals is further demonstrated by their minimal effect on UT's diversity. In 2004, when race was not a factor, 3.6% of non-Top Ten Percent Texas enrollees were African-American and 11.6% were Hispanic. See Supp. App. 157a. It would stand to reason that at least the same percentages of African-American and Hispanic students would have been admitted through holistic review in 2008 even if race were not a factor. If that assumption is correct, then race was determinative for only 15 African-American students and 18 Hispanic students in 2008 (representing 0.2% and 0.3%, respectively, of the total enrolled first-time freshmen from Texas high schools).

The majority contends that "[t]he fact that race consciousness played a role in only a small portion of admissions decisions should be a hallmark of narrow tailoring, not evidence of unconstitutionality." *Ante,* at 15. This argument directly contradicts this Court's precedent. Because racial classifications are "'a highly suspect tool,'" *Grutter*, 539 U.S, at 326, they should be employed only "as a last resort," *Croson*, 488 U.S., at 519 (opinion of KENNEDY, J.); see also *Grutter*, *supra*, at 342 ("[R]acial classifications, however compelling their goals, are potentially so dangerous that they may be employed no more broadly than the interest demands"). Where, as here, racial preferences have only a slight impact on minority enrollment, a race-neutral alternative likely could have reached the same result. See *Parents Involved*, 551 U.S., at 733–734 (holding that the "minimal effect" of school districts' racial classifications "casts doubt on the necessity of using [such] classifications" and "suggests that other means [of achieving their objectives] would be effective"). As JUSTICE KENNEDY once aptly put it, "the small number of [students] affected suggests that the schoo[l] could have achieved [its] stated ends through different means." *Id.*, at 790 (opinion concurring in part and concurring in judgment). And in this case, a race-neutral alternative could accomplish UT's objectives without gratuitously branding the covers of tens of thousands of applications with a bare racial stamp and "tell[ing] each student he or she is to be defined by race." *Id.,* at 789.

. . .

A

First, the Court states that, while "th[e] evidentiary gap perhaps could be filled by a remand to the district court for further fact finding" in "an ordinary case," that will not work here because "[w]hen petitioner's application was rejected, . . . the University's combined percentage-plan/holistic-review approach to admission had been in effect for just three years," so "further fact finding" "might yield little insight." *Ante,* at 9. This reasoning is dangerously incorrect. The Equal Protection Clause does not provide a 3-year grace period for racial discrimination. Under strict scrutiny, UT was required to identify evidence that race-based admissions were necessary to achieve a compelling interest *before* it put them in place—not three or more years after. See *ante,* at 13–14 ("Petitioner is correct that a university bears a heavy burden in showing that it had not obtained the educational benefits of diversity *before* it turned to a race-conscious plan" (emphasis added)); *Fisher I,* 570 U.S., at (slip op., at 11) ("[S]trict scrutiny imposes on the university the ultimate burden of demonstrating, *before* turning to racial classifications, that available, workable race-neutral alternatives do not suffice" (emphasis added)). UT's failure to obtain actual evidence that racial preferences were necessary before resolving to use them only confirms that its decision to inject race into admissions was a reflexive response to *Grutter,* and that UT did not seriously consider whether race-neutral means would serve its goals as well as a race-based process.

B

Second, in an effort to excuse UT's lack of evidence, the Court argues that because "the University lacks any authority to alter the role of the Top Ten Percent Plan," "it similarly had no reason to keep extensive data on the Plan or the students admitted under it—particularly in the years before *Fisher I* clarified the stringency of the strict-scrutiny burden for a school that employs race-conscious review." *Ante,* at 9–10. But UT has long been aware that it bears the burden of justifying its racial discrimination under strict scrutiny. See, *e.g.,* Brief for Respondents in No. 11–345, at 22 ("It is undisputed that UT's consideration of race in its holistic admissions process triggers strict scrutiny," and "that inquiry is undeniably rigorous"). In light of this burden, UT had *every* reason to keep data on the

students admitted through the Top Ten Percent Plan. Without such data, how could UT have possibly identified any characteristics that were lacking in Top Ten Percent admittees and that could be obtained via race-conscious admissions? How could UT determine that employing a race-based process would serve its goals better than, for instance, expanding the Top Ten Percent Plan? UT could not possibly make such determinations without studying the students admitted under the Top Ten Percent Plan. Its failure to do so demonstrates that UT unthinkingly employed a race-based process without examining whether the use of race was actually necessary. This is not—as the Court claims—a "good-faith effor[t] to comply with the law." *Ante,* at 10.

. . .

Notwithstanding the majority's claims to the contrary, UT should have access to plenty of information about "how students admitted solely based on their class rank differ in their contribution to diversity from students admitted through holistic review." *Ante,* at 9. UT undoubtedly knows which students were admitted through the Top Ten Percent Plan and which were admitted through holistic review. See, *e.g.,* Supp. App. 157a. And it undoubtedly has a record of all of the classes in which these students enrolled. See, *e.g.,* UT, Office of the Registrar, Transcript—Official, online at https://registrar.utexas.edu/students/transcripts-official (instructing graduates on how to obtain a transcript listing a "comprehensive record" of classes taken). UT could use this information to demonstrate whether the Top Ten Percent minority admittees were more or less likely than the holistic minority admittees to choose to enroll in the courses lacking diversity.

. . .

C

Third, the majority notes that this litigation has persisted for many years, that petitioner has already graduated from another college, that UT's policy may have changed over time, and that this case may offer little prospective guidance. At most, these considerations counsel in favor of dismissing this case as improvidently granted. But see, *e.g., Gratz,* 539 U.S., at 251, and n. 1, 260–262 (rejecting the dissent's argument that, because the case had already persisted long enough for the petitioners to graduate from other schools, the case should be dismissed); *id.,* at 282 (Stevens, J., dissenting). None of these considerations has any bearing whatsoever on the merits of this suit. The majority cannot side with UT simply because it is tired of this case.

IV

It is important to understand what is and what is not at stake in this case. *What is not at stake* is whether UT or any other university may adopt an admissions plan that results in a student body with a broad representation of students from all racial and ethnic groups. UT previously had a race-neutral plan that it claimed had "effectively compensated for the loss of affirmative action," App. 396a, and UT could have taken other steps that would have increased the diversity of its admitted students without taking race or ethnic background into account.

What is at stake is whether university administrators may justify systematic racial discrimination simply by asserting that such discrimination is necessary to achieve "the educational benefits of diversity," without explaining—much less proving—why the discrimination is needed or how the discriminatory plan is well crafted to serve its objectives. Even though UT has never provided any coherent explanation for its asserted need to discriminate on the basis of race, and even though UT's position relies on a series of unsupported and noxious racial assumptions, the majority concludes that UT has met its heavy burden. This conclusion is remarkable—and remarkably wrong.

Because UT has failed to satisfy strict scrutiny, I respectfully dissent.

SAMUEL ALITO *is an associate justice of the United States Supreme Court. He was appointed in 2005 by President George W. Bush.*

Should Colleges and Universities Be Able to Consider an Applicant's Race When Deciding Whether to Accept a Student? by Miller

151

EXPLORING THE ISSUE

Should Colleges and Universities Be Able to Consider an Applicant's Race When Deciding Whether to Accept a Student?

Critical Thinking and Reflection

1. How do you believe colleges should select students they want to attend?
2. Should race play a role in determining whether someone is accepted to a college?
3. In what cases do you believe it is most appropriate to consider race when making a college admissions decision?
4. Should colleges always admit the most qualified students based on test scores and high-school performance? Why or why not?
5. Do you believe the college admissions process is fair? Why or why not?

Is There Common Ground?

Of all the issues discussed in this volume, perhaps there is the greatest opportunity for common ground to be reached on the question of including race as a factor in college admissions. The Supreme Court, after all, has already created a template by which schools can legally do this, without causing harm to non-minority students, through the Gratz v. Grutter decisions. Yet we can expect to continue to hear discussions about the role of race in college admissions as long as higher education is as emphasized in American society as it is today.

From a college or university's perspective, diversity is a key component of the student experience. Beyond textbook learning, college is a time for young adults to be exposed to new and different situations, people, and ways of thinking. This cannot be easily accomplished in a homogenous setting. Yet, standardized tests have been shown by repeated studies to be easier for white students than minority groups—especially African Americans and Hispanics. As a result, if colleges and universities want to assure diverse student populations—and the greatest potential for well-rounded educations for all students—it may mean admitting students of color with lower academic profiles than white applicants. Through the court's recent rulings, we have witnessed the creation of common ground that has been largely accepted be those impacted.

Additional Resources

Elizabeth Armstrong, *Paying for the Party: How College Maintains Inequality* (Harvard University Press, 2013)

Annette Lareau, *Unequal Childhoods: Class, Race, and Family Life* (University of California Press, 2011)

Lois Weis, Kristin Cipollone, and Heather Jenkins, *Class Warfare: Class, Race, and College Admissions in Top-Tier Secondary Schools* (University of Chicago Press, 2014)

Internet References . . .

Diversity in Admission

http://www.nacacnet.org/issues-action
/LegislativeNews/Pages/Diversity-in-Admission.aspx

Diverse Issues in Higher Education

http://diverseeducation.com/

Why Diversity Matters in Higher Education

http://www.collegexpress.com/counselors-and
-parents/parents/articles/college-journey/why
-diversity-matters-college-admissions/

Selected, Edited, and with Issue Framing Material by:
William J. Miller, *Flagler College*

ISSUE

Should the United States Be More Restrictive of Gun Ownership?

YES: Barack Obama and Joe Biden, from "Gun Control," *Speech or Remarks* (2013)

NO: Jeffrey Goldberg, from "The Case for More Guns (and More Gun Control)," *The Atlantic Magazine* (2012)

Learning Outcomes

After reading this issue, you will be able to:

- Discuss current gun ownership restrictions in the United States.
- Assess the threats gun pose to society.
- Describe efforts by the Obama administration to limit gun ownership.
- Explain why some argue that society would be safer with more guns.
- Identify key political players in the battle over gun control.

ISSUE SUMMARY

YES: President Barack Obama and Vice President Joe Biden, speaking in the wake of the Newtown shooting, discuss why America needs to take a more proactive stance in limiting control to guns to prevent further mass shootings.

NO: Columnist Jeffrey Goldberg presents an argument that Americans own plenty of guns to protect themselves but will only be able to prevent mass shootings if they are more readily able to carry them at all times.

Should Americans have the right to self-defense? Does the Second Amendment not give all Americans a fundamental right to bear arms in order to protect themselves and their property in the pursuit of life and liberty? Without guns, rebellion against a tyrannical government would not have been possible and the American Revolution would not mark the beginning of America's independence from England. In fact, search and seizure of firearms and ammunition were a major catalyst for events leading to the American Revolution. While the Second Amendment laid the foundation for gun rights in America, it was not until recently that courts began to clarify exactly who the Second Amendment impacts. Without such clarification, state and local governments have been slowly stripping away access to firearms and therefore a citizen's right to self-defense with false claims of more guns equals more violence.

The Second Amendment, ratified in 1791, states, "A well-regulated militia, being necessary to the security of a free State, the right of the people to keep and bear Arms, shall not be infringed."

Proponents of gun control believe the word "militia" was specifically used to guarantee the right of states to have an armed militia, like our current National Guard. Of course, opponents of gun control believe it to be an individual right to bear arms and a denial of access to guns is unconstitutional. Prior to *District of Columbia v. Heller* in 2008, the Supreme Court had not reviewed a Second Amendment case since *United States v. Miller* in 1939, which did not answer if the Second Amendment was an individual right or one specifically held by the state militia. Without a Supreme Court standing on the issue, states and local governments spent nearly 70 years with little authoritative guidance and have been able to push gun restrictions to the edge, including all out handgun bans in places like the District of Columbia and the city of Chicago.

In 2008, *District of Columbia v. Heller* finally answered the question as to individual rights granted by the Second Amendment. In 1976, the District of Columbia banned all handguns within the district, and all long guns had to be disassembled and a trigger lock used at all times, ultimately defeating the usefulness of a firearm for self-defense in one's home. In siding with *Heller*, the Supreme Court showed that such stringent controls are unconstitutional and obstruct a person's right of self-defense. The *Heller* case was a monumental movement to solidifying the individual right to bear arms, at least at the federal level, but did not express whether the case was enforceable against the states. In 2010, the Supreme Court heard the case of *McDonald v. Chicago*, in which the Supreme Court ruled that the Second Amendment was enforceable against the state under the Privileges and Immunities Clause of the Fourteenth Amendment. *District of Columbia v. Heller* and *McDonald v. Chicago* have been two of the most influential cases in decades to address the right to bear arms, but as is often the result with major court decisions, the rulings have raised many new questions.

The problem with imposing excessive gun bans like those in Chicago and the District of Columbia is that they may not do much to actually reduce crime. Instead, they hinder the law-abiding citizen's right to self-defense, and at best create unreasonable barriers to access firearms. According to a Harvard study by Don Kates and Gary Mauser, Russia's gun controls are so stringent that very few civilians have access to firearms, yet as of 2002 Russia had the highest murder rate of any developed country. Russia is not alone, ownership of any gun in Luxembourg is minimal and handguns are banned, yet they have a murder rate nine times that of countries with high gun ownership such as Germany, Norway, Switzerland, and Austria. In 1996, Australia banned most guns and made the defensive use of a firearm illegal, which resulted in armed robberies rising 51 percent, unarmed robberies by 37 percent, assaults by 24 percent, and kidnappings by 43 percent in the four years following the ban. England has fared no better, during the late 1990s handguns were banned resulting in a 40 percent increase in firearm-related crimes, yet hundreds of thousands of guns were confiscated from law-abiding citizens. Countries like Australia and England are proving when stringent gun restrictions are imposed, and the right to self-defense is taken away, there are only two people with access to guns: the government and criminals.

The idiom "guns don't kill people, people kill people" is being tested in public opinion in the United States every time a mass shooting occurs within the nation's borders. In recent months, we have experienced two such incidents that returned gun control to the federal agenda. First, on July 20, 2012, James Eagan Holmes killed 12 people and injured 70 others during a mass shooting at a Century theater in Aurora, Colorado during a late screening of *The Dark Knight Rises*. Less than five months later, Adam Lanza shot and killed twenty school children and six adults at Sandy Hook Elementary School in Newtown, Connecticut. He also killed his mother. By the time Lanza took his own life with police closing in, it had become the second deadliest mass shooting by an individual gunman in the history of the United States. In both Aurora and Newtown, there were concerns raised about gun control: how did these men gain access to weapons despite displaying signs of mental illness? Why do we have semiautomatic weapons available? Is there any way to prevent possible criminals from getting access to guns without preventing Americans from protecting themselves?

Speaking after a mass shooting in the Navy Yard, President Obama explained: "By now . . . it should be clear that the change we need will not come from Washington. . . . Change will come the only way it ever has come, and that's from the American people. . . . Part of what wears on . . . is the sense that this has happened before," the president said. "What wears on us, what troubles us so deeply, as we gather here today is this senseless violence that took place in the Navy Yard echoes other recent tragedies. . . . I do not accept that we cannot find a common sense way to preserve our traditions, including our basic Second Amendment freedoms and the rights of law-abiding gun owners while at the same time reducing the gun violence that unleashed so much mayhem on a regular basis." Yet the National Rifle Association remains a significant obstacle to any gun control in the United States. With strong membership numbers, funds, and a knack for lobbying, even after a string of massacres, the NRA has successfully prevented any new restrictions to gun ownership.

In the following selections, we hear from President Barack Obama and Vice President Joe Biden who in the aftermath of the Sandy Hook shooting took to a microphone to ask Americans to be more proactive in trying to limit access to guns in order to prevent future death. Opposing our chief executives is Jeffrey Goldberg, who claims Americans have plenty of guns but need better capabilities for carrying them on their person if they plan to prevent massacres.

YES ⬅

Barack Obama and Joe Biden

Gun Control

THE VICE PRESIDENT: Before I begin today, let me say to the families of the innocents who were murdered 33 days ago, our heart goes out to you. And you show incredible courage—incredible courage—being here. And the President and I are going to do everything in our power to honor the memory of your children and your wives with the work we take up here today.

It's been 33 days since the nation's heart was broken by the horrific, senseless violence that took place at Sandy Hook Elementary School—20—20 beautiful first-graders gunned down in a place that's supposed to be their second sanctuary. Six members of the staff killed trying to save those children. It's literally been hard for the nation to comprehend, hard for the nation to fathom.

And I know for the families who are here that time is not measured in days, but it's measured in minutes, in seconds, since you received that news. Another minute without your daughter. Another minute without your son. Another minute without your wife. Another minute without your mom.

I want to personally thank Chris and Lynn McDonald, who lost their beautiful daughter, Grace, and the other parents who I had a chance to speak to, for their suggestions and for—again, just for the courage of all of you to be here today. I admire the grace and the resolve that you all are showing. And I must say I've been deeply affected by your faith, as well. And the President and I are going to do everything to try to match the resolve you've demonstrated.

No one can know for certain if this senseless act could have been prevented, but we all know we have a moral obligation—a moral obligation—to do everything in our power to diminish the prospect that something like this could happen again.

As the President knows, I've worked in this field a long time—in the United States Senate, having chaired a committee that had jurisdiction over these issues of guns and crime, and having drafted the first gun violence legislation—the last gun violence legislation, I should say. And I have no illusions about what we're up against or how hard the task is in front of us. But I also have never seen the nation's conscience so shaken by what happened at Sandy Hook. The world has changed, and it's demanding action.

It's in this context that the President asked me to put together, along with Cabinet members, a set of recommendations about how we should proceed to meet that moral obligation we have. And toward that end, the Cabinet members and I sat down with 229 groups—not just individuals, representing groups—229 groups from law enforcement agencies to public health officials, to gun officials, to gun advocacy groups, to sportsmen and hunters and religious leaders. And I've spoken with members of Congress on both sides of the aisle, had extensive conversations with mayors and governors and county officials.

And the recommendations we provided to the President on Monday call for executive actions he could sign, legislation he could call for, and long-term research that should be undertaken. They're based on the emerging consensus we heard from all the groups with whom we spoke, including some of you who are victims of this god-awful occurrence—ways to keep guns out of the wrong hands, as well as ways to take comprehensive action to prevent violence in the first place.

We should do as much as we can, as quickly as we can. And we cannot let the perfect be the enemy of the good. So some of what you will hear from the President will happen immediately; some will take some time. But we have begun. And we are starting here today and we're going to resolve to continue this fight.

During the meetings that we held, we met with a young man who's here today—I think Colin Goddard is here. Where are you, Colin? Colin was one of the survivors of the Virginia Tech massacre. He was in the classroom. He calls himself one of the "lucky seven." And he'll tell you he was shot four times on that day and he has three bullets that are still inside him.

And when I asked Colin about what he thought we should be doing, he said, "I'm not here because of what happened to me. I'm here because of what happened to me keeps happening to other people and we have to do something about it."

Colin, we will. Colin, I promise you, we will. This is our intention. We must do what we can now. And there's no person who is more committed to acting on this moral obligation we have than the President of the United States of America.

Ladies and gentlemen, President Barack Obama. (Applause.)

THE PRESIDENT: Thank you, everybody. Please have a seat. Good afternoon, everybody.

Let me begin by thanking our Vice President, Joe Biden, for your dedication, Joe, to this issue, for bringing so many different voices to the table. Because while reducing gun violence is a complicated challenge, protecting our children from harm shouldn't be a divisive one.

Obama, Barack and Biden, Joe. Remarks delivered at South Court Auditorium, The White House, Washington, DC, on January 16, 2013.

Over the month since the tragedy in Newtown, we've heard from so many, and, obviously, none have affected us more than the families of those gorgeous children and their teachers and guardians who were lost. And so we're grateful to all of you for taking the time to be here, and recognizing that we honor their memories in part by doing everything we can to prevent this from happening again.

But we also heard from some unexpected people. In particular, I started getting a lot of letters from kids. Four of them are here today—Grant Fritz, Julia Stokes, Hinna Zeejah, and Teja Goode. They're pretty representative of some of the messages that I got. These are some pretty smart letters from some pretty smart young people.

Hinna, a third-grader—you can go ahead and wave, Hinna. That's you—(laughter.) Hinna wrote, "I feel terrible for the parents who lost their children . . . I love my country and [I] want everybody to be happy and safe."

And then, Grant—go ahead and wave, Grant. (Laughter.) Grant said, "I think there should be some changes. We should learn from what happened at Sandy Hook . . . I feel really bad."

And then, Julia said—Julia, where are you? There you go—"I'm not scared for my safety, I'm scared for others. I have four brothers and sisters and I know I would not be able to bear the thought of losing any of them."

These are our kids. This is what they're thinking about. And so what we should be thinking about is our responsibility to care for them, and shield them from harm, and give them the tools they need to grow up and do everything that they're capable of doing—not just to pursue their own dreams, but to help build this country. This is our first task as a society, keeping our children safe. This is how we will be judged. And their voices should compel us to change.

And that's why, last month, I asked Joe to lead an effort, along with members of my Cabinet, to come up with some concrete steps we can take right now to keep our children safe, to help prevent mass shootings, to reduce the broader epidemic of gun violence in this country.

And we can't put this off any longer. Just last Thursday, as TV networks were covering one of Joe's meetings on this topic, news broke of another school shooting, this one in California. In the month since 20 precious children and six brave adults were violently taken from us at Sandy Hook Elementary, more than 900 of our fellow Americans have reportedly died at the end of a gun—900 in the past month. And every day we wait, that number will keep growing.

So I'm putting forward a specific set of proposals based on the work of Joe's task force. And in the days ahead, I intend to use whatever weight this office holds to make them a reality. Because while there is no law or set of laws that can prevent every senseless act of violence completely, no piece of legislation that will prevent every tragedy, every act of evil, if there is even one thing we can do to reduce this violence, if there is even one life that can be saved, then we've got an obligation to try.

And I'm going to do my part. As soon as I'm finished speaking here, I will sit at that desk and I will sign a directive giving law enforcement, schools, mental health professionals and the public health community some of the tools they need to help reduce gun violence.

We will make it easier to keep guns out of the hands of criminals by strengthening the background check system. We will help schools hire more resource officers if they want them and develop emergency preparedness plans. We will make sure mental health professionals know their options for reporting threats of violence—even as we acknowledge that someone with a mental illness is far more likely to be a victim of violent crime than the perpetrator.

And while year after year, those who oppose even modest gun safety measures have threatened to defund scientific or medical research into the causes of gun violence, I will direct the Centers for Disease Control to go ahead and study the best ways to reduce it—and Congress should fund research into the effects that violent video games have on young minds. We don't benefit from ignorance. We don't benefit from not knowing the science of this epidemic of violence.

These are a few of the 23 executive actions that I'm announcing today. But as important as these steps are, they are in no way a substitute for action from members of Congress. To make a real and lasting difference, Congress, too, must act—and Congress must act soon. And I'm calling on Congress to pass some very specific proposals right away.

First: It's time for Congress to require a universal background check for anyone trying to buy a gun. (Applause.) The law already requires licensed gun dealers to run background checks, and over the last 14 years that's kept 1.5 million of the wrong people from getting their hands on a gun. But it's hard to enforce that law when as many as 40 percent of all gun purchases are conducted without a background check. That's not safe. That's not smart. It's not fair to responsible gun buyers or sellers.

If you want to buy a gun—whether it's from a licensed dealer or a private seller—you should at least have to show you are not a felon or somebody legally prohibited from buying one. This is common sense. And an overwhelming majority of Americans agree with us on the need for universal background checks—including more than 70 percent of the National Rifle Association's members, according to one survey. So there's no reason we can't do this.

Second: Congress should restore a ban on military-style assault weapons, and a 10-round limit for magazines. (Applause.) The type of assault rifle used in Aurora, for example, when paired with high-capacity magazines, has one purpose—to pump out as many bullets as possible, as quickly as possible; to do as much damage, using bullets often designed to inflict maximum damage.

And that's what allowed the gunman in Aurora to shoot 70 people—70 people—killing 12 in a matter of minutes. Weapons designed for the theater of war have no place in a movie theater. A majority of Americans agree with us on this.

And, by the way, so did Ronald Reagan, one of the staunchest defenders of the Second Amendment, who wrote to Congress in 1994, urging them—this is Ronald Reagan speaking—urging them to "listen to the American public and to the law enforcement community and support a ban on the further manufacture of [military-style assault] weapons." (Applause.)

And finally, Congress needs to help, rather than hinder, law enforcement as it does its job. We should get tougher on people who buy guns with the express purpose of turning around and selling them to criminals. And we should severely punish anybody who helps them do this. Since Congress hasn't confirmed a director of the Bureau of Alcohol, Tobacco and Firearms in six years, they should confirm Todd Jones, who will be—who has been Acting, and I will be nominating for the post. (Applause.)

And at a time when budget cuts are forcing many communities to reduce their police force, we should put more cops back on the job and back on our streets.

Let me be absolutely clear. Like most Americans, I believe the Second Amendment guarantees an individual right to bear arms. I respect our strong tradition of gun ownership and the rights of hunters and sportsmen. There are millions of responsible, law-abiding gun owners in America who cherish their right to bear arms for hunting, or sport, or protection, or collection.

I also believe most gun owners agree that we can respect the Second Amendment while keeping an irresponsible, law-breaking few from inflicting harm on a massive scale. I believe most of them agree that if America worked harder to keep guns out of the hands of dangerous people, there would be fewer atrocities like the one that occurred in Newtown. That's what these reforms are designed to do. They're common-sense measures. They have the support of the majority of the American people.

And yet, that doesn't mean any of this is going to be easy to enact or implement. If it were, we'd already have universal background checks. The ban on assault weapons and high-capacity magazines never would have been allowed to expire. More of our fellow Americans might still be alive, celebrating birthdays and anniversaries and graduations.

This will be difficult. There will be pundits and politicians and special interest lobbyists publicly warning of a tyrannical, all-out assault on liberty—not because that's true, but because they want to gin up fear or higher ratings or revenue for themselves. And behind the scenes, they'll do everything they can to block any common-sense reform and make sure nothing changes whatsoever.

The only way we will be able to change is if their audience, their constituents, their membership says this time must be different—that this time, we must do something to protect our communities and our kids.

I will put everything I've got into this, and so will Joe. But I tell you, the only way we can change is if the American people demand it. And by the way, that doesn't just mean from certain parts of the country. We're going to need voices in those areas, in those congressional districts, where the tradition of gun ownership is strong to speak up and to say this is important. It can't just be the usual suspects. We have to examine ourselves and our hearts, and ask ourselves what is important.

This will not happen unless the American people demand it. If parents and teachers, police officers and pastors, if hunters and sportsmen, if responsible gun owners, if Americans of every background stand up and say, enough; we've suffered too much pain and care too much about our children to allow this to continue—then change will come. That's what it's going to take.

In the letter that Julia wrote me, she said, "I know that laws have to be passed by Congress, but I beg you to try very hard." (Laughter.) Julia, I will try very hard. But she's right. The most important changes we can make depend on congressional action. They need to bring these proposals up for a vote, and the American people need to make sure that they do.

Get them on record. Ask your member of Congress if they support universal background checks to keep guns out of the wrong hands. Ask them if they support renewing a ban on military-style assault weapons and high-capacity magazines. And if they say no, ask them why not. Ask them what's more important—doing whatever it takes to get a A grade from the gun lobby that funds their campaigns, or giving parents some peace of mind when they drop their child off for first grade? (Applause.)

This is the land of the free, and it always will be. As Americans, we are endowed by our Creator with certain inalienable rights that no man or government can take away from us. But we've also long recognized, as our Founders recognized, that with rights come responsibilities. Along with our freedom to live our lives as we will comes an obligation to allow others to do the same. We don't live in isolation. We live in a society, a government of, and by, and for the people. We are responsible for each other.

The right to worship freely and safely, that right was denied to Sikhs in Oak Creek, Wisconsin. The right to assemble peaceably, that right was denied [to] shoppers in Clackamas, Oregon, and moviegoers in Aurora, Colorado. That most fundamental set of rights to life and liberty and the pursuit of happiness—fundamental rights that were denied to college students at Virginia Tech, and high school students at Columbine, and elementary school students in Newtown, and kids on street corners in Chicago on too frequent a basis to tolerate, and all the families who've never imagined that they'd lose a loved one to a bullet—those rights are at stake. We're responsible.

When I visited Newtown last month, I spent some private time with many of the families who lost their children that day. And one was the family of Grace McDonald. Grace's parents are here. Grace was seven years old when she was struck down—just a gorgeous, caring, joyful little girl. I'm told she loved pink. She loved the beach. She dreamed of becoming a painter.

And so just before I left, Chris, her father, gave me one of her paintings, and I hung it in my private study just off the Oval Office.

And every time I look at that painting, I think about Grace. And I think about the life that she lived and the life that lay ahead of her, and most of all, I think about how, when it comes to protecting the most vulnerable among us, we must act now—for Grace. For the 25 other innocent children and devoted educators who had so much left to give. For the men and women in big cities and small towns who fall victim to senseless violence each and every day. For all the Americans who are counting on us to keep them safe from harm. Let's do the right thing. Let's do the right thing for them, and for this country that we love so much.

BARACK OBAMA served as U.S. Senator for Illinois prior to defeating John McCain in the 2008 presidential election to become the 44th President of the United States. He is the first African American to hold the position. In 2012, President Obama defeated Republican challenger Mitt Romney to win a second term.

JOE BIDEN is Vice President of the United States. He is a member of the Democratic Party and was a United States Senator from Delaware from January 3, 1973, until his resignation on January 15, 2009, following his election to the Vice Presidency. In 2012, Biden was elected to a second term alongside Obama.

Jeffrey Goldberg

The Case for More Guns (and More Gun Control)

How Do We Reduce Gun Crime and Aurora-Style Mass Shootings When Americans Already Own Nearly 300 Million Firearms? Maybe by Allowing More People to Carry Them

The Century 16 Cineplex in Aurora, Colorado, stands desolate behind a temporary green fence, which was raised to protect the theater from prying eyes and mischief-makers. The parking lots that surround the multiplex are empty—weeds are pushing through the asphalt—and the only person at the theater when I visited a few weeks ago was an enervated Aurora police officer assigned to guard the site.

I asked the officer whether the building, which has stood empty since the night of July 20, when a former graduate student named James E. Holmes is alleged to have killed 12 people and wounded 58 others at a midnight showing of *The Dark Knight Rises,* still drew the curious. "People drive by to look," he said, but "not too many." The Aurora massacre is noteworthy, even in the crowded field of mass shootings, as one of the more wretched and demoralizing in the recent history of American violence, and I was surprised that the scene of the crime did not attract more attention. "I guess people move on," he said.

I walked up a slight rise that provided an imperfect view of the back of Theater 9, where the massacre took place, and tried to imagine the precise emotions the victims felt as the gunfire erupted.

"The shooting started at a quiet moment in the movie," Stephen Barton told me. He was shot in the opening fusillade. "I saw this canister-type thing, a smoking object, streak across the screen. I thought it was a kid with fireworks playing a prank."

Barton is 22 years old. He had been preparing to leave for Russia this fall on a Fulbright scholarship. "The first feeling I remember was bewilderment. I don't remember having a single thought before I was shot, because I was shot early on. I was sitting in the middle of the row, toward the back. I got blasted in my head, neck, and face—my whole upper body—by shotgun pellets."

As he lay wounded on the floor by his seat, he said, his bafflement gave way to panic. "I had this unwillingness to accept that this was actually happening. I wanted to believe that there was no way that someone in the same room as me was shooting at people," he said. "So it was disbelief and also this really strong feeling that I'm not ready to die. I'm at someone else's mercy. I've never felt more helpless."

In the chaos of smoke and gunshots, Barton saw the emergency exit door open, and managed to escape into the parking lot. "If I hadn't seen that door, I might not have made it," he said.

I left the theater and drove into Denver, to meet a man named Tom Mauser, who lost a son in the 1999 massacre at Columbine High School, 19 miles from the Aurora theater.

Daniel Mauser, who was 15 years old when he died, tried to hide from the Columbine killers, Eric Harris and Dylan Klebold. Harris found the boy under a table in the school library. A classmate told *The Denver Post* shortly after the massacre, "Eric shot him once, and Daniel pushed chairs at him to try to make him stop, and Eric shot him again."

After the murder of his son, Tom Mauser became a gun-control activist. In the days after Columbine, advocates of more-stringent controls of firearms thought they could feel a shift in the culture. People were disgusted that Harris and Klebold, neither of whom was of the legal age to buy firearms, had found a way to acquire guns: an 18-year-old woman, a friend of the two shooters, bought three weapons legally at a gun show, where federal background checks were not required.

After Columbine, Colorado closed its "gun-show loophole," but efforts to close the loophole on the national level failed. The National Rifle Association and other anti-gun-control groups worked diligently to defend the loophole—misnamed, because while *loophole* suggests a small opening not easily negotiated, about 40 percent of all legal gun sales take place at gun shows, on the Internet, or through more-informal sales between private sellers and buyers, where buyers are not subject to federal background checks. Though anti-loophole legislation passed the U.S. Senate, it was defeated in the House of Representatives. On top of that, the 1994 ban on sales of certain types of semiautomatic weapons, known as the assault-weapons ban, expired in 2004 and was not reauthorized.

Goldberg, Jeffrey. First published in *The Atlantic Magazine,* December 2012. Copyright © 2012 by The Atlantic Media Co. All rights reserved. Distributed by Tribune Content Agency, LLC.

After the Aurora shooting, gun-control activists who expected politicians to rise up in outrage were quickly disappointed. Shortly after the massacre, John Hickenlooper, the Democratic governor of Colorado, suggested that stricter gun laws would not have stopped the shooter. "If there were no assault weapons available and no this or no that, this guy is going to find something, right?," Hickenlooper said. "He's going to know how to create a bomb."

Hickenlooper's statement helped Mauser realize that his side was losing the fight. "I had deep anger when I heard that," he told me. "I heard the same kinds of statements from some people after Columbine: 'Well, you know, they had bombs, too.' The fact is that the deaths were from guns."

Mauser believes the public has grown numb to mass violence. "People say 'How tragic' and then move on," he said. "They're told by their governor, their political leaders, that there's no solution. So they don't see a solution out there."

According to a 2011 Gallup poll, 47 percent of American adults keep at least one gun at home or on their property, and many of these gun owners are absolutists opposed to any government regulation of firearms. According to the same poll, only 26 percent of Americans support a ban on handguns.

To that 26 percent, American gun culture can seem utterly inexplicable, its very existence dispiriting. Guns are responsible for roughly 30,000 deaths a year in America; more than half of those deaths are suicides. In 2010, 606 people, 62 of them children younger than 15, died in accidental shootings.

Mauser expresses disbelief that the number of gun deaths fails to shock. He blames the American attachment to guns on ignorance, and on immaturity. "We're a pretty new nation," he told me. "We're still at the stage of rebellious teenager, and we don't like it when the government tells us what to do. People don't trust government to do what's right. They are very attracted to the idea of a nation of individuals, so they don't think about what's good for the collective."

Mauser said that if the United States were as mature as the countries of Europe, where strict gun control is the norm, the federal government would have a much easier time curtailing the average citizen's access to weapons. "The people themselves would understand that having guns around puts them in more danger."

There are ways, of course, to make it at least marginally more difficult for the criminally minded, for the dangerously mentally ill, and for the suicidal to buy guns and ammunition. The gun-show loophole could be closed. Longer waiting periods might stop some suicides. Mental-health professionals could be encouraged—or mandated—to report patients they suspect shouldn't own guns to the FBI-supervised National Instant Criminal Background Check System, although this would generate fierce opposition from doctors and patients. Background checks, which are conducted by licensed gun shops, have stopped almost 1 million people from buying guns at these stores since 1998. (No one knows, of course, how many of these people gave up their search for a gun, and how many simply went to a gun show or found another way to acquire a weapon.)

Other measures could be taken as well. Drum-style magazines like the kind James Holmes had that night in Aurora, which can hold up to 100 rounds of ammunition and which make continuous firing easy, have no reasonable civilian purpose, and their sale could be restricted without violating the Second Amendment rights of individual gun owners.

But these gun-control efforts, while noble, would only have a modest impact on the rate of gun violence in America.

Why?

Because it's too late.

There are an estimated 280 million to 300 million guns in private hands in America—many legally owned, many not. Each year, more than 4 million new guns enter the market. This level of gun saturation has occurred not because the anti-gun lobby has been consistently outflanked by its adversaries in the National Rifle Association, though it has been. The NRA is quite obviously a powerful organization, but like many effective pressure groups, it is powerful in good part because so many Americans are predisposed to agree with its basic message.

America's level of gun ownership means that even if the Supreme Court—which ruled in 2008 that the Second Amendment gives citizens the individual right to own firearms, as gun advocates have long insisted—suddenly reversed itself and ruled that the individual ownership of handguns was illegal, there would be no practical way for a democratic country to locate and seize those guns.

Many gun-control advocates, and particularly advocates of a total gun ban, would like to see the United States become more like Canada, where there are far fewer guns per capita and where most guns must be registered with the federal government. The Canadian approach to firearms ownership has many attractions—the country's firearm homicide rate is one-sixth that of the U.S. But barring a decision by the American people and their legislators to remove the right to bear arms from the Constitution, arguing for applying the Canadian approach in the U.S. is useless.

Even the leading advocacy group for stricter gun laws, the Brady Campaign to Prevent Gun Violence, has given up the struggle to convince the courts, and the public, that the Constitution grants only members of a militia the right to bear arms. "I'm happy to consider the debate on the Second Amendment closed," Dan Gross, the Brady Campaign's president, told me recently. "Reopening that debate is not what we should be doing. We have to respect the fact that a lot of decent, law-abiding people believe in gun ownership."

Which raises a question: When even anti-gun activists believe that the debate over private gun ownership is closed; when it is too late to reduce the number of guns in private hands—and since only the naive think that legislation will prevent more than a modest number of the criminally minded, and the mentally deranged, from acquiring a gun in a country absolutely inundated with weapons—could it be that an effective way to combat guns is with more guns?

Today, more than 8 million vetted and (depending on the state) trained law-abiding citizens possess state-issued "concealed carry" handgun permits, which allow them to carry a concealed handgun or other weapon in public. Anti-gun activists believe the expansion of concealed-carry permits represents a serious threat to public order. But what if, in fact, the reverse is true? Mightn't allowing more law-abiding private citizens to carry concealed weapons—when combined with other forms of stringent gun regulation—actually reduce gun violence?

This thought has been with me for nearly two decades. On December 7, 1993, a bitter and unstable man named Colin Ferguson boarded an eastbound Long Island Rail Road train at the Jamaica, Queens, station. As the train pulled into the Merillon Avenue station in Nassau County, Ferguson pulled out a Ruger 9 mm pistol he had bought legally in California (which had a 15-day waiting period) and began walking down the aisle, calmly shooting passengers as he went. He killed six people and wounded 19 others before three passengers tackled him while he was reloading.

I had been an LIRR commuter not long before this happened, and I remember clearly my reaction to the slaughter, and I remember as well the reaction of many New York politicians. Much of the political class, and many editorialists, were of the view that the LIRR massacre proved the need for stricter gun control, and even for the banning of handguns. I shared—and continue to share—the view that muscular gun-control regulations, ones that put stumbling blocks in front of criminals seeking firearms, are necessary. But I was also seized by the thought that, had I been on the train, I would much rather have been armed than unarmed. I was not, and am not, under the illusion that a handgun would have necessarily provided a definitive solution to the problem posed by Colin Ferguson. But my instinct was that if someone is shooting at you, it is generally better to shoot back than to cower and pray.

Would a civilian firing back at Ferguson have wounded or killed innocent people? Quite possibly yes. Is that a risk potential victims quaking under train seats or classroom desks might accept? Quite possibly yes. Especially when you consider the massacres that have been prevented or interrupted by armed civilians before the police arrived.

Many of the worst American massacres end not in the capture of the gunman but in his suicide. In the 2007 mass shooting at Virginia Tech, for instance, the gunman, Seung-Hui Cho, killed himself as the police were set to capture him. But in other cases, massacres were stopped early by the intervention of armed civilians, or off-duty or retired police officers who happened to be nearby.

In 1997, a disturbed high-school student named Luke Woodham stabbed his mother and then shot and killed two people at Pearl High School in Pearl, Mississippi. He then began driving toward a nearby junior high to continue his shooting spree, but the assistant principal of the high school, Joel Myrick, aimed a pistol he kept in his truck at Woodham, causing him to veer off the road. Myrick then put his pistol to Woodham's neck and disarmed him. On January 16, 2002, a disgruntled former student at the Appalachian School of Law in Grundy, Virginia, had killed three

people, including the school's dean, when two students, both off-duty law-enforcement officers, retrieved their weapons and pointed them at the shooter, who ended his killing spree and surrendered. In December 2007, a man armed with a semiautomatic rifle and two pistols entered the New Life Church in Colorado Springs and killed two teenage girls before a church member, Jeanne Assam—a former Minneapolis police officer and a volunteer church security guard—shot and wounded the gunman, who then killed himself.

And so I put a question to Stephen Barton, who described feeling helpless in the Aurora theater: Would he rather have been armed, or at least been in the theater with armed patrons, when the massacre started?

"Intuitively it makes sense for people to have that reaction, to want to defend themselves," he said. "It's easy to say that if more people had guns to defend themselves, they could take criminals down, but I don't think concealed-carry weapons are the answer." In a dark and crowded theater, he said, facing someone wearing bullet-resistant armor on much of his body, a gun, even in trained hands, would have been unlikely to do much good.

I put to Tom Mauser a variation of the question I had asked Barton. What if a teacher or an administrator inside Columbine High School had been armed on the day of the massacre? Unlike the theater in Aurora, the school was brightly lit, and not as densely packed. If someone with a gun had confronted Harris and Klebold in the library, he or she would have been able, at the very least, to distract the killers—perhaps even long enough for them to be tackled or disarmed.

"That kind of speculation doesn't solve anything," Mauser said. "I don't know if that person might have shot my son accidentally."

But the worst thing that could have happened to Daniel Mauser did, in fact, happen. The presence in the Columbine library of a well-trained, armed civilian attempting to stop the killers could hardly have made the situation worse. Indeed, the local police—who waited 45 minutes to enter the school, while a SWAT team assembled—were severely criticized for the delay.

But Mauser remained implacable. "We know that if the country adopts this vision that everyone should be armed—that administrators and janitors in school are armed, that people are walking around armed—we won't be safe," Mauser told me. "In Aurora, if five people in that theater had guns, they could have just ended up shooting each other or innocent people in the crossfire. It just makes sense that if people are walking around armed, you're going to have a high rate of people shooting each other."

Earlier this year, a man who was upset with the anti-gay-rights position of the Family Research Council entered the group's Washington, D.C., headquarters and allegedly shot and wounded the building manager (who subsequently tackled the gunman). At the time, Washington's mayor, Vincent Gray, said: "We don't need to make more guns available to people. . . . The more access they have, the more they threaten people."

The District of Columbia does not allow for concealed carry, though its residents can now apply for a license allowing them to keep handguns at home, thanks to the 2008 Supreme Court ruling in a case brought on behalf of a D.C. man who wanted a gun for self-protection.

I called Gray to ask him about his assertion that more guns mean more violence, noting that he himself travels the city with armed police bodyguards, a service not afforded the typical Washington resident. "Well, first of all, I've never even seen the guns that the security people have. When I travel outside the city, I don't have security. I would be fine without security," he said. "But we have 3,800 police officers to protect people. They may not be at someone's side at every moment, but they're around."

I asked him whether he could envision a scenario in which an armed civilian might be able to stop a crime from occurring. "There are those who believe that if they have a weapon, they can combat crime, but I don't think that way," he said.

The police, of course, have guns to stop crime. So why couldn't a well-trained civilian also stop crime? "If you have a gun on you, that's just another opportunity to use it," Gray said. "It's the temptation of the moment. I just think the opportunity is there to create more violence."

In 2004, the Ohio legislature passed a law allowing private citizens to apply for permits to carry firearms outside the home. The decision to allow concealed carry was, of course, a controversial one. Law-enforcement organizations, among others, argued that an armed population would create chaos in the streets. In 2003, John Gilchrist, the legislative counsel for the Ohio Association of Chiefs of Police, testified, "If 200,000 to 300,000 citizens begin carrying a concealed weapon, common sense tells us that accidents will become a daily event."

When I called Gilchrist recently, he told me that events since the state's concealed-carry law took effect have proved his point. "Talking to the chiefs, I know that there is more gun violence and accidents involving guns," he said. "I think there's more gun violence now because there are more guns. People are using guns in the heat of arguments, and there wouldn't be as much gun violence if we didn't have people carrying weapons. If you've got people walking around in a bad mood—or in a divorce, they've lost their job—and they get into a confrontation, this could result in the use of a gun. If you talk to emergency-room physicians in the state, [they] see more and more people with gunshot wounds."

Gilchrist said he did not know the exact statistics on gun-related incidents (or on incidents concerning concealed-carry permit holders specifically, because the state keeps the names of permit holders confidential). He says, however, that he tracks gun usage anecdotally. "You can look in the newspaper. I consciously look for stories that deal with guns. There are more and more articles in *The Columbus Dispatch* about people using guns inappropriately."

Gilchrist's argument would be convincing but for one thing: the firearm crime rate in Ohio remained steady after the concealed-carry law passed in 2004.

It is an unexamined assumption on the part of gun-control activists that the possession of a firearm by a law-abiding person will almost axiomatically cause that person to fire it at another human being in a moment of stress. Dave Kopel, the research director of the libertarian-leaning Independence Institute, in Denver, posits that opposition to gun ownership is ideological, not rational. "I use gay marriage as an analogue," he said. "Some people say they are against gay marriage because they think it leads to worse outcomes for kids. Now, let's say in 2020 all the social-science evidence has it that the kids of gay families turn out fine. Some people will still say they're against it, not for reasons of social science, but for reasons of faith. That's what you have here in the gun issue."

There is no proof to support the idea that concealed-carry permit holders create more violence in society than would otherwise occur; they may, in fact, reduce it. According to Adam Winkler, a law professor at UCLA and the author of *Gunfight: The Battle Over the Right to Bear Arms in America,* permit holders in the U.S. commit crimes at a rate lower than that of the general population. "We don't see much bloodshed from concealed-carry permit holders, because they are law-abiding people," Winkler said. "That's not to say that permit holders don't commit crimes, but they do so at a lower rate than the general population. People who seek to obtain permits are likely to be people who respect the law." According to John Lott, an economist and a gun-rights advocate who maintains that gun ownership by law-abiding citizens helps curtail crime, the crime rate among concealed-carry permit holders is lower than the crime rate among police officers.

Today, the number of concealed-carry permits is the highest it's ever been, at 8 million, and the homicide rate is the lowest it's been in four decades—less than half what it was 20 years ago. (The number of people allowed to carry concealed weapons is actually considerably higher than 8 million, because residents of Vermont, Wyoming, Arizona, Alaska, and parts of Montana do not need government permission to carry their personal firearms. These states have what Second Amendment absolutists refer to as "constitutional carry," meaning, in essence, that the Second Amendment is their permit.)

Many gun-rights advocates see a link between an increasingly armed public and a decreasing crime rate. "I think effective law enforcement has had the biggest impact on crime rates, but I think concealed carry has something to do with it. We've seen an explosion in the number of people licensed to carry," Lott told me. "You can deter criminality through longer sentencing, and you deter criminality by making it riskier for people to commit crimes. And one way to make it riskier is to create the impression among the criminal population that the law-abiding citizen they want to target may have a gun."

Crime statistics in Britain, where guns are much scarcer, bear this out. Gary Kleck, a criminologist at Florida State University, wrote in his 1991 book, *Point Blank: Guns and Violence in America,* that only 13 percent of burglaries in America occur when the occupant is home. In Britain, so-called hot burglaries account for about 45 percent of all break-ins. Kleck and others attribute America's low rate of occupied-home burglaries to fear among criminals that homeowners might be armed. (A survey of almost 2,000 convicted U.S. felons, conducted by the criminologists Peter Rossi and James D. Wright in the late '80s, concluded that burglars are more afraid of armed homeowners than they are of arrest by the police.)

Others contend that proving causality between crime rates and the number of concealed-carry permits is impossible. "It's difficult to make the case that more concealed-carry guns have led to the drop in the national crime rate, because cities like Los Angeles, where we have very restrictive gun-control laws, have seen the same remarkable drop in crime," Winkler told me. (Many criminologists tend to attribute America's dramatic decrease in violent crime to a combination of demographic changes, longer criminal sentencing, innovative policing techniques, and the waning of the crack wars.)

But it is, in fact, possible to assess with some degree of accuracy how many crimes have been stopped because the intended victim, or a witness, was armed. In the 1990s, Gary Kleck and a fellow criminologist, Marc Gertz, began studying the issue and came to the conclusion that guns were used defensively between 830,000 and 2.45 million times each year.

In only a minority of these cases was a gun fired; the brandishing of a gun in front of a would-be mugger or burglar is usually enough to abort a crime in progress. Another study, the federal government's National Crime Victimization Survey, asked victims of crimes whether they, or someone else, had used a gun in their defense. This study came up with a more modest number than Kleck and Gertz, finding 108,000 defensive uses of firearms a year.

All of these studies, of course, have been contested by gun-control advocates. So I asked Winkler what he thought. He said that while he is skeptical of the 2.45 million figure, even the smaller number is compelling: 108,000 "would represent a significant reduction in criminal activity."

Universities, more than most other institutions, are nearly unified in their prohibition of licensed concealed-carry weapons. Some even post notices stating that their campuses are gun-free zones. At the same time, universities also acknowledge that they are unable to protect their students from lethal assault. How do they do this? By recommending measures that students and faculty members can take if confronted by an "active shooter," as in the massacre at Virginia Tech.

These recommendations make for depressing reading, and not only because they reflect a world in which random killing in tranquil settings is a genuine, if rare, possibility. They are also depressing because they reflect a denial of reality.

Here are some of the recommendations:

- Wichita State University counsels students in the following manner: "If the person(s) is causing death or serious physical injury to others and you are unable to run or hide you may choose to be compliant, play dead, or fight for your life."
- The University of Miami guidelines suggest that when all else fails, students should act "as aggressively as possible" against a shooter. The guidelines, taken from a Department of Homeland Security directive, also recommend "throwing items and improvising weapons," as well as "yelling."
- Otterbein University, in Ohio, tells students to "breathe to manage your fear" and informs them, "You may have to take the offensive if the shooter(s) enter your area. Gather weapons (pens, pencils, books, chairs, etc.) and mentally prepare your attack."
- West Virginia University advises students that if the situation is dire, they should "act with physical aggression and throw items at the active shooter." These items could include "student desks, keys, shoes, belts, books, cell phones, iPods, book bags, laptops, pens, pencils, etc."
- The University of Colorado at Boulder's guidelines state, "You and classmates or friends may find yourselves in a situation where the shooter will accost you. If such an event occurs, quickly develop a plan to attack the shooter. . . . Consider a plan to tackle the shooter, take away his weapon, and hold him until police arrive."

It is, of course, possible to distract a heavily armed psychotic on a suicide mission by throwing an iPod at him, or a pencil. But it is more likely that the psychotic would respond by shooting the pencil thrower.

The existence of these policies suggests that universities know they cannot protect their students during an armed attack. (At Virginia Tech, the gunman killed 30 students and faculty members in the 10 minutes it took the police to arrive and penetrate the building he had blockaded.) And yet, these schools will not allow adults with state-issued concealed-carry permits to bring their weapons onto campus, as they would be able to almost anywhere else. "Possession or storage of a deadly weapon, destructive device, or fireworks in any form . . . is prohibited," West Virginia University's policy states.

To gun-rights advocates, these policies are absurd. "The fact that universities are providing their faculties and students with this sort of information is, of course, an admission that they can't protect them," Dave Kopel told me. "The universities are unable to protect people, but then they disable people from protecting themselves."

It is also illogical for campuses to advertise themselves as "gun-free." Someone bent on murder is not usually dissuaded by posted anti-gun regulations. Quite the opposite—publicly describing your property as gun-free is analogous to posting a notice on your front door saying your home has no burglar alarm. As it happens, the company that owns the Century 16 Cineplex in Aurora had declared the property a gun-free zone.

"As a security measure, it doesn't seem like advertising that fact is a good idea," Adam Winkler says of avowedly gun-free campuses, though he adds that "advertising a school's gun-free status does provide notice to potentially immature youth that they're not allowed to have guns."

In Colorado, the epicenter of the American gun argument, the state supreme court recently ruled that the University of Colorado must lift its ban on the carrying of concealed handguns by owners who have been licensed by local sheriffs. (The university has responded by requiring students who own guns to move to a specified housing complex.) The ruling has caused anxiety among some faculty. The chairman of the faculty assembly, a physics professor named Jerry Peterson, told the Boulder *Daily Camera,* "My own personal policy in my classes is if I am aware that there is a firearm in the class—registered or unregistered, concealed or unconcealed—the class session is immediately canceled. I want my students to feel unconstrained in their discussions."

Peterson makes two assumptions: The first is that he will know whether someone is carrying a concealed weapon in class. The second is that students will feel frightened about sharing their opinions if a gun is present. (I could find no evidence that any American educational institution has ever seen fatalities or serious gun-related injuries result from a heated classroom discussion.)

Claire Levy, a Colorado state legislator, says she intends to introduce a bill that would ban guns once again. "If discussions in class escalated," she argues, "the mere fact that someone is potentially armed could have an inhibiting effect on the classroom, This is genuinely scary to faculty members." The push to open up campuses to concealed-carry permit holders, Levy says, is motivated by ideological gun-rights advocacy, rather than an actual concern for campus safety. Guns, even those owned by licensed and trained individuals, she insists, would simply make a campus more dangerous. "American campuses are the safest places to be in the whole world," she said. "The homicide rate on campuses is a small fraction of the rate in the rest of the country. So there's no actual rational public-safety reason that anyone would need to bring a gun on campus."

However, the University of Colorado's own active-shooter recommendations state:

Active harming incidents have occurred at a number of locations in recent years, and the University of Colorado is not immune to this potential. While the odds of this occurring at CU are small, the consequences are so potentially catastrophic it makes sense for all students, staff, faculty and visitors to CU to consider the possibility of such an incident occurring here.

In making her argument against concealed-carry weapons to me, Levy painted a bit of a contradictory picture: On the one hand, campuses are the safest places in the country. On the other hand, campus life is so inherently dangerous that the introduction of even licensed guns could mean mayhem. "You're in this milieu of drugs and alcohol and impulsive behavior and mental illness; you've got a population that has a high propensity for suicide," she told me. "Theft is a big concern, and what if you had a concealed-carry gun and you're drinking and become violent?"

For much of the population of a typical campus, concealed-carry permitting is not an issue. Most states that issue permits will grant them only to people who are at least 21 years old. But the crime-rate statistics at universities that do allow permit holders on campus with their weapons are instructive. An hour north of Boulder, in Fort Collins, sits Colorado State University. Concealed carry has been allowed at CSU since 2003, and according to James Alderden, the former sheriff of Larimer County, which encompasses Fort Collins, violent crime at Colorado State has dropped since then.

Despite the fact that CSU experienced no violent incidents involving concealed-carry permit holders, the university governing board voted two years ago to ban concealed carry. The ban never went into effect, however, because the state appeals court soon ruled against a similar ban at the University of Colorado, and because Sheriff Alderden announced that he would undermine the ban by refusing to process any violator in the county jail, which serves the university's police department.

Alderden, who recently retired, told me that opponents of concealed carry "make an emotional argument rather than a logical one. No one could show me any study that concealed carry leads to more crime and more violence. My idea of self-defense is not those red rape phones on campus, where you get to the phone and tell someone you're getting raped. I have a daughter, and I'd rather have her have the ability to defend herself. I'm not going to violate a citizen's right to self-defense because someone else has an emotional feeling about guns."

Though Colorado is slowly shading blue, Alderden said he believes most of its residents "still don't rely on the government to protect them." He added: "Maybe in Boulder they do, but most people believe they have a right to self-defense."

Boulder may be the locus of left-wing politics in Colorado, but it is also home to the oversubscribed Boulder Rifle Club, which I visited on a bright early-fall morning with Dave Kopel, of the Independence Institute. The existence of the rifle club surprised me, given Boulder's reputation. But Kopel argued that gun ownership and sport shooting are not partisan phenomena, and he made the plausible assertion that Boulder is home to "the largest population of armed vegans in America."

I wanted to understand from Kopel the best arguments against government intervention in gun ownership, and Kopel wanted to fire some of the many handguns he owns, so we alternately talked and shot. Kopel brought with him a bag of guns: a Ruger Mark II .22 LR pistol; a Springfield Armory XD-9 9 mm; a Glock 9 mm; a Springfield Armory 1911 tactical-response pistol (similar to a Colt .45); and a Ruger Alaskan .45 revolver, powerful enough to drop a bear. The Ruger Alaskan is the most powerful weapon we used, but the act of firing even a .22 underscores for most thinking people the notion that firing a gun is a serious business. Kopel argued that a law-abiding citizen is less likely to get into a confrontation after a traffic accident or an exchange of insults if he or she is carrying a weapon: "You're aware of the power you have, and you naturally want to use that power very carefully."

I expressed to Kopel my concern that the overly lax standards some states set for concealed-carry permitting means that the occasional cowboy gets passed through the system. Florida—which has among the most relaxed standards for gun permitting, and granted a license to George Zimmerman, who famously killed Trayvon Martin, apparently during an exercise in freelance vigilantism—is a case in point. (Zimmerman has pled not guilty, claiming he shot Martin in self-defense.) Applicants in Florida must submit to a background check, take a brief class, and pay $112 to obtain a license.

In Colorado, the standards are slightly more stringent. Permit seekers must submit to criminal checks, fingerprinting, and safety classes, but in addition, they must pass what James Alderden referred to as the "naked man" rule: if a local sheriff learns that a person has no criminal record, and has not been deemed mentally ill, but nevertheless was, say, found naked one night in a field howling at the moon, the sheriff is granted the discretion to deny that person a permit.

Kopel argued, correctly, that Florida, like Colorado, has seen a drop in crime since 1987, when it started granting concealed-carry permits—which suggests to him that permit holders are not, in the main, engaging in crime sprees or taking the law into their own hands. But for Kopel, the rigor, or laxity, of the permitting process from state to state is not his principal concern, because he believes that in most cases, the government has no right to interfere with an adult's decision to buy or carry a weapon. Those who seek to curtail gun rights, he insists, are promoting the infantilization of Americans.

"If they get their way," he said of the anti-gun forces, "people who are the victims of violent crimes wouldn't be able to fight back; women who are abused couldn't protect themselves; criminals will know that their intended victims, who have no access to the black market, will be unable to defend themselves.

"It's more than that," he went on. "Telling the population that they are incapable of owning a tool that can be dangerous means you are creating a population that loses its self-reliance and increasingly sees itself as wards of the state."

James Alderden put it another way: "Your position on concealed-carry permits has a lot to do with your position on the reliability and sanity of your fellow man."

The ideology of gun-ownership absolutism doesn't appeal to me. Unlike hard-line gun-rights advocates, I do not believe that unregulated gun ownership is a defense against the rise of totalitarianism in America, because I do not think that America is ripe for totalitarianism. (Fear of a tyrannical, gun-seizing president is the reason many gun owners oppose firearms registration.)

But I am sympathetic to the idea of armed self-defense, because it does often work, because encouraging learned helplessness is morally corrupt, and because, however much I might wish it, the United States is not going to become Canada. Guns are with us, whether we like it or not. Maybe this is tragic, but it is also reality. So Americans who are qualified to possess firearms shouldn't be denied the right to participate in their own defense. And it is empirically true that the great majority of America's tens of millions of law-abiding gun owners have not created chaos in society.

A balanced approach to gun control in the United States would require the warring sides to agree on several contentious issues. Conservative gun-rights advocates should acknowledge that if more states had stringent universal background checks—or if a federal law put these in place—more guns would be kept out of the hands of criminals and the dangerously mentally unstable. They should also acknowledge that requiring background checks on buyers at gun shows would not represent a threat to the Constitution. "The NRA position on this is a fiction," says Dan Gross, the head of the Brady Campaign. "Universal background checks are not an infringement on our Second Amendment rights. This is black-helicopter stuff." Gross believes that closing the gun-show loophole would be both extremely effective and a politically moderate and achievable goal. The gun lobby must also agree that concealed-carry permits should be granted only to people who pass rigorous criminal checks, as well as thorough training-and-safety courses.

Anti-gun advocates, meanwhile, should acknowledge that gun-control legislation is not the only answer to gun violence. Responsible gun ownership is also an answer. An enormous number of Americans believe this to be the case, and gun-control advocates do themselves no favors when they demonize gun owners, and advocates of armed self-defense, as backwoods barbarians. Liberals sometimes make the mistake of anthropomorphizing guns, ascribing to them moral characteristics they do not possess. Guns can be used to do evil, but guns can also be used to do good. Twelve years ago, in the aftermath of Matthew Shepard's murder, Jonathan Rauch launched a national movement when he wrote an article for *Salon* arguing that gay people should arm themselves against violent bigots. Pink Pistol clubs sprang up across America, in which gays and lesbians learn to use firearms in self-defense. Other vulnerable groups have also taken to the idea of concealed carry: in Texas, African American women represent the largest percentage increase of concealed-carry permit seekers since 2000.

But even some moderate gun-control activists, such as Dan Gross, have trouble accepting that guns in private hands can work effectively to counteract violence. When I asked him the question I posed to Stephen Barton and Tom Mauser—would you, at a moment when a stranger is shooting at you, prefer to have a gun, or not?—he answered by saying, "This is the conversation the gun lobby wants you to be having." He pointed out some of the obvious flaws in concealed-carry laws, such as too-lax training standards and too much discretionary power on the part of local law-enforcement officials. He did say that if concealed-carry laws required background checks and training similar to what police recruits undergo, he would be slower to raise objections. But then he added: "In a fundamental way, isn't this a question about the kind of society we want to live in?" Do we want to live in one "in which the answer to violence is more violence, where the answer to guns is more guns?"

What Gross won't acknowledge is that in a nation of nearly 300 million guns, his question is irrelevant.

JEFFREY GOLDBERG is a national correspondent for *The Atlantic* Magazine and a recipient of the National Magazine Award for Reporting. Author of the book *Prisoners: A Story of Friendship and Terror*, Goldberg also writes the magazine's advice column.

EXPLORING THE ISSUE

Should the United States Be More Restrictive of Gun Ownership?

Critical Thinking and Reflection

1. What are the arguments for placing greater restrictions on gun ownership in the United States? Which argument do you believe is most persuasive, why?
2. What are the arguments for loosening present restrictions on gun ownership in the United States? Which argument do you believe is most persuasive, why?
3. Do you believe mass tragedies like those in Aurora and Newtown can ever be prevented? Why or why not?
4. Cities like Chicago, which have some of the strictest gun control laws in the country, have the highest rates of gun violence in the United States. How does this happen? How can it be prevented?
5. Do you believe the Second Amendment is properly applied and understood in the United States? Why or why not?

Is There Common Ground?

While it may seem that lines are clearly drawn in the sand when it comes to gun control in the United States, in reality there is great potential for middle ground to be discovered. Throughout the history of guns in America, compromises have been reached. There are certain restrictions and purchasing protocols in place currently trying to assure that malintenioned individuals struggle to gain access to a firearm. In another vein, across the country concealed carry laws are becoming prominent, permitting skilled individuals to keep their piece on their person at all times. What these examples show is that both sides of the argument have made certain sacrifices already.

But there are concerns that are perhaps more difficult to bridge the gap on. Those opposed to gun control, for example, routinely point to the fact that criminals are not likely to obey any form of law passed related to access to weapons. In this scenario, law abiding citizens could find themselves vulnerable as only lawbreakers maintain firearms. At the same time, those in favor of curbing access will seemingly always have a fresh mass shooting to use when driving home key arguments. Few Americans are on the fence with regards to gun control, and consequently the sharpness of opinions leads one to believe that middle ground may be more difficult to realize than we originally expected.

Additional Resources

Gregg L. Carter, *Gun Control in the United States: A Reference Handbook* (ABC-CLIO, 2006)

Saul Cornell, *A Well-Regulated Militia: The Founding Fathers and the Origins of Gun Control in America* (Oxford University Press, 2008)

John R. Lott Jr., *More Guns, Less Crime: Understanding Crime and Gun Control Laws* (University of Chicago Press, 2010)

Robert Spitzer, *The Politics of Gun Control* (Paradigm, 2011)

Craig Whitney, *Living with Guns: A Liberal's Case for the Second Amendment* (PublicAffairs, 2012)

Internet References . . .

Brady Campaign to Prevent Gun Violence (BCPGV)

www.handguncontrol.org

Coalition to Stop Gun Violence (CSGV)

www.gunfree.org

National Criminal Justice Reference Service

www.ncjrs.gov/App/Topics/Topic.aspx?topicid=87

National Rifle Association

www.nra.org

Revolution PAC

www.revolutionpac.com

Selected, Edited, and with Issue Framing Material by:
William J. Miller, *Flagler College*

ISSUE

Should "Recreational" Drugs Be Legalized?

YES: Bryan Stevenson, from "Drug Policy, Criminal Justice, and Mass Imprisonment," *Global Commission on Drug Policy* (2011)

NO: Charles D. Stimson, from "Legalizing Marijuana: Why Citizens Should Just Say No," *Heritage Foundation Legal Memorandum* (2010)

Learning Outcomes

After reading this issue, you will be able to:

- Identify different interpretations of what should be classified as recreational drugs.
- Explain how individual choices can impact public well-being.
- Discuss the potential long-term health effects of drug usage.
- Explain why some argue that using certain drugs is not risky behavior.
- Identify the possible impacts to law enforcement of legalizing or not legalizing recreational drugs.

ISSUE SUMMARY

YES: Law professor Bryan Stevenson focuses on how the criminalization of drugs has led to mass imprisonment with negative consequences for law enforcement.

NO: Charles D. Stimson, former Deputy Assistant Secretary of Defense, explains that marijuana is not safe and makes more sense than the prohibition of alcohol did in the early 1900s. Further, he demonstrates that the economic benefits would not outweigh the societal costs.

Prohibition is a word Americans associate with the prohibition of liquor, which was adopted as a national policy with the ratification of the Eighteenth Amendment to the U.S. Constitution in 1920 and repealed with the adoption of the Twenty-first Amendment in 1933. Many states had earlier banned whiskey and other intoxicating beverages, and some states have had various restrictions since repeal.

Similarly, certain categories of illicit drugs were banned in some states prior to the passage of the Controlled Substance Act in 1970, which made the prohibition a national policy. Unlike the Prohibition Amendment, this was achieved by an Act of Congress. Many claimed then, and many still do today, that to do this in the absence of a constitutional amendment exceeds the power of the national government. Nevertheless, it has been upheld by the federal courts and has continued to function for more than four decades.

The principal substances that are banned include opium, heroin, cocaine, and marijuana. Marijuana is also known as cannabis (the plant from which it is obtained) and by a variety of informal names, most familiarly "pot." Its use dates back several thousand years, sometimes for religious or medical purposes. However, it is a so-called recreational drug that a United Nations committee characterized as "the most widely used illicit substance in the world." Because opium, heroin, and cocaine are more powerful, more addictive, and less prevalent, advocates of legalization often restrict their appeal to removing the ban on marijuana.

In the 50 years following an international convention in 1912 that urged the restriction of dangerous drugs, the use in the United States of illicit drugs other than marijuana was consistently below 1/2 of 1 percent of the population, with cocaine rising somewhat in the counter culture climate that began in the late 1950s. Illicit drug use was widely promoted as mind-expanding and relatively harmless. It is estimated that its use peaked in the 1970s. Present estimates for drugs other than marijuana suggest that between 5 and 10 percent of the population at least occasionally engages in the use of some illicit drugs.

In 2006, there were approximately 1.9 million drug arrests in the United States. Of these, 829,625 (44 percent of the total) were marijuana arrests. During the past two decades, the price of marijuana has gone down, its potency has increased, and it has become more readily available. Further, it has begun being mixed with other substances, increasing the potential for unintended side effects.

Studies, principally conducted in Sweden, Holland, and other nations with more tolerant drug policies, conclude that social factors influence drug use. Apart from peer pressure, particularly in the use of marijuana, hard drugs generally become more common in times of higher unemployment and lower income. Apart from cannabis, which is easily grown, the illicit character of hard drugs makes them expensive, but the profit motive induces growers, distributors, and "pushers" to risk arrest and punishment. It has been estimated that as many as one-sixth of all persons in federal prisons have been convicted of selling, possessing, or using marijuana.

The movement to legalize these drugs, often with a focus on marijuana, has existed as long as their prohibition, but in recent years has won recruits from both liberal and conservative ranks. As with the prohibition of alcohol, experience with the unintended consequences of prohibition of drugs led some to wonder whether this has not only failed to eliminate their use but has increased public health problems. Under the Prohibition Amendment, people drank unlicensed alcohol, often adulterated by the addition of poisonous substances. Illicit drug prohibition has led to the sale of toxic ingredients added to the drugs resulting in more impure and more dangerous products. Drug users injecting the drugs employ dirty reused needles that spread HIV and hepatitis B and C. While illicit drug use has never rivaled the widespread public acceptance of alcohol, their use has been extensive enough to spawn new networks of organized crime, violence related to the drug market, and the corruption of law enforcement and governments. We have recently witnessed this in the drug gang wars in Mexico that have slipped over into the American southwest.

Milton Friedman, who was America's most influential conservative economist, reached the interesting conclusion that drug prohibition has led to the rise of drug cartels. His reasoning was that only major retailers can handle massive shipments, own aircraft fleets, have armed troops, and employ lawyers and methods of eluding and bribing the police. Consequently, law enforcement as well as competition drives out smaller, less ruthless, and less efficient drug dealers.

The economic cost of legislating and attempting to enforce drug prohibition is very high. When the national policy went to effect, the federal cost was $350 million in 1971. Thirty-five years later in 2006, the cost was $30 billion. To this should be added the revenue that could be obtained if marijuana were subject to taxation. If it were taxed at the same rate as alcohol or tobacco, it has been estimated that it would yield as much as $7.7 billion. It may be, as advocates of legalization suggest, that the financial costs exceed the damages that the drugs themselves cause.

Against these arguments for repeal, those who support the war on drugs claim that prohibitive drug laws suppress drug use. Compare the large majority of Americans who consume legal alcohol with the very much smaller proportion who use illicit drugs. The Drug Enforcement Administration (DEA) has demonstrated that people under the influence of drugs are more than six times more likely to commit homicides than people looking for money to buy drugs. Drug use changes behavior and causes criminal activity. Cocaine-related paranoia frequently results in assaults, drugged driving, and domestic violence. These crimes are likely to increase when drugs are more readily available.

The point that liberalization advocates miss is that the illicit drugs are inherently harmful. In the short term, illicit drugs cause memory loss, distorted perception, a decline of motor skills, and an increased heart rate and anxiety. Particularly for young people, drug use produces a decline in mental development and motivation, as well as a reduced ability to concentrate in school.

The United States Centers for Disease Control and Prevention has concluded that although there are more than seven times more Americans who use alcohol than drugs, during a single year alone (2000), there were almost as many drug-induced deaths (15,8520) as alcohol-induced (18,539). The DEA concludes that drugs are "far more deadly than alcohol." This is true even for marijuana, which is deemed more potent than it was a generation ago. It contains more than 400 chemicals (the toxicity of some is clear and of many others is unknown) and one marijuana cigarette deposits four times more tar than a filtered tobacco cigarette.

The widespread support for medicinal marijuana seems to be changing public attitudes toward potential legalization. Colorado and Washington voters have sent a message that their respective states will exercise their rights under the Constitution legalizing the recreational use of marijuana. This process began with the legalization of medical marijuana in over a dozen states, opening the doors of debate with regards to the benefits of marijuana and dispelling some misconceptions. Party support has increased across the board. Republican support increased from 33 percent to 35 percent between November 2012 and October 2013, with Democratic changes increases from 61 percent to 65 percent and Independents from 50 percent to 62 percent within the same time period respectively. While marijuana is still illegal at the federal level, the Obama administration has made it clear that they will not go after users in states that choose to legalize. A memo sent from Attorney General Eric Holder to all U.S. attorneys informs them that the federal government will not intervene with state laws as long as the states follow certain protocols and guidelines in regulating product. Perhaps the tides are actually changing.

In the following selections, Bryan Stevenson, Executive Director of the Equal Justice Initiative, focuses on how the criminalization of drugs has led to mass imprisonment with negative consequences for law enforcement. Charles D. Stimson argues, on the other hand, that marijuana is by no means the safe drug some make it out to be and that the economic benefits of legalization will not be able to surmount the societal costs.

YES ⤶

Bryan Stevenson

Drug Policy, Criminal Justice, and Mass Imprisonment

The last three decades have witnessed a global increase in the criminalization of improper drug use. Criminalization has resulted in increased use of harsh punitive sanctions imposed on drug offenders and dramatic increases in rates of incarceration. These policies have had limited impact on eliminating or reducing illegal drug use and may have resulted in adverse consequences for social and community health. The criminal justice system has proved to be an ineffective forum for managing or controlling many aspects of the drug trade or the problem of illegal drug usage. In recent years, some progress has been reported when governing bodies have managed drug use and addiction as a public health problem which requires treatment, counseling and medical interventions rather than incarceration. Primarily as a result of drug policy, the number of people currently incarcerated worldwide is at an all time high of ten million.

In the United States, the prison population has increased from 300,000 in 1972 to 2.3 million people today. One in 31 adults in the United States is in jail, prison, on probation or parole. The American government currently spends over 68 billion dollars a year on incarceration. Drug Policy and the incarceration of low-level drug offenders is the primary cause of mass incarceration in the United States. [Forty percent] of drug arrests are for simple possession of marijuana. There is also evidence that drug enforcement has diverted resources from law enforcement of violent crimes and other threats to public safety.

Incarceration of low-level drug offenders has criminogenic effects that increase the likelihood of recidivism and additional criminal behavior. Enforcement of drug policy against low-level users and small scale trafficking has been racially biased and fueled social and political antagonisms that have undermined support of drug policy.

Growing evidence indicates that drug treatment and counseling programs are far more effective in reducing drug addiction and abuse than is incarceration. Needle exchange, compulsory treatment, education, counseling, drug substitutes like Methadone or Naxolene have proved highly effective in reducing addiction, overdose and the spread of HIV and Hepatitis C.

The last three decades have witnessed a global increase in the criminalization of improper drug use. Criminalization has resulted in increased use of harsh punitive sanctions imposed on drug offenders and dramatic increases in rates of incarceration. These policies have had limited impact on eliminating or reducing illegal drug use and may have resulted in adverse consequences for social and community health. The criminal justice system has proved to be an ineffective forum for managing or controlling many aspects of the drug trade or the problem of illegal drug usage. In recent years, some progress has been reported when governing bodies have managed drug use and addiction as a public health problem which requires treatment, counseling and medical interventions rather than incarceration. Most experts agree that drug-related HIV infection, the spread of infectious diseases like Hepatitis C and related public health concerns cannot be meaningfully addressed through jail and imprisonment and are often aggravated by policies which are primarily punitive. This paper briefly reviews this issue and identifies some of the costs of over-reliance on incarceration and outlines new strategies.

Criminal Justice Policy and Increased Use of Sanctions and Incarceration for Low-Level Drug Offenders

The Criminalization of Drugs and the Legacy of Mass Imprisonment

Criminalization of possession and illegal use of drugs compounded by mandatory sentencing and lengthy prison sanctions for low-level drug use has become the primary cause of mass incarceration. The global prison population has skyrocketed in the last three decades with ten million people worldwide now in jails and prisons. The extraordinary increase in the number of people now incarcerated has had tremendous implications for state and national governments dealing with global recession and a range of economic, social and political challenges. Research indicates that resources that would otherwise be spent on development, infrastructure, education and health care have been redirected over the last two decades to incarcerating drug offenders, many of whom are low-level users. The trend toward mass incarceration has been especially troubling in the United States. In the last thirty-five years, the number of U.S. residents in prison has

From *Drug Policy, Criminal Justice and Mass Imprisonment*, January 2011. Copyright © 2011 by Global Commission on Drug Policies. Reprinted by permission.

increased from 330,000 people in jails and prisons in 1972 to almost 2.3 million imprisoned people today. The United States now has the highest rate of incarceration in the world.

Over five million people are on probation and parole in America. Currently, one out of 100 adults is in jail or prison and one out of 31 adults is in jail, prison on probation or parole. The consequences of increased incarceration and penal control strategies have been dramatic and costly. Many states spend in excess of $50,000 a year to incarcerate each prisoner in a state prison or facility, including non-violent, low-level drug offenders. Corrections spending by state and federal governments has risen from $6.9 billion in 1980 to $68 billion in 2006 in America. During the ten year period between 1985 and 1995, prisons were constructed at a pace of one new prison opening each week.

The economic toll of expansive imprisonment policies has been accompanied by socio-political consequences as well. Mass incarceration has had discernible impacts in poor and minority communities which have been disproportionately impacted by drug enforcement strategies. Collateral consequences of drug prosecutions of low-level offenders have included felon disenfranchisement laws, where in some states drug offenders permanently lose the right to vote. Sociologists have also recently observed that the widespread incarceration of men in low-income communities has had a profound negative impact on social and cultural norms relating to family and opportunity. Increases in the imprisonment of poor and minority women with children have now been linked with rising numbers of displaced children and dependents. Drug policy and the over-reliance on incarceration is seen by many experts as contributing to increased rates of chronic unemployment, destabilization of families and increased risk of reincarceration for the formerly incarcerated.

There are unquestionably serious consequences for community and public health when illegal use of drugs is widespread. Addiction and other behavioral issues triggered by drug abuse have well known consequences for individuals, families, communities and governing bodies trying to protect public safety. Governing bodies are clearly justified in pursuing policies and strategies that disrupt the drug trade and the violence frequently associated with high-level drug trafficking. Similarly, drug abuse is a serious problem within communities that threatens public health and merits serious attention. However, some interventions to address drug abuse are now emerging as clearly more effective than others. Consequently, interventions that reduce drug dependence and improve the prospects for eliminating drug addiction and abuse are essential if measurable improvements on this issue are to be achieved in the coming years.

Drug Policy and the Criminal Justice System

Many countries have employed the rhetoric of war to combat the drug trade. While there are countries where violent drug kingpens have created large militias that have necessitated more militarized responses from law enforcement, most drug arrests are directed at low-level

users who have been the primary targets in the "war on drugs." States have criminalized simple possession of drugs like marijuana and imposed harsh and lengthy sentences on people arrested. Small amounts of narcotics, unauthorized prescription medicines and other drugs have triggered trafficking charges that impose even lengthier prison sentences. The introduction of habitual felony offender laws has exacerbated drug policy as it is not uncommon for illegal drug users to accumulate multiple charges in a very short period of time. Under the notorious "three strikes laws" that have become popular in America, drug offenders with no history of violence may face mandatory minimum sentences in excess of 25 years in prison. Thousands of low-level drug offenders have been sentenced to life imprisonment with no chance of parole as a result of these sentencing laws.

In the United States, drug arrests have tripled in the last 25 years, however most of these arrests have been for simple possession of low-level drugs. In 2005, nearly 43% of all drug arrests were for marijuana offenses. Marijuana possession arrests accounted for 79% of the growth in drug arrests in the 1990s. Nearly a half million people are in state or federal prisons or a local jail for a drug offense, compared to 41,000 in 1980. Most of these people have no history of violence or high-level drug selling activity.

The "war on drugs" has also generated indirect costs that many researchers contend have undermined public safety. The federal government has prioritized spending and grants for drug task forces and widespread drug interdiction efforts that often target low-level drug dealing. These highly organized and coordinated efforts have been very labor intensive for local law enforcement agencies with some unanticipated consequences for investigation of other crimes. The focus on drugs is believed to have redirected law enforcement resources that have resulted in more drunk driving, and decreased investigation and enforcement of violent crime laws. In Illinois, a 47% increase in drug arrests corresponded with a 22% decrease in arrests for drunk driving. Florida researchers have similarly linked the focus on low level drug arrests with an increase in the serious crime index.

In prison, as a result of the increased costs of incarceration, most drug addicts are less likely to receive drug treatment and therapy. The increasing costs of mass imprisonment have eliminated funds for treatment and counseling services even though some of these services have proved to be very effective. In 1991, one in three prison inmates was receiving treatment while incarcerated, today the rate is down to one in seven. The decline of treatment and counseling services makes re-offending once released much more likely. This is one of the ways in which incarceration and criminal justice intervention has proved costly and less effective than other models of managing illegal drug use.

Racially Discriminatory Enforcement of Drug Laws

In the United States, considerable evidence demonstrates that enforcement of drug policy has proved to be racially discriminatory and very biased against the poor. America's criminal justice system is very wealth sensitive which makes it difficult for low-income residents to obtain equally favorable outcomes as more wealthy residents when they are charged with drug crimes. Targeting communities of color for enforcement of drug laws has added to the problems of racial bias in American society and generated some of the fiercest debates about the continuing legacy of racial discrimination. Illegal use of drugs is not unique to communities of color and rates of offending are not higher in these communities than they are in non-minority communities. African Americans comprise 14% of regular drug users in the United States, yet are 37% of those arrested for drug offenses and 56% of those incarcerated for drug crimes. Black people in the United States serve almost as much time in federal prison for a drug offense (58.7 months) as whites serve for a violent crime (61.7 months), primarily as a result of the racially disparate sentencing laws such as the 100-1 crack powder cocaine disparity. For years, the sentences for illegal possession or use of crack cocaine, which is more prevalent in communities of color, were 100 times greater than possession or use of equivalent amounts of powder cocaine, leading to dramatically longer prison sentences for African Americans. In 2010, Congress amended this law and reduced the disparity from 100-1 to 12-1. However, the failure to make the law retroactive has left the costly and troubling racial disparities uncorrected. Hispanic people are also disproportionately at much greater risk of arrest and prosecution for drug crimes than are whites in the United States.

Discriminatory enforcement of drug laws against communities of color has seriously undermined the integrity of drug policy initiatives and frequently these policies are perceived as unfair, unjust and targeted at racial minorities. Enforcement of drug laws tends to be directed at low-income communities or residential and social centers where residents have less political power to resist aggressive policing and engagement. Even some reforms aimed at shielding low-level drug offenders from incarceration have been skewed against the poor and people of color. Some data show that people of color are more likely to be redirected back to the criminal courts if drug court personnel have discretion. Similarly, many community-based programs that permit drug offenders to avoid jail or prison have significant admission fees and costs that many poor people simply cannot afford. Discriminatory enforcement of drug policy has undermined its effectiveness and legitimacy and contributed to continuing dysfunction in the administration of criminal justice.

There Is Growing Evidence that Drug Treatment Is More Cost Effective than Incarceration and Incapacitation Strategies

One of the clear consequences of mass incarceration directed at low level drug offenders has been to acculturate and socialize illegal drug users into criminality through extended incarceration. This criminogenic effect has been seen in studies that examined rates of recidivism among drug offenders who are given probation and not sent to jail or prison and drug offenders who are incarcerated for the same offenses. In purely human terms, these findings reveal that incarceration may be dramatically more costly than other approaches.

However, the economic analysis of approaches to low level drug offending that avoid incarceration are even more compelling. Whatever the measure, data indicates that drug treatment is more cost effective than incarceration. In California, a study has recently shown that spending on drug treatment is eight times more likely to reduce drug consumption than spending on incarceration. Corresponding decreases in drug-related crime were also documented when comparing drug treatment programs with incarceration. In a RAND analysis study, treatment was estimated to reduce crime associated with drug use and the drug trade up to 15 times as much as incarceration. These findings have been reflected in other studies that have also found that drug treatment is more cost effective in controlling drug abuse and crime than continued expansion of the prison system when looking at low level drug offenders.

Consequently, many states have now started to shift their management of drug offenders to drug courts that have discretion to redirect people who illegally use drugs away from jail or prison and into community-based treatment, counseling and therapeutic interventions. The early signs suggest that these innovations are saving states millions of dollars and accomplishing improved public safety. For the first time in 38 years, 2010 saw a slight decrease in the national state prison population in the United States. Significant reductions will need to continue to deal with a global recession and decreasing resources available for incarceration.

New and More Effective Strategies for Managing Low-Level Drug Offenders Are Emerging

Proponents of "Harm Reduction" have long argued that a more effective way to combat illegal drug use is to spend more on public education, treatment and interventions that view illegal drug use as a public health problem rather than continued spending on incarceration and harsh sanctions. Supporters of harm reduction acknowledge that the use of incarceration and sanctions will be necessary when illegal drug trafficking or distribution threatens public safety, however, they contend that most drug arrests don't directly implicate public safety. States are beginning to recognize the benefits associated with harm reduction and in recent years have begun to reallocate resources with surprisingly good outcomes.

Sentencing Reform

In recent years, states have begun to retreat from mandatory sentences and other harsh strategies for enforcing drug laws and moved to alternative models that involve probation, treatment, counseling and education. Between 2004 and 2006, at least 13 states expanded drug treatment or programs which divert drug offenders away from jail or prison into community-based programs. States like Michigan have recently amended statutes that required a mandatory sentence of life imprisonment without parole for distribution of cocaine or heroin. With over 5 million people on probation or parole in the United States, drug use on parole or probation has become the primary basis by which thousands of people are returned to prison. These technical violations of parole or probation account for as many as 40% of new prison admissions in some jurisdictions. In recent years, states have restricted the length of incarceration imposed when formerly incarcerated people test positive for recent drug use. These new statues . . . incarcerated drug users into drug therapy and counseling programs.

The federal government has amended mandatory sentencing laws for drug offenders and seen a dramatic reduction in the number of people facing long-term incarceration for low-level drug use. These sentencing reforms are considered critical to containing the costs of mass imprisonment in the United States and for generating resources necessary to approach drug addiction and abuse as a public health problem.

Drug courts have also emerged in the last decade to play a critical role in redirecting low-level drug offenders away from traditional, punitive models of intervention for illegal drug use. Drug courts have been set up in hundreds of communities. Court personnel have discretion to order drug treatment and community-based programs where offenders must receive counseling and treatment and receive education concerning drug addiction and abuse. By shielding thousands of drug offenders from incarceration and transfer to overcrowded prisons, drug courts have reduced the collateral consequences of illegal drug use, saved millions of dollars and had more favorable outcomes for people who have been identified as illegally using drugs. Drug court participants can avoid a criminal record and all the disabling collateral consequences associated with a criminal record.

Reducing the penalties for some low-level drug crimes, giving judges more discretion to avoid unwarranted and lengthy mandatory sentences and retreating from the rhetoric of war and unscientific policy analysis could substantially reduce incarceration rates and provide additional resources for treatment options that are more effective at eliminating drug abuse.

Medical and Public Health Models for Drug Abuse Intervention

The risk of criminal prosecution has had many unintended consequences, especially for people with addiction problems who also have critical medical issues that require treatment and intervention. HIV infection and AIDS continue to threaten many countries with tragic and devastating effect. Intravenous drug users are primary targets for infection and have extremely elevated risks of illness from sharing needles. Rather than facilitating less hazardous practices for this community, criminal justice interventions have forced people with addiction underground and infection rates have spiraled. Providing clean needles and other strategies associated with needle exchange have had a significant impact on reducing the rate of HIV infection and offering people with addiction issues an opportunity for treatment. Creating safe zones where people struggling with drug addiction can safely come has also greatly increased the ability of public health officials to provide education, counseling and treatment opportunities that are scientifically proven to be effective to the population with the greatest needs. For example, where needle-exchange has been implemented, the results have been extremely promising for controlling illegal drug use and reducing public health threats.

Policies that make it permissible for people to safely admit to drug addiction problems are well established to be more effective at managing drug addiction. In 2006, there were 26,000 deaths in the United States from accidental drug overdose, the highest level ever recorded by the Centers for Disease Control. Accidental death through overdose is currently the leading cause of injury-related death for people between the ages of 35–54. This extraordinarily high level of death through overdose can only be meaningfully confronted with public education efforts and improving treatment options for people who are abusing drugs.

Criminalization has created huge and complex obstacles for people motivated to eliminate their drug dependence to seek or obtain necessary health care and support. When public health options are made available, studies have reported dramatic declines in drug dependence, mortality and overdose. Medical developments have proved extremely effective in reducing drug dependence and addiction. A range of maintenance therapies are available for people with addiction problems. Methadone maintenance has been cited as the primary intervention strategy for people with heroin addiction. Drugs like Naloxone have been utilized in an extremely effective manner to save lives when people ingest too many opiates. However, these very cost effective treatments are not possible without providing safe opportunities to report drug and overdose issues to health care providers who are free to treat rather than arrest people with addiction and drug dependence.

Mass imprisonment, the high economic and social costs of incarcerating low-level drug offenders and the ineffectiveness of criminalization and punitive approaches to drug addiction have had poor outcomes in many countries. Governing bodies have available dozens of new, scientifically tested interventions which have been proved to lower rates of drug abuse and addiction without incarceration. Reducing illegal drug use and disrupting the sometimes violent drug trade will require new and more effective strategies in the 21st century. The politics of fear and anger that have generated many of these policies must be resisted and adoption of scientifically established treatment protocols that have been found effective and successful should be pursued vigorously.

BRYAN STEVENSON is a faculty member of the New York University School of Law and executive director of the Equal Justice Initiative, an organization that focuses on criminal justice reform.

Charles D. Stimson

 **NO**

Legalizing Marijuana: Why Citizens Should Just Say No

The scientific literature is clear that marijuana is addictive and that its use significantly impairs bodily and mental functions. Marijuana use is associated with memory loss, cancer, immune system deficiencies, heart disease, and birth defects, among other conditions. Even where decriminalized, marijuana trafficking remains a source of violence, crime, and social disintegration.

Nonetheless, this November, California voters will consider a ballot initiative, the Regulate, Control and Tax Cannabis Act of 2010 (RCTCA), that would legalize most marijuana distribution and use under state law. (These activities would remain federal crimes.) This vote is the culmination of an organized campaign by pro-marijuana activists stretching back decades.

The current campaign, like previous efforts, downplays the well-documented harms of marijuana trafficking and use while promising benefits ranging from reduced crime to additional tax revenue. In particular, supporters of the initiative make five bold claims:

1. "Marijuana is safe and non-addictive."
2. "Marijuana prohibition makes no more sense than alcohol prohibition did in the early 1900s."
3. "The government's efforts to combat illegal drugs have been a total failure."
4. "The money spent on government efforts to combat the illegal drug trade can be better spent on substance abuse and treatment for the allegedly few marijuana users who abuse the drug."
5. "Tax revenue collected from marijuana sales would substantially outweigh the social costs of legalization."

As this paper details, all five claims are demonstrably false or, based on the best evidence, highly dubious.

Further, supporters of the initiative simply ignore the mechanics of decriminalization—that is, how it would directly affect law enforcement, crime, and communities. Among the important questions left unanswered are:

- How would the state law fit into a federal regime that prohibits marijuana production, distribution, and possession?

- Would decriminalization, especially if combined with taxation, expand market opportunities for the gangs and cartels that currently dominate drug distribution?
- Would existing zoning laws prohibit marijuana cultivation in residential neighborhoods, and if not, what measures would growers have to undertake to keep children from the plants?
- Would transportation providers be prohibited from firing bus drivers because they smoke marijuana?

No one knows the specifics of how marijuana decriminalization would work in practice or what measures would be necessary to prevent children, teenagers, criminals, and addicts from obtaining the drug.

The federal government shares these concerns. Gil Kerlikowske, Director of the White House Office of National Drug Control Policy (ONDCP), recently stated, "Marijuana legalization, for any purpose, is a non-starter in the Obama Administration." The Administration—widely viewed as more liberal than any other in recent memory and, for a time, as embodying the hopes of pro-legalization activists—has weighed the costs and benefits and concluded that marijuana legalization would compromise public health and safety.

California's voters, if they take a fair-minded look at the evidence and the practical problems of legalization, should reach the same conclusion: Marijuana is a dangerous substance that should remain illegal under state law.

The Initiative

The RCTCA's purpose, as defined by advocates of legalization, is to regulate marijuana just as the government regulates alcohol. The law would allow anyone 21 years of age or older to possess, process, share, or transport up to one full ounce of marijuana "for personal consumption." Individuals could possess an unlimited number of living and harvested marijuana plants on the premises where they were grown. Individual landowners or lawful occupants of private property could cultivate marijuana plants "for personal consumption" in an area of not more than 25 square feet per private residence or parcel.

Stimson, Charles D. From *Legal Memorandum No. 56,* September 13, 2010. Copyright © 2010 by The Heritage Foundation. Reprinted by permission.

The RCTCA would legalize drug-related paraphernalia and tools and would license establishments for on-site smoking and other consumption of marijuana. Supporters have included some alcohol-like restrictions against, for example, smoking marijuana while operating a vehicle. Finally, the act authorizes the imposition and collection of taxes and fees associated with legalization of marijuana.

Unsafe in Any Amount: How Marijuana Is Not Like Alcohol

Marijuana advocates have had some success peddling the notion that marijuana is a "soft" drug, similar to alcohol, and fundamentally different from "hard" drugs like cocaine or heroin. It is true that marijuana is not the most dangerous of the commonly abused drugs, but that is not to say that it is safe. Indeed, marijuana shares more in common with the "hard" drugs than it does with alcohol.

A common argument for legalization is that smoking marijuana is no more dangerous than drinking alcohol and that prohibiting the use of marijuana is therefore no more justified than the prohibition of alcohol. As Jacob Sullum, author of *Saying Yes: In Defense of Drug Use*, writes:

> Americans understood the problems associated with alcohol abuse, but they also understood the problems associated with Prohibition, which included violence, organized crime, official corruption, the erosion of civil liberties, disrespect for the law, and injuries and deaths caused by tainted black-market booze. They decided that these unintended side effects far outweighed whatever harms Prohibition prevented by discouraging drinking. The same sort of analysis today would show that the harm caused by drug prohibition far outweighs the harm it prevents, even without taking into account the value to each individual of being sovereign over his own body and mind.

At first blush, this argument is appealing, especially to those wary of over-regulation by government. But it overlooks the enormous difference between alcohol and marijuana.

Legalization advocates claim that marijuana and alcohol are mild intoxicants and so should be regulated similarly; but as the experience of nearly every culture, over the thousands of years of human history, demonstrates, alcohol is different. Nearly every culture has its own alcoholic preparations, and nearly all have successfully regulated alcohol consumption through cultural norms. The same cannot be said of marijuana. There are several possible explanations for alcohol's unique status: For most people, it is not addictive; it is rarely consumed to the point of intoxication; low-level consumption is consistent with most manual and intellectual tasks; it has several positive health benefits; and it is formed by the fermentation of many common substances and easily metabolized by the body.

To be sure, there are costs associated with alcohol abuse, such as drunk driving and disease associated with excessive consumption. A few cultures—and this nation for a short while during Prohibition—have concluded that the benefits of alcohol consumption are not worth the costs. But they are the exception; most cultures have concluded that it is acceptable in moderation. No other intoxicant shares that status.

Alcohol differs from marijuana in several crucial respects. First, marijuana is far more likely to cause addiction. Second, it is usually consumed to the point of intoxication. Third, it has no known general healthful properties, though it may have some palliative effects. Fourth, it is toxic and deleterious to health. Thus, while it is true that both alcohol and marijuana are less intoxicating than other mood-altering drugs, that is not to say that marijuana is especially similar to alcohol or that its use is healthy or even safe.

In fact, compared to alcohol, marijuana is not safe. Long-term, moderate consumption of alcohol carries few health risks and even offers some significant benefits. For example, a glass of wine (or other alcoholic drink) with dinner actually improves health. Dozens of peer-reviewed medical studies suggest that drinking moderate amounts of alcohol reduces the risk of heart disease, strokes, gallstones, diabetes, and death from a heart attack. According to the Mayo Clinic, among many others, moderate use of alcohol (defined as two drinks a day) "seems to offer some health benefits, particularly for the heart." Countless articles in medical journals and other scientific literature confirm the positive health effects of moderate alcohol consumption.

The effects of regular marijuana consumption are quite different. For example, the National Institute on Drug Abuse (a division of the National Institutes of Health) has released studies showing that use of marijuana has wide-ranging negative health effects. Long-term marijuana consumption "impairs the ability of T-cells in the lungs' immune system to fight off some infections." These studies have also found that marijuana consumption impairs short-term memory, making it difficult to learn and retain information or perform complex tasks; slows reaction time and impairs motor coordination; increases heart rate by 20 percent to 100 percent, thus elevating the risk of heart attack; and alters moods, resulting in artificial euphoria, calmness, or (in high doses) anxiety or paranoia. And it gets worse: Marijuana has toxic properties that can result in birth defects, pain, respiratory system damage, brain damage, and stroke.

Further, prolonged use of marijuana may cause cognitive degradation and is "associated with lower test scores and lower educational attainment because during periods of intoxication the drug affects the ability to learn and process information, thus influencing attention, concentration, and short-term memory." Unlike alcohol, marijuana has been shown to have a residual effect on cognitive ability that persists beyond the period of intoxication. According to the National Institute on Drug Abuse, whereas alcohol is broken down relatively quickly in the human body, THC (tetrahydrocannabinol, the main active chemical in marijuana) is stored in organs and fatty tissues, allowing it to remain in a user's body for days or even weeks after consumption. Research has shown that marijuana consumption may also cause "psychotic symptoms."

Marijuana's effects on the body are profound. According to the British Lung Foundation, "smoking three or four marijuana joints is as bad for your lungs as smoking twenty tobacco cigarettes." Researchers in Canada found that marijuana smoke contains significantly higher levels of numerous toxic compounds, like ammonia and hydrogen cyanide, than regular tobacco smoke. In fact, the study determined that ammonia was found in marijuana smoke at levels of up to 20 times the levels found in tobacco. Similarly, hydrogen cyanide was found in marijuana smoke at concentrations three to five times greater than those found in tobacco smoke.

Marijuana, like tobacco, is addictive. One study found that more than 30 percent of adults who used marijuana in the course of a year were dependent on the drug. These individuals often show signs of withdrawal and compulsive behavior. Marijuana dependence is also responsible for a large proportion of calls to drug abuse help lines and treatment centers.

To equate marijuana use with alcohol consumption is, at best, uninformed and, at worst, actively misleading. Only in the most superficial ways are the two substances alike, and they differ in every way that counts: addictiveness, toxicity, health effects, and risk of intoxication.

Unintended Consequences

Today, marijuana trafficking is linked to a variety of crimes, from assault and murder to money laundering and smuggling. Legalization of marijuana would increase demand for the drug and almost certainly exacerbate drug-related crime, as well as cause a myriad of unintended but predictable consequences.

To begin with, an astonishingly high percentage of criminals are marijuana users. According to a study by the RAND Corporation, approximately 60 percent of arrestees test positive for marijuana use in the United States, England, and Australia. Further, marijuana metabolites are found in arrestees' urine more frequently than those of any other drug.

Although some studies have shown marijuana to inhibit aggressive behavior and violence, the National Research Council concluded that the "long-term use of marijuana may alter the nervous system in ways that do promote violence." No place serves as a better example than Amsterdam.

Marijuana advocates often point to the Netherlands as a well-functioning society with a relaxed attitude toward drugs, but they rarely mention that Amsterdam is one of Europe's most violent cities. In Amsterdam, officials are in the process of closing marijuana dispensaries, or "coffee shops," because of the crime associated with their operation. Furthermore, the Dutch Ministry of Health, Welfare and Sport has expressed "concern about drug

and alcohol use among young people and the social consequences, which range from poor school performance and truancy to serious impairment, including brain damage."

Amsterdam's experience is already being duplicated in California under the current medical marijuana statute. In Los Angeles, police report that areas surrounding cannabis clubs have experienced a 200 percent increase in robberies, a 52.2 percent increase in burglaries, a 57.1 percent increase in aggravated assault, and a 130.8 percent increase in burglaries from automobiles. Current law requires a doctor's prescription to procure marijuana; full legalization would likely spark an even more acute increase in crime.

Legalization of marijuana would also inflict a series of negative consequences on neighborhoods and communities. The nuisance caused by the powerful odor of mature marijuana plants is already striking California municipalities. The City Council of Chico, California, has released a report detailing the situation and describing how citizens living near marijuana cultivators are disturbed by the incredible stink emanating from the plants.

Perhaps worse than the smell, crime near growers is increasing, associated with "the theft of marijuana from yards where it is being grown." As a result, housing prices near growers are sinking.

Theoretical arguments in favor of marijuana legalization usually overlook the practical matter of how the drug would be regulated and sold. It is the details of implementation, of course, that will determine the effect of legalization on families, schools, and communities. Most basically, how and where would marijuana be sold?

- Would neighborhoods become neon red-light districts like Amsterdam's, accompanied by the same crime and social disorder?
- If so, who decides what neighborhoods will be so afflicted—residents and landowners or far-off government officials?
- Or would marijuana sales be so widespread that users could add it to their grocery lists?
- If so, how would stores sell it, how would they store it, and how would they prevent it from being diverted into the gray market?
- Would stores dealing in marijuana have to fortify their facilities to reduce the risk of theft and assault?

The most likely result is that the drug will not be sold in legitimate stores at all, because while the federal government is currently tolerating medical marijuana dispensaries, it will not tolerate widescale sales under general legalizational statutes. So marijuana will continue to be sold on the gray or black market.

The act does not answer these or other practical questions regarding implementation. Rather, it leaves those issues to localities. No doubt, those entities will pass a variety of laws in an attempt to deal with the many problems caused by legalization, unless the local laws are struck down by California courts as inconsistent with the underlying initiative, which would be even worse. At best, that patchwork of laws, differing from one locality to another, will be yet another unintended and predictable problem arising from legalization as envisioned under this act.

Citizens also should not overlook what may be the greatest harms of marijuana legalization: increased addiction to and use of harder drugs. In addition to marijuana's harmful effects on the body and relationship to criminal conduct, it is a gateway drug that can lead users to more dangerous drugs. Prosecutors, judges, police officers, detectives, parole or probation officers, and even defense attorneys know that the vast majority of defendants arrested for violent crimes test positive for illegal drugs, including marijuana. They also know that marijuana is the starter drug of choice for most criminals. Whereas millions of Americans consume moderate amounts of alcohol without ever "moving on" to dangerous drugs, marijuana use and cocaine use are strongly correlated.

While correlation does not necessarily reflect causation, and while the science is admittedly mixed as to whether it is the drug itself or the people the new user associates with who cause the move on to cocaine, heroin, LSD, or other drugs, the RAND Corporation reports that marijuana prices and cocaine use are directly linked, suggesting a substitution effect between the two drugs. Moreover, according to RAND, legalization will cause marijuana prices to fall as much as 80 percent. That can lead to significant consequences because "a 10-percent decrease in the price of marijuana would increase the prevalence of cocaine use by 4.4 to 4.9 percent." As cheap marijuana floods the market both in and outside of California, use of many different types of drugs will increase, as will marijuana use.

It is impossible to predict the precise consequences of legalization, but the experiences of places that have eased restrictions on marijuana are not positive. Already, California is suffering crime, dislocation, and increased drug use under its current regulatory scheme. Further liberalizing the law will only make matters worse.

Flouting Federal Law

Another area of great uncertainty is how a state law legalizing marijuana would fit in with federal law to the contrary. Congress has enacted a comprehensive regulatory scheme for restricting access to illicit drugs and other controlled substances. The Controlled Substances Act of 1970 prohibits the manufacture, distribution, and possession of all substances deemed to be Schedule I drugs—drugs like heroin, PCP, and cocaine. Because marijuana has no "currently accepted medical use in treatment in the United States," it is a Schedule I drug that cannot be bought, sold, possessed, or used without violating federal law.

Under the Supremacy Clause of the Constitution of the United States, the Controlled Substances Act is the supreme law of the land and cannot be superseded by state laws that purport to contradict or abrogate its terms. The RCTCA proposes to "reform California's cannabis laws in a way that will benefit our state" and "[r]egulate

cannabis like we do alcohol." But the act does not even purport to address the fundamental constitutional infirmity that it would be in direct conflict with federal law. If enacted and unchallenged by the federal government, it would call into question the government's ability to regulate all controlled substances, including drugs such as Oxycontin, methamphetamine, heroin, and powder and crack cocaine. More likely, however, the feds would challenge the law in court, and the courts would have no choice but to strike it down.

Congress has the power to change the Controlled Substances Act and remove marijuana from Schedule I. Yet after decades of lobbying, it has not, largely because of the paucity of scientific evidence in support of a delisting.

California, in fact, is already in direct violation of federal law. Today, its laws allow the use of marijuana as a treatment for a range of vaguely defined conditions, including chronic pain, nausea, and lack of appetite, depression, anxiety, and glaucoma. "Marijuana doctors" are listed in the classified advertising sections of newspapers, and many are conveniently located adjacent to "dispensaries." At least one "doctor" writes prescriptions from a tiny hut beside the Venice Beach Boardwalk.

This "medical marijuana" law and similar ones in other states are premised on circumvention of the Food and Drug Administration (FDA) approval process. "FDA's drug approval process requires well-controlled clinical trials that provide the necessary scientific data upon which FDA makes its approval and labeling decisions." Marijuana, even that supposedly used for medicinal purposes, has been rejected by the FDA because, among other reasons, it "has no currently accepted or proven medical use."

The lack of FDA approval means that marijuana may come from unknown sources, may be adulterated with foreign substances, or may not even be marijuana at all. Pot buyers have no way to know what they are getting, and there is no regulatory authority with the ability to go after bogus manufacturers and dealers. Even if one overlooks its inherently harmful properties, marijuana that is commonly sold is likely to be far less safe than that studied in the lab or elsewhere.

Marijuana advocates claim that federal enforcement of drug laws, particularly in jurisdictions that allow the use of medical marijuana, violates states' rights. The Supreme Court, however, has held otherwise. In 2002, California resident Angel Raich produced and consumed marijuana, purportedly for medical purposes. Her actions, while in accordance with California's "medical marijuana" law, clearly violated the Controlled Substances Act, and the local sheriff's department destroyed Raich's plants. Raich claimed that she needed to use marijuana, prescribed by her doctor, for medical purposes. She sued the federal government, asking the court to stop the government from interfering with her right to produce and use marijuana.

In 2006, the Supreme Court held in *Gonzales vs. Raich* that the Commerce Clause confers on Congress the authority to ban the use of marijuana, even when a state approves it for "medical purposes" and it is produced in small quantities for personal consumption.

Many legal scholars criticize the Court's extremely broad reading of the Commerce Clause as inconsistent with its original meaning, but the Court's decision nonetheless stands.

If the RCTCA were enacted, it would conflict with the provisions of the Controlled Substances Act and invite extensive litigation that would almost certainly result in its being struck down. Until that happened, state law enforcement officers would be forced into a position of uncertainty regarding their conflicting obligations under federal and state law and cooperation with federal authorities.

Bogus Economics

An innovation of the campaign in support of RCTCA is its touting of the potential benefit of legalization to the government, in terms of additional revenues from taxing marijuana and savings from backing down in the "war on drugs." The National Organization for the Reform of Marijuana Laws (NORML), for example, claims that legalization "could yield California taxpayers over $1.2 billion per year" in tax benefits. According to a California NORML Report updated in October 2009, an excise tax of $50 per ounce would raise about $770 million to $900 million per year and save over $200 million in law enforcement costs per year. It is worth noting that $900 million equates to 18 million ounces—enough marijuana for Californians to smoke one billion marijuana cigarettes each year.

But these projections are highly speculative and riddled with unfounded assumptions. Dr. Rosalie Liccardo Pacula, an expert with the RAND Corporation who has studied the economics of drug policy for over 15 years, has explained that the California "Board of Equalization's estimate of $1.4 billion [in] potential revenue for the state is based on a series of assumptions that are in some instances subject to tremendous uncertainty and in other cases not validated." She urged the California Committee on Public Safety to conduct an honest and thorough cost-benefit analysis of the potential revenues and costs associated with legalizing marijuana. To date, no such realistic cost-benefit analysis has been done.

In her testimony before the committee, Dr. Pacula stated that prohibition raises the cost of production by at least 400 percent and that legalizing marijuana would cause the price of marijuana to fall considerably—much more than the 50 percent price reduction incorporated into the state's revenue model. Furthermore, she noted that a $50-per-ounce marijuana tax was not realistic, because it would represent a 100 percent tax on the cost of the product.

Under the state scheme, she testified, there would be "tremendous profit motive for the existing black market providers to stay in the market." The only way California could effectively eliminate the black market for marijuana, according to Dr. Pacula, "is to take away the substantial profits in the market and allow the price of marijuana to fall to an amount close to the cost of production. Doing so, however, will mean substantially smaller tax revenue than currently anticipated from this change in policy."

The RCTCA, in fact, allows for so much individual production of marijuana that even the Board of Equalization's $1.4 billion per year revenue estimate seems unlikely. Under the law, any resident could grow marijuana for "personal use" in a plot at home up to 25 square feet in size. One ounce of marijuana is enough for 60 to 120 marijuana cigarettes. One plant produces one to five pounds, or 16 to 80 ounces, of marijuana each year, and 25 square feet of land can sustain about 25 plants. Therefore, an individual will be able to produce 24,000 to 240,000 joints legally each year.

Not only is this more than any individual could possibly consume; it is also enough to encourage individuals to grow and sell pot under the individual allowance. Who would buy marijuana from a state-regulated store and pay the $50 tax per ounce in addition to the sale price when they can either grow it themselves or buy it at a much lower price from a friend or neighbor? In this way, the RCTCA undermines its supporters' lavish revenue claims.

Other Negative Social Costs

In addition to its direct effects on individual health, even moderate marijuana use imposes significant long-term costs through the ways that it affects individual users. Marijuana use is associated with cognitive difficulties and influences attention, concentration, and short-term memory. This damage affects drug users' ability to work and can put others at risk. Even if critical workers—for example, police officers, airline pilots, and machine operators—used marijuana recreationally but remained sober on the job, the long-term cognitive deficiency that remained from regular drug use would sap productivity and place countless people in danger. Increased use would also send health care costs skyrocketing—costs borne not just by individual users, but also by the entire society.

For that reason, among others, the Obama Administration also rejects supporters' economic arguments. In his speech, Kerlikowske explained that tax revenue from cigarettes is far outweighed by their social costs: "Tobacco also does not carry its economic weight when we tax it; each year we spend more than $200 billion and collect only about $25 billion in taxes." If the heavy taxation of cigarettes is unable even to come close to making up for the health and other costs associated with their use, it seems doubtful at best that marijuana taxes would be sufficient to cover the costs of legalized marijuana—especially considering that, in addition to the other dangers of smoking marijuana, the physical health effects of just three to four joints are equivalent to those of an entire pack of cigarettes.

Other claims also do not measure up. One of the express purposes of the California initiative is to "put dangerous, underground street dealers out of business, so their influence in our communities will fade." But as explained above, many black-market dealers would rationally choose to remain in the black market to avoid taxation and regulation. Vibrant gray markets have developed throughout the world for many products that are legal, regulated, and heavily taxed. Cigarettes in Eastern Europe, alcohol in Scandinavia, luxury automobiles in Russia, and DVDs in the Middle East are all legal goods traded in gray markets that are wracked with violence. In Canada, an attempt at a $3 per pack tax on cigarettes was greeted with the creation of a black market that "accounted for perhaps 30 percent of sales."

Further, even if the RCTCA were to pass, marijuana would remain illegal in the entire United States under federal law while taxed only in California, a situation that would strengthen both California's gray market and the nationwide black market in illegal drugs. Fueled by generous growing allowances and an enormous supply in California, criminal sales operations would flourish as excess California marijuana was sold outside the state and, at the same time, out-of-state growers attempted to access the more permissive market inside the state.

In sum, legalization would put additional strain on an already faltering economy. In 2008, marijuana alone was involved in 375,000 emergency room visits. Drug overdoses already outnumber gunshot deaths in America and are approaching motor vehicle crashes as the nation's leading cause of accidental death. It is true that taxing marijuana sales would generate some tax revenue, but the cost of handling the influx of problems resulting from increased use would far outweigh any gain made by marijuana's taxation. Legalizing marijuana would serve only to compound the problems already associated with drug use.

Social Dislocation and Organized Crime

The final two arguments of those favoring legalization are intertwined. According to advocates of legalization, the government's efforts to combat the illegal drug trade have been an expensive failure. Consequently, they argue, focusing on substance abuse and treatment would be a more effective means of combating drug abuse while reducing the violence and social ills stemming from anti-drug enforcement efforts.

There is no doubt that if marijuana were legalized, more people, including juveniles, would consume it. Consider cigarettes: While their purchase by people under 18 is illegal, 20 percent of high school students admit to having smoked cigarettes in the past 30 days. Marijuana's illegal status "keeps potential drug users from using" marijuana in a way that no legalization scheme can replicate "by virtue of the fear of arrest and the embarrassment of being caught." With increased use comes increased abuse, as the fear of arrest and embarrassment will decrease.

Legalization advocates attempt to create in the minds of the public an image of a typical "responsible" user of marijuana: a person who is reasonable and accountable even when under the influence of marijuana. And for those few that don't fit that image? Society will treat them and restore them to full health. The facts, however, are much uglier.

The RAND Corporation projects a 50 percent increase in marijuana-related traffic fatalities under the RCTCA. That alone

should weigh heavily on California voters this fall. In a 2008 national survey, approximately 3 million Americans 12 years old or older started using illicit drugs in the past year—almost 8,000 new users per day. The most commonly used illicit drug is marijuana, especially among the 20 million Americans over 12 who were users in 2008. In California, 62 percent of all marijuana treatment cases are already individuals under 21. Legalization will increase the number of underage users.

Keeping marijuana illegal will undoubtedly keep many young people from using it. Eliminate that criminal sanction (and moral disapprobation), and more youth will use the drug, harming their potential and ratcheting up treatment costs.

Educators know that students using marijuana underperform when compared to their non-using peers. Teachers, coaches, guidance counselors, and school principals have seen the negative effect of marijuana on their students. The Rev. Dr. D. Stuart Dunnan, Headmaster of Saint James School in St. James, Maryland, says of marijuana use by students:

> The chemical effect of marijuana is to take away ambition. The social effect is to provide an escape from challenges and responsibilities with a like-minded group of teenagers who are doing the same thing. Using marijuana creates losers. At a time when we're concerned about our lack of academic achievement relative to other countries, legalizing marijuana will be disastrous.

Additionally, making marijuana legal in California will fuel drug cartels and violence, particularly because the drug will still be illegal at the national level. The local demand will increase in California, but reputable growers, manufacturers, and retailers will still be unwilling—as they should be—to produce and distribute marijuana. Even without the federal prohibition, most reputable producers would not survive the tort liability from such a dangerous product. Thus, the vacuum will be filled by illegal drug cartels.

According to the Department of Justice's National Drug Threat Assessment for 2010, Mexican drug trafficking organizations (DTOs) "have expanded their cultivation operations in the United States, an ongoing trend for the past decade.... Well-organized criminal groups and DTOs that produce domestic marijuana do so because of the high profitability of and demand for marijuana in the United States."

Legalize marijuana, and the demand for marijuana goes up substantially as the deterrence effect of law enforcement disappears. Yet not many suppliers will operate legally, refusing to subject themselves to the established state regulatory scheme—not to mention taxation—while still risking federal prosecution, conviction, and prison time. So who will fill the void?

Violent, brutal, and ruthless, Mexican DTOs will work to maintain their black-market profits at the expense of American citizens' safety. Every week, there are news articles cataloguing the murders, kidnappings, robberies, and other thuggish brutality employed by Mexican drug gangs along the border. It is nonsensical to argue that these gangs will simply give up producing marijuana when it is legalized; indeed, their profits might soar, depending on the actual tax in California and the economics of the interstate trade. While such profits might not be possible if marijuana was legalized at the national level and these gangs were undercut by mass production, that is unlikely ever to happen. Nor does anyone really believe that the gangs will subject themselves to state and local regulation, including taxation. And since the California ballot does nothing to eliminate the black market for marijuana—quite the opposite, in fact—legalizing marijuana will only incentivize Mexican DTOs to grow more marijuana to feed the demand and exploit the black market.

Furthermore, should California legalize marijuana, other entrepreneurs will inevitably attempt to enter the marketplace and game the system. In doing so, they will compete with Mexican DTOs and other criminal organizations. Inevitably, violence will follow, and unlike now, that violence will not be confined to the border as large-scale growers seek to protect their turf—turf that will necessarily include anywhere they grow, harvest, process, or sell marijuana. While this may sound far-fetched, Californians in Alameda County are already experiencing the reality of cartel-run marijuana farms on sometimes stolen land, protected by "guys [who] are pretty heavily armed and willing to protect their merchandise."

It is not uncommon for drugs with large illegal markets to be controlled by cartels despite attempts to roll them into the normal medical control scheme. For instance, cocaine has a medical purpose and can be prescribed by doctors as *Erythroxylum coca*, yet its true production and distribution are controlled by drug cartels and organized crime. As competition from growers and dispensaries authorized by the RCTCA cuts further into the Mexican DTOs' business, Californians will face a real possibility of bloodshed on their own soil as the cartels' profit-protection measures turn from defensive to offensive.

Thus, marijuana legalization will increase crime, drug use, and social dislocation across the state of California—the exact opposite of what pro-legalization advocates promise.

Conclusion

Pro-marijuana advocates promoting the Regulate, Control and Tax Cannabis Act of 2010 invite Californians to imagine a hypothetical and idyllic "pot market," but America's national approach to drug use, addiction, and crime must be serious, based on sound policy and solid evidence.

In 1982, President Ronald Reagan adopted a national drug strategy that took a comprehensive approach consisting of five components: international cooperation, research, strengthened law enforcement, treatment and rehabilitation, and prevention and education. It was remarkably successful: Illegal drug use by young adults dropped more than 50 percent.

Reagan was right to make drug control a major issue of his presidency. Illegal drugs such as marijuana are responsible for a disproportionate share of violence and social decline in America. Accordingly, federal law, representing the considered judgment of medical science and the nation's two political branches of government, takes the unequivocal position that marijuana is dangerous and has no significant beneficial uses.

California cannot repeal that law or somehow allow its citizens to contravene it. Thus, it has two options. By far the best option is to commit itself seriously to the federal approach and pursue a strategy that attempts to prevent illegal drug use in the first place and reduce the number of drug users. This may require changes in drug policy, and perhaps in sentencing guidelines for marijuana users charged with simple possession, but simply legalizing a harmful drug—that is, giving up—is not a responsible option.

The other option is to follow the above path in the short term while conducting further research and possibly working with other states in Congress to consider changes in federal law. Although those who oppose the legalization of marijuana have every reason to believe that further, legitimate scientific research will confirm the dangers of its use, no side should try to thwart the sober judgment of the national legislature and sister states.

In short, no state will likely be allowed to legalize marijuana on its own, with such serious, negative cross-state spillover effects. Yet even if California could act as if it were an island, the legalization route would still end very badly for the Golden State. There is strong evidence to suggest that legalizing marijuana would serve little purpose other than to worsen the state's drug problems—addiction, violence, disorder, and death. While long on rhetoric, the legalization movement, by contrast, is short on facts.

CHARLES D. STIMSON is a senior legal fellow in the Center for Legal & Judicial Studies at The Heritage Foundation. Before joining The Heritage Foundation, he served as deputy assistant secretary of defense, as a local, state, federal, and military prosecutor, and as a defense attorney and law professor.

EXPLORING THE ISSUE

Should "Recreational" Drugs Be Legalized?

Critical Thinking and Reflection

1. How harmful are illegal drugs? Are they more dangerous than alcohol? Can we distinguish among them?
2. Is the history of prohibition of alcohol relevant in revealing the consequences of prohibition? Are the indicted substances sufficiently different so that comparisons are not useful?
3. In view of crowded prisons, should we consider alternative means of punishment for some categories of drug offenders? Does prohibition inspire its violation?
4. Why shouldn't we have a civil right to do what may be harmful to ourselves?
5. Do you believe there would be a larger societal impact if recreational drugs were to be legalized? If so, what could it be? If not, why not?

Is There Common Ground?

Advocates of legalization mostly believe that it must be accompanied by restraints on drug usage. Just as alcohol is subject to restrictions regarding its manufacturing and sale, and states vary in their requirements regarding the sale of alcohol, so legal drugs may be subject to strict controls. Absolute libertarians will dissent, arguing that there should be no regulation, but a vast majority of Americans would disagree. It would be likely that legalization would involve laws on purity of contents and other requirements that apply to alcohol and other legal drugs.

It is possible that supporters of prohibition may distinguish among the illicit drugs based on present awareness of their different effects. Defenders of drug prohibition might consent to the sale of medical marijuana, due to the claim that its use can reduce the pain of certain diseases. However, the experience in California and elsewhere is that licensing medical marijuana is likely to lead to the easy medical dispensing of medical marijuana to persons who are not legally entitled to it.

Perhaps the true common ground has already begun to emerge. States are able to legalize within their boundaries and not fear federal crackdowns so long as they regulate the drug within federal guidelines. While such a measure works well for the time being, questions will arise in 2016 when a new president takes office. After all, the current setup keeps recreational drugs illegal at the federal level and relies on policy memos from a political appointee. For the states to feel safe in their status, it will be necessary for a clearer relationship to develop between federal and state authorities on these issues so enforcement does not ultimately become a political whim of the sitting president.

Additional Resources

Jonathan P. Caulkins, Angela Hawken, Beau Kilmer, and Mark A.R. Kleiman, *Marijuana Legalization: What Everyone Needs to Know* (Oxford University Press, 2012)

Larry Gaines, *Drug, Crimes, & Justice* (Waveland Press, 2002)

James A. Inciardi, *The Drug Legalization Debate* (Greenhaven Press, 2013)

Robert J. MacCoun and Peter Reuter, *Drug War Heresies* (Cambridge University Press, 2001)

U.S. Department of Justice and Drug Enforcement Administration, *Speaking Out Against Drug Legalization* (CreateSpace, 2012)

Internet References . . .

Citizens Against Legalizing Marijuana

www.calmca.org/about/

Gallup

www.gallup.com/poll/165539/first-time-americans
-favor-legalizing-marijuana.aspx

Marijuana Policy Project

www.mpp.org/

**National Organization for the Reform
of Marijuana Laws**

http://norml.org/

Public Broadcasting Service

www.pbs.org/wnet/need-to-know/ask-the-experts
/ask-the-experts-legalizing-marijuana/15474/

Selected, Edited, and with Issue Framing Material by:
William J. Miller, *Flagler College*

ISSUE

Should Corporations Be Awarded Religious Freedoms?

YES: Patricia Miller, from "How the Catholic Church Masterminded the Supreme Court's Hobby Lobby Debacle," *Salon* (2014)

NO: Ruth Bader Ginsberg, from "Dissenting Opinion in *Sylvia Burwell v. Hobby Lobby Stores*," Supreme Court of the United States (2014)

Learning Outcomes
After reading this issue, you will be able to: • Explain the Supreme Court's role in determining religious freedom. • Discuss religious freedom in the American context. • Assess the impact of recent Supreme Court rulings on religion. • Explain the freedoms of corporations in the United States. • Assess the relationship between law and religion.

ISSUE SUMMARY

YES: Patricia Miller argues that religious institutions have gone to great measures to help corporations have legal protections in order to promote religious causes.

NO: Ruth Bader Ginsberg argues that the Constitution's protection of religious liberty has been seen as a personal right, and any efforts to extend the right to corporations could come with unforeseen consequences society is not fully prepared for.

Within the United States, a volume of legal scholarship exists deeming that a corporation (an entity consisting of a group of people) may be recognized as having many of the same legal rights—and responsibilities—as an individual. Corporations, for example, can enter contracts or seek legal remedies much the same as individual American citizens can. While corporations are given many rights, they are not viewed by the courts as people. Likewise, they are not provided with all of the same rights as human beings.

This legal phenomenon is not particularly new—despite numerous public claims that corporations have never had such rights in the country's past. In 1819, the Supreme Court—in *Trustees of Dartmouth v. Woodward*—recognized that corporations possess the same rights as natural persons to enforce contracts. Six decades later, in *Santa Clara v. Southern Pacific Railroad*, Justice Morrison White

stated at the beginning of oral arguments that "The court does not wish to hear argument on the question whether the provision in the Fourteenth Amendment to the Constitution, which forbids a State to deny to any person within its jurisdiction the equal protection of the laws, applies to these corporations. We are all of the opinion that it does." Since White's statement was not part of the official opinion, it did not immediately become legal precedent. Shortly thereafter, however, White's proclamation became part of the official record in *Pembina Consolidated Silver Mining v. Pennsylvania*. Within the ruling the Court held that "Under the designation of 'person' there is no doubt that a private corporation is included [in the Fourteenth Amendment]. Such corporations are merely associations of individuals united for a special purpose and permitted to do business under a particular name and have a succession of members without dissolution." In the next century, this finding would be reaffirmed regularly.

If we look at why corporations are viewed as persons, we can turn to the Fourteenth Amendment, which clearly mentions the powers of people. If one is to interpret a group of people (a corporation) as a person, it becomes possible to understand the assumption of some individual rights being granted to the aggregate. After all, if corporations are just organizations of people, how could the courts justify the deprivation of individual constitutional rights simply because of collective action? By treating corporations as people, it becomes easier to legally consider them. They can be sued, taxed, regulated, and observed far more easily. Perhaps even more importantly, corporations are simplified and allow individuals to reap the benefits of working together without being forced to sacrifice their right of association. Not all Americans are accepting of these rules, however. Instead, opponents believe the Constitution should only apply to natural born persons and that only state laws should be permitted to provide corporations with rights and responsibilities.

It is important to remember that not all individual rights are automatically given to corporations; the Supreme Court utilizes cases and selective incorporation to make rulings on an independent basis. As a rough estimate, if groups of people do not possess the protection, odds are corporations do not either. Corporations, for example, cannot claim a Fifth Amendment protection against self-incrimination. Corporations have tried to argue for such protections, but they have yet to succeed (most recently failing in *United States v. Sourapas and Crest Beverage*).

Suffice it to say, corporate personhood was not a particularly controversial concept prior to the Supreme Court's ruling in *Citizens United v. Federal Election Commission* in 2010. In the *Citizens United* case, the Court upheld the rights of corporations to make political expenditures under the First Amendment. Despite making no references to either corporate personhood or the Fourteenth Amendment, public outcry has begun to demand the revocation of individual rights from corporate organizations. Yet, as stated above, the debate was not new when it arose in 2010—with questions of campaign finance and corporate impact on democratic governance leading the considerations. In 1990, the Court ruled in *Austin v. Michigan Chamber of Commerce* that corporations could be prohibited from using money from their aggregate treasury to directly support or oppose federal candidates due to the potential for unfair influence. Ultimately, in the *Citizens United* case, the Court opted to overrule *Austin*. And the influence has not stopped in 2010 as the newly created precedent has already been applied—most notably in *Western Tradition Partnership v. Attorney General of Montana* in 2012. In this case, the Court reversed a Montana Supreme Court ruling that *Citizens United* did not preclude a Montana state law regarding the illegality of corporate spending in election.

At the end of the day, in the past half-decade, the Supreme Court has decided that corporations are entitled to the same free speech protections that individuals received from the *Buckley v. Valeo* ruling in 1976—at least when it comes to campaign donations. Opponents of these recent decisions have argued that if all corporate rights under the Constitution were abolished, it would clear the way for greater regulation of campaign spending and contributions. It should be noted, however, that neither decision relied on the concept of corporate personhood, and the Buckley decision in particular deals with the rights of individuals and political committees, not corporations. But—taken on the whole—the cases show corporations are gaining significantly more rights. Enter the discussion on religion.

The U.S. Supreme Court heard arguments last year in the latest challenge to the Affordable Care Act with Hobby Lobby, a chain of arts and crafts stores owned by Christians who object to certain methods of birth control—IUDs and morning after pills—because they can interfere with the creation of life once an egg is fertilized, resulting in abortion, serving as the lead plaintiff. The issue in the case was clear: can for-profit corporations, citing religious objections, refuse some or potentially all contraceptive services in health plans offered to employees? It's a hot-button issue that had Americans watching carefully for the Court's decision as siding with Hobby Lobby would provide additional freedoms to corporations. Ultimately, the Court ruled with Hobby Lobby for a number of reasons. They discussed how corporations, while having independent legal existences, are formed through individuals. Further, they noted concerns with restricting the First Amendment and removing the private aspect of private enterprise.

At the end of the day, granting individual freedoms to a corporation looks ridiculous on its face. Mitt Romney was mocked from making such claims when campaigning for president in 2012. Yet the U.S. Code defines corporations as people in its opening line. Even if corporations have individual rights—especially those espoused in the First Amendment—there are still questions about exactly how far Americans want the courts to go in expanding freedoms to these created groups. When asked their opinion, Americans consistently agree that religious liberty is important for both individual employees and owners. Yet, in contrast, they were significantly and consistently less willing to grant the same scope of protection to all the for-profit companies we presented them. In the following readings, Patricia Miller argues that religious institutions (specifically the Catholic Church) have done great things for important causes and merit individual rights and protections related to public policy while Justice Ginsberg counters that since corporations cannot express devotion to a God in the same way an individual can, they should not be given religious expression freedoms.

YES ⤹

Patricia Miller

How the Catholic Church Masterminded the Supreme Court's Hobby Lobby Debacle: While Evangelical Christians Ultimately Brought Down the Contraception Mandate, They Had Big Help from Catholics

But while the Green family who filed the *Hobby Lobby* suit objecting to the mandate are evangelical Christians, the road to *Hobby Lobby* wasn't paved by the Christian Right. It was the Catholic Church, more specifically the U.S. Catholic bishops' conference, that largely engineered *Hobby Lobby* to block the legitimization of contraception as a standard health insurance benefit—a last ditch effort to prevent by law what it couldn't prevent from the pulpit: women from using birth control.

The Catholic bishops' interest in "conscience clauses" that would allow employers to opt out of reproductive health care services began in earnest in the late 1990s, with the increased viability at the state and national levels of contraceptive equity measures designed to ensure that health plans covered prescription contraceptives like the Pill just like other prescription medications. For years, insurers had omitted contraceptives from prescription drug plans— the only entire class of drugs routinely and explicitly excluded— which made women's out-of-pocket medical expenses some 70 percent higher than men's. Measures to ensure contraceptive equity had been stalled by male legislators and social conservatives who asserted that employers and insurers shouldn't be forced to pay for what they called a "lifestyle" choice, not a health care need. Despite that fact that nearly all women use contraceptives at some point in their lives—98 percent, according to government surveys— and that at any given moment two-thirds of women of child-bearing age are using a contraceptive method, the implication was that fertility management was frivolous or immoral and that "other people" shouldn't be forced to pay for it.

When Connecticut considered a contraceptive equity measure in 1999, a Catholic priest, the Rev. Joseph Looney of Bethlehem, Connecticut, told the legislature that covering contraceptives would only benefit "playboys" and would fund "craziness and irresponsibility." It was a framework that conservatives had successfully applied to abortion—asserting that it must be segregated from other health services and government funding because it was immoral— and now were trying to apply to birth control.

But the decision of most health insurers to cover Viagra almost immediately after it was approved by the FDA in 1998 largely negated this argument. Suddenly contraceptive coverage measures were sailing through state legislatures. A national contraceptive equity measure was introduced but failed to make it out of committee. The sponsors retooled the bill and reintroduced it as a measure that required insurance plans participating in the health insurance program for federal employees to cover contraceptives. Even this scaled-down measure would set an important precedent because the federal benefits package is often used as a model for private sector health plans. The bishops and social conservatives worked furiously to derail the measure by claiming that it would force health plans to cover abortifacients—which they now defined as anything that worked post-fertilization. Representatives Christopher Smith (R-NJ), who had a track record of introducing legislation favored by the U.S. Conference of Catholic Bishops (USCCB), and Tom Coburn (R-OK) tried unsuccessfully to insert a provision prohibiting "coverage for abortifacients," claiming that newly approved emergency contraceptive pills and the intrauterine device were abortifacients because they could prevent a fertilized egg from implanting.

When charges that contraceptives were abortifacients failed to halt the measure, the bishops turned to a new tack: claiming that contraception equity laws violated the religious freedom of insurers and employers who disapproved of contraception and would be forced to subsidize its use. "They force private health insurance plans and/or employers . . . to cover all 'FDA-approved' methods of contraception . . . regardless of the provider's conscientious objection or long-standing religious beliefs against such coverage," wrote Cathy Deeds of the NCCB. It was a stunning claim, suggesting that anyone who administered or paid for an insurance policy should be free to dictate what coverage was provided to policyholders based on their objection to services that they themselves would not be forced to use.

The Catholic bishops now sought a broad-based conscience clause that would allow any employer or insurer to refuse to cover contraceptives for any religious or moral objection. This represented

Patricia Miller, "How the Catholic Church Masterminded the Supreme Court's Hobby Lobby debacle," *Salon*, September 14, 2014.

a major escalation in the grounds for claiming conscience protections. Traditionally so-called conscience clauses, like the 1973 Church Amendment, protected individuals or health care entities like hospitals only from being compelled to directly perform abortions or sterilizations in violation of their moral or religious beliefs. In 1997, the federal government expanded conscience protections to the payers of abortion-related services when it allowed Medicaid and Medicare managed-care plans to refuse to pay providers for abortion counseling or referral services. Now the bishops were attempting to extend conscience protection to any payer who had a "moral" objection to contraception. Such a measure would make contraceptive coverage mandates useless, because any employer or insurer could opt out. And it would once again leave women's reproductive health care at the mercy of individual employers and insurers and stigmatize contraceptives, like abortion, as a segregated health service that could be carved out of the continuum of women's health needs.

The bishops failed to get a broader conscience clause in the bill mandating coverage of contraceptives for federal employees, but they did manage to get an exemption for the five religiously affiliated plans in the system. Having set the precedent that religious providers would be treated differently concerning the provision of reproductive health care, even in the matter of noncontroversial services such as contraception, the bishops launched a major new effort to create broad conscience exemptions.

The issue was particularly contentious because the FDA recently had approved the first prepackaged "morning after" pill—a high dose of oral contraceptives that worked to prevent pregnancy if taken shortly after unprotected intercourse. Like regular oral contraceptives, emergency contraceptives (ECs) work primarily by preventing ovulation; however, at the time it was believed that this early version might in some cases prevent implantation. Public health advocates praised the widespread availability of EC as a major step forward in preventing unwanted pregnancy and reducing abortion. The Catholic bishops, however, were among the earliest and sharpest critics of EC, asserting that it was an abortifacient because it may prevent implantation and "destroy a developing embryo" despite the fact that the FDA said it could not interrupt an established pregnancy.

"What is striking is how hard the bishops worked to conflate abortion and contraception, particularly around EC," said Lois Uttley, director of MergerWatch, which began tracking religiously based health restrictions in the mid-1990s. "But they said it over and over enough that they actually managed to convince many people," she said.

During the Bush administration, the Catholic bishops found a willing partner in their quest for "conscience clauses." President George W. Bush's PEPFAR anti-AIDS program included an exemption for religious providers who didn't want to distribute condoms, which was custom-made for Catholic agencies like Catholic Relief Services. Bush signed an appropriations bill in 2005 that included the first federal conscience clause. This broadened the abortion

exemption to a wide range of health care entities, including HMOs and other insurers, and included the right to refuse to refer for abortions.

By this time, the issue of conscience refusals was becoming increasingly contentious, as the bishops were joined by elements of the Christian Right in asserting the need for greater conscience protections for health care workers, who they charged were regularly being forced to violate their faith in the provision of certain services. Organizations like Pharmacists for Life campaigned for the right of pharmacists to refuse to dispense or refer for oral contraceptives or EC on the grounds that they were potentially abortifacients. Reports of conscience-based service refusals mushroomed. There were hospital nurses who refused to care for patients before or after emergency abortions, doctors who refused to prescribe the Pill to unmarried women, and infertility clinics that turned away lesbian patients. Conscience exemptions were now being used as a political tool to block access to services to which some objected or to make moral judgments about the provision of care to certain patients.

By the dawn of the Obama administration, however, the bishops were losing ground on conscience exemptions. They lobbied unsuccessfully in Arizona to broaden that state's narrow religious exemption to its contraceptive equity law, which covered only churches, to include any religious employer, such as Catholic hospitals and universities. The bishops in Connecticut lost a bruising two-year battle for an exemption to that state's new "EC in the ER" law despite putting up a fierce fight. The Obama administration undid some sweeping conscience exemptions created during the Bush administration, noting that federal law still protected providers from being compelled to participate in abortions. Then, in August 2011, the Department of Health and Human Services (HHS) announced that all employer-based health plans would be required to provide contraceptives to women at no cost under its proposed rules for the preventive services guaranteed to all individuals under the Affordable Care Act.

In deference to the Catholic bishops, HHS proposed a narrow conscience clause that exempted nonprofit organizations directly involved in the inculcation of religion that primarily employed individuals of the same religion, like Catholic churches and other houses of worship. However, Catholic-affiliated institutions like universities and hospitals that served the general population and employed non-Catholics would have to provide contraception through their plans. Many of these employers had chosen to self-insure—that is, serve as their own insurers—to circumvent state contraception mandates, but they would be required to comply with federal law.

The type of narrowly drawn conscience clause proposed by the administration had been sanctified by two closely watched state supreme court decisions in New York and California. The U.S. Supreme Court let both decisions stand, which was seen as a major victory for a limited application of conscience clauses. But in the ensuring years since the 2006 New York decision, not only had the Christian Right become activated on the issue, but the question of conscience clauses had spilled beyond health care as efforts advanced to ensure equality for same-sex couples. Catholic Charities affiliates in Boston and Illinois closed their well-respected adoption agencies rather than comply with state mandates that they provide adoptions to gay and lesbian couples.

Then in September 2011, shortly after the Obama administration announced the contraceptive mandate, HHS announced that it would not renew a contract with the USCCB to provide assistance to victims of international human trafficking because the bishops' organization refused to provide women who had been subjected to rape or forced prostitution with access to comprehensive reproductive health care, including abortion, EC, and family planning and sexually transmitted disease counseling. Where HHS saw the need to provide all medically appropriate services to these women, the bishops claimed anti-Catholic discrimination, especially because political appointees at HHS had overruled a program evaluation that rated the USCCB as the top-performing contractor in terms of service provision. Sister Mary Ann Walsh, a spokesperson for the USCCB, said that there was a "new, albeit unwritten rule of HHS, the ABC rule—Anybody But Catholics.

It was a dramatic charge and signaled that the bishops were going to make a full-court press on the issue of exemptions for Catholic providers. In mid-November, USCCB president Archbishop Timothy Dolan of Milwaukee, Wisconsin, announced a new Committee for Religious Liberty to counter what he said was a move to "neuter religion" in the public square. The committee was put under the direction of Bridgeport, Connecticut, Bishop William Lori, an outspoken conservative who was formerly the head of the Pro-Life Committee, and staffed by Anthony Picarello, a rising young lawyer at the USCCB who had worked as a litigator for the Becket Fund for Religious Liberty, which had pursued a number of high-profile religious freedom cases.

In addition to the contraceptive mandate, Dolan named the dropping of the USCCB from the HHS contract, state marriage equality laws that required same-sex couples be allowed to adopt, and the Obama administration's failure to defend the Defense of Marriage Act, which prohibited federal recognition of same-sex partnerships, as government actions that "infringe upon the right of conscience of people of faith." The bishops were charging that efforts to make them play by the same rules as other health and social service providers were affronts to religious freedom—their freedom to discriminate against others or deny services in the name of religion.

There was more at stake than just the bishops' authority over services provided by Catholic institutions. Domestic and international social service agencies affiliated with the church, like Catholic Charities USA and Catholic Relief Services, receive hundreds of millions of dollars in government contracts each year to provide social services to the poor, run adoption agencies, and manage international development projects. Catholic Charities affiliates received nearly $3 billion in government funding in 2010, accounting for more than 60 percent of their revenue. Religiously affiliated hospitals in the United States, of which 70 percent are Catholic, receive some $40 billion in government funding each year through Medicare and Medicaid and other government programs.

The bishops were making the preservation of their right to participate in these federally funded programs and discriminate based on religious doctrine their most high-profile crusade since *Roe v. Wade*. Between the launch of the religious freedom committee and the election of Dolan, who was selected over the organization's more moderate vice president, the bishops were trying to reclaim the national leadership role on social issues that they had enjoyed under pugnacious, outspoken conservatives like the late Cardinal John O'Connor.

With the bishops' newly aggressive stance, all eyes turned to the White House to see if Obama would accept the HHS rule, with its narrow conscience exemption, or seek to pacify the increasingly outspoken bishops. He came under ferocious lobbying from the reproductive rights community to maintain the mandate after a private meeting with Dolan at the White House that left the archbishop "feeling a bit more at peace about this issue," which many took to mean that he had received assurances from Obama that he would soften the mandate.

But no one was prepared for the firestorm that broke loose when the mandate, with its narrow religious exemption intact, was announced on January 20. That the bishops screamed bloody murder shouldn't have come as any surprise. They had announced their intention to make this their defining issue. But the mandate was also denounced by Sister Keehan, who had proved such a critical ally to the White House on the health reform bill, and a handful of mostly male, liberal-leaning Catholic columnists and pundits, who seemed to think the administration was asking nuns in habits to stand on street corners handing out condoms rather than proposing a reasonable compromise on the issue that had been affirmed by two influential high courts. Also lost in the debate was the fact that many Catholic health plans like the OSF Health Plan in Illinois already routinely covered birth control through a third-party administrator, an arrangement that proved adequate for these plans for at least a decade.

The Obama administration announced that religiously affiliated employers would be given an additional year to figure out how to apply the mandate, but that didn't mollify the bishops, who contended that the mandate was an affront to rank-and-file Catholics—even though some 98 percent of Catholic women have used birth control and nearly 60 percent of all Catholics supported the mandate. In addition, many of the 650,000 employees of Catholic hospitals aren't Catholic, which meant that the bishops had absolutely no moral authority over their reproductive health choices. Dolan argued in a video made even before the administration released the final rule, however, that the mandate was a violation of religious freedom because it would force Catholics "to go out into the marketplace and buy a product that violates their conscience."

It was a radical new way of viewing conscience rights—not as the right of an individual to decline to use or participate in a service, but as their right to deny that service to others based on their mere participation in an insurance pool in a commercial marketplace.

But with Catholic use of birth control nearly universal, Dolan needed to raise the stakes. He drew on years of efforts by the bishops to conflate abortion and contraception, and particularly abortion and emergency contraception, to charge that the mandate would require Catholic insurers and employers to cover "abortion-inducing drugs" in a reference to EC. He made the charge even though the official journal of the Catholic Health Association had published an article nearly two years earlier saying that Plan B, the most widely used emergency contraceptive, was not an abortifacient—even under the bishops' definition—because it worked to prevent fertilization, not implantation. The general medical community also was increasingly in agreement that post-fertilization effects of EC were virtually nonexistent.

But no sooner had all the parties breathed a sigh of relief than the bishops backtracked and denounced the compromise, saying Catholics were still "being called upon to subsidize something we find morally illicit." It was a rehash of the bishops' long-running contention that funding streams could never be adequately segregated in the case of morally illicit services, but now they were applying it to birth control. Conservative Catholics like Robert George and Mary Ann Glendon took up the bishops' tack and called the compromise a "cheap accounting trick." But many Catholic moral theologians disagreed, saying that Catholic institutions' role in the provision of contraception under the compromise would be remote material cooperation, which was acceptable and widely used in the realm of health care to allow Catholic hospitals to operate in secular society.

But the bishops wouldn't back down. Instead, they took their demands one step further, calling for a broad conscience clause that would allow any employer who had a moral objection to contraception to refuse to provide it. Increasingly it looked as if the fight wasn't about finding a reasonable compromise that would allow Catholic employers to distance themselves sufficiently from the provision of contraception to satisfy at least the letter of the widely ignored Catholic teaching on contraception. It was an attempt to block the federal enshrinement of contraception as a basic women's health care right.

The full scope of the issue didn't become apparent to most people until a few days later, when the Republican-run House Committee on Oversight and Government Reform held a hearing on the mandate and its supposed impediment to religious freedom. Within hours a picture from the first panel of witnesses was ricocheting around the Internet and social media sites like Twitter. It showed five middle-aged men—half in clerical garb—testifying about women's access to birth control. There was Bishop Lori, testifying for the USCCB; the Reverend Matthew Harrison, president of the Missouri Synod of the Lutheran Church, a conservative Lutheran sect that has long been prominent in the anti-abortion movement; Meir Soloveichik, a conservative rabbi; and two conservative Christian theologians. When Georgetown University law student Sandra Fluke, a non-Catholic whose student health insurance excluded contraception, was denied the right to testify on the basis that the hearing wasn't about women's access to birth control but religious freedom, the picture became clear to many for the first time.

Women's health advocates and political pundits expressed amazement that contraception could be so controversial in 2012. But they shouldn't have been surprised. That's because the forty-year fight over reproductive rights had never really been about abortion; it had always been about women and sex—specifically, the ability of women to have sex without the consequence of pregnancy. That's why it was the shot heard 'round the world when in the midst of the flap over the all-male birth control panel radio talk show host Rush Limbaugh called Fluke a "slut" for wanting her insurance to treat birth control like any other prescription medication. Limbaugh had revealed what the right really believed about women and sex: Women who wanted to have sex—especially outside of marriage—and control their fertility were doing something fundamentally illicit and shouldn't expect anyone else to pay for it. To them, birth control was just a lesser form of abortion.

Patricia Miller is the author of *Good Catholics: The Battle Over Abortion in the Catholic Church*. She writes extensively about the intersection of sex, politics, and religion. Her work has appeared in *The Nation*, *Ms.* magazine, and *Religion Dispatches*. She is the former editor-in-chief of *National Journal*'s *Daily Health Briefings* and of *Conscience* magazine.

Ruth Bader Ginsberg

Dissenting Opinion in *Sylvia Burwell v. Hobby Lobby Stores*

Justice Ginsburg, with whom Justice Sotomayor joins, and with whom Justice Breyer and Justice Kagan join as to all but Part III–C–1, dissenting.

In a decision of startling breadth, the Court holds that commercial enterprises, including corporations, along with partnerships and sole proprietorships, can opt out of any law (saving only tax laws) they judge incompatible with their sincerely held religious beliefs. See *ante*, at 16–49. Compelling governmental interests in uniform compliance with the law, and disadvantages that religion-based opt-outs impose on others, hold no sway, the Court decides, at least when there is a "less restrictive alternative." And such an alternative, the Court suggests, there always will be whenever, in lieu of tolling an enterprise claiming a religion-based exemption, the government, *i.e.*, the general public, can pick up the tab.

The Court does not pretend that the First Amendment's Free Exercise Clause demands religion-based accommodations so extreme, for our decisions leave no doubt on that score. See *infra*, at 6–8. Instead, the Court holds that Congress, in the Religious Freedom Restoration Act of 1993 (RFRA), 42 U. S. C. §2000bb *et seq.*, dictated the extraordinary religion-based exemptions today's decision endorses. In the Court's view, RFRA demands accommodation of a for-profit corporation's religious beliefs no matter the impact that accommodation may have on third parties who do not share the corporation owners' religious faith—in these cases, thousands of women employed by Hobby Lobby and Conestoga or dependents of persons those corporations employ. Persuaded that Congress enacted RFRA to serve a far less radical purpose, and mindful of the havoc the Court's judgment can introduce, I dissent. . . .

The exemption sought by Hobby Lobby and Conestoga would override significant interests of the corporations' employees and covered dependents. It would deny legions of women who do not hold their employers' beliefs access to contraceptive coverage that the ACA would otherwise secure. See *Catholic Charities of Sacramento, Inc.* v. *Superior Court*, 32 Cal. 4th 527, 565, 85 P. 3d 67, 93 (2004) ("We are unaware of any decision in which . . . [the U.S. Supreme Court] has exempted a religious objector from the operation of a neutral, generally applicable law despite the recognition that the requested exemption would detrimentally affect the rights of third parties."). In sum, with respect to free exercise claims no less than free speech claims, "'[y]our right to swing your arms ends just where the other man's nose begins.'" Chafee, Freedom of Speech in War Time, 32 Harv. L. Rev. 932, 957 (1919). . . .

Religious organizations exist to foster the interests of persons subscribing to the same religious faith. Not so of for-profit corporations. Workers who sustain the operations of those corporations commonly are not drawn from one religious community. Indeed, by law, no religion-based criterion can restrict the work force of for-profit corporations. See 42 U. S. C. §§2000e(b), 2000e–1(a), 2000e–2(a); cf. *Trans World Airlines, Inc.* v. *Hardison*, 432 U. S. 63, 80–81 (1977) (Title VII requires reasonable accommodation of an employee's religious exercise, but such accommodation must not come "at the expense of other [employees]"). The distinction between a community made up of believers in the same religion and one embracing persons of diverse beliefs, clear as it is, constantly escapes the Court's attention. One can only wonder why the Court shuts this key difference from sight. . . .

The Court notes that for-profit corporations may support charitable causes and use their funds for religious ends, and therefore questions the distinction between such corporations and religious nonprofit organizations. See *ante*, at 20–25. See also *ante*, at 3 (Kennedy, J., concurring) (criticizing the Government for "distinguishing between different religious believers—burdening one while accommodating the other—when it may treat both equally by offering both of them the same accommodation"). Again, the Court forgets that religious organizations exist to serve a community of believers. For-profit corporations do not fit that bill. Moreover, history is not on the Court's side. Recognition of the discrete characters of "ecclesiastical and lay" corporations dates back to Blackstone, see 1 W. Blackstone, Commentaries on the Laws of England 458 (1765), and was reiterated by this Court centuries before the enactment of the Internal Revenue Code. . . .

Importantly, the decisions whether to claim benefits under the plans are made not by Hobby Lobby or Conestoga, but by the covered employees and dependents, in consultation with their health care providers. Should an employee of Hobby Lobby or Conestoga share the religious beliefs of the Greens and Hahns, she is of course under no compulsion to use the contraceptives in question. But "[n]o individual decision by an employee and her physician—be it to use contraception, treat an infection, or have a hip replaced—is in any meaningful sense [her employer's] decision or action." *Grote* v. *Sebelius*, 708 F. 3d 850, 865 (CA7 2013) (Rovner, J., dissenting). It is doubtful that Congress, when it specified that burdens must be "substantia[l]," had in mind a linkage thus interrupted by independent decisionmakers (the woman and her health counselor) standing between the challenged government action and the religious exercise claimed to be infringed. Any decision to use contraceptives made by a woman covered under Hobby Lobby's or Conestoga's plan will not be propelled by the Government, it will be the woman's autonomous choice, informed by the physician she consults. . . .

Perhaps the gravity of the interests at stake has led the Court to assume, for purposes of its RFRA analysis, that the compelling interest criterion is met in these cases. See *ante,* at 40. It bears note in this regard that the cost of an IUD is nearly equivalent to a month's full-time pay for workers earning the minimum wage, Brief for Guttmacher Institute et al. as *Amici Curiae* 16; that almost one-third of women would change their contraceptive method if costs were not a factor, Frost & Darroch, Factors Associated With Contraceptive Choice and Inconsistent Method Use, United States, 2004, 40 Perspectives on Sexual & Reproductive Health 94, 98 (2008); and that only one-fourth of women who request an IUD actually have one inserted after finding out how expensive it would be, Gariepy, Simon, Patel, Creinin, & Schwarz, The Impact of Out-of-Pocket Expense on IUD Utilization Among Women With Private Insurance, 84 Contraception e39, e40 (2011). See also Eisenberg, *supra,* at S60 (recent study found that women who face out-of-pocket IUD costs in excess of $50 were "11-times less likely to obtain an IUD than women who had to pay less than $50"); Postlethwaite, Trussell, Zoolakis, Shabear, & Petitti, A Comparison of Contraceptive Procurement Pre- and Post-Benefit Change, 76 Contraception 360, 361–362 (2007) (when one health system eliminated patient cost sharing for IUDs, use of this form of contraception more than doubled). . . .

Why should decisions of this order be made by Congress or the regulatory authority, and not this Court? Hobby Lobby and Conestoga surely do not stand alone as commercial enterprises seeking exemptions from generally applicable laws on the basis of their religious beliefs. See *e.g, Newman* v. *Piggie Park Enterprises, Inc.*, 256 F. Supp. 41, 945 (SC 1966) (owner of restaurant chain refused to serve black patrons based on his religious beliefs opposing racial integration), aff'd in relevant part and rev'd in part on other grounds, 377 F. 2d 433 (CA4 1967), aff'd and modified on other grounds, 390 U. S. 400 (1968); *In re Minnesota ex rel. McClure*, 370 N. W. 2d 844, 847 (Minn. 1985)

(born-again Christians who owned closely held, for-profit health clubs believed that the Bible proscribed hiring or retaining an "individua[l] living with but not married to a person of the opposite sex," "a young, single woman working without her father's consent or a married woman working without her husband's consent," and any person "antagonistic to the Bible," including "fornicators and homosexuals" (internal quotation marks omitted)), appeal dismissed, 478 U. S. 1015 (1986); *Elane Photography, LLC* v. *Willock*, 2013–NMSC–040, ___ N. M. ___, 309 P. 3d 53 (for-profit photography business owned by a husband and wife refused to photograph a lesbian couple's commitment ceremony based on the religious beliefs of the company's owners), cert. denied, 572 U. S. ___ (2014). Would RFRA require exemptions in cases of this ilk? And if not, how does the Court divine which religious beliefs are worthy of accommodation, and which are not? Isn't the Court disarmed from making such a judgment given its recognition that "courts must not presume to determine . . . the plausibility of a religious claim"? *Ante,* at 37.

Would the exemption the Court holds RFRA demands for employers with religiously grounded objections to the use of certain contraceptives extend to employers with religiously grounded objections to blood transfusions (Jehovah's Witnesses); antidepressants (Scientologists); medications derived from pigs, including anesthesia, intravenous fluids, and pills coated with gelatin (certain Muslims, Jews, and Hindus); and vaccinations (Christian Scientists, among others)? According to counsel for Hobby Lobby, "each one of these cases . . . would have to be evaluated on its own . . . apply[ing] the compelling interest-least restrictive alternative test." Tr. of Oral Arg. 6. Not much help there for the lower courts bound by today's decision.

The Court, however, sees nothing to worry about. Today's cases, the Court concludes, are "concerned solely with the contraceptive mandate. Our decision should not be understood to hold that an insurance-coverage mandate must necessarily fall if it conflicts with an employer's religious beliefs. Other coverage requirements, such as immunizations, may be supported by different interests (for example, the need to combat the spread of infectious diseases) and may involve different arguments about the least restrictive means of providing them." *Ante*, at 46. But the Court has assumed, for RFRA purposes, that the interest in women's health and well being is compelling and has come up with no means adequate to serve that interest, the one motivating Congress to adopt the Women's Health Amendment.

There is an overriding interest, I believe, in keeping the courts "out of the business of evaluating the relative merits of differing religious claims," *Lee*, 455 U. S., at 263, n. 2 (Stevens, J., concurring in judgment), or the sincerity with which an asserted religious belief is held. Indeed, approving some religious claims while deeming others unworthy of accommodation could be "perceived as favoring one religion over another," the very "risk the Establishment Clause was designed to preclude." *Ibid*. The Court,

I fear, has ventured into a minefield, cf. *Spencer* v. *World Vision, Inc.*, 633 F. 3d 723, 730 (CA9 2010) (O'Scannlain, J., concurring), by its immoderate reading of RFRA. I would confine religious exemptions under that Act to organizations formed "for a religious purpose," "engage[d] primarily in carrying out that religious purpose," and not "engaged . . . substantially in the exchange of goods or services for money beyond nominal amounts." See *id.*, at 748 (Kleinfeld, J., concurring).

RUTH BADER GINSBERG is an associate justice of the U.S. Supreme Court. She was appointed by President Bill Clinton in 1993.

EXPLORING THE ISSUE

Should Corporations Be Awarded Religious Freedoms?

Critical Thinking and Reflection

1. What was the contraception mandate? Do you agree with the Court's decision regarding it?
2. What role did Catholics play in the Court's ruling?
3. On what other issues do we see politics and religion intersecting in the United States today?
4. How does the Court typically view corporations? In which ways do they have individual rights? In which ways do they not?
5. Is it possible to have a wall between church and state in America today? Why or why not?

Is There Common Ground?

At the end of the day, corporations are either people or they are not. While the Courts continue to discuss what rights and freedoms these legally constructed groups of citizens should possess, at the end of the day, there is little room for common ground in this debate. After all, citizens will either agree that corporations should have First Amendment freedoms or not—and that decision will largely be based on perceptions of the entities themselves. And, most importantly, this opinion is unlikely to be swayed. What citizens believe about corporations and corporate personhood is typically a steadfast attitude, unable to be swayed or penetrated by new ideas or opinions.

When it comes to matters of religion, the issue becomes even more debatable. We are now taking sensitive issues that hit at the inner core of many Americans and suggesting that legal constructions be provided with similar freedoms. Abortion—for example—is a deeply personal issue for many and one that many seek spiritual guidance for understanding and interpreting. Now, the Courts are suggesting that soulless, heartless, and bodiless organizations are potentially capable of making the same interpretations. If citizens do not believe politics should interfere with religion, the odds are they will not appreciate the ability for corporations to do the same—at least if their side is not winning. Unfortunately, when it comes to religion and politics, issues—in reality—are never black and white, despite citizens doing everything in their power to view them that way. Common ground on this issue will be particularly difficult to find as a result.

Additional Resources

Andrew Koppleman, *Defending American Religious Neutrality* (Harvard University Press, 2013)

Brian Leiter, *Why Tolerate Religion?* (Princeton University Press, 2012)

Ira Luple and Robert Tuttle, *Secular Government, Religious People* (Wm. B. Eerdmans Publishing Co., 2014)

Martha Nussbaum, *Liberty of Conscience: In Defense of America's Tradition of Religious Equality* (Basic Books, 2010)

Steven D. Smith, *The Rise and Decline of American Religious Freedom* (Harvard University Press, 2014)

Internet References . . .

Alliance for Defending Freedom

http://www.alliancedefendingfreedom.org/issues
/religious-liberty

Bill of Rights Institute

http://billofrightsinstitute.org/resources/educator
-resources/headlines/freedom-of-religion/

Center for Religious Freedom

http://www.hudson.org/policycenters/7-center-for
-religious-freedom

International Association for Religious Freedom

https://iarf.net/

International Religious Freedom Report for 2013

http://www.state.gov/j/drl/rls/irf/religiousfreedom
/index.htm

Unit 4

UNIT

America and the World

*A*t one time the United States could isolate itself from much of the world, and it did. But today's America affects and is affected—for good or ill—by what happens anywhere on the planet. Whether the topic is ecology, finance, war, or terrorism, America is integrally tied to the rest of the world. With a globalized economy and instant communication, no nation lives in a bubble, regardless of its intent or desire to. What happens in one country will impact societies across the globe.

The United States, then, simply has no choice but to act and react in relation to a constantly shifting series of events; the arguments turn on over whether it acts morally or immorally, wisely or foolishly, what methods are morally justified in protecting the American homeland from attack? Do they include warrantless wiretapping and indefinite detention of suspected terrorists? What role should the United States take in battling global actors like ISIS? Are diseases like Zika the future of international conundrums? Is it time to revisit old feuds, like President Obama has with Cuba? Where do we go under a new administration?

Selected, Edited, and with Issue Framing Material by:
William J. Miller, *Flagler College*

ISSUE

Should the United States Be More Heavily Involved in Efforts to Defeat ISIS?

YES: Max Boot, from "Defeating ISIS," *Council on Foreign Relations* (2014)

NO: Barack Obama, from "Address to the Nation by the President," *The White House* (2015)

Learning Outcomes

After reading this issue, you will be able to:

- Describe the formation of ISIS.
- Assess the United States' current policy toward ISIS.
- Explain the potential costs and benefits of engaging with ISIS.
- Identify potential strategies for defeating ISIS.
- Assess public opinion toward the American military as it pertains to possible action against ISIS.

ISSUE SUMMARY

YES: Max Boot, Jeane J. Kirkpatrick Senior Fellow for National Security Studies at the Council for Foreign Relations, argues that the United States will need to increase its commitment in a measured way if it wishes to see ISIS defeated in the Middle East. He advocates not ruling out the option of ground-combat troops as it makes the country appear non-committed and reduces available leverage.

NO: President Barack Obama, speaking to the nation in the aftermath of the San Bernardino shooting, reiterates his desire to destroy ISIS. But, in doing so, does not appear willing to change the country's current policy, which has been judged by many to be inadequate in addressing the threat of the Islamic State terrorist group.

The Islamic State is a militant Sunni movement that has conquered territory in western Iraq, eastern Syria, and Libya, from which it has tried to establish the caliphate, claiming exclusive political and theological authority over the world's Muslims. Its state-building project, however, has been characterized more by extreme violence than institution building.

The group traces its lineage to the aftermath of the U.S. invasion of Iraq in 2003, when Jordanian militant Abu Musab al-Zarqawi aligned his militant group, Jama'at al-Tawhid w'al-Jihad, with al-Qaeda, making it al-Qaeda in Iraq (AQI). Zarqawi's organization immediately took aim at U.S. forces, their allies abroad, and all local collaborators. It sought to draw the United States into a sectarian civil war by attacking Shias and their holy sites to provoke them to retaliate against Sunni civilians.

Zarqawi was killed in a U.S. air strike in 2006. Zarqawi's successors rebranded AQI as the Islamic State of Iraq, and later, the Islamic State of Iraq and al-Sham (ISIS). The name refers to a territory that roughly corresponds with the Levant, or eastern Mediterranean, reflecting the group's broadened ambitions with the onset of the 2011 uprising in Syria. The Islamic State's leader, the self-proclaimed caliph Abu Bakr al-Baghdadi, spent time in American-run prisons in Iraq.

The group has capitalized on Sunni disenfranchisement in both Iraq and Syria. In Iraq, the Sunni minority was sidelined from national politics after 2003, first by the U.S.-led occupation leadership and then by politicians from Iraq's Shia majority. Prime Minister Maliki cemented his power as U.S. forces withdrew from Iraq in 2010 by excluding Sunni political rivals and providing Shias disproportionate benefits. Maliki also purged the officer corps of potential rivals, which, combined with desertion and corruption, contributed to the Iraqi military's collapse as Islamic State militants overran Mosul, Iraq's second-largest city, in June 2014.

In Syria, the civil war that emerged from a broad-based uprising against President Bashar al-Assad in 2011, which pitted the ruling minority Alawis, a Shia sect, against the Sunni majority, gave the group new opportunities to expand. Its early battlefield successes attracted militant Sunnis from across the region to join a jihad against the regime. As extremists came to dominate territory in Syria's north and east, Assad claimed it validated his argument that only his government could mount an effective campaign against "terrorists"—a term he has applied to opposition figures of all stripes.

The Islamic State's claim to be a caliphate has raised concerns that its ambitions are not bound by the borders of Iraq and Syria. Insurgent groups in Afghanistan, Bangladesh, Egypt, Indonesia, Nigeria, Pakistan, the Philippines, Saudi Arabia, and Yemen have sworn allegiance to Baghdadi. In 2015, the group seized territory in Libya that spanned more than 150 miles of Mediterranean coastline between Tripoli and Benghazi.

The conflicts in Syria and Iraq have attracted foreign fighters by the thousands. Middle Eastern and Western intelligence agencies have raised concern that their citizens who have joined the fighting in Iraq and Syria will return to their home countries to carry out attacks. U.S. Director of National Intelligence James Clapper estimated in February 2015 that more than 13,000 foreign fighters joined Sunni Arab antigovernment extremist groups, including the Islamic State, in Syria.

Even more worrisome to Western intelligence is the Islamic State's call on its followers worldwide to carry out attacks in Europe and the United States. Following an attack on an LGBT nightclub in Florida in June 2016, FBI Director James Comey remarked on the scale of the counterterrorism challenge: "We are looking for needles in a nationwide haystack, but we are also called up to figure out which pieces of hay might someday become needles." Some analysts say the Islamic State hopes such attacks will draw Western countries into a protracted military conflict, perhaps to fulfill an apocalyptic prophesy. Two of the suicide bombers in the November 2015 attacks in Paris smuggled themselves into Europe through Greece, disguised among refugees. This has helped fuel the anti-migrant backlash across Europe.

President Barack Obama's administration has assembled a coalition of some 60 countries to "degrade and ultimately defeat" the Islamic State. Privately, it has expressed frustration that many of these countries, particularly Sunni Arab states, have contributed little more than rhetorical support. As of late July 2016, the coalition has carried out more than 14,093 air strikes, 77 percent of them by U.S. forces, in Iraq and Syria, the Pentagon said. The administration has cited the post-9/11 Authorization for the Use of Military Force and 2002 Iraq war resolution as the domestic legal justification for this open-ended conflict. Some legal scholars are dubious, however, particularly as U.S. military operations have expanded from Iraq to Syria and Libya.

In Iraq, the United States has deployed more than 3000 uniformed personnel, built up counterterrorism units of the Iraqi army, and armed the Kurdistan Regional Government's paramilitary, the Peshmerga, in a bid to wrest the Islamic State from major cities and strategic points. Ramadi fell in December 2015 and Fallujah in June 2016, and in August 2016 Iraqi forces were gearing up to take Mosul. But with much of the Iraqi army still in disarray, Shia militias known as Popular Mobilization Forces have done much of the fighting, raising concerns that Sunni residents of cities that have been liberated from the Islamic State will find, in its place, forces at least as hostile to them. Rights groups allege that these militias have evicted, disappeared, and killed residents of Sunni and mixed neighborhoods.

In Syria, meanwhile, the Pentagon began a three-year program in early 2015 to train and equip 5000 "appropriately vetted elements of the Syrian opposition" a year to attack Islamic State forces—but not the Assad regime and its allies. But the Obama administration abandoned the $500 million program in October 2015 after it was revealed to have yielded just "four or five" fighters in Syria. In its place, the White House said it would adopt a looser approach, screening just commanders rather than individual fighters.

Regional geopolitics have complicated U.S. efforts in Iraq and Syria. The YPG, a Syrian Kurdish militia, has proven to be one of the forces most effective at rolling back the Islamic State, at least within areas claimed by Kurds. But Turkey, which fears the establishment of an autonomous Kurdish entity in territory contiguous with its own Kurdish-majority regions, says the YPG is an extension of the Kurdistan Workers' Party, which the United States, EU, and Turkey all consider a terrorist organization.

Russia launched air strikes in Syria in late 2015. Though it claimed to be targeting extremist groups like the Islamic State and al-Qaeda, it has largely targeted Syrian opposition forces, helping Assad recapture lost territory as international negotiations were underway. Iran remains committed to the Assad regime's survival, while the Gulf Arab states are more interested in containing Iran than fighting the Islamic State.

The U.S. objective is a negotiated transition that would see Assad gone, while maintaining the structure of the state and Syria's territorial integrity, but the diplomatic process has deadlocked, and the civil war, which has enabled the Islamic State to carve out territory, shows no sign of abating. In Iraq as well, military gains have not been matched by political progress. Maliki's successor, Haider al-Abadi, assumed office in September 2014, pledging to practice a more inclusive brand of politics, but his government has been wracked by protests over widespread corruption; and in many Sunni-majority areas, Shia militias are the most visible face of the government.

The group's momentum in Iraq and Syria withered in 2016 as local forces, backed by a U.S.-led coalition, ousted Islamic State fighters from much of the territory they controlled. But major cities, including Mosul and Raqqa, remain in ISIS hands. In both Iraq and Syria, there are few signs of the political progress that, analysts say, would likely be needed to sustain military gains. Meanwhile, across the region, and as far away as Europe and the United States, followers of the Islamic State have often eluded counterterrorism agencies, raising the possibility that the group will continue to motivate attacks even if it's pushed out of Iraq and Syria.

In the following selections, we see arguments for the United States to become more involved in international efforts to curb ISIS and arguments to stand pat, or maybe even become less directly involved. Max Boot, Jeane J. Kirkpatrick Senior Fellow for National Security Studies at the Council for Foreign Relations, argues that the United States will need to increase its commitment in a measured way if it wishes to see ISIS defeated in the Middle East. He advocates not ruling out the option of ground-combat troops as it makes the country appear non-committed and reduces available leverage. However, President Barack Obama, speaking to the nation in the aftermath of the San Bernardino shooting, reiterates his desire to destroy ISIS. But, in doing so, does not appear willing to change the country's current policy, which has been judged by many to be inadequate in addressing the threat of the Islamic State terrorist group.

YES ⤶

Max Boot

Defeating ISIS

President Barack Obama's strategy in Syria and Iraq is not working. The president is hoping that limited air strikes, combined with U.S. support for local proxies—the peshmerga, the Iraqi security forces, the Sunni tribes, and the Free Syrian Army—will "degrade and ultimately destroy" the Islamic State of Iraq and Syria (ISIS). U.S. actions have not stopped ISIS from expanding its control into Iraq's Anbar Province and northern Syria. If the president is serious about dealing with ISIS, he will need to increase America's commitment in a measured way—to do more than what Washington is currently doing but substantially less than what it did in Iraq and Afghanistan in the past decade. And although President Obama will probably not need to send U.S. ground–combat forces to Iraq and Syria, he should not publicly rule out that option; taking the possibility of U.S. ground troops off the table reduces U.S. leverage and raises questions about its commitment.

A Big Threat

A reasonable goal for the United States would be neither to "degrade" ISIS (vague and insufficient) nor to "destroy" it (too ambitious for the present), but rather to "defeat" or "neutralize" it, ending its ability to control significant territory and reducing it to, at worst, a small terrorist group with limited reach. This is what happened with ISIS' predecessor, al-Qaeda in Iraq, during 2007 and 2008, before its rebirth amid the chaos of the Syrian civil war. It is possible to inflict a similar fate on ISIS, which, for all of its newfound strength, is less formidable and less organized than groups like Hezbollah and the Taliban, which operate with considerable state support from Iran and Pakistan, respectively. Although not as potent a fighting force as Hezbollah or the Taliban, ISIS is an even bigger threat to the United States and its allies because it has attracted thousands of foreign fighters who could return to commit acts of terrorism in their homelands.

What It Will Take to Defeat ISIS

To defeat ISIS, the president needs to dispatch more aircraft, military advisors, and special operations forces, while loosening the restrictions under which they operate. The president also needs to do a better job of mobilizing support from Sunnis in Iraq and Syria, as well

as from Turkey, by showing that he is intent on deposing not only ISIS but also the equally murderous Alawite regime in Damascus. Specific steps include:

Intensify air strikes. So far, the U.S. bombing campaign against ISIS has been remarkably restrained, as revealed by a comparison with the strikes against the Taliban and al-Qaeda in Afghanistan after 9/11. When the Taliban lost control of Afghanistan between October 7, 2001, and December 23, 2001—a period of seventy-five days—U.S. aircraft flew 6,500 strike sorties and dropped 17,500 munitions. By contrast, between August 8, 2014, and October 23, 2014—seventy-six days—the United States conducted only 632 airstrikes and dropped only 1,700 munitions in Iraq and Syria. Such episodic and desultory bombing will not stop any determined military force, much less one as fanatical as ISIS.

Lift the prohibition on U.S. "boots on the ground." President Obama has not allowed U.S. Special Forces and forward air controllers to embed themselves in the Free Syrian Army, Iraqi security forces, Kurdish peshmerga, or in Sunni tribes when they go into combat as he did with the Northern Alliance in Afghanistan. This lack of eyes on the ground makes it harder to call in air strikes and to improve the combat capacity of U.S. proxies. Experience shows that "combat advisors" fighting alongside indigenous troops are far more effective than trainers confined to large bases.

Increase the size of the U.S. force. Military requirements, not a priori numbers dreamed up in Washington, should shape the force eventually dispatched. The current force, even with the recent addition of 1,500 more troops for a total of 2,900, is inadequate. Estimates of necessary troop size range from 10,000 personnel (according to General Anthony Zinni, former head of Central Command) to 25,000 (according to military analysts Kim and Fred Kagan). The total number should include Special Forces teams and forward air controllers to partner with local forces as well as logistical, intelligence, security, and air contingents in support.

Work with all of Iraq's and Syria's moderate factions. The United States should work with the peshmerga, Sunni tribes, the Free Syrian Army, and elements of the Iraqi security forces (ISF) that have not been overtaken by Iran's Quds Force, rather than simply supplying weapons to the ISF. Given Shiite militia infiltration, working exclusively through the ISF would risk empowering the Shiite sectarians whose attacks on Sunnis are ISIS' best recruiter. The United States should directly assist Sunni tribes by establishing

Boot, Max. "Defeating ISIS," Council on Foreign Relations, 2014. Copyright © 2014 by Council on Foreign Relations. Used with permission.

a small forward operating base in Anbar Province, and also increase support for and coordination with the Free Syrian Army. Current plans to train only five thousand Syrian fighters next year need to be beefed up.

Send in the Joint Special Operations Command (JSOC). Between 2003 and 2010, JSOC—composed of units such as SEAL Team Six and Delta Force—became skilled at targeting the networks of al-Qaeda in Iraq. Its success was largely due to its ability to gather intelligence by interrogating prisoners and scooping up computers and documents—something that bombing alone cannot accomplish. JSOC squadrons should once again be moved to the region (they could be stationed in Iraq proper, the Kurdistan Regional Government, Turkey, and/or Jordan) to target high-level ISIS organizers.

Draw Turkey into the war. President Obama should do what he can to increase Turkey's involvement in the anti-ISIS campaign. If the Turkish army were to roll across the frontier, it could push back ISIS and establish "safe zones" for more moderate Syrian opposition members. Turkish President Recep Tayyip Erdogan has said that he will not join the fray without Washington's commitment to overthrowing Syrian President Bashar al-Assad, whom he rightly sees as the source of instability in Syria. Assuming Erdogan has honestly outlined his conditions for Turkish involvement in Syria, a greater U.S. commitment, demonstrated by a no-fly zone and airstrikes on Assad's forces, should be sufficient to entice Ankara to play a greater role.

Impose a no-fly zone over part or all of Syria. Even though U.S. aircraft are overflying Syria, they are not bombing Assad's forces. This has led to a widespread suspicion among Sunnis that the United States is now willing to keep Assad in power. More broadly, Sunnis fear that Obama is accommodating Assad's backers in Tehran to allow Iran to dominate Mesopotamia and the Levant. A no-fly zone over part or all of Syria would address these concerns and pave the way for greater Turkish involvement. The United States should act to ensure that Assad does not take advantage of the anti-ISIS campaign to bomb opposition centers. Obama could announce that no Syrian aircraft will be allowed over designated "safe zones." Such a move would garner widespread support among Arab states, undercutting attempts to portray U.S. action as a war against the Muslim world. There are legitimate concerns that overthrowing Assad now, before the Syrian opposition is ready to fill the vacuum, would be counterproductive and potentially pave the way for a jihadist takeover of all of Syria. But instituting a partial or even a complete no-fly zone would *not* lead to Assad's immediate ouster. It would, however, facilitate the moderate opposition's ability to organize an administration capable, with international help, of governing Syria once Assad finally goes.

Mobilize Sunni tribes. As long as the Sunni tribes of Iraq and Syria continue to tacitly support ISIS, or at least not to resist it, defeating ISIS will be almost impossible. But if the tribes turn against ISIS, as they did against al-Qaeda in Iraq in 2007, a rapid reversal of fortunes is likely. Galvanizing Sunni tribes into action will not be easy; Iraqi Sunnis feel that the United States betrayed them after the

surge by leaving them under Shiite domination in Baghdad. The fact that Haidar al-Abadi replaced former Prime Minister Nouri al-Maliki in September is a good first step. But Abadi is also a Shiite from the same Dawa Party as Maliki, making it unlikely that Sunnis will fight ISIS if they once again find themselves subordinated to Shiite rule. This concern could be allayed if the United States were to engineer a political deal to grant Sunnis autonomy within the Iraqi federal structure, similar to what the Kurdistan Regional Government already enjoys. To assuage Sunnis' fear of betrayal, the United States should pledge to indefinitely maintain advise-and-assist forces in Iraq—even without Baghdad's agreement, U.S. forces could at least remain in the Kurdish area.

Prepare now for nation-building. The United States should lay the groundwork for a postconflict settlement in both Iraq and Syria that does not necessarily require keeping both political entities intact. In the Iraqi context, this means offering greater autonomy to the Sunnis and guaranteeing the Kurds that their hard-won gains will not be jeopardized; the United States should propose to permanently station troops in the Kurdistan Regional Government. This is not necessarily synonymous with Kurdish independence, but the United States should give serious consideration to dropping its long-time opposition to the creation of a Kurdish state or possibly even two—one in Syria and one in Iraq.

Social fragmentation in Syria will make postwar reconstruction difficult; after three years of civil war, it may not be possible to reconstitute the country as it previously existed. The U.S. goal should simply be to ensure that Syrian territory is not controlled by either Shiite or Sunni extremists. The postwar settlement in the former Yugoslavia, which involved the dispatch of international peacekeepers and administrators under United Nations, European Union, and NATO mandates, could be a possible model. The United States should push UN Special Envoy for Syria Staffan de Mistura to work in cooperation with the Arab League, the EU, NATO, the United States, and even Russia to create a post-Assad administration that can win the assent of Syria's sectarian communities. As Kenneth Pollack of the Brookings Institution has suggested, "[T]he U.S. should provide most of the muscle, the Gulf states most of the money, and the international community most of the know-how." This is admittedly an ambitious goal. Neither Assad nor ISIS is in imminent danger of falling, and it will be challenging to impose any kind of order in Syria. But the United States should not repeat the mistake it made in Iraq and Libya of pushing for regime change absent a plan to fill the resulting vacuum. Admittedly even the best-laid plans can fail, but failure is guaranteed if no such plans are in place.

Down the "Slippery Slope"?

Critics will call this strategy too costly, alleging that it will push the United States down a "slippery slope" into another ground war in the Middle East. This approach will undoubtedly incur greater financial cost (dispatching ten thousand troops for a year would cost

$10 billion) and higher risk of casualties among U.S. forces. But the present minimalist strategy has scant chance of success, and it risks backfiring—ISIS' prestige will be enhanced if it withstands half-hearted U.S. air strikes. Left unchecked, ISIS could expand into Lebanon, Jordan, or Saudi Arabia. Greater American involvement could galvanize U.S. allies—the most important being Turkey and the Sunni tribes of Iraq and Syria—to commit more resources to the fight. If this plan is not implemented, a major ground war involving U.S. troops becomes more probable, because the security situation will likely continue deteriorating. By contrast, this strategy, while incurring greater short-term risks, enhances the odds that ISIS will be defeated before Obama leaves office.

Max Boot is Jeane J. Kirkpatrick Senior Fellow in National Security Studies at the Council on Foreign Relations in New York. He is a military historian and foreign-policy analyst who has been called one of the "world's leading authorities on armed conflict" by the International Institute for Strategic Studies.

Barack Obama

 **NO**

Address to the Nation by the President

THE PRESIDENT: Good evening. On Wednesday, 14 Americans were killed as they came together to celebrate the holidays. They were taken from family and friends who loved them deeply. They were white and black; Latino and Asian; immigrants and American-born; moms and dads; daughters and sons. Each of them served their fellow citizens and all of them were part of our American family.

Tonight, I want to talk with you about this tragedy, the broader threat of terrorism, and how we can keep our country safe.

The FBI is still gathering the facts about what happened in San Bernardino, but here is what we know. The victims were brutally murdered and injured by one of their coworkers and his wife. So far, we have no evidence that the killers were directed by a terrorist organization overseas, or that they were part of a broader conspiracy here at home. But it is clear that the two of them had gone down the dark path of radicalization, embracing a perverted interpretation of Islam that calls for war against America and the West. They had stockpiled assault weapons, ammunition, and pipe bombs. So this was an act of terrorism, designed to kill innocent people.

Our nation has been at war with terrorists since al Qaeda killed nearly 3,000 Americans on 9/11. In the process, we've hardened our defenses—from airports to financial centers, to other critical infrastructure. Intelligence and law enforcement agencies have disrupted countless plots here and overseas, and worked around the clock to keep us safe. Our military and counterterrorism professionals have relentlessly pursued terrorist networks overseas—disrupting safe havens in several different countries, killing Osama bin Laden, and decimating al Qaeda's leadership.

Over the last few years, however, the terrorist threat has evolved into a new phase. As we've become better at preventing complex, multifaceted attacks like 9/11, terrorists turned to less complicated acts of violence like the mass shootings that are all too common in our society. It is this type of attack that we saw at Fort Hood in 2009; in Chattanooga earlier this year; and now in San Bernardino. And as groups like ISIL grew stronger amidst the chaos of war in Iraq and then Syria, and as the Internet erases the distance between countries, we see growing efforts by terrorists to poison the minds of people like the Boston Marathon bombers and the San Bernardino killers.

For seven years, I've confronted this evolving threat each morning in my intelligence briefing. And since the day I took this office, I've authorized U.S. forces to take out terrorists abroad precisely because I know how real the danger is. As Commander-in-Chief, I have no greater responsibility than the security of the American people. As a father to two young daughters who are the most precious part of my life, I know that we see ourselves with friends and coworkers at a holiday party like the one in San Bernardino. I know we see our kids in the faces of the young people killed in Paris. And I know that after so much war, many Americans are asking whether we are confronted by a cancer that has no immediate cure.

Well, here's what I want you to know: The threat from terrorism is real, but we will overcome it. We will destroy ISIL and any other organization that tries to harm us. Our success won't depend on tough talk, or abandoning our values, or giving into fear. That's what groups like ISIL are hoping for. Instead, we will prevail by being strong and smart, resilient and relentless, and by drawing upon every aspect of American power.

Here's how. First, our military will continue to hunt down terrorist plotters in any country where it is necessary. In Iraq and Syria, airstrikes are taking out ISIL leaders, heavy weapons, oil tankers, infrastructure. And since the attacks in Paris, our closest allies—including France, Germany, and the United Kingdom—have ramped up their contributions to our military campaign, which will help us accelerate our effort to destroy ISIL.

Second, we will continue to provide training and equipment to tens of thousands of Iraqi and Syrian forces fighting ISIL on the ground so that we take away their safe havens. In both countries, we're deploying Special Operations Forces who can accelerate that offensive. We've stepped up this effort since the attacks in Paris, and we'll continue to invest more in approaches that are working on the ground.

Third, we're working with friends and allies to stop ISIL's operations—to disrupt plots, cut off their financing, and prevent them from recruiting more fighters. Since the attacks in Paris, we've surged intelligence-sharing with our European allies. We're working with Turkey to seal its border with Syria. And we are cooperating with Muslim-majority countries—and with our Muslim communities here at home—to counter the vicious ideology that ISIL promotes online.

Obama, Barack. "Address to the Nation by the President," The White House Office of the Press Secretary, December 2015.

Fourth, with American leadership, the international community has begun to establish a process—and timeline—to pursue ceasefires and a political resolution to the Syrian war. Doing so will allow the Syrian people and every country, including our allies, but also countries like Russia, to focus on the common goal of destroying ISIL—a group that threatens us all.

This is our strategy to destroy ISIL. It is designed and supported by our military commanders and counterterrorism experts, together with 65 countries that have joined an American-led coalition. And we constantly examine our strategy to determine when additional steps are needed to get the job done. That's why I've ordered the Departments of State and Homeland Security to review the visa *Waiver program under which the female terrorist in San Bernardino originally came to this country. And that's why I will urge high-tech and law enforcement leaders to make it harder for terrorists to use technology to escape from justice.

Now, here at home, we have to work together to address the challenge. There are several steps that Congress should take right away.

To begin with, Congress should act to make sure no one on a no-fly list is able to buy a gun. What could possibly be the argument for allowing a terrorist suspect to buy a semi-automatic weapon? This is a matter of national security.

We also need to make it harder for people to buy powerful assault weapons like the ones that were used in San Bernardino. I know there are some who reject any gun safety measures. But the fact is that our intelligence and law enforcement agencies—no matter how effective they are—cannot identify every would-be mass shooter, whether that individual is motivated by ISIL or some other hateful ideology. What we can do—and must do—is make it harder for them to kill.

Next, we should put in place stronger screening for those who come to America without a visa so that we can take a hard look at whether they've traveled to warzones. And we're working with members of both parties in Congress to do exactly that.

Finally, if Congress believes, as I do, that we are at war with ISIL, it should go ahead and vote to authorize the continued use of military force against these terrorists. For over a year, I have ordered our military to take thousands of airstrikes against ISIL targets. I think it's time for Congress to vote to demonstrate that the American people are united, and committed, to this fight.

My fellow Americans, these are the steps that we can take together to defeat the terrorist threat. Let me now say a word about what we should not do.

We should not be drawn once more into a long and costly ground war in Iraq or Syria. That's what groups like ISIL want. They know they can't defeat us on the battlefield. ISIL fighters were part of the insurgency that we faced in Iraq. But they also know that if we occupy foreign lands, they can maintain insurgencies for years,

killing thousands of our troops, draining our resources, and using our presence to draw new recruits.

The strategy that we are using now—airstrikes, Special Forces, and working with local forces who are fighting to regain control of their own country—that is how we'll achieve a more sustainable victory. And it won't require us sending a new generation of Americans overseas to fight and die for another decade on foreign soil.

Here's what else we cannot do. We cannot turn against one another by letting this fight be defined as a war between America and Islam. That, too, is what groups like ISIL want. ISIL does not speak for Islam. They are thugs and killers, part of a cult of death, and they account for a tiny fraction of more than a billion Muslims around the world—including millions of patriotic Muslim Americans who reject their hateful ideology. Moreover, the vast majority of terrorist victims around the world are Muslim. If we're to succeed in defeating terrorism we must enlist Muslim communities as some of our strongest allies, rather than push them away through suspicion and hate.

That does not mean denying the fact that an extremist ideology has spread within some Muslim communities. This is a real problem that Muslims must confront, without excuse. Muslim leaders here and around the globe have to continue working with us to decisively and unequivocally reject the hateful ideology that groups like ISIL and al Qaeda promote; to speak out against not just acts of violence, but also those interpretations of Islam that are incompatible with the values of religious tolerance, mutual respect, and human dignity.

But just as it is the responsibility of Muslims around the world to root out misguided ideas that lead to radicalization, it is the responsibility of all Americans—of every faith—to reject discrimination. It is our responsibility to reject religious tests on who we admit into this country. It's our responsibility to reject proposals that Muslim Americans should somehow be treated differently. Because when we travel down that road, we lose. That kind of divisiveness, that betrayal of our values plays into the hands of groups like ISIL. Muslim Americans are our friends and our neighbors, our co-workers, our sports heroes—and, yes, they are our men and women in uniform who are willing to die in defense of our country. We have to remember that.

My fellow Americans, I am confident we will succeed in this mission because we are on the right side of history. We were founded upon a belief in human dignity—that no matter who you are, or where you come from, or what you look like, or what religion you practice, you are equal in the eyes of God and equal in the eyes of the law.

Even in this political season, even as we properly debate what steps I and future Presidents must take to keep our country safe, let's make sure we never forget what makes us exceptional. Let's not forget that freedom is more powerful than fear; that we have always met challenges—whether war or depression, natural disasters or terrorist attacks—by coming together around our common ideals as one nation, as one people. So long as we stay true to that tradition, I have no doubt America will prevail.

Thank you. God bless you, and may God bless the United States of America.

Barack Obama served as U.S. Senator for Illinois prior to defeating John McCain in the 2008 presidential election to become the 44th President of the United States. He is the first African American to hold the position. In 2012, President Obama defeated Republican challenger Mitt Romney to win a second term.

EXPLORING THE ISSUE

Should the United States Be More Heavily Involved in Efforts to Defeat ISIS?

Critical Thinking and Reflection

1. How do you think ISIS grew to what it is today?
2. Do you believe the United States should be involved in attempts to eliminate ISIS? Why or why not?
3. What do you think ISIS will do if it is not stopped?
4. What other actors should play a direct role in attempting to curb ISIS's influence? Why?
5. How big of a threat do you believe ISIS is to the United States?

Is There Common Ground?

When it comes to becoming involved in international affairs—especially when the engagement of the American military is possible—common ground can be difficult to reach. If we think of Americans as typically being hawks or doves, we can see why trying to find common ground is hard. It's not like we can half commit to attempting to defeat ISIS. But, where common ground is possible is perhaps in how we choose to commit more to defeating ISIS. For example, a dove may oppose sending ground troops into Syria to attempt to overthrow ISIS strongholds in cities lime Aleppo, but they may support providing more extensive training to ally soldiers in Syria. Or they may be more supportive of increased drone attacks as opposed to airstrikes.

What really shapes the debate over American action against ISIS is citizen attitudes toward interventionism, the Middle East, and to some degree radical Islam. It is not simply a question of whether one believes the military should be engaged in conflict, but where they should be dedicating their energies. For Americans that feel terrorism is a domestic concern and one that could directly impact their lives, we are more likely to see a push for intervention. For those who believe ISIS exists only half the globe away and does not pose a direct threat to the United States, an isolationist approach is likely to be preferred. Either way, this is another issue where the dividing lines between those who say yes and those who say no are drawn quite clearly in the sand.

Additional Resources

Jessica Stern and J. M. Berger, *ISIS: The State of Terror* (Ecco, 2016)

Joby Warrick, *Black Flags: The Rise of ISIS* (Anchor, 2016)

Michael Weiss and Hassan Hassan, *ISIS: Inside the Army of Terror* (Regan Arts, 2015)

Internet References . . .

ISIS Fast Facts

http://www.cnn.com/2014/08/08/world/isis-fast-facts/

The Islamic State

http://www.cfr.org/iraq/islamic-state/p14811

What Is the Islamic State?

http://www.pbs.org/newshour/rundown/what-is-islamic-state-iraq-and-syria/

Selected, Edited, and with Issue Framing Material by:
William J. Miller, *Flagler College*

ISSUE

Is the United States Doing Enough to Address the Global Threat of Diseases like Zika?

YES: The White House, from "FACT SHEET: Preparing for and Responding to the Zika Virus at Home and Abroad," *The White House* (2016)

NO: Peter J. Hotez, from "Zika Is Coming," *The New York Times* (2016)

Learning Outcomes

After reading this issue, you will be able to:

- Describe what the Zika virus is.
- Assess the potential for Zika to have an impact in the United States.
- Explain the international reaction to Zika.
- Compare and contrast Zika to other global diseases.
- Describe ways the United States could help combat the spread of Zika, both domestically and abroad.

ISSUE SUMMARY

YES: The White House Fact Sheet on preparing for Zika clearly delineates the steps taken across the country to help mitigate the threat of the Zika virus and handle any responses necessary if the disease were to find itself within the United States. This includes a detailed discussion of available funding and funding priorities.

NO: Peter Hotez, Dean of the National School of Tropical Medicine at Baylor College of Medicine, warns Americans, however, that Zika will likely arrive within our borders soon—especially in major Southern cities—and that we are vastly unprepared to handle any outbreak.

It seems there are an ever-increasing number of global epidemics emerging. As soon as one disease falls off the radar, another seemingly appears to take its place. Just think about recent coverage of Ebola and Zika. Both caused mass panic across the globe, including in the United States where both diseases emerged as viable threats for large segments of the population. Since diseases can easily spread across borders, questions arise regarding who should take charge of handling transnational illnesses.

Zika virus is mostly transmitted through the bite of an infected mosquito, primarily *Aedes aegypti*—the same vector that transmits chikungunya, dengue, and yellow fever. This virus may also be transmitted through sexual intercourse. Zika virus disease has a similar epidemiology, clinical presentation, and transmission cycle in cities and towns as chikungunya and dengue, although the illness is generally milder. Symptoms of Zika virus disease include mild fever, skin rash, conjunctivitis, muscle and joint pain, which normally last for two to seven days. There is no specific treatment but symptoms are normally mild and can be treated with common fever medicines, rest, and drinking plenty of fluids.

Zika virus was first identified in 1947 in a monkey in the Zika forest of Uganda and it was first identified in humans in 1952 in Uganda and the United Republic of Tanzania. Over the following half century, Zika virus has been causing sporadic disease in Africa and Asia. Outbreaks were reported for the first time from the Pacific in 2007 and 2013 in Yap Island and French Polynesia, respectively. The virus subsequently spread to other Pacific islands. The geographical range of Zika virus has been steadily increasing ever since.

The current Zika virus outbreak and its association with an increase in microcephaly, other congenital malformations and Guillain–Barré syndrome (GBS), have caused increasing alarm in countries across the world, particularly in the Americas. Brazil announced a national public health emergency in November 2015. An International Health Regulations Emergency Committee met on February 1, 2016, and WHO declared the recent clusters of microcephaly and other neurological disorders in Brazil (following a similar cluster in French Polynesia in 2014) a Public Health Emergency of International Concern. In the absence of another explanation for the clusters of microcephaly and other neurological disorders, the IHR Emergency Committee recommended enhanced surveillance and research and aggressive measures to reduce infection with Zika virus, particularly among pregnant women and women of childbearing age.

In February 2015, Brazil detected cases of fever and rash that were laboratory-confirmed to be Zika virus in May 2015. In December 2015, there were 56,318 suspected cases of Zika virus disease in 29 states in Brazil. As of June 15, 2016, 60 countries and territories have reported mosquito-borne transmission, of which 46 countries are experiencing the first outbreak of Zika virus since 2015, with no previous evidence of circulation. Non-vector-borne Zika virus transmission, most probably via a sexual route, has been documented in 10 countries: Argentina, Canada, Chile, France, Germany, Italy, New Zealand, Peru, Portugal, and the United States. It is assumed that sexual transmission is ongoing in countries, which report local transmission, by mosquitoes.

The Pan American Health Organization (PAHO) and WHO's operational response began long before the declaration of the Zika outbreak as a Public Health Emergency of International Concern and has accelerated since. On February 14, 2016, WHO launched a global Strategic Response Framework and Joint Operations Plan to guide international coordination.

In February 2016, 23 partners were identified as working with WHO to implement the Strategic Response Framework. This number has now increased to over 60. UNICEF, for example, is working in 21 countries at both community and policy levels to control the spread of Zika virus and mitigate its impact by safely engaging communities and children in mosquito control, provide care and support for affected children and families, and drive the much needed development of easy-to-use tools to diagnose infection and vaccines to prevent Zika virus disease.

The global response to Zika is coordinated from WHO headquarters in Geneva. The agency has activated an Incident Management System (IMS) in its headquarters and regional offices as part of its new Health Emergencies Program. The system enables a dedicated incident manager based at WHO headquarters to draw on expertise and resources from across the entire organization. Since February 2016, the United Nations Deputy Secretary-General has convened monthly coordination meetings to provide a forum at the principals' level for UN system coordination and information sharing. At the working level, WHO has also been holding regular meetings with partners of the Inter-Agency Standing Committee to disseminate information, seek input from partners, and create a transparent approach to the response.

Governments of Colombia, Dominican Republic, Ecuador, El Salvador, and Jamaica have all advised women to postpone becoming pregnant until more is known about the virus and its complications. However, it is important to note that this is not necessarily an option for women who live in contexts where the majority of pregnancies are unplanned, access to contraceptives and sexual and reproductive health services are limited, and sexual violence is prevalent. The U.S. Centers for Disease Control and Prevention (CDC) has issued a level 2 travel warning, which includes recommendations that pregnant women consider postponing travel to any area with ongoing Zika virus transmission.

An effective public health response needs to be consistent with human rights, including the rights of men and women to be informed of, and have access to safe, effective, affordable, and acceptable methods of contraception, without discrimination. These should include emergency contraception, maternal health care and safe abortion services (where it is legal), and post-abortion services. WHO has established a Zika response portal on its website. This is a central point of reference for partners that shows in real time who is doing what, where, and when, at the global, regional, and national levels. More than 500 partner activities and associated budgets are now being tracked through the tool. This helps to ensure that efforts are directed where they are most needed, duplications and deficits are minimized, and the cost-effectiveness of activities is boosted accordingly.

Based on the recommendations from the IHR Emergency Committee meeting on June 14, 2016, WHO has issued no general restrictions on travel or trade with countries, areas, and/or territories with Zika virus transmission. However, WHO is advising pregnant women not to travel to areas with ongoing Zika virus outbreaks, and for all returning travelers to practice safer sex, including through the correct and consistent use of condoms, or abstain from sex for at least eight weeks. If men experience symptoms (rash, fever, arthralgia, myalgia, or conjunctivitis) then they should adopt safer sexual practices or consider abstaining for at least six months. This advice is based on the increased risk of microcephaly and other congenital malformations in babies born to pregnant women infected with Zika virus.

The support already received from donors has been crucial to enable a rapid and effective Zika response during the first months of the response, and WHO and partners are grateful to all donors who have contributed so far. However, funding needs have been largely unmet, both for WHO and for its partners. For instance, WHO and PAHO required US$ 25 million to fund its emergency response to Zika from January to June 2016. From there onwards, WHO has received just over $4 million.

As the Zika response moves from an acute emergency setting to a longer-term programmatic approach, funding sources will also need to shift from emergency to longer-term national and international development and technical assistance programs, especially in the areas of maternal and child care and sexual reproductive health. Therefore, it would be useful to assess the short-, medium-, and long-term economic impact of Zika and to develop an investment case covering all areas of the strategy–in particular, for the care and support of children and families affected. This information should be used to advocate for sustained funding from international and national sources.

As the above description of Zika virus shows, handling transnational disease is a complex issue. No one country can hope to contain such a virus on their own, but there are questions about whether the United States is doing enough to assure citizens are protected and prepared when the threat arrives.

In the following selections, The White House Fact Sheet on preparing for Zika clearly delineates the steps taken across the country to help mitigate the threat of the Zika virus and handle any responses necessary if the disease were to find itself within the United States. This includes a detailed discussion of available funding and funding priorities. Peter Hotez, Dean of the National School of Tropical Medicine at Baylor College of Medicine, warns Americans, however, that Zika will likely arrive within our borders soon—especially in major Southern cities—and that we are vastly unprepared to handle any outbreak.

YES ←

FACT SHEET: Preparing for and Responding to the Zika Virus at Home and Abroad

Since late last year, the Administration has been aggressively working to combat Zika, a virus primarily spread by mosquitoes that has recently been linked to birth defects and other concerning health outcomes. The Federal Government has been monitoring the Zika virus and working with our domestic and international public health partners to alert healthcare providers and the public about Zika; provide public health laboratories with diagnostic tests; and detect and report cases both domestically and internationally.

The Administration is taking every appropriate measure to protect the American people, and today announced that it is asking Congress for more than $1.8 billion in emergency funding to enhance our ongoing efforts to prepare for and respond to the Zika virus, both domestically and internationally. The Administration will submit a formal request to Congress shortly.

The Pan American Health Organization reports 26 countries and territories in the Americas with local Zika transmission. While we have not yet seen transmission of the Zika virus by mosquitoes within the continental United States, Puerto Rico and other U.S. territories in warmer areas with *Aedes aegypti* mosquito populations are already seeing active transmission. In addition, some Americans have returned to the continental U.S. from affected countries in South America, Central America, the Caribbean and the Pacific Islands with Zika infections. The Centers for Disease Control and Prevention reports 50 laboratory-confirmed cases among U.S. travelers from December 2015–February 5, 2016. As spring and summer approach, bringing with them larger and more active mosquito populations, we must be fully prepared to mitigate and quickly address local transmission within the continental U.S., particularly in the Southern United States.

The requested resources will build on our ongoing preparedness efforts and will support essential strategies to combat this virus, such as rapidly expanding mosquito control programs; accelerating vaccine research and diagnostic development; enabling the testing and procurement of vaccines and diagnostics; educating health care providers, pregnant women and their partners; improving epidemiology and expanding laboratory and diagnostic testing capacity; improving health services and supports for low-income pregnant women, and enhancing the ability of Zika-affected countries to better combat mosquitoes and control transmission.

There is much that we do not yet know about Zika and its relationship to the poor health outcomes that are being reported in Zika-affected areas. We must work aggressively to investigate these outbreaks, and mitigate, to the best extent possible, the spread of the virus. Congressional action on the Administration's request will accelerate our ability to prevent, detect and respond to the Zika virus and bolster our ability to reduce the potential for future infectious disease outbreaks.

Department of Health and Human Services—$1.48 billion

Centers for Disease Control and Prevention—$828 million. The request includes funding to support prevention and response strategies through the following activities:

- Support Zika virus readiness and response capacity in States and territories with mosquito populations that are known to transmit Zika virus, with a priority focus on areas with ongoing Zika transmission;
- Enhance mosquito control programs through enhanced laboratory, epidemiology and surveillance capacity in at-risk areas to reduce the opportunities for Zika transmission;
- Establish rapid response teams to limit potential clusters of Zika virus in the United States;
- Improve laboratory capacity and infrastructure to test for Zika virus and other infectious diseases;
- Implement surveillance efforts to track Zika virus in communities and in mosquitoes;
- Deploy targeted prevention and education strategies with key populations, including pregnant women, their partners, and health care professionals;
- Expand the CDC Pregnancy Risk Assessment Monitoring System, improve Guillain–Barré syndrome tracking,

The White House. "FACT SHEET: Preparing for and Responding to the Zika Virus at Home and Abroad," White House Press Release, February 2016.

and ensure the ability of birth defect registries across the country to detect risks related to Zika;

- Increase research into the link between Zika virus infections and the birth defect microcephaly and measure changes in incidence rates over time;
- Enhance international capacity for virus surveillance, expand the Field Epidemiology Training program, laboratory testing, health care provider training, and vector surveillance and control in countries at highest risk of Zika virus outbreaks; and
- Improve diagnostics for Zika virus, including advanced methods to refine tests, and support advanced developments for vector control.

Centers for Medicare and Medicaid Services—$250 million. The request seeks a temporary one-year increase in Puerto Rico's Medicaid Federal Medical Assistance Percentage (FMAP) to provide an estimated $250 million in additional Federal assistance to support health services for pregnant women at risk of infection or diagnosed with Zika virus and for children with microcephaly, and other health care costs. This request does not make any changes to Puerto Rico's underlying Medicaid program, and the additional funding will not be counted towards Puerto Rico's current Medicaid allotment. Puerto Rico is experiencing ongoing active transmission of Zika. Unlike States, Puerto Rico's Medicaid funding is capped, which has limited capacity to respond to these emergent and growing health needs.

Vaccine Research and Diagnostic Development & Procurement—$200 million. The request includes $200 million for research, rapid advanced development and commercialization of new vaccines and diagnostic tests for Zika virus. It includes funding for the National Institutes of Health to build upon existing resources and work to develop a vaccine for Zika virus and the chikungunya virus, which is spread by the same type of mosquito. Funding will accelerate this work and improve scientific understanding of the disease to inform the development of additional tools to combat it. The request also includes resources for the Food and Drug Administration to support Zika virus medical product development including the next generation diagnostic devices.

Other HHS Response Activities—$210 million. The request includes funding to establish a new Urgent and Emerging Threat Fund to address Zika virus and other outbreaks. This funding would be available to support emerging needs related to Zika, including additional support to States for emerging public health response needs should mosquito populations known to be potential Zika carriers migrate to additional States.

In addition, the request includes funding to support Puerto Rico's community health centers in preventing, screening, and treating the Zika virus, expand home visiting services targeting low-income pregnant women at risk of Zika virus, and provide targeted maternal and child health.

U.S. Agency for International Development—$335 million

The request includes investments to support affected countries' ability to control mosquitoes and the transmission of the virus; support maternal health; expand public education on prevention and response; and create new incentives for the development of vaccines and diagnostics. The request would also provide flexibility in the use of remaining USAID Ebola funds. Activities would focus particularly on South America, Central America, the Caribbean, and would:

- Implement integrated vector management activities in countries at-risk of Zika virus;
- Stimulate private sector research and development of vaccines, diagnostics, and vector control innovations through public private partnerships and mechanisms to provide incentives such as advance market commitments or volume guarantees;
- Support training of health care workers in affected countries, including providing information about best practices for supporting children with microcephaly;
- Support for pregnant women's health, including helping them access repellant to protect against mosquitos.
- Establish education campaigns to empower communities in affected countries to take actions to protect themselves from Zika Virus as well as other mosquito-borne diseases; and
- Issue a Global Health Security Grand Challenge calling for groundbreaking innovations in diagnostics, vector control, personal protection, community engagement and surveillance for Zika and other infectious diseases.

U.S. Department of State—$41 million

The funding request includes support for U.S. citizens in affected countries, medical support for State Department employees in affected countries, public diplomacy, communications, and other operations activities. State would also support the World Health Organization and its regional arm, the Pan American Health Organization (PAHO), to minimize the Zika threat in affected countries while reducing the risk of further spreading the virus. These resources will support critical public health actions underway, including preparedness, surveillance, data collection, and risk communication. Activities would also include support for UNICEF's Zika response efforts in Brazil; activities to bolster diagnostic capabilities through deployment of equipment and specialized training.

THE WHITE HOUSE Office of the Press Secretary, or the Press Office, is responsible for gathering and disseminating information to three principal groups: the President, the White House staff, and the media.

Peter J. Hotez  **NO**

Zika Is Coming

Houston—IF I were a pregnant woman living on the Gulf Coast or in Florida, in an impoverished neighborhood in a city like Houston, New Orleans, Miami, Biloxi, Miss., or Mobile, Ala., I would be nervous right now. If mosquitoes carrying the Zika virus reach the United States later this spring or summer, these are the major urban areas where the sickness will spread. If we don't intervene now, we could begin seeing newborns with microcephaly and stunted brain development on the obstetrics wards in one or more of these places.

There are many theories for Zika's rapid rise, but the most plausible is that the virus mutated from an African to a pandemic strain a decade or more ago and then spread east across the Pacific from Micronesia and French Polynesia, until it struck Brazil. There, it infected more than a million people over the last one to two years. Today, the extremely poor cities of Brazil's northeastern states make up the epicenter of the epidemic.

There are three reasons that Zika has slammed this particular part of Brazil: the presence of the main mosquito species that carries the virus and transmits it to humans, *Aedes aegypti*; overcrowding; and extreme poverty.

In crowded places, mosquitoes have lots of access to lots of people. Poor people often live in proximity to garbage, including old tires, plastic containers and drainage ditches filled with stagnant water, where this species of mosquito lives and breeds. And they often have homes with torn screens on their windows. The combination creates ideal conditions for the Zika virus to spread.

The same factors are present in the poorest urban areas of coastal Texas, Louisiana, Mississippi and Alabama, in addition to South Florida, and an area around Tucson. In the Fifth Ward of Houston (a historically African-American neighborhood that was populated by freed slaves after the Civil War), just a few miles from the medical center where I work, there is an astonishing level of extreme poverty. A brief tour reveals water-filled drainage ditches in place of gutters, as well as evidence of dumping—a common practice in which people toss old tires and other garbage into residential areas rather than designated landfill sites—right next to shabby and crumbling housing.

These are also the major areas in the continental United States where Aedes aegypti is found. This mosquito has transmitted viruses such as yellow fever and dengue throughout the Gulf Coast for centuries. Most recently, in 2003, it transmitted an outbreak of dengue here in Houston that was associated with at least two deaths.

It's only April, but temperatures are hitting the 80s in the afternoons, and Aedes mosquitoes are already here. By May or June we will start seeing those mosquitoes in much larger numbers.

I develop vaccines for neglected tropical diseases. Several Zika vaccines are being created, but none will be ready in time for this year's epidemic. In place of a vaccine we need a robust program of mosquito control and environmental cleanup in the poorest neighborhoods of our Gulf Coast cities and in Florida. This should include removing garbage and debris, and installing gutters to replace drainage ditches. We need to improve access to contraception, and provide pregnant women with proper window screens for their homes and information about the risk of Zika. Finally, we will need to train teams to visit homes in poor neighborhoods and instruct occupants on how to empty water containers and spray for mosquitoes, just as we are doing now in Puerto Rico.

At the federal level this effort would need to bring in the Environmental Protection Agency, the Centers for Disease Control and Prevention and the Department of Housing and Urban Development. But we'll also need parallel approaches at the state, county and city levels.

This coordination is labor intensive and will not be easy, but if we don't start working now, by the end of the year, I am afraid we will see microcephaly cases in Houston and elsewhere on the Gulf Coast. This could be a catastrophe to rival Hurricane Katrina or other recent miseries that disproportionately affect the poor. Zika is a potentially devastating health crisis headed for our region, and we might have only a few weeks to stop it before pregnant women become infected.

PETER J. HOTEZ, a pediatrician and microbiologist at Texas Children's Hospital, is dean of the National School of Tropical Medicine at Baylor College of Medicine.

Hotez, Peter. "Zika Is Coming", from *The New York Times*, April 2016. Copyright © 2016 by New York Times. All rights reserved. Used by permission and protected by the Copyright Laws of the United States. The printing, copying, redistribution, or retransmission of this Content without express written permission is prohibited.

EXPLORING THE ISSUE

Is the United States Doing Enough to Address the Global Threat of Diseases like Zika?

Critical Thinking and Reflection

1. Do you believe global epidemics will continue to grow in number? Why or why not?
2. Who should bear responsibility for addressing global health threats?
3. What are the concerns about each individual country handling these issues on their own?
4. How can individual citizens better address global disease?
5. Do international organizations adequately address global disease? Why or why not?

Is There Common Ground?

Like international conflicts, the line in the sand surrounding America's role in global disease seems to fall between isolationists and interventionists. Some individuals would prefer that the United States not take part in international efforts due to the loss of resources, which could be used, perhaps more adequately, at home as opposed to abroad. Yet, this is not the recipe for stopping the spread of potentially deadly epidemics. We can stand at our border and be prepared to react to its arrival, but perhaps it would be more efficient—and effective—to intervene earlier—even if it means being more international in scope—to keep the disease from arriving here at all.

Another component of determining if common ground is possible is to determine who should bear responsibility for global disease. No individual country, after all, can reasonably be expected to single handedly tackle disease. Yet international organizations cannot do much without political and financial support from sovereign states sharing their vision and goals. The benefit when considering global disease is that there is agreement among individuals and governments that the world is better off without Zika, Ebola, and other similar epidemics. The debates will continue, however, on how best to make this vision a reality.

Additional Resources

S. Harris Ali and Roger Keil, *Networked Disease: Emerging Infections in the Global City* (Wiley-Blackwell, 2008)

Donald G. McNeil Jr, *Zika: The Emerging Epidemic* (W.W. Norton, 2016)

David Quammen, *Ebola: The Natural and Human History of a Deadly Virus* (W.W. Norton, 2014)

Internet References . . .

Zika Virus

https://www.cdc.gov/zika/

Zika Virus

http://www.who.int/mediacentre/factsheets/zika/en/

Zika Virus

http://www.nhs.uk/conditions/zika-virus/Pages/Introduction.aspx

Selected, Edited, and with Issue Framing Material by:
William J. Miller, *Flagler College*

ISSUE

Should the United States Accept More Refugees from Syria?

YES: Katy Long, from "Why America Could—and Should—Admit More Syrian Refugees," *The Century Foundation* (2015)

NO: Martin Pengelly, Tom Dart, and Sabrina Siddiqui, from "Cruz and Rubio Lead Republican Charge against Obama over Syria Policy," *The Guardian* (2015)

Learning Outcomes
After reading this issue, you will be able to:
• Describe the Syrian refugee crisis.
• Assess the potential for the United States to accept more refugees from Syria.
• Explain arguments for and against accepting more refugees from Syria.
• Identify other ways the United States could aid Syrian refugees.
• Describe the current political debate over Syrian refugees.

ISSUE SUMMARY

YES: Katy Long, a visiting fellow at Stanford, argues America should work to bring more refugees that are Syrian into its borders. She contends that resettling more refugees that are Syrian quickly and equitably will lead to a moral victory, which in turn will help it persuade allies to do more to help resolve the Syrian war and the attendant humanitarian catastrophe.

NO: Three reporters, Martin Pengelly, Tom Dart, and Sabrina Siddiqui, from *The Guardian* highlight opposition arguments waged by 2016 Republican presidential hopefuls, including Ted Cruz and Marco Rubio. The major arguments against increasing the number of refugees centers on concerns for national safety and security.

Five years since the conflict began, more than 250,000 Syrians have been killed in the war, and almost half the country's pre-war population has been displaced from their homes—with many choosing to flee the country. The conflict's roots began with the Arab Spring revolts in 2011 that toppled Tunisian President Zine El Abidine Ben Ali and Egyptian President Hosni Mubarak. That March, peaceful protests, erupted in Syria as well, after a handful boys were detained and tortured for having written graffiti in support of the Arab Spring. One of the boys, 13-year-old Hamza al-Khateeb, was killed after having been brutally tortured.

The Syrian government, led by President Bashar al-Assad, responded to the protests by killing hundreds of demonstrators and imprisoning many more. In July 2011, defectors from the military announced the formation of the Free Syrian Army, a rebel group aiming to overthrow the government, and Syria began to quickly slide into civil war.

Initially, lack of freedoms and economic woes fueled resentment of the Syrian government, and public anger was inflamed by the harsh crackdown on protesters. Successful uprisings in Tunisia and Egypt energized and gave hope to Syrian pro-democracy activists. Many Islamist movements were also strongly opposed to the Assad's rule. In 1982, Bashar al-Assad's father, Hafez, ordered a military crackdown on the Muslim Brotherhood in Hama, which killed between 10,000 and 40,000 people and flattened much of the city.

Even global warming has been claimed to have played a role in sparking the 2011 uprising. A severe drought plagued Syria from 2007 to 2010, spurring as many as 1.5 million people to migrate from the countryside into cities, which exacerbated poverty and social unrest. Although the initial protests were mostly nonsectarian, armed conflict led to the emergence of starker sectarian divisions.

Minority religious groups tend to support the Assad government, while the overwhelming majority of opposition fighters are Sunni Muslims. Although most Syrians are Sunni Muslims, Syria's security establishment has long been dominated by members of the Alawite sect, of which Assad is a member. The sectarian split is reflected among regional actors' stances as well. The governments of majority-Shia Iran and Iraq support Assad, as does Lebanon-based Hezbollah; while Sunni-majority states including Turkey, Qatar, Saudi Arabia, and others staunchly support the rebels.

Foreign backing and open intervention have played a large role in Syria's civil war. An international coalition led by the United States has bombed targets of the Islamic State of Iraq and the Levant (ISIS) group since 2014. In September 2015, Russia launched a bombing campaign against what it referred to as "terrorist groups" in Syria, which included ISIS as well as rebel groups backed by Western states. Russia has also deployed military advisers to shore up Assad's defenses. Several Arab states, along with Turkey, have provided weapons and materiel to rebel groups in Syria.

Many of those fighting come from outside of Syria. The ranks of ISIS include a sizeable number of fighters from around the world. Lebanese members of Hezbollah are fighting on the side of Assad, as are Iranian and Afghan fighters. Although the United States has stated its opposition to the Assad government, it has hesitated to involve itself deeply in the conflict, even after the Assad government allegedly used chemical weapons in 2013, which U.S. President Barack Obama had previously referred to as a "red line" that would prompt intervention. In October 2015, the United States scrapped its controversial program to train Syrian rebels, after it was revealed that it had spent $500 million but only trained 60 fighters.

The Assad government currently controls the capital, Damascus, parts of southern Syria, portions of Aleppo and Deir Az Zor, much of the area near the Syrian-Lebanese border, and the northwestern coastal region. Rebel groups, ISIS, and Kurdish forces control the rest of the country. Rebel groups continue to jockey against one another for power, and frequently fight each other. The Free Syrian Army has weakened as the war has progressed, while explicitly Islamist groups, such as the al-Nusra Front, which has pledged allegiance to al-Qaeda, and the Saudi-backed Islamic Front, have gained in strength.

In 2013, ISIS emerged in northern and eastern Syria after overrunning large portions of Iraq. The group quickly gained international notoriety for its brutal executions, its ultra-strict interpretation of Islamic law, and its energetic use of social media. Meanwhile, Kurdish groups in northern Syria are seeking self-rule in areas under their control. This has alarmed Turkey's government, which fears its large native Kurdish population may grow more restive and demand greater autonomy as a result. In response to attacks within Turkey, the Turkish government has bombed Kurdish targets in Syria. Kurdish groups have also clashed with al-Nusra Front and ISIS.

The Syrian war is creating profound effects far beyond the country's borders. Lebanon, Turkey, and Jordan are hosting large and growing numbers of Syrian refugees, many of whom have attempted to journey onwards to Europe in search of better conditions. Fighting has occasionally spilled over from Syria into Lebanon, contributing to the country's political polarization.

Several rounds of peace talks have failed to stop the fighting. Although a ceasefire announced in February 2016 has limited fighting in some parts of Syria, recent government air strikes in Aleppo have prompted uncertainty about the ceasefire's future. But with much of the country in ruins, millions of Syrians having fled abroad, and a population deeply traumatized by war, one thing is certain: Rebuilding Syria after the war ends will be a lengthy, extremely difficult process.

For the United States, the question has arisen regarding how many refugees—if any—should be admitted from Syria. Republican governors, lawmakers, and presidential candidates are calling for a halt to federal program that resettles Syrian refugees in the United States. In the aftermath of the Paris attacks, many in the GOP say they are concerned that a terrorist could slip into the country by posing as an asylum seeker, an argument that President Obama and other Democrats reject. All refugees taken in by the United States undergo extensive background checks. The small number from Syria are subject to additional layers of security screening.

The process begins with a referral from UNHCR. The UN's refugee agency is responsible for registering some 15 million asylum seekers around the world, and providing aid and assistance until they are resettled abroad or (more likely) returned home once conditions ease. The registration process includes in-depth refugee interviews, home country reference checks, and biological screening such as iris scans. Military combatants are weeded out. Among those who pass background checks, a small percentage are referred for overseas resettlement based on criteria designed to determine the most vulnerable cases. This group may include survivors of torture, victims of sexual violence, targets of political persecution, the medically needy, families with multiple children, and a female head of household.

The American government performs its own intensive screening, a process that includes consultation from nine different government agencies. They meet weekly to review a refugee's case file and, if appropriate, determine where in the United States the individual should be placed. When choosing where to place a refugee, officials consider factors such as existing family in the United States, employment possibilities, and special factors such as access to needed medical treatment.

Every refugee goes through an intensive vetting process, but the precautions are increased for Syrians. Multiple law enforcement, intelligence, and security agencies perform "the most rigorous screening of any traveler to the U.S.," says a senior administration official. Among the agencies involved are the State Department, the FBI's Terrorist Screening Center, the Department of Defense, and the Department of Homeland Security (DHS). A DHS officer conducts in-person interviews with every applicant. Biometric information such as fingerprints are collected and matched against criminal databases. Biographical informations such as past visa applications are scrutinized to ensure the applicant's story coheres.

In the following selections, we heard both sides of the argument on whether the United States should be doing more to help Syrian refugees relocate into the United States. Katy Long, a visiting fellow at Stanford, argues America should work to bring more refugees that are Syrian into its borders. She contends that resettling more refugees that are Syrian quickly and equitably will lead to a moral victory, which in turn will help it persuade allies to do more to help resolve the Syrian war and the attendant humanitarian catastrophe. However, three reporters from *The Guardian* highlight opposition arguments waged by 2016 Republican presidential hopefuls, including Ted Cruz and Marco Rubio. The major arguments against increasing the number of refugees centers on concerns for national safety and security.

YES

Katy Long

Why America Could—and Should—Admit More Syrian Refugees

In the past forty years, the United States has resettled over three million refugees, offering victims of persecution and conflict the opportunity to build a new life. In Fiscal Year (FY) 2016, the United States will admit up to 85,000 refugees through the United States Refugee Admissions Program (USRAP); the administration plans to admit 100,000 refugees in FY2017. The largest number to arrive—34,000—will be resettled from locations in the Near East and South Asia. This regional quota will include "at least" 10,000 Syrian arrivals, under plans announced by President Barack Obama in September 2015.

However, in the wake of the Paris terrorist attacks, there have been widespread calls for the United States to suspend Syrian refugee resettlement. Further calls to restrict immigration from Muslim regions have been made in the wake of the San Bernardino shootings in California on December 2.

The recent controversy over Syrian resettlement has raised important questions about USRAP. Is refugee resettlement safe? Is it effective? Is resettlement just one form of humanitarian relief, or can it also advance U.S. strategic interests? Should the number of refugees being resettled to the United States be increased? Does USRAP have the capacity to expand its operations? And what additional resources—either pre- or post-arrival—could help to ensure the success of such an expansion?

Refugee resettlement is unequivocally safe. It would be wrong, both morally and politically, to curtail Syrian refugee resettlement, and why it is in fact both ethically imperative and politically expedient to instead expand U.S. commitment to refugee resettlement. Resettlement could help both to meet humanitarian needs in the region and advance the U.S. strategic interests, above all by providing another means of leverage through which to broker regional and EU engagement with Syrian crisis. The United States is already the single-largest donor of humanitarian relief to the Syrian people—having given some $4.5 billion in aid since the beginning of the conflict —but it is increasingly clear that offering more resettlement places is essential to help alleviate the political strain of hosting millions of refugees in the region, and to meet some of the refugees' urgent needs.

The United States can—and should—continue to protect itself against terrorist threats, but it can do so while still admitting a greater number of Syrian refugees for resettlement, and processing applications more quickly than it does now. In resettling more Syrian refugees quickly and equitably, Washington will win a moral victory, which in turn will help it persuade allies to do more to help resolve the Syrian war and the attendant humanitarian catastrophe. Instead of seeking to dismantle refugee resettlement, those interested in ensuring the program is both safe and effective should focus their efforts on securing the resources needed both to reduce delays in processing and to establish strong foundations for community integration upon arrival. . . .

USRAP and the Syrian Refugee Crisis

There currently are over four million Syrian refugees, making the Syrian crisis the largest in the world today. Faced with such acute humanitarian suffering, the moral imperative for accepting more Syrian refugees is obvious. One question that should be asked, however, is: Why only 10,000 additional places? Another question is: Why Syria?

It is important to consider Syria and USRAP's role in the context of a global refugee crisis. At the end of 2014, UNHCR estimates that there were 19.5 million refugees displaced worldwide (as well as 38.2 million internally displaced people and 1.8 million asylum seekers). Although Syrians are the largest group, there are also 2.5 million Afghan, and 1.1 million Somali refugees. Many of these refugees have been waiting decades for a solution to their displacement, with little prospect of a sustainable return "home." This is also true for refugees from other crises: Iraqis, Eritreans, Congolese, Burundians, Burmese, and more.

One reason for focusing on Syria's refugees is urgency. UNHCR have made repeated pleas for additional resettlement places to be offered to Syrians to help meet the unprecedented scope of this refugee crisis. As of November 24, 2015, 160,664 additional places had been offered by thirty states, through various resettlement and humanitarian visa schemes. However, this represents only a small fraction of Syria's resettlement needs—and represents what should be considered at best an optimistic tally, at worst a misleading one. In the case of some states, these numbers are very different,

Long, Katy. "Why America Could—and Should—Admit More Syrian Refugees," *The Century Foundation*, December 2015. Copyright © 2015 by The Century Foundation. Used with permission.

and arrivals will be spread out over a number of years (for example, the United Kingdom has offered to accept 20,000 Syrians by 2020, but has only welcomed 216 Syrians through resettlement to date). UNHCR figures also include the number of resettlement submissions made to USRAP—22,427—conveniently ignoring the fact that U.S. officials only expect to approve about 50 percent of these cases, closer to the "at least 10,000" resettlement pledge. For the United States to withdraw from resettlement now would have serious repercussions in terms of global commitment to Syrian resettlement.

Helping Syrian refugees is also in the United States' own strategic self-interest. Accepting more Syrian refugees gives the United States more credibility with its rivals; the Assad regime and its foreign backers tend to dismiss Washington as a paper tiger, so any evidence of U.S. commitment to its Syria policy helps reverse an unfortunate trend. Furthermore, Syrian resettlement is also strategically important in terms of wide U.S. engagement in the broader region, including with the Gulf monarchies and Turkey, Lebanon, and Jordan; as the United States assumes a greater share of refugee resettlement, it will have an easier time persuading U.S. allies to coordinate policies toward Syria and fall in line with U.S. preferences.

Strategic and humanitarian imperatives are mutually reinforcing. Refugee-hosting countries in the region are overwhelmed. Lebanon—a state close to breaking point—is currently hosting 1.1 million refugees—an astounding one refugee for every four residents. It is projected that Turkey will host 1.7 million Syrian refugees by the end of 2015; Jordan 680,000. Protection space for Syrians is extremely fragile in all these states, with refugees being afforded limited socioeconomic rights and aid budgets having been drastically reduced due to funding shortages. Stagnating refugee camps are often fertile recruitment grounds for armed groups, and this is a risk in the Syrian context. By showing solidarity, U.S. resettlement programs can help to check unrest in host states, offer refugees hope, and in turn the United States can demand more of its partners and allies. However, to make any significant contribution to the prospects for regional stability, resettlement needs to be carried out on a much greater scale.

If the United States assumes a more equitable share of resettlement, Washington will also gain political capital it can use with respect to international organizations and the Europeans. It will also address a very real security threat and humanitarian crisis. In the past six months, Europe's inability to respond in a coordinated and collective fashion to the refugee and migrant crisis unfolding at its borders has underlined the need for an effective American response. The Paris terrorist attacks suggest that ISIS have already exploited the EU's political paralysis: a large-scale, extra-regional, American-led resettlement program could meet humanitarian need, help to reduce this security threat, and—perhaps most importantly of all—demonstrate a real commitment to international protection. In recent months, many of Europe's leaders have questioned the continued viability of a global asylum regime: U.S. action could help to protect vital safeguards for those fleeing tyranny.

There is therefore both a humanitarian and a strategic case for greater scope and speed in resettling Syrians. Only 2,200 Syrians have been resettled to the United States in total since the current conflict began in March 2011. USRAP have rejected the charge that this is too little, too late, arguing that they only began to receive referrals from UNHCR in significant numbers beginning July 2014, and are now processing 500 to 1,000 referrals per month. However, the first arrivals from this expanded program have not even arrived yet, and the slow speed of processing remains a serious concern. In addition, security concerns relating to the lack of safe accommodation available for USCIS interview teams travelling to Beirut mean that there are currently no refugees being resettled through Lebanon. There are plans to resume refugee processing in early 2016 and to open a new processing center in Erbil, Iraq, by the end of the year, but at present, nearly all Syrian resettlement files are processed in Istanbul or Amman.

When it comes to Syrian refugees' integration after their arrival in the United States, it is important to recognise that, relative to recently resettled populations such as the Bhutanese or Burmese, Syrians on average are better educated and more urban. This means that, with proper support, Syrians are well-placed to integrate successfully into American communities: but it also brings new challenges, such as ensuring these refugees are able to find employment commensurate with their skill levels, and dealing with the psychological effects of having recently escaped violent conflict.

Furthermore, USRAP is currently focused on resettling the "most vulnerable" Syrians—"particularly survivors of violence and torture, those with severe medical conditions, and women and children." Coupled with the stringency of TRIG checks and other security requirements, this means 50 percent of the Syrian refugee population arriving in the United States to date have been children. Only 2 percent of Syrian refugees resettled into the United States have been single men of combat age. This undoubtedly addresses short-term security concerns, but in the long-run, lower language and skills capacity may make integration more difficult, and reduce the potential socioeconomic gains (including the potential development benefits accruing from remittances) that resettled men of working age may be better placed to make. In addition, leaving young men behind in resettlement camps without prospects of an alternative solution (other than irregular migration) may fuel long-term radicalization and aid ISIS recruitment efforts.

Some public figures—including Jeb Bush and Ted Cruz—have argued that the United States should do more to help Christian Syrians resettle. Prior to the conflict, approximately three-quarters of the Syrian population were Sunni and 10 percent Christian; but only 2.7 percent of the refugees who have arrived in the United States to date are Christian. However experts suggest that this reflects the targeting of the Sunni community by the Assad regime, and the (relative) protection of the Christian minority. Syrian Christians may also be better able to draw on social networks and community resources in displacement, reducing the need for humanitarian resettlement. This public Islamophobia in the United States will undoubtedly increase the challenges faced by Muslim refugees upon arrival. It will also fuel ISIS' own propaganda claims.

Conclusions and Recommendations

Refugee resettlement in the United States can offer a humanitarian lifeline. Yet in the past seventy years of resettlement, refugees' arrivals in the United States have often been accompanied by suspicion and fear regarding community cohesion. History suggests that such fears are a distortion. Refugees become committed American citizens, not terrorists. They are the victims—not the perpetrators—of persecution and tyranny.

There is no evidence that current Syrian resettlement poses any threat to national security. Robust security checks are already in place. The resettlement program's security checks lean toward preemptive exclusion: refugees are not given the benefit of the doubt. Suspending, scaling back, or halting Syria's USRAP program would be a gross and counter-productive over-reaction.

The United States right now is counting on its allies to make great, destabilizing sacrifices in order to shoulder the lion's share of the Syrian refugee crisis. Allied governments in Lebanon, Turkey, and Jordan are hosting close to four million refugees at tremendous strain to their infrastructure and political fabric. If the United States increases its own role in the refugee crisis, even symbolically, it is better able to ask great sacrifices from its allies in the Middle East. Canada's efforts to resettle 25,000 Syrian refugees by the end of February 2016 has reaped enormous goodwill and political cooperation for Ottawa, and shows one possibility for dramatically accelerating resettlement programs.

Closing the Syrian resettlement program, on the other hand, would certainly hand ISIS a propaganda victory. It would also increase the risk of Syrians—trapped in refugee camps without any solution to exile in sight—becoming radicalized or being recruited by ISIS agents. Furthermore, Syrians looking to escape the region will continue to depend upon expensive and risky smuggling networks to do so irregularly. These journeys can end in human catastrophe—and provide an important stream of revenue for ISIS and Al-Qaeda. Offering Syrians the possibility of resettlement is an important weapon in the fight against global terrorism. Engagement with refugee resettlement may also help to reduce regional instability and will certainly provide the United States with additional political leverage to help shape a coordinated global response to both the refugee crisis and the broader conflict.

There are many reasons why U.S. engagement in refugee resettlement is important in political and symbolic terms. But numbers are important too. Precedent shows that—provided the right resources are put in place—the United States has been able to settle large numbers of refugees. Several hundred thousand Indochinese refugees were successfully resettled during the recessions of the 1970s. Given current favorable labor market conditions and the relatively high skill levels of the Syrian population relative to other recently resettled groups, the United States can certainly afford to resettle 10,000 Syrians—and could be far more ambitious.

Rather than focusing on tightening up an already rigorous security process, the real focus of political energy should be on increasing USRAP's capacity to process cases swiftly and efficiently. Refugees—whether in Syria or elsewhere—should not have to wait two years for processing. Many simply cannot afford the human cost of being asked to wait for so long. Investments in staffing and training, and in appropriate information and communications technology, could help to speed up resettlement without compromising U.S. security. Current projections call for the resettlement quota to rise to 100,000 for FY2017. In order to ensure that this higher ceiling translates into actual departures, and to lay the foundations for much-needed further expansion of USRAP, capacity-building is essential.

It is also vital to ensure that appropriate and well-funded support services are in place to help with community integration after refugees' arrival. If resettlement programs continue to focus on women, children, and the elderly, partly as a means to assuage security fears, it is important to recognize that this has implications in terms of refugees' likely speed in obtaining economic self-sufficiency. In recent years, integration has been under-resourced, and this should be the focus of renewed efforts in Washington.

Isolationist immigration policies will not protect the United States from ISIS, or from ISIS-inspired terrorism. The only real solution is continued engagement. Refugee resettlement offers one way to do this while helping victims of oppression and tyranny—including the victims of ISIS. Offering humanitarian aid need not be at odds with national self-interest. And in the case of Syria, a large refugee resettlement program could undoubtedly do both.

KATY LONG is a refugee and migration expert. She is currently a visiting fellow at Stanford University and an honorary fellow at the University of Edinburgh.

Martin Pengelly, et al.

 **NO**

Cruz and Rubio lead Republican charge against Obama over Syria policy

Ted Cruz led Republican criticism of White House policy on Syria on Saturday, in light of the devastating terror attacks in Paris, deriding Barack Obama's pledge to take more refugees and calling for intensified action against Islamic State. Marco Rubio took a different tack, however, in declaring "a civilizational conflict with radical Islam."

"This is not a grievance-based conflict," Rubio said in a video released by his presidential campaign. "This is a clash of civilizations. And either they win, or we win."

Cruz and presidential candidates including Donald Trump, Bobby Jindal and Mike Huckabee seized on the news to demand drastic action on immigration, a hot-button issue on the campaign trail. Rubio, however, has made foreign policy a central focus of his run for the White House. In that light, he said the attacks in Paris were "a wake-up call."

"They literally want to overthrow our society and replace it with their radical, Sunni Islamic view of the future," the Florida senator said. "They do not hate us because we have military assets in the Middle East.

"They hate us because of our values. They hate us because young girls here go to school. They hate us because women drive. They hate us because we have freedom of speech, because we have diversity in our religious beliefs. They hate us because we're a tolerant society."

Cruz, the senator from Texas who is riding high with right-wing voters, unleashed a scathing indictment of Obama and Democratic frontrunner Hillary Clinton.

"President Obama and Hillary Clinton's idea that we should bring tens of thousands of Syrian Muslim refugees to America: it is nothing less than lunacy," he said, in an interview with Fox News.

He later said the US should "not allow jihadists to come back to America using US passports to murder innocent men and women."

Rubio also criticized the president for lacking a strategy against Isis. The Florida senator called for a more aggressive tack against the militants, although he placed the onus on Sunni countries to defeat Isis "ideologically and militarily" with the US playing a supporting role.

Other candidates kept their focus on the implications of the Paris attacks for immigration policy. The Kentucky senator Rand Paul went directly after Rubio, who two years ago co-authored a comprehensive immigration reform bill. Paul said he had offered an amendment to Rubio's bill that would have applied "special scrutiny" to immigrants coming to the US from countries "that have large jihadists."

He then accused Rubio of having done a "secret deal" with Democrats to block any amendments to the bill.

"My amendment . . . was defeated because Rubio was more intent on working with Chuck Schumer than he was in working with conservatives," Paul said.

Alex Conant, a spokesman for Rubio, disputed the claim.

"I don't know what Senator Paul is talking about. The Senate voted on amendments, including conservative ones," Conant told the Guardian. "It would appear Senator Paul is trying to change the subject away from his dangerous isolationist agenda and proposals to cut defense spending."

But in a sign that the immigration debate would continue to dominate the Republican primary, other contenders reacted to the Paris attacks with calls to ramp up security along US borders.

At a rally in Beaumont, Texas, Donald Trump said: "With the problems our country has, to take in 250,000 people, some of whom are going to have problems, big problems, is just insane."

Elsewhere, Louisiana governor Bobby Jindal said it was time "to close our borders and keep our people safe from these radical, evil terrorists." Former Arkansas governor Mike Huckabee said: "We don't just have open borders like they do in Europe."

In September, the White House said it would accept 10,000 Syrian refugees in the fiscal year starting on 1 October 2015, up from less than 2,000. Refugees fleeing the Syrian civil war have caused a crisis in Europe, where rightwing politicians reacted to the Paris attacks with tough rhetoric.

It was reported on Saturday that one of the gunmen who carried out the Paris attacks was a Syrian who passed through Greece as a refugee last month.

Pengelly, Martin; Dart, Tom; Siddiqui, Sabrina. "Cruz and Rubio Lead Republican Charge against Obama Over Syria Policy," *The Guardian,* November 2015. Copyright © 2015 by Guardian Media Group. Used with permission.

Islamic State claimed responsibility for the suicide bomb and shooting attacks in Paris on Friday night, in which 129 people were killed and 352 wounded, 99 of them critically. The group said it had acted in response to French involvement in Syria.

On Saturday, the US military said an airstrike had killed the Isis leader in Libya.

Speaking to reporters ahead of a "rally for religious liberty" in Greenville, South Carolina, Cruz said of the victims of the Paris attacks: "They were not injured by some faceless menace. They were not injured by some abstract and inchoate violent extremism."

"They were injured by radical Islamic terrorism, an evil that is at war with the people of America, that is at war with freedom-loving people across the globe."

Repeating a common charge against Obama regarding semantics as much as policy, Cruz added: "We need a commander-in-chief willing to utter the words 'radical Islamic terrorism' because it is the Islamists who embrace this extreme political and theological philosophy that … will murder or try to forcibly convert anyone that doesn't share their extreme view of Islam."

Cruz continued: "I call on Congress to pass the Expatriate Terrorist Act, legislation I've introduced that says that any American who goes and takes up arms and joins Isis to wage jihad against the United States of America, that by doing so they forfeit their American citizenship.

"We should not allow jihadists to come back to America using US passports to murder innocent men and women."

Huckabee—who, unlike Cruz, is well off the pace in polls of the 2016 field and missed out on this week's prime-time Republican debate—said Syrian refugees should be provided a safe haven, but it did not have to be in the US.

"We need to have a better process," Huckabee said on CNN. "We don't just have open borders like they do in Europe."

Huckabee also attacked Obama for saying recently that Isis had been "contained" and said the president was more concerned with "image of Islam" than defeating extremist terror groups.

The former Pennsylvania senator Rick Santorum, speaking at the Republican Party of Florida's Sunshine Summit, said he was uniquely qualified to lead the US in the effort against Islamic State because "no other presidential candidate has been in [the] Isis magazine."

Promising a major offensive against Isis if he made it to the White House, he said: "They know who I am and I know who they are."

In South Carolina, Cruz advocated a similar course of action and invoked a familiar Republican exemplar, saying: "What is the answer to radical Islamic terrorism? It is, to paraphrase President Ronald Reagan with regard to the Cold War, very simple. We win, they lose. That is the only appropriate resolution to this."

He continued: "It would start with a commander-in-chief laying out the objective that we will utterly destroy Isis. The next thing that would happen would be using overwhelming air power. You know, in the first Persian Gulf war we launched roughly 1,100 air attacks a day. Overwhelming air power."

"Right now, President Obama is launching between 15 and 30 air attacks a day. It is pinprick air assault. It is photo-op foreign policy. It makes for a good shot on CNN, but it doesn't actually do anything to stop the terrorists."

On Friday, Cruz issued a statement which appeared to suggest that airstrikes that risked killing innocent civilians would be acceptable, given the nature of the threat.

Martin Pengelly is the *Guardian US* weekend editor, based in New York. He has a special interest in rugby union, particularly as played in the United States.

Tom Dart is a Houston-based freelance journalist. Before moving to Texas he was a soccer reporter, editor, and columnist for *The Times* in London, also covering MLB and the NFL.

Sabrina Siddiqui is a political reporter for the *Guardian US* based in Washington, DC. She previously covered U.S. politics for the *Huffington Post* and worked with the White House team at Bloomberg News.

EXPLORING THE ISSUE

Should the United States Accept More Refugees from Syria?

Critical Thinking and Reflection

1. Why do you believe refugees have become such a political topic?
2. Which other nations do you believe should be assisting in the refugee crisis?
3. How do you think the United States should determine whether to accept refugees?
4. Do you believe the United States is compassionate enough in foreign affairs? Why or why not?
5. Do you believe the United States is asked to do too much internationally? Why or why not?

Is There Common Ground?

When Donald Trump's son took to Twitter and compared the Syrian refugee crisis to reaching into a bowl of Skittles and hoping to avoid the poisoned candy in the bowl, he demonstrated exactly why common ground is difficult to find on the issue of refugees in the United States. Despite the terrible domestic situation Syrian refugees are fleeing from, many Americans are questioning the potential impacts of admitting more to the country. From a self-interested standpoint, there are questions of overcrowding, economic impacts, and national security.

Even while recognizing the need for these refugees to have safety and security, there are questions of whether the United States is the proper landing place. Once heralded as a land of opportunity and a place where immigrants were vital and welcomed, today many Americans would prefer to place a sign at Ellis Island informing all those arriving that America is closed. While it is quite possible to come to agreements on the number of immigrants to allow in, the countries to give preference to, and the process for which to admit individuals, this does not equate to reaching common ground on the central question: Do we, as Americans, still want to be viewed as a place that protects the innocent and welcomes all or do we put our own safety and security (both physical and economic) ahead of that of others?

Additional Resources

Wolfgang Bauer and Stanislav Krupar, *Crossing the Sea: With Syrians on the Exodus to Europe* (And Other Stories, 2016)

Hugh Eakin and Lauren Gelfond Feldinger, *Flight from Syria: Refugee Stories* (Pulitzer Center, 2015)

Janine di Giovanni, *The Morning They Came for Us: Dispatches from Syria* (Liveright, 2016)

Internet References . . .

Stories from Syrian Refugees

http://data.unhcr.org/syrianrefugees/syria.php

Syrian Refugees

http://syrianrefugees.eu/

Syrian Refugees

http://ngm.nationalgeographic.com/2015/03/syrian-refugees/salopek-text

Selected, Edited, and with Issue Framing Material by:
William J. Miller, *Flagler College*

ISSUE

Should the United States Launch a Preemptive Strike Against Iran?

YES: Matthew Kroenig, from "Time to Attack Iran," *Foreign Affairs* (2012)

NO: Colin H. Kahl, from "Not Time to Attack Iran," *Foreign Affairs* (2012)

Learning Outcomes

After reading this issue, you will be able to:

- Assess the current political environment in Iran.
- Identify the benefits and costs of a preemptive strike on Iran.
- Explain the procedures for launching a strike.
- Indicate potential outside partners to assist in any attack.
- Ascertain whether an attack is wise given the current political environment.

ISSUE SUMMARY

YES: Defense Department Adviser Matthew Kroenig believes that the United States should launch a preemptive attack on Iran because a policy of deterrence would allow Iran to develop powerful nuclear weapons that would endanger the United States and its allies.

NO: Defense Department Adviser Colin H. Kahl believes that striking Iran now would not prevent future aggression, and it is undesirable as long as economic and diplomatic means to prevent Iran's nuclear armament still hold the possibility of success.

In 2006, the United States National Security Council stated: "We may face no greater challenge from a single country than from Iran." That judgment has never been revised. The radically anti-American Shiite Islamic government of Iran is closely allied with Hamas and Hezbollah, terrorist movements that are dedicated to the creation of an anti-American Muslim Middle East. Ever since revolutionary Shiites and their followers came to power in Iran more than 30 years ago, Friday night services in Iran's capital, Tehran, have repeated the vow, "Down with the United States!"

Paramount among the threats that Iran poses to the United States is its progress toward the development of nuclear energy that can result in the development of nuclear weapons. Nine nations are believed to have the capacity to build nuclear weapons. None is believed to be a formidable threat to the United States, despite the mutual hostility of the United States and North Korea. By contrast, U.S. presidents of both parties have been in agreement that Iran should be prevented from acquiring the capability of enriching uranium and building nuclear bombs. Iran claims that its nuclear program is designed for peaceful domestic use. The United States is skeptical. In late 2012, international nuclear inspectors reported that Iran has installed three-fourths of the nuclear centrifuges it needs in order to complete a deep underground site for the production of nuclear fuel.

In addition to its potential nuclear power, Iran has the naval power to close access to the Strait of Hormuz, a narrow passage that separates Iran from the Arabian Peninsula and through which one-quarter of the world's petroleum (including that from Iran) passes by sea. This could cut off a vital source of oil for other nations. Iran also has established long-range ballistic missiles that threaten Israel and American military assets.

It is impossible to understand the deterioration of relations between Iran and the United States without considering the critical events that have shaped their policies. In 1953, the United States played a minor role in the coup that overthrew the elected government of Iranian Prime Minister Mohammad Mosaddeq and resulted in the return to power of the autocratic Shah Mohammad Reza Pahlavi. In 1979, the Shah was forced to leave Iran when the Iranian revolution drove him from power and installed a Shiite Muslim theocracy. When the Shah was permitted to enter the United States in order to receive medical treatment, enraged radical Iranian students retaliated by taking more than 50 Americans hostage and holding them for 444 days. Good relations have never been restored.

The United States sees Iran as a threat to world peace because it seeks to possess decisive influence in the Middle East, because it effectively controls access to the Straits of Hormuz through which much of the region's oil (much of it from Iran itself) must pass on its way to the rest of the world, because its population is less divided than others in the area and, most threatening to the United States, because it may soon possess the ability to develop powerful nuclear weapons, which could pose an immediate threat to Israel, America's strategic ally in the region, and a long-term threat to the United States.

American Middle East scholars who believe that war with Iran can be avoided argue that the threat of a nuclear Iran can be avoided because it once had more tolerant leadership and it still contains moderate elements, because Israel has the nuclear power to destroy Iran's nuclear weaponry (there is evidence that Iran's nuclear development was set back by several years as a result of sabotage), because American-sponsored economic sanctions already in place have weakened it, and because its rulers are rational enough to know that the United States will destroy their power in any conflict.

In an October 2013 speech during a Knesset commemoration Tuesday of the 40th anniversary of the Yom Kippur War, Israeli Prime Minister Benjamin Netanyahu offered a defense of a possible Israeli preemptive strike on Iran. In the speech, he stated, "The first lesson is to never underestimate a threat, never underestimate an enemy, never ignore the signs of danger. We can't assume the enemy will act in ways that are convenient for us. The enemy can surprise us. Israel will not fall asleep on its watch again." He adds, "A preventive war, even a preventive strike, is among the most difficult decisions a government can take, because it will never be able to prove what would have happened if it had not acted . . . in the Six Day War we launched

a preventive strike that broke the chokehold our enemies had placed on us, and on Yom Kippur the government decided, despite all warnings, to absorb the full force of an enemy attack." Yet Israel and the United States have different attitudes toward dealing with the Iranians. This difference can be largely explained by geographic location. Whereas the Iranians may in fact have capabilities of reaching Israel, they do not have the same when considering the United States.

In November 2013, the United States, Great Britain, France, Germany, Russia, and China (the P5+1 Group) reached a deal with Iran to bring a halt to their nuclear weapons program. For the first time in almost 10 years, the Iranians have agreed to back off their quest for nuclear weapons. This is made even more monumental by the fact that the United States and Iran have had no formal relationship since the Revolution in 1979. Four key provisions were agreed to.

1. No uranium will be enriched above 5 percent U-235 and all uranium presently above that level will be blended down;
2. No new centrifuges will be produced and many current ones will become inoperable;
3. Heavy reactor work will stop immediately;
4. IAEA inspectors will be given full access and daily visitation.

In return, the United States and its partners have agreed to drop some of its sanctions, amounting to about $6–7 billion in relief. While the international community welcomed the agreement, Netanyahu was less satisfied. He remarked, "I think that it would be a historic mistake to ease up on Iran without it dismantling the nuclear capabilities it is developing. . . . Iran is now on the ropes, and it is possible to employ sanctions at their fullest in order to achieve the desired result. I hope that the international community will do this, and I call upon it to do so."

Both Matthew Kroenig and Colin H. Kahl have academic credentials as well as experience as Defense Department advisers on Middle East policy, yet like other thoughtful analysts of Iran both in and out of the U.S. government, they disagree on how and when to confront the challenge that the prospect of a nuclear-armed Iran poses to American national security and world peace.

YES

Matthew Kroenig

Time to Attack Iran

Why a Strike Is the Least Bad Option

In early October, U.S. officials accused Iranian operatives of planning to assassinate Saudi Arabia's ambassador to the United States on American soil. Iran denied the charges, but the episode has already managed to increase tensions between Washington and Tehran. Although the Obama administration has not publicly threatened to retaliate with military force, the allegations have underscored the real and growing risk that the two sides could go to war sometime soon—particularly over Iran's advancing nuclear program.

For several years now, starting long before this episode, American pundits and policymakers have been debating whether the United States should attack Iran and attempt to eliminate its nuclear facilities. Proponents of a strike have argued that the only thing worse than military action against Iran would be an Iran armed with nuclear weapons. Critics, meanwhile, have warned that such a raid would likely fail and, even if it succeeded, would spark a full-fledged war and a global economic crisis. They have urged the United States to rely on nonmilitary options, such as diplomacy, sanctions, and covert operations, to prevent Iran from acquiring a bomb. Fearing the costs of a bombing campaign, most critics maintain that if these other tactics fail to impede Tehran's progress, the United States should simply learn to live with a nuclear Iran.

But skeptics of military action fail to appreciate the true danger that a nuclear-armed Iran would pose to U.S. interests in the Middle East and beyond. And their grim forecasts assume that the cure would be worse than the disease—that is, that the consequences of a U.S. assault on Iran would be as bad as or worse than those of Iran achieving its nuclear ambitions. But that is a faulty assumption. The truth is that a military strike intended to destroy Iran's nuclear program, if managed carefully, could spare the region and the world a very real threat and dramatically improve the long-term national security of the United States.

Dangers of Deterrence

Years of international pressure have failed to halt Iran's attempt to build a nuclear program. The Stuxnet computer worm, which attacked control systems in Iranian nuclear facilities, temporarily disrupted Tehran's enrichment effort, but a report by the International Atomic Energy Agency this past May revealed that the targeted plants have fully recovered from the assault. And the latest IAEA findings on Iran, released in November, provided the most compelling evidence yet that the Islamic Republic has weathered sanctions and sabotage, allegedly testing nuclear triggering devices and redesigning its missiles to carry nuclear payloads. The Institute for Science and International Security, a nonprofit research institution, estimates that Iran could now produce its first nuclear weapon within six months of deciding to do so. Tehran's plans to move sensitive nuclear operations into more secure facilities over the course of the coming year could reduce the window for effective military action even further. If Iran expels IAEA inspectors, begins enriching its stockpiles of uranium to weapons-grade levels of 90 percent, or installs advanced centrifuges at its uranium-enrichment facility in Qom, the United States must strike immediately or forfeit its last opportunity to prevent Iran from joining the nuclear club.

Some states in the region are doubting U.S. resolve to stop the program and are shifting their allegiances to Tehran. Others have begun to discuss launching their own nuclear initiatives to counter a possible Iranian bomb. For those nations and the United States itself, the threat will only continue to grow as Tehran moves closer to its goal. A nuclear-armed Iran would immediately limit U.S. freedom of action in the Middle East. With atomic power behind it, Iran could threaten any U.S. political or military initiative in the Middle East with nuclear war, forcing Washington to think twice before acting in the region. Iran's regional rivals, such as Saudi Arabia, would likely decide to acquire their own nuclear arsenals, sparking an arms race. To constrain its geopolitical rivals, Iran could choose to spur proliferation by transferring nuclear technology to its allies—other countries and terrorist groups alike. Having the bomb would give Iran greater cover for conventional aggression and coercive diplomacy, and the battles between its terrorist proxies and Israel, for example, could escalate. And Iran and Israel lack nearly all the safeguards that helped the United States and the Soviet Union avoid a nuclear exchange during the Cold War—secure second-strike capabilities, clear lines of communication, long flight times for ballistic missiles from one country to the other, and experience managing nuclear arsenals. To be sure, a nuclear-armed Iran would not intentionally

Kroenig, Matthew. From *Foreign Affairs*, January/February 2012. Copyright © 2012 by Council on Foreign Relations, Inc. Reprinted by permission of Foreign Affairs. www.ForeignAffairs.com

launch a suicidal nuclear war. But the volatile nuclear balance between Iran and Israel could easily spiral out of control as a crisis unfolds, resulting in a nuclear exchange between the two countries that could draw the United States in, as well.

These security threats would require Washington to contain Tehran. Yet deterrence would come at a heavy price. To keep the Iranian threat at bay, the United States would need to deploy naval and ground units and potentially nuclear weapons across the Middle East, keeping a large force in the area for decades to come. Alongside those troops, the United States would have to permanently deploy significant intelligence assets to monitor any attempts by Iran to transfer its nuclear technology. And it would also need to devote perhaps billions of dollars to improving its allies' capability to defend themselves. This might include helping Israel construct submarine-launched ballistic missiles and hardened ballistic missile silos to ensure that it can maintain a secure second-strike capability. Most of all, to make containment credible, the United States would need to extend its nuclear umbrella to its partners in the region, pledging to defend them with military force should Iran launch an attack.

In other words, to contain a nuclear Iran, the United States would need to make a substantial investment of political and military capital to the Middle East in the midst of an economic crisis and at a time when it is attempting to shift its forces out of the region. Deterrence would come with enormous economic and geopolitical costs and would have to remain in place as long as Iran remained hostile to U.S. interests, which could mean decades or longer. Given the instability of the region, this effort might still fail, resulting in a war far more costly and destructive than the one that critics of a preemptive strike on Iran now hope to avoid.

A Feasible Target

A nuclear Iran would impose a huge burden on the United States. But that does not necessarily mean that Washington should resort to military means. In deciding whether it should, the first question to answer is if an attack on Iran's nuclear program could even work. Doubters point out that the United States might not know the location of Iran's key facilities. Given Tehran's previous attempts to hide the construction of such stations, most notably the uranium-enrichment facilities in Natanz and Qom, it is possible that the regime already possesses nuclear assets that a bombing campaign might miss, which would leave Iran's program damaged but alive.

This scenario is possible, but not likely; indeed, such fears are probably overblown. U.S. intelligence agencies, the IAEA, and opposition groups within Iran have provided timely warning of Tehran's nuclear activities in the past—exposing, for example, Iran's secret construction at Natanz and Qom before those facilities ever became operational. Thus, although Tehran might again attempt to build clandestine facilities, Washington has a very good chance of catching it before they go online. And given the amount of time it takes to construct and activate a nuclear facility, the scarcity of Iran's resources, and its failure to hide the facilities in Natanz and Qom successfully, it is unlikely that Tehran has any significant operational nuclear facilities still unknown to Western intelligence agencies.

Even if the United States managed to identify all of Iran's nuclear plants, however, actually destroying them could prove enormously difficult. Critics of a U.S. assault argue that Iran's nuclear facilities are dispersed across the country, buried deep underground and hardened against attack, and ringed with air defenses, making a raid complex and dangerous. In addition, they claim that Iran has purposefully placed its nuclear facilities near civilian populations, which would almost certainly come under fire in a U.S. raid, potentially leading to hundreds, if not thousands, of deaths.

These obstacles, however, would not prevent the United States from disabling or demolishing Iran's known nuclear facilities. A preventive operation would need to target the uranium-conversion plant at Isfahan, the heavy-water reactor at Arak, and various centrifuge-manufacturing sites near Natanz and Tehran, all of which are located aboveground and are highly vulnerable to air strikes. It would also have to hit the Natanz facility, which, although it is buried under reinforced concrete and ringed by air defenses, would not survive an attack from the U.S. military's new bunker-busting bomb, the 30,000-pound Massive Ordnance Penetrator, capable of penetrating up to 200 feet of reinforced concrete. The plant in Qom is built into the side of a mountain and thus represents a more challenging target. But the facility is not yet operational and still contains little nuclear equipment, so if the United States acted quickly, it would not need to destroy it.

Washington would also be able to limit civilian casualties in any campaign. Iran built its most critical nuclear plants, such as the one in Natanz, away from heavily populated areas. For those less important facilities that exist near civilian centers, such as the centrifuge- manufacturing sites, U.S. precision-guided missiles could pinpoint specific buildings while leaving their surroundings unscathed. The United States could reduce the collateral damage even further by striking at night or simply leaving those less important plants off its target list at little cost to the overall success of the mission. Although Iran would undoubtedly publicize any human suffering in the wake of a military action, the majority of the victims would be the military personnel, engineers, scientists, and technicians working at the facilities.

Setting the Right Redlines

The fact that the United States can likely set back or destroy Iran's nuclear program does not necessarily mean that it should. Such an attack could have potentially devastating consequences—for international security, the global economy, and Iranian domestic politics—all of which need to be accounted for.

To begin with, critics note, U.S. military action could easily spark a full-blown war. Iran might retaliate against U.S. troops or allies, launching missiles at military installations or civilian populations in the Gulf or perhaps even Europe. It could activate its proxies abroad, stirring sectarian tensions in Iraq, disrupting the Arab Spring, and ordering terrorist attacks against Israel and the United States. This could draw Israel or other states into the fighting and compel the United States to escalate the conflict in response. Powerful allies of Iran, including China and Russia, may attempt to economically and diplomatically isolate the United States. In the midst of such spiraling violence, neither side may see a clear path out of the battle, resulting in a long-lasting, devastating war, whose impact may critically damage the United States' standing in the Muslim world.

Those wary of a U.S. strike also point out that Iran could retaliate by attempting to close the Strait of Hormuz, the narrow access point to the Persian Gulf through which roughly 20 percent of the world's oil supply travels. And even if Iran did not threaten the strait, speculators, fearing possible supply disruptions, would bid up the price of oil, possibly triggering a wider economic crisis at an already fragile moment.

None of these outcomes is predetermined, however; indeed, the United States could do much to mitigate them. Tehran would certainly feel like it needed to respond to a U.S. attack, in order to reestablish deterrence and save face domestically. But it would also likely seek to calibrate its actions to avoid starting a conflict that could lead to the destruction of its military or the regime itself. In all likelihood, the Iranian leadership would resort to its worst forms of retaliation, such as closing the Strait of Hormuz or launching missiles at southern Europe, only if it felt that its very existence was threatened. A targeted U.S. operation need not threaten Tehran in such a fundamental way.

To make sure it doesn't and to reassure the Iranian regime, the United States could first make clear that it is interested only in destroying Iran's nuclear program, not in overthrowing the government. It could then identify certain forms of retaliation to which it would respond with devastating military action, such as attempting to close the Strait of Hormuz, conducting massive and sustained attacks on Gulf states and U.S. troops or ships, or launching terrorist attacks in the United States itself. Washington would then need to clearly articulate these "redlines" to Tehran during and after the attack to ensure that the message was not lost in battle. And it would need to accept the fact that it would have to absorb Iranian responses that fell short of these redlines without escalating the conflict. This might include accepting token missile strikes against U.S. bases and ships in the region—several salvos over the course of a few days that soon taper off—or the harassment of commercial and U.S. naval vessels. To avoid the kind of casualties that could compel the White House to escalate the struggle, the United States would need to evacuate nonessential personnel from U.S. bases within range of Iranian missiles and ensure that its troops were safely in bunkers before Iran launched its response. Washington might also need to allow for stepped-up support to Iran's proxies in Afghanistan and Iraq and missile and terrorist attacks against Israel. In doing so, it could induce Iran to follow the path of Iraq and Syria, both of which refrained from starting a war after Israel struck their nuclear reactors in 1981 and 2007, respectively.

Even if Tehran did cross Washington's redlines, the United States could still manage the confrontation. At the outset of any such violation, it could target the Iranian weapons that it finds most threatening to prevent Tehran from deploying them. To de-escalate the situation quickly and prevent a wider regional war, the United States could also secure the agreement of its allies to avoid responding to an Iranian attack. This would keep other armies, particularly the Israel Defense Forces, out of the fray. Israel should prove willing to accept such an arrangement in exchange for a U.S. promise to eliminate the Iranian nuclear threat. Indeed, it struck a similar agreement with the United States during the Gulf War, when it refrained from responding to the launching of Scud missiles by Saddam Hussein.

Finally, the U.S. government could blunt the economic consequences of a strike. For example, it could offset any disruption of oil supplies by opening its Strategic Petroleum Reserve and quietly encouraging some Gulf states to increase their production in the run-up to the attack. Given that many oil-producing nations in the region, especially Saudi Arabia, have urged the United States to attack Iran, they would likely cooperate.

Washington could also reduce the political fallout of military action by building global support for it in advance. Many countries may still criticize the United States for using force, but some—the Arab states in particular—would privately thank Washington for eliminating the Iranian threat. By building such a consensus in the lead-up to an attack and taking the outlined steps to mitigate it once it began, the United States could avoid an international crisis and limit the scope of the conflict.

Any Time Is Good Time

Critics have another objection: even if the United States managed to eliminate Iran's nuclear facilities and mitigate the consequences, the effects might not last long. Sure enough, there is no guarantee that an assault would deter Iran from attempting to rebuild its plants; it may even harden Iran's resolve to acquire nuclear technology as a means of retaliating or protecting itself in the future. The United States might not have the wherewithal or the political capital to launch another raid, forcing it to rely on the same ineffective tools that it now uses to restrain Iran's nuclear drive. If that happens, U.S. action will have only delayed the inevitable.

Yet according to the IAEA, Iran already appears fully committed to developing a nuclear weapons program and needs no further motivation from the United States. And it will not be able to simply resume its progress after its entire nuclear infrastructure is reduced to rubble. Indeed, such a devastating offensive could well force Iran to quit the nuclear game altogether, as Iraq did after its nuclear program was destroyed in the Gulf War and as Syria did after the 2007 Israeli strike. And even if Iran did try to reconstitute its nuclear program, it would be forced to contend with continued international pressure, greater difficulty in securing necessary nuclear materials on the international market, and the lurking possibility of subsequent attacks. Military action could, therefore, delay Iran's nuclear program by anywhere from a few years to a decade, and perhaps even indefinitely.

Skeptics might still counter that at best a strike would only buy time. But time is a valuable commodity. Countries often hope to delay worst-case scenarios as far into the future as possible in the hope that this might eliminate the threat altogether. Those countries whose nuclear facilities have been attacked—most recently Iraq and Syria— have proved unwilling or unable to restart their programs. Thus, what appears to be only a temporary setback to Iran could eventually become a game changer.

Yet another argument against military action against Iran is that it would embolden the hard-liners within Iran's government, helping them rally the population around the regime and eliminate any remaining reformists. This critique ignores the fact that the hard-liners are already firmly in control. The ruling regime has become so extreme that it has sidelined even those leaders once considered to be right-wingers, such as former President Ali Akbar Hashemi Rafsanjani, for their perceived softness. And Rafsanjani or the former presidential candidate Mir Hossein Mousavi would likely continue the nuclear program if he assumed power. An attack might actually create more openings for dissidents in the long term (after temporarily uniting Iran behind Ayatollah Ali Khamenei), giving them grounds for criticizing a government that invited disaster. Even if a strike would strengthen Iran's hard-liners, the United States must not prioritize the outcomes of Iran's domestic political tussles over its vital national security interest in preventing Tehran from developing nuclear weapons.

Strike Now or Suffer Later

Attacking Iran is hardly an attractive prospect. But the United States can anticipate and reduce many of the feared consequences of such an attack. If it does so successfully, it can remove the incentive for other nations in the region to start their own atomic programs and, more broadly, strengthen global non-proliferation by demonstrating that it will use military force to prevent the spread of nuclear weapons. It can also head off a possible Israeli operation against Iran, which, given Israel's limited capability to mitigate a potential battle and inflict lasting damage, would likely result in far more devastating consequences and carry a far lower probability of success than a U.S. attack. Finally, a carefully managed U.S. attack would prove less risky than the prospect of containing a nuclear-armed Islamic Republic—a costly, decades-long proposition that would likely still result in grave national security threats. Indeed, attempting to manage a nuclear-armed Iran is not only a terrible option but the worst.

With the wars in Afghanistan and Iraq winding down and the United States facing economic hardship at home, Americans have little appetite for further strife. Yet Iran's rapid nuclear development will ultimately force the United States to choose between a conventional conflict and a possible nuclear war. Faced with that decision, the United States should conduct a surgical strike on Iran's nuclear facilities, absorb an inevitable round of retaliation, and then seek to quickly de-escalate the crisis. Addressing the threat now will spare the United States from confronting a far more dangerous situation in the future.

MATTHEW KROENIG is an assistant professor of government at Georgetown University. He is the author of *Expecting the Bomb: Technology Transfer and the Spread of Nuclear Weapons* (Cornell University Press, 2010). He is also the coauthor of *The Handbook of National Legislatures: A Global Survey* (Cambridge University Press, 2009) and coeditor of *Causes and Consequences of Nuclear Proliferation* (Routledge, 2011).

Colin H. Kahl  **NO**

Not Time to Attack Iran

Why War Should Be a Last Resort

In "Time to Attack Iran" (January/February 2012), Matthew Kroenig takes a page out of the decade-old playbook used by advocates of the Iraq war. He portrays the threat of a nuclear-armed Iran as both grave and imminent, arguing that the United States has little choice but to attack Iran now before it is too late. Then, after offering the caveat that "attacking Iran is hardly an attractive prospect," he goes on to portray military action as preferable to other available alternatives and concludes that the United States can manage all the associated risks. Preventive war, according to Kroenig, is "the least bad option." But the lesson of Iraq, the last preventive war launched by the United States, is that Washington should not choose war when there are still other options, and it should not base its decision to attack on best-case analyses of how it hopes the conflict will turn out. A realistic assessment of Iran's nuclear progress and how a conflict would likely unfold leads one to a conclusion that is the opposite of Kroenig's: now is not the time to attack Iran.

Bad Timing

Kroenig argues that there is an urgent need to attack Iran's nuclear infrastructure soon, since Tehran could "produce its first nuclear weapon within six months of deciding to do so." Yet that last phrase is crucial. The International Atomic Energy Agency (IAEA) has documented Iranian efforts to achieve the capacity to develop nuclear weapons at some point, but there is no hard evidence that Supreme Leader Ayatollah Ali Khamenei has yet made the final decision to develop them.

In arguing for a six-month horizon, Kroenig also misleadingly conflates hypothetical timelines to produce weapons-grade uranium with the time actually required to construct a bomb. According to 2010 Senate testimony by James Cartwright, then vice chairman of the U.S. Joint Chiefs of Staff, and recent statements by the former heads of Israel's national intelligence and defense intelligence agencies, even if Iran could produce enough weapons-grade uranium for a bomb in six months, it would take it at least a year to produce a testable nuclear device and considerably longer to make a deliverable weapon. And David Albright, president of the Institute for Science and International Security (and the source of Kroenig's six-month estimate), recently told Agence France-Presse that there is a "low probability" that the Iranians would actually develop a bomb over the next year even if they had the capability to do so. Because there is no evidence that Iran has built additional covert enrichment plants since the Natanz and Qom sites were outed in 2002 and 2009, respectively, any near-term move by Tehran to produce weapons-grade uranium would have to rely on its declared facilities. The IAEA would thus detect such activity with sufficient time for the international community to mount a forceful response. As a result, the Iranians are unlikely to commit to building nuclear weapons until they can do so much more quickly or out of sight, which could be years off.

Kroenig is also inconsistent about the timetable for an attack. In some places, he suggests that strikes should begin now, whereas in others, he argues that the United States should attack only if Iran takes certain actions—such as expelling IAEA inspectors, beginning the enrichment of weapons-grade uranium, or installing large numbers of advanced centrifuges, any one of which would signal that it had decided to build a bomb. Kroenig is likely right that these developments—and perhaps others, such as the discovery of new covert enrichment sites—would create a decision point for the use of force. But the Iranians have not taken these steps yet, and as Kroenig acknowledges, "Washington has a very good chance" of detecting them if they do.

Riding the Escalator

Kroenig's discussion of timing is not the only misleading part of his article; so is his contention that the United States could mitigate the "potentially devastating consequences" of a strike on Iran by carefully managing the escalation that would ensue. His picture of a clean, calibrated conflict is a mirage. Any war with Iran would be a messy and extraordinarily violent affair, with significant casualties and consequences.

According to Kroenig, Iran would not respond to a strike with its "worst forms of retaliation, such as closing the Strait of Hormuz or launching missiles at southern Europe" unless its leaders felt that the regime's "very existence was threatened." To mitigate this risk, he claims, the United States could "make clear that it is interested only in destroying Iran's nuclear program, not in overthrowing the

Kahl, Colin H. From *Foreign Affairs*, March/April 2012, pp. 166–173. Copyright © 2012 by Council on Foreign Relations, Inc. Reprinted by permission of Foreign Affairs. www.ForeignAffairs.com

government." But Iranian leaders have staked their domestic legitimacy on resisting international pressure to halt the nuclear program, and so they would inevitably view an attack on that program as an attack on the regime itself. Decades of hostility and perceived U.S. efforts to undermine the regime would reinforce this perception. And when combined with the emphasis on anti-Americanism in the ideology of the supreme leader and his hard-line advisers, as well as their general ignorance about what drives U.S. decision-making, this perception means that there is little prospect that Iranian leaders would believe that a U.S. strike had limited aims. Assuming the worst about Washington's intentions, Tehran is likely to overreact to even a surgical strike against its nuclear facilities.

Kroenig nevertheless believes that the United States could limit the prospects for escalation by warning Iran that crossing certain "redlines" would trigger a devastating U.S. counter-response. Ironically, Kroenig believes that a nuclear-armed Iran would be deeply irrational and prone to miscalculation yet somehow maintains that under the same leaders, Iran would make clear-eyed decisions in the immediate aftermath of a U.S. strike. But the two countries share no direct and reliable channels for communication, and the inevitable confusion brought on by a crisis would make signaling difficult and miscalculation likely.

To make matters worse, in the heat of battle, Iran would face powerful incentives to escalate. In the event of a conflict, both sides would come under significant pressure to stop the fighting due to the impact on international oil markets. Since this would limit the time the Iranians would have to reestablish deterrence, they might choose to launch a quick, all-out response, without care for redlines. Iranian fears that the United States could successfully disrupt its command-and-control infrastructure or preemptively destroy its ballistic missile arsenal could also tempt Iran to launch as many missiles as possible early in the war. And the decentralized nature of Iran's Islamic Revolutionary Guard Corps, especially its navy, raises the prospect of unauthorized responses that could rapidly expand the fighting in the crowded waters of the Persian Gulf.

Controlling escalation would be no easier on the U.S. side. In the face of reprisals by Iranian proxies, "token missile strikes against U.S. bases and ships," or "the harassment of commercial and U.S. naval vessels," Kroenig says that Washington should turn the other cheek and constrain its own response to Iranian counterattacks. But this is much easier said than done. Just as Iran's likely expectation of a short war might encourage it to respond disproportionately early in the crisis, so the United States would also have incentives to move swiftly to destroy Iran's conventional forces and the infrastructure of the Revolutionary Guard Corps. And if the United States failed to do so, proxy attacks against U.S. civilian personnel in Lebanon or Iraq, the transfer of lethal rocket and portable air defense systems to Taliban fighters in Afghanistan, or missile strikes against U.S. facilities in the Gulf could cause significant U.S. casualties, creating irresistible political pressure in Washington to respond. Add to this the normal fog of war and the lack of reliable communications between

the United States and Iran, and Washington would have a hard time determining whether Tehran's initial response to a strike was a one-off event or the prelude to a wider campaign. If it were the latter, a passive U.S. approach might motivate Iran to launch even more dangerous attacks—and this is a risk Washington may choose not to take. The sum total of these dynamics would make staying within Kroenig's proscribed limits exceedingly difficult.

Even if Iran did not escalate, purely defensive moves that would threaten U.S. personnel or international shipping in the Strait of Hormuz—the maritime chokepoint through which nearly 20 percent of the world's traded oil passes—would also create powerful incentives for Washington to preemptively target Iran's military. Of particular concern would be Iran's "anti-access/area-denial" capabilities, which are designed to prevent advanced navies from operating in the shallow waters of the Persian Gulf. These systems integrate coastal air defenses, shore-based long-range artillery and anti-ship cruise missiles, Kilo-class and midget submarines, remote-controlled boats and unmanned kamikaze aerial vehicles, and more than 1,000 small attack craft equipped with machine guns, multiple-launch rockets, anti-ship missiles, torpedoes, and rapid-mine-laying capabilities. The entire 120-mile-long strait sits along the Iranian coastline, within short reach of these systems. In the midst of a conflict, the threat to U.S. forces and the global economy posed by Iran's activating its air defenses, dispersing its missiles or naval forces, or moving its mines out of storage would be too great for the United States to ignore; the logic of preemption would compel Washington to escalate.

Some analysts, including Afshin Molavi and Michael Singh, believe that the Iranians are unlikely to attempt to close the strait due to the damage it would inflict on their own economy. But Tehran's saber rattling has already intensified in response to the prospect of Western sanctions on its oil industry. In the immediate aftermath of a U.S. strike on Iran's nuclear program, Iranian leaders might perceive that holding the strait at risk would encourage international pressure on Washington to end the fighting, possibly deterring U.S. escalation. In reality, it would more likely have the opposite effect, encouraging aggressive U.S. efforts to protect commercial shipping. The U.S. Navy is capable of keeping the strait open, but the mere threat of closure could send oil prices soaring, dealing a heavy blow to the fragile global economy. The measures that Kroenig advocates to mitigate this threat, such as opening up the U.S. Strategic Petroleum Reserve and urging Saudi Arabia to boost oil production, would be unlikely to suffice, especially since most Saudi crude passes through the strait.

Ultimately, if the United States and Iran go to war, there is no doubt that Washington will win in the narrow operational sense. Indeed, with the impressive array of U.S. naval and air forces already deployed in the Gulf, the United States could probably knock Iran's military capabilities back 20 years in a matter of weeks. But a U.S.-Iranian conflict would not be the clinical, tightly controlled, limited encounter that Kroenig predicts.

Spillover

Keeping other states in the region out of the fight would also prove more difficult than Kroenig suggests. Iran would presume Israeli complicity in a U.S. raid and would seek to drag Israel into the conflict in order to undermine potential support for the U.S. war effort among key Arab regimes. And although it is true, as Kroenig notes, that Israel remained on the sidelines during the 1990–91 Gulf War, the threat posed by Iran's missiles and proxies today is considerably greater than that posed by Iraq two decades ago. If Iranian-allied Hezbollah responded to the fighting by firing rockets at Israeli cities, Israel could launch an all-out war against Lebanon. Syrian President Bashar al-Assad might also try to use the moment to divert attention from the uprising in his country, launching his own assault on the Jewish state. Either scenario, or their combination, could lead to a wider war in the Levant.

Even in the Gulf, where U.S. partners are sometimes portrayed as passive, Iranian retaliation might draw Saudi Arabia and the United Arab Emirates into the conflict. The Saudis have taken a much more confrontational posture toward Iran in the past year, and Riyadh is unlikely to tolerate Iranian attacks against critical energy infrastructure. For its part, the UAE, the most hawkish state in the Gulf, might respond to missiles raining down on U.S. forces at its Al Dhafra Air Base by attempting to seize Abu Musa, Greater Tunb, and Lesser Tunb, three disputed Gulf islands currently occupied by Iran. A strike could also set off wider destabilizing effects. Although Kroenig is right that some Arab leaders would privately applaud a U.S. strike, many on the Arab street would reject it. Both Islamist extremists and embattled elites could use this opportunity to transform the Arab Spring's populist anti-regime narrative into a decidedly anti-American one. This would rebound to Iran's advantage just at the moment when political developments in the region, chief among them the resurgence of nationalism in the Arab world and the upheaval in Syria, are significantly undermining Iran's influence. A U.S. strike could easily shift regional sympathies back in Tehran's favor by allowing Iran to play the victim and, through its retaliation, resuscitate its status as the champion of the region's anti-Western resistance.

The Cost of Buying Time

Even if a U.S. strike went as well as Kroenig predicts, there is little guarantee that it would produce lasting results. Senior U.S. defense officials have repeatedly stated that an attack on Iran's nuclear facilities would stall Tehran's progress for only a few years. Kroenig argues that such a delay could become permanent. "Those countries whose nuclear facilities have been attacked—most recently Iraq and Syria," he writes, "have proved unwilling or unable to restart their programs." In the case of Iraq, however, Saddam Hussein restarted his clandestine nuclear weapons program after the 1981 Israeli attack on the Osirak nuclear reactor, and it required the Gulf War and another decade of sanctions and intrusive inspections to

eliminate it. Iran's program is also more advanced and dispersed than were Iraq's and Syria's, meaning it would be easier to reconstitute. A U.S. strike would damage key Iranian facilities, but it would do nothing to reverse the nuclear knowledge Iran has accumulated or its ability to eventually build new centrifuges.

A U.S. attack would also likely rally domestic Iranian support around nuclear hard-liners, increasing the odds that Iran would emerge from a strike even more committed to building a bomb. Kroenig downplays the "rally round the flag" risks by noting that hard-liners are already firmly in power and suggesting that an attack might produce increased internal criticism of the regime. But the nuclear program remains an enormous source of national pride for the majority of Iranians. To the extent that there is internal dissent over the program, it is a discussion about whether the country should acquire nuclear weapons or simply pursue civilian nuclear technology. By demonstrating the vulnerability of a non-nuclear-armed Iran, a U.S. attack would provide ammunition to hard-liners who argue for acquiring a nuclear deterrent. Kroenig suggests that the United States should essentially ignore "Iran's domestic political tussles" when pursuing "its vital national security interest in preventing Tehran from developing nuclear weapons." But influencing Iranian opinion about the strategic desirability of nuclear weapons might ultimately offer the only enduring way of keeping the Islamic Republic on a peaceful nuclear path.

Finally, if Iran did attempt to restart its nuclear program after an attack, it would be much more difficult for the United States to stop it. An assault would lead Iran to distance itself from the IAEA and perhaps to pull out of the Nuclear Non-proliferation Treaty altogether. Without inspectors on the ground, the international community would struggle to track or slow Tehran's efforts to rebuild its program.

Contain Yourself

Kroenig argues that "a nuclear-armed Iran would not intentionally launch a suicidal nuclear war" but still concludes that it is ultimately less risky to attack the Islamic Republic now than to attempt to contain it later. He warns that containment would entail a costly forward deployment of large numbers of U.S. forces on Iran's periphery for decades.

But the United States already has a large presence encircling Iran. Forty thousand U.S. troops are stationed in the Gulf, accompanied by strike aircraft, two aircraft carrier strike groups, two Aegis ballistic missile defense ships, and multiple Patriot antimissile systems. On Iran's eastern flank, Washington has another 90,000 troops deployed in Afghanistan and thousands more supporting the Afghan war in nearby Central Asian states. Kroenig claims that it would take much more to contain a nuclear-armed Iran. But U.S. forces in the Gulf already outnumber those in South Korea that are there to deter a nuclear-armed North. It is thus perfectly conceivable that the existing U.S. presence in the region, perhaps supplemented by a limited forward deployment of nuclear weapons and additional ballistic missile defenses, would be sufficient to deter a nuclear-armed Iran from aggression and blackmail.

To be sure, such a deterrence-and-containment strategy would be an extraordinarily complex and risky enterprise, and there is no doubt that prevention is preferable. Given the possible consequences of a nuclear-armed Iran, the price of failure would be very high. But Kroenig's approach would not solve the problem. By presenting the options as either a near-term strike or long-term containment, Kroenig falls into the same trap that advocates of the Iraq war fell into a decade ago: ignoring postwar scenarios. In reality, the strike that Kroenig recommends would likely be a prelude to containment, not a substitute for it.

Since a military raid would not permanently eliminate Iran's nuclear infrastructure, the United States would still need to construct an expensive, risky post-war containment regime to prevent Iran from reconstituting the program, much as it did in regard to Iraq after the Gulf War. The end result would be strikingly similar to the one that Kroenig criticizes, requiring Washington to maintain sufficient air, naval, and ground forces in the Persian Gulf to attack again at a moment's notice.

A strike carried out in the way Kroenig advocates—a unilateral preventive attack—would also make postwar containment more difficult and costly. Many countries would view such an operation as a breach of international law, shattering the consensus required to maintain an effective post-strike containment regime. The likelihood that the United States could "reduce the political fallout of military action by building global support for it in advance," as Kroenig suggests, would be extremely low absent clear evidence that Iran is dashing for a bomb. Without such evidence, Washington would be left to bear the costs of an attack and the resulting containment regime alone.

Finally, the surgical nature of Kroenig's proposed strike, aimed solely at Iran's nuclear program, would make postwar containment much harder. It would leave Tehran wounded and aggrieved but still capable of responding. Kroenig's recommended approach, then, would likely be just enough to ensure a costly, long-term conflict without actually compelling Iran to change its behavior.

The Options on the Table

In making the case for preventive war as the least bad option, Kroenig dismisses any prospect of finding a diplomatic solution to the U.S.-Iranian standoff. He concludes that the Obama administration's dual-track policy of engagement and pressure has failed to arrest Iran's march toward a bomb, leaving Washington with no other choice but to bomb Iran.

But this ignores the severe economic strain, isolation, and technical challenges that Iran is experiencing. After years of dismissing the economic effects of sanctions, senior Iranian officials now publicly complain about the intense pain the sanctions are producing. And facing the prospect of U.S. sanctions against Iran's central bank and European actions to halt Iranian oil imports, Tehran signaled in early January some willingness to return to the negotiating table. Washington must test this willingness and, in so doing, provide Iran with a clear strategic choice: address the concerns of the international community regarding its nuclear program and see its isolation lifted or stay on its current path and face substantially higher costs. In framing this choice, Washington must be able to assert that like-minded states are prepared to implement oil-related sanctions, and the Obama administration should continue to emphasize that all options, including military action, remain on the table.

Some will undoubtedly claim that highlighting the potential risks associated with war will lead the Iranians to conclude that the United States lacks the resolve to use force. But in authorizing the surge in Afghanistan, carrying out the raid that killed Osama bin Laden, and leading the NATO air campaign to oust Libya's Muammar al-Qaddafi, President Barack Obama has repeatedly shown that he is willing to accept risk and use force—both as part of a coalition and unilaterally—to defend U.S. interests. And as Martin Dempsey, chairman of the U.S. Joint Chiefs of Staff, told CNN late last December, the United States has a viable contingency plan for Iran if force is ultimately required. But given the high costs and inherent uncertainties of a strike, the United States should not rush to use force until all other options have been exhausted and the Iranian threat is not just growing but imminent. Until then, force is, and should remain, a last resort, not a first choice.

COLIN H. KAHL is an associate professor in the Security Studies Program in the Edmund A. Walsh School of Foreign Service at Georgetown University, where he teaches courses on international relations, international security, the geopolitics of the Middle East, American foreign policy, and civil and ethnic conflict.

EXPLORING THE ISSUE

Should the United States Launch a Preemptive Strike Against Iran?

Critical Thinking and Reflection

1. Why do advocates of an American preemptive strike believe that the United States should strike soon?
2. Why do critics of such action argue that it is prudent or essential that America should wait?
3. How would an American strike affect the world's ability to extract and obtain oil?
4. Should Iran have the ability to develop nuclear weapons if its potential rivals have those weapons? Why or why not?
5. Would American intervention be likely to result in a more widespread war? Why or why not?

Is There Common Ground?

Despite the mutual suspicion and hostility, it can be argued that a long and widespread war between the United States and Iran would not advance the long-range interests of either side. It might lead to tens of thousands of military casualties and uncounted civilian deaths. It would be likely to cost vast sums that would require great economic sacrifices. Both sides must be aware that the superior military and economic strength of the United States and its allies would be certain to prevail and that the present Iranian Shiite theocracy would be removed from power so that there is no possibility of a benefit to Iran. At the same time, the American people are reluctant to engage in another war at this time. If Iran can be persuaded to avoid aggressive action, the question remains as to whether the United States can live in peace and with security with the present Iranian regime.

The recent agreement between world superpowers and the Iranians demonstrate a potential for long-lasting common ground. The Iranians have relaxed their nuclear desires and permitted international observers to have unlimited access to all sites within the country in exchange for America lifting sanctions. The removal of

sanctions will save the Iranians millions of dollars and provide a sense of good faith from the United States. Ultimately, the sanctions were successful. They are never intended to cripple a country, only to force them back to the negotiation table. In that sense, we may be witnessing the development and recognition of a middle ground between two countries that have been fighting since 1979.

Additional Resources

Shahram Chubin, *Iran's Nuclear Ambitions* (Carnegie Endowment for International Peace, 2006)

David Crist, *The Twilight War: The Secret History of America's Thirty-Year Conflict with Israel* (Penguin, 2012)

Trita Parsi, *A Single Roll of the Dice: Obama's Diplomacy with Iran* (Yale University Press, 2012)

Kenneth M. Pollack, *The Persian Puzzle: The Conflict Between Iran and America* (Random House, 2004)

Barbara Slavin, *Bitter Friends, Bosom Enemies: Iran, the U.S., and the Twisted Path to Confrontation* (St. Martin's Press, 2007)

Internet References . . .

CIA World FactBook

www.cia.gov/library/publications/the-world-factbook
/geos/ir.html

International Atomic Energy Agency

www.iaea.org/

Islamic Republic of Iran's President

www.president.ir/en/

Office of the Supreme Leader Sayyid Ali Khamenei

www.leader.ir/langs/en/

U.S. State Department

http://travel.state.gov/travel/cis_pa_tw/cis/cis_1142
.html

Selected, Edited, and with Issue Framing Material by:
William J. Miller, *Flagler College*

ISSUE

Was President Obama's Trip to Cuba a Good Step in Normalizing Relations with the Country?

YES: Barack Obama, from "Remarks by President Obama to the People of Cuba," *The White House* (2016)

NO: Armando Valladares, from "I Was a Prisoner of Castro's Regime: Obama's Visit to Cuba Is a Mistake," *The Washington Post* (2016)

Learning Outcomes
After reading this issue, you will be able to:
• Describe the history of American–Cuban relations.
• Assess the timing of President Obama's visit.
• Identify potential avenues for future collaboration between the United States and Cuba.
• Explain the reactions of Cuban–Americans and Cubans to the potential normalization.
• Assess the potential political impact of this development.

ISSUE SUMMARY

YES: In his address from Havana, President Barack Obama explains why ceasing isolationist policies with Cuba can benefit both the United States and the island nation. He takes time to highlight the strengths of Cuban society and how he envisions normalized relations occurring in the next few years.

NO: Armando Valladares, a poet and artist who spent 22 years in Cuba as a political prisoner under Castro, writes that Obama's trip was misguided as it sends a message of favoritism for the strong at the expense of the weak. In short, he argues that common citizens will never see the benefits of normalized relations with the United States.

Less than a hundred miles from the Florida coast, Cuba and Cuban Presidents Fidel and Raul Castro have been thorns in the side of American presidents since the Kennedy administration. Castro came to power in 1959. He nationalized all American property on the island, and relations between the United States and Cuba have been downhill from there. In 1960, the United States gave weak support to a failed invasion of Cuba at the Bay of Pigs. In 1962, Castro allowed the Soviet Union to install nuclear missiles on the island. The resulting Cuban Missile Crisis led the world to the brink of nuclear war.

The United States had an almost full embargo on Cuba between 1961 and 2016. Travel and trade between the United States and Cuba have been heavily restricted. Supporters of the policy say it is the best way to squeeze Castro out of power. Critics say it is time to try

something new since Castro uses American hostility as a way to rally support for his government. When Condoleezza Rice appeared at her Senate confirmation hearings to become Secretary of State she said, "In our world there remain outposts of tyranny—and America stands with oppressed people on every continent—in Cuba, and Burma, and North Korea, and Iran, and Belarus, and Zimbabwe."

In the nineteenth century, when Cuba was still a colony of Spain, many southern Americans wanted to annex the island as a state to increase American slave territory. In the 1890s, while Spain was attempting to suppress a Cuban nationalist rebellion, the United States intervened on the premise of correcting Spanish human rights abuses. In truth, American neo-imperialism fueled American interests as it sought to create a European-style empire of its own. The United States also bristled when a Spanish "scorched earth" tactic against nationalist guerrillas burned out several American interests.

The United States began the Spanish–American War in April 1898, and by the middle of July had defeated Spain. Cuban nationalists believed they had achieved independence, but the United States had other ideas. Not until 1902 did the United States grant Cuban independence, and then only after Cuba had agreed to the Platt Amendment, which roped Cuba into America's sphere of economic influence. The amendment stipulated that Cuba could not transfer land to any foreign power except the United States; that it could not acquire any foreign debt without U.S. approval; and it would allow American intervention in Cuban affairs whenever the United States thought it necessary. To speed their own independence, Cubans added the amendment to their constitution.

Cuba operated under the Platt Amendment until 1934 when the United States rescinded it under the Treaty of Relations. The treaty was part of Franklin D. Roosevelt's Good Neighbor Policy, which attempted to foster better American relations with Latin American countries and keep them out of the influence of rising Fascist states. The treaty retained American rental of Guantanamo Bay naval base.

In 1959, Fidel Castro and Che Guevara led the Cuban communist revolution to overthrow President Fulgencio Batista's regime. Castro's ascent to power froze relations with the United States. The United States' policy toward Communism was "containment" and it quickly severed ties with Cuba and embargoed trade the island.

In 1961, the Central Intelligence Agency (CIA) orchestrated a failed attempt by Cuban emigres to invade Cuba and topple Castro. That mission ended in a debacle at the Bay of Pigs. Castro increasingly sought aid from the Soviet Union. In October 1962, Soviets began shipping nuclear-capable missiles to Cuba. American U-2 spy planes caught the shipments on film, touching off the Cuban Missile Crisis. For 13 days that month, President John F. Kennedy warned Soviet first secretary Nikita Khrushchev to remove the missiles or face consequences—which most of the world interpreted as nuclear war. Khrushchev backed down. While the Soviet Union continued to back Castro, Cuban relations with the United States remained cold but not warlike.

In 1979, faced with an economic downturn and civilian unrest, Castro told Cubans they could leave if they did not like conditions at home. Between April and October 1980, some 200,000 Cubans arrived in the United States. Under the Cuban Adjustment Act of 1966, the United States could allow arrival of such immigrants and avoid their repatriation to Cuba. After Cuba lost most of its Soviet-block trading partners with the collapse of Communism between 1989 and 1991, it suffered another economic downturn. Cuban immigration to the United States climbed again in 1994 and 1995.

In 1996, the United States arrested five Cuban men on charges of espionage and conspiracy to commit murder. The United States alleged they had entered Florida and infiltrated Cuban–American human rights groups. The United States also charged that information the so-called Cuban Five sent back to Cuba helped Castro's air force destroy two Brothers-to-the-Rescue planes returning from a covert mission to Cuba, killing four passengers. U.S. courts convicted and jailed the Cuban Five in 1998.

In 2008, after a prolonged illness, Castro ceded the presidency of Cuba to his brother, Raul Castro. While some outside observers believed that would signal the collapse of Cuban Communism, it did not happen. However, in 2009 after Barack Obama became president of the United States, Raul Castro made overtures to talk to the United States about foreign policy normalization.

Then Secretary of State Hillary Clinton said that the 50-year American foreign policy toward Cuba had "failed," and that Obama's administration was committed to finding ways to normalize Cuban–American relations. Still, another issue stood in the way of normalized relations. In 2008 Cuba arrested USAID worker Alan Gross, charging him with distributing U.S. government-purchased computers with the intent of establishing a spy network inside Cuba. While Gross, 59 at the time of his arrest, claimed no knowledge of the computers' sponsorship, Cuba tried and convicted him in March 2011. A Cuban court sentenced him to 15 years in prison.

Former U.S. President Jimmy Carter, traveling on behalf of his Carter Center for Human Rights, visited Cuba in March and April 2011. Carter visited with the Castro brothers, and with Gross. While he said that he believed the Cuban Five had been jailed long enough (a position that angered many human rights advocates), and that he hoped Cuba would quickly release Gross, he stopped short of suggesting any type of prisoner exchange. The Gross case seemed capable of halting any further normalization of relations between the two countries until its resolution.

On March 20, 2016, President Obama visited Cuba and announced a new path for U.S.–Cuban relations. His goals are to re-establish diplomatic relations, effectively empower the Cuban people by adjusting regulations, and facilitate an expansion of travel to Cuba. The Obama administration's decision to resurrect diplomatic ties with Cuba after more than 50 years is a step in the right direction, but Washington and Havana have different political objectives that may hinder the normalization process. Meanwhile, the U.S. Congress is unlikely to lift the trade embargo anytime soon. President Obama hopes to use the detente to bring Cuba into the twenty-first century and move it toward democracy, whereas the Cubans' objective is to gain the maximum financial gain while maintaining as much of the Old Castro system as they can. Immediate goals for U.S. and Cuban diplomats will be limited to resolving smaller issues. Washington wants to increase its diplomatic presence in Cuba. Havana wants Cuba removed from the State Department's list of State Sponsors of Terrorism, and demands the United States stop offering Internet access and classes to dissidents.

In the following selections, we read about arguments in favor of Obama's actions and those against his decision to normalize relations. In his address from Havana, President Barack Obama explains why ceasing isolationist policies with Cuba can benefit both the United States and the island nation. He takes time to highlight the strengths of Cuban society and how he envisions normalized relations occurring in the next few years. On the other hand, Armando Valladares, a poet and artist who spent 22 years in Cuba as a political prisoner under Castro, writes that Obama's trip was misguided as it sends a message of favoritism for the strong at the expense of the weak. In short, he argues that common citizens will never see the benefits of normalized relations with the United States.

YES ⬅

Barack Obama

Remarks by President Obama to the People of Cuba

PRESIDENT OBAMA: Thank you. (Applause.) Muchas gracias. Thank you so much. Thank you very much.

President Castro, the people of Cuba, thank you so much for the warm welcome that I have received, that my family have received, and that our delegation has received. It is an extraordinary honor to be here today.

Before I begin, please indulge me. I want to comment on the terrorist attacks that have taken place in Brussels. The thoughts and the prayers of the American people are with the people of Belgium. We stand in solidarity with them in condemning these outrageous attacks against innocent people. We will do whatever is necessary to support our friend and ally, Belgium, in bringing to justice those who are responsible. And this is yet another reminder that the world must unite, we must be together, regardless of nationality, or race, or faith, in fighting against the scourge of terrorism. We can—and will—defeat those who threaten the safety and security of people all around the world.

To the government and the people of Cuba, I want to thank you for the kindness that you've shown to me and Michelle, Malia, Sasha, my mother-in-law, Marian.

"Cultivo una rosa blanca." (Applause.) In his most famous poem, Jose Marti made this offering of friendship and peace to both his friend and his enemy. Today, as the President of the United States of America, I offer the Cuban people el saludo de paz. (Applause.)

Havana is only 90 miles from Florida, but to get here we had to travel a great distance—over barriers of history and ideology; barriers of pain and separation. The blue waters beneath Air Force One once carried American battleships to this island—to liberate, but also to exert control over Cuba. Those waters also carried generations of Cuban revolutionaries to the United States, where they built support for their cause. And that short distance has been crossed by hundreds of thousands of Cuban exiles—on planes and makeshift rafts—who came to America in pursuit of freedom and opportunity, sometimes leaving behind everything they owned and every person that they loved.

Like so many people in both of our countries, my lifetime has spanned a time of isolation between us. The Cuban Revolution took place the same year that my father came to the United States from Kenya. The Bay of Pigs took place the year that I was born. The next year, the entire world held its breath, watching our two countries, as humanity came as close as we ever have to the horror of nuclear war. As the decades rolled by, our governments settled into a seemingly endless confrontation, fighting battles through proxies. In a world that remade itself time and again, one constant was the conflict between the United States and Cuba.

I have come here to bury the last remnant of the Cold War in the Americas. (Applause.) I have come here to extend the hand of friendship to the Cuban people. (Applause.)

I want to be clear: The differences between our governments over these many years are real and they are important. I'm sure President Castro would say the same thing—I know, because I've heard him address those differences at length. But before I discuss those issues, we also need to recognize how much we share. Because in many ways, the United States and Cuba are like two brothers who've been estranged for many years, even as we share the same blood.

We both live in a new world, colonized by Europeans. Cuba, like the United States, was built in part by slaves brought here from Africa. Like the United States, the Cuban people can trace their heritage to both slaves and slave-owners. We've welcomed both immigrants who came a great distance to start new lives in the Americas.

Over the years, our cultures have blended together. Dr. Carlos Finlay's work in Cuba paved the way for generations of doctors, including Walter Reed, who drew on Dr. Finlay's work to help combat Yellow Fever. Just as Marti wrote some of his most famous words in New York, Ernest Hemingway made a home in Cuba, and found inspiration in the waters of these shores. We share a national past-time—La Pelota—and later today our players will compete on the same Havana field that Jackie Robinson played on before he made his Major League debut. (Applause.) And it's said that our greatest boxer, Muhammad Ali, once paid tribute to a Cuban that he could never fight—saying that he would only be able to reach a draw with the great Cuban, Teofilo Stevenson. (Applause.)

So even as our governments became adversaries, our people continued to share these common passions, particularly as so many Cubans came to America. In Miami or Havana, you can find places to dance the Cha-Cha-Cha or the Salsa, and eat ropa vieja. People in both of our countries have sung along with Celia Cruz or Gloria Estefan, and now listen to reggaeton or Pitbull. (Laughter.) Millions of our people share a common religion—a faith that I paid tribute to

Obama, Barack. "Remarks by President Obama to the People of Cuba," White House Press Release, March 2016.

at the Shrine of our Lady of Charity in Miami, a peace that Cubans find in La Cachita.

For all of our differences, the Cuban and American people share common values in their own lives. A sense of patriotism and a sense of pride—a lot of pride. A profound love of family. A passion for our children, a commitment to their education. And that's why I believe our grandchildren will look back on this period of isolation as an aberration, as just one chapter in a longer story of family and of friendship.

But we cannot, and should not, ignore the very real differences that we have—about how we organize our governments, our economies, and our societies. Cuba has a one-party system; the United States is a multi-party democracy. Cuba has a socialist economic model; the United States is an open market. Cuba has emphasized the role and rights of the state; the United States is founded upon the rights of the individual.

Despite these differences, on December 17th 2014, President Castro and I announced that the United States and Cuba would begin a process to normalize relations between our countries. (Applause.) Since then, we have established diplomatic relations and opened embassies. We've begun initiatives to cooperate on health and agriculture, education and law enforcement. We've reached agreements to restore direct flights and mail service. We've expanded commercial ties, and increased the capacity of Americans to travel and do business in Cuba.

And these changes have been welcomed, even though there are still opponents to these policies. But still, many people on both sides of this debate have asked: Why now? Why now?

There is one simple answer: What the United States was doing was not working. We have to have the courage to acknowledge that truth. A policy of isolation designed for the Cold War made little sense in the 21st century. The embargo was only hurting the Cuban people instead of helping them. And I've always believed in what Martin Luther King, Jr. called "the fierce urgency of now"—we should not fear change, we should embrace it. (Applause.)

That leads me to a bigger and more important reason for these changes: Creo en el pueblo Cubano. I believe in the Cuban people. (Applause.) This is not just a policy of normalizing relations with the Cuban government. The United States of America is normalizing relations with the Cuban people. (Applause.)

And today, I want to share with you my vision of what our future can be. I want the Cuban people—especially the young people—to understand why I believe that you should look to the future with hope; not the false promise which insists that things are better than they really are, or the blind optimism that says all your problems can go away tomorrow. Hope that is rooted in the future that you can choose and that you can shape, and that you can build for your country.

I'm hopeful because I believe that the Cuban people are as innovative as any people in the world.

In a global economy, powered by ideas and information, a country's greatest asset is its people. In the United States, we have

a clear monument to what the Cuban people can build: it's called Miami. Here in Havana, we see that same talent in cuentapropistas, cooperatives and old cars that still run. El Cubano inventa del aire. (Applause.)

Cuba has an extraordinary resource—a system of education which values every boy and every girl. (Applause.) And in recent years, the Cuban government has begun to open up to the world, and to open up more space for that talent to thrive. In just a few years, we've seen how cuentapropistas can succeed while sustaining a distinctly Cuban spirit. Being self-employed is not about becoming more like America, it's about being yourself.

Look at Sandra Lidice Aldama, who chose to start a small business. Cubans, she said, can "innovate and adapt without losing our identity . . . our secret is in not copying or imitating but simply being ourselves."

Look at Papito Valladeres, a barber, whose success allowed him to improve conditions in his neighborhood. "I realize I'm not going to solve all of the world's problems," he said. "But if I can solve problems in the little piece of the world where I live, it can ripple across Havana."

That's where hope begins—with the ability to earn your own living, and to build something you can be proud of. That's why our policies focus on supporting Cubans, instead of hurting them. That's why we got rid of limits on remittances—so ordinary Cubans have more resources. That's why we're encouraging travel—which will build bridges between our people, and bring more revenue to those Cuban small businesses. That's why we've opened up space for commerce and exchanges—so that Americans and Cubans can work together to find cures for diseases, and create jobs, and open the door to more opportunity for the Cuban people.

As President of the United States, I've called on our Congress to lift the embargo. (Applause.) It is an outdated burden on the Cuban people. It's a burden on the Americans who want to work and do business or invest here in Cuba. It's time to lift the embargo. But even if we lifted the embargo tomorrow, Cubans would not realize their potential without continued change here in Cuba. (Applause.) It should be easier to open a business here in Cuba. A worker should be able to get a job directly with companies who invest here in Cuba. Two currencies shouldn't separate the type of salaries that Cubans can earn. The Internet should be available across the island, so that Cubans can connect to the wider world—(applause)—and to one of the greatest engines of growth in human history.

There's no limitation from the United States on the ability of Cuba to take these steps. It's up to you. And I can tell you as a friend that sustainable prosperity in the 21st century depends upon education, health care, and environmental protection. But it also depends on the free and open exchange of ideas. If you can't access information online, if you cannot be exposed to different points of view, you will not reach your full potential. And over time, the youth will lose hope.

I know these issues are sensitive, especially coming from an American President. Before 1959, some Americans saw Cuba as something to exploit, ignored poverty, enabled corruption. And since 1959, we've been shadow-boxers in this battle of geopolitics and personalities. I know the history, but I refuse to be trapped by it. (Applause.)

I've made it clear that the United States has neither the capacity, nor the intention to impose change on Cuba. What changes come will depend upon the Cuban people. We will not impose our political or economic system on you. We recognize that every country, every people, must chart its own course and shape its own model. But having removed the shadow of history from our relationship, I must speak honestly about the things that I believe—the things that we, as Americans, believe. As Marti said, "Liberty is the right of every man to be honest, to think and to speak without hypocrisy."

So let me tell you what I believe. I can't force you to agree, but you should know what I think. I believe that every person should be equal under the law. (Applause.) Every child deserves the dignity that comes with education, and health care and food on the table and a roof over their heads. (Applause.) I believe citizens should be free to speak their mind without fear—(applause)—to organize, and to criticize their government, and to protest peacefully, and that the rule of law should not include arbitrary detentions of people who exercise those rights. (Applause.) I believe that every person should have the freedom to practice their faith peacefully and publicly. (Applause.) And, yes, I believe voters should be able to choose their governments in free and democratic elections. (Applause.)

Not everybody agrees with me on this. Not everybody agrees with the American people on this. But I believe those human rights are universal. (Applause.) I believe they are the rights of the American people, the Cuban people, and people around the world.

Now, there's no secret that our governments disagree on many of these issues. I've had frank conversations with President Castro. For many years, he has pointed out the flaws in the American system—economic inequality; the death penalty; racial discrimination; wars abroad. That's just a sample. He has a much longer list. (Laughter.) But here's what the Cuban people need to understand: I welcome this open debate and dialogue. It's good. It's healthy. I'm not afraid of it.

We do have too much money in American politics. But, in America, it's still possible for somebody like me—a child who was raised by a single mom, a child of mixed race who did not have a lot of money—to pursue and achieve the highest office in the land. That's what's possible in America. (Applause.)

We do have challenges with racial bias—in our communities, in our criminal justice system, in our society—the legacy of slavery and segregation. But the fact that we have open debates within America's own democracy is what allows us to get better. In 1959, the year that my father moved to America, it was

illegal for him to marry my mother, who was white, in many American states. When I first started school, we were still struggling to desegregate schools across the American South. But people organized; they protested; they debated these issues; they challenged government officials. And because of those protests, and because of those debates, and because of popular mobilization, I'm able to stand here today as an African-American and as President of the United States. That was because of the freedoms that were afforded in the United States that we were able to bring about change.

I'm not saying this is easy. There's still enormous problems in our society. But democracy is the way that we solve them. That's how we got health care for more of our people. That's how we made enormous gains in women's rights and gay rights. That's how we address the inequality that concentrates so much wealth at the top of our society. Because workers can organize and ordinary people have a voice, American democracy has given our people the opportunity to pursue their dreams and enjoy a high standard of living. (Applause.)

Now, there are still some tough fights. It isn't always pretty, the process of democracy. It's often frustrating. You can see that in the election going on back home. But just stop and consider this fact about the American campaign that's taking place right now. You had two Cuban Americans in the Republican Party, running against the legacy of a black man who is President, while arguing that they're the best person to beat the Democratic nominee who will either be a woman or a Democratic Socialist. (Laughter and applause.) Who would have believed that back in 1959? That's a measure of our progress as a democracy. (Applause.)

So here's my message to the Cuban government and the Cuban people: The ideals that are the starting point for every revolution—America's revolution, Cuba's revolution, the liberation movements around the world—those ideals find their truest expression, I believe, in democracy. Not because American democracy is perfect, but precisely because we're not. And we—like every country—need the space that democracy gives us to change. It gives individuals the capacity to be catalysts to think in new ways, and to reimagine how our society should be, and to make them better.

There's already an evolution taking place inside of Cuba, a generational change. Many suggested that I come here and ask the people of Cuba to tear something down—but I'm appealing to the young people of Cuba who will lift something up, build something new. (Applause.) El futuro de Cuba tiene que estar en las manos del pueblo Cubano. (Applause.)

And to President Castro—who I appreciate being here today—I want you to know, I believe my visit here demonstrates you do not need to fear a threat from the United States. And given your commitment to Cuba's sovereignty and self-determination, I am also confident that you need not fear the different voices of the

Cuban people—and their capacity to speak, and assemble, and vote for their leaders. In fact, I'm hopeful for the future because I trust that the Cuban people will make the right decisions.

And as you do, I'm also confident that Cuba can continue to play an important role in the hemisphere and around the globe—and my hope is, is that you can do so as a partner with the United States.

We've played very different roles in the world. But no one should deny the service that thousands of Cuban doctors have delivered for the poor and suffering. (Applause.) Last year, American health care workers—and the U.S. military—worked side-by-side with Cubans to save lives and stamp out Ebola in West Africa. I believe that we should continue that kind of cooperation in other countries.

We've been on the different side of so many conflicts in the Americas. But today, Americans and Cubans are sitting together at the negotiating table, and we are helping the Colombian people resolve a civil war that's dragged on for decades. (Applause.) That kind of cooperation is good for everybody. It gives everyone in this hemisphere hope.

We took different journeys to our support for the people of South Africa in ending apartheid. But President Castro and I could both be there in Johannesburg to pay tribute to the legacy of the great Nelson Mandela. (Applause.) And in examining his life and his words, I'm sure we both realize we have more work to do to promote equality in our own countries—to reduce discrimination based on race in our own countries. And in Cuba, we want our engagement to help lift up the Cubans who are of African descent—(applause)—who've proven that there's nothing they cannot achieve when given the chance.

We've been a part of different blocs of nations in the hemisphere, and we will continue to have profound differences about how to promote peace, security, opportunity, and human rights. But as we normalize our relations, I believe it can help foster a greater sense of unity in the Americas—todos somos Americanos. (Applause.)

From the beginning of my time in office, I've urged the people of the Americas to leave behind the ideological battles of the past. We are in a new era. I know that many of the issues that I've talked about lack the drama of the past. And I know that part of Cuba's identity is its pride in being a small island nation that could stand up for its rights, and shake the world. But I also know that Cuba will always stand out because of the talent, hard work, and pride of the Cuban people. That's your strength. (Applause.) Cuba doesn't have to be defined by being against the United States, any more than the United States should be defined by being against Cuba. I'm hopeful for the future because of the reconciliation that's taking place among the Cuban people.

I know that for some Cubans on the island, there may be a sense that those who left somehow supported the old order in Cuba.

I'm sure there's a narrative that lingers here which suggests that Cuban exiles ignored the problems of pre-Revolutionary Cuba, and rejected the struggle to build a new future. But I can tell you today that so many Cuban exiles carry a memory of painful—and sometimes violent—separation. They love Cuba. A part of them still considers this their true home. That's why their passion is so strong. That's why their heartache is so great. And for the Cuban American community that I've come to know and respect, this is not just about politics. This is about family—the memory of a home that was lost; the desire to rebuild a broken bond; the hope for a better future the hope for return and reconciliation.

For all of the politics, people are people, and Cubans are Cubans. And I've come here—I've traveled this distance—on a bridge that was built by Cubans on both sides of the Florida Straits. I first got to know the talent and passion of the Cuban people in America. And I know how they have suffered more than the pain of exile—they also know what it's like to be an outsider, and to struggle, and to work harder to make sure their children can reach higher in America.

So the reconciliation of the Cuban people—the children and grandchildren of revolution, and the children and grandchildren of exile—that is fundamental to Cuba's future. (Applause.)

You see it in Gloria Gonzalez, who traveled here in 2013 for the first time after 61 years of separation, and was met by her sister, Llorca. "You recognized me, but I didn't recognize you," Gloria said after she embraced her sibling. Imagine that, after 61 years.

You see it in Melinda Lopez, who came to her family's old home. And as she was walking the streets, an elderly woman recognized her as her mother's daughter, and began to cry. She took her into her home and showed her a pile of photos that included Melinda's baby picture, which her mother had sent 50 years ago. Melinda later said, "So many of us are now getting so much back."

You see it in Cristian Miguel Soler, a young man who became the first of his family to travel here after 50 years. And meeting relatives for the first time, he said, "I realized that family is family no matter the distance between us."

Sometimes the most important changes start in small places. The tides of history can leave people in conflict and exile and poverty. It takes time for those circumstances to change. But the recognition of a common humanity, the reconciliation of people bound by blood and a belief in one another—that's where progress begins. Understanding, and listening, and forgiveness. And if the Cuban people face the future together, it will be more likely that the young people of today will be able to live with dignity and achieve their dreams right here in Cuba.

The history of the United States and Cuba encompass revolution and conflict; struggle and sacrifice; retribution and, now, reconciliation. It is time, now, for us to leave the past behind. It is time for us to look forward to the future together—un future de esperanza. And it won't be easy, and there will be setbacks. It will take time. But my time here in Cuba renews my hope and my confidence in what the Cuban people will do. We can make this journey as friends, and as neighbors, and as family—together. Si se puede. Muchas gracias. (Applause.)

BARACK OBAMA served as U.S. Senator for Illinois prior to defeating John McCain in the 2008 presidential election to become the 44th President of the United States. He is the first African American to hold the position. In 2012, President Obama defeated Republican challenger Mitt Romney to win a second term.

Armando Valladares

 **NO**

I Was a Prisoner of Castro's Regime: Obama's Visit to Cuba Is a Mistake

An Afro-Cuban dissident who spent time in Fidel Castro's gulags, Oscar Biscet is one of many people that represent the real Cuba, the people who will be hidden from sight as President Obama visits this week. While the president basks in the Cuban sun and in photo-ops with its heavy-handed dictator, the fate and freedom of political resisters like Biscet remains grim. Biscet is free now in technical terms, but in reality, he remains among a cohort of dissenters who still live in an invisible prison: a society still very much under the thumb of a totalitarian regime. And this week, Obama will provide that very regime with dangerously unwarranted legitimacy in the form of a diplomatic visit.

Biscet and I were convicted of the same crime: fidelity to our consciences. Biscet, a doctor, blew the whistle on corruption and abuse in Cuba's health-care system. The government called it "disrespect." My crime was in refusing to put a simple sign on my desk that said, "I'm with Fidel." He and I and countless others who refused to go along with the Castro regime's flagrant human rights violations were sentenced to decades in jail, where the government showed no restraint in trying to break us into submission.

And while both of us are technically free men now, Biscet and others like him living in Cuba go about their lives bearing the invisible shackles of a government that tolerates not a word of protest.

The entire island of Cuba lives garroted by these unseen chains. And despite glossy magazine ads inviting travelers to come for the mojitos and pristine beaches, and cheerful state visits from the likes of John Kerry and Obama, nothing has changed. Rather, as countless organizations have attested, human rights abuses have only escalated, and Cuba is in violation of basic stipulations in its diplomatic agreement with the United States by refusing to allow workers from the Red Cross and United Nations to come and lift the palm-studded hood and take a look.

When the president announced his intention to reopen diplomatic relations between the United States and Cuba, he said, "I believe that we can do more to support the Cuban people and promote our values through engagement." What followed was to be expected from a dictatorial government that has reigned through violent oppression with nothing but ruler slaps from world governments. Cuba also has cover from international institutions like the U.N., where it sits on the Human Rights Council ranting yearly about "human rights abuses" in other countries. And now, to secure its rewards like state visits and relaxed sanctions from the United States, it will escalate political crackdowns. The government, which no doubt doesn't want to scare away American tourists with visions of bloodied protesters being dragged from the streets, is sending a message to dissidents louder than ever: Shut up or be locked up. As a Washington Post editorial said, there were more than 8,000 political arrests in 2015, up by thousands from years prior. The crackdown on dissidents is so bad that it prompted Kerry to cancel a trip he had scheduled just weeks before Obama's visit.

The president's decision to go anyway sends a message of favoritism for the strong at the expense of the weak. Dictators dream about friendly visits from heads of state; such a favor from the president of the United States is the ultimate fantasy. It provides an endless trove of propaganda material that helps lend legitimacy to the Castro regime, whose agenda of late consists of courting big corporations desperately needed to boost a failed experiment in socialism on the one hand, and bulldozing house churches on the other.

Antagonizing believers is a particular specialty of the Castro regime. To them, faith is especially dangerous, because it kindles the conscience and keeps it burning when enemies advance. "¡Viva Cristo Rey!" were the last words of so many of my friends who were dragged to the shooting wall. Eventually, the government realized this was a battle cry for freedom, one that came from the deepest part of the men they were killing, and one that was only inspiring more men to die faithful to their consciences and to something greater than Fidel Castro. Their executioners realized that an expression of faith was more powerful than the explosion of a gun. So eventually, they gagged them.

The same men who did this are still in power today. In agreeing to meet with Raul Castro, Obama rewards a regime that rules with brutal force and systemically violates human rights. He shrugs his shoulders at the little man. He shows a callous disregard for the human conscience, the single greatest threat to any ruler.

Valladares, Armando. "I Was a Prisoner of Castro's Regime: Obama's Visit to Cuba Is a Mistake," *The Washington Post,* March 2016. Copyright © 2016 by Armando Valladares. Used with permission.

In a March 10 letter responding to an angry message from the Damas de Blanco, an opposition movement of the mothers, wives and other female relatives of jailed dissidents known for their all-white attire, Obama thanked them for being "an inspiration to human rights movements around the world."

I wonder how many more women will be made into Damas by his trip to Cuba.

Armando Valladares is a Cuban poet, diplomat, and human rights activist. In 1960, he was arrested by the Cuban government for conflicting reasons; the Cuban government alleged that he had been complicit in anti-Castro terrorism, while foreign sources regarded his arrest as being due to his protesting communism, leading Amnesty International to name him a prisoner of conscience.

EXPLORING THE ISSUE

Was President Obama's Trip to Cuba a Good Step in Normalizing Relations with the Country?

Critical Thinking and Reflection

1. What are the benefits of normalized relations with Cuba?
2. What are the costs of normalized relations with Cuba?
3. Why do you believe the normalization has occurred at this time?
4. Do you believe Obama's successor will continue on this trajectory? Why or why not?
5. How do you believe this development will impact Cuban Americans within the United States?

Is There Common Ground?

The decision to reenter a diplomatic relationship with Cuba forced many Americans to look back on the Cold War and determine whether they believed it was simply too soon. But, the less discussed opinions were those held by individuals of Cuba descent who had immigrated to the United States and their family members. As opposed to many issues discussed in this volume, from a policy perspective it is relatively easy to find common ground regarding President Obama's visit to Havana. But on a personal level, it may be quite difficult for those with ties to the island nation to easily abandon their opinion—whether they support the change in approach or oppose it.

For those who suffered under Castro's regime that made their way to the United States, their views may be conflicting even within their own heads. On one hand, the decision of the Obama administration will unquestionably open up doors for Cuban citizens to reenter the world marketplace and advance societally. But,
on the other hand, it adds legitimacy to a government today that many continue to argue is overly focused on self-growth rather than being concerned with all citizens. Thus, the ability to find common ground may very well depend on how personally attached to the situation an individual is.

Additional Resources

Soraya M. Castro Mariño and Ronald W. Pruessen, *Fifty Years of Revolution: Perspectives on Cuba, the United States, and the World* (University Press of Florida. 2012)

Jane Franklin and Noam Chomsky, *Cuba and the U.S. Empire: A Chronological History* (Monthly Review Press, 2016)

Louis Pérez Jr. and Lester Langle, *Cuba and the United States: Ties of Singular Intimacy* (University of Georgia Press, 2003)

Internet References . . .

A Brief History of U.S.–Cuba Relations

http://content.time.com/time/nation
/article/0,8599,1891359,00.html

FACT SHEET: United States–Cuba Relationship

https://www.whitehouse.gov/the-press
-office/2016/03/21/fact-sheet-united
-states-cuba-relationship

U.S.–Cuba Relations

http://www.cfr.org/cuba/us-cuba-relations/p11113